E&L 19 (07/05)

Renfrewshire
Council

EDUCATION AND LEISURE SERVICES

L.H.Q.

LIBRARIES

RESERVE STOCK

Thank you for using _____
Library. Please return by the last date below. Renewals can be requested in person, by telephone or via our website www.renfrewshire.gov.uk/libraries

HANDLE WITH CARE !

More WEST *Highland* TALES

Orally collected
BY THE LATE J. F. CAMPBELL

Transcribed and translated from
the original Gaelic by
JOHN G. MACKAY

Edited by
W. J. Watson, D. MacLean
& H. J. Rose

VOLUME 1

Birlinn

This edition by Birlinn Ltd. 1994

Birlinn Ltd.
13 Roseneath Street
Edinburgh EH9 1JH

With thanks to the Department of Celtic
Aberdeen University for use of original editions.

A CIP record of this book is available from the British Library.

ISBN 1 874744 22 X

More West Highland Tales Volume I was originally published
in 1940 by Oliver and Boyd.

Chuidich Comhairle nan Leabhraichean am foill____ea____
le cosgaisean an leabhair seo.

Printed in Finland by Werner Söderström OY

GENERAL PREFACE

ALL the stories in this book have been transcribed from manuscripts preserved in the Collections of the late John Francis Campbell of Islay, but never published by him. In 1859 this great man, called in Gaelic Iain Òg Île, or Young John of Islay, began collecting the folk-tales and legends that were then still living in the form of oral traditions in the West Highlands of Scotland. He was ably assisted by many Highlanders, Gaelic-speaking men, whom he induced to help him in the labour of collecting. The ability and qualifications that he brought to bear on this great work will probably never again be united together in the person of any single individual. For he was one of the hereditary chieftains of the country, and had an intimate acquaintance with the Highlands and the Highlanders. Being a native, he spoke Gaelic as only a native could, and having the happiest knack of making friends, was always sure of a clear road to the hearts of the Highland people, who, in consequence, gave him of their best, and that freely and unstintedly. Moreover, he thoroughly understood the art of collecting, loved folk-lore and knew the value of it, had the utmost enthusiasm for his work, and scrupulously recorded as far as possible the exact words of his reciters, without subtraction or addition. He rightly thought that to polish a genuine popular tale would be as barbarous as, it would be to adorn the bones of a Megatherium with tinsel, or gild a rare old copper coin,' *W. H. Tales*, intro., xi, or iii.

The genius of this great lover of his people's folk-culture did not meet with much sympathy in his own generation. He never knew of the esteem in which later generations were to hold him, or of the fame that he won in the world of Gaelic folk-lore in which he was an unrewarded pioneer. The fact that in the dark ages of ignorance and contempt he was able to impress upon others the duty of collecting, and of drilling into them the idea that the words of the humble peasants who recited the tales were to be scrupulously recorded without any additions or omissions, speaks worlds for his tremendous personality.[1]

Eventually, this great master of folk-tales[2] amassed a vast and magnificent collection of stories. In 1860-2 he published his famous *Popular Tales of the West Highlands*, hereinafter referred to as *West Highland Tales*, in four volumes. This contained eighty-six tales, as well as many variants or abstracts of variants, some tales having even six variants. In 1890-3 a second edition appeared, under the auspices of the Islay Association.[3]

The publication of these volumes raised Campbell at once to the front rank of folk-lorists. 'The unrivalled combination of knowledge, critical power, and instinctive racial sympathy which gave to its owner his unique position in the study of folk-lore can hardly be expected from any other man. . . . Some among the readers of Folk-Lore may, it is hoped, be able to do the work I have sketched in the foregoing pages, the work of rendering accessible to fellow-students the rich stores of folk-fancy, and of learning so full of life and penetration, as almost to deserve the name of genius, at present hidden away in the MSS. of Campbell of Islay.'[4]

These words refer to the immense number of tales which Campbell of Islay left behind him, and which he did not live to publish. They are domiciled in the National Library, Edinburgh. Nearly eight hundred of them are specified in the two lists given at the end of *W. H. Tales*, iv. They are here called the English List and the Gaelic List. Almost all the tales in the English List are in English, and are bound up in MS. Vol. xiii.[5]

---

[1] He died on 17th February 1885. Obituary notices appeared in *The Athenæum* (1885), i., p. 250, and *The Academy* (1885), xxvii., p. 151.

[2] *Folk-Lore*, i., p. 205.

[3] The pagination of these editions differ. In referring, therefore, it was necessary to quote the page numbers of each.

[4] Alfred Nutt, in *Folk-Lore*, i., p. 383.

[5] Fair copies of these were made in a volume lettered—'HIGHLAND STORIES —Collected in 1859-60—ENGLISH.'

But it is with the tales in the Gaelic List that we have now to do. Almost all are in Gaelic, and are either first-hand transcriptions or fair copies of such transcriptions, and all were taken down from the oral recitation of Gaelic speakers.[1]

Unfortunately, after numbering the tales in his Gaelic List, and including in it several of his published items, Campbell separated them and bound them up in different MS. volumes. Thus there are many gaps between the numbers of the tales in any one of these volumes. There is a gap of twenty-three tales between Nos. 126 and 150. This may, however, be due to the fact that he numbered most of his tales three times, and may have bound up this group of missing ones under some previous system of numbering, or under a later system. In some few places he has quoted wrong references, so that I have not been able to trace the items. Some items have, I fear, been lost. And some have not been mentioned in his Gaelic List, and bear no number.[2] The resulting confusion has been considerable.

The tales of the Gaelic List have been bound up in various MS. volumes, the contents of which are as follows :—

MS. Volumes i. to vi. contain the original MSS. of the published tales (i.e. *West Highland Tales*) as well as proofs, revise, notes, instructions to printers, newspaper clippings, and various odds and ends.

MS. Volume vii. contains correspondence, and an index of Ossianic items.

MS. Volumes viii. and ix. contain variants of his published tales, of which variants he published summaries in *W. H. Tales*, i., ii., iii. MS. Volume viii. also contains two tales, Nos. 106, 203, which he classed as variants of *W. H. Tales*, i., No. 1. But they are much more than mere variants. And Islay did not publish a summary of either.

---

[1] There are several hundred stories not mentioned in his published lists. They are bound up in various MS. volumes and will be dealt with later.

[2] In these cases the item has been given the number of the preceding item, plus a letter, A, B, C, etc.

MS. Volumes x. and xi. contain tales of fresh theme. The latter volume contains about forty tales not mentioned in the Gaelic List.

MS. Volume xii. contains Ossianic Ballads.

On the fly-leaves of tales Nos. 106, 203, respectively, Islay has written: 'To be made into something better for it is worth it,' and 'This story is considered as something great. It is the chief story,' etc. Such opinions expressed by so illustrious an authority are good warrant as to the value and importance of these stories. It was clearly desirable to give them pride of place in this book, and to follow them with tales from MS. Volume x. as containing fresh themes and breaking new ground.

Every tale has been given a new number. At the head of each tale, the number indicating its place in the Aarne-Thompson Classification will be found. And a list of such tales as are represented in that Classification is given at the end of the book.

The overwhelming majority of the tales in Islay's Collections are genuine examples of Scottish Gaelic oral tradition, as will be abundantly apparent to any Gaelic-speaking person. The native speaker, when thinking in Gaelic and unbiassed by any English model, delivers his soul in crisp, picturesque, and idiomatic language of great intensity. Accordingly, short simple sentences that go to the heart of the subject without waste of words are characteristic of these stories, and afford the best guarantee of their genuineness. Nothing is ever laboured, and it is clear that the aim of reciters was to state simply and plainly the facts of the stories.[1] It was not necessary for them to

[1] In these things, Scottish Gaelic folk-tales closely resemble the Irish Gaelic folk-tales. Both kinds are told in short and trenchant sentences. (Not so the Irish literary tales, which are often overburdened with epithet, and abound in long laboured sentences.) The desire to get hold of the unvarnished facts of a story is characteristic. Speaking of the Highlanders, Campbell of Islay says: 'If such as these get hold of the contents of a story book, they seem unconsciously to extract the incidents and reject all the rest— to select the true wood, and throw away foreign ornament,' *W. H. Tales*, i., intro. xix or xi. See also MS. Vol. x., No. 105. Dr Douglas Hyde bears similar witness regarding the many Irish folk-tales he has gathered—'the incidents and not the language were the things to be remembered,' *Beside the Fire*, xxiv.

concern themselves with the method of presentation, for
they spoke a tongue that was comparatively pure, and one
which had not been much mixed with other tongues. The
poorest classes usually speak the language admirably. The
great gulf that exists between spoken and literary English
has no counterpart in Gaelic, in which the everyday speech
of the people is close to the standard of literary excellence.[1]

There are other characteristics which are of a piece
with the brevity of style. For instance, the most striking
incidents are hardly ever commented upon. Epithet is
hardly ever indulged in. Moralizing is rare.[2] The feelings
of the various dramatis personæ are seldom mentioned.[3]
Even the desperate valour of the hero who overcomes all
difficulties and conquers all his enemies seldom receives
a word of praise.

A word as to the character of the reciters of stories
may be desirable. Some stories were obtained from an
old bed-ridden pauper woman, some from rough farmers,
others from boatmen, ferry-boys, herd-boys, young children,
tinkers, dyke-builders, foresters, gamekeepers, and from
the poorest of the poor. One of the raciest tales, told in
exquisite idiom, was obtained from a man of whom Islay
remarks that he had never worn boots or shoes.[4] Elsewhere he says that 'the less instructed the narrator, the
more quaint and complete his version is.'[5] He thought
the 'island tales the oldest,'[6] which is what one might

---

[1] *Waifs and Strays*, ii., p. xix.

[2] MS. Vol. x., No. 117, and a group of tales at the end of MS. Vol. xi.,
contain some moralizing. Hector MacLean tacked on morals to several
stories he collected, morals of a very quaint kind. But he did not insert
them in the text. And with the exceptions noted, native reciters never did
so. This was as well, otherwise the accumulated moralizings of successive
centuries would have been inevitably incorporated with the tales themselves,
and eventually it would have become impossible to distinguish the original
material from the later accretions.

[3] The lamentations of the old Were-wolf King (pp. 13, 33); the praise
given by the fairy godmother to her god-child ('God-child and good god-
child') (MS. Vol. x., No. 83); and the remark by the heroine in MS. Vol. x.,
No. 154, that her courage was 'firmer now,' are the only expressions of feeling
I remember.

[4] MS. Vol. xi., No. 327.   [5] *W. H. Tales*, ii., No. 52, Notes.

[6] *Ibid.*, i., intro. cxxii or cxxvii; iii., p. 243 or 258.

have expected, for in Islay's day Anglicization had had, as yet, little effect in out-of-the-way places.

Campbell of Islay frequently remarks upon the extraordinary powers of memory and the fluency of delivery displayed by the reciters of the stories. Some tales took an hour to recite—others took four. Some reciters could recite at speed for an hour without a break. Some could tell tale after tale, and keep it up for evening after evening. Some recited thousands of lines of ancient heroic poems. One man, after delivering a lengthy story, said that what he had recited was 'but the contents.' Another man, while walking along the road with Islay, told him a tale which lasted several miles. When done, he said he had forgotten much of it.[1] Nineteen stories (there should have been twenty-four) forming the long chain called 'The Story of Kane's Leg,' and occupying almost the whole of MS. Vol. xvii., were recited by one man, Lachlan MacNeill. He recited them to Hector MacLean as fast as the latter could take them down, the process continuing for many days. In another place, Islay says of his recension of the Fenian saga :—'I have done simply my best to fuse into one English story speeches which took at least an hour to deliver—fluent, eloquent, clear, consistent stories told by men who cannot read a word or write their names, so far as I know.'[2]

Islay further says: 'In August and September 1860 I again visited the Western Highlands, carrying with me nearly the whole of these two volumes [*W. H. Tales*, i., ii.] in print. I have repeatedly made the men who told the stories to my collectors repeat them to me, while I compared their words with the book. In two instances I have made men repeat stories which I had myself written

---

[1] See *W. H. Tales*, i., intro. xxvii, cxviii, or xx, cxiii. No. 17c, Notes. ii., No. 40, Notes. No. 44, Notes. MS. Vol. x., No. 105. MS. Vol. xi., No. 268. MS. Vol. xiii., Nos. 326, 340.

[2] *Celtic Review*, i., p. 364. Witness to the powers of memory peculiar to the old Highlanders are to be found elsewhere. Archibald MacTavish, from Mull, then in his seventy-fourth year, recited without any hesitation nine of the twelve tales in *Waifs and Strays*, ii., intro. vii, x. Alexander Cameron of Ardnamurchan recited all the tales in *Waifs and Strays*, iii.

down in English from their Gaelic, and I have found no important variation in any instance. I find that the story is generally much longer as told, but that it is lengthened by dialogue, which has often little to do with the incidents, though sometimes worth preservation. I have now seen most of the men whose names are mentioned, and I have myself heard versions of nearly every story in the book[s] repeated, either by those from whom they were got, or by people who live far from them.' [1] A more searching test no man could have invented, and Islay's words speak volumes for his scribes, and prove for his reciters a reverent and religious fidelity to the letter of the stories as they had been handed down to them by their forbears, a fact which suggests that the latter also were equally accurate, and probably had been for untold generations. The further conclusion of course is, that though some tales may be but the shadows of their former selves, mere summaries or 'but the contents' of more ancient versions, though some again may be gapped and broken, and though various details and incidents may have been forgotten, or left unmotivated or unfinished, we may nevertheless be sure that in them we have records that are very close to a much lower civilization. Herein lies their virtue, the quality that gives them value in the eyes of science. They are a revelation of a much earlier period, a revelation handed down to us by the method which primitive man himself had inaugurated, and which his descendants continued to

---

[1] See *W. H. Tales*, i., end of intro. 'Postscript.' The late Alfred Nutt, commenting on this gift of memory, came to 'the startling conclusion that well-nigh the same stories as were told of Finn and his warrior braves by the Gael of the eleventh century, are told in well-nigh the same way by his descendant of to-day,' *Ossian and the Ossianic Literature*, p. 53 (London: David Nutt, 1890). Nutt says again: 'The existing folk-beliefs go back to the folk-beliefs of 2000 years ago, rather than to the creeds and legends that have come down to us in literature,' *Waifs and Strays*, iii., intro. xx. See also *ibid.*, ii., pp. 415, 430, 468. Gudmund Schütte holds similar opinions regarding the reliability of modern Danish folk-lore, *Folk-Lore*, xxxv., p. 371. The picture given by M. Joseph Déchelette in his *Manuel d'Archéologie Préhistorique Celtique et Gallo-Romaine*, ii., p. 595 (Paris: Auguste Picard, 1913), shows clearly that some at least of the Highland folk-tales (upon which I based my article in *Folk-Lore*, xliii., pp. 144-174, on The Deer- and Deer-Goddess cult) go back to the Halstatt epoch, 600-500 B.C.

practise, and in a few odd places do still practise, even unto this day.

The folk often preserve a myth in a form which is nearer to the primitive, and therefore more accurate and valuable than that preserved among the MSS. of the upper classes. Professor Thomas F. O'Rahilly finds that Scottish oral versions of the famous old chain of stories called 'Leigheas Coise Chéin,' or 'The Healing of Kane's Foot,' are in some respects more accurate than the fifteenth century MS. version.[1] Dr Douglas Hyde notes the discrepancy in style and contents between the Irish MS. stories, and those he had collected among the people.[2] Campbell of Islay, speaking of the Lay of Diarmaid, says: 'There would seem to be two forms of the myth; one the wildest and best known to the people, the other more rational and best known to the educated classes.'[3]

It is obvious that the ability to recite many long stories implies the existence of an art, and a persistence in the practice of that art which must have needed many years to attain to proficiency in it. It is equally clear that such an art could not have grown up in a single century. Exactly how it began we shall never know. But we have some evidence as to how it was continued.

'The manner of preserving the accuracy of tradition is singular and worthy of notice. In the winter evenings a number of Senachies frequently meet together and recite alternately their traditionary stories. If anyone repeats a passage which appears to another to be incorrect he is immediately stopped, when each gives a reason for his way of reciting the passage. The dispute is then referred to a vote of the meeting, and the decision of the majority becomes imperative on the subject for the future.'[4]

That some faculty or school of story-telling formerly existed is suggested by certain facts concerning the various

---

[1] *Gadelica*, i., p. 282 *n.*   [2] *Beside the Fire*, xix.

[3] *W. H. Tales*, iii., p. 90 or 102.

[4] *Statistical Account or Parochial Survey of Ireland, drawn from the communications of the Clergy*, by William Shaw Mason, Dublin, London, and Edinburgh, 1814-19, vol. i., pp. 317-8. Quoted *Folk-Lore Journal* (1884), ii., p. 142.

'runs'[1] or descriptive prose passages that occur in the tales. The 'runs' are of stereotyped form. Each is used in its appropriate connection, and any one of them may occur in tales which are otherwise quite unrelated. As the tales were gathered from all parts of the country and from reciters unknown to each other, it is evident that they could not have borrowed their 'runs' from each other. Many 'runs' are long and could not therefore have gained currency in the manner of proverbs. Their length seems to imply conscious co-operation. Stereotyped passages of some length indicate unanimity among practitioners in the art of story-telling, and possibly point to some period when the story-telling faculty had sufficient cohesion and unity among its members to agree upon what forms of words and what phrases should be used in connection with given incidents. Perhaps the faculty in question is represented by the bardic institutions known to tradition as the *Tromdám*[2] or the *Cliar Sheanchain*.[3] Islay himself seems to have suspected the former existence of such academies, for he says of some tales: 'I believe these to be bardic recitations fast disappearing and changing into prose; for the older the narrator is, the less educated, and the farther removed from the rest of the world, the more his stories are garnished with these passages.'[4] Professor W. J. Watson says of these 'runs' that they 'are the oldest part of the tales, and their form was fixed so long ago that the wording became obscure to the reciters, who therefore were apt, while maintaining the general sound and the number of rhythmical beats, to slur unfamiliar terms, or modify them by analogy. For their understanding a knowledge of the older language is useful, but there is a residuum in them that can only be guessed at.'[5] The late Professor Donald Mackinnon

---

[1] Called in Gaelic *ruith*, or *siubhal*, plu. *ruitheanna*, *siubhlaichean*.

[2] See *Ossianic Soc. Transactions*, vol. v., 'Imtheacht na Tromdhaimhe.'

[3] See Professor W. J. Watson and A. P. Graves for an account of this institution, and the corresponding Irish one, *Celtic Review*, iv., p. 80; vii., p. 174. And see No. 25 (MS. Vol. x., No. 47) Notes.

[4] *W. H. Tales*, intro. xxxiv or xlii. And see Islay's notes to tales Nos. 17c, 35, 36, 38, 52, *ibid.*, i., ii.

[5] *Rosg Gàidhlig*, p. 209. See p. 262 *n*.

also draws attention to the archaic diction of the 'runs.' [1]

Professor W. J. Watson further informs us that 'trained poets and men of learning occupied an honoured position in the social system. Their recompense, always liberal and often munificent, was derived partly from grants of land, partly from dues and privileges, and partly from the fees to which they were entitled for their compositions. They were in close touch with the chief or lord, sat in his council, preserved the history of his family, and on due occasion celebrated his praises. The office of poet, like other offices among the Gael, tended to be hereditary in a family. This family represented learning and culture in the tribe, as the chief represented authority. Its poet-historians through successive generations kept alive the pride of race, and ministered to it, especially by panegyrics.' Professor Watson also says that these men 'used a literary style which, though it changed with the changes of the language, was always more archaic than the vernacular of the day.' [2] Such a state of things had obtained in more ancient times. Says Professor R. A. Stewart Macalister: 'The Ogham inscriptions teach us that even proper names appeared in the epic language in a form quite different from their form in current speech.' [3]

The decay of the old Highland bardic compositions must be attributed to the fact that the upper classes forsook the ancient institutions of their fathers, ceased to keep a bard in their retinue, or to keep any retinue at all, cut themselves off from their own roots, and adopted the manners of another nation. In consequence, the old official bardic class,[4] who gloried and rejoiced in the old classical masterpieces, and in the archaic forms of speech in which they were composed, passed away, and with them also passed away much of the knowledge of the old poetry and of the old classical speech, and what was much

---

[1] *Celtic Review*, i., p. 216 *n*; iv., pp. 89, 109 *n*.
[2] *Bàrdachd Ghàidhlig*, intro. xvii.   [3] *Temair Breg*, p. 315.
[4] The last of the old bards was Donald MacVurich, of Staoiligearraidh in South Uist, who died some time after 1722 (*Bàrdachd Ghàidhlig*, xviii.).

more serious, an amount of traditional lore and history that must have been enormous. In spite of this, it is certain that at one time, say fifty years before the advent of Campbell of Islay, the folk of the West Highlands must have been still fairly well acquainted with the great bardic compositions which had frequently been recited in the houses of their chiefs.[1] Otherwise, these compositions could not have been extant among the people in the days of Campbell of Islay.

Stories and mythologies, if of an aristocratic nature, tend to die out amongst the folk.[2] William Larminie, speaking of Ireland,[3] says: 'Here the heroic cycle has been handed down in remembrance almost solely by the bardic literature. The popular memory retains but few traces of it. Its essentially aristocratic character is shown by the fact that the people have all but forgotten it if they ever knew it. But the Fenian cycle has not been forgotten. Prevailing everywhere, still cherished by the conquered peoples, it held its ground in Scotland and Ireland alike.' Similarly, though the colossal goddess, An Chailleach Bhéarach (Scotice Cailleach Bheurr or Bheur) is the most tremendous figure in Gaelic myth to-day, the ancient Irish MSS., which deal with the heroic and divine cycles of the aristocrats, have only a few marginal notes and references to her. But while the two aristocratic cycles have been forgotten, the Fenian saga and the old Cailleach live on in legend to this day. Both she and the saga must be of great antiquity. They are of the folk and therefore more durable and closer to the primitive.

From the fact that the longest of these tales can easily

---

[1] The vernacular poetry, in some instances, shows that the authors (*e.g.* Mary Macleod, MacCodrum, and others) were acquainted with the bardic poetry and bardic methods.

[2] Gudmund Schütte, speaking of Danish folk-lore, says that 'the superior classes of the mythical society, the gods, have only left feeble traces,' *Folk-Lore*, xxxv., p. 360. The same might be said of the Olympic pantheon. Of the popular Scandinavian Eddic poems, Bertha S. Phillpotts, O.B.E., Litt.D., says that they 'differ *in toto* from the skaldic lays, which are aristocratic in tone, employ a highly artificial poetic terminology, and are of the nature of narrative eulogies of a patron or his family,' *Folk-Lore*, xxxii., p. 142.

[3] *West Irish Folk-Tales and Romances*, intro. xxii.

be read in twenty minutes, it is apparent that some
considerable condensation has taken place. One of the
causes of condensation was that aged individuals (in whose
repertoires the best and most complete stories were usually
to be found) commonly broke down when made to go
slowly, and that when they had warmed to their work
and were declaiming apace, it was of course impossible
for the scribe to keep abreast of them.[1] Hector MacLean
seems to have felt this keenly. It was probably the cause
of a notable gap in No. 2 (MS. Vol. viii., No. 203), p. 41.
Hence no doubt one reason for Islay's occasional complaint
that the 'measured prose passages,' or the 'impassioned
language,' or the curious phrases that were dotted about
in a tale 'like plums in a pudding,' had been lost. Still
the few instances of 'impassioned language' and the like
that remain, are of the same trenchant brevity that belongs
to the tales generally. Among these instances are to be
included the 'runs' mentioned already. A Gaelic-speaker
can easily imagine with what animation such 'runs' would
have been declaimed.[2] However, the collectors were
quite capable of profiting by experience and of becoming
more expert as time went on, and this is shown by the
fact that the tales in MS. Vol. xi. are much longer and
more detailed than those in MS. Vol. x.

Another cause of the fragmentary character of some
tales is to be found in the obliterating effect of modern
civilization. Witness Islay's own statements (already
quoted) that he thought the 'island tales the oldest,' and
that 'the less instructed the narrator, the more quaint

---

[1] Occasionally, however, warming to the work of recitation must have
had an advantageous effect. See No. 25 (MS. Vol. x., No. 47). The 'runs'
in that tale are much more complete at the end than at the beginning,
showing that the act of recitation had gradually quickened the reciter's
memory.

[2] The late Rev. Dr George Henderson informed me that he had seen a
professional story-teller actually perspire when reciting a story. Whether
this was due to dramatic exertion, or the exciting nature of the incidents,
I did not hear. Witness is borne to the reverence as well as to the exultation
with which professionals would recite Ossianic and other poetry, and to
the extraordinary accuracy of their recitations in L. na Féinne, pp. xxxii,
xxxiii, 218, and Waifs and Strays, iv., p. 31.

and complete his version is.' These words imply that the best tales or those nearest to the primitive came from places where, in Islay's day, Anglicization had hardly begun, and that stories found among the educated were not so interesting or complete. The substitution of English for Gaelic must have blotted out treasure wholesale in many places. It is certain that many of the tales in Islay's Collections were saved at the last minute, when on the brink of oblivion, and when the rising tide of Anglicization was just about to overwhelm them.

The condensation of tales already notable for their brevity was bound to result in loss. And this is probably the case with almost every tale. Still there are differences in style and diction that are very apparent (though hardly possible to reproduce in a translation), and this shows that the scribes had kept closely to the original language of the reciters.[1] And this is borne out by the words of Islay's 'Postscript,' already quoted (p. xiii *n.*).

Still, though some of the tales in Islay's Gaelic List are fragmentary, and though a few are but bare outlines, the greater number are fairly complete entities. Gaps appear here and there, confusion on the part of scribe or reciter is often noticeable, especially in the matters of number and time, but seldom to such an extent as to spoil the plot of the story. What is more important is that many of the tales are novel in theme or plot, and on that account it is difficult to overestimate their value, either from the literary or scientific point of view. They constitute a mine of virgin material, unique, refreshing, and in some cases almost startling. A treasure-house for the student of origins, they are full of events and ideas undreamed of by moderns, full of quaint old customs and beliefs, and they afford peeps into the past that could have scarcely been hoped for. Their novelty and diversity abundantly recommend them, and it may be safely said that the gradual publication of so great a mass of material

---

[1] Compare, for instance, No. 14 (MS. Vol. x., No. 28) with MS. Vol. xi., No. 354; also No. 20 (MS. Vol. x., No. 34) with MS. Vol. No. 83; also No. 22 (MS. Vol. x., No. 37) with MS. Vol. No. 126.

will be of considerable value as it will enable science to give us a more complete picture of the primitive, and through that, of European pre-history, than has hitherto been possible. The late Professor Donald MacKinnon, M.A., says: 'The Campbell Collection, although made comparatively recently, thus contains a large amount of hitherto unpublished matter of great value' (*A Descriptive Catalogue of Gaelic Manuscripts*, p. 282).

Besides an English translation, the original Gaelic of every tale is given also. This is clearly what Islay desired.[1]

Islay implies or complains that his education in Gaelic had been neglected. He frequently spelt it very badly, and some of his scribes spelt it still worse.[2] It has been necessary to adopt a uniform orthography of Gaelic, and the eccentricities of Islay and his scribes have been noted only when they give rise to a doubt as to the meaning.

The remaining Tales in MS. Vol. x. will appear in the second Volume of *More West Highland Tales*.

My grateful thanks are due to several: to Mr Cyril J. Inglis for the help he gave me in transcribing the MSS., whereby he saved me at least one year's labour; to the MS. Department of the British Museum, who accepted custody of the MSS. to enable Mr Inglis and myself to continue the transcribing; to the Librarian of the Bank of England who also accepted custody of the MSS., also for the purposes of transcribing; to the Keeper and officials of the National Library, Edinburgh, who allowed me to transcribe there; to Mr George Milne, of Craigellie, Lonmay, Aberdeenshire, for very much assistance, very many kindnesses, advice, and encouragement; to the Scottish Anthropological and Folk-Lore Society, Edinburgh, for undertaking publication; to the Editor of *Béaloideas*, Mr J. H. Delargy, M.A., of the Irish Folk-Lore Commission, University College, Dublin, who brought the project of publishing Campbell of Islay's MSS. to the notice of the Scottish Anthropological and Folk-Lore Society,

---

[1] *W. H. Tales*, v., p. 328 or 359.
[2] *Ibid.*, No. 20, Notes, and *Waifs and Strays*, v., p. 140.

and who did much disinterested work to forward that project; and to Professor W. J. Watson for many corrections and amendments in the matter of the Gaelic.

I am specially indebted to the Marquis of Bute and the Marquess of Ailsa, who most kindly advised and directed me in various ways, and made ultimate success possible and complete.

The thanks of the Scottish Anthropological and Folk-Lore Society are also due to Professor Stith Thompson, of Indiana University, Bloomington, Indiana, for kindly adding to every tale the numbers of the Aarne-Thompson Classification, and those of his own Classification of incidents. For these, see end of book.

J. G. McKAY

FRANWYN
SIDFORD, SIDMOUTH
DEVON

CONTENTS

	PAGE
PREFACE BY J. G. MCKAY	vii
INTRODUCTION BY PROFESSOR W. J. WATSON	xxiv
INTRODUCTION BY PROFESSOR H. J. ROSE	xxvii
LIST OF TALES	xxxi
ADDENDUM	xxxv
ABBREVIATIONS	xxxvii
TALES	2

APPENDICES—

    I. A' CHAILLEACH CHEARC 491
        The Hen-Wife

    II. AN EACHRAIS-URLAIR 492
        The Floor-Mischief

    III. A' MHUIME 500
        The Stepmother or Foster-mother

    IV. BE-SPELLING AND COUNTER-BE-SPELLING INCANTATIONS—
        RESUSCITATION 504

SUBJECT INDEX	515
THE AARNE-THOMPSON CLASSIFICATION	523
THE STITH THOMPSON CLASSIFICATION	525
LIST OF SUBSCRIBERS	539

INTRODUCTION

By Professor W. J. WATSON

HAVING been asked to write a few sentences by way of introduction to this volume, I do so with much pleasure.

The tales contained in this volume will be found not inferior in their varied interest to those published in his own lifetime by John Francis Campbell himself. Their language, their origin, their possible hidden or allegorical meanings, their similarity to and difference from the tales of other peoples, are among the subjects of investigation which these tales provide. In this connexion Campbell's Introduction to his own book is well worth reading. Apart from this, their special interest lies in the light they shed on the intellectual life of the people. The tales were regularly recited to keenly appreciative hearers, and the recitation took several hours or even several nights. And Campbell's Collections, and those of other gleaners in the same field, noble as they are, represent but a part of the mental resources of the Gaelic people ; they had in addition a great and rich store of religious poetry, such as is recorded by Dr Alexander Carmichael, of proverbs, represented by the collections of Donald Mackintosh and Alexander Nicolson, of riddles, of secular poetry and of song.

This intellectual inheritance was by no means confined to the West Coast or the Isles. The stories of the Fiann, for example, were as well known and as firmly localised further east ; the circular forts of Perthshire are in Gaelic *Caistealan nam Fiann* ; in Glen Lyon Fionn had twelve such castles, beside one of which is to be seen *An Conbhacan*, to which his hounds were tied. The grave and stone of Oisean in the Sma' Glen (*An Caolghleann*, part of Glen Almond in Perthshire) are still marked on maps ; about 1728 the stone was removed in the building of Wade's

xxiv

road. " The people of the country, to the number of three or four score men, venerating the memory of the bard, rose with one consent and carried away the bones with bagpipe playing and other funeral rites, and deposited them with much solemnity within a circle of large stones, on the lofty summit of a rock, sequestered and difficult of access . . . in the wild recesses of Wester Glen Almond " (*Ordnance Gazetteer*, i., 262, quoting from Newte, who was here in 1791).

The extraordinary tenacity of Gaelic tradition is illustrated by the fact (related to me by the Rev. Dr Kenneth MacLeod) that in Eigg the people asseverate by Crom Cruaich, the great idol of Magh Slécht (the " Plain of Prostrations "), in County Cavan, who was worshipped long before the coming of St Patrick.

It is safe to say that this ancient culture extended over all the north and northerly midlands of Scotland. The people who possessed this culture may have been, and usually were, unlettered : they were far from being un-educated. It is sad to think that its decay has been partly due to the schools and the Church ! That it is not quite gone is shown by such material as the six Gaelic stories from South Uist and Barra just published by Mr John Lorne Campbell, " typical of the present oral Gaelic literature of these islands."

In this volume it has been attempted to present the Gaelic text in correct and uniform spelling. The original wording has not been departed from ; grammar needed no correction ; and so far as preservation of the dialect of the reciters is concerned, it should be observed that on the one hand no dialectal evidence of any value has been obliterated (if it has been obliterated inadvertently, the original MSS. will continue to preserve it), and, on the other, these tales, as preserved by Campbell and his collaborators, are not and cannot be made reliable bases for phonetic research.

The publication of so many more of Campbell's Tales will be a cause of satisfaction to many ; it will also be, as Mr McKay himself will wish, a stone upon that great collector's cairn. It will be no less a memorial to the labours of the many helpers who made Campbell's work possible, a devoted band whose names should not be lost because they appear on no title-page. Of this band, though later in time, Mr McKay has been one through many years of arduous and disinterested labour. For this he will have the thanks of every student, and our congratulations on the result. His efforts, and the support of the Scottish Anthropological and Folk-Lore Society, have produced a most valuable addition to the literature of Gaelic and of folk-lore.

INTRODUCTION

By Professor H. J. ROSE

It is with a certain complacency that I take my share in presenting these tales to anthropologists and folk-lorists. Mr McKay has sufficiently explained the importance of the work done by Campbell of Islay, and the impossibility of repeating it. The comparatively small amount which he himself was able to publish marked an epoch in these studies ; the Society of which I have the honour to be president hopes to put forth the much larger amount of material which Campbell was obliged to leave in his notebooks, veiled, to the eyes of most students, by being in a tongue so little understood as Gaelic. If the present venture meets with such an amount of success as may repay the costs of publication, it is intended to go on producing a series of volumes, each containing part of this buried treasure, with a translation into English of the tales and such minimum of annotation as shall make them intelligible and enable students who perhaps know nothing of the Highlands of Scotland to assign them their proper place in the great mass of material which the popular imagination has provided. My own part has generally been the humble one of pruning and shortening the notes. Much more might have been said concerning the plots of the stories, the habits, customs and beliefs which they illustrate and the social conditions of the Scotland which gave them birth ; but considerations of bulk and consequent expense have made it necessary to be very brief in our commentary. My standard has been the amount of information which I found necessary for the proper understanding of the narratives, having myself no acquaintance with the Highlands or their language ; what makes a tale intelligible to me will, I hope, prove sufficient for others. With this has been inserted a little in the way of parallels, especially from other Gaelic sources, in order to make some slight beginning of the assignment of these stories to their proper setting.

A few very general remarks may be permitted here. The tales we publish in this volume are of the nature of *märchen* for the most part ; that is to say, they are the Highland Gaelic forms (or to speak more accurately, those forms current last century in certain parts of West Highlands) of a number of traditional narratives which circulate, or at least used to circulate, over vast areas of the world in the mouths of the folk, or in some cases of professional reciters ; the latter indeed have left their traces here and there in the " runs " which form an interesting feature of several items in this book, for example, Nos. 2, 17, 22. Thanks to the kindness of Professor Stith Thompson, full references to the themes of these tales are to be found on our margins. If there were no more than this in the Campbell notebooks, we should think ourselves fully justified in publishing, for new versions of even the best-known *märchen* are material which the folk-lorist needs in his long task of forming a picture of the way the human imagination has worked and been influenced by contacts of one group with another, indirect communications from groups perhaps far removed, and by the environment of the tale-makers and tale-tellers.

But there is much more. Although the general atmosphere of the stories is that of Scotland within the last century or so (hunters use firearms against even the most extraordinary game, as in No. 24 ; the girl in No. 19, after all her adventures, goes to a school in Edinburgh and learns the accomplishments of a young lady of the late eighteenth century at earliest ; the wealth which the orphan in No. 23 romantically acquires is in solid English currency), there is much which is neither of the Lowlands nor of recent date. The weird stories of games played with monstrous and supernatural beings for unstated stakes, as in No. 1 ; the constant intervention of fairies and witches ; the savage revenges and prodigious feats of strength, as in No. 17 ; all these belong to a much earlier and wilder world than the douce Scotland of post-Union days. It is not simply that the narrators have often got hold of very old themes, for many *märchen* have a pedigree stretching to centuries, some few to millennia. The details are often old, part of the mythological heritage of the Kelt. It is not accidental that No. 29 is an offshoot of the Ossianic cycle, an anecdote with whole epics behind it, or at least epic ballads, nor that other stories which we hope to publish later are of the same origin.

Side by side with this we have tales which are incongruously modern. For example, No. 12 has come, presumably via some chapbook, from the mediæval *Lives of Æsop*, which Bentley, in days before the investigation of popular stories became a matter for science, contemptuously compared to " our *Penny-Merriments*, printed at London-Bridge." [1] Indeed, the immediate source may have been the preface to an English Æsop intended for nursery use, such as I well remember from my own childhood. No. 21 cries aloud in its incidents and, I am informed, in the poor quality of its Gaelic, that it owes its being to some English version of part of the *Thousand Nights and a Night.* Yet even here the Highland adapter has managed to put into his telling something of a local and native flavour. There are a few stories (for convenience sake we use the word *novella* to describe them) in which the narrator's own imagination and no traditional material is the chief source. Of these we suspect No. 7 is one, though there is some old material in it ; a flavour of such mediæval collections as the *Gesta Romanorum* may be detected in some of the details, however the narrator came by them. We hope in later volumes to publish quite obvious instances of recent imagination, perhaps stimulated by the cheaper sort of periodicals and novelettes, at work producing original stories of a kind.

In the sharpest possible contrast with this sort of thing are such fragments of comparatively antique lore as No. 10, and the saga-atmosphere of No. 8, another remnant of

Ossianic literature, it would seem ; at all events, the great Fionn plays a part in it.

Thus we have, in the compass of one volume, examples of popular fancy and tradition ranging certainly over some centuries, possibly, if we reckon with the ultimate origin of some of the themes and traditional details, over thousands of years ; yet all from the store of one small part of the country within one lifetime, and that too at so recent a date that there is no doubt but that far more had perished before anyone of Campbell's intelligence and sympathy could hear or record it. I have mentioned the value of the material for comparative study ; but if no such thing as comparative *märchenforschung* or the examination of saga in the light of history and archæology existed, we should still feel fully justified in making known these fragmentary remains of what was once a veritable unwritten library of the memories and poetry of a nation.

LIST OF TALES

TWO TALES FROM MS. VOL. VIII

MS. Vol. viii. is lettered 'Versions of Stories in Vol. i.,' *i.e.* Vol. i. of Campbell of Islay's *West Highland Tales*. It contains two versions of The Chief Story, Nos. 1, 2 (MS. Vol. viii., 106, 203). *Note.*—The numbers in brackets are those of the Gaelic List.

PAGE

1 (106). MAR A CHUIREADH AN TUAIRISGEAL MÓR GU BÀS .   2
How the Great Tuairisgeal was put to death

2 (203). AN TUAIRISGEAL MÓR   28
The Great Tuairisgeal

TALES FROM MS. VOL. X

MS. Vol. x. is lettered 'Unpublished Nos. 1 to 169 Index.' This must be understood as meaning—Nos. 1 to 169 of Islay's Gaelic List, minus those he had sorted out and bound up in other MS. volumes. The volume opens with three lists of tales which were all superseded by the Gaelic List at the end of *W. H. Tales*, iv. For tales Nos. 1*a*, 1*b*, see Addendum.

3 (2). BALGAM MÓR, Great Gulp   48
4 (3). MÓR NIGHEAN SMÙID   62
Mór, the Daughter of Smùid
5 (10). SGEULACHD CHOISE CHÉIN   68
The Tale of Kane's Leg
6 (15). NA TRÌ CHOMHAIRLEAN   74
The Three Counsels
7 (16). MAC AN TUATHANAICH [Ilich] .   .   .   84
The [Islay] Farmer's Son

For some small items bound up here, see Nos. 31*a*-31*d*, p. 486.

8 (18). MAC CUAIN, The Son of the Sea .   .   .   92
9 (19). SGRÌOB LIATH AN EARRAICH .   .   .   104
The Scouring Gray Blast of Spring
10 (20). FRAOCH, Fraoch   114
11 (24). BILIDH, Billy   118
12 (25). IOSBADAIDH, NO, NA TRI GILLEAN NACH DEALAICHEADH   130
Iosbadaidh, or, The Three Lads who would not separate

PAGE

13 (26). An Nighean Bhrèagh Leisg 148
The Handsome Lazy Lass

14 (28). Alasdair, Mac an Impire 168
Alasdair, the Son of the Emperor

15 (29). Grù[th]an an Eòin is an Sporan Oir . . . 188
The Bird's Liver and the Sporran full of gold

16 (30). Gille a' Bhuidseir 210
The Wizard's Gillie

17 (31). Iain Og, Mac Rìgh na Frainge 228
Iain Og, the Son of the King of France

18 (32). An Dà Chraoibh Ghaoil 278
The Two Love Trees

19 (33). An Nighean a reiceadh 292
The Lass who was sold

20 (34). An Leanabh gun Bhaisteadh 308
The Unchristened Child

21 (35). An Duine Bochd, Beairteach . . . 330
The Poor Rich Man

22 (37). Na Trì Léintean Canaich 346
The Three Shirts of Canach Down

23 (40). An Dà Sgiobair 372
The Two Skippers

24 (44). Mac a' Bhreabadair 394
The Weaver's Son

25 (47). Smeuran Dubha 's an Fhaoillteach . . . 410
Bramble Berries in February

Here follows a sheet on which Islay has written: '4 stories from Benbecula told by Donald MacDonald MacCharles MacinTyre,[1] written down first by Miss Torrie sister to John Torrie—copied by John Torrie a student in Glasgow. Recd. Decr. 1859—spelling to be corrected.

48. 1st. Ossianic Poem about the heads on the withies—separate.
49. 2nd. about a poor beggar in Edinburgh, something like the Blind Beggar of Bethnal Green as far as I can remember that ballad.
50. 3rd. Story of a man who took to robbing and robbed robbers—scene laid in Astrilla [recte, Stirling].
51. 4th. The Provost of London. The story of the man who spoke oracular sentences to the travellers—nearly the same as the story told by John MacKenzie.' (See Addendum, p. xxxvi.)

26 (49). Dìol-déirce Dhùn-Éideann 438
The Beggar of Edinburgh

[1] See W. H. Tales, ii., No. 20, Notes. Donald MacinTyre was from Aird, Benbecula. No. 48 was published in Leabhar na Féinne, p. 18, No. Z5. For other versions of No. 48, see Reliquiæ Celticæ, i., pp. 66, 113, 114; ii., p. 365. Irisleabhar na Gaedhilge, xi., p. 63 (Dublin, 1901). Hugh and John MacCallum, Poems of Ossian (1816), p. 129. Donald Mackinnon, Catalogue, p. 341, col. 2.

PAGE

27 (50). AN DUINE A THUG RIS A'MHÈAIRLE, AGUS A CHREACH
           MÈAIRLICH   446
           The Man who took to Robbing, and robbed Robbers

After Nos. 51 and 52 (see Addendum), follows in the handwriting of
Alexander MacDonald, Schoolmaster, Inverasdale, Loch Ewe, a sheet
on which are listed items 53 to 59. The last, a collection of riddles, is
missing. The first two items are both numbered 53, and both have
the same title. They are distinguished here as Nos. 53a, 53b. For
the latter item, see Addendum. Nos. 57, 58 are two unintelligible
songs. See p. 485 n.

28 (53a and 67a). UISDEAN MÓR MAC GILLE PHÀDRUIG, AGUS
                   A' GHOBHAR MHAOL BHUIDHE   454
                   Uisdean Mór Mac Gille Phàdruig, and the Hornless
                   Yellow Goat

With this tale is fused No. 67a.

29 (54). MAC GILLE MHAOIL NA CRUIT   462
           Macmillan the Harpist
30 (55). DONNCHADH EILEIN IÙ, AGUS AN GILLE GLAS .   . 474
           Duncan of Ewe Isle and the Sallow Lad
31 (56). GILLE DUBH LOCHA DRING   480
           The Black Lad of Loch Dring

The following little items are bound up after No. 7 (16).

31a (17a). Notes on No. 36 (MS. Vol. x., No. 17) . .   . 486
            A' BHANTRACH, The Widow. See p. xxxvi.
31b (No Number). AN DONN MARA MÓR MACMHOIREIN   . 486
            The Great Brown MacMorran (or Morrison) of
            the Sea
31c (No Number). AN SAC BÀN, The White Sack .   . 488
31d (No Number). A' GHLAISRIG 488
            The Glaishrig or Glaistig

ADDENDUM

THE following tales were bound up by Islay in MS. Vol. x., but are not reproduced here for the reasons shown below.

32 (1a). The Spirit of Eld
(1b). SPIORAD NA H-AOISE

Hector Urquhart, in March 1859, got this story from an old man building dykes in Ardkinglass, Loch Fyne. Being the same as that published and translated by the two Rev. Drs Norman MacLeod, grandfather and grandson, it is not given here. See *Caraid nan Gàidheal*, p. 273 (ed. 1899, Norman MacLeod, Edinburgh), and *Reminiscences of a Highland Parish*, p. 360 (Alex. Strahan, 1867, London). For a very different version, see No. 117, MS. Vol. x. The two items bear no numbers; but I have distinguished them as 1a and 1b, the one being a translation of the other.

33 (6). COMHAIRLE CHARMAIC D'A MHAC
Cormac's Advice to his Son

Called in Islay's Gaelic List 'Proverbs metrical.'   J 171
Didactic verses, all of which have been published in Sheriff Alexander Nicolson's *Gaelic Proverbs*, pp. 394-404. They are therefore not given here. For other or similar verses, see Kuno Meyer, *The Instructions of King Cormac Mac Airt*, Roy. Irish Acad., Todd Lectures, xv. (Dublin: Hodges, Figgis). *Irische Texte*, iv., pp. 17, 277 (Leipzig, 1900), of which a translation is given *Silva Gadelica*, ii., p. 115. Malcolm MacFarlane, *The Fernaig Manuscript*, pp. 51, 328 (Dundee: Malcolm C. MacLeod, 1933). Professor Donald MacKinnon, *Catalogue of Gaelic MSS.*, pp. 7, 186, 187, 269. *Bàrdachd Ghàidhlig*, pp. 29, 267, 268 (ed. 1932). Dr George Henderson, *Leabhar nan Gleann*, p. 291 (Inverness, 1898). Rev. Donald MacLean of Dunvegan, *Typographia Scoto-Gadelica*, p. 167 (Edinburgh: John Grant, 1915). *Reliquiæ Celticæ*, ii., pp. 25, 358. John Gillies, *Collection of Poems* (Perth, 1786). *Zeitschrift für Celtische Phil.* (1925), xv. p. 187. *Celtic Review*, vii., p. 94. *Trans. Gael. Soc. Inverness*, xxxii., p. 284.

34 (7). GAELIC PROVERBS

To be published in a later volume.

35 (14). NIGHEAN RÌGH NA FRAINGE
The Daughter of the King of France

See Notes to No. 23 (40) of which this is a very corrupt version. No. 14 appeared in *Béaloideas* (1934), iv., p. 292.

36 (17). A' BHANTRACH, The Widow

Summarized *W. H. Tales*, ii., No. 41, Var. 2. For the Gaelic, see *Béaloideas* (1934), iv., p. 396.

37 (27). NIGHEAN RÌGH FO THUINN
The Daughter of King Under Waves

For the Gaelic, see *An Ròsarnach*, i., p. 211 (Glasgow: MacLaren & Sons, 1917). For a translation, see *W. H. Tales*, iii., No. 86. A tale bearing the same name, but related to No. 52, *W. H. Tales*, ii., is at end of MS. Vol. ix. It is numbered 82.

38 (51). BAILLIDH LUNNAINN
The London Baillie or Provost

Islay has summarized the opening incidents in *W. H. Tales*, i., No. 17*a* (22). Apart from these and apart from a difference in sequence of some of the other incidents, No. 51 is, as Islay says, nearly the same as *W. H. Tales*, No. 17*b*. The Gaelic will appear in *Béaloideas*, viii., No. II.

39 (52). EACHDRAIDH A' CHEATHARNAICH
The Adventures of the Champion

Published *W. H. Tales*, i., No. 17*c*, Version 2. (Version 1 is the one numbered 79 in the Gaelic List.) For a valuable list of versions, see *Gadelica*, i., pp. 188, 204, 304 (Dublin: Hodges, Figgis, 1913).

40 (53 [*b*]). UISDEAN MÓR MACGILLE PHÀDRUIG
Uisdean Mór MacGille Phàdruig

Islay translated this in *W. H. Tales*, i., No. 7, Var. 4. The Gaelic original will appear in *Béaloideas*, June 1939, Vol. ix., No. 1.

ABBREVIATIONS

Am Bàrd. See Camshron, Alasdair.

Am Faclair : Faclair Gàidhlig, a Gaelic Dictionary (Lyminge, Kent : E. MacDonald & Co., 1909). Also spoken of as *Dwelly's Dictionary*.

An Deò Gréine. The Official Magazine of An Comunn Gàidhealach, Glasgow. The title of the magazine was changed in 1923 to *Gàilig*, and afterwards to *An Gàidheal*, q.v.

An Gàidheal. See *An Deò Gréine*. The organ of An Comunn Gàidhealach. Still proceeding. Glasgow. Distinguish from next item.

An Gàidheal, a monthly magazine. Vols. i.-vi., 1873-77. (Published at first in Toronto, afterwards by MacLachlan and Stewart in Glasgow.) Distinguish from preceding item.

An Ròsarnach, Vols. i.-iii. (Glasgow : Alex. MacLaren & Sons, 1917).

An Sgeulaiche, Vols. i.-iii. (Glasgow : Alex. MacLaren & Sons, 1909-11).

Bàrdachd Ghàidhlig. See Watson, Professor W. J.

Cameron, Rev. Alex. *Reliquiæ Celticæ*, Vols. i., ii. (Inverness, 1892-4).

Campbell, John Francis, of Islay. *Popular Tales of the West Highlands orally collected.* 4 vols. Two editions, 1860-62, 1890-93. The pagination of these being different, it is sometimes necessary to quote two page numbers. Also *Leabhar na Féinne*, Heroic Gaelic Ballads collected in Scotland chiefly from 1512 to 1871 (London : Spottiswoode & Co., 1872).

Campbell, Rev. John Gregorson. *Superstitions of the Highlands and Islands of Scotland* (Glasgow : James MacLehose and Sons, 1900). Also *Witchcraft and Second Sight in the Highlands and Islands of Scotland* (Glasgow : James MacLehose and Sons, 1902).

Camshron, Alasdair, Bàrd Thùrnaig, and I. M. Moffatt-Pender. *Am Bàrd* (U. M. Urchardainn agus a Mhac, Dun-Eideann, 1926).

Celtic Annual, 1912-1919, Year Book of Dundee Highland Society.

Celtic Dragon Myth. See Henderson, Rev. Dr George.

Celtic Magazine (Inverness, 1875-88), 13 Vols.

Celtic Monthly (Glasgow, 1892). Still in progress.

Celtic Review, a Quarterly Magazine, Vols. i.-x. (Edinburgh : T. & A. Constable, 1904-16).

Cuairtear nan Gleann, edited by Rev. Dr Norman MacLeod (Glasgow, 1840-43).

Dwelly's Dictionary. See *Am Faclair*.

Folk-Lore Journal (London, 1883-89), 7 Vols.

Folk-Lore. Organ of the Folk-Lore Society, London. In progress.

FFL : Folk-Tales and Fairy Lore. See MacDougall, Rev. James.

Gadelica, *A Journal of Modern-Irish Studies,* edited by Thomas F. O'Rahilly. Vol. i., all published (Dublin : Hodges, Figgis & Co., Ltd., 1912-13).

Guth na Bliadhna, a Quarterly Gaelic Magazine (Glasgow : Alex. MacLaren & Sons).

Henderson, Rev. Dr George. *The Norse Influence on Celtic Scotland* (Glasgow, 1910). Also, *Survivals in Belief among the Celts* (Glasgow, 1911). Also, *The Celtic Dragon Myth* (Edinburgh: John Grant, 1911.)

Hyde, Dr Douglas. *Beside the Fire* (London : David Nutt, 1890).

Inverness Courier, a bi-weekly newspaper (Inverness).

Irische Texte, edited by Stokes and Windisch (Leipzig, 1900).

Larminie, William. *West Irish Folk-Tales and Romances* (London : Eliot Stock, 1898).

L. na F., Leabhar na Féinne. See Campbell, J. F., of Islay.

Macalister, Professor R. A. Stewart. *Temair Breg, Proc. Roy. Irish Acad.,* January 1919.

MacDonald, Keith Norman, M.D. *Puirt-a-beul,* Mouth-Tunes, or Songs for Dancing. Reprinted from the *Oban Times,* 1901.

MacDougall, Rev. James. *Folk-Tales and Fairy Lore in Gaelic and English.* Collected from Oral Tradition. Edited by Rev. George Calder (Edinburgh : John Grant, 1910).

Macfadyen, John. *Sgeulaiche nan Caol* (Glasgow : Archibald Sinclair, 1902).

McKay, J. G. *The Wizard's Gillie* ; ten Gaelic tales and translations from the MS. Collections of the late J. F. Campbell of Islay (London : Saint Catherine Press, 1914).

Mac Talla (a Scottish Gaelic Weekly), 12 Vols. Edited by J. G. MacKinnon (Sydney, Cape Breton, Canada, 1892-1904).

Nicolson, Alexander, M.A., LL.D. *Gaelic Proverbs* (Edinburgh, 1881).

Norse Influence. See Henderson, Rev. Dr George.

Northern Chronicle, a weekly newspaper, Inverness.

Oban Times, a weekly newspaper, Oban.

O'Grady, Standish Hayes. *Silva Gadelica,* 2 Vols. (London : Williams & Norgate, 1892).

Puirt-a-beul. See MacDonald, Keith Norman, M.D.

Rel. Celt. See Cameron, Rev. Alex.

Robertson. The MS. Collections of the late Rev. Charles Moncrieff Robertson, now housed in the National Library, Edinburgh, thanks to the foresight, energy and generosity of Dr W. J. Watson, Professor of Celtic Languages in the University of Edinburgh. Enormous and valuable Collections.

S.C.R. : Scottish Celtic Review, i.-iv. (Glasgow : Robert MacLehose, 1881-85).

Sgeulaiche nan Caol. See Macfadyen, John.

Silva Gad. See O'Grady, Standish Hayes.

Superstitions. See Campbell, Rev. John Gregorson.

Survivals. See Henderson, Rev. Dr George.

Temair Breg. See Macalister, Professor R. A. Stewart.

The Wizard's Gillie. See McKay, J. G.

T.G.S. Inverness : *Transactions of the Gaelic Society of Inverness*, 1870, in progress. This Society has done splendid work, and has gathered together an immense amount of traditions and tales that must otherwise have been lost.

Waifs and Strays *of Celtic Tradition.* 5 Vols. Series initiated and directed by Lord Archibald Campbell (London : David Nutt, 1889-95).

Watson, Professor William J. *Bàrdachd Ghàidhlig* (Inverness, 1918 ; Stirling, 1932). *Rosg Gàidhlig* (Inverness, 1918 ; Glasgow, 1929).

W. H. Tales, *West Highland Tales.* See Campbell, J. F., of Islay.

Witchcraft. See Campbell, Rev. John Gregorson.

Z.C., *Zeitschrift für Celtische Philologie*, i., 1897, in progress (London : David Nutt).

More West Highland Tales

AM PRÌOMH SGEUL

MAR A CHUIREADH AN TUAIRISGEAL MÓR GU BÀS

No. 1.   *Campbell, MS. Vol. viii., No. 106*

BHA rìgh air Eirinn uair, agus bha e a mach aig tulaich, agus choinnich marcaiche aig an tulaich e, 's thuirt e ris, 'Có thusa ?'

'Is mise,' ars esan, 'an Tuairisgeal Og,[1] Mac an Tuairisgeil Mhóir.'

Dh' iarr an Tuairisgeal [Og] air an Rìgh tighinn a chumail cluiche ris am màireach. An là-'r-na-mhàireach, chaidh an Rìgh a dh'iomairt cluiche ris an Tuairisgeal Og. Dh'iomair iad an cluich, agus chaidh an cluich air an Tuairisgeal.

N 2·0·1*   'Tog [buaidh] do chluiche, a Rìgh Eireann,' ars an Tuairisgeal Og.

N 2·6   'Is e buaidh mo chluiche am boirionnach a tha comhla riut fhaotainn.' Fhuair e am boirionnach, agus thug e leis i.

N 831   'Nis,' ars ise ris an Rìgh, 'théid thu a dh'iomairt cluiche ris an Tuairisgeal [Og] am màireach a rithist, agus ma bhuidhneas tu, iarr airson buaidh do chluiche, an fhalaire a tha aige.'

Chaidh an Rìgh an là-'r-na-mhàireach a choinneachadh
N 2·0·1*   an Tuairisgeil [Oig]. Choinnich iad a chéile aig an tulaich. 'An téid thu a dh'iomairt cluiche air tàileasg rium an diugh ?' ars an Tuairisgeal Og.

'Théid,' ars an Rìgh.

Dh'iomair iad an cluich, agus chaidh an cluich air an Tuairisgeal [Og]. 'Tog buaidh do chluiche,' ars an Tuairisgeal Og.

F 531·   [1] The *Tuairisgeal* is a particular species of giant, of the kind called
1·6·3·1*   *Samhanaich*, who lived in caves by the sea-shore, the strongest and coarsest of any, and noted for their clumsiness and unshapeliness.

2

THE CHIEF STORY

HOW THE GREAT TUAIRISGEAL [1] WAS PUT TO DEATH

No. 1.   *[Vol. viii., No. 106]*

THERE was once a King of Erin, who was out of doors one day and had come to a certain hillock, when a rider met him there. 'Who art thou ?' said the King.

'I,' said he, 'am the Young Tuairisgeal,[1] the Son of the Great Tuairisgeal.'

The [Young] Tuairisgeal asked the King to come and gamble with him on the morrow. On the morrow, accordingly, the King went to gamble with the Young Tuairisgeal. They played the game through, and the game went against the Tuairisgeal.

'Take [the winnings of] thy gaming, King of Erin,' N 2·0·1* said the Young Tuairisgeal.

'The stake of my gaming is that I get the young woman N 2·6 whom thou hast there with thee.' He got the woman, and took her away with him.

'Now,' said she to the King, 'to-morrow thou wilt go N 831 again to engage in a gambling with the [Young] Tuairisgeal, and if thou win, demand from him as the stakes of thy gaming, the palfrey he has.'

On the morrow, the King went to meet the [Young] Tuairisgeal. They met each other at the hillock. 'Wilt come and play a game of chess with me to-day ?' said the N 2·0·1* Young Tuairisgeal.

'I will,' said the King.

They played the game through, and the game went against the [Young] Tuairisgeal. 'Take the stakes of thy gaming,' said the Young Tuairisgeal.

'Is e buaidh mo chluiche an fhalaire a tha agad fhaotuinn,' ars an Rìgh. Thug an Tuairisgeal Og an

B 181   fhalaire air cheann do Rìgh Eireann.

Chaidh e dhachaidh. 'Nis,' ars am boirionnach, 'théid thu a dh'iomairt cluiche ris an Tuairisgeal Og am

C 650   màireach, agus buidhnidh e ort, agus cuiridh e mar gheasaibh ort brath a thoirt d'a ionnsuigh, ciod e mar a

H 1388   chaidh a athair, an Tuairisgeal Mór, gu bàs, agus cuiridh thusa mar gheasaibh airsan, e bhi 'na shìneadh air a uilinn

D 5·1   air a' chnoc gus an tig thusa.'

An là-'r-na-mhàireach, chaidh Rìgh Eireann gus an tulaich a chumail cluiche ris an Tuairisgeal Og. Choinnich iad a chéile aig an tulaich.

N 2·0·1*   'An téid thu [a dh'iomairt cluiche air an tàileasg rium an diugh?' ars an Tuairisgeal Og.]

'Théid,' [ars an Rìgh. Chaidh iad anns a' chluich, agus mar bhuaidh mhallachd do'n Rìgh, bhuidhinn an Tuairisgeal Og an cluich an là sin.][1]

'Tog buaidh do chluiche,' thuirt Rìgh Eireann.

H 942*   'Is e buaidh mo chluiche, thusa chur fo gheasaibh,
H 1252   brath a thoirt do m' ionnsuigh, ciod e mar a chuireadh
H 1337   m' athair, an Tuairisgeal Mór, gu bàs, [agus an claidheamh
D 1273   soluis aige a thoirt leat, cuideachd].'
H 951·1*   'Tha mise 'gad chur-sa fo gheasaibh, thu bhi 'nad
Z 85*   shìneadh air t'uilinn air a' chnoc so, gus an till mise.'
D 1273

Chaidh Rìgh Eireann dhachaidh. 'Nis,' thuirt am boirionnach ris, 'théid thu air muin na falaire, agus ruigidh tu rìoghachd na Gréige far am faigh thu a mach mar a chuireadh gu bàs an Tuairisgeal Mór. Chan 'eil duine

B 181·9*   beò 's an rìoghachd nach coinnich thu[2] an uair a dh'aithnicheas iad an fhalaire.'

An là-'r-na-mhàireach, chaidh e air muin na falaire, is ghabh e air falbh. Bha e falbh gus an do ràinig e tigh

---

[1] In order to clear up the meaning, this sentence is interpolated from J. F. Campbell, *W. H. Tales*, i., No. 1.

[2] In 'Morraha,' *West Irish Folk-Tales and Romances*, p. 10, by Wm. Larminie (London, 1898), the advent of the magic steed, Brown Allree, makes the bells

'The stakes of my gaming are that I get that palfrey
of thine,' said the King. The Young Tuairisgeal gave the
King of Erin the palfrey by the bridle (*lit.* the head).   B 181

Home went the King. 'Now,' said the woman,
'to-morrow thou wilt go again to gamble with the Young
Tuairisgeal, but he will defeat thee, and he will lay binding C 650
spells upon thee that thou bring him word as to how his
father, the Great Tuairisgeal, was put to death. And H 1388
thou on thy part, shalt lay binding spells upon him that
he shall lie stretched out on the hillock and propped up D 5·1
on his elbow until thou return.'

On the morrow, the King of Erin went to the hillock
to hold a gaming with the Young Tuairisgeal. They met
each other at the hillock.

'Wilt thou come [and play a game of chess with me N 2·0·1*
to-day?' said the Young Tuairisgeal.]

'I will,' [said the King. They engaged in the game,
but the Young Tuairisgeal won the game that day, and,
for the King, that was indeed a curséd victory.] [1]

'Take the stakes of thy gaming,' said the King of Erin.

'These are the stakes of my gaming—to lay thee under H 942*
binding spells to bring me word how my father, the Great H 1252
Tuairisgeal, was put to death [and to bring his sword of H 1337
light with thee, also].'   D 1273

'Then I lay thee under binding spells, that thou lie H 951·1*
there stretched out on this hillock, and propped up on Z 85*
thine elbow, till I return.'   D 1273

Home went the King of Erin. 'Now,' said the woman
to him, 'thou must mount the palfrey's back, and visit
the kingdom of Greece, and there thou wilt discover how
the Great Tuairisgeal was put to death. There is not a
living man in that kingdom who will not come to meet thee [2] B 181·9*
when they recognize the palfrey.'

On the morrow, the King mounted the palfrey, and
departed. He travelled on till he came to the house of

---

to ring, and the king of the country knows by this that Brown Allree is in the
land. See *Trans. Gael. Soc. Inverness*, xxxiv., p. 101. In No. 106, the people
gather to meet the hero when they recognize the palfrey.

an Ridire Bhàin. Dh'aithnich an Ridire Bàn an fhalaire,
is thàinig e 'na choinnimh.

'Ciod an naidheachd a tha agad? a bheil naidheachd
mo pheathar-sa agad ?' thuirt an Ridire Bàn.

'Tha,' thuirt esan, 'tha i a stigh agam-sa.'

'Fanaidh tu leam-sa a nochd,' thuirt an Ridire Bàn.
Rug an Ridire Bàn air an fhalaire,[1] agus dh'òrduich e a
stigh do'n stabull i, agus thug e Rìgh Eireann leis a stigh
do'n chaisteal. Dh'òrduich e biadh 's deoch a chur air
a bheulaibh. Rinneadh siod. Ghabh e biadh 's deoch,
agus chuir e seachad an oidhche gu toil-inntinneach leis
an Ridìre Bhàn. Moch 'sa mhaduinn, dh'éirich e gu bhi
falbh. Dh'éirich an Ridìre Bàn 'ga fhaicinn air dòigh.
Ghabh e biadh, agus thug iad an fhalaire d'a ionnsuigh.
H 1235   'Nis,' thuirt an Ridire Bàn, 'bidh tu an tigh an Ridire
Fhinn a nochd, agus an uair a chì e an fhalaire, bidh
flath agus fàilte romhad.' Dh'fhàg e fhéin agus an Ridire
Bàn beannachd aig a chéile, is dh'fhalbh e.

Bha e falbh gu luath, sunndach, gun stad, gus an
do ràinig e tigh an Ridire Fhinn. Choinnich an Ridire
Fionn e, agus fhuair e gréim air an fhalaire. 'A bheil
naidheachd mo pheathar agad?' thuirt an Ridire Fionn.
'Tha sin agam; dh'fhàg mi a stigh agam fhéin i,' thuirt
Rìgh Eireann. 'Fanaidh tu leam fhéin a nochd,' ars an
Ridire Fionn. 'Fanaidh,' arsa Rìgh Eireann. [Dh'òrduich
an Ridire Fionn an fhalaire a stigh do'n stabull, agus thug
e Rìgh Eireann leis a stigh do'n chaisteal. Dh'òrduich e
biadh is deoch a chur air a bheulaibh. Rinneadh siod.
Ghabh e biadh is deoch, agus chuir e seachad an oidhche
gu toil-inntinneach leis an Ridire Fhionn]. Moch 'sa'
mhaduinn, [dh'éirich e gu bhi falbh. Dh'éirich an
Ridire Fionn g'a fhaicinn air dòigh. Ghabh e biadh,
agus thug iad an fhalaire d'a ionnsuigh. 'Nis,' thuirt an
Ridire Fionn,] 'bidh tu an tigh an Ridire Dhuibh a nochd,
agus innsidh am fear sin duit ciod e is còir duit a dhèanamh.
An uair a chì e an fhalaire, bidh flath agus fàilte romhad.'

---

[1] No. 203, the second variant of 'The Chief Story,' may be said to begin
at this juncturė.   For the last five words of this page, see p. 27.

the Fair Knight. The Fair Knight recognized the palfrey, and came forward to meet the King.

'What news hast thou? hast thou tidings of my sister?' * said the Fair Knight.

'I have,' said he, 'I have her at home in my house.'

'Thou must stay with me to-night,' said the Fair Knight. The Fair Knight laid hold of the palfrey,[1] and ordered it into the stable, and took the King of Erin with him into the castle. He ordered food and drink to be set before him. This was done. The King ate and drank, and passed the night very pleasantly with the Fair Knight. Early in the morning, the King rose to depart. The Fair Knight also rose to see that he was well provided for. The King took food, and then they brought him the palfrey. 'Now,' said the Fair Knight, 'thou wilt be in the house H 1235 of the White Knight to-night, and when he sees the palfrey, thou wilt be hailed as a chief, and welcome will await thee.' The King and the Fair Knight left farewell blessings with each other, and the King went off.

On and on he travelled, swiftly and cheerily, and never a stay did he make till he came to the house of the White Knight. The White Knight met him, and laid hold of the palfrey. 'Hast thou tidings of my sister?' said the White Knight. 'That have I; I left her at home in my own house,' said the King of Erin. 'Thou shalt stay with me to-night,' said the White Knight. 'I will,' answered the King of Erin. [The White Knight ordered the palfrey into the stable, and took the King of Erin with him into the castle. He ordered food and drink to be set before him. This was done. The King ate and drank, and passed the night very pleasantly with the White Knight.] Early in the morning, [the King rose to go. The White Knight rose also to see that he was well provided for. The King took food, and then they brought him the palfrey. 'Now,' said the White Knight,] 'to-night thou wilt be in the house of the Black Knight, and he is the one who will tell thee what thou oughtest to do. When he sees the

---

* Story appears to be defective here as there has been no hint that the woman won at gaming had a brother.

Dh'fhàg e fhéin agus an Ridire Fionn beannachd aig a
chéile, agus chaidh e air muin na falaire, agus dh'fhalbh e.

Bha e falbh gu luath, sunndach, gun stad, gun fhuras,
gus an do ràinig e tigh an Ridire Dhuibh. [Dh'aithnich
an Ridire Dubh an fhalaire, agus thàinig e 'na choinnimh.]
'A bheil naidheachd mo pheathar agad?' [thuirt an
Ridire Dubh.[1]
'Tha sin agam; dh'fhàg mi a stigh agam fhéin i,' thuirt
Rìgh Eireann. 'Fanaidh tu leam fhéin a nochd,' ars an
Ridire Dubh. 'Fanaidh,' arsa Rìgh Eireann. Rug an
Ridire Dubh air an fhalaire, agus dh'òrduich e a stigh do'n
stabull i, agus thug e Rìgh Eireann leis a stigh do'n chaisteal.
Dh'òrduich e biadh is deoch a chur air a bheulaibh.
Rinneadh siod. Ghabh e biadh 's deoch, agus chuir e
seachad an oidhche gu toil-inntinneach leis an Ridire
Dhubh.] Moch 'sa' mhaduinn [dh'érich e gu bhi falbh.
Dh'éirich an Ridire Dubh 'ga fhaicinn air dòigh. Ghabh
e biadh, agus thug iad an fhalaire d'a ionnsuigh].

'Nis,' thuirt an Ridire Dubh, 'tha abhainn romhad
mun ruig thu rìoghachd na Gréige. Bheir thu leat naoidh
botuil fhìona, agus naoidh muilnean cruithneachd, agus
an uair a ruigeas tu an abhainn, bheir thu do'n fhalaire
trì muilnean cruithneachd agus trì botuil fhìona, agus
cìridh tu an aghaidh na gaoisid i agus leis a' ghaoisid,
mura leum i an abhainn, bheir thu tuilleadh dhi gus an
leum i i.' Dh'fhàg e fhéin agus an Ridire Dubh beannachd
aig a chéile, is ghabh e air falbh.

Bha e falbh gu luath, sunndach, gun stad, gun fhuras,
gus an do ràinig e an abhainn. An uair a ràinig e an
abhainn, thàinig e bhàrr na falaire, agus thug e dhi trì
botuil fhìona agus trì muilnean cruithneachd, agus chìr

Z 71·1

Z 71·6
Z 71·1

D 1835·2*
D 1335·1

---

[1] The hero's newly won bride is sister to all three knights, in this version,
and in the Tiree version. She is the daughter of the Black Knight in the
next version.

palfrey, thou wilt be hailed as a chief, and welcome will await thee.' The King and the White Knight left farewell blessings with each other, and the King mounted the palfrey, and was off.

On and on he travelled, swiftly and cheerily, never stopping nor taking ease till he came to the house of the Black Knight. [The Black Knight recognized the palfrey, and came forward to meet the King.] 'Hast thou tidings of my sister?' [said the Black Knight.[1] ＿ ＿ 3 71·1

'That have I; I left her at home in my own house,' said the King of Erin. 'Thou shalt stay with me to-night,' said the Black Knight. 'I will,' said the King of Erin. The Black Knight laid hold of the palfrey, and ordered her into the stable, and took the King of Erin with him into the castle. He ordered food and drink to be set before him. This was done. The King ate and drank, and passed the night very pleasantly with the Black Knight.] Early in the morning [the King rose to go. The Black Knight rose also to see that he was well provided for. The King took food, and then they brought him the palfrey.]

'Now,' said the Black Knight, 'there is a river before thee or ever thou come to the kingdom of Greece. Thou art to take with thee nine bottles of wine, and nine wheaten ＿ Z 71·6 loaves, and when thou arrivest at the river, thou shalt give the palfrey three loaves of bread and three bottles ＿ Z 71·1 of wine, and thou shalt comb her hair the wrong way ＿ D 1835·2* and then the right way, and if she will not then leap the ＿ D 1335·1 river, thou must give her more [food and combing] until she does leap it.' The King and the Black Knight then left farewell blessings with each other, and the King set forth.

On and on he travelled, swiftly and cheerily, never stopping nor taking ease until he came to the river. When he arrived there, he dismounted and gave the palfrey three bottles of wine and three wheaten loaves, and combed her

e an aghaidh na gaoisid agus leis a' ghaoisid i.[1] An uair
a ghabh i siod, chaidh e air a muin, is thug e làmh air an
abhainn a leum, is cha do rinn i ach a ceann a thumadh
innte. Thàinig e a nuas, agus thug e dhi trì botuil fhìona
agus trì muilnean cruithneachd eile, agus chìr e [an aghaidh
na gaoisid agus leis a' ghaoisid i]. Agus chaidh e air a
muin a rithist, agus dh'fhiach e a rithisd ris an abhainn a
leum, is cha do rinn i ach dol d'a broinn innte. Thàinig
e a nuas a rithist, agus thug e dhi trì botuil [fhìona agus trì
muilnean cruithneachd eile], agus chìr e [an aghaidh na
gaoisid agus leis a' ghaoisid i.] Agus chaidh e air a muin
a rithisd, agus dh'fhiach e a rithist ris an abhainn a leum,
agus chaidh i thairis oirre, an turus so.

<table>
<tr><td>B 181·9*</td><td>Chunnaic Rìgh Og [2] na Gréige an fhalaire a' leum na
h-aibhne, agus chaidh [e] 'nan coinnimh.</td></tr>
<tr><td>B 401</td><td>[Chunnaic an fhalaire a' tighinn e, agus is math a
dh'aithnich i ciod e bha bhuaidh.] 'Thoir dha mise airson
brath fhaotuinn mar a chaidh an Tuairisgeal Mór [a chur]
gu bàs,' thuirt an fhalaire ri Rìgh Eireann.</td></tr>
</table>

Thug e an fhalaire do Rìgh na Gréige, agus thug Rìgh
na Gréige brath dha c'àite an robh an duine chuir an
Tuairisgeal Mór gu bàs.

Chaidh e a stigh do'n tigh a leig Rìgh na Gréige fhaicinn
da, agus bha seann duine an sin 'na laighe ann an creathaill.
F 571·4* Dh'éirich e, agus dh'fhalbh e leis. Cha do stad iad gus
an do ràinig iad tigh a bha ann an gleann. Dh'fhosgail
am bodach an dorus,[3] is chaidh iad a stigh. Thug e
cathair òir do Rìgh na h-Eireann, is shuidh e fhéin air
F 786·1* cathair airgid, is thòisich e air innseadh mar a chaidh an
Tuairisgeal [Mór a chur] gu bàs.[4]

<hr>

[1] In MS. *leis a 'ghaoisid agus an aghaidh na gaoisid*, with the hair and against
the hair. This is probably a mere clerical error : for the Black Knight's
instructions were to do the combing the wrong way first and the right way
afterwards. In other tales also, where combing the magic filly occurs, the
order of procedure is to comb the hair the wrong way first. See *W. H. Tales*, ii.,
No. 51 ; *Celtic Review*, v., p. 264 ; Wm. Larminie, p. 13.

[2] The only place in this version where there is mention of a *Young* King
of Greece. In other versions the Young King purchases the palfrey, not

hair the wrong way, and then the right way.[1] When she had taken all that (wine, loaves, and the combing) he mounted her back, and made an attempt to leap the river, but all she did was to dip her head in it—nothing more. He dismounted, and gave her three more bottles of wine and three more wheaten loaves, and combed [her hair the wrong way and then the right way]. Again he mounted her back, and again he tried to leap the river, but all she did was to go up to her belly in it. Down he came again, and gave her three more bottles [of wine and three more wheaten loaves], and combed [her hair the wrong way and then the right way]. Then once more he mounted her back and tried again to leap the river, and this time she went over it.

The Young [2] King of Greece saw the palfrey leaping the river, and set off to meet them.   B 181·9*

[The palfrey saw him coming, and well she knew what he wanted.] 'Thou must hand me over, thou must give me to him in exchange for information as to how the Great Tuairisgeal was put to death,' said the palfrey to the King of Erin.   B 401

The King of Erin gave the palfrey to the King of Greece accordingly, and the King of Greece informed him where the man was who had put the Great Tuairisgeal to death.

He went into a house which the King of Greece had pointed out to him, and there [he found] an old man lying in a cradle. The old man arose, and set forth with him. They never stopped till they came to a house situated in a certain glen. The old man opened the door, and they went in. He gave the King of Erin a golden chair, but seated himself in a silver one, and then did he begin to tell how the [Great] Tuairisgeal was [put] to death.[4]   F 571·4*   F 786·1*

by selling a story but by selling the man who tells it, who is his own ancestor, and a very remote one.—*Trans. Gael. Soc. Inverness*, xxxiv., p. 71. It is to be noted that this ancient person is found in a house separate from other houses.

[3] MS. *dorusd.*

[4] Version No. 106 is very corrupt in this paragraph—so much so as to be misleading. See the corresponding paragraph in No. 203, which puts a very different colour on the incidents of the gold and silver chairs, p. 34.

'Sgeul is cruaidhe chuala cluas a tha mise dol a dh'innseadh duit-se. Bha aig Rìgh na Gréige triuir mhac, agus dh'eug a bhean, agus phòs e bean eile. Bha a' Bhanrighinn Og 'na droch mhuime: agus rinn i triuir mhadaidh-allaidh de thriuir chloinn an Rìgh.[1] Chaidh iad an sin gu beinn.

Thuirt ise gun robh na madaidh-allaidh a' marbhadh nan caorach aice-se, 's gum b'éiginn am marbhadh.

Chuir i mìolchoin agus geurchoin air falbh gu ruig a' bheinn. Lean na mìolchoin iad, agus mharbh iad dithis diubh. Chaidh an t-aon a bha beò ann an creig, ann an nead Gire-mhìnich,[2] agus bha e an sin deich laithean. Bha soitheach a' dol seachad, agus thàinig i teann air a' chreig. Rinn e burral mór caoinidh an uair a chunnaic e an soitheach. An uair a chuala an caibtinn e, chuir e dithis[3] làmhan le geòla dh'a iarraidh. Chunnaic iad e a' cur a theangaidh[4] a mach, agus thug iad a' gheòla fo'n àite anns an robh e. An uair a chunnaic esan a' gheòla a' tighinn foidhe, leig e [e] fhéin sìos leis a' chreig, agus thuit e innte. Dh'fhalbh iad an sin leis a' gheòla chun an t-soithich. Lean a' ghire-mhìneach an soitheach, ach rug a h-aon de na làmhan air handspike 'na dhórn, agus chum e air falbh i. Thug iad suas air bòrd e. Thug iad brot da, agus cha bheanadh e dha.[5] Thug iad biadh ceart da, agus dh'ith e rud deth sin.

Ann an rìoghachd eile anns a' Ghréig, chaidh an soitheach gu tìr. Is e bràthair athar dà-san [do'n mhadadh-allaidh] a bha 'na rìgh an sin. Thug bràthair a athar o mhaighstir an t-soithich e, agus thug e leis gus an teaghlach aige fhéin e, agus bha e air ùr-phòsadh.

Bha a bhean [bean an Rìgh] leatromach anns an am, agus an ùine ghoirid, thuisleadh i air leanabh nighinn. Bha trì mnathan-glùine a' feitheamh air a' Bhan-righinn agus air an leanabh.[6] Thàinig Cràg Mhór a stigh air mullach an tighe,

[1] After the children have been turned into wolves, the King ought to miss them and to wonder where they had gone. It is a significant fact that a king seldom misses or mourns for such of his children as have been metamorphosed, though he is usually concerned about those who are stolen from him.

[2] MS. Cri-mhinich, Creveenach, W. H. Tales, ii., No. 44. Gìre-Mhìneach in this tale a few sentences further on. Cri-bhìnneach, in No. 203, p. 34. Other forms are Cro mhineach, Ghri Mhineach, Greeveen-ach, names which Islay supposed meant a griffin, W. H. Tales, iii., 252 or 237. A' ghré-bhinneach, Trans. Gael. Soc. Inverness, xxv., p. 242. This huge bird is probably own brother to the carrying eagle, for which see W. H. Tales, i., Nos. 9, 16.

D 683·2
S 31
D 113·1

R 322*

D 686·1*

G 261·1

B 31·1

'A tale more painful than ear ever heard am I now going
to tell thee. There was once a King of Greece who had three D 683·2
sons. His wife died, and he married another. The Young S 31
Queen was a bad step-mother: and she turned the King's three D 113·1
children into three wolves.[1]

At that, the three fled to a mountain.

She told [people] that there were three wild wolves killing
the sheep belonging to her, and that these wolves must be
killed.

She sent blood-hounds and terriers off to the mountain.
The blood-hounds followed the wolves, and killed two of them.
The one who survived went to a rock, and got into the nest
of a Geere-veenach, and stayed there for ten days. A ship R 322*
went by, and passed close to the rock. The wolf gave a great
howl of grief when he saw the ship. When the captain heard
him, he sent two of the hands in a yawl to fetch him. They
saw the wolf putting out his tongue,[4] and they brought the
yawl close in and under the place where he was. When he
saw the yawl coming close in under him, the wolf let himself
fall down the rock, and into the yawl. They then took the
yawl back to the ship. The Geere-veenach followed the vessel,
but one of the hands snatched up a handspike in his fist, and
kept her away. Then they fetched the wolf on board. They
gave him some broth, but he would not touch that.[5] Then D 686·1*
they gave him the proper food (for dogs), and of that he ate
some.

It was in another kingdom situated in Greece, that the
vessel came to land. It was his [the wolf's] own father's
brother who was King there. His father's brother, who was
newly married, took the wolf from the master of the ship, and
brought him to his own household.

His [the King's] wife was pregnant at the time, and in a
short time she was delivered of a girl-child. There were three
midwives waiting upon the Queen and upon the child.[6] In
came a Great Claw-like Hand [7] through the roof of the house, G 261·1

But in No. 11 Cro-mhinich is a talking bird, small enough to carry about with
one in a box. See p. 141.   [3] MS. dithisd.   [4] bhial, mouth, in MS.
   [5] The enchanted hound always refuses food that was not thought suitable
for animals, such as broth, thereby showing his human sense, as in the next
story. See also Norse Influence, p. 301.
   [6] The mysterious music that sweeps round the house and puts everyone D 1364·24
in it (including the midwives but not the mother) to sleep, ought to be
mentioned here. But it is not mentioned, nor in the next version.
   [7] Parallel to the 'hand' incident in the Mabinogi of Pwyll, Prince of Dyved.
See also Waifs, ii., p. 62 ; ibid., iii., p. 5.

agus rug i air an leanabh, agus thug i air falbh e. Cha robh
fios aig na mnathan-glùine ciod e dhèanadh iad, a thaobh
gun do leig iad air falbh an leanabh. Dh'fhalbh iad, agus

K 2155·1 mharbh iad isean coilich, agus shuath iad an fhuil ri a fhiaclan-
san. Thuirt iad ri bràthair a athar gun d'ith e an leanabh,
agus gum bu chòir a losgadh.

Thuirt bean bhràthair a athar leigeil leis [1] gus am biodh ise
leatromach a rithist, agus gum faicteadh ciod e mar a bhiodh.
Ann an ùine, dh'fhàs i leatromach a rithist, agus bha leanabh
gille aice. Bha na mnathan-glùine feitheamh oirre fhéin, agus
air an leanabh. Cha do smuainich iad mar a thachair roimhe.[2]
Thàinig a' Chràg a stigh air mullach an tighe, agus thug i

G 261·1 leatha an leanabh. Mharbh na mnathan-glùine isean coilich
mar a rinn iad roimhe, agus bhuail iad am basan, agus ghlaodh
iad gun d'ith am madadh maol [3] an leanabh. Bha e an so ri
a chur gu bàs co dhiùbh.

Thuirt bràthair a athar gun rachadh e do'n cheardaich,
is gum faigheadh e ceangal iaruinn a dhèanamh dha, is gun
leigeadh iad leis air an t-siubhal ud fhathast. Chaidh bràthair
a athar do'n cheardaich, agus thug e air a' ghobha lomhainn
làidir iaruinn a dhèanamh, agus chuir e siod air-san. Ann an
ùine, thuislicheadh a' Bhan-righinn a rithist. Bha na mnathan-
glùine feitheamh oirre fhéin, agus air an leanabh mar a b'
àbhaist. Cha robh smuaineachadh aca mar a thachair roimhe.
Thàinig a' Chràg a stigh air mullach an tighe, is thug i leatha

G 261·1 an leanabh. Chunnaic esan a' Chràg. Bhrist e an lomhainn
iaruinn, agus leum e a dh'ionnsuigh na Cràige, agus ghearr e
leis i le a fhiaclan [bho'n ghualainn].

[Thuit a' Chràg is e fhéin a nuas air an ùrlar, is mun do
dhùisg e as a' phairileis sin, chuir an Tuairisgeal Mór a bha
a muigh, a' Chràg eile a stigh, is thug e leis an leanabh. A'
Chràg a ghearr e leis, shlaod e a stigh fo'n leabaidh, is chuir e

H 105·3* ann an soitheach i. Mharbh na mnathan-glùine isean coilich,
is bhuail iad am basan, is ghlaodh iad gun d'ith am madadh
an leanabh.] [4]

Bha e nis gu bhi air a losgadh, co dhiùbh. An là-'r-na-
mhàireach, bha iad a' fadadh teine airson a losgaidh, is bha

---

[1] In some versions of this incident, the bereaved mother observes the
Claw-like Hand stealing away the child, but is prevented by some taboo of
silence from disclosing anything. She probably witnessed the theft in this
tale too, and hence her befriending of the wolf.

[2] MS. *roimhid*.

[3] The only mention in this version of the animal being crop-eared. See
p. 37.

which seized the child, and took it away. The midwives did
not know what to do, for it was they who had let the child go.
They went, and killed a young cockerel, and rubbed the blood   K 2155·1
upon the wolf's teeth. They told his father's brother that the
wolf had eaten the child, and that it ought to be burnt.

But his father's brother's wife said that the wolf should be
let alone [1] until she should be pregnant again, and that then
they would see what would happen. In time, she became
pregnant again, and had a man-child. The mid-wives were
waiting upon her and upon the child. They never took any
thought about what had happened before. In through the
roof of the house came the Claw-like Hand and took the   G 261·1
child away. The midwives killed a young cockerel as they
had done before, and then clapping their hands (in grief),
cried out that the crop-eared [3] wolf had eaten the child. So
now in any case, the wolf was to be put to death.

But his [the wolf's] father's brother said that he would go
to the smithy, and have an iron fastening made for him, and
that they would forgive him on this occasion also. So his
father's brother went to the smithy, and got the smith to make
a strong iron leash, with which he fastened him. In course
of time, the Queen was delivered again. The mid-wives were
attending upon her and the child as usual. They never took
a thought about what had happened before. In through the
roof of the house came the Claw-like Hand and took the   G 261·1
child away. But the wolf saw it. And breaking the iron
leash, he leaped at the thing, and biting it through with his
teeth, tore it off [from the shoulder].

[He and the Claw-like Hand fell down on the floor, and
before he could awake from his stunned condition, the Great
Tuairisgeal, the giant who was outside, put in his other Claw-
like Hand, and took away the child. The wolf dragged the
Claw-like Hand he had bitten off under the bed, and put it   H 105·3*
in a vessel. The midwives killed a cockerel, beat their palms,
and shouted that the wolf had eaten the child.] [4]

He was now to be burnt in any case. On the morrow,
they began kindling a fire to burn him, and he was hiding under

---

[4] This paragraph, adapted from the Islay version (*Trans. Gael. Soc.
Inverness*, xxv., p. 224), is inserted here in order to clear up subsequent points,
which otherwise would be unintelligible. In the Islay and Tiree versions,
in the next, No. 203 (and also in the related tales, *Waifs and Strays*, iii., p. 5;
iv., p. 206), the Giant puts down his second hand and carries off the third
child, and must have done so in this version also, to judge from what follows.

esan a' dol fo'n chleòc aig bràthair a athar. [Thug e a' bheinn
air.] An uair a chunnaic e gun robh an teine deas airson e

H 105·3* fhéin a chur ann, thàinig e dhachaidh, agus thug e a' Chràg
a mach á soitheach is chuir e air beulaibh bhràthair a athar i.[1]
'Tha sin ag innseadh gur tusa bha dìleas domhsa,' arsa
bràthair a athar. Cha robh iomradh an so air a losgadh.

Fhuair bràthair a athar geòla an là-'r-na-mhàireach, agus
chuir e a dh'ionnsuigh na fairge i. Chunnaic e eilean, agus
chaidh e gu ruig an t-eilean. Chaidh e air tìr, agus chunnaic
e caisteal air an eilean. Ràinig e an caisteal, agus chaidh a
stigh. Ciod e chunnaic e, ach an Tuairisgeal Mór 'na chadal,
is a chlann fhéin còmhla ris. Chunnaic e [an] claidheamh
D 1081 soluis [2] air sgeilp. Rug e air a' chlaidheamh sholuis, agus
D 1645·4 ghearr e an sgornan aige, agus chuir e an ceann bhàrr a'
D 1254 mhuineil aige.[3]   Fhuair e slacan druidheachd anns a' chaisteal.
Thug e leis a thriuir chloinne agus an claidheamh soluis, agus
H 1337 an slacan druidheachd, is ceann an Tuairisgeil Mhóir, is chuir
R 169·3 e anns a' gheòla iad. Thill e dhachaidh.
An uair a ràinig e tìr, choinnich am madadh-allaidh e.
Bhuail e an slacan-druidheachd air, agus dh'fhàs e 'na òganach
D 712·3 brèagh, sgiamhach. An uair a dh'fhàs e 'na òganach brèagh,
D 771·4 sgiamhach, thuirt bràthair a athar ris, 'Is tusa Rìgh na Gréige.'

An là-'r-na-mhàireach, dh'fhalbh bràthair a athar agus e
fhéin, agus ràinig iad rìoghachd na Gréige. Mharbh iad a
h-uile duine anns a' Ghréig a chuir làmh 'nan aghaidh, agus
Q 414 loisg iad a' mhuime. Chrùnadh e 'na rìgh air a' Ghréig an
latha sin.[4]
Falbh ! fiach am faigh sinn ceann an Tuairisgeil Mhóir.'

Chaidh iad gu bad luachrach, agus bha coire fo'n
bhad luachrach,[5] agus bha ceann an Tuairisgeil Mhóir
anns a' choire. Spìon am bodach a nìos e, is shìn e do
Rìgh Eireann e, is thug e dha an claidheamh soluis leis—

---

[1] Why the Were-wolf did not bring the Claw-like Hand out till the fire
was ready, does not appear. It is probable that some incident has been
lost which related that the execution of the Were-wolf was delayed, and
explained why it was so delayed.
[2] MS. *soluisd*.
[3] Observe that in this version it is not the Were-wolf but the Were-wolf's
uncle who slays the Giant.

the cloak of his father's brother. [Then he fled to the hill.]
When he perceived that the fire was now ready for him to be
thrown on to it, he came back home, fetched the Claw-like
Hand out of the vessel and placed it before his father's brother.[1] H 105·3*

'That shows that it was thou who wert faithful to me,'
said his father's brother. There was now no mention of burning
him.

His father's brother got a yawl the next day, and put out
to sea. He saw an island, and went to it. Upon going ashore,
he saw a castle in the island. He made for the castle, and
went in. What should he see there, but the Great Tuairisgeal, D 1081
asleep, and his own children along with him. He saw [the
or a ?] sword of light on a shelf. He seized the sword of light, D 1645·4
cut the Tuairisgeal's throat, and struck his head from off his D 1254
neck.[3] In the castle he found a magic wand. He took his H 1337
three children, the sword of light, the magic wand, and the
head of the Great Tuairisgeal, and put them on board the R 169·3
yawl. Then he returned home.

When he returned to land, the wolf met him. The King
struck him with the magic wand, and he turned into a handsome D 712·3
and comely youth. When he had become a handsome and D 771·4
comely youth, his father's brother said to him, 'Thou art the
King of Greece.'

On the morrow, he and his father's brother set forth, and
arrived in the kingdom of Greece. They killed every man in
Greece who raised a hand against them, and they burnt the Q 414
stepmother. He [the late wolf] was crowned King over Greece
that day.[4]

Come ! let us go over, and see if we can find the head of
the Great Tuairisgeal.'

They went over to a clump of rushes. Underneath
the clump of rushes [5] there was a cauldron, and in the
cauldron was the head of the Great Tuairisgeal. With
a heave, the old man lugged it up out of the cauldron,
and handed it to the King of Erin, and with it he gave him

---

[4] What became of the Were-wolf's father, who was King of Greece at the
opening of this inset story, does not appear.

[5] 'There is something mysterious about rushes. The fairies are found in
a bush of rushes ; the great cauldron of the Feen is hidden under a bush of
rushes ; and in a great many other instances (*Tom Luacharach* [a tuft of rushes])
appears.'—*W. H. Tales*, intro., xcvi. or lxxxviii.

H 1337 'Abair ris an Tuairisgeal Og,' thuirt esan, 'gur mise a mharbh an Tuairisgeal Mór !' [1]

Thug e leis an ceann is an claidheamh soluis. Choinnich an fhalaire aig abhainn na Gréige e. Chaidh e air muin na falaire, agus leum i an abhainn. Bha e an tigh an Ridire Dhuibh an oidhche sin, agus fhuair e gabhail roimhe gu maith ann. Chuir e fhéin is an Ridire Dubh seachad an oidhche gu h-aighearach, sunndach, le h-òl, is le ceòl is le h-itheadh. Anns a' mhaduinn, dh'éirich e, is ghabh e air falbh, is bha e an àth-oidhche an tigh an Ridire Fhinn, agus cha b'ann a bu mhiosa a fhuair e gabhail roimhe. Anns a' mhaduinn dh'éirich e agus ghabh e air falbh, agus bha e, an treas oidhche, an tigh an Ridire Bhàin. Ma fhuair e gabhail roimhe gu maith aig an dà Ridire eile, fhuair e gabhail roimhe gun taing cho maith aig an Ridìre Bhàn. Chuir iad seachad [an oidhche gu h-aighearach, sunndach, le h-òl is le ceòl is le h-itheadh. Anns a' mhaduinn dh'éirich e].

'A nis,' thuirt an Ridìre Bàn ris, 'an uair a ruigeas tu, gheibh thu an Tuairisgeal Og air tuiteam 'na chnàmhan air a' chnoc. Eubh gun tàinig thu—eubh a rithist gun

E 55·1·1* tàinig thu—eubh an treas uair gun tàinig thu. Eirichidh e an sin air a uilinn air a' chnoc, agus iarraidh e claidheamh a athar a thoirt da.[2] Sìnidh tu an claidheamh da, is an am a shìnidh da, cuiridh tu an ceann deth, air neò, is tu fhéin fear saoghail ghoirid.' Dh'fhàg e fhéin agus an Ridire Bàn beannachd aig a chéile.

---

[1] The old man found in the cradle, who has been reciting the inset tale, here says that it was he who slew the Giant. He must therefore be the Were-wolf's uncle. In the other four Scottish versions it is the Were-wolf himself who slays the Giant and recites the inset story, and this is the more likely course of events. However in this version, the old man drops out of the story at this point without any apology, though in two other versions he is thrown, at the end of his recital, either into a boiling cauldron or into a fire.—The return journey. Leaping the river on the return journey, and revisiting the three knights, occur in this version only. And even in this version, the incidents of meeting the Young King of Greece, of giving the palfrey food and of combing her, are not mentioned in connection with the return journey.—In the Eigg version, the palfrey escapes from her purchaser in order to succour the hero, and comes to him before the Old Were-wolf King begins his tale. Her brother, the great black horse, also appears in that version, and in *W. H. Tales*, i., No. 1.

the sword of light—'Tell the Young Tuairisgeal,' said he, H 1337
'that it was I who slew the Great Tuairisgeal.' [1]

The King of Erin, taking the head and the sword with
him, departed. At the river of Greece, he met the palfrey.
He mounted her back, and over the river she sprang.
The same evening he was in the house of the Black Knight,
and right hospitably was he treated there. He and the
Black Knight spent the night gaily and merrily, with
drinking and with music and with feasting. In the
morning, the King arose and set out, and the next evening
he was in the house of the White Knight, and was treated
there no less hospitably. In the morning he rose and
departed, and the third evening he was in the house of the
Fair Knight. If he was treated hospitably by the other
two Knights, he was certainly treated every whit as well
in the house of the Fair Knight. They passed [the night
gaily and merrily, with drinking, with music, and with
feasting. In the morning the King arose].

'Now,' said the Fair Knight, 'when thou comest to the
end of thy journey thou wilt find that the Young Tuairisgeal
has become a mere heap of bones on the hillock. Shout
at him that thou hast come—shout again that thou hast
come—shout the third time that thou hast come. He E 55·1·1*
will then raise himself up [2] on his elbow on the hillside,
and demand that the sword of his father be given to him.
Do thou then hand him the sword; but when doing so,
strike off his head; otherwise, it is thou who wilt get short
shrift.' The King and the Fair Knight then left farewell
blessings with each other.

---

[2] In No. 2 (MS. vol. viii., No 203) instructions for resuscitating and then
killing the Young Giant are given by the Were-wolf, not by the Fair Knight.
In other versions of the resuscitating incident the hero, before killing his
enemy, always faithfully relates the story he had been sent to get, being bound
to do so by the tenor of the spells laid upon him. Whereas in No. 1 (MS.
vol. viii., No. 106) and No. 2 (MS. vol. viii., No. 203) the hero only shouts at the
enemy, and relates nothing. But it is quite possible to suppose that the incident
of relating the story has been forgotten, while the incident of the shouting has
been preserved, and that in more ancient versions the hero related his story
over his enemy's remains, and gave the shouts either at the end of it, or at
various times during the recital.

E 55·1·1

Ràinig e an cnoc far an robh an Tuairisgeal Og. Dh'eubh e ris tri uairean gun tàinig e. Air an treas uair, dh'éirich an Tuairisgeal [Og] air a uilinn, agus dh'iarr e claidheamh a athar air. Shìn e dha an claidheamh, agus an uair a bha e 'ga shìneadh dha, chuir e an ceann deth.

H 1385·3

Chaidh e an so dhachaidh, agus an uair a ràinig e, cha robh bad de'n mhnaoi aige.

Dh'fhalbh e air tòir na mnatha, agus ghabh e air aghaidh gus an do ràinig e Seobhag Sùilghorm Shliabh Brat. Chuir Seobhag Sùilghorm Shliabh Brat e a dh'fhuireach leis an oidhche sin, is thuirt e gum bu mhaith an aoidheachd leis e bhi a stigh, seach am Fuamhaire Mór [1] is aobharrach a mhnatha is a leannain aige. Dh'fhuirich e an oidhche sin an tigh Seobhag Sùilghorm Shliabh Brat.

B 459·1*

Anns a' mhaduinn, an uair a bha e a'falbh, thuirt Seobhag Sùilghorm Shliabh Brat ris, 'Ma thig càs sam bith ort, cuimhnich orm-sa is bidh mi agad.' Dh'fhàg e beannachd aig an t-Seobhaig, is dh'fhalbh e.

An am na h-oidhche ràinig e tigh Madadh Gearr Glas na Coille Uaine. Chuir Madadh Gearr Glas na Coille Uaine a stigh e, is thuirt e gum bu mhaith an aoidheachd leis e bhi aige seach [am Fuamhaire Mór is aobharrach a mhnatha 's a leannain aige. Dh'fhuirich e an oidhche sin an tigh Madadh Gearr Glas na Coille Uaine. Anns a' mhaduinn, an uair a bha e falbh, thuirt Madadh Gearr Glas na Coille Uaine ris, 'Ma thig càs sam bith ort,

B 421

cuimhnich ormsa is bidh mi agad.'] Dh'fhàg e beannachd [aig a' Mhadadh, is dh'fhalbh e.]

An am na h-oidhche, ràinig e Dóbhran Sruth an t-Siubhail. Chuir [Dóbhran Sruth an t-Siubhail a stigh e, is thuirt e gum bu mhaith an aoidheachd leis e bhi aige a stigh seach am Fuamhaire Mór is aobharrach a mhnatha is a leannain aige. Dh'fhuirich e an oidhche sin an tigh

---

[1] Presumably, the Hawk had entertained the kidnapping Giant the previous night, as in a corresponding incident in W. H. Tales, i., No. 1, and in the next, p. 45. See also Waifs, iii., p. 106.

The King came to the hill where the Young Tuairisgeal lay. Three times did he shout at him that he had come. E 55·1·1 At the third shout, the [Young] Tuairisgeal sat up on his elbow, and desired him to give him his father's sword. The King handed him the sword, but when in the act of doing so, struck off his head.

Then he [the King] went home, but when he arrived, H 1385·3 not a trace of his wife could he find.

He went off in pursuit of his wife, and pressed on till he came to the house of the Blue-eyed Hawk of Slieve Brat. The Blue-eyed Hawk of Slieve Brat invited him to stay with him that night, and said that he thought the King a much better subject for hospitality than the Great Giant [1] who had had with him the King's prospective wife and lover. The King stayed that night in the house of the Blue-eyed Hawk of Slieve Brat.

In the morning when he was going, the Blue-eyed Hawk of Slieve Brat said to him, 'If any crisis come upon thee, remember me and I will be with thee.' He left a farewell B 459·1* blessing with the Hawk, and went off.

At night he came to the house of the Short-tailed Gray Hound of the Green Wood. The Short-tailed Gray Hound of the Green Wood invited him in, and said that he thought the King a much better subject for hospitality than [the Great Giant who had had with him the King's prospective wife and lover. He stayed that night in the house of the Short-tailed Gray Hound of the Green Wood. In the morning, when he was departing, the Short-tailed Gray Hound of the Green Wood said to him, 'If any crisis come upon thee, remember me and I will be with thee].' B 421 He left a farewell blessing [with the Hound, and set forth].

At night time, he came to the house of the Otter of Rapid Stream. [The Otter of Rapid Stream] invited [him in, and said that he thought him a much better subject for hospitality than the Great Giant who had had with him the King's prospective wife and lover. He stayed

Dóbhran Sruth an t-Siubhail.   Anns a' mhaduinn, an
uair a bha e falbh, thuirt Dóbhran Sruth an t-Siubhail ris,
B 449·3   'Ma thig càs sam bith ort, cuimhnich ormsa is bidh
mi agad.']   Dh'fhàg e beannachd [aig an Dóbhran is
dh'fhalbh e].

Ràinig e an oidhche sin tigh an Fhuamhaire, is chunnaic
G 532   e a bhean fhéin a stigh.   Chuir i am falach e.

An uair a thàinig am Fuamhaire dachaidh, thuirt i
K 975·2*   ris, 'Nam biodh fios agam c'àite a bheil t'anam 'ga
ghléidheadh, chuirinn craobhan is dealbhannan air.'

Dh'ainmich e àite dhi, agus an uair a dh'fhalbh am
Fuamhaire o'n tigh an là-'r-na-mhàireach, rinn ise agus
esan obair ghasd air an àite.

An uair a thàinig am Fuamhaire, chòrd an obair ris gu
maith.   Thuirt e nach ann an siod a bha a anam 'ga
E 710   ghléidheadh, ach ann an stoc craoibhe; gun robh reatha
am broinn an stuic; lach am broinn an reithe; ugh am
E 713   broinn na lach; agus gur h-ann anns an ugh a bha a anam.

An uair a chaidh am Fuamhaire o'n tigh an là-'r-na-
mhàireach, thug esan [Rìgh Eireann] leis tuagh, agus
thòisich e air an stoc a chur as a chéile.   Leum reatha as
an stoc, is thug e aghaidh air a' bheinn.

B 571·1   'Nam biodh agamsa nis Madadh Gearr Glas na Coille
Uaine, cha b'fhad a bhiodh e a' breith air an reatha.'

D 2074·2·1   Mun do rinn e ach am facal a ràdh, thàinig Madadh Gearr
Glas na Coille Uaine, agus an reatha leis 'na bheul.

Rug iad air an reatha agus sgoilt iad e, agus an uair a
sgoilt iad e, leum lach a mach a bhroinn.   'Bu mhaith a
nis Seobhag Sùilghorm Shliabh Brat,' ars esan.   Mun
do leig e am facal as a bheul, thàinig Seobhag Sùilghorm
Shliabh Brat, agus an lach leis.

An uair a sgoilt iad an lach, fhuair iad ugh 'na broinn,
agus an uair a bhrist iad an t-ugh, leum breac [1] a mach

---

[1] The Giant had said nothing about the trout.   But the Irish conception
bradan na beatha, or the salmon of life, suggests that the trout was the Giant's
life or soul.

that night in the house of the Otter of Rapid Stream. In the morning, when he was going, the Otter of Rapid Stream said to him, 'If any crisis come upon thee, remember B 449·3 me and I will be with thee.'] He left a farewell blessing [with the Otter, and departed].

That night he came to the house of the Giant, and there indoors he saw his own wife. She put him into a G 532 hiding place.

When the Giant came home, she said to him, 'If I only knew where thou keepest thy life [or soul] I would K 975·2* cover the place with branching tracery and pictures.'

The Giant named a place to her, and on the morrow, when he had left the house, she and the King of Erin decorated the place splendidly.

When the Giant came home, the ornamental work pleased him greatly. He said that that was not the place where his life was kept, but that it was in the stump of a E 710 tree; that there was a ram inside the stump; a wild duck inside the ram; an egg inside the duck; and that his life E 713 was in the egg.*

When the Giant had left the house on the morrow, he [the King of Erin] took an axe, and began to split that stump to pieces. Out of the stump leaped a ram, and the ram headed straight for the mountain.

'If I only had the Short-tailed Gray Hound of the Green B 571·1 Wood now, he would not be long in catching the ram.' He had scarcely said the word, when the Short-tailed Gray D 2074·2·1 Hound of the Green Wood came, bringing the ram with him in his mouth.

They seized hold of the ram and split it open, and when they had done so, a wild duck leaped out of it. 'How useful would the Blue-eyed Hawk of Slieve Brat be now,' said he. Scarcely had he allowed the word to pass his lips when up came the Blue-eyed Hawk of Slieve Brat, bringing the wild duck with him.

When they had split the duck open, they found an egg inside it, and when they broke the egg, a trout [1] leaped

---

* A lacuna here. The Giant should name the trout as well. See *infra*.

D2074·2·1 as [1] anns an abhainn. 'Bu mhaith a nis Dóbhran Sruth an t-Siubhail,' ars esan. Mun do rinn e ach am facal a ràdh, thàinig Dóbhran Sruth an t-Siubhail, agus am breac leis 'na bheul. Rug e air a' bhreac, agus mharbh e e, G 510 is thuit am Fuamhaire marbh aig a' cheart am.

Thug e leis am boirionnach, is thàinig e dhachaidh gu h-Eirinn. Chuir e fios air a bhràithrean,[2] agus phòs i fhéin agus esan. Bha banais aighearach, shunndach aca, biadh is deoch gu leòir, toil-inntinn, is ceòl is dannsadh.

From Donald MacFie, Iochdar, South Uist, who says he learnt it in his boyhood from John MacDonald, Aird a'Mhachair, who was an old man at that time. Reciter is seventy-nine years of age.

NOTES

MS. Vol. viii., No. 106. On the flyleaf of this tale, Islay has written :—

'An t-Uairasgeul Mor
Gaelic Index 106.

From Donald MacFie, Iochdar, South Uist, who learned it in his boyhood from John MacDonald, Aird a'Mhachair, who was an old man at the time—The reciter is 79—July or August, '59. [Written down from MacFie's dictation by] Hector MacLean—Referred to in Note [3] No. 1. Printed, but to be made into something better for it is worth it.' Islay never printed the tale. Below this he has pasted a cutting from West Highland Tales, i., No. 1, Var. 3 :—

'3. I have a third version of this written [recited?] by John [corrigenda give Donald] MacPhie, in South Uist. The old man was very proud of it, and said it was "the hardest" story that the transcriber had ever heard. He told me the same.

'As often happens with aged reciters, when he repeated it a second time slowly for transcribing, nearly all the curious, "impassioned and sentimental" language was left out. This is MacLean's account, and it entirely agrees with my own experience of this man, who is next thing to a professional reciter (see introduction). This version [No. 106] is the most curious of the three, etc.'

In the MS. of No. 105 occurs a loose sheet on which Islay has written :—" The great uairisgeul—MacFie—a version of the King of

out of it into the river. 'Good were now the Otter of D2074·2·1
Rapid Stream,' said he [the King of Erin]. He had
scarcely said the word, when up came the Otter of Rapid
Stream, bringing the trout with him in his mouth. He
seized the trout, and killed it, and the Giant fell dead at G510
that very moment.

The King then took his wife with him, and came home
to Erin. He sent word for his brothers to come,[2] and she
and he married. They had a merry and cheerful wedding,
food and drink in plenty, inward contentment, music and
dancing.

[1] *aisde* (out of her) in MS.

[2] The King of Erin's brothers were not mentioned before. Perhaps the
sentence ought to be—*Chuir i fios air a bràithrean*—'She sent word for *her*
brothers,' the three knights.

Asair Ruadh [= Easaidh Ruaidh] but very curious—The good old
language lost—Referred to in Notes in No I. Ja[nuar]y [18]60.'

H. MacLean, the transcriber, added the following note to the MS.
of No. 106 :—'In writing this tale, I was much disappointed. The
reciter at first recited it with great fluency, but when obliged to dictate
slowly, he completely lost a great many of the expressions [he] formerly
used. He gave the matter-of-fact narration, but all the impassioned
and sentimental language in which the tale abounds was completely
lost, and though I tried all means that I could, I could not get him
to recite it as he had previously. I have found the most of very old
men fail in this manner. The young and middle-aged can recite
either slow or fast, but the old get quite stupefied if they are not allowed
to recite in their usual way. Were the person able to write pretty fast
the thing might be done.' The inability of (probably) the same
reciter to go slowly is noted by Islay in *West Highland Tales*, ii., No. 44,
notes.

In the *Trans. Gael. Soc. Inverness*, xxxiv. p. 7, will be found a list of
versions of " The Chief Story." Those versions to which it will be
necessary to refer in this book, are mentioned below. For convenience,
they have been numbered as in the *Transactions*.

No. 1. The Eigg version.—Reciter, Angus MacKay, Galmasdale,
Isle of Eigg—Collector, Donald C. MacPherson. *An Gàidheal* (1875,
Edinburgh) iv., p. 303. Contributed with a translation by J. G. McKay
to *Trans. Gael. Soc. Inverness*, xxxiv., p. 1.

No. 2. The Tiree version.—Reciter, John Campbell, Hianish, Isle of Tiree—Collector, Rev. J. G. Campbell. *The Scottish Celtic Review* (1881-85, Glasgow), i., p. 61 ; ii., p. 137.

No. 3. The Islay version.—Reciter, Lachlin MacNeill, Bowmore, Isle of Islay—Collectors, Hector MacLean and J. F. Campbell, both also of Islay. *Trans. Gael. Soc. Inverness*, xxv., pp. 211-229. Not translated.

No. 4. South Uist version, No. 106, and

No. 5. Another South Uist version, No. 203, both given with translations in this book.

Nos. 8 and 9, 'Morraha.'—Reciters, P. McGrale, Achill Island, Mayo, and Terence Davis, Renvyle, Galway.—Collected and published, English only, by William Larminie, *West Irish Folk-Tales and Romances*, viii., pp. 10, 252 (London, 1898).

Closely related, No. 16, 'The Young King of Easaidh Ruadh.'—Reciter, James Wilson, Islay—Collectors, Hector MacLean and J. F. Campbell, both of Islay. *W. H. Tales*, i., No. 1.

See also Dr Robin Flower, *Catalogue of Irish MSS. in the British Museum*, ii., p. 271 (London, 1926) : R. A. Stewart Macalister, *Two Irish Arthurian Romances*, Irish Texts Society, x., p. 2 (London, in progress) ; *The Gaelic Journal*, xix., p. 355 (Dublin, 1882-1909) and *Béaloideas*, iii., p. 140 ; iv., pp. 330, 453 (two instances) : p. 163, for 'An An-Sgéalaidhe' —for a Werewolf, *ibid.*, iii., p. 326.

In the Eigg version, the magic filly shows an intense loathing for the Old King, and instructs the hero to roast the soles of his feet at the fire, and afterwards to throw him into it.

In the Tiree version, she tells the hero how he is to defeat the Old King. Finally, the Old King commands the hero to pitch him into a cauldron, but it is far more likely that it was the filly who gave the command.

In the Islay version, though the Old King detests telling his story (as he does in every version), he lives at peace with the hero after telling it, and is not tortured. This is also the case in the Irish versions. In these, however, the wolf begins by cutting the hero's horse in half, and so evinces a hatred of horses as inveterate as the filly's hatred of the were-wolf in the Eigg version. Nevertheless he afterwards lives at peace with the hero, and all rivalry appears to be forgotten.—*Trans. Gael. Soc. Inverness*, xxv.

In South Uist version, No. 1, the palfrey or filly tells the hero how to get the Wolf's uncle into his power. It may be inferred that she also tells him how to counter the uncle's moves, as she does in the next. What becomes of the uncle is not told.

In South Uist version, No. 2, she not only tells the hero how to get the Old King into his power, but also how to counter his moves. The Old King curses her, and after telling his story, says he must die. It is not stated that he does die, but it seems probable that he comes to a terrible end in this version as he does in the Eigg and Tiree versions. In all three versions (South Uist 2, Eigg and Tiree) the Old King tries to get the hero into his power, and the incident of the gold chair and the silver one in version No. 1, though corrupt, implies that he does so in that version also. He dreads his approaching end in four versions, but not in the Islay one, and in all five versions he detests telling his story.

His hatred of horses in the Irish versions is paralleled by the filly's loathing of him in the Eigg version, and by the pains she takes for his undoing in the other versions.

Flath agus fàilte romhad. This strange expression occurs on p. 6 (twice) and p. 28 ; also in the text of the Tales already published. I suggest that the real original must have been *fiath agus fàilte*, "honour and welcome." The term *fiath* or *fiadh* is well attested in Irish at all stages, and *fiath agus fàilte* is a regular phrase. With us it is now rare, but it is known in Raasay and probably elsewhere. The Rev. Dr Kenneth MacLeod informs me that an aged farmer near Campbeltown, whom he used to visit once a week, always greeted him with the words, *"Féidh agus fàilte, a dhuine."* Here *féidh* is an oblique case of *fiadh* or *fiath,* and is to be explained by reference to the ancient standard expression *airmitiu féid* (or *féith*), as in *"amal do-m-beir in ben airmitin féith don fiur,"* "even as the woman gives due respect to the man" (*Würz. Glosses,* 11, c. 14). The phrase is discussed by Zeuss (*Gramm. Celt.,* p. 918). From *fiadh,* Old Irish *fiad,* we have *fiadhaich,* to invite, welcome, as to a wedding or funeral ; still in fairly common use.   W. J. W.

See also *W. H. Tales,* ii., p. 436 or 447.   J. G. M.

AM PRÌOMH SGEUL

AN TUAIRISGEAL MÓR

No. 2. *Campbell MS., Vol. viii., No. 203*

1* .   .   .   .   .   .

B 181·9* CHUIR an fhalaire a ceann ann an achlais an Ridire
Bhàin. Ghabh an Ridire Bàn roimhe le flath agus le
B 577* fàilte. Chaidh calman a ghairm [2] air gach gualainn aige,
is bha iad a caitheamh na cuirme gu subhach, suilbhearra,
H 1235 sòlasach. This is repeated with the different knights.

* .   .   .   .   .   .

Spor e chun na h-aibhne i, is leum i an abhainn a chasa
tiorma. [Cha robh duine 'sa Ghréig nach tàinig 'nan
coinnimh an uair a chunnaic iad i a' leum na h-aibhne,
agus Rìgh Og na Gréige air an ceann.]
Ars an fhalaire, 'Bidh e a' dol am cheannach, is abraidh
e, ''D è a ghabhas tu oirre?' is abair thusa nach gabh thu
oirre ach e a thoirt duit fios de mar a chuireadh an
Tuairisgeal Mór gu bàs.'

---

[1] The first sheet of this MS. begins as shown here with an asterisk and a
dotted line, next a paragraph ending in a sentence in English, and then
another asterisk and another dotted line. On the opposite side of this first
sheet, Hector MacLean the transcriber has written the following note, which
he may have intended to refer to the asterisk :—

'What I think I took down correctly before is omitted, a Righ na Greige
[Oh King of Greece].'

I have searched the MS. volumes for some page or pages which should
contain what Hector had taken 'down correctly before,' and have tried every
plan that suggested a clue, but in vain. The fact that Islay himself has
numbered the flyleaf to this tale as page 1, and the page which begins as above
with the asterisk and dotted line as page 2, proves that the missing sheets were
lost before they could be bound up. As a result, the hero's adventures before
his first visit to the Fair Knight, though given in detail in the previous version

THE CHIEF STORY

THE GREAT TUAIRISGEAL

No. 2.   *Campbell MS., Vol. viii., No. 203*

1 *   .   .   .   .   .   .

THE palfrey [lovingly] pushed her head under the Fair   B 181·9*
Knight's arm. The Fair Knight received him [= the
King of Erin] as a chief and with welcoming. A dove [2]   B 577*
was called [to abide or settle] upon each of the King's
shoulders, and they plied the feast merrily, cheerfully,
delightedly. This is repeated with the different knights.   H 1235

*   .   .   .   .   .   .

He spurred her [the palfrey] towards the river, and
she leaped it dry-shod. [There was not a man in Greece
who did not come to meet them when they saw her leaping
the river, and at their head came the Young King of Greece.]
Quoth the palfrey, 'He [the Young King of Greece]
will come and want to buy me. He will say, 'What wilt
thou take for her?' and say thou that thou wilt take
nothing for her except this—that he tell thee how the
Great Tuairisgeal was put to death.'

(Tale No. 1) are lost from this one. The feeding and combing of the palfrey are
also omitted. Nevertheless, this version contains much that is very valuable,
and Islay thought very highly of it. The words 'a Righ na Greige' suggest
that Hector was going to have written more, or perhaps the words constituted
one of his land marks.

  [2] Possibly an echo of some ancient mode of doing honour to a guest.
But compare the honeybird on Trembling's shoulder, in Curtin's *Myths of
Ireland*, p. 78, and the three starlings twittering on each of the Snow-white
Maiden's shoulders, *Celtic Magazine*, xiii., p. 455. For the signs of a son or   H 41
daughter of a king on the breast of a hero or heroine, *Larminie*, p. 14, *Zeits. Celt.*   H 71
Phil., i., p. 153; Meave's pet bird and squirrel (Miss Hull, *Cuchulain*, p. 95),
Caithreim Conghail Clairinghnigh, p. 135 (Irish Texts Society) and *Celtic Review*,
i., pp. 367-8.

Thàinig Rìgh [Og] na Gréige far an robh e, is mar a
thuirt an fhalaire, dh'fheòraich e, "D è ghabhas tu oirre?'
—'Cha ghabh mi oirre,' arsa Rìgh Eireann, 'ach thu
dh'innseadh dhomh cia mar a chaidh an Tuairisgeal Mór
gu bàs.'

Chaidh Rìgh [Og] na Gréige far an robh a athair,[1]
is dh'innis e dha mar a leum an fhalaire abhainn na Gréige,
is gun robh e ag iarraidh a ceannach; is gur h-e an luach
a bha e ag iarraidh oirre, 'ciamar a chaidh an Tuairisgeal
H 1388   Mór gu bàs.'

Thuirt a athair ris an Rìgh Og, 'Chan 'eil brath air.'

Thill e an sin far an robh Rìgh Eireann, is thuirt e ris,
'Chan 'eil brath air.'

'Tha brath air,' ars an fhalaire.

Thill an Rìgh Og air ais a rithist far an robh a athair,
Q 414·3   is thuirt e ris, 'Tha brath air, is mur an innis thu e, beiridh
mi ort is loisgidh mi thu, is leigidh mi an luaith leis a'
ghaoith—mur an coisinn thu an fhalaire dhomh.'[2]

[B'eudar do'n t-Seann Rìgh strìochdadh, agus gabhail
os làimh leigeil le Rìgh Eireann a thoirt leis, agus gun
innseadh e an sgeul da. Sin an uair a ghabh an Rìgh
Og boch mór, agus a chinnt aige a nis gum faigheadh e an
fhalaire. Bha fios glé mhaith aig an fhalaire mar a thachair
eadar an Rìgh Og agus an Seann Rìgh, agus gun tigeadh
Rìgh Og na Gréige dh'a h-iarraidh, agus thòisich i air
comhairle a sparradh air Rìgh Eireann.]

'Abair ris,' ars an fhalaire ri Rìgh Eireann, 'an uair a
thig e a mach, gum faigh e mise; ach tha ubhal air ceann
C 837   na sréine; thoir dhìom i, is cuir ann ad phoca i.[4] Tha
F.571·4* a athair 'na sheann duine 'na laighe ann an creathaill leis
an aois. Iarraidh e ort a thoirt leat air do mhuin, is dèan

---

[1] '[a] athair,' (= his father) in MS. But the character in question is
probably a much more remote ancestor. See *Trans. Gael. Soc. Inverness,*
xxxiv., p. 71.

[2] In the related story of 'The Cotter's Son and the Half Slim Champion,'
Trans. Gael. Soc. Inverness, xxxiv., p. 111, the king's son puts his father, who had

The [Young] King of Greece came up to the King of Erin, and as the palfrey had said, he asked, 'What wilt thou take for her?'—'I will take nothing for her,' said the King of Erin, 'but this—that thou tell me how the Great Tuairisgeal was put to death.'

The [Young] King of Greece went off to where his father [1] was, and told him how the palfrey had leaped the river of Greece, and that he wanted to buy her; and that the price which the King of Erin wanted for her, was [the story called] 'How the Great Tuairisgeal was put to H 1388 death.'

His father replied to the Young King, 'There is nothing known of it.'

The Young King then returned to the King of Erin, and said, 'There is nothing known of it.'

'There *is* something known of it,' said the palfrey.

The Young King went back once more to where his father was, and said to him, 'Something *is* known of it, and unless thou tell what it is, I will seize thee and burn Q 414·3 thee, and let thine ashes be scattered by the wind—if thou wilt not win the palfrey for me.' [2]

[The Old King was obliged to submit, and he undertook to allow the King of Erin to carry him off, and agreed to tell him the story. Then it was that the Young King took great joy, being now certain that he would get the palfrey. The palfrey knew very well what had happened, between the Young King and the Old King, and knew too that the Young King of Greece would come to claim her, and so she began to urge advice upon the King of Erin.] [3]

'Say to him,' said the palfrey to the King of Erin, 'when he comes out—that he shall have me; but see, there is an apple-like knob at the end of the rein; take it off me, C 837 and put it in thine own pocket.[4] His father is an old man who has to lie in a cradle because of his great age. The old F 571·4*

also been a were-wolf, on a red-hot griddle and tortures him three times, to make him tell the answer to the riddle propounded by the Cotter's Son.

[3] Conjecturally inserted to make sense of what follows (J. G. McK.).

[4] In order to be able to summon her to his assistance when necessary, as in the Eigg version. But in this version, he fails to do so, which indicates D 1441 corruption.

D 1783·4* sin. Iarraidh e ort an rathad leathan ìseal [1] a ghabhail:
is gabh thusa an rathad àrd aimhleathan. Iarraidh e
F 786·1* ort esan a chur 'na shuidhe 'sa' chathair airgid, is thu
fhéin a shuidhe anns a' chathair òir; ach cuir thusa esan
'na shuidhe anns a' chathair òir, agus suidh fhéin anns a'
chathair airgid.'

Thàinig Rìgh Og na Gréige air a ais [bho a athair],
is fhuair e an fhalaire [bho Rìgh Eireann]; ach ghléidh
esan an ubhal a bha air an t-sréin. Ghabh e chun an
tighe, 's fhuair e athair an Rìgh anns a' chreathaill, is
thug e leis air a mhuin e. An uair a ràinig iad far an robh
an rathad mór a' dol 'na dhà mheanglan, thuirt am bodach
ris, 'Gabh thusa an rathad mór ìseal; is e as réidhe.'

Ghabh esan an rathad àrd, aimhleathann.
'Carson a ghabh thu mar so?' arsa athair Rìgh na
Gréige.
'Is e so rathad as taitniche leam,' arsa Rìgh Eireann.

'Beannachd dhuit-sa, is mallachd do t'oide-ionnsachaidh,'
ars am bodach. 'Is e so [an] aon sgeul as puirsgeula [2]
a chuala cluas no a chaidh a stigh ann an cridhe, a tha
mise a' dol a dh'innseadh dhuit-se an dràsd! Mac rath
thu-sa: is mac mìorath mise an uair a dh'amais mi riut-sa.'

Bha iad a' gabhail air falbh, is gun iad a' faighinn dad
no a' faicinn dad.
'An uair a chì thu tom luachrach am bràigh monaidh,'
ars athair Rìgh na Gréige ris, 'gabh thu-sa d'a ionnsuigh, 's
chì thu tigh os a chionn gu h-àrd. Gabh thusa a dh'ionnsuigh an tighe. Cuir do làmh os cionn an àrd-doruis, is
gheibh thu iuchair ann. Fosgail an dorus, is theirig a
stigh. Chì thu an sin cathair òir is cathair airgid. Cuir
mise anns a' chathair airgid, agus suidh fhéin anns a'
chathair òir.'

Chunnaic e an tom luachrach, is ghabh e d'a ionnsuigh,
is chunnaic e an sin tigh os a chionn, mar a thuirt an seann

---

[1] Dial. for ìosal.
[2] 'Puirsgeal, melancholy, mournful.—Reciter.' Note on opposite page

man will ask thee to carry him on thy back, and mind that D 1783·4*
thou do so.   He will also ask thee to take the broad low
road: but do thou take the high narrow road.   He will F 786·1*
ask thee also to seat him in the silver chair, and to seat
thyself in the golden chair; but do thou put him in the
golden chair, and seat thyself in the silver chair.'

The Young King of Greece came back [from seeing his
father], and got the palfrey [from the King of Erin]; but
he, [the King of Erin,] retained the apple-like knob on
the rein.   He set off to the house, and found the father
of the King [of Greece] in the cradle, and carried him off
on his back.   When they came to where the high road
split into two branches, the old man said to him, 'Take
thou the broad low road; it is the easier one.'

But he [the King of Erin] took the upper narrow road.

'Why hast thou gone this way ?' said the father of the
King of Greece.

'This is the road that pleases me better,' said the King
of Erin.

'A blessing to thee and a curse to thy teacher,' said the
old man.   'What I am now going to tell thee is the most
singularly melancholy and mournful [2] tale that ear ever
heard or that ever was laid to heart ! A son of good
fortune thou: but a son of bad fortune am I in the hour
that I lighted upon thee.'

On and on they went, but without finding anything
or seeing anything.

'When thou seest a clump of rushes on a certain moorland
brae,' said the father of the King of Greece, 'go towards
it, and thou wilt see a house beyond the rushes and higher
up the brae.   Make for that house.   Put thine hand above
the lintel of the door, and there thou wilt find a key.   Open
the door and go in.   There thou wilt see a golden chair
and a silver chair.   Place me in the silver chair, and seat
thyself in the golden chair.'

He saw the clump of rushes, and went towards it, and
then he saw the house standing higher up the brae and

of MS.   This paragraph appears to anticipate a later one.   It is possibly
out of place here.

F 786·1

Rìgh ris. Ràinig e an tigh, is fhuair e an iuchair os cionn an ard-doruis. Dh'fhosgail e an dorus, is chaidh iad a stigh. Shuidh e fhéin anns a' chathair airgid, is chuir e am bodach anns a' chathair òir.

'Carson a rinn thu so ?' ars am bodach.

'Nach do chuir mi anns a' chathair a b' urramaiche thu ?' ars esan.[1]

'Beannachd dhuit-se, ach mallachd do t'oide-ionn-sachaidh. Mac rath thusa; is mac miorath mise an uair a dh' amais mi riut-sa. Sin naidheachd as puirsgeula a chuala cluas no a ràinig cridhe.

'Bu mhise Mac Rìgh na Gréige.

Phòs e mo mhàthair, is rug i triuir mhac da.

S 31

An uair a chaochail mo mhàthair, phòs m'athair bana-bhuidseach, is cha tugadh i greim bìdh dhuinn. Fhuair

G 200

i baobh de Eachlach Urlair, is bha i a stigh aice. Bha sinn a' toirt arain bho 'n teine, is sinn air acras.

D 683·2
D 113·1
D 565·2

D 1254

R 322*

B 31·1

R 188*

'Bhuail an Eachlach Urlair an slacan druidheachd oirnn, is rinn i trì madaidh-allaidh dhinn. Chaidh sinn do'n t-sliabh, is cha robh sinn a' beantail ach do na caoraich aice-se. Fhuair i mìolchoin, agus gearrchoin, is chuir i as ar déidh iad, is mharbh iad dithis de mo bhràithrean.[2] Chaidh mise gu bearradh creige far an robh cri-bhìnneach is chuir mi na h-iseanan as an nead, is cha robh de chridhe aig a' chri-bhìnnich tighinn 'nam chòir. Bha mi seachduinn anns a' chreig. Chunnaic mi soitheach a' seòladh, agus bàta tighinn gu tìr. Thug mi burral asam, is leig mi mi fhéin sìos anns a' bhàta, is thuit na daoine a bha innte ann an neul.[4] [Nuair a dhùisg iad as an neul, thug iad am

---

[1] Observe that the hero disobeys the Old Were-wolf's commands dia-metrically.—*Trans. Gael. Soc. Inverness*, xxxiv., p. 81. In the next sentence it is clear that the Were-wolf hates the palfrey, the hero's teacher.

[2] Probably a clerical error for *mo dhithis bhràithrean*, my two brethren.

[3] It is a mournful noise—whatever the best English word may be.

S 145

[4] The men were horrified at the Wolf's appearance. Marooned men also

beyond the clump of rushes, as the Old King had told him. He went up to the house, and found the key above the lintel of the door. He opened the door, and they went in. F 786·1 He seated himself in the silver chair, and placed the old man in the chair of gold.

'Why hast thou done this?' said the old man.

'Have I not set thee in the most honourable chair?' replied the other.[1]

'A blessing to thee, and a curse to thy teacher. A son of good luck art thou; but I alas! a son of bad luck am I, seeing that I have lighted upon thee. Here followeth the most melancholy and mournful story that ear ever heard or that ever was laid to heart.

'I was the Son of the King of Greece.

He married my mother, and she bore him three sons.

When my mother died (*lit.* changed), my father married S 31 a witch. She would not give us a bite of food. She got hold of a sorceress, an Eachlach Urlair [= the Floor G 200 Mischief] whom she kept in the house. We were constantly taking bread from the fire [where it was baking] as we were so hungry.

'The Eachlach Urlair struck us with the witch wand, D 683·2 and turned us into three wolves. We went off to the D 113·1 mountains, but we did not touch anything but the sheep D 565·2 belonging to her. She procured blood-hounds and terriers, D 1254 and set them after us, and they killed two of my brothers.[2] I went off to a precipitous rock where a *cri-bhìnneach* lived, R 322* and I threw her nestlings out of the nest, and the *cri-bhìnneach* did not dare to come near me. I spent a week B 31·1 in that rock. Then I saw a vessel sailing along, and a boat coming to land. I gave a whine,[3] and let myself fall down into the boat, but the men in the boat swooned away.[4] [When they recovered from their swoon, they R 188*

uusally strike terror or horror into those who see them. See p. 199.—It will be noted that this paragraph shows that in this version as in the Eigg, Tiree and Islay versions the old man who is found in the cradle, and who recites the inset story, is the Were-wolf himself and not, as in Tale No. 1, the Were-wolf's uncle.

bàta chun an t-soithich.] Tharruing an fheadhainn a
bha air bòrd maidean a dhol dh'am mharbhadh, ach chaidh
mise fo chleòc a' mhaighstir.

"Leigibh tàmh leis a' chreutair," ars esan, "is creutair gun
lochd e; thugaibh biadh dha."

D686·1* Thug iad domh brot, is cha bheanainn da. Thug iad domh
an sin, feòil, is dh'ith mi beagan dith. Bheirinn fhéin air
ball-coirce an sin, le m' spògan. Chunnaic mi na leabhraichean,
D682·3 is rug mi air peann ann am spòig, is cha robh ball a bha ann
nach do sgrìobh mi. Dh'fheuch iad an leabhar a sgrìobh mi,
H62·2* is thug iad domh peann is dubh.[1]
"Tha thu-sa, a ghalad [= ghalghad],[2] fo gheasan," ars an
caibtinn. Thug e mi gu rìgh a bha'n sin, agus b'e bràthair
m'athar e. Bha bràthair m'athar air ùr-phòsadh. Chuireadh
mise ann am bocsa.
An uair a bha bean bhràthair m'athar chun a h-asaid,
fhuaradh trì mnathan-glùine a dh'fheitheamh oirre. Dh'asaideadh i air leanabh-nighinn; is thàinig Cràg Mhór a stigh
air druim an tighe, is thug i leatha an leanabh![3] Mharbh
na mnathan-glùine cat, is shuath iad an fhuil ri mo bheul is ri
K2155·1 mo spògan-sa. Leig iad beum sgéithe asda gun do mharbh
am madadh maol an leanabh.

"Tha siod dèanta," arsa bean bhràthair m'athar, "is leigidh
sinn leis air an turus so."
An ath uair a bha i chun a h-asaid, fhuaradh na mnathan-
glùine. Dh'asaideadh i air leanabh-nighinn a rithist, is thàinig
G261·1 a' Chràg, is thug i leatha an leanabh. Dh'eubh na mnathan-
glùine gun d'ith am madadh maol an leanabh. Bha iad ag
iarraidh mo losgadh, is thuirt bean bhràthair m'athar leigeil
leam air an turus so fhathast, gun robh siod dèanta. Chaidh

---

[1] Giving the Were-wolf pen and ink ought to have been placed earlier in
the paragraph. He probably did something also with the rope to show
human intelligence.
[2] *galad* in MacBain, but that does not indicate pronunciation which is
gal-a-ad. M.Ir. *galgat*.
D1364·24 [3] The incident of the mysterious music coming round the house and
putting all in it, including the midwives, to sleep, has been omitted, as in
the preceding Tale No. 1. The incident of the midwives awaking, and dis-
covering their loss, has also been forgotten. As in No. 2 the mother protects
the animal, which suggests that she had witnessed the kidnapping of her
child, and knew the animal to be innocent. The uproar made by the midwives was such as to be comparable with the noise made by heroes who

brought the boat to the ship.] The people on board [the ship] fetched blows at me with sticks in order to kill me, but I slipped under the master's cloak.

"Let the creature be," said he, "it is quite harmless; give him food."

They gave me broth, but I would not touch it. Then D 686·1* they gave me some flesh, and of that I ate a little. With my paws I laid hold of a rope. Seeing some books, I took up a D 682·3 pen in my paw, and there was not a letter there that I did not write. They examined the book I had written, and gave me H 62·2* pen and ink.[1]

"Thou, my beauty, art enchanted," said the captain. He brought me to the king of the place, who was my father's brother. He was newly married. I was put into a box.

When my father's brother's wife was about to be delivered, three midwives were procured to attend upon her. She was delivered of a girl-child; but a great Claw-like Hand came through the roof of the house, and took away the child![3] The midwives killed a cat, and rubbed the blood over my mouth and paws. Then they raised an outcry like the sound K 2155·1 of shields being clashed, and said that the crop-eared wolf had eaten the child.

"The thing is done now," said my father's brother's wife, "we will forgive him on this occasion."

The next time she was about to be delivered, the midwives were procured. She was delivered of a girl-child again, but the Claw-like Hand came, and stole the child away. The G 261·1 midwives shouted that the crop-eared wolf had eaten the child. They wanted to have me burnt, but my father's brother's

strike their shields and make them ring when challenging or demanding combat, as in No. 17, p. 245. Like No. 1, this tale does not explain why the wolf is *crop-eared* (see p. 15, Tale No. 1). The Eigg version says that he and his brother wolves were driven over a high rock by hunters, and that after the fall he recovered consciousness, only to find his two brothers lying drowned by his side, and his own ears eaten off. It is very possible that some incident has been lost here which related that the wolf had been punished for killing sheep or marauding, by having his ears cut off. There was an old highland custom of punishing cats for raiding the cream-dish by cutting off their left Q 451·6 ears as close to the roots as possible. 'Nether Lochaber,' the late Rev. Alex. Stewart, contributed a long article on the custom to the *Inverness Courier*, 24th October 1878.

bràthair m'athar do'n cheardaich, is fhuair e lomhainn iaruinn
a dhèanamh dhomh, is chaidh siod a chur orm.

Bha bean bhràthair m'athar chun a h-asaid a rithist, is
fhuaradh na mnathan-glùine a dh'fheitheamh oirre. Dh'
asaideadh i air leanabh-gille air an turus so. Thàinig a' Chràg
G 261·1   a stigh air druim an tighe, is thug i leatha an leanabh. Bhrist
mise an lomhainn iaruinn is rug mi air a' Chràig, ach spìon
e [1] leis mi gus an toll. Air an ath spìonadh, thug e a mach
mo cheann is mo dhà spòig air druim an tighe, is air an treas
spìonadh thug e a mach mi uile gu léir. Ghearr mi an làmh
o'n ghualainn deth; ach thug e [1] leis an leanabh anns an
làimh eile. Thug mise leam an làmh do'n bhocsa agam
fhéin. Leig na mnathan-glùine beum sgéithe asda, gun do
mharbh am madadh maol an leanabh. Leig iad dàil seachduinn
domh,[2] is an ceann seachduinn, dh'fhadaidh iad teine airson
mo losgadh ann.

Thug mi a mach a' Chràg 'nam bheul, is chuir mi eadar
H 105·3*   dà làimh bhràthair m'athar i. "Is fhìor e," ars esan, "is tusa a
bha dìleas domh-sa, is cha b'e na mnathan-glùine."

Lean mi sràbh na fala, is chaidh mi chun a'chladaich, is
thug mi burral caoinidh asam.[3] Chuir iad geòla leam gus an
taobh eile. Ghabh mi suas mo thurus gu caisteal mór a bha
an sin. Chaidh mi a stigh, is bha an Tuairisgeal Mór 'na chadal.
H 1337   Rug mi air a' chlaidheamh sholuis aige fhéin eadar m' fhiaclan,
D 1645·4   is thug mi an ceann deth. Thug mi dà latha is dà oidhche
D 1081   eadar an ceann is a' choluinn, 'gan cumail o chéile, gus an do
E 783   reoth [4] an smior-chailleach. Chan fhuilingeadh clann bhràthair
m'athar m' fhaicinn. Rug an nighean a bu shine air an t-slacan
R 169·3   druidheachd airson mo bhualadh,[5] ach thug mi uaipe e, is
cheangail mi an sin an triuir chloinne, is thug mi leam do'n
gheòla iad.

[1] e, he, i.e. the Giant, the Great Tuairisgeal to whom the Claw-like Hand
belonged.

[2] In No. 1, only one day's respite.

[3] The wolf's grief was the grief of disappointment at finding that the
blood traces stopped at the water's edge, so that further tracking was impossible.

G 635·1   [4] Giants and others possess the disconcerting power of replacing their
severed heads upon their bodies, and effecting complete re-union. Hence
the necessity, which occurs twice in this tale, of keeping their heads and
bodies apart until quite cold. Otherwise they would suffer nothing but a
slight temporary inconvenience, and would be able to renew hostilities
immediately.—Waifs and Strays, ii., p. 367; iv., p. 262; Dr Geo. Henderson,
Celtic Dragon Myth, p. 126; W. H. Tales, i., No. 4, Var. 3; ii., No. 41, Var. 2,

wife said that I should be forgiven on this occasion also, for
that the thing was done. My father's brother went to the
smithy, and had an iron leash made for me, and I was secured
by it.

Again my father's brother's wife was about to be delivered,
and the midwives were procured to attend upon her. On
this occasion, she was delivered of a man-child. In through G 261·1
the roof of the house came the Claw-like Hand, and took the
child away. I broke the iron leash and seized the Hand, but
it dragged me with it to the hole in the roof. With the next
wrench, it pulled me out through the roof as far as my head
and paws, and with the third struggle, it pulled me out completely. I bit the arm off from the shoulder; but he [1] took
the child away in the other hand. I dragged the arm into my
own box. The midwives made an uproar like the sound of
clashing shields, saying that the crop-eared wolf had killed the
child. They allowed me a week's delay,[2] and at the end of a
week, they kindled a fire to burn me.

But I fetched the Claw-like Hand out in my mouth, and
placed it in my father's brother's hands. "True enough," said H 105·3*
he, "it is thou who wert faithful to me—not the midwives."

I followed the blood traces to the shore. When I got there,
I gave a whine of grief.[3] So they provided me with a yawl,
which took me over to the other side of the water. I went up
to a great castle that stood there. In I went, and there was H 1337
the Great Tuairisgeal asleep. With my teeth, I seized his own D 1645·4
sword of light, and took off his head. For two days and two D 1081
nights did I stay between the head and the body, keeping them E 783
apart until the spinal marrow froze.[4] My father's brother's
children could not bear the sight of me. The eldest daughter
took the magic wand to strike me,[5] but I took it from her, and R 169·3
bound the three children, and took them with me to the yawl.

No. 52, Var. 2 ; iii., No. 76 ; Campbell MS., x., No. 158 ; *Trans. Gael. Soc.*
Inverness, xvi., p. 117; xxv., p. 228 ; Rev. J. G. Campbell, *Superstitions*, p. 224.
A decapitated head may fly up in the air and try to fling itself upon the hero
who has performed the act of decapitation, *W. H. Tales*, ii., No. 52, notes,
end; iii., p. 259 or p. 244. In a story in *Trans. Gael. Soc. Inverness*, xix., p. 34,
a skull comes down a chimney *mar eun air iteig, like a bird on the wing*, and fights
another skull which enters by the window.

[5] The children were probably angry with the wolf for killing one whom
they supposed to be their parent. The wolf does not let the eldest girl strike
him with the magic wand, probably because he wanted the striking to be
done by his uncle, who would then observe the change from wolf to man,
and be thus convinced of the wolf's identity.

D 712·3 Thill mi air m'ais, agus bhuail bràthair m' athar an slachdan
D 771·4 druidheachd orm, is bha mi cho maith is a bha mi riamh.
D 1254

Chaidh bràthair m'athar leam do'n Ghréig, is fhuair mi
[a bhi] 'nam rìgh orra. Loisgeadh mo mhuime is an Eachlach
Q 414·3 Urlair, is leigeadh an luaith leis a' ghaoith.

Theirig sìos gus a' bhad luachrach ud, is gheibh thu coire
ann, is a bheul fodha. Tog an coire, is gheibh thu ceann an
Tuairisgeil Mhóir [agus a chlaidheamh] foidhe.[1] [Thoir leat
an dà chuid, an ceann agus an claidheamh soluis.] Abair
ri mo mhac-sa, an uair a thilleas tu, tighinn agus tòrradh a
dhèanamh orm-sa; cha bhi mise beò n'as fhaide.[2] An uair
a thilleas tu, eubhaidh tu trì uairean ris an Tuairisgeal Og.
E 55·1·1* Air a' cheud eubh, tòisichidh na cnàimhean air leantuinn ri
chéile—air an dara eubh, thig feòil air na cnàimhean—is air
an treas eubh, éirichidh e air a uilinn. Ma bheir thusa an
claidheamh da, tha thu dheth. Cha dearg muir air—cha
G 510·1* dearg teine air—cha dearg faobhar claidheimh air; cha dearg
Z 312 sìon air ach buille de'n cheann; is marbhaidh sin e. An uair
E 783 a bheir thu dheth an ceann, feumaidh tu a bhi dà latha is dà
oidhche eadar an ceann is a' choluinn gus an reoth an smior
G 635·1 chailleach, agus an fhuil anns na cuislean.'[3]

Shiubhail am bodach an uair a chuir e crìoch air an
sgeul, is ghabh esan air falbh [a' toirt a' chinn 's a'
chlaidheimh sholuis leis] is dh'innis e do Rìgh [Og] na
Gréige gun do bhàsaich a athair, is gun d'iarr e air dol
agus tòrradh a dhèanamh air.
[Dh'fhàg Rìgh Eireann Rìgh Og na Gréige, is ghabh
e roimhe. An uair a ràinig e abhainn na Gréige, crathar
an ubhal a bha air ceann sréine na falaire, agus thàinig
i 'na choinnimh. Chaidh e air a muin, agus leum i thairis

---

[1] So MS.
[2] In the Tiree version (*Scot. Celt. Rev.*, i. (1881), p. 77), the Old Were-wolf
King of Greece tells the hero to throw him into the cauldron which has been
boiling during the telling of the tale. In the Eigg version (*Trans. Gael. Soc.
Inverness*, xxxiv., pp. 43, 107) the magic filly tells the hero to 'pitch the wretch
into the fire.' In No. 1 preceding, the Old King's fate is not mentioned. In
the Islay version, he remains on good terms with the hero.
[3] For killing the Young Giant by striking his head with his giant father's
head, see No. 17, p. 275, where the hero kills a Cailleach by striking her on the
head with her own brother's head. In No. 1, p. 21, the hero strikes off his

When I went back again, my father's brother struck me D 712·3
with the magic wand, and I was as right as ever I was [= I D 771·4
recovered my original human shape]. D 1254

My father's brother accompanied me to Greece, and I got
[to be] king over them [the Greeks]. My stepmother and the
Eachlach Urlair were burnt, and their ashes were let fly with Q 414·3
the winds.

Go down to yonder clump of rushes, and thou wilt find a
cauldron there, lying mouth downwards. Lift it up, and thou
wilt find the head [and the sword] of the Great Tuairisgeal
beneath it. [Take with thee both the head and the sword of
light.] When thou art on thy homeward journey, tell my
son to come and bury me ; for I shall not live any longer.[2]
When thou returnest to the Young Tuairisgeal, shout at him
thrice. At the first shout, his bones will begin to join together E 55·1·1*
—at the second shout, flesh will come upon the bones—and at
the third shout, he will prop himself up on his elbow. If thou
give him the sword, thou art done for. The sea cannot affect
him—fire will not hurt him—the edge of the sword can make G 510·1*
no impression on him ; nothing can injure him except a blow Z 312
with that head.[3] That will kill him. And when thou hast E 783
cut off his head, thou must stay for two days and two nights
between the head and the body, until the spinal marrow and G 635·1
the blood in the veins, freeze.' [4]

The old man died when he had made an end of the
tale, and the King of Erin went off [taking the head and
the sword of light with him]. He told the [Young] King
of Greece that his father had died, and had desired him
to go and bury him.

[The King of Erin left the Young King of Greece,
and pressed on. When he came to the River of Greece,
he shook the apple-like knob that had been attached to
the end of the palfrey's rein, and she came to meet him.

---

enemy's head with the task-sword. That method of dealing with him, being
different from the method described here, is one of the points that prove the
two tales, Nos. 1 and 2, to have been delivered by different reciters.

[4] There is some confusion in the tale at this point between two methods
of killing the Tuairisgeal. For it is stated first of all that he is killed by being
hit with the head, and can be killed, apparently by that method only. Then
it transpires that he is not dead till head and body have been severed and
kept apart for two days and nights. Was there a version which stated that
he was merely *stunned* by being hit with the Old Tuairisgeal's head ?

air an abhainn. Agus bha e oidhche ann an tigh gach
aon de na Ridirean an déidh a chéile.

Thug e an sin air an cnoc air an d'fhàg e an Tuairisgeal
Og. Bha am fear ud air tuiteam 'na thòrr ruadh chnàmh
air a' chnoc, agus dh'eubh Rìgh Eireann ris trì uairean.
E 55·1·1* Air a' cheud eubh, thòisich na cnàimhean air leantuinn
ri chéile—air an dara eubh, thàinig feòil air na cnàimhean
—is air an treas eubh, dh'éirich an Tuairisgeal Og air a
uilinn. Dh'fhaighnich e ciamar a fhuair Rìgh Eireann
an claidheamh. Ghabh an Rìgh cothrom air; agus
tharruing e ceann an Tuairisgeil Mhóir, agus bhuail e
siod air an Tuairisgeal Og ann an taobh a' chinn aige,
's mharbh e e. Thug e an sin an ceann deth le claidheamh
an Tuairisgeil Mhóir, agus dh'fhuirich e dà là 's dà oidhche
eadar an ceann is a' choluinn, gus an do reoth an smior-
chailleach, is an fhuil anns na cuislean.

Chaidh e an so dhachaidh, agus an uair a ràinig e,
cha robh bad de'n mhnaoi aige. Dh'fhalbh e air tòir na
H 1385·3 mnatha.] [1]

Z 85*
Bha e a' falbh gus an robh
Dubhadh air a bhonnaibh,
Agus tolladh air a ghruaidhean.
'S gach eun beag, clocharra, donn,
A' gabhail tàimh ann am bun nam preas,
'S am bàrr gach dos,
'S am bàrr gach craoibhe coise gallda [2]
A b'fhaisge dhaibh.
Neòil dhùdaidh, dhorcha na h-oidhche tighinn,
'S neòil sheididh, shèimhidh an latha falbh.

[1] Guided by the words of the old man on p. 41, I have interpolated the
three paragraphs between the square brackets for the sake of sequence and
in amplification of the following note in the MS., from which it seems probable
that the transcriber was unable to obtain the exact Gaelic words of this part
of the story, and only caught the general drift of it.—'He [the King of Erin]
went with the sword and head to the Urraisgeal Og [= the Young Tuairisgeal]
and addressed him thrice. He [the Young Tuairisgeal] asked how he got
the sword. He [the King of Erin] took an advantage and struck him [the
Young Tuairisgeal] with his father's head, and killed him. On his [the

He mounted her back, and she leaped over the river.
And he visited the Knights one after the other, and spent
a night in the house of each of them.

He then betook himself to the hill on which he had left
the Young Tuairisgeal. But the Young Tuairisgeal had
fallen to pieces there on the hill, and had become nothing
but a reddish heap of bones. The King of Erin shouted
at him three times. At the first shout, the bones began   E 55·1·1*
to join themselves together—at the second shout, flesh
came upon the bones—and at the third shout, the Young
Tuairisgeal sat up leaning on his elbow. He asked how
the King of Erin had obtained the sword. But the King
took advantage of him; and bringing the head of the Great
Tuairisgeal into play, struck the Young Tuairisgeal on the
side of the head with it, killing him. He then cut off his
head with the Great Tuairisgeal's sword, and stayed for
two days and two nights between the head and the body,
until the spinal marrow, and the blood in the veins also,
froze.

After this he went home, but when he got there, not a
trace could he find of his wife. He set forth in search of   H1385·3
her.] [1]

> He travelled and travelled until
> The soles of his feet were getting black,   Z 85*
> And his cheeks were falling in.
> And every little chirping brown bird,
> Was going to rest at the roots of the bushes,
> And in the tops of the branches,
> And in the top of every walnut [?] tree
> That was nearest to them.
> The dark dismal clouds of night were coming on,
> And the soft, downy clouds of day departing.

King of Erin's] return [home, he found that] the wife was carried off, and
so he went in pursuit of her.' The note commences with a caret. But the
caret in the text of the MS. to which the note refers, has been placed in error
at the end of the travelling 'run,' which follows here.—*Note*. The MS. does
not state anywhere that the Young Giant was the *son* of the Big Giant, but
these words of Hector MacLean's prove that he was, as also is the case in
Tale No. 1. In some versions they are brothers.—*Trans. Gael. Soc. Inverness*,
xxxiv., p. 56.

[2] So MS.

B 421   Ràinig e tigh Madadh Gearr na Coille.

G 361·1

'Is tu aoidh a' mhi-àidh,' ars am Madadh; 'bha fuamhair mór nan cóig ceann is nan cóig meall is nan cóig muineal an so an raoir, is chan 'eil dad a chruinnich mi o cheann bliadhna nach d'ith e; is bu tùrsach do bhean-sa air falbh leis; ach dèan suidhe—dh'fhaoidte gu bheil rud againn duit-se fhathast.'

Dh'fhan e an oidhche sin aig Madadh Gearr na Coille, is fhuair e deagh bhiadh is deagh leabaidh.

An uair a bha e falbh 'sa' mhaduinn, thuirt am Madadh ris, 'Càs sam bith anns am bi thu, cuimhnich orm-sa is gheibh thu mo chuideachadh.'

B 459·1*   Ràinig e an oidhche sin Seobhag Sùilghorm Shliabh Brat, etc., etc.[1]

G 532   Dh'fhalbh e, is ràinig e caisteal an fhuamhair; 's bha Nighean an Ridire Dhuibh [2] a stigh, 's chuir i am falach fo'n talamh e.

G 84   [Thàinig am fuamhair dachaidh.] 'Tha boladh an fharbhalaich a stigh,' ars esan.

'O ! bhìdh is aodaich !' [3] ars ise, 'thàing eun beag a stigh is thonn [4] e a itean anns an teine.'

K 975·2*   Dh'iarr i fios air c'àite an robh a anam 'ga ghleidheadh, is gun cuireadh i an òrdugh le dealbhannan gu brèagh e.

E 713   'Dèan sin fhéin,' ars esan, agus dh'innis e gun robh e ann an cnagairneach mhóir dharaich a bha a muigh an siod.

E 710   Chuir ise an òrdugh a' chnagairneach gu ciatach an oidhche sin, is chunnaic am fuamhair mar a rinn i, is chòrd e ris gu maith.

B 449·3

[1] 'etc., etc.' So in MS. On the opposite page of the MS. there is the following note—'[1] Here the otter is wanting. In righ og Easuidh ruaidh (sic, see W. H. Tales, i., No. 1) the egg leaps out, but there is one tale I sent, in which a trout leaps out of the egg into the water, and the otter catches the trout.' The transcriber is referring to No. 1, in which this incident occurs.

[2] This paragraph shows that in this tale the hero's bride is not the sister of all three Knights, as in No. 1, but the daughter of one of them, the Black Knight.

[3] The Black Knight's Daughter is addressing the Giant as her treasure, or as the one to whom she looked for food and clothing. Compare a love-song in An Gàidheal (1925), xx., p. 70 :—

He came to the house of the Short-tailed Hound of the B 421
Wood.

"Tis thou who art the unlucky guest,' said the Hound;
'the great Giant of the five heads and of the five humps G 361·1
and of the five necks was here last night, and there was
not a scrap [of food] I had gathered during the year that
he did not eat; and very tearful was thy wife when she
went away with him; but sit thee down—perhaps we may
yet find something for thee to eat.'

That night he stayed with the Short-tailed Hound of
the Wood, and good was the food he got and good the bed.

When going away in the morning, the Hound said to
him, 'Whenever thou art in any strait, remember me, and
thou shalt have my help.'

He came the next night to the Blue-eyed Hawk of Slieve B 459·1*
Brat, etc., etc.[1]

He left him, and arrived at the Giant's castle; and G 532
the Black Knight's Daughter [2] was indoors, and she hid
the King away underground.

[The Giant came home.] 'The smell of a stranger is G 84
about the house,' said he.

'O ! food and clothing !' [3] said she, 'it was just a wee
bird that came in and dipped his wings in the fire.'

She asked the Giant where his life [5] was kept, so that K 975·2*
she might furbish the place up and ornament it with
pictures. 'Do so,' said he, and told her that his life was E 713
in a great gnarled oak trunk that stood outside there.
And that night she furbished up the gnarled trunk very E 710
charmingly, and the Giant saw what she had done, and
it pleased him right well.

> "S gur tusa mo riaghailt,
> Mo bhiadh agus m' aodach.'

[4] 'Tonn, to dip. Thaddeus Connellan's Easy Lessons. Not in Scotch
Gaelic dictionaries.' Note on opposite page of MS. These words show
that Hector MacLean, the scribe, had studied Irish as well as Scottish Gaelic.
In Scottish Gaelic it is usually *thom*, probably by confusion between similar
sounds *m* and *nn*.

[5] This is further evidence of mutilation. The Giant names the correct
place at once, instead of upon the second occasion, as in Tale 1, or on the third,
as is more usual.

An uair a dh'fhalbh am fuamhair o'n tigh an là-'r-na-
mhàireach, thug esan leis tuagh is ghearr e a' chnagairneach,
D2074·2·1 is leum reatha a mach as. Chuimhnich e air Madadh
Gearr na Coille, is bha e aige, is rug e air an reatha.
B571·1 Sgoilt e an reatha, is an uair a sgoilt, leum lach a mach as
anns an iarmailt. Chuimhnich e air Seobhaig Sùilghorm
Shliabh Brat, is bha i aige, is rug i air an lach. Sgoilt e
an lach, is fhuair e ugh, is phronn e 'na dhòrn i, is an uair
G510 a phronn, thuit am fuamhair marbh. Dh'fhalbh iad an
sin, is ràinig iad tigh an Ridire Dhuibh. Rinn iad banais
sheachd latha agus sheachd oidhche gun fuaradh, gun
fao[tha]chadh.

[from] Donald M'Phie, Iochdar, South Uist.

NOTES

MS. vol. viii., No. 203.—On the flyleaf of the MS. Islay has
written as follows :—

'Gaelic Index 203.   Vol. I [No] 1.
    No. 12.   T-8.
            An t-Urraisgeal Mór.
        W. H. Tales, Vol. 1st, page 21.
        From Donald MacPhie, Iochdar, South Uist
            November 30 [18]60.

This must be compared with the other version [No. 1 preceding]
and compounded with No. 1 [W. H. Tales]. It contains a vast number
of curious words and phrases, and traces of many other stories, the
framework is very nearly the same as No. 1, but it differs very widely ;
one bit is like the Arabian Nights. This is evidently very old and very
mythical, but the man who tells it is clearly failing ; he has the old
phrases, but the thread is broken. This story is considered as something great. It is the chief story, and is said to be very long. It is
hard to get men to tell it, and though I met many who said they knew
it, I never got it told, something always came in the way.'
    It is difficult to tell what Campbell means by 'T-8.' 'No 12'
probably means the twelfth story that Hector MacLean transcribed
in South Uist, in November 1860.
    There is much in this version that is not in No. 1. But it is very
corrupt, especially at the beginning and at the end. The fact that
No. 1 was recited by Donald MacFie, and No. 2 by Donald MacPhie,
both of Iochdar, South Uist, and both aged and failing, might lead

When the Giant left the house on the morrow, he (the
King of Erin) took an axe and split the gnarled trunk, and
out leaped a ram. He remembered the Short-tailed D2074·2·1
Hound of the Wood, and the Hound was instantly beside
him, and caught the ram. He cut the ram open, and B571·1
when he did, a wild duck sprang forth on the wing and
away to the skies. The King remembered the Blue-eyed
Hawk of Slieve Brat, and she was with him at once, and
caught the duck. He cut the duck open, found an egg,
and crushed it in his hand, and as soon as he did so, the
Giant fell dead. They [the King and his wife] then set G510
forth, and came to the house of the Black Knight. And
they made a wedding for seven days and seven nights with
an ardour that did not cool or seek respite.

to thinking that there was only one reciter, whose name happened to
have been spelt in two different ways. But all who know the Highlands
know how frequently one meets two individuals who both bear the
same Christian name and surname,[1] and who are therefore distinguished
by some sobriquet.[2] To suppose, then, that there were two Donald
MacFies or MacPhies, both of Iochdar, South Uist, and both aged
and failing, were to suggest something quite commonplace. In any
case, the differences between the two versions prove conclusively that
there were two reciters. This is confirmed by the implications of one
of the notes made in the MS. of No. 2 by the scribe, Hector MacLean,
where he, undoubtedly referring to No. 1, says : 'Here the otter is
wanting . . .' etc. Had No. 2 been recited by the reciter of No. 1,
Hector would surely have said instead something to the following
effect : 'Here the reciter omitted the otter which he mentioned when
telling me the story before.' The rest of his note clearly shows that
he thought of No. 2 as a story different from No. 1, and not a re-telling
of it by the same man.

Curiously enough, in *W. H. Tales*, i., No. 1, Var. 3, Islay says that
Var. 3 (= No. 106) was recited by John MacPhie. But in his list of
'Errata' he corrects this to Donald, and marks the entry—'*passim*.'
This correction therefore applies to the text of tales No. 4, Var. 2, and
No. 44 (*W. H. Tales*, i. and ii.), and to *The Celtic Dragon Myth*, intro.,
xiv., pp. 131, 133.

[1] This was the case even in ancient times. See the case of Fergus, three
of whose sons were each called Illann. *Celtic Review*, iii., p. 15.
[2] And still oftener by the name of their father and grandfather, sometimes
even farther back than that.

BALGAM MÓR

No. 3.   Campbell MS. Vol. x., No. 2

Aarne-Thompson, Nos. 513, 514

F 112   Bha nighean aig Rìgh Eilean nam Ban,[1] a bha anabarrach
F 134   brèagha.

Agus mar a tha tachairt do na gruagaichean sgiamhach,
bha móran shuirgheach aice.

H 335   Ach a h-aon cha phòsadh i, ach fear a dhèanadh long
D1533·1·1 a sheòladh air muir is tìr, ach so cha robh e an comas a
h-aon diubh a dhèanamh, ged a dh'fheuch cuid dhiùbh
ris.

L 111·3   Bha bantrach bhochd an sin, aig an robh triuir mhac.
Thuirt am fear a bu shine ri a mhàthair,

'Eirich, a mhàthair, is deasaich dhomh-sa bonnach,
is falbhaidh mi, feuch an dèan mi long a sheòladh air muir
is tìr, gus feuch am faigh mi Nighean an Rìgh.'

Dh'éirich a mhàthair, is rinn i dà bhonnach, fear
beag is fear mór. Is thuirt i ris, 'Có is fhearr leat—am
J 229·3   bonnach mór le mo mhallachd, no am bonnach beag le mo
bheannachd ?'

'Beannachd no mallachd—thoir dhomhsa am bonnach
mór,' thuirt esan, agus dh'fhalbh e leis a' bhonnach.

Thòisich e air togail an t-soithich, ach cha robh e
Q 2   fada ag obair, an uair a thàinig seann duine liath an
rathad, is thuirt e, 'Tha thu trang, a Mhic na Bantraich !'

'Tha mi sin,' thuirt esan.

---

[1] *Beann* in MS. (of bens). But this is probably wrong. 'The Isle of
Bens' would not be a distinctive name, as it is applicable to many Scottish
islands. Besides Campbell in his summary, *W. H. Tales*, iv., p. 260, refers to
it as 'the island of women' which would be 'Eilean nam Ban.' This latter
A 692   name was that of one of the islands in the Happy Otherworld of Celtic
myth, and is probably the island referred to here. The fact that there was
a well in the isle, a green well, and that the well was situated 'at the outer
embankments of the world,' or as Campbell usually translates it 'about the heaps

GREAT GULP

Aarne-Thompson, Nos. 513, 514

THE King of the Isle of the Women,[1] had a daughter,   F 112
who was exceedingly lovely.   F 134
And as usually happens to beautiful maidens, she had
many suitors.
But not one would she marry, unless he could make   H 335
a ship that could sail on sea and on land. But this was   D1533·1·1
not in the power of any of them, though some of them had
a try at it.
There was a certain poor widow living there, who had   L 111·3
three sons. The eldest one said to his mother,
'Arise, mother, and make a bannock ready for me, and
I will go and see if I can make a ship that will sail both
on sea and land, and see if I can win the King's Daughter.'
His mother arose, and she made two bannocks, a
small one and a big one. And she said to him, 'Which
dost thou prefer—the big bannock with my curse, or the   J 229·3
little bannock with my blessing?'
'Be it a blessing or a curse—give me the big bannock,'
said he, and off he went with it.
He began to build the ship, but he had not been long
working, when a gray-haired old man came that way, and   Q 2
said, 'Thou art busy, O Son of the Widow!'
'That I certainly am,' said he.

---

of the deep,' makes it certain that the isle was one of the Happy Isles. Most
tales locate the green well in the *Green* Isle, another of the Happy Isles, which
were supposed to lie far out to sea in the Atlantic. In this story there seems
to be only one island spoken of, but it is very possible that in more ancient
versions, there were more than one island, perhaps several.—For 'The Isles
of the Blest,' see *Folk-Lore*, xxxii., p. 150 ; *W. H. Tales*, iv., p. 322 or 294. Eilean
nam Ban Móra, the Isle of the Big Women, is another name for the Isle   F 531·6·2
of Eigg.

'Ma bheir thu dhomhsa cuid de do bhonnach mór,
nì mi do chuideachdainn.'

'Gu dearbh, cha toir—tha e beag n'a[s] leòir dhomh
fhéin, mun cuir mi crìoch air an t-soitheach so.'

Agus mar a thuirt, b'fhìor. Cha b'fhada 'na dhéidh
so, gus an tug e suas an obair, is thug e an tigh air.

'Ma tà,' ars an darna bràthair, 'théid mi féin 'ga
fheuchainn cuideachd,' agus air a' cheart dòigh mar a
thachair d'a bhràthair, thachair dà-san.

L 10   Ach latha de na làithean, thuirt am fear a b'òige ri a
mhàthair, i a dheasachainn bonnaich dha-san, agus gun
rachadh e a dh'fheuchainn an dèanadh e long.

J 229·3   Rinn a mhàthair an so, dà bhonnach. 'A nis,' ars ise,
'gabh do roghainn, am fear mór le mallachd do mhàthar,
no am fear beag le a beannachd.'

L 222   'Thoir thusa dhomhsa do bheannachd, a mhàthair,
agus beag no mór am bonnach, tha mise toilichte,' agus is
ann mar so a thachair.

Fhuair e bonnach beag agus beannachd 'na chois, is
thug e cùl do'n bhaile 's an robh e, agus ràinig e an t-àite
anns an robh aige ris an long a thogail.

Thòisich e air obair, agus an ceann beagan làithean,
thàinig an seann duine liath a rithist, is thuirt e, 'Tha thu
trang, a Mhic na Bantraich.'

'Tha mi,' ars esan.

'An toir thu dhomh roinn de do bhonnach, is nì mi do
N 825·2   chobhair.'

Q 2   'Ach ! gheibh thu sin, ged nach 'eil e ro mhór,' thuirt
esan.

Thòisich iad air togail na luinge, is cha b'fhada gus an
robh i ullamh.[2]

Dh'fhalbh iad a nise 'ga seòladh, is a shealltuinn a
F 601   mach airson sgioba.

Bha iad an so là 'ga seòladh, (is b'e an seòladair i, bu
choingeis leatha muir no monadh), bha iad an so a'

---

¹ I shall need it all.
² For a similar ship, see *Waifs and Strays*, iii., p. 289, and *W. H. Tales*, i.,
No. 16.

'If thou wilt give me some of that big bannock of thine, I will help thee.'

'Indeed I won't—it will be little enough for myself[1] before I finish this ship.'

And as he said, so it happened. For it was not long afterwards that he gave up his task, and went home.

'Well,' said the second brother, 'I also will go and have a try at it,' but that which had befallen his brother, befell him too, in exactly the same way.

But on a day of days, the youngest one asked his mother L 10 to prepare a bannock for him, so that he might go and try whether he could make a ship.

Upon this his mother made two bannocks. 'Now,' J 229·3 said she, 'take thy choice, the big one with thy mother's curse, or the little one with her blessing.'

'Give me thy blessing, mother, and whether the bannock L 222 be little or big, I shall be happy,' and things were done accordingly.

He got the little bannock and a blessing to follow and attend it, and he turned his back on the town where he lived, and arrived at the place where he had to build the ship.

He began working, and at the end of a few days, the gray-haired old man came again, and said, 'Thou art busy, thou Son of the Widow.'

'I am indeed,' said he.

'If thou wilt give me a share of thy bannock, I will help thee.' N 825·2

'O ! that shalt thou have, though it is none too big,' Q 2 said he.

They began building the ship, and it was not long before she was ready.[2]

They now went off sailing the ship, and looking out for a crew. F 601

So there they were sailing her one day, (and she *was* a good sailor; sea or moorland, it was all the same to

seòladh ri taobh coille, agus a mach thàinig as a' choillidh
fiadh 'na dheann.

F 681 Cha deach am fiadh fad air aghaidh, an uair a thàinig
Ceatharnach [1] 'na dhéidh, is rug e air an fhiadh.
'Is maith a ruitheas tu,' ars an sgiobair.
'Seadh,' thuirt an Ceatharnach.
'Is fhearr dhuit gabhail agam fhéin 'san t-soitheach so.'

'Nì mi sin,' thuirt esan.
'C'ainm a th'ort?'
'Is ainm dhomh Lurga Luath.'

Cha deach iad fad air an aghaidh mar so, an uair a
chunnaic iad fear eile agus a aghaidh ris a' ghrunnd, agus
e mar gum bitheadh e ag éisdeachd.
Dh'fheòraich e dheth, ciod è bha e 'dèanamh mar siod.

F 641·1 'Tha,' thuirt esan, 'tha mi ag éisdeachd [5] an fheoir a'
tighinn [t]roimh [an] talamh.'
'Is fearr dhuit tighinn leam fhéin 'san t-soitheach so.'
'Nì mi sin.'
'C'ainm a th' ort?'
'Is e is ainm dhomh, Clàistneachd [2] Mhaith.'

Cha robh iad fada a' seòladh, dar a chunnaic iad fear
F 626·1* eile, is e sgealbadh na creige le a thòin.
Ciod e tha thu dèanamh mar sin?'
'Tha mi cur seachad an là mar so.'
'Is fhearr dhuit tighinn leam fhéin 'san t-soitheach so.'
'Nì mi sin.'
'C'ainm a th' ort?'
'Is e Tòn Chruaidh as ainm dhomhsa.'

Cha deach iad fada mar so, an uair a chunnaic iad fear
F 661 eile, is gunna ri a shùil.
'Ciod e tha thu ag amharc mar sin?'
'Tha mi dèanamh cuimse air eun a tha thall an Eirinn.'
'Is fhearr duit tighinn leam fhéin 'san t-soitheach so.'
'Nì mi sin.'

---

[1] *Ceatharnach*, champion, hero, stout robust man; robber, whence
'cateran.'
[2] MS. éistneachd.   [3] MS. clarsneachd.

her), they were sailing by the side of a wood, when out of the wood dashed a deer at full speed.

The deer had not gone very far, when a Champion [1] F 681 came after it, and caught it.

'Thou art indeed a fine runner,' said the skipper.

'Yes,' said the Champion.

'Thou hadst better take service with me and join me in this ship.'

'That will I,' said he.

'What name dost thou bear ?'

'Nimble Shanks is my name.'

They had not travelled very far in this way, when they saw another man with his face to the ground, and he [seemed] as if he were listening.

They asked him, what he was doing by acting in that way.

'I,' said he, 'am listening to the grass coming up through F 641·1 the earth.'

'Thou hadst better come with me then in this ship.'

'That I will.'

'What is thy name ?'

'My name is Good Hearing.'

They had not been sailing long, when they saw another man, and he was splintering the rocks with his haunches. F 626·1*

'What art thou doing, going on in that way ?'

'I am passing the day in this manner.'

'Thou hadst better come with me in this ship.'

'That will I.'

'What is thy name ?'

'Hard Haunches is my name.'

They had not gone far thus, when they saw another man, with a gun to his eye. F 661

'What art thou looking at in that way ?'

'I am aiming at a bird that is over in Ireland yonder.'

'Thou hadst better come with me in this ship.'

'That will I.'

'C'ainm a th'ort ?'

'Is ainm dhomh Cuimse Dhìreach.'

F 633 'Na dhéidh so, chunnaic iad fear eile a' srupladh lochain, is 'ga spùtadh a mach a rithist.

'Is fhearr dhuit do spùtadh a leigeil dhìot, agus tighinn leam fhéin 'san t-soitheach so.'

'Nì mi sin,' ars esan.

'C'ainm a th'ort ?'

'Is ainm dhomh BALGAM MÓR.'

Air an aghaidh ghabh iad, gus an do ràinig iad tigh an Rìgh, agus an uair a chunnaic an Rìgh an long a' tighinn, cha robh e ro dheònach a nighean a thoirt gu Mac na Bantraich.

Is e a bh'ann, gun do chruinnich an Rìgh uaislean a' bhaile mhóir gu léir, chum is gun gabhadh iad comhairle, ciod e dhèanadh iad mu Nighean an Rìgh.

Bha, an sin, gach fear a' toirt a chomhairle is a theanga 'na ghob, ach le còir is ceartas, bha Mac na Bantraich ri Nighean an Rìgh fhaotainn, [a chionn gun do thog e an long a bha i ag iarraidh].

G 200
H 910 Thàinig an Earchlais-Urlair [1] agus thuirt i gum feuchadh
H 301 ise ri dòigh a dhèanamh air Mac na Bantraich. Agus is
H 935
H 1321 e a bh'ann, gum feumadh Mac na Bantraich neach fhaotainn
A 692 a bheireadh botul uisge á tobair uaine an iomall tòrra an
H 1109·1 domhain, an toiseach air Nighinn Duibh na Luideig. [2]

'Tha mi cluinntinn nì,' thuirt Clàistneachd Mhaith.

'Ciod e tha thu cluinntinn ?' ars esan.

H 335 'Tha—mur toir thu botul uisge á tobar uaine an iomall
F 601·2 tòrra an domhain, an toiseach air Nighinn Duibh na Luideig, nach faigh thu Nighean an Rìgh.' [3]

---

[1] So spelt in MS. See note on Appendix II., p. 492.

[2] This character, to judge by her name, seems to be the much-dreaded washing-fairy, or *Bean-Nighe*.—J. G. McKay, *Bean-Nighe* (Alex. MacLaren & Son, Glasgow).—The green well is usually situated in the Green Isle, one of the islands of the Happy Otherworld.

[3] It will be noticed that Good Hearing speaks as if his master, the hero,

'What is thy name ?'

'My name is Straight Aim.'

After this they saw another man sucking up a little F 633
loch, and spouting it out again.

'Thou hadst better leave off thy spouting, and come
along with me in this ship.'

'That will I,' said he.

'What is thy name ?'

'My name is GREAT GULP.'

Forward they pressed until they came to the King's
house. But when the King saw the ship coming, he was
not very willing to give his daughter to the Widow's Son.

So what happened was that the King gathered all the
nobles of the great town together, in order that they might
take counsel as to what to do concerning the King's
Daughter.

So there they were, every man giving his advice with
his tongue in his prattling mouth, but right and justice
prevailing, the Widow's Son was to have the King's
Daughter, [because he had built the ship she wanted]. G 200

But the Floor-Mischief [1] came, and said that she would H 910
try a stratagem that should settle the Widow's Son. And H 301
so it was, that the Widow's Son must find some one who H 935
could fetch a bottle of water from the green well that was H 1321
situated at the outermost embankments of the world, more A 692
quickly than the Black-Lass-of-the-Ragged-Clout [2] could H 1109·1
fetch it.

'I hear something,' said Good Hearing.

'What dost thou hear ?' said the Widow's Son.

'Why this—that if thou canst not fetch a bottle of water H 335
from the green well at the outermost embankments of the F 601·2
world before Black-Lass-of-the-Ragged-Clout can do so,
thou art not to win the King's Daughter.' [3]

was the person who had to perform the task of fetching the water. The
probability is that in every instance the hero was indeed asked to perform,
and that one of his magic servants then proposed to act as proxy, and that
this proposal was accepted. That this was the original trend of the tale
appears from a comparison of all the incidents. See p. 251 n.

H 331·5·4 'Leig a mach mise,' thuirt Lurga Luath. ['Théid mise 'sa' chomh-ruith rithe.']

Agus air falbh gabhar iad.

Bha Nighean Dubh na Luideig gu maith luath. Ach cha dèanadh i stàth air Lurga Luath.

Ràinig Lurga Luath an tobar, agus thog e soitheach uisge: thachair Nighean Dubh na Luideig ris air an rathad. Smuainich i gum feuchadh i ris an t-soitheach a thoirt uaidh leis an teanga, bho'n a dh'fhairtlich e oirre le luathas nan cas.

'Dèan suidhe, is leig t'anail, is slìogaidh mi do cheann.'
D 1962·3 Rinn e so, is cha robh e fad air a glùn, dar a thuit e 'na throm chadal.

Rug i air claigeann eich mhairbh a bha làimh rithe, is chuir i gu socrach fo a cheann e, is thug i na buinn aisde leis an t-soitheach uisge.

'Tha mi cluinntinn rud,' thuirt Clàistneachd Mhaith.

'Ciod e tha thu cluinntinn?' thuirt esan.

'Tha mi cluinntinn srann Lurga Luaith; chaidil e, agus tha Nighean Dubh na Luideig air an t-soitheach uisge a thoirt uaidh, is tha i tighinn 'na deann.'

'Nì mise gnothuch ris a sin,' thuirt Cuimse Dhìreach. Is loisg e peileir air, is buailear claigeann an eich a bha fo a cheann.

Dhùisg Lurga Luath, is cha b'fhada bha e cur ri Nighinn Duibh na Luideig. [Spìon e an soitheach uisge uaipe, is dh'fhalbh e dhachaidh 'na làn luathas. An uair a ràinig e,] thug esan an so an soitheach do Nighean an Rìgh.

Dh'iarr e an so Nighean an Rìgh ri a pòsadh, 'ach cha leig sinn air falbh i mar sin fhathast,' thuirt an Earchlais-Urlair.

Is e a bh'ann, le comhairle na h-Earchlais-Urlair,
H 331·1 gum feumadh e torc nimhe a bha anns a' choillidh ubhal
H 1154·3 ud shuas, a mharcachd beò, slàn, gu dorus Lùchairt an Rìgh, 'is chan 'eil duine aige as urrainn sin a dhèanamh,' thuirt an Earchlais-Urlair.

* * * * * *

'Let me go forth,' said Nimble Shanks. ['I will run H 331·5·4 in the race against her.']

And away they raced.

Black-Lass-of-the-Ragged-Clout was very speedy. But she could do nothing against Nimble Shanks.

Nimble Shanks arrived at the well, and drew a vessel of water : Black-Lass-of-the-Ragged-Clout met him on the road. She determined to try and get the vessel away from him by the use of her tongue, seeing that she had been utterly unable to do so by swiftness of foot.

'Be seated, and take breath, and I will stroke thy locks.' He did so, but he was not long on her knee, when he fell D 1962·3 fast asleep.

Then she got hold of the skull of a dead horse that was beside her, and having placed it comfortably under his head, took to her heels with the water-pot.

'I hear something,' said Good Hearing.

'What hearest thou ?' said the Widow's Son.

'I hear the snoring of Nimble Shanks; he has gone to sleep, and Black-Lass-of-the-Ragged-Clout has taken the water-pot away from him, and she is coming at great speed.'

'I will settle that,' said Straight Aim. And firing a bullet at the horse's skull that was under Nimble Shanks' head, hit it.

Nimble Shanks awoke, and he was not long in dealing with Black-Lass-of-the-Ragged-Clout. [He wrenched the water-pot away from her, and set off home at his utmost pace. When he got back], he gave the vessel to the King's Daughter.

The Widow's Son then asked for the King's Daughter in marriage, 'but we cannot yet let her go like this,' said the Floor-Mischief.

Accordingly, upon the advice of the Floor-Mischief, [it was agreed that] the Widow's Son must ride a wild and H 331·1 deadly boar, which was in yonder wood of apple trees. H 1154·3 The boar was to be ridden alive and uninjured, right up to the door of the King's Palace, 'and he has not a man who can do that,' said the Floor-Mischief.

*   *   *   *   *   *

'Tha mi cluinntinn rud,' arsa Clàistneachd Mhaith.
'Ciod e tha thu cluinntinn?'
'Tha—gum feum thu torc nimhe a tha 'sa' choillidh
[ubhal] ud shuas, a thoirt beò, slàn, gu Lùchairt an Rìgh,
mum faigh thu Nighean an Rìgh.'

Air falbh gabhar Lurga Luath is Tòn Chruaidh, Lurga
Luath gu beireachd air an torc, is Tòn Chruaidh gu a
mharcachd, is thug iad an torc gu Lùchairt an Rìgh.
Dh'iarr e, an sin, Nighean an Rìgh, ri a pòsadh.

Thuirt an Earchlais-Urlair ris an Rìgh gum feuchadh
i dòigh eile air. 'Thoir cuireadh dha do dhinnear an
diugh, is bheir thu air suidhe air a' chathair mhóir anns a
bheil am bior nimhe, is cuiridh sin ás da.' [1]

H 1531

Chuala Clàistneachd Mhaith so; thuirt Tòn Chruaidh
gum bruicheadh esan lus an so.[2] Chaidh Tòn Chruaidh
'na ghille le a mhaighstir do'n Lùchairt, agus do sheòmar
na dinnearach.
Chuir an Rìgh furan is fàilte air, is sheall e dha a'
chathair mhór gu suidhe oirre.
Thuirt Tòn Chruaidh gun robh e 'na chleachduinn
aige-san suidhe anns gach cathair air an robh a mhaighstir
gu suidhe, feuch an robh i làidir n'a[s] leòir.
Shuidh Tòn Chruaidh anns a' chathair, is bhrist e
gach bìor agus gach cathair 'na phronnagan.
An déidh na dinnearach, bha sùil aige ri Nighean an
Rìgh fhaotainn, ach thuirt an Earchlais-Urlair nach
faodadh sin tachairt.
'Feuchaidh sinn dòigh eile air.'
Is e a bh' ann, gum feumadh e lochan uisge a bha am
mullach na beinne seilge, a thoirt gu lagan bòidheach a
bha fa chomhair dorus mór Tigh an Rìgh.

H 1023
·2·2

Chuala Clàistneachd Mhaith so.

---

[1] This sentence speaks of only one spiked chair. But later on, there
appear to have been several.

'I am hearing something,' said Good Hearing.

'What dost thou hear?'

'Why—that thou must bring the deadly wild boar that is in yonder wood of [apple] trees, alive and uninjured to the King's Palace, before thou mayest win the King's Daughter.'

Away went Nimble Shanks and Hard Haunches together, Nimble Shanks to catch the boar and Hard Haunches to ride him, and they brought the boar to the King's Palace.

Then the Widow's Son asked for the King's Daughter in marriage.

But the Floor-Mischief said to the King that she would try another plan with the Widow's Son. 'Give him an invitation to dinner to-day, and make him sit in the big H 1531 chair in which the deadly spike is fixed. That will kill him.' [1]

Good Hearing heard this; Hard Haunches said that he would cook a herb at this point.[2] So in the rôle of a servant, Hard Haunches went with his master to the Palace, and to the dining-room.

The King welcomed and saluted the Widow's Son, and showed him the big chair that he might sit in it.

Hard Haunches said that it was his custom to sit in every chair in which his master was to sit, to see if it were strong enough.

So Hard Haunches sat in the chair, and smashed every spike and every chair to little bits.

After dinner, the Widow's Son expected to get the King's Daughter, but the Floor-Mischief said that could not be.

'We will try another plan with him.'

The thing that happened next was, that he must bring the freshwater loch that was on the summit of the hunting H 1023 hill, to a beautiful dell facing the great door of the King's ·2·2 House.

Good Hearing heard this.

---

[2] Metaphorical. Probably equivalent to 'cooking one's goose for him,' 'dishing one's enemy,' 'settling his hash,' 'stewing him in his own juice,' culinary metaphors all.

'Leig mise 'na caraibh,' thuirt BALGAM MÓR, 'is [ma]
tha iad am feum an uisgeachadh, is maith a dh'fhaoidte,
gum faigh iad an sàth.'

D 2151
·1·3*

Thug Balgam Mór am monadh air, is thòisich an spùtadh
uisge tighinn.

Bha gach nì a bha mun chaisteal air snàmh an so. Bha
a choslas mur stadadh an t-uisge, gum biodh gach ni a
bha mu'n Lùchairt air a mhilleadh gu tur.

Ach is e a bh'ann, gun d'iarr an Rìgh air Mac na
Bantraich òrdugh a thoirt do Bhalgam Mór, gun tuilleadh
uisge a dhòrtadh, is gum faigheadh e fhéin a nighean gu

H 1242

pòsadh a nochd fhéin.

Is chaidh an Earchlais-Urlair a losgadh, bho'n is i

G 275·3
Q 414

bu chiontach ris an uisge a mhilleadh gach nì, mar a
rinneadh.

Phòs iad an sin, agus rinn an Rìgh banais mhór, ghreadhnach, agus dh'fhàg mise an Caisteal an Rìgh iad le chéile.

Copy[d] From John McKenzie, Kenmor near Inverary. Hector
Urq[t'] [= Urquhart].

NOTES

'Copy[d],' at the end of the MS., probably implies the existence of
a first rough transcription.
Islay summarized this tale in *W. H. Tales*, iv., p. 259 or 283. He
referred to it in No. 16, *ibid.*, i., where the only character who helps
to build the magic ship is a Urisk. But after procuring his complement
of magic helpers, the hero embarks upon adventures different from
those in 'Balgam Mór.'
Similar narratives appear in Islay's English List, No. 275 :

'Let me tackle it,' said GREAT GULP, 'and if they are in need of being watered, it may well be that they will get enough to satisfy them.'

Great Gulp betook him to the mountain, and then indeed the water-spouts began. D 2151 ·1·3*

Everything about the castle was now swimming in water. And it seemed very likely that unless the water stopped, everything in and about the Palace would be utterly ruined.

So what happened was, that the King requested the Widow's Son to order Great Gulp not to shower down any more water, and that the Widow's Son should get the King's Daughter in marriage that very night. H 1242

And the Floor-Mischief was burned, as it was she who was to blame for the water having spoiled everything as it had been spoiled. G 275·3

Q 414

Then they married, and the King made a great joyous wedding, and I left them there in the King's Castle.

Béaloideas, ii. p. 194 ; Dr Douglas Hyde, *Beside the Fire* (London, 1890), pp. 18, 179, 'The King of Ireland's Son,' a tale which is also closely related to Campbell's MS. vol. x., No. 97, and in some respects to *W. H. Tales*, iii., No. 58, 'Ridire Ghrianaig.' *Cf.* Grimm, *Kinder und Hausmärchen*, p. 71.

See MS. vol. xi., No. 310 ; MS. vol. xiii., No. 275 ; *Waifs and Strays*, ii., p. 445 ; iii., p. 2 ; iv., pp. 177, 183, 205.

MÓR NIGHEAN SMÙID

No. 4. [Vol. x., No. 3]

Aarne-Thompson, No. 20, C, and 2033

Z 41·4   ROIMHE so, bha cailleach ann ris an abradh iad, Mór
Nighean Smùid,[1] agus bha i dol as a' bhaile agus shleamh-
nuich i, agus thuit i, agus shaoil i gum b'e am Bàs a bh'ann.

Agus dh'fhalbh i agus dh'fhalbh i, gus an do choinnich
i fear ris an abradh iad, Eòghann MacAlk. 'Eòghann
MacAlk, bò chugad am Bàs,' thuirt Mór Nighean Smùid.
'Am faca thu e no an cuala ?' thuirt Eoghann MacAlk.
'Mo chluas a chuala, mo shùil a chunnaic, mo bhonn
a mhothaich,' thuirt Mór Nighean Smùid, agus dh'fhalbh
Mór Nighean Smùid, agus Eòghann MacAlk gus an do
choinnich iad Sagart Gille Breac.[2] 'A Shagairt Ghille
Bhric ! bò chugad am Bàs,' thuirt Mór Nighean Smùid.
'Am faca thu e no an cuala ?' thuirt Sagart Gille Breac.

'Mo chluas a chuala, mo shùil a chunnaic, mo bhonn
a mhothaich,' arsa Mór Nighean Smùid, agus dh'fhalbh
Mór Nighean Smùid, agus Eòghann MacAlk, agus Sagart
Gille Breac, gus an do choinnich iad 'Aon Sùil Fhear.'
'Aon Sùil Fhear, Bò chugad am Bàs !' arsa Mór Nighean
Smùid.
'Am faca thu e no an cuala ?' thuirt Aon Sùil Fhear.
'Mo chluas a chuala, mo shùil a chunnaic, mo bhonn
a mhothaich,' thuirt Mór Nighean Smùid, agus dh'fhalbh
Mór Nighean Smùid, agus Eòghann MacAlk, agus Sagart
Gille Breac, agus Aon Sùil Fhear, gus an do choinnich iad
an Uiseag a bha air an nead.
'Uiseag a tha air an nead, Bò chugad am Bàs,' arsa
Mór Nighean Smùid.

---

[1] Pronounced Smootch.

MÓR, THE DAUGHTER OF SMÙID

No. 4.   *[Vol. x., No. 3]*

Aarne-Thompson, No. 20, C, and 2033

BEFORE this, there was an old woman whom they called z 41·4 Mór the Daughter of Smùid,[1] and when going away from home she slipped and fell, and she thought that Death had come.

And she went on and went on, until she met a man whom they called Ewan MacAlk. 'Ewan MacAlk, look out, beware of Death,' said Mór the Daughter of Smùid.

'Hast thou seen him or heard him?' said Ewan MacAlk.

'My ear has heard, my eye has seen, and my foot has felt,' said Mór the Daughter of Smùid, so Mór the Daughter of Smùid and Ewan MacAlk went on till they met Priest Speckled Boy.[2] 'Priest Speckled Boy! look out, beware of Death,' said Mór the Daughter of Smùid.

'Hast thou seen or heard him?' said Priest Speckled Boy.

'My ear has heard, my eye has seen, and my foot has felt,' said Mór the Daughter of Smùid, so Mór the Daughter of Smùid, and Ewan MacAlk, and Priest Speckled Boy went on till they met the One-eyed Man.

'One-eyed Man, look out, beware of Death,' said Mór the Daughter of Smùid.

'Hast thou seen or heard him?' said the One-eyed Man.

'My ear has heard, my eye has seen, my foot has felt,' said Mór the Daughter of Smùid, so Mór the Daughter of Smùid, and Ewan MacAlk, and Priest Speckled Boy, and the One-eyed Man went on till they met the Lark that was on the nest.

'Thou Lark that art on the nest, look out, beware of Death,' said Mór the Daughter of Smùid.

[2] Compare a name for the frog, Gille Chriosda MacDhughail, Gilchrist MacDugald, *W. H. Tales*, i., No. 17*a*, 13.

'Am faca thu e no an cuala?' thuirt an Uiseag a bha air an nead. 'Mo chluas a chuala, mo shùil a chunnaic, mo bhonn a mhothaich,' thuirt Mór Nighean Smùid, agus dh'fhalbh Mór Nighean Smùid, agus Eòghann MacAlk, agus Sagart Gille Breac, agus Aon Sùil Fhear, agus an Uiseag a bha air an nead gus an do choinnich iad an Dreòlan a bha anns a' chreig, etc.,

> agus Tughadair na h-Atha,
> *Grinder* a' Mhuilinn,
> Ruairidh Beag na Creige,
> Ruairidh Mór na Creige,
> Cailleach a' Bhothain,
> Agus Each an Triubhais Bhàin,

agus dh'fhalbh iad gus an do ràinig iad abhainn.

Z 31·2·1   'Ciod e mar a gheibh sinn thar na h-aibhne?' thuirt Mór Nighean Smùid, agus Ewan MacAlk, agus Sagart Gille Breac, agus Aon Sùil Fhear, agus an Uiseag a bha air an nead, agus an Dreòlan a bha anns a' chreig, agus Tughadair na h-Atha, *Grinder* a' Mhuilinn, Ruairidh Beag na Creige, Ruairidh Mór na Creige, agus Cailleach a'Bhothain.

'Thigeadh sibhse air mo mhuin,' thuirt Each an Triubhais Bhàin, 'agus bheir mise thairis sibh,' agus dh'fhalbh Mór Nighean Smùid, agus Eòghann MacAlk, agus Sagart Gille Breac, agus Aon Sùil Fhear, agus Uiseag a bha air an nead, agus an Dreòlan a bha anns a' chreig, agus Tughadair na h-Atha, agus *Grinder* a' Mhuilinn, agus Ruairidh Beag na Creige, agus Ruairidh Mór na Creige, agus Cailleach a' Bhothain, agus chaidh iad air fad air muin Each an Triubhais Bhàin, agus dh'fhalbh iad leis an abhainn, agus dhealaich mise riutha !!

NOTES

MS. vol. x., No. 3. The MS. bears two numbers—3 and 24. It is probably the item called 'No. 3. Procession and death,' in Islay's Gaelic List, *W. H. Tales,* iv., end, where we read that it was narrated by a nursemaid in Islay and was collected by Miss Ord Campbell.

'Hast thou seen or heard him?' said the Lark that was on the nest. 'My ear has heard, my eye has seen, and my foot has felt,' said Mór the Daughter of Smùid, so Mór the Daughter of Smùid, and Ewan MacAlk, and Priest Speckled Boy, and the One-eyed Man, and the Lark that was on the nest went on till they met the Wren that was in the Rock, etc.,

> and The Thatcher of the Kiln,
> The Grinder of the Mill,
> Little Rory of the Rock,
> Big Rory of the Rock,
> The Old Woman of the Bothy,
> And the Horse with the White Trews,

and on they went till they came to a river.

'How shall we get across the river?' said Mór the Z 31·2·1 Daughter of Smùid, and Ewan MacAlk, and Priest Speckled Boy, and the One-eyed Man, and the Lark that was on the nest, and the Wren that was in the Rock, and the Thatcher of the Kiln, the Grinder of the Mill, Little Rory of the Rock, Big Rory of the Rock, and the Old Woman of the Bothy.

'Get ye up on my back,' said the Horse with the White Trews, 'and I will take you across,' and so Mór the Daughter of Smùid, and Ewan MacAlk, and Priest Speckled Boy, and the One-eyed Man, and the Lark that was on the nest, and the Wren that was in the rock, and the Thatcher of the Kiln, and the Grinder of the Mill, and Little Rory of the Rock, and Big Rory of the Rock, and the Old Woman of the Bothy, went, and the whole lot of them got up on the back of the Horse with the White Trews, and they were carried away by the river, and I parted from them !!

A translation is also bound up, but there is no signature, nor any clue as to reciter or provenance, in the MS. *Aon Suil Fhear* is bad Gaelic. It appears in the translation as the One-eyed Man. It may be a misapprehension for *an Sùlair*, the Solan Goose.

Dr R. C. MacLagan, *The Games and Diversions of Argyleshire*, p. 3, gives an 'Articulation Test' which is evidently a close relation to the foregoing, though in a different dress, and much curtailed. But the names of two of the characters have been preserved by Dr MacLagan as Mór Niall Smuilc and Eoin MacCuilc.

An Irish version is given in *The Gaelic Journal* (1889), ix., p. 339. For a similar tale, see *Béaloideas*, I, p. 94 (Aa 130 not 125) iv. (1934), p. 10, Supplt. part iv. It is in essence a well-known droll, 'Henny-Penny.' For the sky falling, see *Waifs and Strays*, iv., p. 206 ; *Superstitions*, p. 132.

The Irish Folklore Commission, University College, Dublin, have collected for S.W. Waterford, W. Kerry, and S.W. Donegal one, three and two versions respectively.

SGEULACHD CHOISE CHÉIN

BHA rìgh air Eirinn ris an canadh iad Iarl Antruim, is bha buachaille each aige do am b'ainm O'Cròleagann. Agus bha móran each aig Iarl Antruim, agus is e an dòigh chunntaidh bha aig O'Cròleagann [orra] taod mu choinnimh na h-uile each; is cha robh clann aig O'Cròleagann ach aon mhac.

Agus bhàsaich an seann duine, agus o'n a bha O'Cròleagann cho measail aig an Iarla, bha am mac aige an àite a athar a' buachailleachd nan each. Agus air latha àraidh agus mac O'Cròleagann a' buachailleachd nan each is breacan ruadh air, chunnaic e maigheach is thòisich e air a ruith, is chaidh i a steach ann an tom luachrach. Dar a bha e ag iarraidh na maighich 'san tom

F 234
·1·7*

luachrach, leum i fo'n bhreacan air a dhruim. Theannaich e am breacan gu maith air a dhruim, is thàinig e dhachaidh leatha, is thuirt e ri a mhàthair, 'Dùin na h-uile toll a tha air an tigh, tha maigheach agamsa 'sa' bhreacan.' Agus

D 323

an uair a dh'fhuasgail e am breacan, thuit am boirionnach bu bhriagha a chunnaic e riamh de a dhruim. Agus bha Iarl Antruim airson gum pòsadh mac O'Cròleagann

F 234
·1·8*

i. Rinn Iarl Antruim banais mhór dhaibh, agus dar a chaidh am pòsadh, mar a tha daonnan a' tachairt, chaidh

F 302
D 131
F 221·2*

ise a laighe an toiseach. Agus dar a thàinig esan gu dol a laighe, leum ise as an leabaidh 'na lothaig [1] ghuirm, agus thog i cas agus rinn i dà chruinn leth air cnàimh na sléisde aige-san. Agus sùil de'n tug e, bha e anns a' ghleann luachrach anns an d'fhuair e an toiseach i. Bha Iarl Antruim anabarrach brònach airson mar a dh'éirich do mhac O'Cròleagann, agus chuir e fios air a h-uile lighich a bha'n Eirinn, ach cha robh iad a' dèanamh feum sam bith da.

---

[1] MS. lothain.

THE TALE OF KANE'S LEG

THERE was a king over Ireland whom they called the
Earl of Antrim, and he had a herd called O'Cròleagann,
who managed his horses for him. And the Earl had many
horses, and O'Cròleagann's method of counting the horses
was to have a halter for each one [to act as a tally?], and
O'Cròleagann had no children except one son.

And the old man died, and because the Earl had held
him in high esteem, O'Cròleagann's son was to have his
father's place and manage the horses. And one day,
when the son of O'Cròleagann was wearing a red plaid
and herding the horses, he saw a hare and began to chase
it, and it fled into a clump of rushes. While searching for
the hare among the rushes, she leaped under the plaid on F 234
his back. He wrapped the plaid very tightly about him, ·1·7*
and brought the hare home, and said to his mother—'Shut
every opening there is in the house, I have a hare in my
plaid.' And upon loosening the plaid, the most beautiful D 323
woman he had ever seen fell off his back, and the Earl of
Antrim was desirous that the son of O'Cròleagann should
marry her. The Earl made them a great wedding, and F 234
when they were married, she, as is always done, went to ·1·8*
bed first, and when he came to go to bed, she leaped out F 302
of bed, changed into a blue [or dark gray?] filly, and D 131
lifting her foot [kicked him, and] made two exact halves
of his thigh-bone, [and vanished,] and upon glancing round, F 221·2
he found himself in the glen of rushes where he had first
found her. The Earl of Antrim was greatly grieved
because of what had happened to O'Cròleagann's son, and
he sent for every doctor in Ireland, but they were doing
him no good.

Thàinig seann duine an rathad, is thuirt e gun robh lus
ann an Eilean Iar-thuath an Domhain Mhóir [1] [is gun
leighseadh an lus e]. Ach cha b'aithne do dhuine bha an
Eirinn an lus. Agus chuir Iarl Antruim sgioba is birlinn
leis an duine leònta do Eilean Iar-thuath an Domhain
Mhóir, agus dar a ràinig iad, cha b'aithne dhaibh an lus.
Agus is e a rinn iad, thòisich iad air [an duine] a shlaodadh
as an déidh troimh fheur is lusan an Eilein.

Thòisich an duine leònta air sgriachail is air rànail,
agus dar a chunnaic iad nach [robh] a choltas orra feum
air bith a dhèanamh do'n duine leònta, is nach robh a
choltas a bhi beò air, dh'fhàg iad ann an siod e, is thug
iad fhéin an tigh orra. Agus an ceann trì làithean 'na
dhéidh so, chunnaic e curachan beag bàta a' tighinn do'n
eilean, is aon duine innte. Thàinig e far an robh an duine
leònta, agus thuirt e ris, 'Sìn do chas, a Chéin,[2] ach an
cuir mise barra-léigh [3] is barra-leighis, ciaran furtachd
agus slàinte [rithe].' 'Ma tà,' ars am fear leònta, 'nar
bu chas dhomh féin i, 's nar bu chas do Chéin i, ma
théid barra-léigh [4] no barra leighis rithe, fhiach [5] an dèan
thu aon sgeulachd [6] bheag eile dhomh air sin,' agus tha

D 965

H 1324

S 145

D 1500
·1·19

P 331*

---

[1] MS. *Eillan iar odha domhain Mhoir properly Eillan iarthuath a domhainn
Mhoir, the island of Lewis.* [Recte, Eilean Iar-thuath an Domhain Mhóir.]
The late Rev. Dr George Henderson, *Trans. Gael. Soc. Inverness*, xxv., p. 265,
gives the following footnote to the word 'Lewis': 'In Norway so far as actually
reminiscent of place-names; cf. *iruade, iruath*, of the older sagas.—G.H.'
Obscure to me; *iruath* seems sometimes to mean Norway itself, and in earlier
times was probably vague and mythical like Tìr nan Og, etc. In his *Norse
Influence*, p. 171, he writes: 'Eilean *Iubhard*, Lewis, is seemingly for Eu-ord,
N[orse] *ey-fjörðr*, "isle-firth," transferred from the firth to the island.'—
The wounded man is dragged along in order that sooner or later he may
happen to touch the herb, and thus be cured. The incident occurs in version
B (see Notes).

[2] MS. at this point occur in brackets '*this was his name.*'

[3] MS. *barra-lithi.*

[4] MS. *barra léith.*

[5] MS. *ach,* and so pronounced.

D 1338·7

A 692

An old man came that way, and he said that there was a herb in 'Eillan Iar odha Domhain Mhóir,' the Northwest Island of the Great World, [and that the herb would D 965 heal him]. But not a man in Ireland knew the herb. So the Earl of Antrim sent the wounded man and a crew with him in a ship to the Northwest Island of the Great H 1324 World, and when they got there, they did not know the herb. So what they did was to begin dragging the wounded man after them through the grass and herbs of the Island.

The wounded man began to shriek and roar, and when they saw that there was no likelihood of their doing the wounded man any good, and that he was not likely to live, they left him there, and took themselves off home. S 145 And at the end of three days after this, he (the wounded man) saw a little coracle of a boat with one man in it coming to the Island. This man came to where the wounded man was, and said to him, 'Stretch forth thy leg, O Kane, until I put a leech's dressing and a healing-dressing on it, D 1500 a plaster of comfort and of health.'—'Well then,' said the 'I·19 wounded man, 'may it never be a foot of mine or a foot of Kane's either, if a leech's dressing or healing-dressing be applied to it, until you tell me another little story P 331*

---

* MS. *aon sgeulachd.*

This seems to be a 'run,' perhaps corrupted.

> 'Sìn do chas a Chéin   Z 85*
> Ach an cuir mise barra-léigh
> Is barra-leighis,
> Ciarom furtachd
> Agus slàinte
> Rithe.'

'Ma tà,' ars am fear leonta,

> 'Nam bu chas dhomh féin i,
> 'S nam bu chas do Chéin i,
> Ma theid barra-léigh
> No barra-leighis rithe,
> Fhiach an dèan thu sgeulachd
> Bheag eile dhomh air sin.'

Z 20   an sgeulachd a' dùnadh is ri ràdh gun tàinig e ceithir latha
fichead agus sgeulachd ùr aige na h-uile latha dhiubh sin.

> From John Campbell, Strath Gairloch, Ross-shire. He learned
> this sgeulachd from a very old man, who only died two years
> ago ; this old man had the four and twenty other sgeulachds
> that [formerly] follow[ed], but John Campbell does not
> remember them.
>
> H[ector] Urq[uhar]t.

NOTES

MS. vol. x., No. 10. On the flyleaf Islay has written 'June 27,'
the date he received it. The year was probably 1859. The Gaelic
of this version appeared *Trans. Gael. Soc. Inverness*, xxv., pp. 264-265.
We may call this version 'A.'

Islay's MS. vol. xvii. is entirely occupied by three other versions
which have appeared in the following volumes of *Trans. Gael. Soc.
Inverness* :—

    (B) Gaelic only, xxv., pp. 189-262.
    (C) Gaelic and English, xiv., pp. 78-100.
    (D) Gaelic only, xxv., pp. 262-264.

B is one of the most considerable specimens of Gaelic tales. Islay's
Abstract of it is given, *ibid.*, xxv., p. 181. The late Alfred Nutt deals with
it, *Folk-Lore*, i. (1890), pp. 373 ff. The tale clamours for translation.

Other versions are :—

    (E) *Waifs and Strays*, ii., pp. 206-277, 464-473.
    (F) *Superstitions*, p. 127.
    (G) *Silva Gadelica*, i., p. 296 ; ii., p. 332.
    (H) Harleian MS. 3756, British Museum, notices of which appear
        in *Waifs and Strays*, v., p. 149 ; *Gadelica*, i., p. 281.

This tale, No. 5 (Version A) is a miserably corrupt version of
what once was one of the best, the longest, and the most complex tales.
But it is well worth giving, because when compared with better versions
(such as B *ut supra*) it shows the lines on which story-decay takes place ;
it may therefore act as a guide to reconstruction when decay is suspected
elsewhere. Reference to any of the other versions will clear up the
confusion which in this version has overtaken the identities of
O'Cròleagann and Kane.

about that;' and the narrative concludes saying that he Z 20 [the stranger] came on twenty-four [successive] days, and brought a fresh tale with him every time.

The last words of the tale show that the reciter knew that the stranger had told the wounded man a story when first meeting him, and had broken that story off short—and that thereupon the sufferer had demanded that the sequel should be related, or he would refuse to allow his leg to be healed. The stranger complies, and sequel after sequel is recited, until twenty-four tales have been told. Other versions prove that in the most ancient recension this must have been the course of events. But the reciter of the story (No. 5) cannot remember any of the twenty-four.

The refusal of the wounded man to allow his leg to be healed until all the tales have been told, and the fact that the stranger seems to feel that he is under an obligation to heal him, and to fall in with his humour of demanding tales, may be paralleled by the curious conventions that regulated relations between a host and his guest. For a guest might and often did compel his host to grant him any request upon pain of having his hospitality refused. Rather than have his hospitality slighted or impugned, the host would comply. Similarly in this No. 5, rather than have his desire to heal the sufferer frustrated, the stranger complies with the latter's demands no less than twenty- P 320 four times. An illustration this, of the immense importance attached to story-telling, and of the interest taken in a new one. However, *Superstitions*, p. 132, says that the stranger was either the King of Lochlin or of Ireland and that he was bound not to allow any one to remain in distress whom he could relieve. As to hospitality, see p. 216 n. Similarly, a laird supplies some tinkers with work, and *afterwards* asks what payment they require. See p. 223. Similarly again, characters gamble, but the stakes are not named until *after* the game is won. See pp. 5, 231, 235.

NA TRÌ CHOMHAIRLEAN

No. 6.   *Campbell MS. Vol. x., No. 15*

Aarne-Thompson, No. 910, B

BHA duine bochd ann roimhe so, agus bha bliadhna
anabarrach dhaor, ghortach ann, agus cha robh tighinn
mu làimh aca, ach a bhean a bhi 'g iarraidh an t-saoghail.

Bha nàire oirre mu dheireadh a bhi cur dragha tuilleadh
is bitheanta air an aon fheadhainn, agus smaointich i gun
rachadh i féin agus a mac, balachan beag a bha aice, na
b'fhaide air astar, agus thuirt i ri a fear, 'Iain, is fhearr
dhuit-sa bhi dèanamh air do shon fhéin, agus bidh sinne
'strìth ri sinn fhéin a thoirt [t]roimhe, mar as fhearr a
dh'fhaodas sinn.'
[Ach thuirt Iain nach b'iadsan a rachadh a mach ach
esan.]
Fhuair e beagan léintean is stocaidh, is ghabh e air
falbh. An déidh dha astar maith a chur seachad, choinnich
tuathanach taobh an rathaid mhóir [e], agus thuirt e
ris, an robh e airson fàsdadh, agus thuirt e gun robh.
Dh'fhasdaidh an tuathanach e, agus chaidh e [Iain] leis
chun a thighe.
Chuir e seachad seachd bliadhna aig an tuathanach.
An ceann nan seachd, thuirt e ris an tuathanach, 'Bidh
mi nis a' falbh; tha toil agam mo bhean is mo mhac
fhaicinn.'
'A bheil bean agus mac agad ?' ars an tuathanach.
'Tha,' ars esan.
'C'arson nach d'innis thu sin domhsa is gheibheadh tu
am faicinn roimhe so !'
'Cha tàinig e man ear domh,' ars esan.
'Tha tuarasdal seachd bliadhna dligheach dhuit,' ars
an tuathanach; 'có aca is fhearr leat—tuarasdal nan
seachd bliadhna, no trì chomhairlean maith fhaotainn ?'

THE THREE COUNSELS

No. 6.   *[Vol. x., No. 15]*

Aarne-Thompson, No. 910, B

ONCE upon a time there was a very poor man. A year of great famine came, when everything was so dear that they could hardly get along at all, and his wife had to go out begging for a living.

At last she became ashamed of troubling the same people so frequently, and she determined that she and her son, a little boy that she had, would go farther afield, and so she said to her husband, 'Iain, thou hadst better be doing for thyself, while we strive to make shift for ourselves, as best we may.'

[But Iain said that it should be he and not they who should go out into the world.]

He procured a few shirts and stockings, and went off. After putting a considerable distance behind him, a farmer met him by the side of the high road, and asked him if he wished to be hired, and he said he did. The farmer hired him, and Iain went with him to his house.

He spent seven years with the farmer. At the end of the seven, he said to the farmer, 'I must now be going; I wish to see my wife and my son.'

'Hast thou a wife and a son?' said the farmer.

'Yes, I have,' said he.

'Why didst thou not tell me that before, thou shouldst have had leave to see them before this !'

'It never occurred to me,' said he.

'Seven years' wages are due to thee,' said the farmer; 'which dost thou prefer—the wages of the seven years, or to have three good counsels ?'

Bha e [Iain] smaointeachadh gun robh e mór tuarasdal
seachd bliadhna a chall, ach gum bu mhór a b'fhiach
comhairlean matha, agus thuirt e gun rachadh e mach
do'n t-sabhal gu h-am *breaceafas* agus gum biodh e 'ga
chomh-chomhairle gus an sin.[1]

J 163·4 An uair a thàinig e a stigh aig am [breaceafas], roghnaich
e na trì chomhairlean.

'Nis,' ars a mhaighstir, 'is e so na trì chomhairlean.
J 21·5 A' dol gu baile mór no gu h-àite eile, na fàg an rathad mór
J 21·3 airson ath-ghoirid.   Na fan ann an tigh anns am bi bean
J 21·2 òg posda aig seann duine.   Ma chì thu fear 'na laighe le
do bhean, na marbh i gus am bruidhinn thu rithe.'

'So dhuit,' arsa bean an tighe, '*loaf*, agus na boin dhi
C 320 gus an ruig thu do bhean is do mhac, agus an uair a ruigeas
tu iad, gearr 'na dà leth i, agus thoir leth do gach aon
diubh.'

Dh'fhàg e beannachd aig a mhaighstir, is aig a bhanmhaighstir, is dh'fhalbh e.

An uair a bha e treis mhaith air aghaidh, dh'amais
trì marsandan air, is pac air muin gach fir dhiubh.   Bha
e féin is iad-san a' gabhail air an aghart, gus an tàinig iad
gu ceann rathaid a bha dol a mach o'n rathad mhór.
'Nis, gabhaidh sinn mar so,' arsa na marsantan, 'agus
bheir e móran n'as clise sinn chun a' bhaile mhóir.'

Smaointich esan air comhairle a mhaighstir, agus
thuirt e nach fàgadh e an rathad mór.

Bha na marsantan cho maith is a b'urrainn iad a' strìth
r'a aomadh leò, ach cha tugadh nì sam bith air an rathad
mór fhàgail.

Ghabh na marsantan an ath-ghoirid, agus ghabh esan
an rathad mór.   Bha an rathad a ghabh na marsantan
a' dol troimh bheinn.   Anns a' bheinn so, choinnich
mèirlich iad, agus cha d'fhàg iad stuth aca nach tug iad
uatha.

Choinnich esan is na marsantan a chéile aig a' bhaile
mhór, agus cha robh aca na ghabhadh fàrdach oidhche

---

[1] *lit.* that he would be co-counselling = weighing, considering the pros
and cons.   Contrast, *ann an tigh comh-agail*, in the house of co-doubting, which

Iain thought that it was a serious matter to lose the wages of seven years, but that good counsels were worth much; so he said that he would go out to the barn till breakfast-time, and that he would think over the matter till then.[1]

When he came in at breakfast-time, he chose the three counsels.   J 163·4

'Now,' said his master, 'these are the three counsels. When going to a big town or other place, do not leave the high road for a short-cut. Do not stay in any house where there is a young woman married to an old man. If thou see a man in bed with thy wife, kill her not till thou hast spoken to her.'   J 21·5   J 21·3   J 21·2

'Here is a loaf for thee,' said the goodwife. 'Do not meddle with it till thou meet thy wife and thy son. And when thou dost, cut it in two halves, and give a half to each of them.'   C 320

Iain left a farewell blessing with his master and mistress, and departed.

When he had gone a good way forward, he met three pedlars, each of whom had a pack on his back. He and they pressed on together, till they came to a road that turned off from the high road. 'Now, we will go in this direction and turn off here,' said the pedlars, 'it will take us to the big town much quicker.'

But Iain recollected his master's counsel, and said he would not leave the high road.

The pedlars strove as hard as they could to incline him to take their view of the matter, but nothing would make him leave the high road.

So they took the short-cut, but he took the high road. The road the pedlars took went over a mountain. In this mountain, robbers met them, who robbed them of all they had.

He and the pedlars met each other again in the big town, but the pedlars had not anything with which to

implies uncertainty as to what was the best course to pursue, 'this way and that dividing the swift mind.'

dhaibh. 'Thigibh leam-sa,' ars esan, 'agus pàidhidh mi
cuid na h-oidhche air bhur son.'

Chaidh iad a stigh do thigh-seinnse.

Ghabh iad am biadh, agus chaidh esan a chomhnadal
ri bean an tighe do'n cheairn, boirionnach òg, gasda.

An ceann tacain, chuala esan casadaich.

'Ciod e tha'n siod ?' ars esan.

'Tha an siod,' ars ise, 'm'fhear-sa, seann duine truagh
a thug iad orm a phòsadh airson a bheairteis, agus b'fhearr
leam gun robh mi marbh mun do phòs mi riamh e: is
truagh an gno[thuch] bhi ceangailte ri seann duine.'

An uair a chuala e so, smuainich e air an dara comhairle
a thug a mhaighstir air, agus thuirt e ris féin nach fanadh e
'san tigh an oidhche sin. A mach a ghabh e gu sabhal
feòir a bha cùl an tighe, agus laigh [e] anns an fheur,
agus chàraich e am feur timchioll air féin. An ceann
tacain mhaith, thàinig [fear] mór, gasda, a stigh, is cleòca
breacain air, is bha e spaisdearachd air ais is air aghaidh
feadh an t-sabhail.

Treis 'na dhéidh sin, có thàinig a stigh ach bean an
tighe. Shuidh i féin is fear a' chleòca bhreacain comhla
gu maith dlùth air [Iain], agus bha iad a' pògadh a
chéile agus a' suirghe an sin. Am feadh is a bha iad
comhla mar so, thug esan [Iain] sgian a phoca, agus ghearr
e pios ás a' chleòca bhreacain. 'Nis,' arsa bean an tighe
ri fear a' chleòca bhreacain, 'so an t-am, marbh am bodach.
Tha trì marsantan a' laighe a stigh, is cha bhi ach maoir
is fianuisean a ghlaodhach, is a fhàgail orra.'

H 117
K 2213·3

'Cha dèan mi sin,' ars esan, 'a thaobh gur mi àrd fhear-
lagha a' bhaile, ach marbhaidh thu féin e, is dìtidh mise na
marsantan.'

A stigh a ghabh i, agus mharbh i am bodach, agus
ghlaodh i daoine a stigh airson fianuis. Bha am fear-lagha
a làthair, is cha robh ach breith air na marsantan, is an
toirt air falbh do'n phrìosan.

An là-'r-na-mhàireach, chaidh na marsantan a dhìteadh

get themselves a night's lodging. 'Come with me,' said Iain, 'and I will get you a night's entertainment, and pay for it.'

They went in to the change house.

They all took their food, and Iain went to talk to the goodwife in the kitchen, a very nice woman and a young one.

After a little while, he heard coughing.

'What is that?' said he.

'That,' said she, 'is my husband, a wretched old man whom they made me marry for the sake of his riches, but I wish I had died before I married him: it is very miserable to be tied up to an old man.'

When he heard this, he remembered the second counsel that his master had impressed upon him, and said to himself he would not stay in that house that night. So out he went to a hay barn at the back of the house, and lay down in the hay, and covered himself over with it. Some long time after that, a fine big man came in, wearing a tartan cloak, and began walking up and down in the barn.

A while after that, who should come in but the goodwife. She and the man with the tartan cloak sat down together close to Iain, and there began kissing each other and courting. While they were engaged with each other in this way, Iain took a knife out of his pocket, and cut a piece out of the tartan cloak. 'Now,' said the goodwife H 117 to the man with the tartan cloak, 'now is the time; kill K 2213·3 the old carle. There are three pedlars sleeping in the house, and there will be nothing to do but just to call for officers and witnesses, and accuse the pedlars of the crime.'

'I will not do that,' said he, 'seeing that I am the supreme law-man of the town, but do thou kill him, and I will condemn the pedlars.'

In she went, and killed the old carle, and called people in as witnesses. The law-man was present, and there was nothing to be done but seize the pedlars, and take them away to prison.

On the morrow the pedlars were condemned to death

gu bàs airson mort, is bha iad ri an crochadh aig dà uair
dheug an là'r-na-mhàireach a rithist.

Chaidh esan [Iain] gu tigh seinnse eile, agus chuir e
seachad an oidhche ann.

Anns a' mhaduinn, thuirt e ri fear an tigh sheinnse,
gun robh e a' falbh.

'Na falbh,' ars esan, 'gus am faic thu an crochadh.
Tachraidh e aig dà uair dheug an diugh.'

Bha so 'na aire fhéin.

Dh'fhalbh e fhéin is fear an tigh sheinnse a dh'fhaicinn
a' chrochaidh, agus bha iad aig an àite, mu aon uair dheug.

'Ciod e,' arsa fear a' chleòca bhreacain ris na marsantan,
'a th'agaibh ri ràdh air bhur son féin?'

'Chan 'eil ach gu bheil fios aig Nì Maith gu bheil sinn
neo-chiontach.'

'Cha dèan sin feum; bidh sibh air bhur crochadh, tha
n'as leòir de fhianuis 'nur n-aghaidh.'

'Chan 'eil,' ars Iain, 'ach tha na's leòir de fhianuisean
na t'aghaidh-sa. Tha na daoine sin,' ars esan, 'neo-
chiontach; agus is i a' bhean sin, bean an tigh-sheinnse,
comhla ris an fhear-lagha a rinn am mort, agus tha mise
làn-chomasach air a dhearbhadh.'

Chaidh e an sin suas; dh'innis e a h-uile nì mar a
thachair, agus mar dhearbhadh, thug e a mach am pìos
ás a phòca. Dhìteadh an dithis, am fear-lagha agus bean
an tigh-sheinnse gu bàs. Chrochadh esan, agus loisgeadh
ise ann am baraille tearra.

H 117

Fhuair Iain cuid an t-seann duine chaidh a mhort air
fad. Thug e roinn mhaith do na marsantan, agus ghabh
e air aghart a dh'fhaicinn a mhnatha.

Nuair a chaidh e a stigh, chunnaic e a bhean agus gille
òg bòidheach 'nan laighe 'san aon leabaidh.

Is e an ceud smaoin a thàinig 'na cheann, breith air

for murder, and they were to be hanged at twelve o'clock on the morrow after that.

Iain went away to another change-house, and there passed the night.

In the morning, he said to the goodman that he was going away.

'Do not go,' said he, 'till thou see the hanging. It will happen at twelve o'clock to-day.'

This was just what Iain had intended doing.

He and the goodman of the change-house went off to see the hanging, and they arrived at the place about eleven o'clock.

'What,' said the man of the tartan cloak to the pedlars, 'have you to say on your own behalf?'

'Nothing but that the Good Thing knows that we are innocent.'

'That will not do; you must be hanged, there is abundant evidence against you.'

'Not so,' said Iain, 'but there is abundant evidence against thee. Those men,' said he, 'are innocent; but it is that woman, the goodwife of the change-house, who, together with the law-man, committed the murder, and I am perfectly able to prove it.'

He then came forward; he related all that had happened, and as proof, drew forth from his pocket the piece [of H 117 tartan cloak that he had cut off]. The law-man and the goodwife of the change-house were condemned to death, the pair of them. He was hanged, and she was burnt in a barrel of tar.[1]

Iain received all the goods of the old man who had been murdered. He gave a good deal of it to the pedlars, and went on to see his wife.

Upon going in, he saw his wife and a beautiful young boy lying in the same bed.

The first thought that came into his head was to seize

---

[1] The usual punishment for husband-murder. As late as 1782, in England, a woman who had murdered her master was burned. See *The Star*, 12th December 1922. See also L. T. Hobhouse, *Morals in Evolution*, p. 124. The woman would be strangled first.

J 21·2

furm na croise [1] agus an t-eanchainn a chur aisde, ach chuimhnich e air an treas comhairle a thug a mhaighstir air, agus bhruidhinn e [rithe].

'Och Iain, an tu tha an sin ? nach fhaic thu t'athair ?' ars i ris a' ghille òg a bha 'na laighe 'san aon leaba.

Bha toil-inntinn mhór orra an so r'a chéile.

Rug esan air an *loaf* a thug a bhana-mhaighstir dha: rinn e dà leth oirre 'na meadhon, mar a dh'iarr i air, agus thàinig a thuarasdal a mach a a broinn. Bha iad gu maith, agus gu ro mhaith as a dhéidh so.

[1] *Furm na croise*, the handle (?) or main-piece (?) of the hank-reel or yarn-windlass.

NOTES

MS. vol. x., No. 15 (renumbered 42 by Campbell, for some unknown reason).

The name of the reciter, Hugh Macindeor, is not given at the end of this MS. But it is given in *W. H. Tales*, iv., p. 402, and at the end of MS. vol. x., No 17A.

Executions always take place at noon in these tales. See p. 328.

Related tales :—

MS. vol. xvi. (Journal, 1870), pp. 16, 206.
Celtic Magazine, xii., pp. 42, 423.

the handle of the hank-reel,[1] and dash out her brains, but he bethought himself of the third counsel his master gave him, and spoke to her.   J 21·2

'Och Iain, is that thou? seest thou not thy father?' said she to the young boy who was lying in the same bed.

At this, they rejoiced over each other greatly.

Seizing the loaf his mistress had given him, he made two halves of it [dividing it evenly] in the middle as she had desired him, and his wages fell out of the inside of it. Thereafter, they were well-to-do, and very well-to-do.

Kuno Meyer's *Merugud Uilix Maic Leirtis* (Nutt, London, 1886).
J. Jacob's *Celtic Fairy Tales*, p. 195, 'Ivan.'
Proc. Royal Irish Acad., xxxiv., C8, p. 348.
Béaloideas, ii., p. 50.

For a Burmese story about three counsels or precepts, and how they were obeyed, see *Folk-Lore*, xxxii., p. 93.

MAC AN TUATHANAICH [ILICH]

No. 7.   *Campbell MS. Vol. x., No. 16*

BHA mac tuathanaich anns na h-Earadh [1] a fhuair sgoil agus ionnsachadh maith, agus smaointich e gun rachadh e a dhèanamh air a shon fhéin.

Ràinig e Dùn-Eideann, agus bha e an sin an seòmar le a chlaidheamh, agus le a leabhraichean.

Thàinig bean-an-tighe far an robh e, agus thuirt i ris, nam b'e a thoil e an seòmar fhàgail tacan is dol a ghabhail [àite eile]; gun robh cuideachd an siod a bha toil aice a chur a stigh ann tacan.

Thuirt esan nach robh e eòlach 'sa' bhaile, ach gun rachadh e a stigh do'n leabaidh, is gun leigeadh e e fhéin 'na shìneadh innte, an fheadh is a bhiodh iad a stigh, is nach cuireadh iad umhail gum biodh e ann.

Chaidh e a stigh do'n leabaidh, is thàinig a' chuideachd a stigh, is 'd è bha an so ach dorlach cheardan.

N 455   Bha iad a' comhnadal an sin air iomadach nì: am measg ghnothuichean eile, thug iad iomradh air Ban-Righinn na Ròimhe; is thuirt a h-aon diubh, 'Is i Ban-Righinn na Ròimhe boirionnach is bòidhche air an t-saoghal,' is dh'aidich càch air fad gum b'i.

An uair a dh'fhalbh iad, bha esan a' smaointeachadh T II·I   gun stad air Ban-Righinn na Ròimhe. Dh'fhàs e gu bochd, is thàinig lighich dh'a amharc, is thuirt an lighich ris nach robh nì sam bith air ach gaol, agus e a ruigheachd ge b'e àite 'san robh an té air an robh a ghaol.

Dh'fhalbh e, is thug e Lunnuinn air.

Bha e an so ann an seòmar mar a bha e roimhe.[2] Thàinig sè saighdearan agus seirdsein a stigh, 's chaidh esan a stigh do'n leabaidh.

---

[1] The last sentence in the tale describes the hero as 'Mac an Tuathanaich Ilich' = the Son of the Islay Farmer. The first sentence probably means

THE [ISLAY] FARMER'S SON

No. 7.   *[Vol. x., No. 16]*

THERE was a farmer's son in Harris [1] who had received a good schooling and education, and who determined to go and fend for himself.

He arrived at Edinburgh, and there he stayed in a room, having his sword and his books with him.

The goodwife came to where he was, and asked if he would be so good as to leave the room for a while and go and take [some other place], for that there was a party of people in the house whom she wished to put into the room for a little while.

He replied that he did not know the town well, but that he would go in to bed and lay himself down there, while they were in the house, and that in this way they would never notice that he was there.

So he went in to bed, and the company came in, and who were they but a handful of tinkers.

They conversed together of many a thing: amongst N 455 other matters, they made mention of the Queen of Rome; and one of them said, 'The Queen of Rome is the most beautiful woman in the world,' and the others all agreed that she was.

When they had departed, he began to think unceasingly of the Queen of Rome. He at last became poorly, and a T 11·1 leech came to see him, and told him that there was nothing the matter with him but love, and that he was to go to whatever place the woman he loved was in.

He set off, and betook himself to London.

He stayed in a room here as he had done before. Six soldiers and a sergeant came in, and he went off to bed.

---

that this Son of the Islay Farmer had been living in Harris. In Islay's List the tale is called 'Mac an Tuathanach Ilach.'

[2] MS. roimhid.

Nuair a bha iad a' bruidhinn tacan, chuir iad an umhail
gun robh rud-eigin 'san leabaidh is thuirt iad ris o'n a bha
e cluinntinn a h-uile rud a bha aca, gum feumadh e an
t-òl air fad a phàidheadh.

Thuirt esan nach pàidheadh, ach gum pàidheadh e
roinn a h-aon deth.

Chuir an seirdsein a dhruim ris an dorus, agus thuirt e
nach biodh a' chùis mar siod, ach gum pàidheadh e a h-uile
peighinn deth.

Tharruing iad an claidheamhaichean is tharruing esan
a chlaidheamh cuideachd, is mun do stad e, thug e na
cinn de'n t-seachdnar.

Dh'fhàg e an so an tigh, agus thug e air gus an acarsaid.
Fhuair e an sin soitheach Frangach a bha trì ràithean a'
feitheamh soirbheis, is thuirt e ris a' Chaiptein, gun robh
e dol do'n Ròimh.

'Gheibh thu an Ròimh as an Fhraing,' ars an Caiptein.

Ann an tiota beag, thàinig soirbheas gasda orra, is chuir
an caiptein fo sheòl. An uair a bha e fo sheòl, thàinig
buidheann a dh'iarraidh an fhir a thàinig air bòrd, a
thaobh gun robh mort air a chur as a leth.

'Biodh sin is a roghainn da,' ars an caiptein, 'thàinig
soirbheas leis, agus bha mi glé fhada 'ga fheitheamh, is
chan fhaigh sibh e.'

Ràinig e an Fhraing agus bha e an sin treis, agus as an
Fhraing chaidh e do'n Ròimh.

An uair a thàinig e do'n Ròimh, bha am *factor* a bha
aig an Impire an déidh siubhal, is bha duine a dhìth orra
a dhèanamh a àite.

Chaidh an gnothuch mu a choinnimh-san, is ghabh e
os làimh e, is bha e còrdadh ris an Impire gu fuathasach.

An ceann bliadhna bha e dol a dh'fhalbh, is bha an

---

¹ A ship-captain and a mate hide a fugitive in their ship in MS. vol. x.,
No. 112. But the idea at the back of the captain's mind in this tale is closely
related to that of the smith in *Waifs and Strays*, ii., pp. 5, 435, who tells a newcomer that he will be a lucky man, because, just as he knocked at the door, the
smith succeeded in making the eye of a needle, a matter which had, up to then,
defeated him. See Nicolson's *Gaelic Proverbs*, pp. 67, 287, 365, 'Bidh tu beo am

When the others had been talking for a while, they noticed that there was something in the bed; they found him and said to him that since he had heard everything, he must pay for all the drink.

He said he would not, but that he would pay one share only of it.

The sergeant set his back against the door, and said that the matter should not remain on that footing, that the farmer's son must pay every penny of it.

The others drew their swords, and he drew his sword too, and before he stopped fighting he had taken off the heads of all the seven.

Thereupon he left the house, and betook himself to the harbour. There he found a French vessel that had been waiting nine months for a breeze, and he told the Captain that he intended to go to Rome.

'You can get to Rome by way of France,' said the Captain.

In a trice a splendid breeze came upon them, and the Captain set sail. When the ship was under sail, a band of men came to look for the man who had just come on board, because he was charged with murder.

'Be that as it may,' said the Captain, 'with him came the breeze, and as I had been a very long time waiting for it, you shall not have him.' [1]

The farmer's son went to France where he stayed for a while, and from France he went to Rome.

When he arrived in Rome, the Emperor's factor had just died, and they wanted a man to fill his place.

The berth was offered to him, and he took it on hand, and his doings pleased the Emperor immensely.

At the end of a year, he made ready to depart; the

---

bliadhna. *You will survive this year.* Said to a person who suddenly appears when being spoken of.'—'Is sona a' chailleach a thig ri linn an fhaothachaidh. *Lucky is the old wife that comes at the turn of the disease.* She would get credit for the cure.' But contrast, 'Thig an donas ri iomradh. *Evil comes by talking of it.* Al[ternate]. Thig an t-olc ri iomradh. Speak o' the Deil, and he'll appear.—*Scot.* Talk of the Devil, and see his horns.—*Eng.*'

t-Impire fìor dhuilich air a shon so, ach cha b'urrainn da
toirt air fantail.

Dh'innis e do'n Bhan-Impire [1] nach b'urrainn da toirt
air fantail. 'Cuir thusa [e] far a bheil mise,' ars ise, 'is
cha lughaide gun toir mise air fantail.'

Chuir an t-Impire far an robh a' Bhan-Impire e, is
dh'aom ise e gu fantail, is ghabh an dithis [2] taitneachd d'a
chéile.

Bha iad a' faicinn a chéile tric.

K 2111

Mu dheireadh, ars ise ris, 'Their mise ris an Impire
gun robh thu cur gnothuich mhìomhail mu m' choinnimh,
agus comhairlichidh mi e airson gun òrduicheadh e duine
bhi feitheamh airson do chuipidh. Bidh thusa ann an
àite falaich, agus an uair a dh'éireas an t-Impire feadh na
h-oidhche a dh'fhaicinn có bhios ann, éirichidh thu air

K 2213·3 leis a' chuip, is an uair a gheibh e gabhail air mar so, cha
bhi e fada beò as a dhéidh.'

An ath oidhche, chaidh esan am falach mar a dh'iarr
i air, is nuair a dh'éirich e feadh na h-oidhche, dh'éirich
an t-Impire a dh'amharc có a bh' ann.

K 1514·4 Thòisich am *factor* air leis a' chuip, agus chuip e cho
goirt is gur ann air éiginn a choisich e do'n leabaidh.

Cha robh ach gur h-ann am mearachd a thachair e,
is gun do ghabhadh an t-Impire an àite an fhir a bha tighinn
a choinneachadh na Ban-Impire.

S 122 Cha robh an t-Impire beò thar cupall latha an déidh
a' chuipidh so. An uair a shiubhail e, bha iad ag amharc
a mach airson Impire.

'Tha dùil agam,' ars a' Bhan-Impire, 'gur còir dhomh
fhéin facal a bhi agam ann an taghadh impire ùir.'

'Is còir,' ars a h-uile h-aon.

'Có as fhearr a fhreagras na am *factor*?'

'Chan 'eil gin,' ars iadsan.

Phòs i fhéin is am *factor*, is bha Mac an Tuathanaich
Ilich 'na Impire air an Ròimh.

<hr />

[1] Previously spoken of as a Queen.
[2] MS. dithisd.

Emperor was very sorry for this, but could not make him stay.

The Emperor told the Empress [1] that he could not make the man stay. 'Send him to me,' quoth she, 'perhaps I can make him stay.'

So the Emperor sent him to the Empress, and she induced him to stay, and the two took a fancy to each other.

They used to see each other often.

At last she said to him, 'I shall tell the Emperor that thou didst make an immodest proposal to me, and I shall K 2111 advise him to order a man to lie in wait to flog thee. Be thou in some hiding-place, and when the Emperor arises during the night to see who is there, thou shalt rise and fall upon him with the whip, and after getting such a K 2213·3 drubbing he will not live long afterwards.'

The next night, he went into hiding as she had asked him, and when in the course of the night he arose, the Emperor arose too, to see who was there.

The factor began at him with the whip, and flogged him K 1514·4 so sorely, that it was with difficulty the Emperor could get back to bed.

There was nothing to be done or said, but that it had all happened in mistake, and that the Emperor had been taken for the man who was coming to hold a meeting with the Empress.

The Emperor did not live more than a couple of days S 122 after this flogging. When he died, they began to look for another Emperor.

'I think,' said the Empress, 'that I myself have a right to say a word regarding the choosing of a new Emperor.'

'You have a right indeed,' said everyone.

'Who then would be more suitable than the factor ?'

'There is no one more so,' they answered.

So she and the factor married, and the Son of the Islay Farmer became Emperor of Rome.

NOTES

MS. vol. x., No. 16. Reciter, Hugh MacIndear or MacIndeoir of Bowmore, Islay.—Scribe, Hector MacLean.

This is a novella, completely non-moral, like many of its kind. That the woman is Queen or Empress of Rome is an example of the survival of the greatness of the Empire in folk-tale long after it had ceased to be a political fact. Journeys in search of a hero or heroine occur elsewhere. See MS. vol. x., Nos. 44, 118. MS. vol. xi., Nos. 185, 216. *W. H. Tales*, i., Nos. 17a (22) 17b; ii., Nos. 44, 51. *Proc. Scot. Anthrop. Soc.*, vol. i., No. 1 (1934), p. 7.

MAC CUAIN

No. 8.

Bha duine uasal mór an Eirinn, is bha triuir nigheanan aige, is chaidh an triuir dh'am falcadh.

B 612·2*
B 631

Chaidil té dhiubh, is mhothaich i i fhéin fuathasach iongantach an déidh dùsgadh, is chunnaic i ròn air falbh treis uaithe. Dh'fhàs i leatromach. Agus an uair a rugadh am pàisde, bha e cho giobach ri gobhair. Thugadh sgoil is ionnsachadh dha, is thugadh pac dha airson a bhi marsantachd feadh na dùthcha. [Agus thug iad MacCuain mar ainm air.]

Bha e falbh leis a' phaca gus an do rinn e beairteas, agus chuir e suas an sin bùth is rinn e tuillidh airgid, is cheannaich e baile o'n Rìgh.

Thàinig an Rìgh latha a shealgaireachd air a ghrunnd, is chuir MacCuain 'na aghaidh, is thuirt e ris nach fhaigheadh [e] sealgaireachd air a ghrunnd, nach robh còir aige air.

Thuirt an Rìgh gum b'e a chòir sealgaireachd air a h-uile grunnd 'san rìoghachd.

Cha robh ach là blàir a shuidheachadh.

Bha an Rìgh is MacCuain a' cruinneachadh dhaoine airson a' bhlàir, ach a thaobh gun robh MacCuain na b'eòlaiche na an Rìgh feadh na dùthcha, fhuair e barrachd dhaoine na fhuair an Rìgh.

Chuir iad blàr garbh, is chaill an Rìgh.

Bha an tòir air an Rìgh, is thàinig e gu tigh gobhainn, is cha robh a stigh ach nighean a' ghobhainn, is bha i gu maith bòidheach.

Bha e 'ga pògadh, is bha iad fìor mhór aig a chéile.

THE SON OF THE SEA

No. 8.   [*MS. Vol. x., No. 18*]

THERE was once a great gentleman in Ireland, who had three daughters, and they went to bathe.

One of them went to sleep, and when she awoke, she felt a most amazing sensation. She saw a seal making B 612·2* off a little way from her. She became heavy. And when B 631 the child was born, he was as hairy as a goat. Schooling and education were given to him, and a pedlar's pack, with which he might travel about the country selling goods. [And the name they gave him was MacCuain, *i.e.* the Son of the Sea.]

So he travelled about with the pack until he had made some money, and then he set up a shop and made more money, and he bought a township from the King.

The King came one day to hunt on his ground, but the Son of the Sea withstood him, and told him he should not be allowed to hunt on his ground, that he had no right to do so.

The King said that he had a right to hunt over all the lands in the kingdom.

So there was nothing for it, but to arrange a day of battle.

So the King and the Son of the Sea began gathering men for the battle, but because the Son of the Sea was better acquainted with the country than the King, he got together a greater number of men than the King did.

They fought a desperate battle, and the King lost.

The King was pursued; he came to a smith's house, and there was no one indoors but the smith's daughter, and she was exceedingly beautiful.

He fell to kissing her, and they were making much of each other.

An uair a thàinig a h-athair a stigh, thuirt e rithe,
'Ciod e thàinig ort? Bha sùil maighdinn agad an uair a
chaidh mi a mach, is tha nis sùil bean leatromaich agad.'

Thuirt ise nach robh nì sam bith cearr oirre.

Dh'innis an Rìgh mar a bha a' chùis, agus dh'iarr e
air a h-athair a falach, chionn gum marbhadh iad i nan
robh fios aca gun robh gnothuch aige-san rithe.

Laigh an Rìgh is i féin comhla an oidhche sin.

Bha ise bruadar feadh na h-oidhche.

Bhruid esan i, is dhùisg e i, is thuirt e rithe, ciod e bha
oirre?

Thuirt i gun robh i bruadar air craoibh mhóir chaoruinn
a bhi aig ceann an tighe.

D 1812·
3·3

'Sin,' ars esan, 'far an croch iad mise.'

Bhruadair i a rithist, is thuirt an Rìgh rithe ciod e
bha i bruadar, is thuirt i gun robh craobh mhór mhór
a bha dol thar an tighe is 'ga chomhdach.

'Tha tighinn air mo shliochd-sa na chuireas an rìoghachd
fopa féin.'

Thàinig an tòir, rug iad air, thug iad a mach e, is
chroch iad e far an do bhruadair ise an do chinn a' cheud
chraobh.[1] [Agus fhuair MacCuain an rìoghachd dha féin.]

R 315

Airson a dìon o nàimhdean an Rìgh, rinn a h-athair
uamh fo'n ghrunnd eadar an tigh agus a' cheardach, is
bha i fuireachd an sin.

Bha a bhean leatromach anns an àm cuideachd, agus
anns an aon àm, bha mac aig a nighinn agus nighean aig
a bhean.

K 1921·2
K 514

Chuir e am mac an uchd a mhnatha, agus an nighean
an uchd a nighinn, thaobh nach marbhadh iad am pàisde
bhiodh aig a nighinn nam bu nighean a bhiodh ann.

---

[1] These incidents are similar to some in 'Conall,' *W. H. Tales*, ii., No. 35;
iii., No. 74. *Waifs and Strays*, iv., p. 16 foll.

When her father came in, he said to her, 'What has come over thee? Thou hadst the glance of a maiden when I went out, but now thou hast the glance of a woman heavy with child.'

She said there was nothing whatever wrong with her.

The King now informed them how matters stood, and he asked her father to hide her, because they [the pursuers] would kill her if they knew that he had had anything to do with her.

The King and she went to bed together that night.

She was dreaming during the night.

He nudged her hard and awoke her, and asked her what was the matter with her?

She said she had been dreaming that a great rowan tree stood at the end of the house.

'That,' said he, 'is where they will hang me.'   D 1812·3·3

She dreamed again, and the King asked her what she was dreaming about, and she said that [she had dreamed that] there was a great big tree that was spreading all over the house and covering it.

'[That dream betokens] that there shall come of my race those who will conquer the kingdom for themselves again.'

Then came the pursuers and seized him. They took him out and hanged him where she had dreamed that the first tree had grown.[1] [And the Son of the Sea got the kingdom to himself.]

In order to protect her from the enemies of the King, her father made a cave under the ground between the   R 315 house and the smithy, and there she lived.

The smith's wife was heavy with child at the time also, and so at the same time, his daughter had a son, and his wife had a daughter.

He laid the son in his wife's lap, and the daughter in his daughter's lap, because they [the King's enemies] would   K 1921·2 not kill his daughter's child, if it were a girl.   K 514

Chuir e a nighean air falbh, an earalas gum faodadh
nì sam bith a bhi air a dhèanamh oirre.

Bha am balach a' cinntinn suas gu gasda, is bha an
gobha a' toirt dha gach foghluim a b'urrainn da.

An uair a bha e ['na ghille bàn] mu ochd no naoi deug
de bhliadhnachan, leis mar a fhuair e air aghart 'san
t-saoghal, thàinig carachadh air ceann agus air cridhe
MhicCuain. [Rachadh e 'na uaireannan air an dearg-
chuthach, agus ri a linn sin, dh' atharraicheadh fiamh a
ghnùis gu h-eagalach.]

Bha buidheann 'g a fhaire oidhche mu seach,[1] agus
oidhche bha an sin, bha aig a' ghobhainn ri dol dh'a
fhaire.

'Théid mise dh'a fhaire a nochd air bhur son,' ars am
balach.

'Cha téid, a laochain, ciod è bheir[eadh] thusa ann?
Nam biodh fhios agad mar a tha na cùisean, is tu a h-aon
mu dheireadh a bu chòir smaointeachadh air dol ann,
chionn faodaidh [e?] t'aithneachadh, is ma dh'aithneachas
e thu, faodaidh tu bhi cinnteach gum bi e airson do
mharbhadh, o'n is tu Mac an Rìgh a bha an so roimhid
is a mharbh esan.'

An uair a chuala am balach gum b'e Mac an Rìgh,
ghlac e misneach na bu mhó, is thuirt e gun rachadh e
ann, co dhiùbh.

Chaidh e a dh'fhaire Mhic Cuain, is bha an tigh làn
de luchd faire.

Thàinig teumannan garbh air MacCuain, is dh'fhàs
dà shùil na béisde cho mór ri sùilean muice-mara, is theich
a h-uile h-aon a mach ach Mac an Rìgh.

H 41
Dh'amhairc MacCuain air a bhalach, is thuirt e ris,
'Ciod e chuir nach do theich thusa mar a theich càch?'

G 308
'Cha b'fhiach leamsa teicheadh romhad, chionn chan
fhaca mi nì riamh cho uamhasach coltas riut, ach Meall
Mór a' Chuain.'[2]

---

[1] *Lit.* There was a group or band watching him night about, or on each
alternate night.

[2] mial-mhór-a'-chuain, *s.f.* Sea-serpent. *Am Faclair.* 'mial-mhór-mhara,

And he sent his daughter away, lest anything might be done to her.

The boy was growing up splendidly, and the smith gave him all the education he could.

When the boy [now a fair-haired lad] had become eighteen or nineteen years old, [it happened that] a great change came over the head and heart of the Son of the Sea, as a result of his having got on so well in the world. [He would at times be seized with a frenzy, and then the appearance of his face would change most horribly.]

There were groups of people to watch him at night. The groups took it in turn, night about.[1] One night, the smith [amongst others] had to go and watch him.

'I will go to-night to watch him for you,' said the lad.

'Thou must not go, my little hero, what couldst thou do there? [or what should make thee go there?] If thou didst but know how matters stand, thou art the last who shouldst think of going, because [he] may recognize thee, and if he does, thou mayst be certain that he will be all for killing thee, because thou art the Son of the King who reigned here before, and whom he killed.'

When the lad heard that he was the Son of the King, his courage became all the greater, and he said that he would go, in any case.

So he went to watch the Son of the Sea, and [he found] the house full of watchers.

[Presently] a wild frenzy seized the Son of the Sea, and the two eyes of the brute became as big as the eyes of a whale and every one fled out of doors, all except the Son of the King.

The Son of the Sea glared at the boy, and said to him, 'How is it that thou didst not flee as the rest did?'   H 41

'I would not condescend to flee before thee, because I have never seen anything so awful in appearance as thou art, except the Great Sea-Monster.'[2]   G 308

---

s. f. Sea-monster. Seachd ròin sath mial-mhór-mhara, *seven seals make a meal for the Sea-monster.* This cannot represent the whale, as it is generally translated, for whales could not swallow seals.' *Ibid.*

An uair a chuala MacCuain so, thug e tionndadh garbh air, is bha a choltas fiadhaich.

Rinn e seòrsa aithneachaidh air Mac an Rìgh, is le oilltealachd a choltais, b'éiginn da teicheadh.

Ghabh e air falbh, is o'n a dh'aithnich MacCuain có e, cha robh maith dha fuireachd ro dhlùth air.

Bha e dol seachad air fearann duine uasail a bha gu maith mór le MacCuain, is bha e 'na alach [òlach?] anabarrach saoghalta.

Bha buachaillean aige a' gléidheadh chaorach air cnocan lom bochd, agus a thaobh gun robh am feur cho dona, cha robh stad no fois air a' bhuachaille ach 'gan ruith o chnoc gu cnoc.

'Carson a tha thu 'gad mharbhadh a' ruith nan caorach mar sin?   Nach leig thu a stigh do na pàircean iad?'

'Chan fhaod mi sin a dhèanamh le mo mhaighstir.'

'An daor shlaoightire,' ars esan, 'coma leat e.'

Thug e leis na caoraich, is spàrr e a stigh anns na pàircean iad.

An uair a mhothaich a mhaighstir gun robh na caoraich a stigh anns na pàircean, chuir e na maoir as déidh a' bhuachaille.   'Cha mhise,' ars am buachaille, 'a leig a stigh iad, ach fear a thàinig an rathad an sin.'

[Chuir a mhaighstir na maoir an déidh Mac an Rìgh.]

An uair a mhothaich [e] gun robh an tòir as a dhéidh, theich e, is thug e air Gleann Arm far an robh na Fianntan.

Choinnich Fionn MacCumhail e a' gabhail sràid, agus thuirt e ris, cia as a thàinig e.

Dh'innis e so.

Thuirt e ris, c'à'n robh e a' dol.[2]

Thuirt e gun robh e dol a dh'iarraidh maighstir, gum bu ghille maith ag iarraidh maighstir e.

'Tha sin a dhìth ormsa,' arsa Fionn, 'gille airson

---

[1] The sentence may be reflexive.   If so, it would mean that the monster changed and altered in an awful way.

When the Son of the Sea heard this, he turned furiously at him,[1] and his appearance became terrible.

In some dim way he recognized [that the other was] the Son of the King. But so horrifying did he seem, that the Son of the King must needs flee also.

Away he went, and seeing that the Son of the Sea had recognized him, [he thought] that it would be better not to remain near him.

It so happened that he was passing by the land of a gentleman with whom the Son of the Sea was very friendly, a man who was an exceedingly worldly churl.

He had shepherds who herded his sheep for him on a bare and wretched hill-side, and because the pasture was so poor, the shepherd could get neither rest nor respite, because he had to keep driving the sheep from hill to hill.

'Why art thou killing thyself chasing the sheep in that way? Why dost thou not let them in to the parks?'

'I may not do that because of my master.'

'The niggardly rogue,' said he, 'never thou mind him.'

He took the sheep away with him, and drove them into the parks.

When the master noticed that the sheep were in the parks, he sent officers after the shepherd. 'It was not I,' said the shepherd, 'who let them in, but some man who happened to pass that way.'

[His master sent the officers after the Son of the King.]

When [he] (the fair-haired lad, the Son of the King), perceived that the pursuit was after him, he fled, and betook himself to Glen Arm where the Fenians were.

Fionn Mac Cumhail when taking a walk, met him, and asked him whence he came.

He told him.

He then asked him where he was going.[2]

He said he was going to seek for a master, that he was a good servant looking for a master.

'That is just what I want,' said Fionn. 'I want a lad

---

[2] or, what he was going to do. See for idiom, No. 167. And *Waifs and Strays*, v., p. 54—'What business has brought you, and where are you going when you have come here?'

feitheamh air a' bhòrd, is tha thusa cosmhuil ri h-aon a dhèanadh feum.'

Rinn e còrdadh gu ceann là is bliadhna.

Bha fleadh aig an Fhéinn r'a thoirt do'n Rìgh is d'a chuideachd uair 'sa' bhliadhna, is bha a h-uile gnothuch iongantach a bhiodh ri fhaotainn aig seilg ri bhi aig an fhleadh.   Bha so de chìs aig an Rìgh air na Fianntan.

An ceann latha is bliadhna, rinn an Fhiann deas airson latha mór seilge.

B'e so latha Ghuill a bhi aig an tigh, e fhéin is an gille bàn.

'Is mithich dhomhsa bhi falbh,' ars an gille bàn.

'Chan fhalbh thu,' arsa Goll, 'gus an téid am fleadh seachad.'

'Is mise,' ars esan, 'Mac an Rìgh bha an so roimhid, is ma dh'aithnicheas Mac Cuain mi, marbhaidh e mi.'

'B'e sin,' arsa Goll, 'an Rìgh, 's cha b'e MacCuain. Caillidh mise mo bheatha airson do bheatha, mun téid beud a dhèanamh ort.' [1]

An uair a thàinig Fionn dachaidh, dh'innis Goll gum b'e an gille Mac an Rìgh a bha ann roimhe.[2]

Thuirt an Fhéinn air fad gun cailleadh iad am beatha as a leth, is gun rachadh gach riobag de a ghruaig a dhìon.

[Chaidh an fhéisd a chur a suas, agus thàinig MacCuain chuice.]

Bha an gille bàn gu maith clis a' freasdail timchioll a' bhuird.

Bha MacCuain ag amharc air gu maith geur.

'C'à'n d'fhuair thu,' arsa MacCuain, 'an gille bàn ? Có è ?'

'Cha robh mi cho mìomhail is gun d'fhaighnich mi dheth,' arsa Fionn.

---

[1] Compare the enthusiasm of the enslaved Fenians, when Fionn is first made known to them in *Waifs and Strays*, iv., p. 27. *Celtic Review*, ii., pp. 15, 262; iii., p. 56.   [2] MS. *roimhid*.

to wait at table, and thou lookest like one who would do
well.'

He made an agreement with him that was to last a
year and a day.

The Fenians had to give a feast to the King and his
retinue once a year, and every uncommon kind of game
that was to be got by hunting was to figure at the feast.
This was by way of tribute, a tribute which the King levied
on the Fenians.

At the end of a year and a day, the Fenians made ready
for a great day's hunting.

Now that day it was Goll's turn to stay at home, his
and the fair lad's.

'But it is time for me to go,' said the fair lad.

'Thou shalt not go,' said Goll, 'until the feast be over.'

'I,' he replied, 'am the Son of the King who reigned
here before, and if the Son of the Sea recognize me, he will
kill me.'

'[True],' said Goll, 'that other was indeed the King,
and the Son of the Sea was not. I will lay down my life
for thine, ere harm be done to thee.' [1]

When Fionn came home, Goll told him that the lad was
the Son of the King who had reigned there before.

The Fenians all said that they would lay down their
lives on his behalf, and that every hair of his head should
be protected.

[So the feast was prepared, and the Son of the Sea
came to it.]

The fair lad was very rapid and dextrous at waiting
at table.

The Son of the Sea regarded him very intently.

'Where didst thou find that fair lad?' said the Son of
the Sea.   'Who is he?'

'I was not so unmannerly as to ask him,' answered
Fionn.

'Bidh a bheatha agamsa,' arsa MacCuain.

'Cha bhi, ach bidh do bheatha-sa agamsa,' arsa Fionn.

Shuidheachadh latha blàir eadar MacCuain is na Fianntan.[1]

Chruinnich MacCuain a dhaoine—chuireadh cath doirbh,—mharbh Fionn MacCuain, agus chuireadh mac an Rìgh 'na shuidhe ann an cùirt agus an cathair a shinnsearan.

Bha an gobha, is a bhean, is a nighean gu maith dheth.

---

[1] The custom of amicably settling beforehand a day of battle occurs twice in this tale. It occurs in others also, as in the tale of Eoghann a' Chinn Bhig. J. G. McKay, *A' Bhean Nighe* (Alex. MacLaren & Sons, Glasgow). It is

NOTES

MS. vol. x., No. 18. The reciter was Alexander MacAlister, Islay. The scribe was probably Hector MacLean.

This tale clearly makes Fionn and the Fenians subordinates of the King.

For legends regarding seals, see Campbell's English List, Nos. 250

'I will have his life,' said the Son of the Sea.

'Not so, but I will have thy life,' answered Fionn.

So a day of battle was arranged between the Son of the Sea and the Fenians.

The Son of the Sea gathered his men—a desperate battle was fought—Fionn killed the Son of the Sea, and the King's Son was placed on the throne and in the court of his ancestors.

The smith, and his wife, and his daughter were all well off.

typically Keltic ; *cf. e.g.* Plutarch, *Marius*, 25 (Boiorix proposes a time and place for a battle).

to 260. Rev. Dr George Henderson, *The Norse Influence on Celtic Scotland*, p. 261. David MacRitchie, *The Testimony of Tradition*. *Folk-Lore*, xxxii., pp. 118-120. *Celtic Magazine*, xiii., p. 107. For a possibly related tale, *Celtic Review*, ii., p. 256. For connected matters, see Dr John Arnott MacCulloch, *The Religion of the Ancient Celts*, p. 223.

SGRÌOB LIATH AN EARRAICH

No. 9.   [*Vol. x., No. 19*]

Aarne-Thompson, Nos. 1386, 1541, 1653 A

BHA duine bochd ann roimhe so ann an Ragh Monaidh
an Eirinn, is bha e daonnan a' ruamhar is a' dèanamh
dìchill airson poc a bhi aige a dhol do'n mhuileann.   Is e
a theirte ris fhéin Bodach an Ruamhair, agus Corra
Chriosag [1] ri a bhean.

Bha a bhean a' snìomh, is cha robh aice ach an aon
cheairsle daonnan, is bhiodh i 'ga tilgeil a nis is a rithist
ann an cùil, is ag ràdh, 'Bi thusa an sin comhla ri càch.
Tha móran an siod de do sheòrsa.'   [Cha robh i glic; is
ann a bha car dh'a dìth.]

'A bheil thu brath dol chun an fhigheadair idir?'
theireadh a fear; 'tha dùil agam fhéin gur mithich dhuit
dol chun an fhigheadair.'
'Tha mi dol ann gu goirid,' ars ise.

Là bha an sin, lìon i poca làn mòine, is chuir i a' cheairsle
a bha aice air a h-uachdar, is dh'fhalbh i.   An uair a bha
i tighinn dlùth air tigh an fhigheadair, chunnaic i a' bhò
ag ionaltradh fagus do eas, is dh'fhalbh oirre, is chuir i
a' bhó am bogadh, is ghlaodh i, is i a' greadadh a basan
gun robh a' bhó am bogadh.

Thàinig am figheadair a mach agus daoine leis a thoirt
na bà as a' bhogadh, agus leig ise dhi am poca taobh
gàraidh, is chaidh i a chuideachadh leò.

An uair a thug iad a' bhó as a' bhogadh, chaidh ise
chun a' phoca, is ghlaodh i is ghread i a basan, gun robh iad
an déidh nan ceairslean a thoirt as a poca, is mòine a
chur 'nan àite.

J 2325·1
K 251

---

[1] Alasdair Ross of Colbost, Skye, says that 'Corra chriosag' is a name for
a small insect like a leather-jacket. Similar insect names are *corra-bhainne,*

THE SCOURING GRAY BLAST OF SPRING

No. 9.   [Vol. x., No. 19]

Aarne-Thompson, Nos. 1386, 1541, 1653 A

THERE was formerly a poor man living in Ragh Monaidh in Erin, and he was always delving and doing his best to have a sack [well filled with grain] with which to go to the mill. People used to call him The Delving Bodach, and his wife they called Corra Chriosag.[1]

His wife used to spin, but she never got further than the same old hank, and she used to throw it into a corner now and again, saying, 'Stay thou there along with the rest. There are many more there like thee.' [She was not quite wise: indeed there was something wanting about her.]

'Hast thou no word of ever going to the weaver at all?' her husband would say; 'I certainly think it is high time for thee to do so.'

'I am going there shortly,' she would reply.

One day, she filled a poke full of peats, put the hank that she had on top of everything, and started off. When she was getting near the weaver's house, she saw his cow grazing near a waterfall; she set to work and drove the cow into a bog, and then striking her hands together, cried out that the cow was stuck in a bog.

The weaver came out with some other men to extricate the cow, while she laid the poke down by the side of a dyke, and went to help them.

When they had got the cow out of the bog, she went back to the poke, and smiting her hands together, cried out that they had taken the hanks out of the poke, and put peats in their place.

J 2325·1*

K 251

crane-fly, daddy-long-legs; *corra-chaoghal*, a grasshopper; *corra-chòsag*, a cheslip (?) a small insect found in chinks.

'O'n is ann timchioll air mo ghnothuch-sa thachair [e],' ars am figheadair, 'bheir mi fhéin dhuit snàth 'na àite.'

Thill i dhachaidh, agus an uair a bha an eige réidh [aig an fhigheadair], chaidh i dh'a h-iarraidh.

Thug i leatha air a muin i, is an uair a bha i tighinn seachad air rucan mòine, chunnaic i feannag air ruc, is i a' glaodhach, 'Gòrag! gòrag!'[1] is ciod è shaoil ise ach gur h-e bha i glaodhaich, 'Is mise am fùcadair, is mise am fùcadair !'

J 1851 'Ma's tu,' ars ise, 'sin agad e, is fùc e.'

Dh'fhàg i am poc an siod aig an fheannaig air ruc, is chaidh i dhachaidh.

'Dh'fhàg mise [am poc] an siod aig an fhùcadair, agus e air ruc mòine,' ars ise [ri a fear].

'Cha bhi thu glic gu bràth,' ars esan.

Rinn Bodach an Ruamhair a h-uile dìchioll, gus an d' fhuair e dòigh air mart a mharbhadh aig an t-Samhuinn.

Mharbh e i, agus ghearr e 'na mìrean beaga i airson dol 's a' phoit a h-uile là, mar a fhreagradh do dhuine bochd.

Bha an deagh ghàradh-càil aige. Smuaintich Corra
J 1856·1 Chriosag gun caomhnadh i dragh dhi féin, le a mhìr feòla féin a cheangal ris gach gais, air alt 's nach bitheadh ach an gais agus an fheòil a thoirt a stigh comhla agus an cur 'sa phòit.

Rinn i so.

An uair a thàinig a fear dachaidh, chuala e tabhann gun chiall 'sa ghàradh.

'Is fiadhaich an tabhann a tha 'sa ghàradh,' ars esan ri a bhean.

'Cha lughaid,' ars ise, 'gu bheil iad ag itheadh na feòla agam-sa.'

'Ciod e an fheòil ?' ars esan.

'O,' ars ise, 'tha, an fheòil a bha 'sa bharaille ! Thug mise a mach do'n ghàradh [e], agus cheangail mi a mhìr féin ri bun gach gais.'

---

[1] See *W. H. Tales*, i., No. 17a, Var. 12. Gòrag, pronounced approximately *gawrack*, means *silly woman*.

'Seeing that it has happened through an affair of mine,' quoth the weaver, 'I will give thee worsted myself to make up for it.'

She returned home, and when [the weaver] had the web [of worsted] ready, she went to fetch it.

She carried it away on her back, and when she was passing a peatstack, she saw a hoodie crow on it, calling out, ' Gawrack ! Gawrack !' [1] but she thought that what it was saying, was 'I am the fuller; I am the fuller !'

'If thou art,' said she, 'there it is for thee ! take it and full it !' J 1851

She left the poke with the hoodie on the peatstack, and went home.

'I left the poke yonder with the fuller, who was on a peatstack,' said she [to her husband].

'Thou wilt never have any sense,' he replied.

Well, the Delving Bodach, by working his hardest, at last managed to get a cow to kill at Martinmas time.

He killed it, and cut it into small pieces, small enough for putting into the pot every day, as befitted a poor man.

Now he had a very good kail yard, and Corra Chriosag thought that she would save herself trouble by tying to every kail stump its own piece of meat, so that there would J 1856·1 be nothing to do but fetch them both in at the same time and put them in the pot together.

This she did accordingly.

When her husband came home, he heard an inordinate amount of yelping in the garden.

'What a wild yelping is going on in the garden,' said he to his wife.

'Very likely they are eating that meat of mine,' said she.

'What meat ?' said he.

'O,' said she, 'why, the meat that was in the barrel. I took it out to the garden, and tied a piece to every kail stump.'

'Tha dùil 'm fhéin nach bi thu glic gu bràth,' ars esan.
'Tha an fheòil a nise aig na coin. Gléidh a h-uile mìr
ime a bhios air bainne na bà agus cuir e ann an crog, agus
gléidh an crog gus an tig Sgrìob Liath an Earraich, feuch
am bi e 'na leasachadh air call na feòla.'

Lìon i an crog, agus chuir i seachad e, agus bha e aice
car treis mar so.

Feasgar a bha an sin, thàinig seann duine bochd liath
an rathad, agus thuirt ise ris—

K 362·1 'An tusa SGRÌOB LIATH AN EARRAICH?'
'Ma tà,' ars esan, 'tha mi cinnteach gur mi; tha mi
bochd, ànraideach gu leòir.'
'Ma tà, ma 's tu,' ars ise, 'tha crog ime an so a
dh'iarr[adh] ormsa a ghléidheadh gu'n tigeadh tu, agus is
fhearr dhuit a thoirt leat, chionn chan 'eil dòigh agamsa ort.'

Dh'fhalbh am bodach, is thug e leis an crog ime.

An uair a thàinig a fear dachaidh, thuirt i ris,
'Thàinig Sgrìob Liath an Earraich.'
'Cha tàinig,' ars esan, 'chan 'eil e a chòir an ama sin
fhathast.'
'Thàinig,' ars ise; 'thug mise dha an crog ime.'

'Cha tig an latha bhios tu glic: fàgaidh mi thu, agus
bheir mi an saoghal orm.'
'Théid mise leat.'
'Ma tà, tarruing an dorus 'nad dhéidh.'

K 1413 Thug i leatha an dorus air a muin.
Ghabh iad air falbh, agus an ám na h-oidhche, thàinig
iad gu coillidh. Smuaintich e gun rachadh e suas am
bàrr craoibhe airson gum biodh e sàbhailt o fhiadh-

'It seems to me that thou wilt never be sensible,' said he. 'The dogs have now got all the meat.—Well, keep every particle of butter that comes from the cow's milk. Put it all away in a jar, and keep it there till the Scouring Gray Blast of Spring come, and see if that will help to compensate for the loss of the meat.'

She filled the jar and put it away, and kept it by her for some time in this manner.

One evening, a poor gray-haired old man came that way. Said she to him—

'Art thou the SCOURING GRAY BLAST OF SPRING ?'   K 362·1

'Why,' said he, 'I am sure I am; for I am poor and miserable enough.'

'Well then, if thou art,' said she, 'I have a jar of butter here, which I was asked to keep till thou shouldst come, and thou hadst better take it with thee, for I have no accommodation for thee here.' [1]

The old man went away, taking the jar of butter with him.

When her husband came home, she said to him,

'The Scouring Gray Blast of Spring has been.'

'No, that it has not,' quoth he, 'it is not near the time yet.' [2]

'Ah ! but he has been,' said she; 'I have given him the jar of butter.'

'The day will never come that thou wilt be wise: I shall simply leave thee, and wander forth into the world.'

'I will go with thee.'

'Well then, draw the door behind thee' [= shut the door behind thee].

But she took the door away on her back.[3]   K 1413

Off they went, and at night time, they came to a wood. He determined to go up into the top of a tree that he might be safe from wild-beasts. He took the door up with him,

---

[1] I cannot give thee house-room here, all I can do for thee is to give thee this jar of butter.

[2] See notes at end.

[3] She misunderstood a common idiom. Parallels are to be found as far apart as France and Greece. See *La France*, 6 Mai 1925 (*renez la porte*), Argenti-Rose, *Folklore of Chios*, chap. viii., No. 26 ('pull the door [to] after you').

bheathaichean. Thug e suas a' chomhla, agus chuir e trasd air meanglan [i], agus shuidh iad 'nan dithis air a' chomhla.

An uair a bha iad 'nan suidhe an sin, ciod e thàinig ach trì mèirlich, agus mart maol odhar leò. Mharbh iad i, agus chuir iad air ann an coire i, aig bun na craoibhe.

An uair a bha an fheòil bruich, is a shuidh iad timchioll oirre dh'a h-itheadh, bha Corra Chriosag ag amharc a nuas, agus a' dol na bu teinne is na bu teinne air oir na comhla, gus an do chuir i car dhith, agus thuit i fhéin agus K 335·1·1 a' chomhla agus a fear air na mèirlich.

Shaoil na mèirlich gur [a] h-olc a bha ann,[1] is air falbh a ghabh iad, is dh'fhàg iad an fheòil an siod. Thòisich ise air gabhail òrain.

'An do chaill thu do chiall, a bhean? an toir nì sam J 581 bith mothachadh dhuit? Bheir thu na mèirlich air n-ais !'

'Biodh sin is a roghainn da,' ars ise, 'gabhaidh mise òran.'

Chuala na mèirlich an t-òran.

'Tillibh,' arsa fear dhiùbh, 'is bidh fios againn có tha gabhail an òrain.'

Thill e.

'Is math a ghabhas tu òran, a bhean !'

'Is math,' ars ise, 'ach cha mhór a b'fhiach mi roimhe !'

'Ciod é mar a dh'ionnsaich thu ?'

'Le mo theanga a sgrìobadh.'

'Ma sgrìobar mo theanga, an gabh mi òran gu math ?' [2]

'Gabhaidh.'

'An sgrìob thu mo theanga-sa ?'

'Sgrìobaidh.'

---

[1] Bogles or evil spirits sometimes dwell in trees.   Others affect lofts and attics.—*Trans. Gael. Soc. Inverness*, xxxiv., p. 76.

[2] To be able to sing a song well or tell a tale well, were arts or accomplishments that were highly prized.   He who knew these arts could shine in a

and put it across a branch, and they both seated themselves upon it.

While they were sitting there, who should come that way but three robbers, having with them a dun polled cow, which they killed, and put in a cauldron, at the foot of the tree.

When the meat was cooked, and they were sitting round to eat it, Corra Chriosag kept looking down, and going closer and closer to the edge of the door, until at last she completely overturned it, and she and the door and her husband fell down upon the robbers.

K 335·1·1

The robbers thought that it was some bogle,[1] and they bolted, leaving the meat there. Thereupon she began to sing a song.

'Hast thou lost thy wits, woman? will [no]thing whatever give thee sense? Thou wilt bring the robbers back!'

J 581

'Be that as it choose,' said she, 'sing a song I will.'

The robbers heard the song.

'Let us return [*lit.* return ye],' said one of them, 'and we shall know who is singing the song.'

So he returned.

'It's brawly thou canst sing a song, woman!'

'Brawly indeed,' quoth she, 'though at first I was not much good.'

'How didst thou learn?'

'By having my tongue scraped.'

'If my tongue be scraped, shall I be able to sing a song well?'[2]

'Oh yes.'

'Wilt thou scrape my tongue?'

'I will.'

---

company when his turn came round to contribute to the general entertainment; but he who knew neither song or tale or even riddle, was liable to forfeit, or even to expulsion from the house. Hence the anxiety of the robber to sing well. For the custom of telling tales, see Tale No. 12, p. 133.

K 825   Chuir e a mach a theanga, is bha i 'ga sgrìobadh, agus an uair a fhuair i làn chothrom, ghearr i as i.

Air falbh a ghabh e as déidh chàich, is gun smid aige ach [1] 'blìù, blèù,' is mar a bu mhó a ghlaodhadh e, is ann a bu mhó a theicheadh càch roimhe.

Chaidh Bodach an Ruamhair is Corra Chriosag dhachaidh, is bha an leòir de fheòil aca, is bha i 'na bean ghlic tuilleadh as a dhéidh so.

[1] *'blia, 'blia*, is another word indicating inarticulate screaming on the part of a person who had been hurt. Hence *blialum*, confused speech, stammering, gibbering—*Scotticé*, blellum.

NOTES

MS. vol. x., 19. Hector MacLean, the transcriber, says in a note that Alexander MacAlister, tailor, Bowmore, Islay, aged 84, was the reciter. This is no doubt correct, though in his Gaelic List, Islay makes Hugh MacIndeor (who recited MS. vol. x., Nos. 14, 15, 16, 17) the reciter. The tale was known to Hector Urquhart. And J. G. McKay heard a very abbreviated version in Colbost, Skye, in May 1922. It is largely identical with Grimm 59, and is essentially a droll with the usual amount of variation. But the episode of the crow seems corrupt or taken from some other language; how could even the completest fool mistake *gòrag* for *fùcadair*?

For Irish versions, see Dr Douglas Hyde, *An Sgeuluidhe Gaodhalach*, p. 259 (Rennes, 1901). *The Gaelic Journal* (1895-6), vi., pp. 7, 151. *Béaloideas*, ii., pp. 17 and 25 for a list of similars, and p. 342 *n*, and vii., p. 205.

For other tales of foolish characters, MS. vol. x., Nos. 85, 86 and *W. H. Tales*, ii., No. 48.

For the meaning of the title, see Nicolson's *Gaelic Proverbs*, p. 347:—

'Sgrìob liath an Earraich.
The gray track of Spring.

He put out his tongue, and she began to scrape it, but K 825
when she got a good opportunity, she cut it out.

Away he rushed after the other robbers, shrieking [1]
'blew ! blayoo !' the only sound he could make, and the
more he shrieked, the more the others fled from him.

So the Delving Bodach and Corra Chriosag went home,
having now plenty of meat, and she became a wise woman
thenceforth and ever afterwards.

Al[*ternative*].   Bheir sgrìob ghlas Earraich cairt bharrach Foghair—
A green Spring will fill the cart in Autumn.'   I would rather translate—
'The scouring biting weather of Spring makes a well-filled cart at
harvest-time.'   The sense shows that the expression was sometimes
used of Spring generally.   But Hector MacLean, in a note to No. 19,
says that 'Sgrìob liath an Earraich' meant the end of Spring, by which
he probably meant a period at the end of Spring, for Spring was divided
into many periods.   The lengths of these periods and the order in
which they occurred, varied greatly.   No two authorities agree about
them.   The names of some might be used in a broad, as well as
in a narrow sense.   Hence probably the difference between Nicolson's
conception of the meaning of *Sgrìob liath an Earraich*, and Hector
MacLean's notion of it.

Duncan MacDonald, Headmaster, Sandwickhill Public School,
Stornoway, in his *Gaelic Idioms and Expressions* (Glasgow, 1932), says
that 'Sgrìob liath an Earraich' means 'disaster, or, destitution.'   Annag
Nic Iain, Isle of Barra, writing in *Béaloideas*, ii., p. 342 n., says that
it is 'literally the Hoary Scrape of Spring, Hunger personified.   Hunger
time was February and March, when food for man and beast was
scarce, and the whole earth was scraped bare.'   Rev. Charles M.
Robertson, MS. notebook No. 468, says that 'sgrìob liath' meant the
'gray furrow.'

FRAOCH

LEAGADH le h-anacain mhór,
Nighean Domhnaill nan còir fiar,
Chaidh an sin fios air Fraoch,
4   'S dh'fhidir an laoch ciod e a miann.
'Caora meala a Locha Luaim,
H 1333   'S gun aon duine am buain ach Fraoch.'
·3·1*   'S dh'fhalbh Fraoch an ainm an àigh,
F 516·3   8   Dhol a shnàmh air linne mhuir.
B'fhaide dhà làimh na crainn shiùil,
'S bu bhinne na cruit-chiùil a ghuth.
Rug e air bhàrr air a' chraoibh,
12   'S bhuain e làn a dhà làimh de'n lus.

'Cia maith so cha dean e feum
Gus an snagain thu an crann as a bhun.'
Dh'fhalbh Fraoch mar dhuine tinn
16   Dhol a shnàmh na linne a ris.
B'fhaide dhà làimh na crainn shiùil,
Bu bhinne na cruit-chiùil a ghuth.
D 950·0·1   'S fhuair e 'bheisd 'na siorram suain,
20   'S a craos suas ri bun an stuic.
Bheir e bhàrr air a' chraoibh,
'S shnagain e'n crann as a bhun.
Rug i air Fraoch air an t-snàmh,
24   'S leadair i e le là[i]mh 'na bial.
'S thuit iad an sin bonn ri bonn,
26   Aig clachan an àth dhonn ma dheas.

FRAOCH

No. *10*.   [*Vol. x., No. 20*]

WITH a great illness was laid low
The Daughter of Donald of the unjust laws,
Then word was sent for Fraoch,
4 And the hero enquired what her wishes were.
'Honey sweet berries from Loch Luaim,
And they are to be plucked by none save Fraoch.'   H 1333
And Fraoch set forth in the name of good luck,   ·3·1*
8 To swim over the sea linn.
His two arms were longer than a mast with sails,   F 516·3
Sweeter his voice than the musical lute.
He seized the tree by the top,
12 And plucked as much as his two hands could hold of
     the fruit.
'Though this be good, it will not suffice,
Unless thou wrench the tree up from its root.'
Fraoch set forth like a sick man
16 And went to swim the linn again.
His two arms were longer than a mast with sails,
Sweeter his voice than the musical lute.
And he found the monster, sound asleep,   D 950·0·1
20 And its wide open jaws were close to the tree trunk.
He seized the tree by the top,
And slowly dragged it out from its root.
But the beast seized Fraoch while swimming,
24 And rent him, having seized his arm in its mouth.
And there they fell, side by side,
26 At the stepping stones of the brown ford that lies to
     the south.

NOTES

MS. Vol. x., No. 20. The following note is written at the end of the song.

'This piece seems to have survived a great many similar pieces. It is pretty well known still. It was at one time a favourite one for children. I remember it being often sung to myself when young. It must have been much longer at one time. The woman who sent Fraoch was his stepmother, and she wished to destroy him, there being a fearful serpent at the root of the tree. The first time he [Fraoch] brought with him some of the fruit but that would not do, [= it did not content the woman]. Shnagain e'n crann as a bhun is a metaphorical expression. Snagan is to move along very slowly. Had these lines from Ann Darroch [of Ballygrant, Islay] who heard them from her father and several others. I have heard them often myself. H[ector] McLean. June 30th 1859.'—Lines 17 and 18 are the same as lines 9 and 10.

The foregoing poem and note are *litteratim* from MS. No. 20. It is so ill-spelt and corrupt that the translation is sometimes conjectural, and partly based on other versions. At the end of the MS. are two notes in Islay's own hand—'Copied and put with Mrs MacTavish version'—'Copied Nov 17/59 with Mrs MacTavish.'

This is plainly a very worn-down ballad, and should be compared with the following from Islay's MS. vol. xii.:—

No. 220, Mrs MacTavish's version of Fraoch.
—— Music for Dan Fhraoich.
No. 289, Laoidh Fhraoich.
No. 221, Bàs Fhraoich.

Other versions.—Celtic Magazine, xiii., p. 280. *Leabhar na Féinne,* v. (E), vi. (G), viii. (Z), p. 29. *Celtic Dragon Myth, passim. Reliquiæ Celticæ,* i., pp. 62, 224, 261, 411. *An Gàidheal* (1931), xxvii., p. 39. John Gillies, *A Collection of Ancient and Modern Gaelic Poems, etc.* (Perth, 1786), p. 107. *Am Bàrd,* i., p. 37 (Norman MacLeod, Edinburgh, 1901). *Journal Folk-Song Society* (1911), iv., part III., p. 246. Mackinnon's *Catalogue,* p. 332. *Trans. Gael. Soc. Inverness,* xxvi., p. 49.

Am Bàrd mentions the 'MS. Collection of Rev. John MacDonald Harris, taken down in Nist [*sic*] *c.* 1860.'

BILIDH

No. 11.   *[Vol. x., No. 24]*

Aarne-Thompson, No. 1525

BHA tuathanach roimhe so, agus bha baile fearainn aige
o dhuine uasal, is bha e fhéin is an duine uasal a' fuireach
dlùth air a chéile.

    Bha mac aig an tuathanach air an robh Bilidh, is bhiodh
e goid rud air daoine, is chan fhàgadh e nì gheibheadh e
cothrom air nach biodh e goid, agus bhiodh e a' goid air
an duine uasal. Thàinig an duine uasal far an robh an
tuathanach, agus thuirt e ris gum bu chòir da dìol ceaird
ionnsachadh d'a mhac, agus nach b'urrainn e ceaird na
b'fhearr ionnsachadh da, na a' mhèirle.

    'Nach co maith leam marbh e,'[1] ars an tuathanach,
'agus dol a dh'ionnsachadh mèirle dha—is e bu docha
leam.'

    'Chan eadh, idir,' ars an duine uasal, 'leigidh sinn dh'a
thoil fhéin e, fiach 'd è 's roghnaiche leis fhéin ionnsachadh.'

    Chuireadh fios air Bilidh, is an uair a thàinig e a stigh,
thuirt an duine uasal ris, am biodh e deònach dol a
dh'ionnsachadh na mèirle. Thuirt Bilidh gum biodh gu
dearbh, nach robh ceaird sam bith a bu docha leis na i.

    O'n a bha e fhéin cho toileach, smaointich a athair
gun robh e cho maith leigeil leis, chionn o'n a bha déidh
aige oirre, nach cuimte uaithe e có dhiùbh, is gun robh e
cho deas e bhi 'na mhèirleach maith is 'na mhèirleach dona,
o'n a bha e brath a bhi 'na mhèirleach.

K 301·1   Chuir a athair an òrdugh e, airson falbh a dh'ionnsachadh na mèirle.

    Ghabh Bilidh air falbh. Choinnich duine air an rathad

---

[1] *Co = equally*, is not aspirated after the verb *is*, present tense. See *An
Deò-Gréine*, vii., p. 161—'cha mhór nach *co* math dhuit,' it were almost as

BILLY

No. *11.*   [*Vol. x., No. 24*]

Aarne-Thompson, No. 1525

THERE was formerly a farmer, who had (rented) a farm
from a gentleman, and he and the gentleman lived near
each other.

The farmer had a son called Billy, who used to be
stealing things from people. He would not leave anything
that he could steal if he only got an opportunity of doing K 301
so, and besides, he used to steal from the gentleman. The
gentleman came to the farmer, and told him that he ought
to give his son a thorough training in a trade, and that he
could not teach him a better trade than thieving.

'Would I not as soon wish him dead,' said the farmer,
'as to go and teach him thieving—I would prefer it [that
he were dead].'

'Not so, not at all,' said the gentleman, 'we will leave
it to his own inclination, and see what he himself would
prefer to learn.'

Word was sent for Billy, and when he came in, the
gentleman asked him whether he would be willing to go
and learn thieving. Billy said he would be willing indeed,
that there was no trade he liked better than thieving.

Since he himself was so keen, his father determined
that it would be as well to let him have his own way, seeing
that as he had a great desire for it, there would be no
keeping him from it in any case, and that it were just as
well for him to be a clever thief as to be an awkward, clumsy
one, since he intended to be a thief.

So his father got him ready to go away to learn thieving. K 301·1

So Billy started forth. On the road he met a man,

well for thee. And see *Nicolson*, p. 222, 'Is co fad' oidhch' 'us latha, Là Fheill
Pàdruig.' Night and day are equal on St Patrick's Day.

e, agus thuirt e ris c'à'n robh e dol. Thuirt e ris gun robh
e dol a dh'ionnsachadh na mèirle, is gun robh maighstir
a dhìth air.

'Is dona a' cheaird a tha thu dol a dh'ionnsachadh,'
ars an duine, 'ach chan eagal nach fhaigh thu maighstir.'

Leig e seachad an duine sin.

Cha b'fhada a chaidh e air aghaidh an uair a choinnich
triuir dhaoine e, is thuirt iad ris c'à'n robh e 'dol.

Thuirt e gun robh e dol a dh'ionnsachadh na mèirle,
is gun robh e airson nan amaiseadh a h-aon air, air an robh
gille a dhìth airson a leithid de cheaird [gun gabhadh e
'na ghille aige].

'Ciod è?' arsa fear dhiubh, 'is ann a' dol a dh'iarraidh
gille airson na ceairde sin a tha mi fhéin, agus bidh mi
toileach t'fhasdadh.'

'Tha mise deònach,' arsa Bilidh. Dh'fhalbh Bilidh leis.

Bha tigh-seinnse dlùth, is bha toil aig an duine so gach
rud a b'fhearr na chéile [1] a ghoid. Chuir e an òrdugh air
a shon, agus thug e leis Bilidh gus an tigh-sheinnse.

Bha ball chainbe leò airson dol sìos air an t-simileir.
'Nis,' ars a mhaighstir ri Bilidh, 'théid thusa sìos an simileir
air a' bhall chainbe, is cuiridh tu a h-uile nì as luachmhoire
na chéile nìos dha'm ionnsuigh-sa air a' bhall, agus bheir
mise an sin a nìos thu fhéin as an déidh.'

Chaidh iad air mullach an tighe anns an oidhche, nuair
a ghabh muinntir an tighe tàmh, agus leig a mhaighstir
Bilidh a sìos air an t-simileir, agus an uair a chaidh e
sìos, chuir e suas a h-uile rud a bu luachmhoire na chéile
bha 'san rùm, agus an uair a bha a h-uile rud shuas, ghabh
am fear a bha shuas air falbh, leis gach nì a fhuair e, is
dh'fhàg e Bilidh shìos 'san rùm.

Bha Bilidh an so 'na éiginn is gun fhios aige ciod è
dhèanadh e. Sheall e mun cuairt, 's ciod e chunnaic e ach
seiche mairt agus na h-adhaircean oirre. Rug e oirre,
is chuir e timchioll air i, is thòisich e air sgreadail agus air
sgriachail feadh an rùm.

Dh'éirich a' bhean-mhuinntir, is las i solus, is dh'fhosgail

_____
[1] *Lit.* everything that was better than another.

K 316

K 484

who asked him where he was going. He told him that
he was going to learn thieving, and that he wanted a
master [to teach him].

'It is a bad trade thou art going to learn,' said the
man, 'and there is no fear but that thou wilt find a master.'

He let that man pass.

He had not gone much farther when three men met him,
who asked him where he was going.

He replied that he was going to learn thieving, and
that his intention was, if any one met him, who wanted a
lad [an apprentice] for such a trade [to take service with
him].

'What?' said one of them, 'I am looking for a lad
for that trade myself, and I am willing to engage thee.'

'I am quite willing,' said Billy. So Billy set off with
him.

There was a change-house near, and this man wanted
to steal all the most valuable things. He got ready for it,
and took Billy with him to the change-house.

They had a rope with them with which to slip down
the chimney. 'Now,' said his master to Billy, 'thou must
go down the chimney on the rope, and send up to me all K 316
the most valuable things, and after sending them up, I will
haul thee up thyself.'

In the night, when the people of the house had gone
to rest, they got up on the roof of the house, and Billy's
master let him down the chimney, and when he had got
down, he sent up all the most valuable things that there
were in the room, and when everything had been sent
up, the man above bolted with all he had got, and left
Billy down below in the room.

Billy was now in a tight fix, and could not think what
to do. He looked round about him, and what should he
see but a cow's hide with the horns attached. He seized
it, and put it over himself, and began to scream and shriek K 484
up and down the room.

The maid-servant arose, and lit a light, and opened the

i dorus an rùm, is an uair a chunnaic i e, thill i air a h-ais
leis an eagal, is ghlaodh i r'a maighstir.

'Ciod è tha ort?' ars a maighstir.

'Tha gu leòir,' ars ise: 'chunnaic mi an donas—tha e
stigh 'san rùm.'

"D è mar a bhiodh e ann?' ars a maighstir, 'is cinnteach
gur ann air an t-simileir a thàinig e a stigh.'

Chaidh fear an tigh-sheinnse a stigh do'n rùm, is chunnaic
e coslas an donais.

'Ciod è chuir an so thu?' arsa fear an tigh sheinnse.

'Is ann an so a bu chòir dhomh bhi, agus is tric leam
a bhi ann,' arsa coslas an donais, 'agus an uair a thig mi
air an turus mu dheireadh, chan fhàg mi fiach snàthaid
agad.'

'Ciod è ghabhas tu, agus gun tighinn tuilleadh? an
gabh thu leth cheud punnd Sasunnach?'

'Cha ghabh: tha ceud beag gu leòir; ma gheibh mi
ceud, falbhaidh mi is cha tig mi tuilleadh.'

K 152*   Thug fear an tigh-sheinnse dha ceud punnd Sasunnach,
agus dh'fhalbh e.

Thàinig e dhachaidh a dh'ionnsuigh a athar, agus
ghabh a athair iongantas e thighinn cho luath. Chuala
an duine uasal gun tàinig Bilidh. Chuir e fios aır.

'A bheil thu ionnsaichte, a cheana, Bhilidh?' ars an
duine uasal.

'Thà,' ars esan.

'Cha chreid mi gu bheil. Ma tha thu ionnsaichte,
cuiridh mise fiachainn mu do choinnimh, agus ma's
mèirleach maith thu, nì thu e. Tha mi cur chairtean is
chairtearan air falbh o'n tigh, agus ma's mèirleach maith
thu, goididh tu a h-aon de na h-eich uatha a té de na
cairtean.'

Arsa Bilidh, 'Is ioma rud a thug mi fiachainn da, cho
doirbh [ris] an sin.'

Chaidh na cairtearan air falbh, agus dh'fhalbh Bilidh,
ach chaidh e cùl cnuic, taobh an rathaid a bhiodh na
cairtearan a' tilleadh. Bha toll choineanan an sin. An
uair a bha na cairtean a' tilleadh, is a' tighinn an dlùths,
rug e air coinean, is bhrist e a chas, ís leig e air falbh cùl

door of the room, and when she saw him, she went back again in a fright, and shouted to her master.

'What ails thee?' said her master.

'A great deal,' said she: 'I have seen the devil—he is in the room.'

'How could he be there?' said her master, 'surely it must be through the chimney that he came in.'

The change-house man went into the room, and saw what seemed to be the devil.

'What brought thee here?' said the change-house man.

'It is here that I ought to be, and where I often am,' said the seeming devil, 'and when I come for the last time, I will not even leave thee as much as a needle is worth.'

'What wilt thou take for not coming any more? will thou accept fifty pounds sterling?'

'I will not: a hundred is little enough: if I get a hundred, I will go away and come no more.'

The change-house man gave him one hundred pounds K 152* sterling, and he went away.

He went home to his father, and his father was astonished at his returning so soon. The gentleman also heard that Billy had returned, and sent for him.

'Art thou trained and proficient already, Billy?' said the gentleman.

'I am,' he replied.

'I do not believe that thou art. If thou be indeed proficient, I shall set thee a certain test, which, if thou be a clever thief, thou wilt accomplish. Now, I am sending off some carts and carters, and if thou be a good thief, thou wilt steal one of the horses from them [= the carters] out of one of the carts.'

Said Billy, 'Many a thing have I attempted, quite as difficult as that.'

The carters departed, and so did Billy; he went to the back of a hillock, by the side of the road by which the carters would return. There was a rabbit hole there. When the carters were returning and getting near, Billy caught a rabbit, broke its leg, and then let it go at the

K 341·5·1 a'chnuic e; an uair a chunnaic na càirtearan an coinean a'
leumartaich, as a dhéidh a bha iad.

Leig e air falbh a h-aon no dhà mar sin, is bha na
cairtearan 'gan ruith.

An uair a bha na cairtearan air cùl a' chnuic as déidh
nan coinean, is gun duine aig na cairtean, thàinig Bilidh
is dh'fhuasgail e a h-aon de na h-eich as na cairtean. Air
a mhuin a bha e, is ràinig e tigh an duine uasail leis.—
An uair a thill na cairtearan, bha an t-each air falbh, is
cha robh fios aca ciod è dhèanadh iad. Thàinig iad
dachaidh, is dh'innis iad gu'n do ghoideadh an t-each orra.
'Tha mi faicinn gun do ghoideadh,' ars am maighstir.
'Tha mi faicinn gur mèirleach maith thu,' ars an
duine uasal ri Bilidh, 'ach cuiridh mi fiachainn eile ort.

H 1151·2 Cuiridh mi each ann an stàbull, agus cóig 'ga dhìon,
ceathrar air an ùrlar,[1] agus a h-aon an taobh a muigh.'

'Sin,' ars Bilidh, 'rud cho doirbh is a dh'fhiach mi
fhathast ris.'

Chaidh an cóignear a ghleidheadh an eich. Thug
Bilidh an tigh-seinnse air, agus thug e as ceithir botuil
uisge-bheatha. Bha treud mhuc dlùth air an stabull.
Chaidh Bilidh sìos far an robh na mucan, is na botuil
'na phoca, is laigh e an sin mar gum biodh e marbh.
Mhothaich an fheadhainn a bha gleidheadh an eich rud-
eigin a' dol rathad nam muc. Arsa a h-aon diubh, 'Seall
sìos, mun téid gin de na mucan a thoirt as an treud, gun
fhios d'ar maighstir.'

Chaidh iad sìos: fhuair iad duine marbh timchioll
nam muc. Thug iad suas an duine marbh, is chunnaic
iad botuil 'na phoca. Thug iad as a' phoca sin dà bhotul,
is thòisich iad air òl, is cha d'fhàg iad deur annta. Chuir
iad an so car de'n duine mharbh, agus fhuair iad dà
bhotul eile anns a' phoca air an taobh eile.

K 332 Thòisich iad orra, is cha d'fhàg iad deur annta, is bha
iad an so gu h-iomlan [air mhisg]. Chan fhanadh iad
a' faire na b'fhaide, ach dh'fhàg iad an t-each an siod,

---

[1] Cf. 'Am freiceadan ùrlair,' the guardians of the floor (John MacFadyen,
Sgeulaiche nan Caol, p. 164).

back of the hill; and when the carters saw the rabbit
limping, away they went after it.   K 341·5·1

He let slip one or two rabbits in that way, and the
carters went on chasing them.

When the carters were at the back of the hill, after the
rabbits, and no one near the carts, Billy came and un-
harnessed one of the horses from the carts. On to its
back he got, and came to the gentleman's house with it.—
When the carters got back, the horse had gone, and they
did not know what to do. So they came home, and said
that the horse had been stolen from them. 'I see that it
has been stolen,' said their master.

'I see that thou art indeed a good thief,' said the
gentleman to Billy, 'but I will set thee another test. I
will put a horse in a stable, with five people to guard, four H 1151·2
on the floor [= in the stable], and one outside.'

'That,' said Billy, 'is as difficult a thing as any I have
yet tried.'

The five men went to guard the horse. Billy betook
himself to the change-house, and brought away four bottles
of whiskey. There was a herd of pigs near the stable, and
Billy went down to where the pigs were, with the bottles
in his pocket, and laid himself down there as if he were
dead. The people who were guarding the horse noticed
something going on where the pigs were. So one of them
said, 'Go down and have a look, lest one of the pigs be stolen
from the herd, without our master's knowledge.'

So they went down: and they found a dead man
amongst the pigs. They brought back the dead man, and
then they noticed some bottles in his pocket. They took
two bottles out of that pocket, and began drinking. They
did not leave a drop in them. Then they turned the dead
man over, and found two other bottles in the pocket on
the other side.

They began on these, and never left a drop in them,
and now they were completely [drunk]. No longer would K 332
they stay to watch, but they left the horse and the dead

agus an duine marbh, agus ràinig iad an tigh-seinnse. An
uair a dh'fhalbh iad, air a bhonn bha Bilidh, agus thug e
leis an t-each, is ràinig e tigh a athar.

Chuala an duine uasal gun do ghoid e an t-each, is
chuir e fios air Bilidh.

'Ghoid thu an t-each,' ars an duine uasal.

'Ghoid,' ars Bilidh.

'Bheir mi fiachainn eile dhuit fhathast. Bidh
claidheamh agam air a' bhòrd, agus daga, is i làn urchair,
H 1151·3 agus mur an toir thu leat an lìon anart fo dhruim na mnatha,
cha bhi tuilleadh saoghail agad.'

'Gu dearbh, tha e cheart cho maith dhuibh mo
mharbhadh far a bheil sinn.'

'Mur an dèan thu siod, cha bhi móran saoghail agad as
a dhéidh so.'

'Sin rud is cruaidhe chaidh mu mo choinnimh riamh.'

Dh'fhalbh Bilidh an oidhche sin, agus chaidh e do'n
chladh, is thog e leis corp a bha air ùr-thiodhlacadh, is
chuir e aodach air. Thug e leis e. Ràinig e tigh an duine
uasail, is chaidh e suas air a' mhullach. Leig e an corp a
K 362
·2·1* sìos air an t-simileir.

Dh'éirich an duin' uasal, is las e solus, is chunnaic e
casan a nuas an simileir. 'Mac an fhir ud![1] tha am
fear so a' tighinn ! Bheir mise air nach bi tuilleadh saoghail
aige. Cha bhi mi aig an dragh losgadh air a chasan,
ach an uair a nochdas e a chorp, is ann a loisgeas mi an
urchair.'

An uair a thàinig an corp a nuas, loisg e an urchair.
'Falbh ! fanadh e an siod. Leigidh mi leis an siod, gus
an tig an latha.'

'Air ghaol Dia, na dèan,' ars a bhean; 'falbh leis, agus
tiodhlaic e, mum bi e 'na choireach ri do bhàs fhéin.'

Chuir e air a mhuin e, is ghabh e a mach leis. An
uair a mhothaich Bilidh gun robh an duine uasal air falbh
leis a' chorp, a stigh a ghabh e.

man there, and arrived at the change-house. When they had gone, Billy was on his feet at once, and taking the horse with him, came to his father's house.

The gentleman heard that Billy had stolen the horse, and sent word for him.

'So thou didst steal the horse,' said the gentleman.

'Yes, I did,' said Billy.

'I shall try thee with another test yet. I shall have a sword on the table, and a pistol, full of shot, and unless thou canst carry off the bed-sheet from under my wife, H 1151·3 thou shalt live no longer.'

'Truly, you might just as well kill me where we now stand.'

'Unless thou do what I said, thou shalt not have long to live after this.'

'It is the hardest thing that was ever set before me.'

That night Billy set forth, and went to the church-yard, and dug up a body that had been newly buried, and dressed it up. Then he carried it off. He came to the gentleman's house, and ascended to the roof. Then he let the corpse down the chimney. K 362 ·2·1*

The gentleman arose, and lit a light, and saw feet coming down the chimney. 'The son of yon one ! [1] here comes this fellow ! I'll see to it that he shall not live any longer. I shall not take the trouble of firing at his feet, but when he shows his body, it is then, then, that I will fire.'

When the corpse had come right down, he fired. 'There ! let him stay there. I shall let him remain there, till day comes.'

'For the love of God, do not do so,' said his wife; 'carry him away, and bury him, lest he be the cause of thine own death.'

So he hoisted him on to his back, and carried him out of the house. When Billy observed that the gentleman had gone off with the corpse, in he went.

---

[1] The son of yon one, *i.e.* of the one whom we would rather not mention—the Fiend.

'Tha e cho trom,' ars esan ri bean an duin' uasail,
'chan urrainn mi falbh leis an dràsd.'
[Chreid ise Bilidh an riochd a fir fhéin.] Chaidh e
do'n leabaidh le bean an duine uasail. A lìon beagan agus
beagan, dh'oibrich e an lìon anart leis. An uair a fhuair
H 1151·3 e leis e, dh'éirich e, is ghabh e a mach.

Thàinig an duine uasal an déidh an corp a thiodhlacadh.
'Tha mise sgìth, agus air mo shàrachadh.'
'Ciod e, a ghràidh, a dh'fhàgadh sgìth thu ? chan 'eil
dà mhionaid o'n a dh'fhàg thu mi anns an leabaidh.'
Sheall an duine uasal, agus mhothaich e gun robh an
lìon anart a dhìth. 'Biodh e [1] fhéin agad cuideachd, agus
bidh mise falbh.'
Dh'fhalbh an duine uasal, is bha an tigh is a' bhean
aig Bilidh.

Roderick MacNeill,

Labourer, Glen, Barra. Learnt this and his other tale from
John MacNeill, Ken Tangval, Roderick MacNeill, Minglay,
Donald MacNeill, Glen, Barra. Heard them recited by
numerous persons.

NOTES

MS. vol. x., No. 24. Islay refers to this tale as 'Very Highland.'
Other tales of clever thieves are:—W. H. Tales, i., Nos. 17, 17d; ii.,
Nos. 40, 45. English List, No. 315. Béaloideas, ii. (1930), pp. 10, 348;
vii., pp. 64, 72.

'He is so heavy,' said he to the gentleman's wife, 'I cannot carry him away just now.'

[She supposed that Billy was her own husband.] And Billy went to bed with the gentleman's wife. Little by little, he worked away until he had got the bed-sheet to himself. When he had got it quite away, he arose, and H 1151·3 went out.

The gentleman returned, having buried the corpse. 'I am tired, and quite worn out.'

'What, my love, could have made thee tired? it is not two minutes since thou didst leave me in the bed.'

The gentleman looked, and noticed that the bed-sheet was wanting. 'Thou mayest have him[1] also. I shall be off.'

The gentleman departed accordingly, and Billy had the house, and the wife.

[1] The gentleman may be apostrophizing the absent Billy here, and telling him he may have the bed-sheet—or, he may be addressing his wife, and telling her she may have Billy. The concluding paragraph suggests this as the meaning.

See Grimm, No. 192, *The Master Thief: Folk-Lore*, xxxiv., p. 123, and Islay's MS. vol. xvi. (Journal, 1870), p. 66. A typical story of a Master Thief. As usual, there is some one who sets him tests, and as usual, the thief passes them, at the examiner's expense.

IOSBADAIDH [1]

no, Na Trì Gillean nach Dealaicheadh

No. 12.   [*Vol. x., No. 25*]

Bha trì gillean ann, a bha 'nan companaich aig a chéile,
agus chuir iad rompa nach dèanadh iad fasdadh ach
comhla, agus nach dealaicheadh iad idir air chor sam
bith. Ghabh iad air falbh a dhol a dh' ionnsuigh fasdaidh.
Bha iad a' falbh, is air an rathad choinnich duine iad, is
thuirt e riu c'à'n robh iad a' dol. Thuirt iad ris gun robh
iad a' dol a dh'iarraidh maighstir.

'Ma tà, is ann ag iarraidh gille a tha mi féin a' dol,'
ars esan.

'Nì sinne fasdadh riut.'

'Chan 'eil a dhìth orm ach a h-aon dhibh.'

'Cha dèan aon fhear againn fasdadh, mura dèan an
triuir e. Tha sinn a' cur romhainn nach dealaich sinn
bho chéile.'

'Chan e sin as fhearra dhuibh. Is iomadh h-aon a
dh'fhasdaidheadh 'nur triuir sibh, nach pàidheadh bhur
tuarasdal. Tha mise deònach air a h-aon agaibh fhasdadh.
Fhir is sine, ciod è an obair a nì thusa?'

'Nì mise a h-uile obair air an t-saoghal is urrainn duibh
a smuaineachadh.'

'Seadh, a laochain, tha thu glé mhath. Ach fhir is
meadhonaiche, ciod e an obair a nì thusa?'

'A h-uile h-obair mar a nì e fhéin.'

L 10   'Sibh tha math. Fhir eile ! ciod e an obair a nì thusa?'

L 114·1   'Ma tà, cha dèan mise car.'

'Nach dèan, a laochain?'

'Cha dèan: ciod chuige nì mi e? tha iad fhéin a' dol

---

[1] *Æsop?* See Notes.

IOSBADAIDH [1]

OR, THE THREE LADS WHO WOULD NOT SEPARATE

No. 12.   [*Vol. x., No. 25*]

THERE were three lads who were companions, and who
had made up their minds that they would only hire
themselves in a body, and that they would not separate
under any conditions. They set off to hire themselves.
While travelling, they met a man on the road, who asked
them where they were going. They said they were going
to look for a master.

'Well, I myself am going about looking for a serving
lad,' said he.

'We will take service with thee.'

'I only want one of you.'

'Not one of us will hire himself, unless all three of us
do. We have determined that we will not separate from
each other.'

'That is not the best thing for you to do. Many a man
would hire the three of you who would not pay your wages.
I am willing to engage one of you. Thou that art the
eldest, what work canst thou do ?'

'I can do every kind of work in the world which you
can think of.'

'Indeed, my little hero, thou art very clever. And
thou, the middle one, what work canst thou do ?'

'Every kind of work, just as much as he can.'

'Well, you *are* good. And now thou other chap ! L 10
what work canst thou do ?'

'Well then, I will not do a single hand's-turn.'   L 114·1

'Wilt not, my little hero ?'

'No: why should I ? it is they who are going to do every

a dhèanamh a h-uile h-obair air an t-saoghal, is cha d'fhàg iad car idir agamsa.'

'Ma thà, tha mi coma ged a dh'fhasdaidhinn thusa, is leigidh mi càch seachad.' Dh'fhasdaidh e e, is thug e leis dhachaidh e.[1]

Ars am maighstir ris a' ghille, 'Tha cuireadh a' tighinn orm chun bainnse, is feumaidh tu dol a dh'ionnsuigh na bainnse leam.'—'Tha mi deònach,' ars Iosbadaidh, 'dol a dh'ionnsuigh na bainnse gun teagamh.'

Dh'fhalbh iad chun na bainnse, agus ciod è an t-am a ràinig iad chun na bainnse, ach an uair a bha muinntir na bainnse aig a' phòsadh. Bha iad a' cur seachad na h-ùine an sin, is iad cho sàmhach, is cha robh facal cainnt idir aca. 'Chan fhaca mi féin riamh,' arsa Iosbadaidh, 'tigh bainnse cho sàmhach ris a so, anns nach robh sgeulachd no òran 'ga ghabhail.'

'Siuthad féin, is gabh sgeulachd.'

'An leabhara, gabhaidh mise sgeulachd; an comain fir na bainnse ghabhas mi i.

Bha sinn uair 'sa' Ghréig an siod,' arsa Iosbadaidh, 'agus bha a' Ghréig cho gann is cho gortach, is na h-uile creutair a' fàs cho gann, is nach robh dad ann a chumadh beò iad. Bha aon loch anns a' Ghréig, is bha gu leòir de bhiadh ann. Bha biastan beaga anns an loch, agus aon bhiasta mhór. Agus an uair a theirig am biadh air a h-uile creutair, agus a bha am biadh cho gann air an té mhóir 'sa bha e air an fheadhainn bheaga, dh'fhalbh a' bhiast mhór is smuainich i gun tòisicheadh i air itheadh nam biastan beaga. Thòisich i air an itheadh air alt 's nach robh i fàgail gin beò de na biastan beaga a bha 'san loch. Bha an fheadhainn bheaga 'gam falach fhéin ann an tuill feadh nan creag. Bha àl aig an té mhóir, agus bha an t-àl a' dol a steach as déidh nam biastan beaga anns na tuill, is bheireadh iad orra, is mharbhadh iad iad, is dh'itheadh iad iad.

---

[1] Notwithstanding the title of the tale, the companions separate here, and two of them do not appear again. This points to corruption, very visible elsewhere in the tale.

kind of work in the world. They have not left me a single hand's-turn to do.'

'Well then, I don't mind if I engage thee, and let the others go.' So he hired him, and took him home with him.'

Said the master to the lad, 'There is an invitation coming to me for a wedding, and thou must go there with me.'—'I am willing,' said Iosbadaidh, 'to go to the wedding with thee, without a doubt.'

They went to the wedding, and when did they arrive but at the time the wedding party were occupied with the marriage ceremony. But the people were passing the time in utter silence, without speaking a word. 'Never have I seen,' said Iosbadaidh, 'a house where a wedding was going on, so quiet as this is, where neither a story is being told, nor a song being sung.'

'Well then, do thou begin and tell a tale.'

'By the books, I will tell one. And it is as a compliment to the bridegroom that I will tell it.

We were in Greece at one time,' said Iosbadaidh, 'and Greece had become so stricken with famine and so short of food, and every living thing had become so scarce, that there was nothing to be had to keep people alive. But there was a certain loch in Greece, in which there was plenty of food. In that loch there were some little beasts, and one big beast. And when the supplies of food had run out and no creature had anything, and when there was as little food for the big beast as there was for the little ones, the big beast thought that she would begin eating the little ones. And she began to eat them to such an extent that she was not leaving one of the little beasts in the lake alive. The little beasts were hiding themselves in holes among the rocks. But the big one had a brood of young ones, and her young were going into the holes after the little beasts, and catching and killing and eating them.

Sin agaibh mar a dh'éireas duibh an so. Is e mèirleach a tha dol a phòsadh a nochd againn, is tha e fhéin glé mhath gu goid, is an uair a thig àl a' mhèirlich air an aghaidh, chan fhàg iad dad idir.'

Cò thàinig a steach air an dorus, ach fear na bainnse. 'Tapadh leat, Iosbadaidh ! chan 'eil dùil 'm féin nach ann a' gabhail sgeulachd a bha thu,' arsa fear na bainnse.

'Ma tà,' ars Iosbadaidh, 'is ann gun teagamh, agus is ann air comain fir na bainnse tha mi 'ga gabhail cuideachd.' [1]

Thàinig muinntir na bainnse air fad, agus chuireadh 'nan suidhe iad, agus thòisich iad ri òl. 'Nis,' arsa maighstir Iosbadaidh ri Iosbadaidh, 'an uair a ghabhas mise dram, chan 'eil fhios agam ciod è their mi. Bi thusa furachail umam-sa, agus na leig leam móran dhram a ghabhail.'

Bha Iosbadaidh a' furachail [2] cho math 'sa b'urrainn da, ach a dh'aindeoin ciod è dhèanadh e, an uair a bha an t-òl a' dol air aghaidh, ghabh a mhaighstir daorach, is cha robh fios aige gu ceart ciod è bha e ag ràdh no ciod è bu chòir dha a ràdh. Bha e fhéin is daoine eile a' bruidhinn ri chéile, is bha iad ri bòilich thall is a bhos.

Ciod è rinn maighstir Iosbadaidh ach geall a chur riu, nach robh deur sàile air uachdar an t-saoghail nach òladh e. Is chuir iadsan cóig ceud punnd Sasunnach ris, nach òladh.

An uair a bha a' chuirm seachad, chaidh Iosbadaidh agus a mhaighstir dhachaidh.

Anns a' mhaduinn an là-'r-na-mhàireach, an uair a dh'éirich Iosbadaidh, chaidh e far an robh a mhaighstir, is dh'iarr e air éirigh. 'Och ! chan éirich mise gu bràth; chuir mi thusa 'nad mhothachadh mar a dhèanadh an deoch orm, is dh'iarr mi ort mo chumail uaipe, is cha d'rinn thu e.'

---

[1] Some robber bridegroom story like MS. vol. x., No. 113 and MS. vol. xi., No. 172, or a story like that in *Waifs and Strays*, v., pp. 29-32, ought to follow here. But we read nothing further about the robbers, though the entry of the alleged robber at the end of Iosbadaidh's tale suggests that he had been engaged outside in taking note of the cattle that he intended stealing, and that Iosbadaidh had taken advantage of his absence to tell the tale against him,

That is just what will happen to you here. He whom J 88* we have with us and who is going to be married to-night, K 1916 is a robber. He himself is very good at stealing, but when the thief's brood appear on the scene, they will take everything and leave nothing at all.'

Who should now come in at the door, but the bridegroom. 'Good luck to thee, Iosbadaidh ! I will not believe but what thou wert reciting a story,' said the bridegroom.

'Well then,' said Iosbadaidh, 'that is so without doubt, and it was as a compliment to the bridegroom that I was telling it, too.'

All the folk of the wedding party now came, and they were made to sit down. They began drinking. 'Now,' said his master to Iosbadaidh, 'when I take a dram, I never know what I may say. Keep thou a vigilant watch over me, and do not allow me to take many drams.'

Iosbadaidh was as vigilant as he was able, but as the drinking proceeded, no matter what he did, and in spite of all he could do, his master got drunk, and he did not quite know what he was saying nor yet what he ought to say. He and other men were talking together, and blustering here and blustering there. And what should Iosbadaidh's master do but lay a wager with them that there was not a drop of salt water on the surface of the earth H 1142·3 that he would not drink. And they laid a bet of five hundred pounds sterling with him that he could not.

When the feast was over, Iosbadaidh and his master went home.

On the morning of the next day, when Iosbadaidh arose, he went to where his master was, and asked him to rise. 'Och ! I will never rise again; I warned thee how the drink would serve me, and desired thee to keep me from it, but thou didst not do it.'

---

afterwards pretending to him that he had told it in honour of him. The next incident resembles the one in Mac-a-Rusgaich, *W. H. Tales*, ii., No. 45, where a master tells his servant to cast ox-eyes at him when it was time for him to leave a wedding, instructions which the servant carries out too literally, to the great damage of his master's cattle.

² So MS.

'Do chumail uaipe ! Moire, sin an rud nach b'urrainn domhsa a dhèanamh.'

Dh'éirich e, is cha do rinn e ach éirigh an uair a thàinig chun an tighe na daoine uaisle ris an do chuir e an geall. Dh'éigh iad a mach air maighstir Iosbadaidh as an tigh. Fhreagair Iosbadaidh iad.

'Do mhaighstir a tha sinn ag iarraidh, is cha tusa,' ars iad-san.

'Agam fhéin tha gnothuch mo mhaighstir r'a dhèanamh,[1] agus an uair a dh'fhairtlicheas orm féin a dhèanamh, thig mo mhaighstir. Ciod è an gnothuch a tha agaibh ri mo mhaighstir an diugh ?'

'Tha, gun do chuir e geall ruinn na bha de shàil air uachdar an t-saoghail òl.'

'A dhaoine gòrach! is fhearr dhuibh dol dhachaidh na bhi bruidhinn air a leithid sin de fhaoineas ! Có is urrainn na tha de fhairge air an t-saoghal òl ?'

'A roghainn sin is da,[2] chuir e an geall, is bidh a cheann againne mura dèan e e.'

'Ma chuir e geall gun òladh e a h-uile deur sàile air uachdar an t-saoghail, cha do chuir e geall gun òladh e an t-uisge. Falbh sibhse, is caisgibh a h-uile sruthan uisge a tha dol a dh'ionnsuigh na fairge, is òlaidh mise an sin an sàil, is òlaidh mo mhaighstir 'nam dhéidh e !'[3]

H 951
H 1142·3

'Tha sin ro dhuilich dhuinn a dhèanamh.'

'Biodh sin is a roghainn da, cha do gheall mo mhaighstir ach an sàil òl. Cuiribh-se an sàile glan mu a choinnimh, is mura h-òl e e, bidh an geall air, is mura dèan sibh sin, biodh an geall oirbh. A bheil sibhse a' smuaineachadh gu bheil mo mhaighstir a' dol a dh'òl sàil is uisge air feadh a chéile is nach do gheall e ach sàil òl ! Caisgibh-se an t-uisge, no pàidhibh an geall.'

Cha robh aca ach an cóig ceud punnd Sasunnach a phàidheadh, chionn cha b'urrainn daibh an t-uisge a chasg. (Nach b'e am balach Iosbadaidh !)

---

[1] See No. 3, p. 55 *n.*
[2] A roighinn sin 's da, *in MS. lit.* the choosing of that is for him.

'To keep thee away from it ! By Mary, that was a thing I was quite unable to do.'

The master arose, and had only just done so, when there came to the house the gentlemen with whom he had laid the wager. They shouted for Iosbadaidh's master to come out of the house. Iosbadaidh answered them.

'It is thy master we want, and not thou,' said they.

'But it is for me to do my master's business,[1] and if it is too much for me then will my master come. What is the business that ye have with my master to-day ?'

'Just this, that he laid a wager with us that he would drink all the salt-water on the surface of the earth.'

'Ye silly men ! Ye had far better go home than talk about the like of such nonsense ! Who is able to drink up all the sea-water there is in the world ?'

'Be that his affair.[2] He laid the wager, and we will have his head if he does not do as he wagered.'

'If he wagered that he would drink every drop of salt-water on the surface of the earth, he did not wager that he would drink up all the fresh-water. Set ye to work, H 951 go and shut off every little fresh-water stream that runs into the sea, and then I will drink up the salt-water, and H 1142·3 my master will drink it after me !'[3]

'That is too difficult for us to do.'

'Be that as it may, my master did not promise to do anything but drink the salt-water. Put ye the salt-water before him, pure and clear, and if he drink it not, the loss of the wager shall come upon him, but if ye cannot do so, the loss must come upon you. Do you think that my master is going to drink salt-water and fresh mixed together, when he only promised to drink the salt ! Keep back the fresh-water, or pay the wager.'

There was nothing now for them to do but to pay the five hundred pounds sterling, because they could not keep back the fresh-water. (Was not Iosbadaidh the boy !)

---

[3] This sentence may perhaps mean—my master will drink what I leave.

An uair a fhuair e an t-airgiod, chaidh e far an robh a
mhaighstir. 'Faodaidh tu éirigh a nis, chan 'eil iad siod
a' dol a chur dragha ort tuilleadh.' Thug e an cóig ceud
punnd Sasunnach d'a mhaighstir.

Ciod e a bh'ann, goirid 'na dhéidh sin, ach là mór
féille. Chaidh maighstir Iosbadaidh is e féin chun na
féille. Có dh'amais air maighstir Iosbadaidh ach na
daoine uaisle a chuir an geall ris, is bha toil mhór aca a
chur an sàs air dòigh air chor-eiginn. Bha iad ag òl
còmhla, is an uair a bha maighstir Iosbadaidh gu math air
aghaidh leis an deoch, cha robh nì sam bith nach dèanadh e.

'Ciod è an tùrn as fhearr a dhèanadh tu an dràsd?'
'Tùrn sam bith a dh'iarras sibh orm, nì mise.'
'Is e a dh'iarras sinn ort, ma thà, tigh geal a thogail
anns na speuran ann a so.'

H 951 'Ma tà, an leabhara, nì mise sin, ma chumas sibh
luchd-freasdail rium.'
'Cumaidh sinn.'

Chuireadh geall. Dhealaich maighstir Iosbadaidh agus na
daoine uaisle, agus chaidh e fhéin agus Iosbadaidh dhachaidh.

An là-'r-na-mhàireach, có ràinig an tigh ach na daoine
uaisle, is dh'éigh iad a mach air maighstir Iosbadaidh ás
an tigh. Chaidh Iosbadaidh a mach far an robh iad.
'Cha tusa tha sinn ag iarraidh, ach do mhaighstir.'
'An uair a dh'fhairtlicheas orm féin gnothuch mo
mhaighstir a dhèanamh, thig mo mhaighstir an sin, agus
nì e e. Ciod è gheall mo mhaighstir a dhèanamh?'

H 1036
H 951 'Gheall e tigh geal a thogail anns na speuran, ach
daoine bhi aige dhèanamh freasdail da.'
'A dhaoine gòrach! A bheil sibh a' smuaineachadh
gur h-urrainn duine sam bith tigh a thogail anns na
speuran? No a bheil sibh a' smuaineachadh gun
dèanadh sibh fhéin freasdal da?'
'Tha sinn a' smuaineachadh gun dèan sinn fhéin a
h-uile dad a bhios a dhìth air.'
'Is fhearr dhuibh dol dhachaidh, is a leigeil as bhur
ceann.'
'Cha dèan sinn idir e.'

When he had got the money, he went off to his master.
'Thou mayst rise now, those fellows are not going to
trouble thee any more.' He gave the five hundred sterling
to his master.

What should take place shortly afterwards but a fair.
It was a great day. Iosbadaidh and his master went to
the fair. Whom should his master meet but the gentlemen
who had laid the wager with him, and very anxious they
were to lay him in the bilboes in some way or another.
They were drinking together, and when Iosbadaidh's
master had got some way on with the drink, there was
nothing that he could not do.

'What is the greatest feat thou couldst do this time?'

'Anything whatever you ask me to do, I will do.'

'What we want thee to do, then, is to build a white
house in the skies at this spot.'

'Well then, by the books, I will, if you will supply me   H 951
with helpers.'

'We will.'

The bet was made. Iosbadaidh's master parted from
the gentlemen, and went home with Iosbadaidh.

On the morrow, who should come to the house but the
gentlemen, and they shouted for Iosbadaidh's master to
come out. Iosbadaidh went out to them.

'It is not thou we want, but thy master.'

'When my master's business has baffled *me*, then my
master himself will come, and manage the matter. What
did my master promise to do?'

'He promised to build a white house in the skies, provided   H 1036
he had men to help him.'   H 951

'Oh ye silly men! Do ye think that there is any man
who is able to build a house in the skies? Or do ye think
that ye yourselves could help him?'

'We think we can do everything he wants done.'

'Ye had better go home, and put all that out of your
heads.'

'We certainly will not.'

Ciod e bha ach seòrsa de pheata beag, Cro mhìnich
B 451·1* aig Iosbadaidh ann am bocsa, is bha bruidhinn aig gach
B 211·9 seòrsa creutair 'san uair sin, is bha bruidhinn aig an eun
so cho math ris gach creutair eile. 'Falbh thusa nis,' ars
Iosbadaidh, 'is éighidh tu 'Clach is aol ! clach is aol !'
a chur chugad.'

Leig e as am peata, is dh'it[eala]ich am peata suas
H 1142·4* anns na speuran, is shiuthad e air éigheach, 'Clach is aol !
clach is aol !'
'So, so,' ars Iosbadaidh, 'suas clach is aol an so a
thiotamh.'
Cha b'urrainn daibh-san clach no aol a chur a suas,
is b'éiginn daibh an geall a phàidheadh do Iosbadaidh air
an darna siubhal.
'Tapadh leat, Iosbadaidh,' ars a mhaighstir, 'tha mi
móran 'nad chomain; shàbhail thu air an darna siubhal
mi.'
Ciod è bha tacan o thigh maighstir Iosbadaidh ach
cruinneachadh mór, agus na h-uiread de luibhean is de
mheasan, is de gach seòrsa dh'a réir ann. Chaidh maighstir
Iosbadaidh is e fhéin ann. Cheannaich maighstir
Iosbadaidh làn mias de fheòil agus de mheasan cho brèagha
'sa bha r'a fhaotainn ann. 'Falbh,' ars esan ri Iosbadaidh,
H 1065 'is thoir a' mhias ud a dh'ionnsuigh an aona chreutair
leis an docha mise air an t-saoghal.'
Chaidh Iosbadaidh dachaidh, is dh'amais mìolchu [2] ris
a bha aig a mhaighstir a stigh, is dhòirt e na bha air
a' mhèis dh'a h-ionnsuigh. Thill e a dh'ionnsuigh na
féille, is thàinig e fhéin is a mhaighstir dhachaidh.
'An do chòrd an rud a chuir mi chugad riut ?' arsa
maighstir Iosbadaidh ri a bhean, 'an rud a chuir mi chugad
le Iosbadaidh ?'
'Ciod e an rud a chuir thu chugam le Iosbadaidh ?—
chan fhaca mise dad fhathast dheth.'
'Iosbadaidh, c'à'n do chuir thu e ?'
'Dh'iarr sibh fhéin ormsa a thoirt do'n aona chreutair

---

[1] See p. 12, footnote.
[2] The context shows that a female animal is meant.

Now what was it that Iosbadaidh had in a box but a little pet, a bird called a Cro veenich.[1] And as at that B 451·1* time every kind of creature had the power of speech, this B 211·9 bird also had that power like any other creature. 'Away with thee now,' said Iosbadaidh [to the bird], 'and shout for 'Stone and lime ! Stone and lime !' to be sent up to thee.'

He let slip the pet bird, and away it flew up into the skies, and began shouting, 'Stone and lime ! Stone and H 1142·4* lime !'

'Come, come,' said Iosbadaidh, 'send stone and lime up instantly.'

But they could send up neither stone nor lime, and so they were obliged to pay the wager to Iosbadaidh for the second time.

'Good luck to thee, Iosbadaidh,' said his master, 'I am greatly indebted to thee; thou hast saved me for the second time.'

What should there be a little way from the house of Iosbadaidh's master but a great [market] gathering, and there was ever such a lot of herbs and fruit, and similar things there. Iosbadaidh and his master went there. His master bought a dishful of meat and fruit as fine as there was to be got in the market. 'Go,' said he to Iosbadaidh, 'and carry that dishful to the creature who above all others H 1065 loves me more than anyone else in the world.'

Iosbadaidh went home, and indoors he met his master's greyhound (bitch),[2] and he emptied all there was in the dish out before her. Then he returned to the fair, and came back home again with his master.

'Wert thou pleased with what I sent thee ?' said Iosbadaidh's master to his wife, 'I mean what I sent thee by Iosbadaidh ?'

'What didst thou send me by Iosbadaidh ?—I have seen nothing of it yet.'

'Iosbadaidh, where didst thou put it ?'

'You yourself asked me to give it to the creature who

leis am bu docha sibh air an t-saoghal, agus thug mise
dha'n tigh mhìolchon e.[1] Bha mi 'smuaineachadh gur
h-i [am mìolchu] creutair leis am bu docha sibh a bh'ann.
Ged a bhuaileadh sibh i, cha teicheadh i, is nan gabhadh
sibh air a' mhnaoi, dh'fhalbhadh i uaibh a' rànaich agus
a' caoineadh, is cha taobhadh i tuilleadh sibh.'

'O'n a bha thu cho math is a bha thu, falbh agus thoir

H 1305
·1*

chugam-sa làn na mèise de'n fheòil a b'fhearr a bha air an
fhéill,' arsa bean a mhaighstir ri Iosbadaidh.

Dh'fhalbh e, is chaidh e chun na féille, is cheannaich
e làn na mèise de theangannan, is thug e siod d'a
h-ionnsuigh.[2] 'An i so feòil as fhearr a th'ann?'

H 1305
·1·1*

'Tha mi smuaineachadh gur h-i.'

'Fhalbh a nis, thoir chugam-sa làn na mèise de'n
fheòil a's miosa.'

Dh'fhalbh e, is ràinig e an fhéill, is cheannaich e làn
na mèise de theangannan, agus thug e dh'a h-ionnsuigh
iad. 'An i so feòil as miosa a th'ann?'

'Chan fhaca sibh-se riamh [dad] is miosa na droch
theanga, is chan fhaca sibh riamh [dad] is fhearr na deagh
theanga, is tha iad agaibh an sin le chéile, is togaibh fhín
bhur roghainn.'

'An rud a th'ann, tha e ann,' ars ise: 'fhir an tighe!
cha bhi a stigh ach mise no Iosbadaidh,[3] agus cum agad
do roghainn, mise no esan.'

'Ma tà,' ars esan, 'shàbhail Iosbadaidh domh mo
cheann dà uair, is cha dealaich mise ri Iosbadaidh gu
bràth—falbh no fuirich thusa.' (Làn cheart, fhir an tighe,
gabhadh i roimpe gus an toir a sròn comhairle oirre.)

Dh'fhalbh ise, is thug i a casan leatha, is theich i.

Dh'fhan Iosbadaidh, agus a mhaighstir le chéile.

Thug Iosbadaidh is a mhaighstir cóig no sia làithean

---

[1] MS. *mhial-choin.* But apparently genitive plural is intended, otherwise
the definite article would come after, and not before, *tigh.*

[2] This incident is taken from the traditional life of Æsop, but in that
Æsop gives a rhetorical proof that the tongue is the best of things. This is
here replaced by a bare assertion, though the corresponding proof that it is
the worst is retained.

[3] *Lit.* there shall not be indoors but I or Iosbadaidh. Compare for idiom,

above all others loved you more than anyone else in the world, so I took it to the greyhound's kennel. I am thinking that she [the greyhound bitch] among all other creatures loves you most. Even if you struck her, she would not run away, but if you beat the wife, she would run away from you crying and weeping, and would never more go near you.'

'Since thou hast been as clever as thou hast been, go and bring me a dishful of the best flesh meat there was at the fair,' said his master's wife to Iosbadaidh.

H 1305
•1*

Off he went, and betook him to the fair, and there he purchased a dishful of tongues, and brought them back to her.[2] 'Is this the best kind of flesh there is?'

'I think it is.'

'Go now, and bring me a dishful of the worst kind of flesh.'

H 1305
•1·1*

Off he went, and having arrived at the fair, purchased a dishful of tongues, and brought them back to her. 'Is this the worst kind of flesh there is?'

'Never did you see anything worse than a bad tongue, and never did you see anything better than a good tongue. There you have both together, so take your choice.'

'That which is, is,' quoth she: 'goodman! either Iosbadaidh or I must leave this house,[3] so take thy choice, and keep either me or him.'

'Well then,' said he, 'Iosbadaidh has saved my head twice, and I will never part with him—go thou or stay.' (Quite right, goodman, let her go away and keep straight on until her nose gives her counsel.)

She went away, and took her feet with her,[4] and bolted.

Iosbadaidh and his master remained there together.

Iosbadaidh and his master spent five or six days

'cha bhi buaidh ach ortsa no ormsa cho luath 's a gheabh mi fuasgladh': *An Gàidheal*, iv., p. 81. *Lit.* there shall not be victory but on thee or on me as soon as I get release : *i.e.* thou and I must fight till one of us gets the victory, and that as soon as I am freed.

[4] *Cf.* for idiom—'Thoir do chasan leat,' *i.e.* be gone, *lit.* 'Take thy feet with thee.'

comhla mar so, is thàinig dubh-thiamhas is mulad air
maighstir Iosbadaidh a' caoidh na mnà. 'Nach bu ghòrach
sibh !' ars Iosbadaidh, 'a chaidh a chur uaibh na mnà
air mo shon, agus an rud a gheibh mise duibhse, gheibh e
duibh neach eile, agus ma thogras sibh, bheir mise dhachaidh
a' bhean chugaibh fhathast.'

'Bheir mi dhuit ceud punnd Sasunnach, is thoir
dhachaidh i.'
Dh'fhalbh Iosbadaidh, is bheairtich e each is cairt.
Bha fhios aige far an robh ise gabhail tàimh, is ghabh e
sìos a dh'ionnsuigh an tighe, is ghlaodh e gun robh tunnagan
is geòidh a dhìth air, làn na cartach, is gun tugadh e an
uibhir so de phrìs orra. Thàinig ise a mach do'n
dorus.
'An tu so, Iosbadaidh?'
'O ! is mi.'
'Ciod è tha thu ag iarraidh?'
'Cha bhean sin duit-sa an dràsd, ach bheanadh e
roimhe duit—tha mo mhaighstir a' dol a phòsadh a nochd,
agus tha mise dol a chruinnicheadh feòla airson na bainnse—
chan 'eil gnothuch sam bith agadsa ris a sin.'
'An deomhan gin a phòsas e am feasd ach mise—bheir
K 441·4*   mi ceud punnd Sasunnach duit, is faic aige mi.'

'Thig thusa a steach do'n chairt, ma thà, air alt is
gum faicinn aige fhathast thu, is fàgaidh sinn na cearcan,
na geòidh, is an fheòil.' [1]
Dh'fhalbh Iosbadaidh leatha, is an uair a thàinig e
dlùth air an tigh, thuirt e rithe-se, 'Nis, fanaidh sibhse an
so cùl cnuic gus an cuir mise mo chomhairle ri mo mhaighstir,
is thig mi fhìn dh'ur n-iarraidh a rithist.'
Dh'fhalbh Iosbadaidh an so, is chaidh e dhachaidh,
is dh'innis e d'a mhaighstir gun d'fhuair e a bhean.
Thill e an sin air a son, is thug e dhachaidh i.
Rinneadh banais shunndach éibhinn d'a mhaighstir is
d'a bhana-mhaighstir. Bha iadsan aig a chéile mar a

_____
[1] Ducks and geese are what were mentioned before.

together in this way, and black-melancholy and grief
came upon Iosbadaidh's master lamenting for the wife.
'Were you not foolish !' quoth Iosbadaidh, 'to go and
send the wife away on my account, seeing that the thing
[*i.e.* payment] that will get me [and my services] for you,
will get some one else for you. However, if you wish, I
will bring the wife back home to you yet.'

'I will give thee one hundred pounds sterling if thou
wilt bring her back.'

Isobadaidh went off and harnessed a horse and cart.
He knew where she was living, and he went down to her
house, and shouted that he wanted enough ducks and geese
to fill the cart, and that he would give such and such a
price for them. Out she came to the door.

'Is it thou, Iosbadaidh ?'

'O ! yes, it is.'

'What dost thou want ?'

'That concerns thee not, not now, though it might
have concerned thee at one time—my master is going to
marry to-night, and I am going to collect meat for the
wedding—but that is no affair of thine.'

'Devil a one shall he ever marry but me—I will give
thee a hundred pounds sterling, if thou wilt see me safely K 441·4*
in his hands once more.'

'Come thou into the cart then, so that I may yet see
thee with him at home again, and we will leave the hens,
the geese, and the meat alone.' [1]

Iosbadaidh set off with her, and when coming near the
house, he said to her, 'Now, wait thou here at the back
of the hillock until I have taken counsel with my master,
and I will come to fetch thee again myself.'

Hereupon Iosbadaidh departed, and going home, told
his master that he had recovered his wife.

Then he returned for her, and fetched her home.

A merry joyful wedding was made for his master and
mistress. They lived together as they had done before,

bha iad roimhe, is bha Iosbadaidh comhla riu, fhad is a
thogair e fhìn.

From Roderick MacNeill, Glen, Barra, who heard it from John
MacNeill, Kentangval, Roderick MacNeill, Minglay, Donald
MacNeill, Glen, and numerous others.

NOTES

MS. vol. x., No. 25. Scribe—Hector MacLean.
Iosbadaidh. The name and doings of this hero suggest Æsop.
In his MS. vol. xvii. (published *Trans Gael. Soc. Inverness*, xxv., p. 179),
Islay speaks of one of his reciters who 'knows, or did know almost the
whole of the Arabian Nights from a book which was given to him in
Islay: ditto Æsop,' *ibid.*, p. 188. This man was Lachlin MacNeill,
who was born in Islay in 1788 (*ibid.*, p. 262). He recited to Hector
MacLean the longest Scottish Gaelic story known, Sgeulachd Cois'
O'Céin. Such a man might well be responsible for bringing a tale
about Æsop, as well as tales derived from the Arabian Nights, like the
following Tale No. 21, into current Gaelic lore. Such tales do not
resemble the native Gaelic tales, in either style or incident; in language
and style they are very dissimilar. Islay himself remarks of one of
them (MS. vol. x., No. 105), 'I cannot understand how this got here

and Iosbadaidh stayed with them as long as he himself
pleased.

[S. Uist], but there is no doubt it is the Arabian Nights and nothing
else. In this there was none of the old language, it was narrative and
dialogue.' The introduction of such tales was probably the cause
of a certain amount of corruption. This is noticeably the case with
this Tale, No. 12. The title and opening sentences speak of three
lads who had made up their minds never to separate. Yet they do
separate, and that very early in the story. It seems as if at least two,
and perhaps three unrelated tales had been joined together, and that
the reciter was apparently unconscious of any incongruity. Some of
the incidents of the tale, such as that concerning the talking bird
(whose name is very like that of the Creveenach, or carrying eagle,
which appears in several tales) may, however, be genuine pieces of
Gaelic oral tradition. But some incidents strike one as foreign. And
there is very little of the old language in the tale, though the Gaelic is
fairly idiomatic and good.

AN NIGHEAN BHRÈAGH, LEISG

No. 13.   [*Vol. x., No. 26*]

Aarne-Thompson, Nos. 901, 956 B

BHA duine uasal ann aig an robh baile fearainn, agus bha e
gléidheadh ghillean agus nigheanan, agus bha tuathanach
dlùth air aig an robh trì nigheanan, agus chuir e roimhe
gun rachadh e a dh' iarraidh té de chlann an tuathanaich
a phòsadh.

Ràinig e tigh an tuathanaich.

Bha dithis de nigheanan an tuathanaich a bha maith
agus dèanadach, agus bha té dhiubh bha brèagha agus
leisg; roghnaich an duine uasal an té leisg, bhrèagh, a
phòsadh.

Ars an tuathanach ris, 'Cha leig mi call ort,[1] cha dèan
W 111·3   i tùrn leis an leisg.'

'Mura dèan, biodh sin orm fhéin,' ars an duine uasal,
T 251·2   is phòs e i, is thug e leis dachaidh i.

'Nis,' ars an duine uasal, 'cuiridh sibh biadh nan gillean
dh'a m'ionnsuigh-sa, agus mo bhiadh-sa chun nan gillean
gu ceann seachduinn.'

Rinneadh siod, agus bha biadh nan gillean aig am
maighstir, agus biadh am maighstir aig na gillean.

'A Rìgh, nach nèonach an rud a th'ann,' ars ise,
'biadh cho maith aig na gillean is a leithid so de bhiadh
againn fhéin.'

'Is ann aig na gillean a tha feum air a' bhiadh mhaith;
tha iad 'ga chosnadh, is o nach 'eil sinne 'g obair, fògh-
naidh am biadh is miosa dhuinn.'

---

[1] *Lit.* I will not allow loss [to come] upon thee; she will not do a turn with
the laziness.

THE HANDSOME LAZY LASS

No. 13.   *[Vol. x., No. 26]*

Aarne-Thompson, Nos. 901, 956 B

THERE was once a gentleman who had a farm, and kept serving-men and serving-women. There was a farmer living near him who had three daughters, and the gentleman made up his mind that he would seek one of the farmer's children in marriage.

He arrived at the farmer's house.

Two of the farmer's daughters were good and industrious. But the other one was handsome and lazy. And the gentleman chose this lazy and handsome one.

The farmer said to him, 'I do not [1] wish thee to suffer loss. She will not do a hand's turn, she is so lazy.'   W III·3

'Even if she will not, let that be my affair,' said the gentleman, and he married her, and took her home with T 251·2 him.

'Now,' said the gentleman [to his servants], 'you are to give me the food that the serving-men eat, and give the serving-men the food that I have. You are to do this for a week.'

This was done, and the master had the food of the serving-men, and the serving-men were supplied with the master's food.

'Oh King! is it not an extraordinary thing,' said she, 'that the serving-men should have such good food, while we have such food as this.'

'It is the serving-men who have need of good food; they earn it, but seeing that we do not work, food that is not so good will suffice for us.'

'Ciod è am feum air biadh cho maith a thoirt do na gillean ? ciod è an obair as trioblaidich is as sàraichte bhios aca ?'

'Treabhadh, bualadh, agus cairtearachd.'

'Ciod è an obair is trioblaidiche dhiubh sin ?'

'Bualadh.'

'Gu dearbh, théid mi fhéin a bhualadh an diugh, ma gheabh mi biadh maith.'

'Gu dearbh, cha téid; chan ann airson sin a fhuair mise thu.'

'Nis,' ars esan ris a' bhean-mhuinntir, 'cuiridh tu mo bhiadh fhéin dh'a m'ionnsuigh-sa, is am biadh fhéin a dh'ionnsuigh nan gillean a rithist.[1] Tha mi fhéin is a' bhean a' falbh as a' bhaile, is glasaidh tu gach àite, is fiach nach leig thu duine sam bith a stigh gus an till sinn.'

Dh'fhalbh iad-san.

Ghabh iad mu'n bhaile cho maith is a dh'fhaodadh a bhi.

Am beul na h-oidhche, có thàinig an rathad ach bean-uasal mhór, agus dh'fhaighnich i de 'n bhean-mhuinntir, am faigheadh i seòmar anns an sgrìobhadh i litir. Thuirt a' bhean-mhuinntir gum faigheadh. Dh'fhosgail i seòmar di, is chuir i coinneal laiste a sìos. An uair a chaidh i sìos, dhùin i an dorus, is ghlas i e.

Bha a' bhean-mhuinntir a' gabhail mulaid, fhad is a bha a' bhean-uasal shìos. Sheall i sìos, is ciod è chunnaic i ach firionnach an déidh aodach boirionnaich a chur deth. Bha e an sin le a chasaig ghuirm, is le a bhriogais chaoil a' dèanamh garadh chùl-chas.

K 311

Ars ise ris a' ghille, 'Feumaidh tu tapadh a dhèanamh nach do rinn thu riamh.'

Sheall iad sìos a rithist, is chunnaic iad esan a' dol a chadal.

'A bheil dad luaidhe agad a stigh ?'

'Tha,' ars an gille.

[1] The restoration of the *status quo* as regards food probably implies that some incidents which related how the lazy woman was completely cured of her laziness, have been lost. Though she has given her name to the story she drops out of it at this point, and another woman becomes the heroine. Two stories have probably been fused.

'What need is there to give such good food to the serving-men? what is the hardest and most exhausting work that they have to do?'

'Ploughing, threshing, and carting.'

'And which of those is the hardest?'

'Threshing.'

'Then certainly I myself will go and thresh to-day, if I get good food.'

'Thou certainly shalt not; it is not for that purpose that I took thee.'

'Now,' said he to the serving-woman, 'thou art to send me my own food again, and theirs to the serving-men.[1] I and my wife are going away from home, and thou art to lock every place up, and remember not to let any man in until we return.'

They departed.

The servants made everything about the place as secure as it could be made.

At night-fall who should come that way but a tall lady, who enquired of the serving-woman if she might have a room in which she might write a letter. The serving-woman said she might. She opened a room for her, and set down a lighted candle. When the lady had gone in [2] the serving-woman shut the door, and locked it.

The lady remained there so long, that the serving-woman began to weary. She looked in, and what did she see, but a man. He had taken off his woman's dress. There he K 311 was in a blue long-coat and a fine pair of breeks, warming the backs of his legs.

Said she to the serving-lad, 'Thou hast a doughty deed to do such as thou never hadst to do before.'

They looked into the inner room again, and saw that he was going to sleep.

'Hast thou any lead in the house?'

'I have,' said the gillie.

---

[2] *Lit.* down. The room would be farther in (*i.e.* farther from outside door) than the room in which she talked with the serving-maid.

'Tha uait taosg sgeileid [1] a leaghadh.' Rinn e siod.

S 112·3 Thug ise leatha an luaidhe, is chaidh i sìos, agus thaom i siod a sìos 'na bheul, is bha e glan marbh far an robh e.

Rannsaich i e, agus fhuair i fìdeag agus claidheamh. 'Nis,' ars ise, 'có aca is fhearr leat-sa—cur seachad mar a leagas mise, no leagail mar a chuireas mise seachad?' 'Gabhaidh mise os làimh, cur seachad mar a leagas tusa.' Chuir i as an solus, chaidh i chun an doruis, is sheinn i an fhìdeag.

K 912
G 510 Thàinig iad-san, companaich an fhir a bha marbh, fuamhairean agus mèirlich. Thàinig deich air an aghaidh. Mharbh i an deich. Bha aon fhear air deireadh, 's cha robh e cluinntinn fuaim sam bith a stigh. Stad e tacan a chluinntinn mar a bha dol daibh. An uair a chunnaic ise e, lean i e, is theich e. Tharruing i an claidheamh, is ghearr i an deireadh dheth. Thill i an so dhachaidh, is chaidh i a chadal.

An là-'r-na-mhàireach, thàinig a maighstir, is chunnaic e mar a thachair. 'Cha bhi thu ann ad bhean-mhuinntir tuilleadh,' ars esan, 'ach bidh té fo do làimh.'

Bha tochar aice ri a fhaotainn o'n duine uasal, is bha na h-uibhir a' tighinn a dh'iarraidh a pòsadh, is cha robh i gabhail gin.

Thàinig stàta fuathasach urramach, a thaobh coslais, an rathad. Dh'fhan e seachduinn an tigh an duine uasail. Thuirt e gun cuala e iomradh air a' ghnìomh a rinn an
K 1916 nighean so, is airson a tapadh, gun robh e airson a pòsadh.

Thuirt an duine uasal o'n a bha i cho tapaidh, nach bu mhaith leis gum faigheadh fear sam bith i ach fear a bhiodh fìor mhaith dhi.

---

[1] MS. taosg 's gileid: *sgeileid*—regular word for sauce-pan (skellet?) *Taosg*—No exact English equivalent. It means that a vessel is holding a fair amount of what it can hold, without being full to the brim.

'Thou must melt as much as will almost fill a sauce-pan.'[1]
He did so accordingly. She took the lead with her, went
into the inner room, and emptied it down his mouth, and S 112·3
there he was, stone dead where he lay.

She searched him, and found a whistle and a sword.
'Now,' said she, 'which dost thou prefer—to clear [2] away
as I cut down, or to cut down as I clear away?'

'I will undertake to clear away, as thou cuttest down.'

She then put out the light, went to the door, and blew
the whistle.

They came, the companions of the dead man, giants and K 912
robbers. Ten of them came along. She killed all the ten. G 510

One of them was behindhand. He could not hear a
sound inside the house, so he stood still for a while to try
and hear how they were getting on. When she saw him,
she followed him, and he fled. She slashed at him with the
sword, and cut off his haunches. Then she returned home,
and went to sleep.

On the morrow, her master returned, and saw what
had happened. 'Thou shalt be a serving-woman no
longer,' said he; 'but shalt have a woman under
thee.'

She was to have a marriage portion from the gentleman;
and ever so many people came to seek her in marriage, but
she would not take one.

A nobleman came that way, who was, to all outward
appearance, exceedingly distinguished. He stayed for a
week in the gentleman's house. He said he had heard
the report of the deeds the lass had done, and that he
wished to marry her, because of her courage and K 1916
resourcefulness.

The gentleman said that seeing she had been so heroic,
he would not like any man to win her except one who would
be exceedingly good to her.

---

[2] Part of the interest of these tales is often to find out by listening to the
subsequent narrative, what cryptic sentences such as this mean.

'Ma gheibh mise i, chan eagal dhi, chionn is e a leithid de bhoirionnach tapaidh a bha dhìth orm.'

Chòrd iad, is rinn an duine uasal banais chridheil daibh. Dh'fhan iad an sin fad seachduinn, agus an ceann na seachduinn, thuirt a fear rithe-se,
'Is fhearr dhuinn a nis falbh, agus bidh banais eile againn aig an tigh againn fhéin.' 'Tha sin ceart gu leòir,' ars ise.

Chaidh e air muin eich, is chaidh ise air a chùl. Bha iad a' falbh gus an tàinig an oidhche orra, is bha iad a' dol troimh choillidh làn de dhraighionn is de dhreasan, is bha a h-aodach-se air a shracadh, is a craicionn air a reubadh leis an draighionn is leis na dreasan.

'Dèan air do shocair leis an each,' ars ise, 'chionn tha mi air mo ghortachadh, is tha m'aodach air a shracadh.'

'Mo thruaighe,' ars esan, 'chan 'eil sin gu maith, ach nam bu chuimhne leat-sa mar a mharbh thu mo dheich bràithrean, is a ghearr thu an deireadh de'n fhear eile, cha chanadh thu sin rium.'

$Q411·1*$

'Mo chreach! an ann mar sin a tha an gnothuch?'

Ràinig iad far an robh an t-àite aige-san, taobh creige. Ghlaodh esan, 'A bheil thu a stigh, fhir a thugadh an deireadh dheth?'

Thàinig duine a mach an uair a chuala e so, is rug e air a' bhoirionnach, is thug e a stigh i.

'A nis,' ars e r'a luchd-muinntir, 'có aca as fhearr leibh, spòrs a bhi againn air a bàs mun gabh sinn ar biadh, no an uair a ghabhas sinn e?'

'Is ann an déidh ar bìdh is mó a nì sinn de ghàireachdaich is de aighear timchioll air a bàs.'

Rug iad oirre, is rùisg iad 'na seasamh i.

'Leigibh orm mo léine,' ars ise. Dh'fhàg iad uimpe a léine, is cheangail iad an sin i, is thilg iad am measg chat, is chon, is mhuc i.

Shuidh iad an sin air am biadh, agus ciod e chuala iad ach stoirm chroachachan[1] a' dol seachad air an toll

[1] So MS.

'If I win her, there need be no fear for her welfare, because it is just such a heroic woman as she that I wish for.'

They were betrothed, and the gentleman had a hearty wedding prepared for them. They remained there for a week, and at the end of the week, her husband said to her,

'We had better depart now, and we will have another wedding at our own house.' 'That would be very proper,' said she.

He mounted a horse, and she got up behind him. They travelled till night came upon them. They went through a forest full of thorns and of brambles, and her clothes were being torn, and her skin was being cut with the thorns and the brambles.

'Go more slowly with the horse,' said she, 'because I have been sorely hurt and my clothes have been torn.'

'Alas,' said he, 'that is not well, but if thou didst but remember how thou killedst my ten brethren, and how Q411·1* thou didst slash the haunches off the other one, thou wouldst not say that to me.'

'My ruin ! is it thus that the matter stands ?'

They arrived at the place where he had his house, at the side of a rock. He shouted, 'Art thou within, thou from whom the haunches were cut ?'

Upon hearing this, a man came out, seized upon the woman, and took her in.

'Now,' said he to his servants, 'which do ye prefer— to amuse ourselves by killing her before we take our meal, or to do so afterwards ?'

'The laughter and sport that we shall have in killing her would be greater if we did it after our food.'

They seized her, and stripped her where she stood.

'Let me have my shift to wear,' said she. So they left her shift on her, and then they bound her, and threw her amongst cats, and dogs, and pigs.

Then they sat down to their food, when what should they hear but a storm of croachachan [?] going past the

anns an robh iad. A mach a ghabh a h-uile fear riamh
as an déidh.[1]

Bha gille glas a stigh a bha aca 'na chòcaire. 'Thig
an so, a ghille òig, agus fuasgail mi.'—'Cha téid,' ars an
gille òg, 'tha seachd bliadhna o'n a ghoid iad mi fhéin,
is tha mi aca ris an obair so, agus cha téid mi a ghiorrachadh
mo shaoghail airson thusa a leigeil mu sgaoil.'

'Falbh, agus fuasgail mise, is bheir mi mi féin is thu
fhéin o'n bhàs fhathast.' Dh'fhuasgail e i. Rug i air
poca, is lìon i làn feòla bhàrr a' bhùird e, agus chuir i
siod air muin a' ghille ghlais, agus dh'fhalbh i fhéin, is
lìon i a sgùird làn de fheòil.

Dh'fhalbh i fhéin agus an gille glas, is thog iad ris a'
mhonadh.

Fada goirid gun robh iad air falbh, an uair a thàinig
na mèirlich, cha d'fhuair iad duine a stigh. Leig iad na
coin mhóra mu sgaoil, is chuir iad as an déidh iad, is cha
b'fhada bha na coin an uair a rug iad orra. An uair a
rug na coin orra, dhòirt i rud de'n fheòil a dh'ionnsuigh
nan con, agus stad na coin ag itheadh na feòla, is ghabh
iad-san air an aghaidh.

An uair a thàinig na mèirlich air an aghaidh, fhuair
iad na coin 'nan stad ag itheadh na feòla, is bhreab iad
iad, is chuir iad air falbh iad.

Rug na coin a rithist orra, is thaom iad tuilleadh de'n
fheòil orra. Stad na coin aig an fheòil, is choisich iad-san
air an aghaidh cho luath is a dh'fhaodadh iad.

Rug na mèirlich air na coin, is fhuair iad iad ag itheadh
na feòla, is bhreab iad as an déidh a rithist iad.

An uair a thàinig na coin orra air an turus so, thilg
iad orra na bha aca de dh'fheòil, is ghabh iad air an aghaidh
cho luath is a b'urrainn daibh. An uair a rug na mèirlich
air na coin, is gann a b'urrainn daibh an cur ri astar,

R 231

---

[1] Similar incident in *W. H. Tales*, ii., No. 30, Var. 7.   *Croachachan* is not
in the dictionary.

cave in which they were. And out after the croachachan every one of them dashed.[1]

There was a young lad in the place whom they kept as a cook. 'Come here, young lad, and release me.'—'I will not,' said the young fellow, 'seven years have passed since they stole me, and they keep me here at this work. And I am not going to shorten my life through having let thee loose.'

'Come on, be quick, come and release me, and I will save both myself and thee from death.' He released her. She seized on a bag, and filled it full of flesh-meat from the table, and put it on the young lad's back, and then she went and filled her own skirt full of flesh-meat.

Then she and the young lad set off for the moors.

Whether they had been away for a long time or a short time [is not told, but] when the robbers returned, they found no one indoors. So they unleashed their great hounds, and set them after them, and it was not long before the hounds came up with them. When they came up with them, she threw some of the flesh-meat to them, and R 231 the hounds stopped to eat the flesh-meat, while she and the young lad pressed onwards.

When the robbers came up, they found that the hounds had stopped to eat the flesh-meat, so they kicked them and drove them on.

The hounds caught up with them again, and they threw them some more of the flesh-meat. The hounds stopped to eat it, while they tore onwards as quickly as they could.

The robbers came up with the hounds, and found them eating the flesh-meat, so they kicked them and drove them after the fugitives again.

When the hounds caught them up on this occasion, they threw them all the flesh-meat they had, and dashed on as quickly as they could. When the robbers came up with the hounds, they were hardly able to make them

bha iad a' fàs sàthach. Lean na mèirlich iad, is bha dà earrann diubh rompa, is earrann 'nan déidh.

Cha robh fios aca 'd è dhèanadh iad. Dh'amais blàr mòna orra, agus gearradh 'na aodann. Dh'fhalaich iad iad féin an so, agus an uair a ràinig na mèirlich an t-àite, cha rachadh na coin seachad air a' bhlàr mhòna. Thòisich iad air gabhail orra, is chan fhàgadh iad siod.

'Tillidh sinn dachaidh,' ars a h-aon diubh. 'Mura ruig sinn an tigh-seinnse,' arsa fear eile, 'cha téid iad-san seach sin. Gheibh sinn a mach o fhear an tigh-sheinnse a bheil iad aige, is mura bi e toileach innseadh, cuiridh sinn air a mhionnan e. Mura bheil iad ann an nochd, is glé chosmhuil gum bi iad ann an ath-oidhche, agus thig sinn an ath-oidhche, is fanaidh sinn 'san tigh-sheinnse,
K 312 is bidh sinn ann am pocaichean,[1] agus feadh na h-oidhche, éiridh sinn agus beiridh sinn orra, agus bheir sinn leinn iad agus robaidh sinn an tigh.' [Chuala ise a h-uile facal, is i a' farchluais air.]

Ràinig iad far an robh an tigh-seinnse.

'An tàinig gin sam bith ad chòir an so a nochd?'

'Cha tàinig duine,' arsa fear an tigh-sheinnse.

'Thàinig: innis duinn e, thàinig nighean agus gille an so a nochd. Tha sinn ag iarraidh nighinn agus gille, agus feumaidh tu innseadh a bheil iad a stigh agad.'

'Bheir mise mo mhionnan duibh, nach 'eil fhios agam-sa
K 640 c'à' bheil nighean no gille tha sibh ag iarraidh air uachdar talamhannda.'

'Na bithibh a' sàrachadh an duine chòir,' arsa fear diubh, 'nam biodh fios aige, dh'innseadh e air ball e.' Dh'fhalbh iad, is thill iad dachaidh. Cha d'fhuair iad gin dhiubh.

Mu thrì uairean 'sa' mhaduinn, thàinig ise agus an gille glas gus an tigh-sheinnse. Bhuail iad 'san dorus, agus dh'iarr iad fosgladh agus an leigeil a stigh. 'Chan

---

[1] So in MS. But 'pocannan,' the word which appears further on, is more probably the one mentioned by the reciter.

hurry, so satiated had they become. The robbers followed
them, two bands of them keeping before the hounds, and
one crew behind them.

The fugitives did not know what to do. They came to
a flat grassy plot among the hills or moors, in the face of
which there was a gorge or ravine. They hid themselves
there, and when the robbers came to the place, the hounds
would not leave the flat grassy spot. The robbers began
beating them, but they would not stir.

'Let us return home,' said one of them. 'Unless we
go to the change-house,' said another, 'they certainly will
not go past that. We shall find out from the change-house
man whether they are with him or not, and if he be not
willing to tell, we will put him on his oath. If they do not
go there to-night, it is very likely that they will go there
to-morrow night, and we will come to-morrow night and
stay in the change-house, and we will hide in some sacks, K 312
and during the night, we will rise and capture them, carry
them away with us, and rob the house.' [But she was eaves-
dropping, and so she heard every word.]

They came to where the change-house was.

'Has anyone been near thee here to-night ?'

'Not anyone,' answered the change-house man.

'Yes, some one has been: tell us all about it, a young
woman and a lad have been here to-night. We are looking
for a young woman and a lad, and thou must say whether
thou hast them indoors with thee.'

'I will give you my oath that I do not know where on
the face of the earth are the young woman and the lad you K 640
are looking for.'

'Don't be harassing the honest man,' said one of the
robbers, 'if he knew about it, he would have said so at
once.' So the robbers went away, and returned home,
without finding one of them.

About three o'clock in the morning, she and the young
lad came to the change-house. They knocked at the
door, and asked that it might be opened, and that they

fhosgail mise an dorus, gus am buailear e trì uairean.' [1]
Bhuail e trì uairean anns an am, agus leig e a stigh iad.

'Chan 'eil fhios 'm nach sibh an fheadhainn a bha na
daoine móra ag iarraidh ann a so o chionn uair !'
'An robh daoine sam bith 'gar n-iarraidh-ne ?'
'Bha—cheasnaich iad mise gu maith air ur son.'

'Bheir thu dhuinn fasgadh o'n bhàs ann ad thigh gus
an tig an là, agus bheir mise o'n bhàs thu féin a màireach.'
An uair a dh'éirich iad 'sa' mhaduinn, bha fear an tighe
a' faighneachd dith, 'd è mar a bheireadh i o'n bhàs
esan.
'A bheil duine a bhuineas duit 'san arm ?' ars ise.
'Tha mac bràthar domh ann, 'na sheanailear.'

'Sgrìobh dh'a ionnsuigh mura bi e agad fo naoi uairean
a nochd gu bheil e cosmhuil gum bi do bheatha air a call,
agus na th'agad air a thoirt air falbh.' Sgrìobh e chun
an t-seanaileir.

Aig ochd uairean 'san fheasgar, co thàinig ach cairtear
mór [2] le trì chairtean làn bathair, agus ceithir pocaichean

K 312

anns a h-uile cairt. Dh'fhaighnich e de fhear an tigh-
sheinnse am faigheadh e fardoch uaidh anns an oidhche.
Thuirt fear an tigh-sheinnse gum faigheadh. Thòisich e
air cur a stigh a bhathair. Thòisich fear an tigh-sheinnse
leis. Thuirt e ri fear an tigh-sheinnse nach ruigeadh e
leas a bhi cuideachadh leis, gum b'fhearr leis e fhéin dh'a
chur a stigh.

Chuir e a stigh na pocaichean ann an seòmar. Chuir
e fios air fear an tigh-sheinnse, agus dh'iarr e siola, agus
bha iad ag òl is a' comhnadal, is a' cur seachad na h-ùine

K 1817·4

comhla. Ghabh iad an tràth-feasgair. Aig deich uairean,
thuirt am marsanta gun robh toil aige dol mu thàmh,
gun robh e sgìth.

Z 71·1

[1] Some incident relating how a signal had been pre-arranged has been
lost. The number 3 appears everywhere. It is a number of totality, completeness. Witches give sailors strings on which are three knots, a hero shouts
three times at a giant to resurrect him (see this book, p. 19) etc., etc. The

might be let in. 'I will not open the door, till it be struck thrice.' [1] He [they?] knocked three times instantly, and the change-house man let them in.

'I don't know but that you are the people for whom those big fellows were searching here an hour ago !'

'Were there any people looking for us ?'

'Yes, there were—they questioned me thoroughly about you.'

'Thou shalt protect us in thy house from death, until day comes, and I will rescue thee from death to-morrow.'

When they arose in the morning, the goodman asked her how she would rescue him from death.

'Hast thou any relation in the army ?' said she.

'Yes, I have. My brother's son is in the army, a general.'

'Write and tell him that if he be not with thee by nine o'clock to-night, thy life will probably be lost, and all that thou hast, taken away.' So he wrote to the general.

At eight o'clock in the evening, who should come but a great carter [2] with three carts full of merchandise, and four sacks in every cart. He enquired of the change-house K 312 man whether he might have a night's shelter of him. The change-house man said he might. So he began to take the merchandise indoors. The change-house man began to help him. He told the change-house man that he need not help him, that he would rather take the merchandise in himself.

He put the sacks into a room. He sent for the change-house man, and asked for a gill, and they were drinking and talking and passing away the time together. They took their evening meal. At ten o'clock, the merchant K 1817·4 said that he wished to go to rest, that he was tired.

---

fact that *e.g.* in modern Greece, three knocks cannot be given by an evil being because it is the number of the Trinity, is irrelevant here. In Gaelic folk-lore the Trinity is never thought of. But in charms and blessings the Trinity often appear.   [2] Spoken of later as a merchant.

'Faodaidh tusa dol a laighe—cha téid duine a chur dragha ort, is faodar do ghlasadh 'nad sheòmar fhéin.'

'Chan fhaigh mise cadal idir ma bhios gluasad sam bith feadh an tighe, agus is còir an tigh a ghlasadh is gabhail mu thàmh.'

'Chan 'eil an tigh agam-sa r'a ghlasadh no r'a dhùnadh, gus am buail e dà uair dheug a dh'oidhche.'

Aig aon uair deug, cha tàinig duine air fear an tigh-sheinnse. 'C'arson nach 'eil thu a' glasadh an tighe, agus a' dol a laighe ?' ars am marsanta.

'Gus am bi e dà uair dheug, cha ghlasar an dorus is cha téid mise a laighe,' arsa fear an tigh-sheinnse.

Cha robh duine a' tighinn, is bha fear an tigh-sheinnse a' gabhail eagail. Bhuail e dà uair dheug, agus cha tàinig duine. Dhùineadh an dorus. Cha do rinneadh ach an dorus a dhùnadh, an uair a chualas buille ann.

'Fosgail an dorus,' ars am fear a bha a muigh.

'Chan fhosgail,' arsa fear an tigh-sheinnse.

'Feumaidh tu a fhosgladh, air neò nì mise dorus dhomh fhéin.'

Dh'fhosgail fear an tigh-sheinnse an dorus, is thàinig an seanailear a stigh fo lùirichean. Chunnaic e solus an uinneag a' mharsanta. Dh'fhosgail e an dorus agus chaidh e sìos. Dh'iarr e dram is fhuair e siod. Dh'òl e air slàinte a'mharsanta.

'Ol air do shlàinte fhéin,' ars am marsanta.

Lìon e a' ghloine a rithist, is thairg e do'n mharsanta e. Cha ghabhadh am marsanta e. 'An e gun gabhainn-sa uait fhéin e ?'

Rug e air a' ghloine is na bha 'na broinn, agus tilgear air a' mharsanta mu'n dà shùil e, agus mun d'fhosgail e a shùilean gu ceart, bha an seanailear an déidh na lùirichean a thilgeil deth, agus e fo bhriogais ghuirm is fo chasaig chaoil.[1] 'So a nis, gabhaidh tu a nis dram uam ! A bheil bathar maith agad anns na pocannan [2] so ?'

---

[1] The robber's dress, after throwing off his disguise, was a blue long-coat and a fine pair of breeks.

'[Oh yes]—thou mayest go to bed—no one will trouble thee, and thou mayest be locked in thine own room.'

'I shall not get any sleep at all, if anyone be moving about the house. The proper thing to do is to lock up the house and go to bed.'

'This house of mine is not to be locked or shut until it strikes twelve o'clock at night.'

Eleven o'clock came, but no one had called upon the change-house man. 'Why art thou not locking up the house, and going to bed?' said the merchant.

'Until twelve o'clock comes, the door shall not be locked, and I shall not go to bed,' said the change-house man.

Nobody was coming, and the change-house man began to be afraid. It struck twelve, but nobody came. The door was then shut. They had only just shut the door, when they heard a knock at it.

'Open the door,' said he who was without.

'I will not open it,' said the change-house man.

'Thou must open it, or else I will make a door for myself [= I will burst into the house somehow].'

The change-house man opened the door, and in came the general in rags. He noticed a light in the merchant's K 1815 window, so he opened the door, and went into the inner room. He asked for a dram, and having got it, drank to the merchant's health.

'Drink to thine own health,' said the merchant.

The general filled another glass, and offered it to the merchant. The merchant would not take it. 'Do you think I would take it from thee?'

The general seized the glass with its contents, and pitched it into the merchant's two eyes, and before he could open his eyes properly, the general had thrown off his rags, and now appeared in blue breeks and in a fine long-coat.[1] 'Come now, thou wilt take a dram from me now! Hast thou some good merchandise in these sacks?'

---

[1] This is better than *pocaichean* ante, and is probably the form really used by the reciter.

'Tha, ach cha bhi sinn 'ga fhiachainn a nochd gu toiseach an là.'

'Chan e sin a tha dhìth orm-sa, ach a fhaicinn a nochd.'

'Gheibh mi fhéin dram, is cuiridh sinn seachad an oidhche mar a tha sinn, is chan fhiach sinn am bathar a nochd: cha léir dhuinn e gu ceart—tha e ro luachmhor.'

'Feumaidh mi am bathar fhiachainn.' Ghabh e gu beul a' phoca. 'Mura fosgail thusa e, fosglaidh mi féin e,' ars an seanailear.

Dh'fhuasgail e beul a' phoca, agus a mach a chuir duine a cheann ! 'An do chaidil iad ?' ars am fear a bha 'sa' phoca.

'Chaidil [', ars an seanailear. '] Gu cinnteach, a mharsanta ! faodaidh tu a ràdh gun robh bathar maith agad ! tha e anabarrach feudalach !'

Thug e fìdeag as a phòca, agus sheinn e i, agus thàinig buidheann shaighdearan a bha leis a stigh. Rug iad air na pocaichean is dh'fhosgail iad iad, agus mharbh iad na robh annta. Cha d'fhàg iad gin beò, ach am marsanta mór 'na ònrachd.

'Fhir an tigh-sheinnse,' ars an seanailear, 'a bheil feadhainn sam bith agad am falach a stigh an so a nochd ?'

'Tha,' arsa fear an tigh-sheinnse.

'A nuas an so iad.'

Thug e a nuas an gille glas agus an nighean.

'O bhéist,' ars ise, [ris a' mharsanta] 'tha thusa an so !'

'Mise ! chan fhaca mise riamh thu !'

'Chunnaic, a dhearg shlaightire ! is tu chunnaic ! agus bu léir a bhlàth dhomh-sa gum faca !'

'Ciod è mar a chunnaic e thu ?' ars an seanailear.

Dh'innis i a h-uile nì, mar a phòs e i, is mar a thug e leis i, is mar a bha e dol a dhèanamh oirre, is am bàs a bha iad a' dol a thoirt dith. Gun do rùisg iad i, is gun do thilg iad a measg chon is chat is mhuc i, is gun robh iad a'

'Yes, I have, but we will not examine it to-night, not till day begins.'

'That is not what I want, but to see it to-night.'

'I myself will fetch a dram and we will pass the night as we are. We will not examine the merchandise to-night —we shall not be able to see it properly—it is exceedingly precious.'

'I needs must examine the merchandise.' He stepped up to the mouth of a sack. 'If thou wilt not open it, I will open it myself,' said the general.

He unfastened the mouth of the sack, and a man put his head out at once. 'Have they gone to sleep?' said the man in the sack.

'Yes, they have,' [said the general]. 'Certainly, merchant! thou mayest well say that thou hast some good merchandise! It is exceedingly precious!'

He took a whistle from his pocket, and blew it, and in came a band of soldiers who belonged to him. They seized the sacks, and they opened them, and they killed all who were in them. They did not leave one alive, save only the big merchant.

'Man of the change-house,' said the general, 'hast thou any people with thee who are hiding in thy house to-night?'

'Yes, I have,' said the change-house man.

'Bring them here.'

He brought forth the young lad and the lass.

'Wretch,' said she [to the merchant], 'art *thou* here?'

'I! I have never seen thee before!'

'Thou hast, thou desperate villain! 'tis thou who *hast* seen me! And the result of thy having seen me was for me only too clear!'

'How, under what circumstances did he see thee?' said the general.

She related everything, how he had married her, how he had taken her away, and what he had been going to do with her, and the death they had intended to give her. That they had stripped her, and thrown her among dogs

dol a chur dà shleagh iaruinn air an dèanamh dearg 'san teine troimpe.

'Am bheil a[o]n sleagh iaruinn a stigh?' ars an seanailear.

'Tha,' arsa fear an tigh-sheinnse.

'Thugaibh an so i, is deargaichibh i 'san teine, agus 'na dhéidh sin, cuiridh sinn an duine so gu bàs.' Rinn an gille glas an t-sleagh dearg anns an teine. Chroch iad tarsuing air sleagh e, agus chuir iad an t-sleagh dhearg troimhe; is do'n nighinn, is e ràn a' bhodaich a bu ghoirte leatha a chluinntinn a stigh na na rinn e riamh de chron oirre.[2]

Q 581
S 112·2

'Is e a nì sinn a nis,' ars an seanailear, 'pòsaidh mi fhìn thu, agus faodaidh an gille glas dol dachaidh gu a athair fhìn.' Phòs an seanailear agus ise, agus chaidh an gille glas dhachaidh gu a athair fhìn.

From Roderick MacNeill, Glen, Barra, who heard it recited by a great many old men in his youth. This tale is pretty common and various versions of it abound.

NOTES

MS. Vol. x., No. 26. Scribe—probably Hector MacLean. On the flyleaf, Islay has written—'Compare 40 thieves.' Compare also the story of Evnissyen in the Mabinogion.

For other robber stories, see No. 12 (MS. vol. x., No. 25), No. 27

and cats and pigs, and that they had intended thrusting two iron spears through her, two iron spears that had been made red-hot in the fire.[1]

'Is there any iron spear in the house ?' said the general.

'Yes, there is,' said the man of the change-house.

'Bring it here, and make it red-hot in the fire, and after that, we will put this man to death.' The young lad made the spear red-hot in the fire. They hung the Q581 merchant on a spear, and thrust the red-hot spear through S112·2 him; and to the lass to hear the shriek of the wretch in the house seemed more agonizing than all the evil and harm he had ever done to her.[2]

'This is what we will now do,' said the general, 'I will marry thee myself, and the young lad may go home to his own father.' So the general and she married, and the young lad went home to his own father.

[1] Nothing was said about the spears before.

[2] *Cf.* the reply of Gràinne in the tale of Diarmaid and Gràinne. When asked by Fionn whether Diarmaid's dying shout (*sic*) was the hardest (*sic*) shriek she had ever heard, Gràinne replies in effect that the shriek of the Ciuthach when Diarmaid killed him was still harder.—*W. H. Tales*, iii., p. 65, or p. 55. *Celtic Review*, ix., p. 201.

(MS. vol. x., No. 50) and MS. vol. x., Nos. 111, 113, 168, and MS. vol. xi., No. 172.

For stopping pursuing hounds, see No. 25 (MS. vol. x., No. 47), *W. H. Tales*, ii., No. 26, and J. G. McKay, *The Tale of the Cauldron* (M. C. MacLeod, Dundee, 1927). See also *Béaloideas*, iii., p. 145.

ALASDAIR, MAC AN IMPIRE

No. 14.   *[Vol. x., No. 28]*

Aarne-Thompson, No. 517

BHA Impire ann roimhe so, agus is e Alasdair a bha air a mhac, agus cha robh duine cloinne aige ach è.

Thug e sgoil is ionnsachadh da, thar móran de chlann ridirean, agus rìghrean eile, air chor is gun tuigeadh e na h-eòin.

Chaidh iad a mach a ghabhail sràide latha, as déidh an tràth-nòin, agus ciod e thachair orra ach eun air craoibh, a' bruidhinn.

Dh'fhaighnich an t-Impire de a mhac, ciod è bha an t-eun a' cantuinn.

'Is coma leam ciod è tha an t-eun a' cantuinn: is motha chuir sin de mhiothlachd orm, na a atharrach.'

'Innis ciod è tha e cantuinn !'

'Innsidh mi sin duibh o'n a tha sibh 'ga iarraidh,' ars a mhac, 'is e tha e cantuinn gum bi sibh-se fhathast a' cumail a *bhason* rium, agus mo mhàthair a' cumail an *rubair*, fhad is a bhios mi glanadh m' aodainn.'

Chaidh iad an so thar a chéile.

Dhealaich a mhac ris an Impire, is ghabh e air falbh. Dh' fhàg e an rìoghachd, is chaidh e do rìoghachd eile. Stad e ann am baile bha an sin, is ghabh e 'na mhaighstir-sgoile. Bha iad a' faighneachd deth, ciod e an t-ainm is an sloinneadh a bha air, agus cha d' innis e nì mu a dheidhinn fhéin, ach thuirt e riu gur e 'Domhnall Sgoilear' a theireadh iad ris anns an àite a dh' fhàg e.

Bha e trì bliadhna 'sa bhaile sin, agus bha an ùine aige a mach. Dh'fhalbh e gu baile eile, is chaidh e gu tigh duine uasail. Thachair an duine uasal a muigh ris.

'Seadh,' ars an duine uasal, 'cia as a thàinig an coigreach nach 'eil mi ag aithneachadh?'

ALASDAIR, THE SON OF THE EMPEROR

No. *14.*   [*Vol. x., No. 28*]

Aarne-*Thompson, No. 517*

THERE was ere now an Emperor, whose son was called
Alasdair, and he had no children but him.

He gave him schooling and education, more than most
children of other knights and kings receive, so that he   B 215·1
could even understand [the language of] birds.   B 216
One day after dinner they went out to take a walk,
and what did they meet but a bird perched on a tree,
talking.
The Emperor asked his son what the bird was saying.

'I dislike what the bird says very much: it has caused   M 312·0·2
me more displeasure than the reverse.'
'Tell me what it is saying.'
'I will tell you since you desire it,' quoth the son.   B 141
'What it says is, that you in time to come will hold the
basin for me, and my mother will hold the towel, while I   M 312·2
wash my face.'
Thereupon they quarrelled with each other.
His son parted from the Emperor, and went away.
He left the kingdom, and went to another. He stopped
in a certain town and became a schoolmaster. People
used to ask him what his name and surname was, but he
would never say anything about himself, but merely told
them that he had been called 'Donald Scholar' in the place K 1831
he had left.
He spent three years in that town, and his time had
now run out. He set off to another town, and went to
the house of a gentleman. While out of doors the gentleman
met him.
'Well,' said the gentleman, 'whence comes the stranger
whom I do not recognize?'

'Thàinig mi as a leithid so de bhaile.'

'Chan 'eil fhios nach tu am maighstir sgoile a bha 'sa bhaile sin.'

'Is mi.'

'Bha moladh mór aca air a' mhaighstir sgoile a bha 'sa bhaile sin.'

'Bha mi meadhonach maith.'

'Chan 'eil cànain nach 'eil aig a' mhaighstir sgoile a bha an siod.'

'Bha roinn agam diubh.'

'Ciod è an t-ainm a th' ort ?'

'Tha orm—Domhnall Sgoilear.'

'B' fhearr leam gun dèanadh tu fasdadh rium fhéin airson mo chlann ionnsachadh ann an sgoil.'

'Tha mi coma ged a nì.'

Rinn e fasdadh thrì bliadhna ris an duine uasal. Bha triuir nigheanan aig an duine uasal, agus dithis ghillean ri sgoil fhaotainn. Thuirt e ris an duine uasal gun robh an tuath airson an clann a chur d'a ionnsuigh, agus gum b'e an aon rud dà-san e, agus gum biodh am pàidheadh aige [aig an duine uasal] fhéin.

'Gabh iad, agus biodh am pàidheadh agad fhìn,' ars an duine uasal. Ghabh e clann an tuath a stigh 'na sgoil, comhla ri clann an duine uasail.

T 31·1 Bha an nighean a b' òige a bha aig an duine uasal déidheil air ionnsachadh, is bha i fuireach a stigh an déidh chàich. Thuirt càch ri am màthair gun robh Domhnall Sgoilear a' cumail a stigh am peathar 'nan déidh-san. Dh' innis a bhean do'n duine uasal e. Thug an duine uasal an aghaidh air Domhnall.

'Cha robh mise 'ga cumail a stigh,' [thuirt Domhnall,] 'ach gun robh toil aice fhìn cuairt a bhi aice a bharrachd air gin diubh, is cha robh nì sam bith an aire dhuinn anns an dòigh sin idir.'

'Tha mi creidsinn ; cha chreidinn a chaochladh ort.'

'Cha robh dad de dhroch nì fainear domh.'

Ann an ceann ùine eile, thàinig neach is thuirt e ris an duine uasal gun robh e 'ga cumail a stigh.

'I come from such and such a town.'

'I don't know but that thou art the schoolmaster who dwelt in that town.'

'I am.'

'They spoke highly of the schoolmaster of that town.'

'I was fairly good.'

'There is no language that the schoolmaster in question does not know.'

'I knew a few of them.'

'What is thy name?'

'I am called—Donald Scholar.'

'I would that thou wouldst accept service with me, in order to educate and school my children.'

'I don't mind if I do.'

He engaged to serve for three years with the gentleman. The gentleman had three daughters and two sons, who were all to be educated. The schoolmaster told the gentleman that the tenantry were desirous of sending their children to him [for schooling] and that as it was all one to him, the gentleman might have the payment.

'Take them and have the payment thyself,' quoth the gentleman. So he took the children of the tenantry into his school along with those of the gentleman.

The gentleman's youngest daughter was very fond of T 31·1 learning, and used to stay in after the others. The others told their mother that Donald Scholar was keeping their sister in after they had gone. The lady told her husband, who accordingly took Donald to task about the matter.

'I have not been keeping her in,' [said Donald,] 'but the fact was that she herself wished to have more lessons than any of the others, and we had no intention of that [the thing to which you refer] at all.'

'I well believe it; I would never believe the reverse of thee.'

'I had no evil in view at all.'

At the end of some time after that, some one else came and told the gentleman that Donald was keeping her in.

Thug an duine uasal an aghaidh air a rithist.

'Chan 'eil mise 'ga cumail a stigh.'

'Tha thusa 'ga cumail a stigh—is fearr leam do phàidheadh deth, is thu bhi falbh.'—'Domhsa mo phàidheadh, ma tà, is bidh mi 'falbh.'

Chaidh iad gu trod.

'Chan 'eil fhios 'm,' arsa Domhnall, 'nach tugadh tu dhomh i, air dheas làimh fhathast.'[1] Dhealaich iad, is dh'fhalbh Domhnall. Dh'fhalbh ise ás a dhéidh. Dh'fheòraich i dheth ciod e an taobh a bha e dol. 'Tha mi dol do na h-Innsean an Iar,' ars esan. Thuirt i ris an so, ' Sgrìobhaidh mise litir do d' ionnsuigh cho luath is a dh'fhaodas mi, agus sgrìobhaidh tusa do m' ionnsuigh-sa.'

'C' àite an cuir mi i ?'

'Cuiridh tu a dh'ionnsuigh mo mhuime i.'

Ràinig e am baile mór, agus sheól e do na h-Innsean an Iar. An uair a ràinig e, fhuair e deagh àite leis an sgoil a bha aige. Sgrìobh e d'a h-ionnsuigh-sa. Chuir ise litir air a h-ais d'a ionnsuigh-san. Bha e trì bliadhna aig an aon mhaighstir, is bha litir air a h-ais is air a h-aghaidh fad nan trì bliadhna. An ceann trì bliadhna chuir e brath d' a h-ionnsuigh i bhi dèanamh deiseil air a shon, gun robh e dol a thilleadh.

Thàinig e an so a nall, is thàinig e do 'n cheart bhaile mhór. Chuir e air deise seòladair [gus e fhéin a chur as aithne], is chaidh e air tìr. An uair a chaidh e air tìr, ciod e thachair ris ach cairtear a' dol a mach as a' bhaile, agus dithis dhaoine uaisle leis anns a' chairt.—'Ghille,' ars esan ris a' chairtear, 'nam biodh tu cho math is gun leigeadh thu mo mhàileid anns a' chàirt—tha e gu math trom.'

'Chan 'eil òrdan agam ; ach iarr air na daoine uaisle a leigeil innte.'

Arsa fear de na daoine uaisle, a thaobh cho modhail is a labhair an seòladair bochd,

'Cuir a stigh e, is faodaidh tu fhéin tighinn a stigh comhla ris. Cia as a sheòl thu mu dheireadh, a sheòladair ?' arsa na daoine uaisle.

<hr>
[1] Alasdair, alias Donald, prophesies.

The gentleman took him to task again on the matter.

'*I* am not keeping her in.'

'Thou *art* keeping her in. I had rather pay thee off and that thou shouldst go away.'—'Give me my pay, then, and I will be going.'

They began to quarrel.

Says Donald, 'I would not be too sure that thou wilt not yet give her to me by her right hand.' [1]

They separated, and Donald went away. She went after him. She asked him in which direction he was going. 'I am going to the West Indies,' quoth he. She thereupon said to him, 'I will write a letter to thee as soon as ever I may, and do thou write to me.'

'Where shall I send it ?'

'Send it to my foster-mother.'

He came to the big town, and sailed for the West Indies. When he got there, he obtained a good place on account of his fine education. He wrote to her. She sent a letter back to him. He was three years with the same master, and letters were going backwards and forwards all those three years. At the end of the three years he sent her word to be getting ready for him, that he was going to return.

He presently returned from abroad and arrived at the same big town [as before]. He put on a sailor's dress [to disguise himself] and went ashore. Upon going ashore, whom did he meet but a carter going out of the town, and a couple of gentlemen with him in the cart. 'My lad,' said he to the carter, 'wouldst thou be so good as to allow my portmanteau to be put in the cart ; it is very heavy.'

'I have no orders ; but ask the gentlemen to allow it to be put in.'

So politely had the poor sailor spoken, that one of the gentlemen said,

'Put it in, and thou mayst come in too along with it. Whence didst thou sail last, sailor ?' quoth the gentlemen.

'Sheòl mi as na h-Innsean an Iar.'

Bha an so móran naidheachdan aig an t-seòladair, agus e fuathasach modhail leò.

Bha iad a' casadh air tigh mór a bha aig duine uasal, is bha tigh-seinnse shìos fodha, agus is ann dlùth air an tigh-sheinnse a bha an tigh aig muime na nighinn.

'Nam biodh sibh cho math, a dhaoine uaisle, is gun rachadh sibh leam fhìn do 'n tigh-sheinnse a ghabhail dheochannan, bhithinn fuathasach fada 'nur comain.'— Ars an darna duine uasal ris an fhear eile, 'Théid sinn comhla ris an t-seóladair, agus gheibh sinn naidheachdan dheth.'

Dh'fhalbh iad comhla ris. Ràinig iad an tigh-seinnse, is chaidh iad a stigh, is dh'iarr esan deochannan freagarrach air daoine uaisle. Thuirt an darna fear de na daoine uaisle ris an t-seòladair gun robh pearsa eaglais comhla ris.

'An è pearsa eaglais a th'ann?' ars an seòladair.

'Is è,' ars am fear eile.

'Tha mise fada cearr—is dòigh leam gun robh mi ro mhìomhail 'nur lathair,' ars an seòladair ris a' phearsa eaglais, 'is tha mi ag iarraidh maitheanais. Tha rud agam r' a innseadh dhuibh,' ars e ris a' phearsa eaglais.

'Ciod è a tha an sin?' ars esan.

'Thà,' ars esan, 'caileag a dh'fhàg mise 'sa' bhaile so o cheann trì bliadhna is bha cumhnanta pòsaidh eadaruinn, agus is ann anns a' bhaile so fhìn a tha i, is chan 'eil màthair no athair aice[2]; is ma's e ur toil e, tha mi deònach dol dh' a h-iarraidh, is gum pòsadh sibh mi.'

Ars am pearsa eaglais, 'Is ann is fhearr dhuit falbh, is nì sinne fuireach gus an tig thu.'

'Fàgaidh mi m'ad air a' bhòrd, is bheir mi leam mo mhàileid, chionn chan e an t-aodach so bhitheas orm, chor is gum faic sibh nach bi an seòladair bochd briagach.'

---

1 'Soldiers and sailors have many stories.'—*Waifs and Strays*, ii., p. 127.

2 The hero says this, in order probably, to prevent the gentlemen from guessing who his lady love was. But he commits a sad defection from the truth in saying so, unless we are to infer confusion on the part of the reciter,

'I sailed from the West Indies.'

The sailor now began to tell some of the many tales he had [1] and the gentlemen thought him very well-mannered.

They were now drawing near to a big house belonging to a gentleman, and there was a change-house further on or below it, and close to the change-house was the house of the foster-mother of the girl.

'If you would be so good, gentlemen, as to go with me to the change-house to take drinks, I should be exceedingly obliged to you.'—Quoth the one gentleman to the other, 'We will go along with the sailor, and hear him tell tales.'

They went along with him accordingly. They came to the change-house and went in, and he called for drinks suitable for gentlemen. One of the gentlemen told the sailor that it was a clergyman who was along with him.

'Is he indeed a clergyman?' said the sailor.

'He is,' said the other.

'I have been very far wrong—I have been far too presumptuous in your presence,' quoth the sailor to the ecclesiastic, 'and I entreat forgiveness. I have something to tell you,' he said to the clergyman.

'What is that?' said the other.

'Why,' said he, 'there is a lass that I left in this town three years ago. There was plighted troth between us. She is in this very town, and she has neither father nor mother[2] ; and if it please you, I am desirous of going to fetch her in order that you may marry me.'

Quoth the clergyman, 'Certainly; thou hadst better set off, and we will wait till thou come.'

'I will leave my hat on the table, but I will take my portmanteau with me, because I shall not wear this dress. Then you will see the poor sailor is not lying.'

---

which is indeed quite possible. The reason probably is that he wanted to prevent the suspicion which the absence of the girl's parents from the proceedings would otherwise cause. It is also part of his plot to trap his prospective father-in-law, as appears later on.

'Tha barail n'as fhearr againn ort ; thoir leat t' ad.'

Ràinig e tigh muime na nighinn.[1] Dh'innis e dhi gur h-e a bh'ann :—'falbh thusa, is abair ris a' chaileg tighinn an so, is gun i a dh'atharrachadh a h-aodaich ; gu bheil mise ann 'ga feitheamh.'

Dh' fhalbh ise, is dh' innis i siod.

T 30 Thàinig an nighean gun atharrachadh, ach mar a bha i.

Bha esan 'san am a' cur air a aodaich ann an tigh na cailliche. Thug e deise d' a h-ionnsuigh-se as [na h-Innsean] an Iar, is bha i fuathasach annasach, an deise, is chuir i uimpe i, is bha esan air a sgeadachadh gu gasda; chuir e aodach an duine uasail air.

Ghabh e fhìn agus ise gus an tigh-sheinnse. Dh' fhaighnich e de'n phearsa eaglais agus de'n fhear eile, an robh iad a' gabhail mulaid o'n a dh'fhalbh e.

'U ! cha robh,' ars iadsan, 'cha robh thu fada.'

'Nis,' ars an seòladair, 'tha mi toileach duine uasal a' bhaile a thoirt chun a' phòsaidh—tha sibh fhìn eòlach air ?'

Ars am pearsa eaglais, 'Tha duine uasal a' bhaile so eòlach orm fhìn, 's ma chluinneas e gu bheil mi an so a nochd, bidh e diombach mura cuir sinn brath air.'

Chuireadh brath d'a ionnsuigh, is thàinig an duine uasal. Cha robh fios aig an duine uasal gun robh a nighean ann idir. Ars am pearsa eaglais, 'Tha seòladair agam r'a phòsadh, is tha mi deònach gum biodh tu comhla ruinn a nochd.'—'Glé thoilichte,' ars athair na nighinn.

'Eiribh, agus gum pòsainn sibh.'

'Chan 'eil athair no màthair aig an nighinn so,' ars an seòladair, ''s bhithinn ro thoilichte nan tugadh duine uasal a' bhaile domh air làimh i.'

---

[1] In these tales the heroine frequently has a foster-mother who protects her and helps her to win her sweetheart.

[2] Perhaps in older versions the bride was closely veiled in the rich dress which the hero had given her. This would explain why her father fails to recognize her. In W. H. Tales, i., No. 17b, the heroine, we are told, does actually disguise herself, with the result that her father unsuspectingly gives

'We have a better opinion of thee than that; take thy hat with thee.'

He arrived at the house of the foster-mother of the lass.[1] He told her that it was he who had come; 'Go and tell the lass to come here, and not to change her dress; that I am waiting for her.'

Off she went, and delivered the message.

So the lass came just as she was, without changing [her T 30 dress].

He was by this time arraying himself in the old woman's house. He had brought a dress for her from the West [Indies], a dress that was exceedingly rare. She put it on. As for him, he was handsomely dressed; he had put on a gentleman's dress.

He and she then repaired to the change-house. He asked of the ecclesiastic and of the other man whether they had been wearying since he had gone.

'U ! no, we have not,' they replied; 'thou hast not been long.'

'Now,' said the sailor, 'I am desirous of bringing the Laird of the place to the wedding; do you yourselves know him ?'

Said the ecclesiastic, 'The Laird of this place is acquainted with me personally, and if he hear that I have been here to-night, he will be annoyed, if we do not send word for him.'

Word was sent to him, and the Laird came.

The Laird had no idea that it was his own daughter.[2] The clergyman said, 'I have a sailor here whom I have to marry, so I am desirous that thou shouldst be present with us to-night.' 'Very pleased,' quoth the father of the lass.

'Rise ye, that I may marry you.'

'This lass has neither father or mother,' quoth the sailor, 'and so I should be very pleased if the Laird of the place gave her to me by the hand.'

her away to the hero, before the Saxon, for whom she was intended, could K 1371·2* come and claim her. In MS. vol. x., No. 73, the hero brings home from abroad one beautiful dress for the heroine, and two for his sisters. In MS. vol. x., No. 104, he brings home the three dresses for his sweetheart. See pp. 185 n, xxxvi., No. 38 (51).

Ars an duine uasal, 'Nì mi sin, a sheòladair !'

Rug e air làimh air a nighinn, is thug e air làimh do 'n t-seòladair i.

Phòs iad.

Thòisich esan an so air dèanamh naidheachd.

'A dhuine uasail, nach robh maighstir sgoile 'san àite, ris an abradh iad Domhnall Sgoilear ?'

'Bha a leithid sin ann.'

'An aithnicheadh sibh e ?'

'Tha mi smaointeachadh gun aithnicheadh. B' aithne dhomhsa fìor mhath an duine sin.'

'Bha e 'g ràdh riumsa gun deachaidh e fhìn agus duine uasal thar a chéile, mu leanabh caileig a bha aige.'

'Bha a leithid sin ann.'

'Is mise,' ars esan, 'Domhnall Sgoilear, agus am bheil beachd agad mar a thuirt mi riut aig ceann do thighe fhéin gun tugadh thu do nighean domh air làimh fhathast? [Chan fhaic thu tuillidh i].' [1]

Mhionnaich an duine uasal do'n droch àite e. Agus cha d' innis e do'n duine uasal có è, no dì-se ; cha b' fhiach leis innseadh ! Bha e coma !

Laigh iad 'san tigh-sheinnse an oidhche sin.

An là-'r-na-mhàireach thuirt esan rithe-se, 'Fuirichidh tusa an so gus an tig mise air m' ais.'

'Ciod è fhad 's a ruigeas tu ?'

'Coma leatsa ciod è fhad 's a ruigeas mi, ach na teirig thusa gu tigh t'athar gus an tig mi, is na fàg mise breugach. Bidh mi agad mu d[h]à uair a màireach, is pàidhidh mi na h-uile sgáth air do shon.'

Dh'fhalbh e, is fhuair e gigachan agus carbadan, agus ràinig e an oidhche sin tigh a athar. Cha robh duine a stigh, ach a mhàthair an uair a ràinig e. Chuir e fàilt air an t-seana bhoirionnach, an uair a chaidh e dhachaidh.

---

[1] Thou shalt see her no more. The hero's conversation with the offending Laird on a later occasion justifies the insertion of this sentence.

[2] He—*i.e.* Alasdair, the Emperor's son—masquerading for the moment as Donald Scholar.

Said the Laird—'That I will, sailor.'

He took the lass by the hand and gave her by the
hand to the sailor.

They [were] wedded.

It was at this point that the sailor began to speak, and
reveal things.

'Sir Laird, was there not a schoolmaster in this place,
whom they called Donald Scholar?'

'There was indeed such a one.'

'Would you recognize him?'

'I should think I should.   I knew that man very well.'

'He was telling me that he quarrelled with a gentleman
about a young lass that the gentleman had.'

'There was, indeed, such an occurrence.'

'Well then, I,' said he, 'am Donald Scholar, and hast
thou any recollection of how I said to thee at thine own
house end, that thou shouldst yet give me thy daughter
by the hand?   [Thou shalt see her no more.]' [1]

The Laird cursed him to the bad place.   But he did [2]
not tell the Laird who he was, neither did he tell her; he
scorned to do so!   He cared not!

That night they slept in the change-house.

On the morrow, he said to her, 'Stay thou here till
I come back.'

'How far art thou going?'

'Never mind how far I am going, but go not to thy
father's house till I return, and do not make me a liar.[3]
I will be with thee about two o'clock on the morrow, and
I will pay for everything on thy behalf.'

Away he went, and procured gigs and carriages, and
arrived at his own father's house that night.   When he
came, there was nobody indoors but his mother.   He
saluted the old dame when he came home.

---

[1] I have told thy father he should see thee no more.   If thou go to his
house, thou wilt make my words untrue.

'Càite a bheil an t-Impire?' ars esan, 'a bheil e aig
an tigh?'

'Chan 'eil,' ars ise, 'tha e gabhail sràide.'

'An robh mac no nighean riamh agaibh?'

'Bha [mac], is cha bu nàrach domh iomradh air
cuideachd.'

'An e bàsachadh a rinn e?'

'Ma tà, chan e bàsachadh a rinn e. Chaidh e fhìn
is an t-Impire a ghabhail sràide, is [cha] chuala sinn
iomradh riamh tuillidh air.'

[Thàinig an t-Impire dhachaidh, agus chaidh an
teaghlach air fad mu thàmh an oidhche sin.

N 682   An uair a dh'éirich e 'sa' mhaduinn, thàinig an t-Impire
agus a' Bhan-Impire a chur onoir air : bha an t-Impire a'
cumail a' *bhasoin* ris, agus a' Bhan-Impire a' cumail an
rubair fhad 's a bha e glanadh a aodainn.

Chunnaic Alasdair an so cainnt an eòin air a
choimhlionadh. Ach cha do leig e dad air gus an d'
fhalbh an t-Impire a mach a ghabhail sràide. Thug e an
sin far an robh a mhàthair air.

'An aithneachadh sibh ur mac?'

'Tha mi 'smaointeachadh gun aithneachadh.' [1]]

'Ma tà, a mhàthair,' ars esan, 'is mise Alasdair.'

Phòg ise e, a mhic cridhe, leis an t-sòlas, is dh'fhuaim
i a h-uile clag a bha stigh, is chuala an t-Impire so, agus
N 731·1   thill e. An uair a thill e, dh'innis iad da gun tàinig Alasdair.
An uair a chuala e so, theab e an caothach a ghabhail
leis an t-sòlas. 'Nis, Alasdair,' ars esan, 'is leat a h-uile
sgàth an so : bidh thu air impireachd 'nam àite fhìn!'

'Chan 'eil mi ag iarraidh ach aon iarrtuis, ma bheir
sibh dhomh e—is e sin, an carbad mór a chur air shiubhal
nach deach air shiubhal o'n a dh'fhalbh mise.'

'Alasdair, gheibh thu sin, is cha dragh leamsa sin idir.'

'Agus a h-uile bratach as còir a bhi ris, a bhi ris am
màireach, agus e a dhol leamsa.'

---

[1] In this tale either the reciter or the scribe most unaccountably forgot
to give the incident of the fulfilling of the bird's prophecy. As this is the

'Where is the Emperor ?' quoth he; 'is he at home ?'

'He is not,' said she; 'he is taking a walk.'

'Did you ever have son or daughter ?'

'I had [a son], and no disgrace to me to speak of him, either.'

'Did he die ?'

'Well, then, die he did not. He and the Emperor went out to take a walk, and we never heard mention of him again.'

[The Emperor presently came home, and the entire household then went to rest for that night.

When he rose in the morning, the Emperor and the Empress came to do him honour; the Emperor held the basin for him, and the Empress held the towel while he was washing his face. N 682

Thereupon Alasdair beheld the bird's prophecy fulfilled. But he never disclosed anything until the Emperor had gone out to take a walk. Then he betook himself to his mother.

'Would you recognize your son ?'

'I think I should.' ¹]

'Well then, mother,' said he, 'I am Alasdair !'

She kissed him, Oh son of my heart ! for very joy, and pealed every bell in the house, and the Emperor heard the sound and returned. When he returned, they told him that Alasdair had come. Upon hearing this, he nearly became frenzied with joy. 'Now, Alasdair,' quoth he, 'everything here is thine; thou shalt rule as Emperor in my own place.' N 731·1

'I only ask for one request, if you will grant it to me— it is to get the big chariot ready for travelling that never travelled since I went away.'

'Alasdair, thou shalt have that, and I shall think it no trouble at all.'

'And that it be equipped to-morrow with every banner with which it ought to be equipped, and that it carry me.'

point at which the incident ought to occur, it has been placed here between the usual square brackets.

'Bidh a h-uile nì dheth sin air a dhèanamh,' ars an t-Impire.

An là-'r-na-mhàireach, chaidh a h-uile bratach a chur suas ris a' charbad—gorm, is uaine, is dearg, is a h-uile seòrsa bu chòir, is a ainm-san air a h-uile té, gur h-e a leithid so de Impire a bh' ann. Dh'fhalbh e, is cha do rinn e stad no fois gus an do ràinig e an tigh-seinnse.

An uair a ràinig e an tigh-seinnse, dh'fhosgail e an carbad, thàinig e am mach, is ruith e a stigh d'a h-iarraidh-se. Phàidh e a h-uile sgàth a chosg ise. Cha robh fios ciod e bu chiall do'n Impire bhi tighinn. Chualas iomradh 'san àite gun robh a leithid ann, ach cha robh tuilleadh air.

'Seadh,' ars Alasdair ri a bhean, 'a bheil fios agad có am fear a th' agad?'—'Chan 'eil,' ars ise.—Dh'innis se e an uair sin, agus cha bu rud dì-se gun rachadh i a ghlanadh a bhròg.

Dh'fhalbh iad an uair sin, a suas gu tigh a h-athar. 'Gabhaidh mi leat a dh'ionnsuigh tigh t' athar, agus innsidh mi dha nach e do ghoid a tha mi dol a dhèanamh.'

[Ràinig iad tigh a h-athar.]

Cha robh duine riamh a bha 'sa chaisteal nach robh ag amharc a mach air na h-uinneagan air a' charbad. Chan fhac iad riamh an t-Impire, ach gun cuala iad gun robh a leithid ann. Thàinig an duine uasal a mach, is chaidh e air a ghlùn do'n charbad.

'Fosgail an dorus, is thig leam a mach,' [ars Alasdair ri a bhean].

Bha ise leis air làimh an so.

'Seadh, a dhuine uasail, a bheil thu ag aithneachadh do nighinn?'

'Tha,' ars esan.

'Smaointich mi tighinn leatha do d' ionnsuigh an diugh, ged a thuirt mi riut an oidhche ud nach faiceadh tu tuillidh i.'

Thàinig an t-Impire a mach, is rinn e modh dha.

'All that shall be done, every detail of it,' said the Emperor.

On the morrow, every banner was displayed about the chariot, blue and green, and red, and every other kind that was correct and suitable, and his name was on every one of them, to the effect that he was such-and-such an Emperor. Off he went, and neither stop nor stay did he make until he reached the change-house.

When he came to the change-house, he opened the chariot, and came out, and ran in to look for *her*. He paid for everything she had spent. Now none knew what the meaning of the Emperor's coming could be. People in the place had heard that there was such a man, but that was all.

'Well,' said Alasdair to his wife, 'dost thou know who thy husband is?'—'I do not,' replied she. Then it was that he told her, and it seemed to her that it would be a mere nothing for her to go and clean his shoes.

Then they went up to her father's house. 'I will go with thee to thy father's house, and tell him that stealing thee is not what I am going to do.'

[They arrived at her father's house.]

There was never a man in the castle who was not craning out of the windows to look at the chariot. They had never seen the Emperor, but had heard that there was such a person. The gentleman came out, and went down on his knee to the chariot.

'Open the door, and come out with me,' [said Alasdair to his wife].

He was now holding her by the hand.

'Well, fair sir, dost recognize thy daughter?'

'I do,' replied the gentleman.

'I determined after all to bring her with me to thee to-day, notwithstanding my having said to thee the other night that thou shouldst see her no more.'

The Emperor now came out, and the gentleman made him obeisance.

'A bheil fios agad, a nis, c'àite a bheil do nighean a' dol, no có am fear a tha aice ?' [ars Alasdair an t-Impire]. 'Tha mi 'ga fhaicinn air na brataichean.'

'Bidh mise, nis, 'gam éubhach 'nam Impire Og, is cha téid mi a stigh air do dhorus.'

'O ! théid sibh a stigh, agus gabhaidh sibh gloine ás mo làimh, is bidh e 'na mheas mór domh anns an àite gun tàinig an t-Impire a stigh, is gun do ghabh e gloine as mo làimh.' Dh'iarr an duine uasal maitheanas air an Impire Og. Fhuair e siod.

'Air a leithid so de latha de'n mhìos, théid thu gu m' shealltuinn-sa, agus a shealltuinn c'àite a bheil i fuireach.'

Dh'fhàg iad beannachd aig a chéile, is gheall an duine uasal siod da ; dh'fhalbh iadsan leis a' charbad, is ràinig iad an lùchairt.

NOTES

MS. vol. x., No. 28. From Roderick MacLean, Ken Tangval, Barra. Scribe, Hector MacLean.

The tale ends as if more were to follow. The fulfilment of the bird's prophecy is forgotten by either the scribe or the reciter. Yet Islay had a high opinion of the tale, for on the flyleaf of the MS. he wrote :— 'It is a curious mixture of ideas of grandeur and the reverse—Barra and the Emperor. It is in that respect about the best I have yet read.'

In a note to this, No. 14, the scribe, Hector MacLean, has written:— 'The dialogue through this tale would seem to be bare. Thuirt esan and thuirt ise [he said and she said] not often occurring, but there has been no pruning. In reciting this tale, the reciter used very few of them indeed, and hearing him recite it, it would be perceived at once that they would have destroyed the point and dramatic effect of the dialogue.'

Across this note of Hector's, Islay has written:—'This note in reply to a suggestion of mine that MacLean had pruned his stories in writing them after an experience of sundry reciters who were very diffuse.'

In Islay's MS. vol. xi., No. 354 (Canain nan Eun, The Language of Birds, brother-story to this tale, No. 14, MS. vol. x., No. 28), events occur as follows:—The hero is the son of a knight, not of an Emperor. He quarrels with his father for the same reason as in this tale, becomes king and marries the king's daughter in virtue of an entirely different set of adventures, and overthrows his father's pride as well as his father-in-law's.

'Dost thou now know where thy daughter is going, or who her husband is ?' [quoth Alasdair, the Emperor].

'I know from the banners.'

'I shall now be proclaimed as the Young Emperor, but thy threshold I will not cross.'

'O ! but you shall, you shall come in, and take a glass out of my hand too, and it will be a great honour to me in this place that the Emperor came in, and took a glass out of my hand.' The gentleman asked forgiveness of the young Emperor, which was granted him.

'On such-and-such a day of the month, thou shalt come and see me, and see also where she dwells.'

They left blessings with each other, and the gentleman promised to come; and they [the young Emperor and Empress] went away in the chariot, and arrived at the palace.

See *Scottish Gaelic Studies*, 1931, iii., p. 160. For learning the language of birds, MS. vol. x., No. 107—*The Celtic Monthly*, xii., p. 13.

Both MS. vol. x., No. 28 and MS. vol. xi., No. 354, brother-tales, were transcribed by Hector MacLean. But the style of No. 354 is of a very different stamp, and the idiom is far more picturesque, as becomes a tale derived, as No. 354 was, from the bard of a famous Highland chief. Hector could scarcely have invented styles so different. The conclusion, therefore, is, that we have, in his transcriptions, records which, though not perfect, are fairly close to the originals; which is satisfactory, and may be held to clear him of the accusation of 'pruning.' He was one of Islay's most careful collectors, though given to moralizing on the tales he collected. However, he only did this in notes which he tagged on to the ends of the tales.

See *The seuin Seages*, intro., xxx., by Geo. F. Black, Ph.D. (Scottish Texts Society, Blackwood, Edinburgh and London, 1932), for a version of No. 354 (MS. vol. xi.). Dr Black kindly notified me of this. Another version is noted in Professor Donald MacKinnon's *Catalogue*, p. 153.

In 'Baillie Lunnain,' or The Provost of London (*W. H. Tales*, i., No. 17*b*) we read the following statement:—'It is the law that no man may be married here unless the Bail[l]ie gives him the bride by the hand.' The existence of this law seems to be reflected also in this Tale No. 14 and in No. 51, MS. vol. x.[1] and in *Larminie*, p. 124. In all four tales

[1] Which is not published in this volume as it was partly summarized in *W. H. Tales*, i., No. 17*a* (22), being nearly the same as No. 17*b*, *W. H. Tales*, and also because it will appear in *Bealoideas*, viii., No. II.

it is either stated or implied that the heroine's father, who is either the Baillie, or laird, or king of the place, is (as in tales of the Married Children theme, see this book, p. 390) unwilling to allow his daughter to marry the hero.   But the heroine puts on a dress probably brought **K 1371·2*** from abroad by her lover (see MS. vol. x., No. 73).   In doing this, it is clear that she wishes to disguise herself, in order that her father shall fail to recognize her when coming to be married;   for the result is that her father, as headman of the place, unsuspectingly bestows her hand upon the hero, only to find, when too late, that he has unwittingly assented to the marriage of his own daughter.   In some cases, however, he is honestly glad to find that she has married such a smart lad.   See pp. 177 *n*, 392 end.

GRÙ[TH]AN AN EÒIN IS AN SPORAN ÒIR

No. 15.   [*MS. Vol. x., No. 29*]

Aarne-Thompson, No. 567

BHA an toiseach ann duine, is bha e 'na bhantrach, is
phòs e a rithist, is bha dithis bhalach aige ris a' cheud
mhnaoi, is thuirt am fear a b' aosda dhiubh ri a athair,
'Athair! falbhaidh sinn feadh an t-saoghail a dhèanamh
air ar son fhìn—chan 'eil mo mhuime maith dhuinn.'
Thòisich an athair air caoineadh airson iad a bhi dealachadh
ris. Dh'fhàg iad beannachd aig an athair, is bha e ro
dhuilich 'nan déidh.

Dh'fhalbh iad, is bha iad a' coiseachd air an aghaidh.
Bha iad a' dol seachad air gàradh, agus 'd è chunnaic iad
ach eun rompa taobh a' ghàraidh. 'D è bha an t-eun ach
fuathasach brèagh, chan fhacas a leithid riamh. Ruith
iad an t-eun, agus rug iad air an eun. Bha e an achlais
an fhir a b' òige, agus 'd è thachair orra ach duine uasal os
cionn a thighe fhìn.

Dh' fhaighnich an duine uasal 'd è an t-eun a bha aige
'na achlais. Thuirt e gun robh eun a rug e air o cheann
ghoirid. 'Leig fhaicinn e,' ars an duine uasal. Leig am
balach fhaicinn an t-eun. Rug an duine uasal air an
eun, sheall e air a uchd, agus spìon e ite as. Bha e air a
sgrìobhadh air uchd an eòin, ge b'e dh' itheadh a chridhe,
gum faigheadh e 'n aon bhean a b' fhearr a bha ri fhaotainn,
is ge b' e dh' itheadh a ghrùthan, gum faightheadh sporan
òir fo a cheann a h-uile latha dh' éireadh e.

'D è ghabhas tu air an eun?' ars an duine uasal.
'Chan 'eil fhios agam,' ars am balach.
'An gabh thu cóig puinnd Shasunnach air?'

THE BIRD'S LIVER AND THE
SPORRAN FULL OF GOLD

No. 15.   *[Vol. x., No. 29]*

Aarne-Thompson, No. 567

FIRST of all, there was once a man, and he was a widower. And he married again. He had two boys by the first wife, and the eldest one of them said to his father,—'Father! we are going to travel through the world in order to do what we can for ourselves,—my stepmother is not good S 31 to us.' Their father began to lament because they were parting from him. They left a farewell blessing with their father, and very sorrowful was he when they had gone.

They set off, and, walking, pressed onwards. As they were passing by a dyke wall, what should they see ahead of them but a bird by the side of the dyke wall. Now the bird was wonderfully beautiful, the like of it had never been seen. They chased the bird and caught it. The N 774 younger one had tucked it under his arm, when whom should they meet but a gentleman, a little way above his own house.

The gentleman enquired what bird it was which the boy had there, tucked under his arm. He said that it was a bird which he had caught a little while ago. 'Let me see it,' said the gentleman. The lad showed him the bird. The gentleman took hold of it, looked at its breast, and plucked a feather from it. It was written on the bird's D 1015 breast, that whoever should eat its heart should get the D 1015 best wife there was to be got, and that whoever should ·4·1 eat its liver, a sporran full of gold would be found under M 312·3 his head every day he rose. D 1451

'What wilt thou take for the bird?' said the gentleman.

'I don't know,' said the boy.

'Wilt take five pounds sterling for it?'

'Gabhaidh.'

Ghabh e na cóig puinnd Shasunnach o 'n duine uasal, is thug e dha an t-eun. Chaidh an duine uasal dachaidh.

'Rachaibh sìos do 'n chidsin,' ars e ris na balaich, 'is dèanaibh bhur gàradh.'

Chaidh na balaich a stigh do 'n chidsin. Thuirt an duine uasal ri té d' a shearbhantan, 'So dhuit an t-eun so, is cuir air dòigh e. Bruich an cridhe is an grùthan dhomhsa, is dèan do roghainn ris a' chuid eile.' Thug an t-searbhanta leatha an t-eun, chaidh [i] do 'n chidsin, is thug i an cridhe is an grùthan as an eun, is chuir i air pann iad.

Bha na balaich anns a' chidsin, agus iad a' faicinn a' chridhe agus a' ghrùthain air a' phanna. Ghliong esan an clag shìos, agus sìos a ghabh ise. An uair dh' fhalbh i, 'O,' ars am fear a b' òige, 'is ann orm a tha an t-acras !' 'D è rinn e an fheadh is a bha ise shìos ach an grùthan a thoirt leis agus a itheadh.

D 859·4*

D 859 ·4·2*

'Dh' ith thu siod, 's cha d' thug thu sgàth domhsa dheth.'

'O, bha e cho beag.'

Dh'fhalbh am fear a b' aosda is thugar an cridhe leis, is dh' ith e fhìn e.

D 859 ·4·1*

Thàinig an t-searbhanta a nìos, is dh' fhaighnich i c'àite an robh an rud a bha air a' phanna.

'O,' ars iadsan, 'thuit e [1] anns an luaith, is thog sinne e —bu mhór leinn a chur air tuillidh—bha e cho beag.'

'Bheir sibh 'ur casan asaibh cho luath 'sa rinn sibh riamh, mum marbh e sibh.'

'Thoir duinn rud-eigin a ghabhas sinn.'

Thug i rud-eigin daibh a bhiodh iad a' gabhail air an rathad. Thug iad an casan as cho luath is a b' urrainn iad. Ghliong esan an clag a rithist, is dh' fheòraich e an robh siod deiseil aice.

---

[1] In MS. *e*, = it, the singular being used for both the heart and liver throughout this paragraph, and in other places in the tale.

'I will.'

He took the five pounds sterling from the gentleman, and gave him the bird. The gentleman went home [taking the boys with him].

'Go down to the kitchen,' said he to the boys, 'and warm yourselves.'

The boys went into the kitchen. The gentleman said to one of his servants, a woman,—'Here, take this bird, and get it ready. Cook the heart and the liver for me, and do as thou please with the rest.' The servant took the bird away, went to the kitchen, took the heart and liver out of the bird, and put them in a pan.

The boys were in the kitchen looking on. They saw the heart and the liver in the pan. The gentleman rang the bell at the other end of the house, and away went the serving-woman. When she had gone, 'O,' said the younger lad, 'how hungry I am!' And what did he do while she was away at the other end of the house, but take the liver and eat it. D 859·4* D 859 ·4·2*

'So then thou hast eaten that, and hast never given me a bit of it.'

'O, but it was such a little bit.'

The elder lad went, took the heart, and ate it himself. D 859 ·4·1*

Back came the serving-woman, and asked where the things were that had been in the pan.

'O,' said they, 'they [1] fell into the ashes, and we picked them up. We thought it would never do to put them on again,—and they were so small.'

'Be off and take your feet with you as quickly as ever you did in your lives, lest he kill you.'

'Give us something that we may eat.'

She gave them something for them to eat on the road. They took their feet away as quickly as ever they were able. The gentleman clinked the bell again, and asked whether she had got that (the heart and liver) ready.

'An uair a thàinig mise a nuas chugaibh fhìn, thàinig an dithis bhalach, is dh' ith iad e.'
'D è an rathad a ghabh iad?'

'Ghabh an rathad a thàinig iad.' Cha b' è idir. [Is ann a dh' fhalbh iad an rathad eile.] Thàinig e mach an cabhaig, feuch am faigheadh e iad, ach cha d' fhuair e gin dhiùbh, is thill e dhachaidh. Am beul na h-oidhche, ràinig iadsan tigh caillich, agus dh' fhuirich iad ann an oidhche sin. An déidh dhaibh éirigh 's a' mhaduinn, fhuair a' chailleach sporan òir fo 'n chluasaig anns an leabaidh. Is è a bh' ann, thuirt i riu, —'A bheil sgoil agaibh, a ghillean?'

'Chan 'eil,' ars iadsan.
'Nach fhearr dhuibh fuireach an so, is dol do 'n sgoil? Tha tigh sgoile shìos fodhaibh, is gum biodh sgoil is ionnsachadh agaibh.'
'Có an sin a chumas biadh ruinn?'
'Cumaidh mi fhìn biadh ruibh.'
Thug iad bliadhna aig an sgoil 'nan dithis. An ceann na bliadhna, thuirt iad gum falbhadh iad.
'Tha sibh a' cur roimhibh gum falbh sibh,' ars a' chailleach.
'O, thà,' ars am fear a b' aosda, 'tha sgoil againn a nis, is bidh sinn a' falbh.'
'O 'n a tha sibh a' falbh a nis, tha rud agam r' a innseadh dhuibh.'
'Ciod è sin?'
'Tha buaidh air fear agaibh,[1] is a bheil fhios agaibh có air a bheil a' bhuaidh?' ars a' chailleach.

'Chan 'eil,' ars iadsan.
'Fuirichibh a nochd, is laigheadh fear agaibh aig gach ceann de 'n leabaidh, is bidh fhios againn 's a' mhaduinn có air a tha a' bhuaidh.'

---

[1] Note by Hector MacLean, who transcribed. 'Tha buaidh air fear agaibh. There is a virtue attaching to one of [you], or there is a valuable quality attached to one of [you]. Buaidh is here used for buadh [victory]. In the Isles, buaidh is always used in the singular. Tha buaidh air [*lit.* there is a virtue on him]. Tha buaidh air an uisge-bheatha [*lit.* there is a virtue

'When I had gone out of the kitchen to wait upon you, the two boys began and they ate everything up.'

'Which way have they gone?'

'They went the way they came.' But it was not so at K 646* all. [They had gone the other way.]

Out he went in haste to try if he could find them, but he never found one of them, and so returned home.

In the mouth of the night, they arrived at the house of an old woman, and there they stayed that night. In the morning, after they had got up, the old woman found a purse full of gold under the pillow in the bed. So what happened was that she said to them,—'Have you had any schooling, lads?'

'No,' said they.

'Would it not be better for you to stay here and go to school? There is a schoolhouse down below there, where you might have schooling and education.'

'Who then would supply us with food?'

'I will supply you with food myself.'

They spent a year at the school, both of them. At the end of the year, they said they would now depart.

'You have made up your minds to go?' said the old woman.

'O, we have,' said the elder one, 'we have some education now, and we must go.'

'Since you are now going away, I have something to tell you.'

'What is it?'

'There is a virtue attaching to one of you,[1] and do ye yourselves know which of you has this virtue?' said the old woman.

'We do not,' said they.

'Stay here to-night then, and let one of you lie at one end of the bed, and the other one at the other end, and we shall know in the morning which of you has the virtue.'

on the whisky]. Seamrag nam buadh [= the shamrock of the virtues] a D 1323·14 clover leaf with four blades, said to grow where a foal is born, which if found by any will prove very lucky. If the fortunate finder put it under his tongue, D 1561·7 it will impart to him very rare gifts, similar to clairvoyance.'

Rinn iad siod, is bha a' bhuaidh air an fhear a b' òige.

'Tha làn ciste de òr agamsa air ur tàilleabh, agus thoiribh leibh bhur toil dheth.'

Thug iad làn duirn an t-aon leotha, 's dh' fhàg iad beannachd aig a' chaillich, is dh' fhalbh iad.   Bha iad a' falbh 's a' falbh gus an tàinig iad fo thigh rìgh a bha 'san àite.   Ghabh iad seachad, is cha robh iad fad air falbh, an uair a chuir nighean an rìgh teachdaire as an déidh. Thill iad.   Thuirt nighean an rìgh ris an fhear a b' aosda, gur e 'n gnothuch a bha aice ris, a fhaotainn r' a phòsadh. Phòs e fhìn agus nighean an rìgh.

Ars am fear a b' òige,—" Ciod è nì mise nis ? bidh mi ann am ònrachd.'

'Nach 'eil airgiod agad na dh'fhoghnas duit ri d'bheò, is nach 'eil thu coma !'

'Chan 'eil: is e nì mi, pòsaidh mi nighean bantraich a tha 'n taobh shìos diom, is ged a tha i bochd, is furasda domh a dèanamh beairteach.'

Phòs e 'n so.   A h-uile maduinn a dh' éireadh e, bha 'n sporan làn.   Dh' fhaighnich a màthair d' a mhnaoi,— 'C'àite an robh a fear a' faotainn na robh an siod de airgiod !'

'Chan 'eil fhios 'm air a sin, chan fhaca mi tronca leis no an àite sam bith, is cho mór is cho beag is a [bha] de airgiod pòca a bhiodh leis, shaoilinn gun teirigeadh e roimhe so.'

'Feuch am faigh thusa a mach c' àite a bheil e 'ga fhaotainn.'

Dh'fhaighnich i dheth,—'C' àite a bheil thu faotainn an airgid a tha agad a h-uile maduinn ?'

'Nach 'eil thu coma c' àite a bheil mi 'ga fhaotainn, ma chumas mi airgiod riut fhìn !'

Bha bruidhinn thall 'sa bhos aca mar so, a h-uile latha, gus an d'innis e dhi mu dheireadh mar a bha e 'ga fhaotainn. Dh' fhalbh ise, agus dh' innis i d' a màthair e.

They did so, and found that the virtue belonged to the L 10 younger one.

'I have a kist full of gold which I got through you ; so take as much as you please of it.'

So they took away a fistful, each of them, left a farewell blessing with the old woman, and went off. They travelled on and on until they came to the house of a King who reigned in the place. The house was above them. They went past it, but had not gone much farther on, when the King's daughter sent a messenger after them. They went back. The King's daughter said to the elder lad that her business with him was to win him in marriage. So he and the King's daughter married.

The younger lad then said, 'What now shall I do ? I shall be all alone.'

'Hast thou not money sufficient to last thee all thy life, and therefore needest not to care !'

'But I do care: so this is what I will do. I will marry the daughter of a widow who dwells down there, and, though she be poor, it is easy for me to make her wealthy.'

So he now married. Every morning that he rose, the purse was full. Her mother asked his wife,—'Whence was her husband getting all that money ?'

'Of that I know nothing. I have never seen a trunk in his possession or anywhere about the place ; and as to the travelling money that he might have had with him, whether it was much or little, I should have thought it would have come to an end before this.'

'Try if thou canst find out whence he is getting it.'

So she asked him,—'Whence art thou getting the money that thou hast every morning ?'

'Does it matter to thee where I get it, if I keep thee supplied with money ?'

Thus they bandied words with one another every day, until at last he told her how he was getting it. Away she went, and told her mother.

Dh' iarr a màthair cliabh-sgei[th]reach [1] a thoirt dà.

D 861·5 Thug i dà so, is chuir e a mach a h-uile nì bha 'na mhionach. Chuir e grùthan an eòin a mach, agus fhuair a bhean fhìn e, agus dh' ith i e, is bha a' bhuaidh oirre fhìn. An uair a fhuair ise a' bhuaidh oirre fhìn, cha robh ach an ceann trì làithean gun do chuir i a mach esan, 's thuirt i ris

K 2213 nach biodh i cosd air na b' fhaide (nach bu laghach i !).

Thug e tigh muilleir, bha an taobh shìos [2] diùbh, air. Thug e leth-bhliadhna an tigh a' mhuilleir. Thog ise tigh geal leis an òr a bha i faotainn 'san sporan.

Thuirt bean a' mhuilleir ris-san, latha,—'Nach truagh mar a dh' éirich dhuit, a dhuine bhochd?'
'Chan 'eil comas air,' ars esan.
Arsa bean a' mhuilleir ris,—'Innsidh mise duit ciod è nì thu.'
'Seadh,' ars esan.
'Théid thu suas an ceartuair an déidh na dìnnearach, is bidh ise gabhail sràide a muigh. Gheibh thu stigh air taobh cùil an tighe aice, agus théid thu a stigh dh' a leithid so de sheòmar ann, agus gheibh thu currachd mór, dubh, crochte a stigh 'san t-seòmar. Thoir leat e, is an uair a chì thu ise tighinn, sparraidh tu an currachd m'a ceann le do dhà làimh, agus guidhidh tu bhi far an togair thu, agus bi thu ann.'
Dh' fhalbh esan, agus rinn e mar a dh' iarr bean a'

D 1520·11 mhuilleir air. Fhuair e 'n currachd, choinnich e leis a muigh i, sparr e m' a ceann e, agus ghuidh e bhi anns

A 692 an Eilean Uaine ann an iomall an domhain mhóir, agus bha e ann, an ùine fìor ghoirid, e fhìn 's i fhìn.[3] Ars ise,—
'Nach truagh an rud a rinn thu !'

<hr>

[1] In MS. the word *cliabh-sgeireach* is written on the line. It is not run through, but immediately above it the word *momantair* is written, and on the opposite page of the MS. occurs the following note by Hector MacLean, the transcriber,—'*Momantair* used by reciter. This is a very singular corruption of the English word *vomit*. The *v* is changed into *m*, and a long tail added to the word. These corruptions are interesting, as they illustrate how language undergoes change and how new languages are formed. *Cliabh-sgeithreach*, from *cliabh* the chest, and *sgéith* to vomit, is the proper Gaelic, and a very expressive word it is, not only in meaning, but the very sound nearly expresses the idea.'

Her mother desired that an emetic [1] be given to him. She gave it to him, and he brought up everything there D 861·5 was in his stomach. He vomited the bird's liver forth, and his wife got it and ate it, and thenceforth the virtue was hers. When she got it to herself, there was no more about it but that in three days she drove him away, and told him that she was not going to spend money on him K 2213 any longer (what a nice girl !).

He betook himself to a miller's house, situated lower down [2] the country. He spent half a year in the miller's house. She [the hero's wife] built a fine white house with the gold she used to get out of the purse.

The miller's wife said to him one day,—'How wretchedly things have happened for thee, poor man !'

'There is no help for it,' he replied.

The miller's wife said to him, 'I will tell thee what do do.'

'Well,' said he.

'Thou shalt go up there [to thy wife's house] immediately after dinner. She will be taking a walk out of doors. Thou shalt get into her house at the back, and go into such and such a room, where thou wilt find a great black hood, hanging up in the room. Take it with thee, and when thou seest her coming, clap the hood upon her head with thy two hands, and wish thyself in whatever place thou please, and thou shalt be there.'

He went off, and did as the miller's wife had desired him. For he found the hood, met his wife out of doors, D 1520·11 clapped it upon her head, and wished himself in the Green A 692 Isle at the outer edge of the great world, and he was there in a very short time, both he and she.[3] Said she,—'What a wretched deed thou hast done !'

[2] *Shìos*, down, refers to the direction towards which the various rivers of a country flow, and therefore implies that the place in question was nearer the sea than the hero then was.

[3] Presumably he clung to her, while the magic hood, which he himself had placed on her head, carried her through the air to the famous Green Isle, one of the Isles of the Blest. But we presently hear that the wind blows the hood off *his* head. This implies the omission of some incident which related how he, upon reaching the Green Isle, snatched the hood off her head, and put it on his own, intending that it should take him back home alone, and leave her there to die of starvation.

'Cha truagh,' ars esan, 'fàgaidh mi thusa an so agus
falbhaidh mi fhéin, is cha bhi thu fada beò, is cha do thoill
thu a atharrach.'

Ars ise,—'Ruighidh tu air an dà ubhal ud shuas 's a'
chraoibh, agus miann agam orra, is bheir thu dha m'
ionnsuigh iad.'

Dh' fhalbh esan suas do 'n chraoibh, is thàinig oiteag
ghaoithe agus shéid i dheth an currachd, is rug ise air a'
D 1765   churrachd, is dh' òrdaich [1] i i fhìn a bhi air falbh, is bha i
aig an tigh gun dàil.

S 145   Bha esan 'na onrachd anns an eilean, gun duine ach e
fhéin. Dh' amais ùbhlan dearg air, agus dh' ith e iad,
agus dh' fhàs dà chabar mhór fhéidh air, is cha b' urrainn
D 1375   e a cheann a thogail. Bha e feuchainn 'd è mar a gheibh-
·1·1·1   eadh e dheth iad le bhi feuchainn a h-uile seòrsa, is dh'
D 1375   ith e seòrsa eile dh' ùbhlan, agus thuit na cabair dheth.[2]
·2·1·1

D 551·2   Bha e a' falbh feadh an eilein, agus 'd è thachair air ach
biolair dhearg. Dh' ith e a' bhiolair, agus thionndaidh
D 131   i e 'na lothaidh ghlais,[3] is bha e 'g itheadh feòir an siod
mar each no mar mhart eile. Ged a bha e 'na lothaidh,
D 682·3   bha tùr duine ann. Bha e feuchainn 'd è bheireadh air ais
D 764   gu cruth duine e, agus dh' amais biolair ghorm air, am
bàrr sruthain, agus dh' ith e i, is bha e 'na dhuine mar a
bha e roimhid.

Thug e leis a neapaigin pòca, agus chruinnich e a h-uile
sgàth a bha an sin a bha gu cron no maith a dhèanamh.
Bha e smuaineachadh gum faiceadh e soitheach air taobh
air choreigin. Bha e sealltuinn mun cuairt, is chunnaic
e soitheach dlùth air an eilean, agus dh' éigh e, is dh'
éigh e dhi. Thàinig am bàta gu tìr, is an uair a chunnaic
iad e, shaoil iad gur h-e an droch chreutair a bh' ann,[4] is
R 188   thill iad a mach. Thòisich esan ri eubhach as an déidh.
Thill am bàta a rithist, is thill am maighstir innte. Dh'

---

[1] *Lit.* ordered, commanded. An invocation, but, as in this story, seldom
addressed to any particular supernatural, or god. See p. 312.

[2] Similar incident in *W. H. Tales*, i., No. 10, vars. 1, 2, 3.

[3] *Loth* means a filly. *Lothaidh*, an old form of the dative, is used here.

'Not at all,' said he, 'I shall leave thee here and go
away, and thou wilt not live long; thou hast not deserved
anything else.'

Said she,—'See if thou canst reach the two apples up
there in that tree, for I have a desire for them. And
bring them to me.'

Up into the tree he went, but there came a gust of wind
which blew the hood off him. She seized it, and wished [1] D 1765
herself away from the place, and, without delay, she found
herself (*lit.* was) at home.

So there he was in the island alone, no one with him S 145
but himself. He came across some red apples, and ate
them, and two huge deers' antlers grew upon him, [so heavy] D 1375
that he was unable to raise his head. He endeavoured ·1·1·1
to find out how to get them off by trying every sort [of
living plant], and he ate another sort of apple, and the D 1375
antlers fell off.[2] ·2·1·1

He wandered about the island, and what should he D 551·2
meet with but some red water-cress. He ate the cress, and it
turned him into a gray filly,[3] and there he was, eating grass D 131
like any horse or cow. Yet though he was in the shape of
a filly, he still had human sense. He tried to find out D 682·3
what would bring him back to human shape, and he came
across some green water-cress, floating on the top of a D 764
streamlet; he ate this cress, and became a man as he had
been before.

He took his pocket-handkerchief, and gathered together
every [magic] thing there was in the place, everything that
could be used to work either evil or good. He thought
that he would see some vessel in some direction or other.
He kept on looking abroad and around him, and seeing a
vessel near the island, shouted and shouted to her. A boat
came to land, and when they [the people in it] saw him,
they thought he was the Evil One,[4] and went back out to sea. R 188
He began to shout after them. The boat came back again,

It is strange that, after metamorphosis, a man should become, not a male
animal, but a female. *Loth*, always *fem.*, is strictly a filly, but is often loosely
used of an animal of one to two years without regard to sex, as *digeach* is
now chiefly used in sense of *stallion*.   [4] See p. 35 *n.*

fhaighnich am maighstir deth, an e duine a bh' ann. Thuirt
e gur h-eadh.
'D è an dòigh air an tàinig thu an so?'
'Chuireadh ann le buidseachas mi.'
'Faodaidh sin a bhi, ach thig anns a' bhàta, is bheir
mise as an so thu.'
Dh' fhalbh e, is chaidh e sìos, is thug iad an t-aiseag
dha as an eilean. An uair a ràinig iad, is a fhuair e air

K 1616 tìr, cha do rinn e stad gus an do ràinig e am baile 'san robh
ise, is i air fàs 'na baintighearna mhóir, chothromaich, is
dùil aice gun do bhàsaich esan o chionn fada 'san eilean,
is nach robh sgeul air.

Cheannaich e cliabh, is chuir e h-uile sgàth a thug e
leis 's a' chliabh. Bha e dol a reic nan ùbhlan ri mnathan
uaisle 's ri daoine uaisle. Chaidh e mu choinneamh an
tighe aice-se latha. Chuir i searbhanta sìos, is a ceann
fhín a mach air uinneig, a dh' fhaighneachd 'd è bha air na
h-ùbhlan.
'Tha dà sheòrsa agam,' ars esan. 'Tha feadhainn ann
airson mhnathan uaisle móra, agus is e cóig puinnd
Shasunnach a bhios air a h-uile té dhiùbh.'
Chuir ise sìos an sin an t-searbhanta, agus cóig puinnd
Shasunnach leatha a dh' iarraidh té de na h-ùbhlan. Thug
e dhi ubhal dearg. Chaidh an t-searbhanta suas leis
an ubhal. Rug ise air an ubhal, is a ceann a mach air an

D 1375 uinneig. Dh' ith i i, is dh' fhàs dà chabar fhéidh oirre, is
·I·I·I cha b' urrainn di a ceann a thoirt a stigh.[1] Cha robh aice
ach a bhi rànaich, is ag eubhach. Bha lighichean a'
tighinn dh' a faicinn, 's cha b' urrainn iad stuth a dhèanamh
dhith. Thàinig esan mun cuairt, is thilg e uaidh an
cliabh.[2] Chaidh e far an robh i.

'A bheil fad o 'n a dh' éirich so duit, a bhoireannaich?'
ars esan.

---

[1] Similar incidents in W. H. Tales, i., No. 10, vars. 1, 2, and 3.
[2] In order, presumably, that he might not be recognized as the man who
had sold her the apples.

and in her came the master of the vessel. The master
asked him if he were a man. He said he was.

'In what way didst thou come here?'

'I was carried here by witchcraft.'

'That is quite possible, but come into the boat, and I
will take thee away from this place.'

He roused himself, and went down to the shore, and
they gave him a passage on the boat and took him away
from the island. When they arrived home, and he had K 1616
got ashore, he never made a stop until he came to the
place where she [his wife] was; she had become a
great lady, and well-to-do, thinking to herself that he
had died long ago in the island, for there were no tidings
of him.

He purchased a basket, and put everything he had
brought with him into the basket. He was going to sell
the apples to ladies and gentlemen. He came up to her
house one day, and stood in front of it. She put her head
out of a window and sent down a serving-woman to him,
to ask what was the price of the apples.

'I have two kinds,' said he. 'Some of them are for
great ladies, and every one of that sort are five pounds
sterling a-piece.'

Then she sent down the serving-woman, with five
pounds sterling to get one of the apples. He gave her
a red one. Back again upstairs went the serving-woman
with the apple. His wife seized the apple, her head being
still out of the window. She ate it, and two deer's antlers
grew upon her head, and she could not draw her head in D 1375
again.[1] She could do nothing but scream and shout. '1'1'1
Doctors kept on coming to see her, but they were not able
to do anything for her. [Another day came, and] he
came round [again], having thrown away the basket.[2]
He went to where she was.

'Is it a long time since this happened to thee, woman?'
said he.

'Chan 'eil,' ars ise, 'is goirid o 'n a dh' éirich e domh.'

'D è bheireadh tu do dhuine chuireadh sin dìot?'

'Bu mhór sin. Bheirinn da na dh' iarradh e.'
'Gabhaidh mise beagan airson a chur dhìot. Gabhaidh
tu purgaid [1] uam airson na cabair a chur dhìot.'

'Cha ghabh, cha ghabh,' ars ise.
'Bi mar sin fhìn, mata.'
'Till,' ars ise, 'is bheir thu dhomh purgaid.'

D 881·1
Rinn e cliabh-sgeithreach gu maith làidir dhi is thug e
oirre a h-uile boinne dheth òl. Chuir i a mach a h-uile
nì bha 'na goile. Fhuair esan grùthan an eòin, is ghlan e
e, is dh' ith e e.

D 1375
·2·1·1
Thug e té de na h-ùbhlan glasa di, 's thuit na cabair
dhith gun dàil an uair a dh' ith i i. Dh' aithnich i gur h-e
esan a bh' ann. Thòisich i air, i fhéin 's a màthair ag
iarraidh air cur leatha, is gum biodh e cho maith is a bha
e roimhe. Dh' aontaich [2] e leis an so, is chaidh e leò.

D 551·2
D 131
Latha bha an sin aig an dinneir, thuirt e riu gun robh
rud aige bhiodh iad a' gabhail an déidh an dinnearach.
Thug e suas a' bhiolair dhearg a rinn loth ghlas [3] dheth
fhìn, is thug e orra a gabhail, air a bhean is air a' chaillich,
a màthair. An uair a dh' ith iad i, dh' fhàs iad 'nan dà
D 661
loth ghlais.
Fhuair e an so cuip, is dh' éirich e orra a mach as an
t-seòmar. Fhuair e strian do na h-uile té dhiùbh. Chaidh
e leotha chun a' mhuilleir, is thug e dha a nasgaidh iad.
Phòs esan, is bha e anns a' chaisteal, is bha e 'na thighearna
mór mu dheireadh.

For annotation, see *Folk-Lore*, xxxvi. (1925), pp. 151 *seq.*, and
Revue Celtique, xlv., part 1, pp. 134-6, for a review by
Professor J. Vendryes, who gives bibliographical details.

'It is not,' she replied, 'it is but a short time since it happened to me.'

'What wouldst thou give to anyone who would take those antlers off thee?'

'A great deal. I would give him,—all he might ask.'

'I shall only want a very little for taking them off. Thou shalt take a purge [1] from me in order to remove the antlers from thy head.'

'I will not, I will not,' said she.

'Remain then in the same condition.'

'Come back,' said she, 'and thou shalt give me a purge.'

He gave her a very strong emetic, and made her drink every drop of it. She vomited up everything in her stomach. D 881·1 He obtained the bird's liver, cleaned it, and ate it.

He next gave her one of the green apples, and the antlers fell off her head without delay when she had eaten it. She then knew that it was he. She began at him, both she and her mother, urging him to cast in his lot with her, saying that he would then be as well off as before. He agreed [2] to this, and joined himself to them. D 1375 ·2·1·1

One day at dinner he told them that he had something which they were to take after dinner. He brought forth the red water-cress which had made a gray filly of him,[3] D 551·2 and induced them both, his wife and the old woman, her D 131 mother, to eat it. Upon eating it, they became two gray D 661 fillies.

He next got a whip and fell upon them with it, and drove them out of the room. He got a bridle for both of them. He took them to the miller, and gave them to him for nothing. He married, and dwelt in the castle, and finally became a great Laird.

---

[1] *Purgaid*, purge, in MS. But in a later sentence it is not a purge but an emetic he administers. He is trying to conceal his design, probably.

[2] *Dh' aidich e* in MS., which is obviously a clerical error, as it means, *he avowed, admitted, confessed.*   [3] *Loth* is used here, being the accusative case.

NOTES

MS. vol. x., No. 29.   Campbell of Islay wrote the following summary at the end of the MS.:—

'Gru[th]an an Eoin 's an Sporan Oir.
Gaelic Index, No. 29.
Pages 242 and 258.   Barra MSS.
Printer's Index.[1]

Two boys go to seek their fortune—catch a bird—A gentleman comes, plucks a feather from its breast, and then reads [from the writing on the breast of the bird [2]] that he who eats the heart shall marry the best wife—he who eats the liver shall have riches.   He buys the bird and orders the heart and liver to be cooked.   The boys eat it [they eat only the heart and the liver] and bolt.—They go to an old woman who makes merry[?] but keeps them for a year, then tells them the secret, and they go away.   [This does not quite correspond with the text of the tale in the MS.   The old woman does indeed admit that the boys had brought her much gold, ascertains by experiment that this was due to a virtue attaching to the younger boy, and informs him of the fact; but she certainly says nothing about either the bird's liver or heart, and seems to know nothing of the virtue attaching to the elder boy.   It is, however, quite possible that Campbell of Islay had himself heard the story recited, and remembered some sentence to the effect that the old woman had told the boys all the facts of the case.]

One marries the Emperor's daughter [recte, the King's daughter. Campbell was thinking of the preceding tale from the same reciter, tale No. 14 (MS. vol. x., No. 28), Alasdair, the son of the Emperor], the other a poor girl who wheedles him out of his secret, gives him an emetic, and gets the liver which she eats.   [She then drives him away.]

By the advice of a miller['s wife], he puts a black hood [which he finds there, and of which no explanation is given, so that one suspects the omission of some important incident] over her head, and wishes them [himself and his wife] to the [Gr]een Island.   [Some other incident has been lost at this point.   He had put the hood on her head at first, but must have taken it off hers and must have put it on his own head afterwards, for]   The wind blows the hood off [his head].   She seizes it [wishes herself away, is transported home] and leaves him there [in the Green Isle].

He eats apples and horns grow, other apples and they fall off.   He eats grass of a certain kind and becomes a gray horse, other grass and becomes a man.   He gets away in a ship, gives his wife red apples

[1] 'Printer's Index.'   Islay probably intended to fill in after these words some number for the guidance of his printers.

[2] We are not told how the gentleman got to know either about the existence of such a bird, or whereabouts on its body writing would be found. Some incident has probably been lost.

[so that the deer's horns grow upon her head] and then an emetic and gets the liver once more. [He next gives her one of the other kind of apples, which at this point in the story, and only at this point, are described as being green; and the horns fall off her head. He now goes to live with her and her mother.] Then he gives the herb [= the red water-cress] to his wife and mother-in-law, who become grey mares. Nothing further is said as to his brother. [The younger is the more important hero].

> 'See Grimm, p. 384. Donkey. Cabbages.
>   „   „   p. 192. Two Brothers.
> German, Vol. 2, 173⎱ No. 122.
>   „   Vol. 3, 201⎰
>   „   Vol. 3, p. 203, long nose.
>   „   Der Krautegel.'

[Islay spells this last word correctly *Krautesel* in his *Popular Tales of the West Highlands*, i., No. 10, Notes. He continues:—]

'This story [No. 15, MS. vol. x., No. 29] is not exactly like any one of the numerous revisions given or referred to in Grimm's 3rd vol., but some bits of it are to be found scattered in nearly all. The horns are in one, in another it is a long nose that grows. Cabbages do the mischief in one case, apples in another. The people are changed into donkeys in one case, a gray horse in another, but through all this haze of incidents the bird's entrails confer gifts, and there are three magic articles which appear everywhere, the cap or cloak for travelling,[1] the purse, and the whistle.' Thus far Campbell of Islay's summary of the tale.

In a list of Gaelic folktales which he gives at the end of vol. iv. of his *Popular Tales of the West Highlands*, Islay refers to No. 15, MS. vol. x., No. 29, as follows:—'Like three soldiers (Grimm), and Arabian

---

[1] The cap is a black hood in MS. x., No. 29. The black hood also appears in 'An t-Each Dubh,' or The Black Horse, MS. vol. xi., No. 353, summarized by Islay in MS. vol. 'Oral Mythology,' and published by J. Jacobs, *More Celtic Fairy Tales*. The Black Horse in MS. vol. xi., No. 353, instructs the hero that he must go through seven doors, and that, after opening the seventh, he will find the hood on top of a press. The hero possesses himself of the hood, and having mounted the Black Horse, rides all night. In the morning he comes to the Land-under-Waves, which, like the Green Isle in MS. vol. x., A 692 No. 29, is one of the Islands of the Blest. In his notes to the Black Horse, Islay says that the black hood was to render its wearer invisible. But at the end of the summary he speaks of the hood as 'the cap for travelling,' D 1520·11 as he does above in his summary of MS. vol. x., No. 29. Nothing is said as to invisibility in either MS. vol. x., No. 29, or in The Black Horse. A 'cap for travelling' appears in some other tale, where a man about to be hanged puts the cap on his head and, saying 'Hurrah for London,' is immediately transported thither, bringing the gallows with him hanging round his neck. See for a similar incident, *Folk-Lore*, xxxiii., pp. 209-10. A green cloak confers invisibility in MS. vol. x., No. 97.

Nights; good.' (For 'The Three Soldiers,' see *ibid.*, vol. i., tale No. 10.) He refers to MS. vol. x., No. 29 again (*ibid.*, vol. ii., No. 47), where tasting the bree of the magical serpent occurs, a proceeding which conferred magical knowledge on the eater. He there says:—'There are varieties of the same incident scattered through Grimm; for instance in the *Two Brothers*, where children eat the heart and liver of a golden bird, and find gold under their pillows; and this story has a relation in Gaelic also.' He gives another story in which tasting the magic trout also confers magical knowledge (*ibid.*, vol. iii., No. 82).[1]

D 1015
·1·1
There may be a connection between the magic powers ascribed to the bird's heart and liver in MS. vol. x., No. 29, and the fact that Highland superstition had an aversion to the liver as food, as well as an aversion to other parts of animals. See the following translations of proverbs given by Sheriff Alexander Nicolson, *Gaelic Proverbs*, pp. 118, 389, 388,—

'Lights are not meat, nor buttermilk milk.
Liver is not meat, nor bran-juice sowens.

D 1793
E 714·4·1
E 714
·4·2*
Eat not eye, or udder, or liver, and thy breasts shall ail thee never.
If you eat the bird's heart, your heart will palpitate for ever.
If you eat the sheep's tongue, you will bleat for ever.'

Nicolson says the last two are meant for children, but the belief may date from a long-lost past, when all in the Highlands believed it.

Even the Water-Horse seems to have shared in the general objection to liver and lungs as food. It was supposed to make away with men, children, and even domestic horses, carrying or dragging them down beneath the waters of the loch or river which it haunted. The presumption was that when in the depths, it devoured its victims, but rejected their livers, for the next day these parts are found floating on the surface of the water. In one tale, the liver of a Water-Horse which had carried a man into a loch, comes ashore the next day, 'the animal, it is supposed, having been killed by the other Water-Horses tenanting the lake, when they felt the smell of a man off it.' In another tale of a man who had been carried into the water by a Water-Horse, it is the victim's lungs and not his liver which come ashore the next day. See the Rev. J. G. Campbell, *Superstitions of the Highlands and Islands of Scotland*, pp. 205-209. Similarly vampires, green fairy women with bone beaks or with cloven hoofs, who in some tales crack men's bones and drink their blood, reject the lungs of their victims in a tale given in *The Celtic Magazine*, xii. (1886-7), p. 513.

In a tale preserved in *The Folk-Lore Journal*, vi. (1888), p. 247, and in Islay's MS. volume, lettered 'Highland Stories, collected in

[1] For other versions of this tale, see the Rev. J. G. Campbell, *The Fians, Waifs and Strays of Celtic Tradition*, iv., p. 19; *The Celtic Review*, i. (1905), p. 360; ii. (1906), pp. 14, 246; Dr George Henderson, *The Norse Influence on Celtic Scotland*, pp. 90, 316, 321; *Béaloideas*, vii., p. 225. For other Highland tales having a resemblance to the *Arabian Nights*, MS. vols. x. and xi., Nos. 35, 105, 327, 383.

1859-60, English,' tale No. 49, the Water-Horse, in this case spoken of as a golden horse, carries some boys away into the depths. An hour afterwards, the hair and entrails of the boys are seen floating about, scattered all over the water.

In No. 173 (Islay's MS. vol. xi.) a giant kills all a king's followers except one, by throwing a brazen ball at them. The giant takes the heart and liver out of the last of the king's followers, while the man yet lives, pounds them up, and forces the king to swallow them. The giant probably thought that the heart and liver were the parts the king would least like to eat.

In No. 113 (Campbell of Islay's MS. vol. x.) a heroine kills a band of robbers, and gives their captain a desperate wound. The captain escapes, and is afterwards informed by a leech that he will never recover till he gets the heart and liver of the maiden who had wounded him. Presumably, he was to have eaten these things, but the heroine is one too many for him, and eventually kills him. In another tale, a jealous queen desires to have the heart and liver of her rival to eat. (*The Celtic Magazine*, xiii. (1887-8), p. 213.)

There are various Highland tales in which, just before being enchanted or dis-enchanted, persons vomit gulps of blood. When, later on, the blood is administered to them, they experience a partial recovery from enchantment, or complete recovery to health. See Islay's MS. vol. x., No. 126 ; Islay's *Popular Tales of the West Highlands*, iii., No. 86 ; *The Celtic Monthly*, xxiv. (Glasgow, 1916), pp. 167-8. Similarly, in No. 52 of Islay's *Popular Tales*, ii., the hero recovers the three teeth which had been knocked out of his father's head and carried away by an enemy, and administers them to his father in a can of water. The teeth thereupon resume their proper place in the sufferer's head. In another tale (*ibid.*, iv., p. 270 or 295,—there are two editions), a mother is able, when her three stolen children are restored to her, to cure them of squinting, by replacing in their eyes the drops that had fallen therefrom when they were being stolen from her.[1] In these cases, the restoration of what had been lost meant restoration indeed.

These instances and the tale of 'The Bird's Liver' seem to show that primitive man looked upon the living subject as something mechanical, a mere collection of parts, which might be sundered and joined together again or replaced, without much prejudice to the individual, who would suffer nothing more than a mere temporary pain or inconvenience. The parts or the whole body might even be eaten, as in the case of the children of Kronos, and as in the tale of the fox and the kids; or they might be eaten and re-eaten, as in the case of 'The Bird's Liver,' and yet retain their original character and coherence. This mechanical conception of the living subject is illustrated in several Highland tales in which one of the dramatis personæ crumbles away to dust, and yet afterwards gathers himself together again and resumes his original shape, when tales are recited over the spot where his dust lay. The

[1] For a very similar incident, see *Zeitschrift für Celt. Philologie*, i., p. 154.

head of many a Highland giant persists in trying to join itself again to the body from which it had been struck, so that the hero who has performed the act of decapitation is obliged to place his sword on the severed neck and keep the head away until the spinal marrow of the monster's body becomes finally cold in death, and the blood freezes in his veins. See this book, pp. 38 n, 41 n.

The Green Isle, one of the Isles of the Blest, where the magic apples grew, is referred to in many Highland tales. But 'The Bird's Liver' is the only tale known to me which tells of the red water-cress and the green water-cress growing there, or speaks of these herbs as possessing magical qualities. Another magical plant, the four-leaved clover, is also new to me as far as its singular properties are concerned, but it is not said to have been one of the flora of the Green Isle. See Hector MacLean's note.

Hector MacLean, the transcriber of No. 15, a euhemerist, adds the following quaint note:—'He who ate the heart of the bird got the best of wives. The heart is typical of courage and generosity, and these qualities are always admired by the fair sex. There is something sour about the liver, something more or less spiritless, perhaps covetous. The very sound in Gaelic is lugubrious, gru[th]an ! The gentleman buys the bird, seeing its value, and gives the boys what they, no doubt, considered a handsome sum, and what no doubt quieted his own conscience. The gentleman is typical of a numerous class in society who, taking advantage of the weak and ignorant, calm their conscience[s] by certain charities, or some other such donations. The old woman is more conscientious than the gentleman,—though she keeps the secret of the purse, she sends them to school and, ultimately, freely confesses the secret. The apples no doubt symbolize intellectual and refined pleasure, ambition, display and luxury. Red is not the right colour of apples, it is the colour of blood, and the red apples are false intellectual pleasures, false ambition, excessive and false refinement which bring people's heads into difficulties of which the deer's antlers are very properly typical. The cresses, growing low and supposed to counteract the bad effects of high feeding, represent physical enjoyment. The red cresses which convert human beings into fillies are sensual vices, which degrade mankind and give preponderance to the animal part of their nature, so as in a manner to convert them into inferior animals.' Hector MacLean added similar notes to many tales. See Folk-Lore, i. (1890), p. 381, where the late Alfred Nutt notes that Campbell of Islay remarks upon the 'common malady of his collectors, who insist upon explaining things they cannot possibly understand.' [1] The collector or transcriber of No. 15 has erred greatly in this respect. His moralizing is worthless and very confused. He had apparently never seen apples that were red. He speaks of the cresses growing low, but the tale does not refer to the fact. But his remark that the

---

[1] The rash interpretation of myths without adequate knowledge is dangerous. See Folk-Lore, xxxi., pp. 278, 282; xxxiv., pp. 178, 180, 243; xxxv., p. 100; xxxiii., pp. 63, 65, 101, 126.

red cresses convert human beings into fillies, is important. He does not say *foals*. And in No. 15, the form of the Gaelic adjective in all cases of metamorphosis into equine shape shows that a female animal is meant. Whether it was the hero, or his wife, or her mother, the D 1793 sex of the subject, when transformed to equine shape, was feminine. It was natural that this should be so in the case of a woman, but it is strange indeed that after the metamorphosis of a male person the resulting animal shape should be feminine. Shape-shifting is a commonplace of mythology, but sex-shifting is unusual. There are three other Highland tales, however, in which sex-shifting occurs, but on the part of women. In one, a queen and her attendant maidens are all changed into white stags ; in another, a royal stag becomes a D 10 woman; and, in a third, a woman becomes a water-horse (Islay, English List, *Popular Tales of the West Highlands*, iv., end, No. 73; Rev. J. G. Campbell, *Superstitions of the Highlands and Islands*, p. 129; Islay, English List, No. 174, referred to in his *Popular Tales*, i., intro., lxxix or lxxxvii. A Skye version of this last is given in *Folk-Lore*, xxxiii. (1922), p. 307).

It is possible that the ideas concerning sex-shifting may be reflected in the Scandinavian belief that men's souls are always female, in the Welsh belief that the fairies were all women, and in the Irish tradition that fairyland was inhabited entirely by women. (See G. Schütte, *Folk-Lore*, xxxv. (1924), p. 362; Sir John Rhys, *Celtic Folk-Lore, etc.*, pp. 245, 661).

The deer's antlers are probably to be referred to memories of a deer-cult. There are abundant indications of the former existence in the Highlands of such a cult. There was also a cult of gigantic deer-goddesses, who owned the herds of deer, and there are several tales of witches who are obviously priestesses of the deer-cult or of the deer-goddesses, for in some cases they bear the names of their patronesses. Some of the witches or priestesses appear to live in distant islands. In Islay's *Popular Tales*, iv., p. 270 or 296, the Island of Deer is mentioned. A 692 In it was a magic well, by washing in the waters of which the heroine's skin, which had been coloured green by 'Druids,' recovers its natural colour. The Seven Big Women of the Isle of Jura, who are undoubtedly deer-goddesses, occur *ibid.*, ii., Tale No. 46, and the name Jura is known to be derived from Old Norse *dýr-ey*, deer isle (Prof. W. J. Watson, *Rosg Gàidhlig*, p. 268, 1st ed.). For the antler incident, see *Béaloideas*, iii., p. 148.

GILLE A' BHUIDSEIR

No. 16.   *Campbell MS. Vol. x., No. 30*

Aarne-Thompson, No. 325

BHA tuathanach ann an Eirinn, agus bha gille crosda aige, agus thuirt e ri a mhàthair, 'Tha cho math leam a bhàthadh; cha bhi e ceart, co dhiùbh.'

Dh'fhalbh e leis, a dh'ionnsuigh a' chladaich. Bha leisg air an so, a chur a mach, an uair a ràinig e.

Ciod è chunnaic e, ach bàta, agus duine 'na shuidhe innte. Thàinig am fear a bha 'sa' bhàta air tìr, agus thuirt e ris an tuathanach, 'An ann a' dol a bhàthadh do mhic a bha thu ?'

'Is ann.'

'Ma leigeas tu leamsa e gu ceann bliadhna, gheabh thu fichead punnd Sasunnach air a shon—is e as fhearr dhuit na a bhàthadh.'

S 212

'Leigidh,' ars an tuathanach.

'An ceann bliadhna, coinnich mise ann an so, agus thig do mhac air ais, agus gheabh thu an fhichead punnd Sasunnach.'

An uair a chaidh an tuathanach dhachaidh, 'Ciod è,' ars a' bhean, 'a rinn thu ris a' ghille ?'

Dh'innis e mar a bha.

'Is math sin,' ars ise, 'seach a bhàthadh.' Bha màthair a' ghille an so toilichte nach do bhàthadh e.[1]

An ceann bliadhna, thàinig am Bodach, 's mac an

---

[1] In other versions, the mother deplores the idea of handing her son over to a Wizard. In the MS. the sentence, 'Is math sin,' that is well indeed,

THE WIZARD'S GILLIE

No. 16.   *Campbell MS. Vol. x., No. 30*

Aarne-Thompson, No. 325

THERE was a farmer in Erin, who had a froward ne'er-do-well of a son. One day he said to the boy's mother, 'I think I may just as well drown him; he will never be fit for anything, in any case.'

So he took him to the shore. But when he got there, he felt, after all, loath to throw him into the sea.

What should he now see but a boat, with a man sitting in it. The man came ashore and said to the farmer, 'Wert thou really about to drown thy son?'

'Yes, I was indeed.'

'If thou wilt let me take him with me for a year, thou shalt have twenty English pounds for him—better do that than drown him.' S 212

'Very well, I will,' quoth the farmer.

'At the end of a year, then, meet me here, and thy son shall come back, and thou shalt have the twenty English pounds.'

When the farmer came home, 'What,' quoth the wife, 'didst thou do with the lad?'

He told her how matters stood.

'That is well indeed,' quoth she, 'much better than drowning him,' and right glad was she that the lad had not been drowned.[1]

At the end of the year, the Bodach, or old man, came,

---

is followed by 'ars esan,' quoth *he.* But the mother seems by the context to be the person in whose mouth the words would be more appropriate.

tuathanaich leis. Choinnich an tuathanach e, 's fhuair
e an fhichead punnd Sasunnach.—Bha iongantas air an
tuathanach cho eireachdail, cho mór, 's cho foghainteach
's a dh'fhàs a mhac.

'An leig thu leam e bliadhna eile, 's gheabh thu fichead
punnd Sasunnach eile ?' [ars am Bodach].

'Leigidh.'
'Coinnich mise an ceann na bliadhna, 's gheabh thu
an fhichead punnd Sasunnach.'
'Coinnichidh.'
An ceann na bliadhna, thàinig am Bodach a rithisd
agus mac an tuathanaich leis, 's fhuair an tuathanach an
fhichead punnd Sasunnach, 's chan aithnicheadh e a
mhac an uair sin, leis cho mór 's cho eireachdail 's a
dh'fhàs e.

'Leigidh tu leam treis eile dheth,' ars am Bodach ris
an tuathanach.

'Leigidh,' ars an tuathanach, [ach cha do chuimhnich
e air ùine ainmeachadh, no air gealladh fhaotainn gun
tilleadh a mhac.] [1]

An ceann na bliadhna, chaidh e sìos chun a' chladaich,
's thug e sùil 's chan fhaca e duine tighinn.

Bha e dol sìos fad seachduinn, 's cha robh duine
tighinn.

Bha e dol sìos fad seachduinn eile, 's cha robh a mhac
no am Bodach a' tighinn.

Dh'fhalbh e an so, 's ràinig e seann duine air a' bhaile.
Dh'innis an seann duine dha a h-uile car mar a dh'éirich
d'a mhac. 'Chan fhaic thu do mhac tuilleadh, chionn
chan 'eil 'san t-saoghal so ach treis. Thug am Bodach
an car asad.'

Thug e gu rànaich 's gu caoineadh, a bhean 's e fhéin.
Chuir e air gu falbh, 's dh'fhalbh e an là-'r-na-mhàireach.
Chaidh e feadh gach àite, a' siubhal feadh an t-saoghail,
feuch am faiceadh e e. Nuair a bha e tilleadh dhachaidh,

---

[1] From other versions which are clearer at this point. The father's
forgetfulness is a characteristic feature.

and with him the farmer's son. The farmer met him and received the twenty English pounds. So handsome, so big and so stalwart had his son grown that the farmer was astonished.

'Wilt thou let me have the lad for another year? and take twenty English pounds more for doing so?' [quoth the Bodach.]

'Yes, I will.'

'Meet me then, at the end of the year, and thou shalt have the twenty English pounds.'

'Very good, I will.'

At the end of the year, the Bodach came, and with him the farmer's son. The farmer received the twenty English pounds, and on this occasion he could not recognize his son, so tall and so handsome had he grown.

'Wilt thou let me have him for another while?' quoth the Bodach to the farmer.

'I will,' quoth the farmer, [but he forgot to name a time, or to get a promise that his son should return.] [1]

At the end of the year, the farmer went down to the shore, and gazed abroad, but could see no one coming.

For a week he kept going down there, but still no one came.

For yet another week he kept going down there, but neither his son nor the Bodach appeared.

Then he went and visited an old man in the township, and this old man told him everything that had happened to his son. 'Thou'lt see thy son no more,' said he, 'for this world is but for a while. The Bodach hath cheated thee.'

Then the farmer gave himself up to lamenting, he and his wife also. He made himself ready for a journey, and on the morrow he departed. All over the world ho travelled, through every country he roamed, seeking to 's gun e an déis brath fhaotainn air, am beul na h-oidhche choinnich duine mór ris.

'Ciod è an taobh a bha thu mar so?' ars an duine mór ris.
'Bha mi ag iarraidh mo mhic feuch am faighinn a mach e. Dh'fhalbh e le duine o chionn bliadhna is còrr, 's chan fhaca mi fhathasd e.'
'Is e treis a tha do mhac 'san t-saoghal so air fad : reic thu fhéin ris e, 's chan fhaic thu tuilleadh e.'

'Chan 'eil comas air.'
'Am faca tu an caisteal a dh'fhàg thu as do dhéidh, an Caisteal Mór?'
'Chunnaic.'
'Ciod è bheireadh tu do dhuine a dh'innseadh dhuit far a bheil do mhac?'
'Rud sam bith a dh'iarradh e, bheirinn da e.'
'Tha do mhac a' fuireach 's a' Chaisteal Mhór ud a dh'fhàg thu 'nad dhéidh—is mise do mhac a tha bruidhinn riut!'
'O! chan fhàg thusa mo làmhan-sa!' [ars an tuathanach].
'Dèan stad beag: tha mise air mo cheangal aige-san. A bheil fios agad có ris a reic thu do mhac?'
['Chan 'eil.']
'Reic thu ri buidsear e, agus bidh sinn [mi féin 's mo chompanaich], a h-uile h-oidhche aige 'nar calmain. Chan 'eil seòrsa air an t-saoghal de chreutair nach bi sinn 'na chruth, agus tha mise pong os cionn chàich. Is e a dhà dheug a tha sinn ann.—Théid thusa a dh'ionnsuigh a' Chaisteil an ceartair; 's bidh mise a stigh romhad. Agus bidh sinn 'nar calmain a nochd, a h-uile gin againn, agus fàgaidh mise ite briste ann am earball, 's bidh sin agad-sa mar chomharradh ormsa; agus buailidh tu an dorus a' Chaisteil, 's thig e fhéin is fosglaidh e dhuit. An uair a bheir e a stigh thu, their e riut biadh a ghabhail; 's their thusa nach gabh—nach gabh thu biadh no deoch gus am faigh thu do chùnnradh. Feòraichidh esan ciod

N 731

Z 71·8

D 610
D 1273
·1·4
D 154·1

find his son. But as he was returning home, without having yet obtained any tidings of him, he met, in the dusk of the evening, a huge man.

'Whence comest thou hither ?' the huge man asked him.

'I have been seeking my son and trying to find him. He went away with a man more than a year since, and I have not seen him again.'

'Thy son is in this world for but a short time at the longest; thou thyself didst sell him to that man; thou'lt see him no more.'

'Then there is no help for it.'

'Sawest thou the castle thou didst leave behind thee, the Great Castle ?'

'Yes, I did.'

'What wouldst thou give to any man who would tell thee where thy son is ?'

'Whatsoever he might ask, that would I give him.'

'Thy son dwells in the Great Castle over there that thou didst leave behind thee—and I that am speaking to N 731 thee, am he !'

'O !' [cried the farmer,] 'now shalt thou never leave mine arms again !'

'Stay a moment: I have been bound to him. Dost thou know to whom thou didst sell thy son ?'

['No, I do not.']

'Thou didst sell him to a Wizard, and every night [my companions and I] are with that wizard in the form of doves. There is no sort of creature in the world whose Z 71·8 shape we do not [at some time] take. There are twelve of D 610 us, and I am a point above the rest in skill.—Go thou D 1273 forthwith to the Castle; I shall be there before thee. For ·1·4 to-night also we shall be in the form of doves, every one D 154·1 of us, but I shall have a broken feather in my tail, and by that sign shalt thou know me. Thou must knock at the door of the Castle, and the Wizard himself will come and open it to thee. When he bringeth thee in, he will ask thee to take food, but thou must say that thou wilt not— that thou wilt take neither food nor drink till thou get thy

è an cùnnradh. Abair thusa gu bheil calman, is ite
briste 'na earball. Bheir esan sin duitsa an uair sin, airson
thu ghabhail bìdh. Beiridh tusa an sin ormsa, is falbhaidh
tu leam.'
    Chaidh an tuathanach gus a' Chaisteal, mar a dh'iarr
a mhac air. Bhuail e aig a' Chaisteal, agus dh'fhosgail
Fear a' Chaisteil an dorus da.
    'Gabhaidh tu biadh,' arsa Fear a' Chaisteil ris, an uair
a chaidh e a stigh.
    'Cha ghabh mi biadh no deoch,' ars esan, 'gus am faigh
mi mo chùnnradh.'
    'Ciod è do chùnnradh?'
    'Tha, calman, le ite briste 'na earball,' ars an tuathanach.

    Thug Fear a' Chaisteil siod da.
    Ghabh e an sin biadh, agus dh'fhalbh e leis. An uair
a bha e treis o'n Chaisteal, leig e ás an calman. An uair a
fhuair an Calman ás, dh'fhàs e 'na dhuine.

    'Coisicheamaid gu math,' ars a mhac ris an tuathanach,
'feuch am bi sinn 's a' bhaile so romhainn mun caidil iad.
Bidh féill 'sa bhaile so a màireach.'
    'Am bi?'
    'Bithidh.'
    'Ciod è an fhéill a bhios ann?'
    'Bidh—féill chon. Théid mise ann am chù am
màireach, 's cha bhi gin air an fhéill cho brèagh rium,
's bidh bann buidhe mu m' amhaich. Reicidh tu air an
fhéill mi am màireach, 's gheabh thu fichead punnd
Sasunnach air mo shon. Ach an uair a reiceas tu mi,
cha reic thu am bann a bhios mu m'amhaich idir. Bidh
mise anns a' bhann a bhios mu m' amhaich.[2]—An uair a
bheir thu seachad an cù, tilgidh thu am bann air cnoc,
is leumaidh mise ann am dhuine còmhla riut fhéin.'

H 62

D 630

D 610
D 612

P 320

---

[1] The laws of hospitality were so imperative and overruled other considerations so supremely, that a host would be glad to grant almost any
request, if by so doing he might induce his guest to accept of his cheer: a
motive in several tales. Supernaturals were, of course, conceived as being
bound by similar obligations.—The College of Magic seems to be a respectable
native institution for there is no word of its being situated in Italy as is the

boon and bargain. He will ask what the bargain is.
Thou must say—a dove with a broken feather in its tail. H 62
That will he then give thee in return for thy taking food.[1]
Then thou must snatch me up and make off with me.'

So off to the Castle went the farmer, as his son had
bidden him. He knocked at the door, and the Laird of
the Castle opened it to him.

When he had come in, the Laird of the Castle said to
him, 'Thou must have some food.'

'Neither food nor drink will I take,' quoth he, 'until I
get my boon and bargain.'

'What is thy boon and bargain ?'

'Why—a dove with a broken feather in its tail,' quoth
the farmer.

This the Laird of the Castle gave him accordingly.

After having taken food the farmer went away taking
the dove with him. Then, when he was a little way from
the Castle, he let the dove go, and the dove as soon as it
was free, turned into a man.   D 630

'Let us walk smartly,' said his son to the farmer, 'and
try to reach the town that lies in front of us before the
people go to sleep. There will be a fair there to-morrow.'

'Will there ?'

'Yes, indeed there will.'

'What sort of a fair will it be ?'

'Why—a dog fair. I shall become a hound to-morrow, D 610
and I shall have, on my neck, a yellow band, and there will D 612
be none at the fair as handsome as I. To-morrow at that
same fair thou shalt sell me, and shalt get twenty English
pounds for me. But when thou sellest me, sell not the
band that is round my neck upon any account, for I shall
become that band [2] myself.—And when thou hast delivered
over the hound, thou must cast the band on a hillock,
and I shall instantly become a man, and accompany thee.'

case with such colleges in other tales: the apprentices to the Black Art are
equally worthy of notice.

[2] An interesting variant: usually a band or collar around the neck simply
prevents the beast from regaining human form—it is magically bound by it. D 722
That the shape-shifter *is* the band and the dog, etc., at the same time, is
certainly strange.

An là-'r-na-mhàireach, chaidh an tuathanach chun na féille leis a' chù. Bha móran chon air an fhéill, ach cha robh gin ann cho brèagh ri cù an tuathanaich. Bha iomadh aon a' sealltuinn air a' chù. Thàinig aon fhear far an robh an tuathanach.

'Ciod è ghabhas tu air a'chù?' ars esan.

'Fichead punnd Sasunnach,' ars an tuathanach.

D 612   Fhuair e siod. An uair a thug e seachad an cù, thug e dheth am bann buidhe a bha mu a amhaich. Thilg

D 722   e am bann buidhe air cnoc, 's leum e suas 'na dhuine còmhla ris.

Dh'fhalbh iad an so 'nan dithis, an tuathanach 's a mhac, is ghabh iad air an aghaidh gu baile eile.

'Bidh féill anns a' bhaile so am màireach,' arsa mac an tuathanaich ri a athair.

'Ciod è an fhéill a bhios ann?' ars a athair.

D 612   'Bidh—féill tharbh. Bidh mise ann am tharbh, reicidh

D 610   tu mi, agus gheabh thu trì fichead punnd Sasunnach orm. Bidh fàinne ann am shròin, 's cha reic thu am fàinne, 's an uair a bheir thu seachad an tarbh, leumaidh am fàinne air do bhois. Tilgidh thu uait am fàinne [air an làr], is leumaidh e 'na dhuine.'

An là-'r-na-mhàireach, chaidh mac an tuathanaich 'na tharbh, agus chaidh a athair leis gus an fhéill.

Cha robh tarbh air an fhéill cho brèagh ris an tarbh so, is bha na h-uibhir a'sealltuinn air. Thàinig fear an rathad, is thuirt e ris, 'Ciod è ghabhas tu air an tarbh?'

'Trì fichead punnd Sasunnach,' ars an tuathanach.

Fhuair e siod, is thug e seachad an tarbh, is leum am fàinne air a bhois. Thilg e am fàinne air an làr, is leum am fàinne 'na dhuine.

Dh'fhalbh iad, is ghabh iad air an aghaidh gu baile eile.

'Bidh féill anns a' bhaile so am màireach!'

'Ciod è an fhéill a bhios ann?'

'Bidh—féill each, agus théid mise ann am each, agus is mi bhuidhneas an geall—cha bhi gin ann cho luath rium,

On the morrow, the farmer went to the fair with the hound. There were a great many dogs at the fair, but not one so handsome as the farmer's hound.

Many a man looked with all his eyes at the hound, and one in particular coming up to where the farmer was, said—

'What will thou take for the hound?'

'Twenty English pounds,' quoth the farmer.

He got the money, but when he handed over the hound, D 612 he took off the yellow band that was about its neck. Then he threw the yellow band upon a hillock, and it instantly D 722 leaped up a man and accompanied him.

The two of them then departed, the farmer and his son, and journeyed on to another town.

'There will be a fair in this town to-morrow,' said the farmer's son to his father.

'What sort of fair will it be?' said his father.

'Why, it will be a bull fair, and I shall be a bull, and D 612 thou must sell me. Three score English pounds shalt D 610 thou take for me. In my nose will be a ring; but this thou shalt not sell, for when thou handest over the bull, the ring will spring into thine hand. Then shalt thou throw the ring from thee [to the ground], and it will instantly become a man.'

On the morrow, the farmer's son became a bull, and his father went with him to the fair.

Not a bull at the fair was as handsome as he, and there were many that kept gazing at him. At last, a certain man came up, and said to the farmer, 'What wilt thou take for the bull?'

'Three score English pounds,' quoth the farmer.

He got the money and handed over the bull. Immediately the ring sprang into his hand, and when he cast the ring on the ground, it instantly leaped up a man.

They departed, and journeyed on to another town.

'To-morrow there will be a fair in this town also.'

'What sort of fair will it be?'

'Why, a horse fair, and I shall become a horse, and it is I who will win the prize—there'll be none there so

no cho brèagh rium. Gheabh thu sia fichead punnd
Sasunnach orm am màireach—ach tha mi toirt comhairle
ort a nis.[1] A bheil fios agad có tha 'gam cheannach air
a h-uile siubhal ?'

'Chan 'eil.'

'Tha—am Buidsear Mór—sin am fear a tha 'gam
cheannach a h-uile siubhal, agus is ann am màireach a
tha an gnothuch agad r'a dhèanamh. Bidh mise anns an
t-sréin am màireach, is na reic an t-srian idir.'

An là-'r-na-mhàireach, chaidh mac an tuathanaich 'na
each brèagh, is chaidh a athair leis gus an fhéill.—Bha
na ceudan a' tairgse air an each leis cho brèagh 's a bha e,
is cha tugadh esan seachad e gun sia fichead punnd
Sasunnach.

Thàinig an so fear far an robh e.

'So,' ars esan, 'sia fichead punnd Sasunnach.'

Ghabh an tuathanach siod mun robh e 'na mhothachadh, 's mun dubhairt e facal, ghlac am fear eile an t-srian,
is leum e air muin an eich, 's dh'fhalbh e.

Cha robh smaointinn aig an duine bhochd air an t-sréin,
leis mar a chuir am fear eile 'na bhoil e, [agus na h-uibhir
airgid a fhuair e uaidh].

*   *   *   *   *   *

Ràinig am Buidsear Mór an tigh, 's bha a thrì nigheanan an sin agus trì choireachan aca, 's a h-uile té cumail
a coire teth gu esan a bhruich ann.—Dh'fhàg am Buidsear
aig a' chloinn e.

'Nach truagh thu,' arsa té aca, "dol dh'ad bhruich
an so ?'

Bha na trì choireachan làn de uisge goileach.

'Agus an cuala thu aig t'athair riamh nach dèanadh
uisge goileach coire do bhuidsear ?' ars esan.

'Cha chuala,' ars ise.

'Tha mise ag ràdh riut-sa, nach dèan uisge goileach
coire do bhuidsear.'

'Is ann aige fhéin is fhearr a tha brath,' arsa té.

C 837

D 1841·2

---

[1] The son evidently forebodes his father's careless forgetfulness.

swift or so handsome as I. Six score English pounds wilt thou get for me to-morrow—and now must I give thee important counsel.[1] Knowest thou who it is that is buying me each time?'

'No, I do not.'

'Well—it is the Great Wizard—he it is who buys me every time. Now it is to-morrow that thou wilt have the most important task to perform, for I shall be the rein to-morrow, and on no account must thou sell the rein.'   C 837

On the morrow, the farmer's son became a handsome horse, and his father went with him to the fair. Hundreds of people made offers for the horse because it was so handsome, but he would not part with it for less than six score English pounds.

Presently a man came up to the farmer.

'Here,' quoth he, 'are six score English pounds.'

The farmer had accepted that sum before he quite knew what he was about, and ere he could say a word, the other grasped the rein, leaped on the back of the horse, and was off.

The poor man never gave the rein a thought, such excitement had the other caused him, [with the greatness of the sum of money he had received from him].

*   *   *   *   *   *

The Great Wizard arrived home, and his three daughters were ready there with three cauldrons, each one keeping her cauldron hot in order to boil the farmer's son therein.— The Wizard left him with his children.

'How dire and sad thy plight,' said one of them, 'about to be boiled thus?'

Now the three cauldrons were full of boiling water.

'And hast thou never heard thy father say that boiling water will do no harm to a wizard?' quoth he.

'Never,' said she.

'Well, then, I now tell thee that boiling water will do no harm to a wizard.'   D 1841·2

'He is the one that knows best about it,' said one of

'Tha e fhéin pong os cionn a h-uile gin a bha a stigh riamh.' [1]

Dh'fhalbh iad a dh'iarraidh trì chuinneagan de uisge fuar. An uair a dh'fhalbh iadsan mar so, [thòisich e air tachas a lethchinn ri peirceall an doruis, gus an d'fhuair e an t-srian ás a cheann, agus dh'fhàs e 'na dhuine mar a bha e riamh].

D 722

Dh'fhalbh e [an so] 'na easgainn chaoil. Ghabh e sìos an srath, 's thug e allt air.

An uair a thill iadsan, lean iad fhéin 's an companaich [agus am Buidsear Mór] e, is e a cóig deug a bh'ann diubh, 'nan cóig easgainn deug. Bha iad 'ga leantainn gu teann.[3]

D 615·1

Bha tighearna an taobh shìos dheth, 's có bha gabhail sràide a nuas taobh an uillt dlùth air, ach a' bhaintighearna. An uair a mhothaich esan di, ciod è ghabh e ach 'na bhreac, 's leum e air tìr, 's chuir ise 'na h-apran e.

'A bhéistean, seachnaibh e,' ars ise ris na h-easgannan.

An uair a dh'fheuch i a h-apran, bha e 'na fhàinne òir, 's chuir i air a meur e, 's chaidh i dhachaidh.

D 263

Chaidh iadsan 'nan cóig ceaird deug, 's ràinig iad tigh an duine uasail, 's dh' iarr iad obair air. Thug an duine uasal sabhal daibh, 's thug e obair daibh.

An là-'r-na-mhàireach, bha iad ullamh, agus dh' fhaighnich an duine uasal dhiubh, ciod è bhitheadh iad ag iarraidh airson an oibre.

Thuirt iad, nach bitheadh ach fàinne òir a bha mu mheur na Baintighearna.

'An gabh sibh ach fàinne òir? Gabhaibh mar so 's gheabh sibh e.'

[1] Reference is to the apprentices to the Black Art, that had attended the Great Wizard's College of Magic. Sir William Soulis, the wicked Seneschal of Scotland, who wrought evil by art magic, could only meet deserved death by being boiled alive in molten lead.—*Castles and Historic Homes of the Border* by Alexander Eddington, Edinburgh: Oliver and Boyd. The sentences setting forth the hero's method of recovering his human shape by fidgeting with the bridle until he gets it off his head were supplied from the tale of 'The Lady of Assynt.' In other versions it is one of the Wizard's daughters,

them. 'For truly he is a point above all who ever came here.' [1]

So they departed to fetch three pails of cold water. When they had gone, [he began to rub the side of his head against the door-jamb, until he had rubbed the bridle off his head, whereupon he became a man once more].[2]   D 722

Away he now went in the form of a slender eel. Down the strath he went, and then to a burn.

When the Wizard's daughters returned, they and their companions, making [with the Great Wizard,] fifteen in all, gave chase in the guise of fifteen eels, and sorely did D 615·1 they press him.[3]

Lower down the burn lived a Laird, and who should be walking down by the burn side, close to the farmer's son, but the Laird's lady. As soon as ever the farmer's son saw her, what did he do but become a trout, and leap on land, whereupon she put him in her apron.

'Avaunt, ye wretches!' cried she to the eels, ' let him alone.'

But when she peeped into her apron, lo ! he had become a golden ring; so she put him on her finger, and went home. D 263

The others became fifteen tinkers. They came and called at the Laird's house, and desired work of him. The Laird lodged them in a barn, and supplied them with work.

On the morrow, when they had finished, the Laird asked them what payment they required for their work.

They said that they wanted no payment but the golden ring that was on the lady's finger.

'Only a golden ring ? Will you indeed take nothing but a golden ring ? Come this way and you shall have it.'

---

or his only daughter, who take the bridle off for him, a form of the incident which would not fit this version.

[2] Here the band or bridle reverts to its original function.

[3] The eels are metamorphoses, not of the bodies but of the 'souls' of the combatants, for the 'soul' or life principle was believed to be separable from E 710 the body at will. But if while absent from the body, the 'soul,' in no matter what shape died, the body died too, and that instantly.

Ràinig iad an seòmar aice féin. Dh'iarr an duine
uasal oirre am fàinne òir a thoirt do na daoine, gur h-e
gheall esan daibh airson an oibre.

'Gheabh iad sin,' [ars ise], 's i 'ga thoirt bhàrr a meòir.
An uair a thug ise bhàrr a meòir e, leum e anns
a' ghealbhan. [Chaidh am Buidsear Mór 's a chompan-
aich nan cóig builg-shéididh dheug, 's thòisich iad air
séideadh an teine.¹]

D 615·1 Bha pocan peasrach an taobh eile de'n t-seòmar. Leum
esan 'na shìlean anns a' pheasair.

Leum iadsan 'nan cóig calmain dheug, 's chaidh iad a
dh'itheadh na peasrach.
Bha a' bhean uasal a' gabhail iolla ris na calmain.
Chaidh i a dh' iarraidh duine a bheireadh orra.
An uair a mhothaich esan gun d'fhalbh a' bhean uasal,
leum e 'na mhadadh ruadh. Rug e air na calmain, 's
mharbh e a h-uile gin mun tàinig ise, ach an t-aon a
thug e leis 'na bheul.
Dh'fhalbh e, 's ràinig e am Buidsear Mór, agus dh'éigh
E 710 e ris—
'Mharbh mi do aon bhuidsear deug [agus do thriùir
nighean,] 's marbhaidh mi thu fhéin a nis.'
'Airson Nì Maith, na bean domh-sa, 's bi falbh, 's
cha chuir mi dragh ort am feasd, 's na cuir dragh orm.'

[Ach bha fios aig mac an tuathanaich nach bu tear-
munn da mur marbhadh e e, 's thug e ceann a' chalmain
ás a amhaich, agus thuit am Buidsear Mór sìos marbh,
G 275·2·1 's cha do chàraich e ás a sin fhathasd. Bha, an so, mac
an tuathanaich sàbhailte.]
Thug e Eirinn air a rithisd; agus cheannaich iad [e
fhéin agus a athair] dà bhaile fhearainn an uair a ràinig iad.

¹ At this place, the MS. has, 'Chuir iad a mach a h-uile sgàth a bha
'sa ghealbhan, 's iad 'ga iarraidh, they cleared everything out of the fireplace to find him,' but these words have been suppressed and the sentence
between square brackets substituted. Substitution seems to be well warranted
because in five of the other versions there occurs at this point the fine incident

They went to her own room accordingly, and the Laird
requested her to give the men the golden ring, because he
had promised them that for their work.

'They shall have it,' [said she], taking it off her finger.
As she took it off her finger, it leaped into the fireplace.
[The Great Wizard and his companions immediately
became fifteen bellows, and began to blow up the fire.] [1]

Now there was a pock of pease on the other side of the D 615·1
room.   One leap and the lad had become a grain of pease
amongst the rest.

At a bound, they turned themselves into fifteen doves,
and flew to eat the pease.

The lady who had been looking at the doves with
interest, went out to fetch a man to catch them.

When the lad saw that the lady had gone, he instantly
turned himself into a red fox, and, seizing the doves, killed
them all before she returned, all but one, and that one he
took away with him in his mouth.

Off he set to where the Great Wizard['s body] was, E 710
and having arrived, he shouted at him,

'I have killed thine eleven wizards, [and thy three
daughters], and now will I kill thee.'

'For the sake of the Good Thing, touch me not, but
begone; nevermore will I trouble thee, and see thou trouble
not me.'

[But the farmer's son knew there would be no safety
for him till he had killed the Great Wizard, so he severed
the dove's head from its neck, and down fell the Great G 275·2·1
Wizard dead, nor has he ever stirred thence yet.   So the
farmer's son at length found safety.]

He [and his father] went to Erin once more, and when
they got there, they purchased two farms.

---

of the enemy first of all turning themselves into either bellows or pincers,
the number of which differs for different versions, and then either blowing
up the fire or searching for the hero therein.   It seems fairly reasonable to
suppose that such an incident once formed part of this version also.

NOTES

MS. vol. x., No. 30.   There are six other versions.

MS. vol. xiii., No. 348.   The Collier's Son.

MS. vol. xi., No. 199.   Mac an Fhùcadair.

MS. vol. x., No. 107.   Fiachaire Gobha.

MS. vol. xi., No. 173.   An t-Amadan Mór.

MS. vol. xi., No. 174.   Biataiche na Boine.

(The Great Wizard is called 'Fiachaire Gobha' in these last three versions.)   In the seventeenth volume of the Gaelic Society of Inverness, on page 58, is published the only other version known to me.   It was called:

Sgoil nan Eun, the School of Birds.

B 215·1   A school of birds at which a hero is educated occurs also in two tales, both in the MS. Collections.   Though quite different in theme and framework, and forming a separate group, the first one, MS. vol. xi., No. 354, is related by its opening incidents to Nos. 173 and 174, and both are related to the first group through the 'School of Birds.'

MS. vol. xi., No. 354.   Canain nan Eun, the Language of Birds.

MS. vol. x., No. 28.   Alasdair, Mac an Impire.   (No. 14 in this volume, p. 168.)

The story as a whole begins as Wizard's Apprentice, and goes on quite normally with a shape-changing magical contest, a theme familiar from Wales (Taliesin in the *Mabinogion*) to Arabia (*e.g.* the Story of the Second Royal Mendicant in the *Thousand and One Nights*).

'This world is but for a while,' appears to be an instance of popular philosophy.

The meeting of the father with his lost son is very closely paralleled in *W. H. Tales*, iii., p. 210, or p. 196.

In the future tense, the verb 'to sell' is written in the MS. as 'creicidh,' though the forms 'reiceas' and 'cha reic' also appear. The spelling with initial 'c' is frequent in Canada.   See p. 292 *n.*

The laird in the story is represented as giving the Wizard's apprentices a barn to work in.   This was quite in accordance with actual custom, and suggests a pretty picture of the old patriarchal Gaelic times, when the 'Cliar Sheanchain' and various professional craftsmen visited places in bodies and were merrily entertained.

That the laird refrains from asking the tinkers beforehand what their charges are is equally in keeping with the Gaelic character of this tale.   Fionn does the same in several tales, and in the gaming incidents that occur in so many legends, the players never dream of mentioning

N 2·0·1*   the stakes till the game is lost and won, and similarly, fights are fought before ever the combatants disclose their respective identities to each other.

Iolla, interest: gabhail iolla, looking on with interest or pleasure. Note by transcriber.

Gabh iolla ris, gabh ealla ris, *i.e.* Observe it, watch it, but have nothing to do with it. Some use not 'iolla' but 'ealla' when meaning 'observe, watch.'

Airson Nì Maith, not airson Nì Mhaith.

The number of apprentices or doves is always twelve in the MS., whether the Great Wizard and his daughters are included or not. Even when the hero has killed all but one, he is made to say he has killed twelve.

In three other versions he kills the Great Wizard in dove shape in the house of the laird. But in this version, he carries the dove shape away in his mouth to his enemy's house, in order, probably, to exult over him before killing him, which he can safely do, for with his enemy in his mouth, he has him completely at his mercy with no chance of escape. Though that part of the tale stops suddenly, without saying whether the hero kills the Great Wizard or not, the translator has made him do so, as will be seen by the paragraph in square brackets.

In another note, Hector MacLean, the transcriber, says he obtained this tale as well as Nos. 14, 15 (MS. vol. x., Nos. 28, 29), from Roderick MacLean, tailor, Ken Tangval, Barra, who had learned them from old men in South Uist about fifteen years before, *i.e.* about fifteen years before 1860; it was probably in 1860 that the tales in question were transcribed. One of these old men was Angus MacIntyre of Bornish, South Uist, who was about 80 years of age at the time and has since died. For an Irish version, *Béaloideas*, vii., p. 213.

IAIN OG, MAC RÌGH NA FRAINGE

No. 17.   [*Vol. x., No. 31*]

BHA Rìgh anns an Fhraing agus phòs e, agus bha gaol
mór aige air a' Bhanrighinn, agus bha iad a' cur ann am
mór thoil-inntinn le chéile.

Dh'fhàs a' Bhanrighinn trom, agus aig ceann a h-ùine,
rug i leanabh mic. Bhaist iad an leanabh, agus is e Iain
Og, Mac Rìgh na Frainge, a thug iad air a' ghille.

Thug i clòch is glùn an so dha gus an robh e bliadhna
a dh' aois.

An ceann bliadhna, dh'fhàs i fhìn tinn, bochd. An
ùine ghoirid, fhuair i bàs, agus bha an Rìgh fo leann-dubh
is fo mhulad mór, a' caoidh na Banrighinn.

Bha e ag aithneachadh gun robh am bàs a' tighinn air
fhéin. Chuir e fios air fear air an robh e fhéin fìor eòlach
a thighinn chuige. Thàinig am fear so.

'Chan 'eil e cosmhuil gum bi mise fada beò,' ars an
Rìgh ris, 'is bheir thusa sùil air an rìoghachd gus an tig
Iain mo mhac gu aois dà bhliadhna deug. An uair a
thig e gus an aois sin, fàgaidh tu an rìoghachd is a h-uile
rud a th'ann, aige fhéin.' 'Nì mise sin,' ars am fear so.

Shiubhail [1] an Rìgh, is dh'fhàg e am fear so a' toirt
sùla air an fhearann.

Bha Iain 'ga àrach aig banaltrum gus an robh e sia
F 611·3·2 bliadhna a dh'aois. 'Na shia bliadhna, chaidh e a
dh'ionnsuigh an uachdarain a dh'fhàg a athair air an
fhearann. Dh'iarr e airm a athar is gun rachadh e a
shealg.

'Cha toir mise sin duit,' ars an t-uachdaran, 'is gun
fhios nach marbh thu thu fhéin.'

---

[1] *Lit.* travelled [to the other world].

[2] In *W. H. Tales*, iii., No. 58, a hero appears to become capable of bearing
arms at sixteen. See also *An Gàidheal* (1875), iv., p. 8—'Na 'm bithinn fhéin

IAIN OG, SON OF THE KING OF FRANCE

No. 17.   [*Vol. x., No. 31*]

THERE was once a King in France who married, and great was the love he had for the Queen, and they dwelt together in much happiness.

The Queen became pregnant, and when her time had come, she bore a son. They baptized the child, and the name they gave him was Iain Og [= Young John] the Son of the King of France.

She suckled him and dandled him until he was one year old.

At the end of a year, she became ill and ailing. In a short time, she died. The King was oppressed with melancholy and great grief, lamenting for her.

He began to perceive that death was coming upon himself also. So he summoned a man with whom he was well acquainted. The man accordingly came to him.

'It is unlikely that I shall be long alive,' the King said to him, 'do thou watch over the kingdom until Iain my son comes to the age of twelve years. When he comes to that age, leave all to him, the kingdom and everything in it.' 'That will I do,' said the other.

The King died,[1] and left this man watching over the land.

Iain was reared by a nurse until he was six years old.[2] When he was six, he went to the governor whom his father F 611·3·2 had left in charge of the land, and asked for his father's weapons, that he might go hunting.

'I will not give them to thee,' said the governor, 'for there is no knowing but that thou wilt kill thyself.'

am shia bliadhn' déug, Gu'm falbhainn fhéin le Teàrlach'—'If only I were sixteen years, I'd march away with Charlie,' a song of the '45. Welsh young men of the olden time came of age at fourteen.—*Celtic Review*, iv., p. 312.

'Cha lughaide nach bithinn-sa fada 'gan iarraidh ort;
gum faighinn fhéin iad.'

Ma bha glas air na h-airm, bhrist esan i, is thug e a
mach claidheamh agus gunna. Chaidh e a dh' ionnsuigh
an uachdarain a dh'fhàg a athair air an fhearann, is ghearr
e a chluas deth.

Q451·6

Ghabh e roimhe is chaidh e do'n bheinn-sheilge. Bha
e fad an latha a' sealg feadh na beinne. Am beul na
h-oidhche, an uair a bha e tighinn dachaidh, ciod e a
chunnaic e ach Laoch mór Bodaich [1] air leathad na beinne
ag eubhach da.

G 101

'Trobhad an so, fhir òig, is gun tugamaid cluich air na
dìsnean.' Chaidh e far an robh am Bodach is thòisich
iad air cluich. Chuir Iain an cluich air an Laoch.

N 2·0·1*

'Tog buaidh do chluiche,' ars an Laoch Bodaich.

N 2·0·2*

'Chan ['eil] fhios 'm fhéin ciod e thogas mi. Chan
'eil dùil 'm gu bheil airgiod agad. Chan 'eil aodach ort,
is chan 'eil airm agad a bheir mise uait am buaidh cluiche,
ach leigidh sinn seachad an cluich ud mar a tha, is théid
sinn ann fhathast.'

Chaidh iad ann a rithist, is chuir an Laoch an cluich
an uair sin air Iain Og.

'Tog buaidh do chluiche,' ars Iain Og.

'Ma tà, gu dearbh, nì mise sin,' ars an Laoch Bodaich.

H 935·1*

'Is e sin——

Z 85*
D 1273

THUSA CHUR FO GHEASAN IS FO CHROISEAN—
Fo naoidh buaraichean mnatha sìdhe, siùbhlaiche, seachranaiche,

F 360

An laogh beag is meataiche 's is mi-threòraiche na thu fhìn

H 942*

A thoirt do chinn 's do chluais 's do chaitheamh beatha
dhìot,

C 650

Mur a toir thu chugam-sa aig dà uair dheug am màireach,
Iain Og, Mac Rìgh na Frainge.' [3]

---

[1] Bodach, an old man, but frequently a name for a male supernatural.

[2] Similar magnanimity shown by hero in *W. H. Tales*, ii., No. 51.

[3] The meaning of this curious incantation or be-spelling 'run' is, that
if the hero failed to perform the task thus laid upon him by his adversary,
evil would meet him in the shape of the dreaded fairy-woman, who is for
ever going to and fro upon the earth, seeking opportunity for mischief, and
leading wayfarers astray. She would strike him with her nine deadly cow-

'It is likely that I shall be a long time asking thee for them ; until I get them for myself.'

As the weapons were locked up, he broke the lock, and fetched out a sword and a gun. He went back to the governor whom his father had left over the land, and cut off his ear.

Q 451·6

Then he went his ways to the hunting-hill. All day long he hunted over it in all directions. At nightfall, when he was coming home, what should he see but a great Champion Bodach [1] on the slope of the hill, shouting at him.

G 101

'Come hither, young fellow, that we may have a game with the dice.' He went over to the Bodach, and they began to play. Iain won the game against the Champion.

'Claim the stakes of thy gaming,' said the Champion Bodach.

N 2·0·1*

'I scarcely know what to claim. I hardly expect that thou hast any money. Thou hast neither raiment nor arms that I might take from thee as the fruits of victory, but we will let that game pass, and engage in the game again.' [2]

N 2·0·2*

So again they engaged in play, and the Champion won the game that time against Iain Og.

'Claim the stakes of thy gaming,' said Iain Og.

'Well then, I will indeed do so,' said the Champion Bodach. 'The stakes are these——

H 935·1*

To LAY THEE UNDER SPELLS AND CROSSES,

Z 85*

Under [pain of being struck by] the nine cowfetters of the wildly-roaming, traveller-deluding fairy-woman,

D 1273

So that some sorry little wight more feeble and misguided than thyself

F 360

Take thy head, thine ear and thy life's career from thee

H 942*

Unless at the morrow's noon thou bring to me,

C 650

Iain Og, the Son of the King of France.' [3]

fetters, and he would thereby be rendered so fey and unlucky, so awkward and silly that the most contemptible persons would be able to overcome him in battle and behead him. See Tale No. 25 (MS. vol. x., No. 47). *W. H. Tales,* i., No. 1; ii., Nos. 46, 51. *Superstitions,* p. 133. *Waifs and Strays,* ii., pp. 347, 487; iii., pp. 2, 35, 260; iv., pp. 177, 212, 233, 261-4. *Trans. Gael. Soc. Inverness,* xvii., p. 235; xxv., p. 214; xxxiv., p. 21. Some of the incantations to be found under these references have been wrongly and meaninglessly translated. ·

'Nì mi sin,' ars esan.

Dh'fhalbh e dhachaidh an oidhche sin, ghabh e a
thràth-oidche, is chaidh e a thàmh.—An là-'r-na-mhàireach,
dh'éirich e is ghabh e a bhiadh, is thug e air falbh air.
Ràinig e an t-àite 'san robh e an dé, is bha an Laoch
roimhe air cnoc an uair a ràinig e.

'An robh thu cho math is do ghealladh?' ars an Laoch.

'Bha mi sin—is e fhéin a tha agad ann an so an diugh,'
ars Iain Og.

'Nam biodh fios agam air an sin, cha deach thu dachaidh
mar a chaidh thu an dé,' ars am Bodach.

'Ma tà, dà thrian de t'eagal ort fhéin, agus a h-aon
ormsa dheth,' ars Iain Og.

Cha robh Iain ach bog, lag, gòrach, ann an ceann
nan sia bliadhna.[1] Thòisich e fhéin agus am Bodach air
a' chéile, agus is ann an sin a bha an gleac aig a' Bhodach is
aig a' bhalach.

G 317

F 943

DHÈANADH IAD BOGAN AIR A' CHREAGAN,
Agus creagan air a' bhogan.

Z 85*

An uair a b'ìsle rachadh iad fodha,
Rachadh iad fodha gu an sùilean,
'S an uair a b'àirde rachadh iad fodha,
Rachadh iad fodha gu an glùinean.
Ach smuaintich Iain Og an so
Gun robh e fad o a chàirdean,
Agus goirid o a nàimhdean.
Thug e an togail shunndach, shanntach, aighearach ud da,
'S chuir e seachad air mullach a chinn e,
'S bhuail e a chliathach ris an talamh,

G 510

'S bhrisd e dà aisinn fodha, 's té os a chionn.[2]

For Irish examples, see *Béaloideas*, iii., p. 144; vii., pp. 135, 180. See also for
connected matters, including the cowfetter, *The Wizard's Gillie*, p. 136, foll.
Witchcraft, pp. 11, 12. *Rosg*, p. 209. *Superstitions*, p. 219. *Survivals*, pp. 29,
296. A. R. Forbes, *Gaelic Names*, p. 97. *Scot. Celt. Rev.*, i., p. 71 (1881).
An Gàidheal, iv., p. 304; v., p. 262 (1875-6). *Larminie*, pp. 101-2, 203. *Celtic
Magazine*, xiii., p. 275. Hyde, *Beside the Fire*, p. 21. In speaking of the
various *runs* that occur in this story, sailing runs, fighting runs, be-spelling
runs, etc., Hector MacLean, the transcriber, says in a note to No. 31, that
they 'resemble the chorus of a song, and are repeated in these tales for the
same purpose, that is, to give spirit and animation to the whole. They are
called *siùbhlaichean*, or rapid parts. . . . They are repeated generally in a

'Very good, I will,' he answered.

He went home that night, took his supper, and went to bed.—On the morrow, he rose, took his food, and set forth. He went to the same place where he had been the day before, and when he got there, found the Champion was there on a hillock before him.

'Hast thou been as good as thy word?' said the Champion.

'That I have—[he whom thou didst desire me to bring] he it is whom thou hast here to-day,' said Iain Og.

'Had I known that, thou hadst not gone home yesterday as thou didst,' said the Bodach.

'Well then, two-thirds of the fear of thee be upon thyself, and one-third be upon me,' said Iain Og.

Now Iain was but soft, weak, and silly at the time, being only at the end of his sixth year.[1] But he and the Bodach attacked each other, and then and there the Bodach and the boy had a mighty wrestling.
G 317

> THEY WOULD MAKE A MARSH OF THE ROCK,   F 943
> And a rock of the marsh.
> When they sank into the earth most deeply,   Z 85*
> They would sink to their eyes,
> And where they sank the least,
> They would sink to their knees.
> But now Iain Og remembered,
> That he was far from his friends,
> And near to his enemies.
> And giving the other such a cheerful, eager, merry heave,
> Pitched him over the top of his head,
> Dashed him upon his side to earth,
> And broke two ribs under him, and one above him.[2]   G 510

half-serious, half-humorous, rapid tone.' Other Highland reciters called these passages *ruitheanna*, runs. Formerly the words *retoric* and *rosg* were applied to them.—*Celtic Review*, iv., p. 90. See Appendix, p. 504.

[1] The suggestion is that though a mere child, he gave promise of prodigious strength.—*Waifs and Strays*, ii., pp. 359, 486. Fionn was enormously strong at seven, some say twelve years.—*Celtic Review*, ii., p. 137. *Cf.* Zeus, Herakles.

[2] The last two lines of this 'wrestling run' have been explained to me to mean that the hero threw his enemy to the ground upon his side, broke two of the ribs of that side, and one of the ribs of the other or uppermost side. For 'wrestling runs,' see *Waifs and Strays*, ii., pp. 297, 345, 359, 365, 486. *Rosg Gàidhlig*, 2nd ed., p. 212. *Bèaloideas*, vii., p. 201.

'Tha am bàs os do chionn ! ciod è t'éirig ?' ars Iain.

'Chan 'eil éirig agamsa duit,' ars am Bodach ; 'is dona
as fhiach duit mo bhàs ; b'fhearr duit aon bhuille a bheirinn
air do shon na mo bhàs air fad. Bheir mise mionnan duit
fo fhaobhar do chuid armaibh, nach 'eil buille a bhuaileas
mi gu bràth nach ann leat a bhuaileas mi, is nach buail
mi gin 'nad aghaidh am feasd.'

Q 82
N 812

'Ma tà, is fhearr domhsa sin na do bhàs ; ach cha leig
mi as thu am feasd, gus am bi fhios 'm ciod è an t-ainm
a th'ort,' arsa Iain Og.

C 432·2*

'Tha orm,' ars am Bodach, 'Ladhar Dubh [1] Mac Brian
[Gàrraidh].'

'Ma tà, gu dearbh, tha ainm iongantach ort, gun
teagamh,' ars Iain Og. Dh'fhalbh iad is bha iad a' dol
dachaidh le chéile. Chaidh Ladhar [Dubh] dachaidh
comhla ri Iain Og.

An là-'r-na-mhàireach, chaidh Iain Og do'n bheinn a
shealg daimh, is dh'fhan Ladhar [Dubh] aig an tigh.
An uair a bha e tighinn dachaidh as a' bheinn-sheilge am
beul na h-oidhche, ciod e chunnaic e ach Cailleach Mhór
os a chionn shuas, is i air leth-shùil, is air leth-chois, is
air leth-làimh.

F 510

'Thig a nuas, Iain Oig, Mhic Rìgh na Frainge, is gun
cuireamaid cluich air na cairtean,' ars a' Chailleach.

'Tha mi fhéin coma, o'n a tha fios agaibh gu bheil
rìoghachd ann, ged a rachainn suas comhla ruibh,' ars
Iain Og.

Chaidh e suas, is chaidh e fhéin is a' Chailleach a
dh'iomairt.

Chuir Iain Og an cluich air a' Chaillich.

N 2·0·1*

'Tog buaidh do chluich,' ars a' Chailleach.

N 2·0·2*

'Chan fhios 'm fhéin ciod e am buaidh cluich a thogas

[1] The name might also be translated *Black Shank*, *Black Hoof*, etc. Many
characters derive their names from some peculiarity of foot, foot-gear, or
from their speed of foot. Without knowing the other's name, the hero would
not have obtained complete mastery over him. Black Toe later on turns
out to be sister's son to the Queen of Lochlann, who lives underground. His
father, Brian, may have been a sun-god. Another Brian marries a sun-

'Death is above thee! with what wilt thou ransom thee?' said Iain.

'Ransom have I none to give thee,' said the Bodach; 'my death is of no value to thee; far better for thee were any single blow that I might strike on thy behalf than all the good there might be in my death. I will swear to thee by the edges of thy weapons, that I will never strike a blow that shall not be on thy behalf, and that I will never strike a blow against thee.'

Q 82

N 812

'Certainly, that would profit me more than thy death; still I will never let thee go, till I know what name thou bearest,' said Iain Og.

C 432·2*

'The name I bear,' said the Bodach, 'is Black Toe,[1] Mac Brian [Gàrraidh].'

'Truly thou bearest a strange name, without a doubt,' said Iain Og. They set off and went home together. Yes, [Black] Toe went home with Iain Og.

On the morrow, Iain Og went to the hill to hunt the deer, and [Black] Toe stayed at home. When Iain was coming home from the hunting-hill at night-fall, what should he see but a Great Cailleach [2] above him, having only one eye, one foot [or leg] and one hand [or arm].

F 510

'Come hither, Iain Og, thou Son of the King of France, that we may have a game at cards,' said the Cailleach.

'Since thou knowest that there really is a kingdom, I don't mind if I do go up and join you,' said Iain Og.

He went up, and he and she engaged in play.

Iain Og won the game against the Cailleach.

'Claim the stakes of thy gaming,' said the Cailleach.

N 2·0·1*

'I do not know what stakes to claim of thee; I see not

N 2·0·2*

---

goddess.—*W. H. Tales*, ii., No. 46, var. 4. For the incident of allowing a vanquished enemy to become a retainer or follower, see *W. H. Tales*, i., No. 6; iii., pp. 242, 247, 267, or 228, 232, 252; *Waifs and Strays*, iv., p. 184.

[2] *Cailleach*, old woman, witch, sorceress: frequently a name for a feminine supernatural, sometimes of colossal size.

G 200

mi uait ; chan fhaic mi rud sam bith agad a bheir mi
uait, ach théid sinn ann fhathast,' ars Iain Og.[1]
Chaidh iad ann an sin a rithist, is chuir ise an cluich
air Iain. 'Tog a nis buaidh do chluich,' ars Iain.

H 942*   'Ma tà, gu dearbh, nì mi sin,' ars a' Chailleach;

Z 85*   'CUIRIDH MI THUSA FO GHEASAN 'S FO CHROISEAN,
H 935   Fo naoidh buaraichean mnatha sìdhe, siùbhlaiche, seach-
D 1273   ranaiche,
F 360   An laogh beag is meataiche 's is mi-threòiriche na thu fhìn,
           A thoirt do chinn, 's do chluais, 's do chaitheamh beatha
             dhìot,
C 650   Mura faigh thu a mach dhomhsa
H 1378·2* Fios aigheir agus mi-aigheir Rìgh Eireann.'

           'Tha sin gu math,' ars Iain, 'ach—

H 951·1*   CUIRIDH MISE THUSA FO GHEASAN 'S FO CHROISEAN,
           Fo naoidh buaraichean mnatha sìdhe siùbhlaiche, seach-
F 360   ranaiche,
           An laogh beag is meataiche 's is mi-threòiriche na thu fhìn,
           A thoirt do chinn, 's do chluais, 's do chaitheamh beatha
             dhìot
           Mura bi thusa
           Air a' cheart àite air a' chnoc so air a bheil thu a nis
           Gus an till mise air m'ais;
           Ma thàirneas tu chugad an làmh is faide uait
           N' as giorra na tha i,
           No an té as giorra dhuit
           A chur uait n' as faide na tha i;
D 5·1   Còta stobach glas a bhi os cionn do dhà ghuaille,
           'S t'aghaidh anns a h-uile sian a thig á athar,
           Gus an till mise air m'ais le naidheachd.' [2]

       Chaidh e dachaidh.   An uair a chaidh e a stigh, shuidh
   e, is chuir e a uileann air a' bhòrd, is leig e osann.—'Osann
   mhic rìgh fo gheasaibh,' ars an t-uachdaran ; 'ma's ann
   airson a' chluas a chur dhìomsa tha thu ag osnaich, tha
   toil do ghnothuich agad.'

       [1] Gambling, at which the Hen-wife, a sorceress, loses, occurs in *Larminie*,
   p. 206.
       [2] After the hero has been be-spelled to the performance of the task, he
   sometimes, as in the above instance, counter-be-spells his mysterious enemy,
   who is as much at the mercy of the incantations of mortals, as mortals are

anything about thee that I might take from thee, but we will engage in play again,' said Iain Og.[1]

They engaged in it again, and this time she won the game against Iain Og. 'Claim the stakes of thy gaming,' said Iain.

'Verily, I will,' said the Cailleach;   H 942*

'I LAY THEE UNDER SPELLS AND CROSSES,   Z 85*
Under [pain of being struck by] the nine cowfetters of the wildly- H 935
    roaming, traveller-deluding fairy-woman,   D 1273
That some sorry little wight more feeble and misguided than F 360
    thyself
Take thy head, thine ear, and thy life's career from thee,
Unless thou find out for me   C 650
All there is to know about the King of Erin's joy and woe.'   H 1378·2*

'That is all very well,' quoth Iain, 'but—

I NOW LAY THEE UNDER SPELLS AND CROSSES,   H 951·1*
Under [pain of being struck by] the nine cowfetters of the wildly-
    roaming, traveller-deluding fairy-woman,   F 360
That some sorry little wight, more feeble and misguided than
    thyself,
Take thy head, thine ear, and thy life's career from thee
If thou do not remain
On the same place in this hill where now thou art
Till I come back again ;
Or if thou dost draw the hand that is farther from thee
Closer to thee than it is,
Or put the hand that is nearer to thee
Farther from thee than it is ;
A short gray cloak must be over thy two shoulders,   D 5·1
And thy face fronting every storm that blows from heaven,
Till I come back again with tidings.' [2]

Home then went Iain. When he went in, he sat him down, put his elbow on the board, and heaved a sigh.— 'The sigh of a king's son under spells,' said the governor; 'but if it is for having cut off my ear thou art sighing, it serves thee right.'

under the compulsion of supernaturals. The enemy honourably observes the conditions or obligations laid upon her. This is the rule, no matter how dire the counter-spells may be. In laying them upon her, the hero takes the first step towards turning the tide of affairs in his own favour. For the whole situation, *cf.* pp. 5, 19, *n*, and Appendix, p. 504.

'Ma tà, droch comdhail ort, a thrusdair ! Nam
biodh mo chlaidheamh aig mo làimh, chuirinn a' chluas
eile dhìot, chionn dùil a bhi agad fhéin gun rachainn-sa a
dh'osnaich airṣon a' chluas a chur dhìot !'

Arsa Ladhar [Dubh], 'Osann mhic rìgh fo gheasaibh !
Tha mi ag aithneachadh gur h-i a' Chailleach Ghlas a
choinnich thu.[1]†† Ciod e na geasan a chuir i ort ?'

'Chuir i orm gun tugainn fios aigheir agus mi-aigheir
Rìgh Eireann d'a h-ionnsuigh,' ars Iain.

'An do chuir thu fhéin geasan oirre ?' arsa Ladhar
[Dubh].

'Chuir,' arsa Iain.

'Ciod e na geasan a chuir thu oirre ?' arsa Ladhar
[Dubh].††

Dh' innis e siod.

'Glé mhath,' arsa Ladhar Dubh, 'ach is beag cron a
nì sin oirre-se. Bidh ise air a' chnoc an sin 'na cual
chnàmh, gus an till thu, ma thilleas tu. Is an uair a thilleas

E 55·1·1*   tu, is a bhios tu ag innseadh do naidheachd, bidh na
cnàmhan a' cruinneachadh r'a chéile gus am bi i cho beò

E 31   's a bha i riamh.

'Tha nighean loth fhiadhaich[2] aig t'athair ann an
stàbull, is chan fhac i leus de thalamh no de athar riamh,
mura faca i a mach air uinneig e. Feuch ri dol air a
muin is gum marcaicheadh tu air falbh i, is mura fuirich
thu air a muin, cha ruig thu leas dol air an astar.'

B 181   Chaidh e a dh' ionnsuigh na loth, is thòisich e ri dol air
a muin, is a cheud turus a chaidh e air a muin, thilg i air
an làr e. [B'e a leithid eile dha air an dara turus.]

'Dona e ! dona e ! Feumaidh tu a feuchainn an treas
uair, is mura fuirich thu air a muin an treas uair, cha
ruig thu leas dol air an astar.' Chaidh e air a muin an

---

[1] The sentences between these daggers and the next two occur twice in
the MS. suggesting that it is a fair copy of another. Similar reduplications
occur in the MSS. of other tales.

[2] Lit. the daughter of a wild foal. In W. H. Tales, i., No. 2, var. 2 (see

'Then may evil meet thee, rascal ! Were my glaive
at hand, I would strike off thine other ear, merely for
thinking that I would so much as sigh for having cut off
an ear of thine.'

Quoth [Black] Toe, 'The sigh of a king's son under
spells ! I perceive that the Gray Cailleach has met
thee.[1]†† What spells has she laid upon thee ?'

'She bespelled me to find out and bring her all there
is to know about the King of Erin's joy and woe,' said
Iain.

'Didst thou also lay spells upon her ?' said [Black] Toe.

'I did,' said Iain.

'What spells didst thou lay upon her ?' said [Black]
Toe.††

He related what they were.

'Very good,' said Black Toe, 'yet that will do her little
harm. She will but remain on that hill, a mere heap of
bones, until thou return, if return thou dost. And when E 55·1·1*
thou dost return and art telling thy tidings, the bones will
begin to gather themselves together again till she be as much
alive as ever she was. E 31

'Now there is in a stable a young filly,[2] a wild one,
belonging to thy father, and she has never seen a glimpse
of earth or sky, unless it were through a window. Try
to mount her and ride off on her, but if thou canst not
keep on her back, thou needest not undertake the
journey.'

Off he went to the filly, and began to try and mount B 181
her, but the first time he got on her back, she threw him
to the ground. [The same thing happened to him the
second time.]

'That is bad ! bad ! Yet thou must try again the
third time, for if thou canst not stick on to her back
the third time, thou needest not undertake the journey.'

MS. vol. x., No. 83 (2)), occurs a 'steed, that had never seen a blink of earth
or air [recte, sky].' See also Béaloideas, i., pp. 76, 273. For the prison of
Liath Macha, Cuchulainn's divine steed, see Proc. Royal Irish Academy, xxx.,
p. 81.

treas uair, is bha e slaodadh ris a' ghath mhuinge aice,
gus an d'fhuair e e fhéin a chur ceart air a muin.

'Trobhad a nis air mo chùl,' ars Iain Og ri Ladhar Dubh,
'is bidh sinn a' falbh.'
'Falbh thusa! Cho math is gun coisich thusa leis an
fhalaire, coisichidh mise le mo chois.'[1]
Dh'fhalbh iad is bhuail iad air coiseachd is air
astarachadh. Bha iad an so an déidh falbh is an rìoghachd
fhàgail ás an déidh air fad. Bha iad a' dol gus a bhi a
stigh ann an rìoghachd Eireann. Dh' amais cnoc maol
gorm riu an sin, is chunnaic iad beagan toit as. An uair
a chunnaic iad an toit as—

'Ma tà, gu dearbh,' ars Iain Og, 'seachad air a so cha
téid mi, gus am bi fhios 'am ciod è tha gabhail còmhnuidh
anns a' chnoc. [Is] ceart cho dòcha gur h-ann an so a
tha an rud a tha sinn ag iarraidh, is an àite eile.'
Dh' fhalbh iad is ghabh iad a dh' ionnsuigh an àite an
robh an toit.
Fhuair iad rathad a' dol a sìos, is ghabh iad a sìos, is
F 721·5   bha an aitreabh a bu bhrèagha chunnaic duine riamh
air a dhèanamh fo'n talamh an sin.
Bha dorsair an sin aig an dorus, is dh' iarr iad cead air
an leigeil a stigh.
'Gu dearbh cha leig mise a stigh sibh, ach innsibh domh
có tha ag iarraidh cead dol a stigh, is théid mi a dh' iarraidh
cead air mo mhaighstir is air mo bhanmhaighstir.'
'Abair thusa gu bheil [Iain Og] Mac Rìgh na Fraing
ag iarraidh fosglaidh anns an dorus,' ars Iain.

Chaidh e suas is thuirt e gun robh Iain Og, Mac Rìgh
na F rainge, ag iarraidh fosglaidh anns an dorus.
'Ma tà! beul sìos ort! an uair a chaidh thu a chumail
a leithid de fhadal air Iain Og Mac Rìgh na Frainge
nach do leig thu a stigh e!' ars a bhanmhaighstir ris an
dorsair.

---

[1] The filly, or palfrey, now drops out of the story, an obvious defect;
contrast the large part played by the horse in Nos. 1 and 2.

He mounted her the third time, and managed to cling on to the part of her mane next her withers, until he had got himself fairly settled on her back.

'Come up now behind me,' said Iain Og to Black Toe, 'and we will be off.'

'Be off thyself! However fast thou goest with the palfrey, I can go as fast on foot.' [1]

Off they went, and applied themselves to hard going and rapid travelling. They were now well on their way, and had left the kingdom completely behind them. They were travelling with the intention of entering the kingdom of Erin. They came to a blue, bluff hillock, and observed a little smoke issuing from it. When they saw the smoke coming forth—

'Well, truly,' said Iain Og, 'past this hill I will not go until I know what dwells in it. The thing we are seeking is just as likely to be here, as in any other place.'

So they went to the place where the smoke was.

They found a path going downwards; down it they went, and there, built under ground, was the most beautiful F 721·5 dwelling that man ever saw.

There was a doorkeeper at the door, and they asked him for leave to enter.

'Indeed I will not let you in; but tell me who is asking for leave to enter, and I will go and ask leave of my master and mistress.'

'Say thou that [Iain Og] the Son of the King of France is at the door and asking that it may be opened,' said Iain.

He went in and said that Iain Og, the Son of the King of France, was at the door asking that it might be opened.

'Well then! mayest thou be laid on thy face dead! for having wearied Iain Og the Son of the King of France so much as not to let him in!' said his mistress to the doorkeeper.

Fhuair iad a stigh, is an uair a chaidh iad a stigh, bha fàilte
rompa aig a' Bhan-righ a bha gabhail còmhnuidh an sin.[1]
Bhuail iad air cur seachad na h-oidhche le toil-inntinn leis a'
Bhan-righ. Dh'fhaighnich a' Bhan-righ de Iain ciod è
an turus air an robh e. Thuirt e gun robh e dol a dh'
fhaotainna mach fios aigheir agus mi-aigheir Rìgh Eireann.

'Ma tà, Iain Oig, a Mhic Rìgh na Frainge, is iomadh
mac rìgh agus ridire air thoiseach ortsa a dh' fhalbh air an
astar sin nach do thill ; ach chan 'eil fios, air a shon sin,
an do ghiorraich sin do shaoghal-sa.

'Ach,' ars ise, 'bheir mise ceud fear sleagh, agus ceud
fear cruit, [agus ceud fear] saighead dhuitsa gu do dhìon
agus gu do ghleidheadh gus an till thu air t' ais. Tha
mise an so o chionn bliadhna 'gam fhalach,' ars ise, 'o'n
a b'éigin domh mo rìoghachd fhagail. Is mise Ban-righ
Rìgh Lochlainn.[2] An uair a thilleas tusa air t'ais, fàgaidh
tu agam na daoine a rithist.'

Dh' fhalbh iad is thog iad orra gu lùchairt Rìgh Eireann.

'Ciod è tha mi smuaineachadh ?' arsa Ladhar [Dubh].
'Ciod è tha thu smuaineachadh ?' arsa Iain Og.
'Tha mi smuaineachadh,' arsa Ladhar Dubh, 'gur co
math dhomh na daoine so mharbhadh, is iad a bhi falbh as
mo dhéidh mar so.'
'O ! na leigeadh am fortan gun dèan thusa sin,' ars
Iain, 'an rud a thug a' Bhan-righ domh fhéin, thusa dol
a mharbhadh is a chur a dhìth orm.'
'Chan e sin rud a nì mi,' arsa Ladhar [Dubh], 'ach
falbhaidh thusa is coisichidh tu gu math, agus tillidh mise
is faighnichidh mi de'n bhoirionnach ciod e am feum a
tha annta, is mur 'eil feum annta, cuiridh mi gu bàs iad.'

---

[1] The doorkeeper's master, who is presumably the King of Lochlann, is
not mentioned again, and does not appear nor act any part. It may be
mere coincidence, but there is another of Islay's tales, in which the King of
Lochlann fails to appear or do anything, though mentioned as the father or
husband of other characters. See *Folk-Lore* (1890), i., p. 373 and *Trans. Gael.
Soc. Inverness*, xxv., p. 182.

[2] The Queen gives no reason for having to leave her kingdom, suggesting
that some incident has been omitted. The fact that she dwells underground

They got in, and when they got in, the Queen who was dwelling there, had a welcome awaiting them. They set themselves to passing the night with the Queen in pleasure of mind.[1] The Queen enquired of Iain upon what errand he was bent. He said he was going to find out all there was to know about the King of Erin's joy and woe.

'Well then, Iain Og, thou Son of the King of France, many a king's son and many a knight's son have there been before thee who set out on that errand, and never returned; nevertheless, it is not at all certain that that has shortened thy life.

'But,' said she, 'I will give thee one hundred spearmen, one hundred crowders (players on the crowd) [and one hundred] bow[men] to protect and preserve thee till thou return. I have been here for a year hiding myself,' said she, 'for I was compelled to leave my kingdom. I am the Queen of the King of Lochlann.[2] When thou comest back, bring those men back also, and leave them with me.'

They went away, and made for the King of Erin's palace.

'[Knowest thou] what I am thinking?' said [Black] Toe.

'What art thou thinking?' said Iain Og.

'I am thinking,' said Black Toe, 'that it is as well for me to kill these men as for them to be following me like this.'

'O ! may fortune [3] forbid that thou shouldst do that,' said Iain, 'that thou shouldst by killing them deprive me of what the Queen gave me.'

'Well then, I will not do so,' said [Black] Toe, 'but do thou go on, and go hard, while I return and ask that woman what is the use of them; then if they are of no use, I will put them to death.'

---

seems to confirm the theory that at one time Lochlann represented some other world. See Alfred Nutt, *Ossian and the Ossianic Literature*, p. 72, quoting Prof. Sir John Rhys (*Hibbert Lectures*, 1886, p. 355) who thought that 'Lochlann, like the Welsh Llychlyn, before it came to mean the home of the Norsemen, denoted a mysterious country in the lochs and seas.' In Denmark, Valhall means Dead-hall, and was originally an underground locality. See Gudmund Schütte, *Folk-Lore*, xxxv., pp. 364, 371.

A 661·1

[3] Providence.

Thill e, is cha robh e ri saothair faighneachd airson an dorsair. Thilg e an dorus roimhe air an ùrlar is ghabh e a steach.

'Ciod e am feum a tha anns na daoine ud a chuir thu leam an siod?' arsa Ladhar Dubh ri Ban-rìgh Lochlainn. 'O! dunaich ort![1] ged is tu mac peathar mo mhàthar, chan ann leat a chuir mi iad, ach le Iain Og, Mac Rìgh na Frainge,' ars a' Bhan-righ.

'O! is coma leamsa gleogaireachd ghrannda cainnt, ach innis domh ciod e am feum a tha annta,' arsa Ladhar [Dubh].

'Tha sin annta, feum gu leòir,' ars ise; 'ma thig nàmhaid sam bith as do dhéidh, no 'nad chòir, cuiridh tu an ceud fear sleagh romhad, cuiridh tu an ceud fear cruit air gach taobh dhìot, is an ceud fear saighead as do dhéidh. Chan 'eil dad a thig romhad nach marbh an ceud fear sleagh. Chan 'eil dad a thig air gach taobh dhìot nach marbh an ceud fear cruit. Le ceòl agus le aighear, bheir iad an leann-tàth[2] is an lùth asda. An ceud fear saighead, bidh iad as do dhéidh, is chan 'eil dad a thig ort a thaobh do chùil nach marbh an ceud fear saighead.'

'Na creutairean bochda, tha feum annta gu dearbh.'
Dh'fhalbh e an so, is cha b'fhada bha e air falbh an uair a rug e air Iain.
'O! na truaghain!' arsa Ladhar [Dubh] ri Iain, 'cha mharbh sinn idir iad, tha feum annta.'
Ghabh iad air an aghaidh, is dh' astaraich iad gus an do ràinig iad lùchairt Rìgh Eireann.

Z 85*   BHUAIL IAD BEUM SGEITHE—
Cath, air neo comhrag,
H 1378·2*   Air neo fios aigheir no mi-aigheir Rìgh Eireann
A chur d'an ionnsuigh.

---

[1] *dunaidh*?

[2] Hector MacLean, the scribe, has made a note in the MS. here, about *leann-tàth*, the word translated *cohesion*. 'Leann-tàth. The humours of the body, the very vital juice of the body. A sarcastic hint at the enervating effect of soft music.' Dr H. C. Gillies, *Gaelic Names of Diseases and of Diseased States*, pp. 8, 32, gives *lionn-tàthaidh* as meaning *callus-fluid*, and says it is a very fine expression. The recognition, as this is, of a special healing or repairing fluid was a very clear step indeed into pathological knowledge, and the

He went back, but never troubled to ask for the door-keeper. He hurled the door in before him upon the floor, and in he went.

'What is the use of those men that thou didst send with me ?' said Black Toe to the Queen of Lochlann.

'O ! pest upon thee ! [1] though thou art the son of my mother's sister, I sent them to help, not thee, but Iain Og, the Son of the King of France,' said the Queen.

'O ! I have no liking for unseemly aimless talk; tell me what is the use of them,' said [Black] Toe.

'Useful they certainly are, useful enough,' said she; 'whatever enemy come after thee or near thee, place the hundred spearmen before thee, the hundred crowders on each side of thee, and the hundred bowmen behind thee. There is nothing that can meet thee in front that the hundred spearmen will not kill. There is nothing that can come upon thee on either side that the hundred crowders will not kill. With music and mirth, they will take the very cohesion [2] and strength out of them [= the enemies' bodies]. The hundred bowmen will be behind thee, and there is nothing that will come upon thee from behind that the hundred bowmen will not kill.'

'The poor creatures ! they are of use indeed.'

Upon this he went off, and had not been going long, when he overtook Iain.

'O ! the poor things !' said [Black] Toe to Iain, 'we will not kill them at all, there is some use in them.'

On they pressed, and travelled hard till they came to the palace of the King of Erin.

THEY SOUNDED A BOOMING SHIELD-CLASHING CHALLENGE—   Z 85*
[Demanding] a battle, or else a combat,
Or else that the story of the joy and woe of Erin's King   H 1378·2*
Should be sent forth to them.

---

word *tàthadh* in this connection is an exceedingly graphic and correct statement. It means to join or rather to weld together, as a smith welds two pieces of red-hot iron. In fact, the word is now limited to this special signification.' The auxiliaries granted by the Queen of Lochlann never come into action or act any part, suggesting that incidents have been omitted. Black Toe's rudeness to his maternal aunt suggests that some other incident has been omitted. As it stands, his rudeness seems to be quite unmotivated.

Siod an rud a gheibheadh iad—
Cath, air neo comhrag,
'S cha b'e fios aigheir no mi-aigheir Rìgh Eireann.

H 1378·2*

Chuireadh a mach
Cóig ceud lùth-ghaisgeach,
Cóig ceud treun-ghaisgeach,
Agus cóig ceud làn-ghaisgeach.

Chuir Iain Og agus Ladhar Dubh as do na bha an siod.

Z 85*

Bhuail iad beum sgéithe an darna uair—
Cath, air neo comhrag,
Air neo, fios aigheir agus mi-aigheir Rìgh Eireann
A chur d'an ionnsuigh.

Siod an rud a gheibheadh iad—
Cath, air neo comhrag,
'S cha b'e fios aigheir no mi-aigheir Rìgh Eireann.

Chuireadh a mach uibhir eile de ghaisgich, agus chuir
Iain agus Ladhar [Dubh] ás daibh sin.

Z 85*

Bhuail iad an treas uair beum sgéithe—
Cath, air neo comhrag,
Air neo, fios aigheir agus mi-aigheir Rìgh Eireann
[A chur d'an ionnsuigh.] [1]

Arsa Rìgh Eireann, 'Cha bhi mi fhéin a' cosd mo chuid
daoine airson fios m' aigheir agus mo mhi-aigheir a thoirt
daibh. Thugaibh a stigh na daoine is gun tugainn fios
m'aigheir agus mo mhi-aigheir daibh.' Thugadh an sin a
stigh Iain Og, Mac Rìgh na Frainge, agus Ladhar Dubh
Mac Brian Gàrraidh.

Thòisich iad air caitheamh na cuirme le aighear is le
toil-inntinn, [agus thòisich Rìgh Eireann air innseadh
naidheachd].[2]

---

[1] For similar challenging-and-fighting runs, and for different fighting runs,
see W. H. Tales, ii., Nos. 35, 36, 38, 52; iii., Nos. 76, 84, 86. Trans. Gael. Soc.
Inverness, xiii., p. 69, foll. Leabhar na Féinne, p. 114. An Gàidheal (1876), v.,
p. 262. Waifs and Strays, ii., p. 497; iii., pp. 39, 60, 239; iv., p. 292.

[2] After most desperate fighting, fraternization may succeed and all quarrel
be forgotten. See W. H. Tales, iii., No. 86. With the King's tale, compare
Waifs and Strays, ii., pp. 77, 87, 454; iii., No. 4. Fionn ann an Tigh a' Bhlàir-

This is what they should have—
A battle, or else a combat,
But not the story of the joy and woe of Erin's King.   H 1378·2*

Then there were sent out
Five hundred lusty heroes,
Five hundred mighty heroes,
And five hundred complete heroes.

Iain Og and Black Toe killed all of them.

A second time they sounded a booming shield-clashing challenge Z 85*
[Desiring] a battle, or else a combat,
Or else, that the story of the joy and woe of Erin's King
Should be sent forth to them.

This is what they should have—
A battle, or else a combat,
But not the story of the joy and woe of Erin's King.

There were sent out as many warriors as before, but
Iain and [Black] Toe killed them.

A third time they sounded a booming shield-clashing challenge— Z 85*
[Desiring] a battle, or else a combat,
Or else, that the story of the joy and woe of Erin's King,
[Should be sent forth to them.]¹

Said the King of Erin, 'I will not waste my men any
more over this matter of telling them the story of my joy
and my woe. Bring the strangers in, that I may tell them
the story of my joy and my woe.' Then were brought
in Iain Og, the Son of the King of France, and Black Toe,
MacBrian Gàrraidh.

Then they began to ply the feast with merriment and
delight, [and the King of Erin began to tell his story].²

Bhuidhe, A. MacLaren & Sons, Glasgow. *W. H. Tales*, ii., Nos. 29, 38.
Islay's MS. vol. xi., No. 173. 'Neart,' *Imtheachta an Oireachtais*, 1899 (Dublin,
Gaelic League). The Shee an Gannon and the Gruagach Gaire, J. Curtin's
Myths and Folk-Lore of Ireland, p. 114 (Boston, 1906). *Celtic Review*, vi.,
p. 370. *Revue Celtique*, i., p. 194. *Folk-Lore* (1925), xxxvi., p. 314. *Béaloideas*,
ii., pp. 134, 414; iii., p. 444; vii., p. 202. Eating a wild boar occurs in
several of these.

'Ma tà, bha mi fhéin uair an so,' arsa Rìgh Eireann,
'is bha sia comhdhalta deug agam, agus bha toil-intinn
agus aighear ann fhad is a bha iad agam, agus bha sinn
latha brèagh, grianach 'nar suidhe an so mu'n bhòrd so
fhéin. Bha latha brèagh, grianach ann, agus bha an
uinneag ud air a togail agam mar a tha i an diugh fhéin,
agus ciod è leum a stigh air an uinneig ach àilleagan féidh.[1]

Bhuail e air siubhal an t-seòmair, is chan fhaca mi
fhéin riamh na bu bhrèagha 's na b'fhearr leam agam
fhéin na e. Ghabh e a mach air an uinneig is ghabh mi
fhéin a mach as a dhéidh.

Bhuail mi air a ruith leam fhéin, agus an uair a bhuail
mi air a ruith, dh'fhalbh mo chomhdhaltan as mo dhéidh.
Bha mise ann an uisge sàiltean an àilleagain fhéidh, agus
bha mo chomhdhaltan-sa ann an uisge mo shàiltean-sa.[2]

Ghabh e an sin sìos an cladach, chaidh e iom[r]all orm
aig beul uamha anns a' chladach.

Chaidh mi a stigh do'n uaimh an sin, is chaidh mo
chomdhaltan a stigh as mo dhéidh. Bha aona Bhodach
Mór a stigh anns an uaimh sin, agus coire mór làn feòla
aige a' goil air an teine, agus bòrd mór air a chomhdach
ann an taobh na h-uamha.

Cha robh mi fhéin is mo chomhdhaltan fada a stigh,
an uair a thàinig a dhà dheug de mhèirlich dachaidh.
Ghabh iad gu dàna a dh' ionnsuigh a' bhìdh sin air a'
bhòrd.

Ma chreideas sibh mise, bha an t-acras ['gam tholladh,]
is cha robh a chridhe agam éirigh a ghabhail greim de'n
bhiadh.

Cha robh sinn fad a stigh an uair a chualas eubhach a

Z 85*

N 774

---

[1] The King, or one of his foster-brothers, had probably been boasting of
his glory or wealth. In several tales, boasting during revelry is presently
followed by the appearance of supernatural animals or adversaries, who insult
or maltreat some one of the revellers, and compel him or others to various
adventures, as in *W. H. Tales*, ii., No. 52, and *Rosg Gàidhlig*, p. 78, 1st ed.
[2] For chasing the deer, and other chasing runs, see *W. H. Tales*, i., No. 17;
ii., No. 38. *Celtic Review*, vi., p. 373. *Waifs and Strays*, iv., p. 197. MS.
vol. x., No. 97, notes.

'Well, I was in this place at one time,' said the King of Erin, 'when I had with me my sixteen foster-brothers, and much pleasure of mind and mirth there was while they were with me, and one fine sunny day we were all seated here, about this very table. Yes, a fine sunny day it was, and I had yonder window raised just as it is to-day, when what should leap in through the window but a pet deer.[1]

It began to traverse the room, and truly I had never seen anything more beautiful or that I would more desire to possess. Out it went again through the window, and out after it went I.

I set to work to chase it by myself, but when I did so, my foster-brothers came after me. I was [treading] in Z 85* the water [that gathered] in the foot[prints] of the pet deer, and my foster-brothers were [treading] in the water [that gathered] in mine.[2]

The deer went down to the shore, but I lost it N 774 at the mouth of a cave on the shore.[3]

Into the cave I went, and in after me came my foster-brothers. Inside that cave there was a single huge Bodach, with a vast cauldron full of flesh which he had boiling on the fire, and there was a great table laid, which stood at one side of the cave.

My foster-brothers and I had not been long inside, when twelve robbers arrived. And right boldly they fell to at the food on that table.

If you will believe me, [though] hunger was [piercing me], I did not dare rise to take a bite of food.

We had not been long inside when a halloo was heard

[3] In another story, Paudyeen O'Kelly chases a weasel into a hut. Upon entering the hut he finds an old hag, but no weasel. The conclusion of course is, that the hag had put off weasel-shape. Dr D. Hyde, *Beside the Fire*, p. 77. Contrariwise, in another tale, Oscar, who on looking into a house had seen a hero inside, finds upon entering a large buzzard, but cannot find any man. On a similar occasion he finds an eagle, and on a third, a winged dragon, but fails to find the men whom he, before entering, had seen inside.—*Waifs and Strays*, iii., pp. 59-61.

muigh, fear de na farbhalaich [1] a dhol a mach a thogail
an tuirc nimhe bhàrr muin an fhir a bha a muigh.

Dh'éirich fear de mo chomhdhaltan fhéin is chaidh e a
mach d'a ionnsuigh, is an déidh dol a mach, cha togadh
e aon ròinnean de na bha anns an torc.

Dh' fhalbh an Gille Dubh air an robh an torc an sin,
is buailear an torc air an fhear a bha a muigh is marbhar
e.   Dh' fhalbh e is thug e fhéin a stigh an torc an uair sin,
is thilg e air an ùrlar e.   Thuirt e rium fhéin,

G 310

"A Rìgh Eireann, mura feann thu an torc le do
làmhan agus le do chasan, chan 'eil thu ri biadh fhaotainn
an so a nochd.   Chan 'eil thu ri sgian no ri iaruinn
'fhaighinn gus an torc a fheannadh."

Dh'éirich dithis de mo chomhdhaltan fhéin, is cha
tugadh iad aon ròin[neag] de na bha 'san torc ás.

Dh' éirich e fhéin 's chuir e pìos 'na làmhan 's pìos na
chasan [3]; spìon e dheth an t-seiche is chuir e anns a' choire
dh'a bhruich e.

"A Rìgh Eireann," ars am Fear Dubh, "ma tha toil
agad do bhiadh fhaotainn a nochd, feumaidh tu an torc
a thoirt ás a' choire le t'fhiaclan, agus mura dèan thu sin,
chan 'eil thu ri sgàth bìdh fhaotainn an so a nochd."

Dh' éirich fear no dhà de mo chomhdhaltan airson siod
a dhèanamh, is cha tugadh iad aona bhìdeag aisde,[4] 's
cha chuireadh iad mìr de'n bhrochan a mach.

Dh' éirich e fhéin an sin, is chuir e séideag leis a' ghoil,
is séideag 'na h-aghaidh, is chuir e a h-uile boinne bha
innte a mach air druim na h-uamha 'na cheò uaine, is
thug e aisde an torc, is chuir e siod a dh'ionnsuigh nan
gillean air a' bhòrd.

---

[1] h-arbhalaich in MS.

[2] See Waifs and Strays, iv., pp. 194, 200, 288, and W. H. Tales, ii.,
No. 29.

[3] Lit. put a piece [of the hide] in his hands and a piece in his feet.   If he
asked the King to flay the boar without implements, the assumption is that
he could do so himself.

without, [and a shout] that one of the strangers was to go forth and lift a deadly boar from off the back of the man who was outside.

One of my own foster-brothers arose, and went out to him, but he was unable to lift so much as a single hair of all the hairs on that boar.[2]

Thereupon the Dark Fellow, he who was carrying the boar, dashed it upon that man [of mine] who had gone outside and killed him. Then he himself fetched the G 310 boar in, and banged it down on the floor. And he said to me,

"King of Erin, unless thou flay the boar with thy hands and feet, thou wilt get no food here to-night. And neither knife nor iron mayest thou have with which to skin him."

Two of my foster-brothers arose, but of all the hairs on that boar, not one could they take off.

Then he himself [the Dark Fellow] arose and grasped a part [of the hide] with his hands and part with his feet[3]; he wrenched off the hide and put [the carcase] into the cauldron to boil.

"King of Erin," said the Dark Fellow, "if thou wish to have thy food to-night, thou must fetch the boar out of the cauldron with thy teeth, but if thou canst not, thou wilt not get a morsel of food here to-night."

One or two of my foster-brothers arose to do this, but they were unable to take a single morsel out of the cauldron,[4] nor could they force out a drop of the broth.

He himself [the Dark Fellow] then rose, and blowing the steam first in the direction it was going and then against it, he drove every drop in the cauldron out of the cave through the roof like a cloud of green reek. Then he fetched the boar out of the cauldron, and placed it on the table before the others.

---

[4] *aisde*, out of her, in MS.—Cauldron is masculine, but both in this place and others in this tale it is referred to with a feminine prepositional pronoun. Contrariwise, even MacMhaigstir Alasdair is known to have used *as* where *aiste* or *aisde* should have been written.—*Celtic Review*, v., p. 24. The foster-brothers undertake for the King; passionate devotion and self-sacrifice are frequent in the old Highland tales. See p. 55 *n*.

Thòisich iad air gabhail am bìdh,[1] is gun teagamh,
mura robh iad a' lomadh chnàmh,[2] 's chà robh cnàimh a
lomadh no a spioladh iad, nach ann orm fhéin a bha iad
'ga bualadh is air mo chomhdhaltan, a' fanaid oirnn.

An uair a bha iad réidh de am biadh, dh'fhaighnich am
Fear Dubh dhiom fhéin an robh mi eòlach air cluich na
h-ubhail. Thuirt mi fhéin gu dearbh gun robh, is mi
gabhail moran misnich gun dèanainn feum leatha.[3]

Dh'fhalbh e an sin is thàinig e agus an ubhal leis, is
bhuail e air fear de mo chomhdhaltan i, agus mharbh e e.
Bha an sin dithis a dhìth orm. Chaith mi fhéin an ubhal
air, agus ghlac an Gille Dubh an cùl an duirn i, agus chaith
e a nall i, agus mharbh e fear eile.

Chaith mise a null i, is ghlac esan an cùl a dhuirn i an
darna uair.

Thuirt e rium ma bha mi sgìth de'n chluich ud, gum
feuchadh e cluich eile rium. Thuirt mise gun robh mi
deònach.

Thuirt esan gun robh cluich aige ris an canadh iad
cluich na h-eige, ma bha mi deònach fheuchainn.

Thuirt mi fhéin gun robh.

Dh'fhalbh e is thug e a nuas sail daraich 's móran
eagannan 'na taobh.[4] Thuirt e an sin ri mo chomhdhaltan,
"Cuiridh sibh ur cinn anns a h-uile h-eig an siod, is cuiridh
mise mo cheann anns a h-uile h-eig m' ur coinnimh."—
Chuir e a cheann anns an eig, is chuir mo chomhdhaltan
an cinn anns na h-eagannan mu a choinnimh. Spìon
e na cinn ás a h-uile gin dhiubh, is thug e fhéin a cheann
as sàbhailte. Cha robh duine agam an so ach mi fhéin
'nam ònrachd.

Rug esan an sin orm fhéin, is thuirt e rium, co dhiùbh
a b'fhearr leam mionnachadh air faobhar arm dà nach

K 864*
F 813·1·4

K 865*

---

[1] Eating the flesh of a deadly, or venomous, or wild boar, occurs in several
tales. Yet pork was an abomination to the old Highlanders. See MS. vol. x.,
No. 159, notes. Cooking a magic deer or salmon under curious conditions
occurs in *W. H. Tales*, ii., No. 51; iii., Nos. 80, 82.

[2] An aposiopesis. Supply, for instance, 'I don't know what they were
doing.'

[3] Throwing a brazen apple at an enemy, who did his best to catch it and
hurl it back, may have been one of the accomplishments of a great warrior,
and the King may have been an adept at the game. See notes at end.

They began taking their food,[1] and certainly, if they were not stripping bones, [well] . . .[2] and there was never a bone that they stripped or picked that they did not fling at me and my foster-brothers, making sport of us.

When they had finished eating, the Black Fellow asked me if I were acquainted with the apple game. I said I certainly was, and my courage began to revive again greatly, thinking that I should do right well at that game.[3]   K 864* F 813·1·4

He went away, and came back with the apple, and hurling it at one of my foster-brothers, killed him. So that I had now lost two of them. I myself now threw the apple at him, but the Black Fellow caught it in his fist, and throwing it back again, killed another.

I threw it across again, but he caught it in his fist a second time.

He said to me that if I were tired of that game, he would try another game with me. I said I was willing.

He said he had a game which they called the game of the notch, if I were willing to try it.

I said I was.

He went and produced an oaken beam with many notches in the side of it.[4] He then said to my foster-brothers, "Do you put your heads in every one of those notches, and I will put mine in every notch opposite yours."—He put his head into a notch, and my foster-brothers put their heads into the notches opposite him. He tore off the heads of every one of them, and took his own head safely out again. So now I had not a man left to me but myself alone.   K 865*

He then seized hold of me, and asked me whether I would prefer to swear to him by the edges of his weapons

---

[4] 'na taobh, in its side, in MS. This part of the tale is obscure, but it would appear that there were notches on both sides of the beam, and that while facing each other in the notches, each player tried to pull off his opponent's head. I know of no other instance of the game of the notch. A somewhat similar contest occurs in Caithreim Conghail Cláiringhnigh, p. 125 (Irish Texts Society, 1904, David Nutt, London), where two combatants play. Each puts his neck in a ring, the two rings being connected by an iron chain which passes over a pillar stone. Each tugs at the chain, until one of them pulls the head of the other off.

rachainn gu bràth tuilleadh far an robh iad, no bàs fhulang
far an robh mi. Thuirt mise gum b'fhearr leam mionnachadh nach rachainn gu bràth tuilleadh far an robh iad.
—Mhionnaich mi an uair sin daibh, is leig iad mo bheò
leam, ach an uair a fhuair mise a mach, ged a bhiodh na
bha a stigh as mo dhéidh, cha bheireadh iad orm. Agus
sin agaibh fios m' aigheir an uair a bha mo chomhdhaltan
leam, is fios mo mhi-aigheir an uair a dh'fhalbh iad.'

'Agus an téid thusa ann tuilleadh?' ars Iain Og, Mac
Rìgh na Frainge.

'O, cha téid mise gu bràth air an àraich.'

'O! thig thu ann, is bheir mi trì gàirean ort o
[gh]run[nd] do chridhe,' ars Iain Og, 'ma théid thu comhla
rium.'

'Chan fhaca mise dad a bheireadh sin orm, o nach
fhaicinn mo chomhdhaltan a' tighinn beò, is an Gille
Dubh is am Bodach 'gam marbhadh,' arsa Rìgh Eireann ;
'cha téid mi idir air an àraich.'

Ach mun do leig e am facal as a bheul, ciod e leum
a stigh air an uinneig ach an t-àilleagan féidh, is chaidh
e mun cuairt ceithir oiseannan an t-seòmair. A mach a
bha e a rithist air an uinneig, is a mach a bha Iain as a
dhéidh, agus lean Ladhar Dubh Iain, agus lean Rìgh
Z 85*   Eireann Ladhar. Bha Iain ann an uisge sàil an àilleagain
fhéidh, is bha Ladhar Dubh ann an uisge sàil Iain, agus
bha Rìgh Eireann ann an uisge sàil Ladhair. Chaidh an
t-àilleagan féidh am falach orra am beul na h-uamha aig
N 774   a' chladach. Ghabh iad a stigh do'n uaimh. Bha bòrd
comhdaichte an sin, agus coire air ghoil air teine aig
Bodach Mór.

'Aha! a Rìgh Eireann,' ars am Bodach, 'shaoilinn
gach neach a thigeadh chun m' fhardaich, nach tigeadh
tusa ann !'

'A mhic an fhir ud ! ma's ann a' dol a dhèanamh
tuilleadh bruidhinn a tha thu, bheir mi an ceann asad o'n
bhràghad', [arsa Ladhar Dubh].

never to return to the place, or to suffer death where I was. I answered that I would rather swear never to return to the place.—I swore to them in that hour accordingly, and they let me depart alive. But once I got out, though all who were in that cave had chased me, they could not have caught me. So there you know all the story of my joy when my foster-brothers were with me, and all the story of my woe when they had gone.'

'And wilt thou go there any more?' said Iain Og, the Son of the King of France.

'O, never more will I go to that place of slaughter.'

'O ! yes, thou shalt go, and I will make thee laugh three laughs from the bottom of thy heart,' said Iain Og, 'if thou wilt go with me.'

'I have never seen anything that would make me laugh, since I cannot see my foster-brothers restored to life, and the Dark Fellow and the Bodach killed,' said the King of Erin; 'I will certainly not go to that stricken place.'

But before he had let the words out of his mouth, what should leap in through the window but the pet deer, and it traversed the room and all the four corners of it completely. Then out of the window it bolted, and out went Iain after it, Black Toe following Iain, and the King of Erin following Black Toe. Iain was [treading] in the water z 85* [that gathered in] the pet deer's foot[prints], Black Toe was [treading] in the water [that gathered in] Iain's foot-[prints], and the King of Erin was [treading] in the water [that gathered in] Black Toe's foot[prints]. But it went into the mouth of the cave on the shore, and vanished from them. Into the cave they went. There was a table N 774 there, laid, and a huge Bodach who had a cauldron boiling on a fire.

'Aha ! thou King of Erin,' said the Bodach, 'I had thought that no matter what other person might come to my hearth, thou wouldst not !'

'Thou son of yon one ! [1] if thou art going to talk any more, I will tear thy head from off thy body,' [said Black Toe].

---

[1] Thou son of him we would rather not mention, *i.e.* the Fiend.

'Siuthadaibh, a ghillean,' ars Iain, 'is gabhaibh ur
biadh. Tha n'a[s] leòir mu ur coinnimh.' Ghabh iad am
biadh, is cha robh iad fada an déidh am biadh a ghabhail,
an uair a thàinig an dà mhèirleach dheug dhachaidh. Cha
b'fhada a bha iad air tighinn, an uair a chualas eubh aig
an dorus, fear de na farbhalaich a dhol a mach a thogail
tuirc nimhe bhàrr muin fir a bha tighinn. Dh' éirich
Rìgh Eireann gu falbh. 'Fois bheag ort! cha tu a dh'fhalbhas ach mise!'
ars Iain. Dh'fhalbh Iain, agus ràinig e fear an tuirc, agus
ciod è bha aige-san ach iris[1] mu a amhaich. Thug Iain
spìonadh air, is thug e leis an ceann bhàrr a amhaich. Thilg
e ceann an Fhir Dhuibh agus ceann an tuirc air an ùrlar,
is an uair a chunnaic Rìgh Eireann ceann an Fhir Dhuibh,
rinn e sgal gàire.

'Tha e an siod a nis,' ars Iain ris na mèirlich, 'is an cleas
a rinn sibh fhéin air Rìgh Eireann roimhid, nì mise a nis
oirbhse e. Is e sin an torc so fheannadh, gun sgian, gun
cheaba, ach ur làmhan is ur casan.' Dh' éirich iadsan,
is cha tugadh a h-aon aca ròin-[neag] as. Dh'éirich Iain
is rug e air, 's chuir e pìos 'na chois, 's pìos 'na làimh, is
dh'fheann e e, is chuir e anns a' choire e, agus bhruich e e.

'Nis, tha siod bruich, is mura toir sibh as a' choire e le
ur fiaclan, chan 'eil sgàth bìdh agaibh r'a fhaotainn.'
Thòisich iad air, is cha b'urrainn gin aca an torc a thoirt
as a' choire. Dh'éirich Iain is chuir e séideag leis a' ghoil
is séideag 'na aghaidh, is chuir e a h-uile boinne bha 'sa
choire 'na thoit uaine a mach air druim na h-uamha, is
thug e an torc ás a' choire.

'A bheil cluich sam bith agaibh?' ars Iain. 'Tha,' ars
iadsan, 'cluich ris an can iad cluich na h-ubhail.'

'Feuchaibh a nall i,' ars Iain.

---

[1] *iris.* I have translated this word provisionally as *a twisted withe*, not
being sure of the exact meaning. Why the hero casts, not the boar but its
head, on the floor, does not appear.

'Begin, lads,' said Iain, 'and take your food. There is plenty before you.' They took their food, but not long after doing so, the twelve robbers arrived. And not long after these had come, a halloo was heard at the door, [and a shout] for one of the strangers to go out and lift a deadly boar from the back of the newcomer. The King of Erin rose to go [and do so].

'Wait a little ! it is not thou who shalt go but I !' said Iain. Iain went up to the man with the boar. What should he have about his neck but a twisted withe.[1] Iain gave it a wrench, and took his head right off his neck. He took the head of the Dark Fellow and the head of the boar, and cast them down on the floor, and when the King of Erin saw the head of the Dark Fellow, he gave a skirl of a laugh.

'There it [he ?] is now,' said Iain to the robbers, 'and the trick you played on the King of Erin before, will I now play upon you. That is, that you flay this boar with your hands and feet, without either a knife or a scalpel.' [2] They rose, but not one of them could so much as pluck a bristle out of it. Then up got Iain. He seized it, and grasping a piece in his hand and a piece in his foot, flayed it, put it in the cauldron, and boiled it.

'Now, there it is boiled, but unless you can take it out of the cauldron with your teeth, not a morsel of food shall you have.' They began at it, but not one of them was able to take the boar out of the cauldron. Iain arose, and blowing the steam first in the direction it was going and then against it, drove every drop in the cauldron out of the cave through the roof like a cloud of green reek, and then he fetched the boar out of the cauldron.

'Have you any game to play at ?' said Iain. 'Yes,' said they, 'we have—a game which they call the game of the apple.'

'Throw it over here,' said Iain.

---

[2] *ceaba* is a spade, according to a note in the MS., but scalpel would fit better. The hero uses neither knife nor scalpel.

Thilg iad an ubhal is ghlac Iain 'na dhorn i. Thilg e
Q581·1* a null i is mharbh e fear aca. Thilg iad a nall a rithist i,
is ghlac Iain 'na dhorn i. Thilg e a null a rithist i, is mharbh
e fear eile. 'Tha sinn sgìth de'n chluich ud,' ars iadsan.

'A bheil cluich sam bith eile agaibh?' ars Iain. 'Tha,'
ars iadsan, 'cluich ris an can iad cluich na h-eige.'

'Feuchamaid a nuas e,' ars Iain.
Thug iad a nuas an t-sail. Chuir esan a cheann ann
an eig, is chuir iadsan an cinn ann an eagannan mu a
choinnimh, agus spìon e na cinn as na h-amhaichean aig
a h-uile gin aca, is thug e fhéin a cheann as sàbhailte.
Cha robh an so gin aca beò ach am Bodach.
Q581·1* Rug e an sin air a' Bhodach, is chuir e glùn air an
amhaich aige. Thuirt e ris, 'Tha am bàs os do chionn :
ciod è t'éirig?'
'Ma tà, is mór sin,' ars am Bodach; 'is iomadh éirig
F531·6·7 duine bhochd agus duine bheairtich a tha fo'n fhardaich
a tha an so.'
'Tha sin agamsa, agus am bàs os do chionn-sa ; ciod è
t'éirig?'
'Och ! chan eil tuilleadh éirig agam, ach innsidh mi
dhuibh mar a bheir sibh beò sia comhdhaltan deug Rìgh
Eireann, ma leigeas sibh leam mo bheatha.'

'D è mar a bheir sinn beò iad?' ars Iain.
'Tha sia comhdhaltan deug Rìgh Eireann marbh shìos
an siod, is an cnàmhan ann am ballan puinnsein. Chan
E 102 'eil ach an togail is an cur anns a' bhallan ioc-shlaint làimh
F 531·6 ris, is bidh iad beò,' ars am Bodach.
·5·3

'Tha sin agam agus do bhàs. Am bheil tuilleadh agad ?'
ars Iain.
'O ! chan 'eil tuilleadh,' ars am Bodach.
'Mura bheil, a mhic an fhir ud, bidh do bhàs agam,'
G 510 ars Iain, is e a' tilgeil a chinn deth.
Rinn Rìgh Eireann an darna gàire.

They threw the apple, and Iain caught it in his fist.
He threw it back again, and killed one of them. They Q581·1*
threw it from their side again, and Iain caught it in his
fist. Again he threw it back, and killed another man.
'We are tired of that game,' said they.

'Have you any other game?' said Iain. 'Yes, we
have,' said they, 'a game which they call the game of the
notch.'

'Let us bring it forth and try it,' said Iain.

They brought forth the beam. He put his head in a
notch, and [each of] them put his head in [whatever]
notch was opposite his,[1] and he tore off every one of their
heads from their necks, and took his own head out safely. Q581·1*
So now there was not one of them alive but the old Bodach.

Then he seized the Bodach, and setting his knee on his
neck, said to him, 'Death is above thee; what ransom hast
thou to offer?'

'Well then, the ransom is a great one,' said the Bodach; F531·6·7
'the ransom got from many a poor man and many a rich
one is beneath this roof.'

'All that is mine, but death hangs over thy head yet:
with what wilt thou ransom thyself?'

'Och! no further ransom have I, but I will tell you how
you can bring the King of Erin's sixteen foster-brothers
to life again, if you will but let me take my life away with
me.'

'How can we bring them to life again?' said Iain.

'The King of Erin's sixteen foster-brothers are down
yonder, dead, and their bones are sunk in a vessel full of
poison. All that has to be done is to lift them out and
plunge them into a vessel of balsam close to it and they E102
will be alive again,' said the old Bodach. F531·6

'That [knowledge] is mine, and I'll have thy life too. ·5·3
Hast thou anything else?' said Iain.

'O! I have nothing more,' said the Bodach.

'If thou hast not, thou son of yon one, I'll have thy
life,' said Iain, striking off his head. G510

The King of Erin laughed for the second time.

---

[1] *Lit.* they put their heads in the notches opposite to him.

Ghabh iad an sin a dh'ionnsuigh comhdhaltan Rìgh
Eireann, agus thug iad beò iad. Bha an so an treas gàire
aig Rìgh Eireann 'ga dhèanamh an uair so.

'Siuthad a nis, a Rìgh na h-Eireann, is thoir leat do thoil
de na bheil de ionmhas fo'n fhàrdaich a tha an so, 'ars
Iain.

'Cha toir mi fhéin leam e, biodh e agaibh fhéin.'

'Cha toir mise dad leam deth, ach beagan a bheir an
rathad domh,' ars Iain.

Dh'fhalbh Rìgh Eireann an so dachaidh ro thoilichte.
Dh'fhalbh Iain Mac Rìgh na Frainge dachaidh, agus
thadhail e aig Bàn-righ Rìgh Lochlainn air an rathad, is
dh'fhàg e an cuideachadh a fhuair e aice. Chaidh e
dhachaidh do rìoghachd na Frainge.

'Nis,' arsa Ladhar [Dubh], 'falbhaidh thu, agus théid
thu gus a' Chaillich a dh'fhàg thu air a' chnoc, is tha ise
'na torradan marbh an sin. Tòisichidh tu air innseadh
do naidheachd di mu aighear agus mu mhi-aighear Rìgh
E 55·1·1*   Eireann, agus bidh ise tighinn air a h-aghaidh is ag at,
is an uair a bhitheas tu ullamh de innseadh do naidheachd,
bidh ise cho beò is a bha i riamh. Tha i an sin a' dol gu
do chur fo na h-ath gheasaibh.'

Dh'fhalbh e, is ràinig e an cnoc air an robh a' Chailleach,
is bhuail e air innseadh a naidheachd di, agus an uair
E 31   a bha e ullamh de innseadh a naidheachd, bha ise cho
beò is cho slàn is a bha i riamh, mar a thuirt Ladhar Dubh.
Thòisich e air falbh.

'Fuireachd bheag ort,' ars a' Chailleach, 'tha tuilleadh
agad a chuireas mise mu do choinnimh a dh' fheumas tu
H 935   a dhèanamh fhathast.

Z 85*   CUIRIDH MI THU FO GHEASAN 'S FO CHROISEAN,
D 1273   'S fo naoidh buaraichean mnatha sìdhe, siùbhlaiche, seach-
ranaiche,
F 360   An laogh beag is meataiche 's is mi-threòiriche
[na thu fhéin,]
A thoirt do chinn 's do chluais 's do chaitheamh beatha dhìot,
C 650   Mura faigh thu dhomhsa 's an toir thu do m'ionnsuigh,
H 1377   Ceann an Fhir Bhig agus ceann an Fhir Mhóir.'

They then went over to the King of Erin's foster-brothers, and restored them to life. At this the King of Erin laughed for the third time.

'Begin now, thou King of Erin, and take with thee what thou please of the treasure beneath this roof,' said Iain.

'I will not take it; let it be yours.'

'None of it will I have, except a little to take me on my way,' said Iain.

Hereupon the King of Erin went home well pleased. Iain, the Son of the King of France, went home too, and visited the Queen of Lochlann on the way, and left with her the auxiliaries he had received from her. He then went home to the Kingdom of France.

'Now,' said [Black] Toe, 'thou shalt set out and visit the old Cailleach whom thou didst leave on the hill, where she has now become only a little heap of dead drift. Thou shalt begin telling her thy story concerning the joy and woe E 55·1·1* of the King of Erin, but [while thou art doing so] she will become more and more invigorated and will get larger in size, so that when thou hast finished telling thy story, she will be as much alive as ever she was. She is then going to lay thee under further spells.'

Away he went, and came to the hill where the Cailleach lay, and commenced telling his story to her, and when he had finished telling his story, she was as much alive and E 31 as well as ever she had been, just as Black Toe had said. He began to move away.

'Bide thee yet a little,' said the Cailleach, 'there is something further which I shall require of thee to perform, H 935 and which thou must yet do.

I LAY THEE UNDER SPELLS AND CROSSES,   Z 85*
And under [pain of being struck by] the nine cowfetters of the D 1273
    wildly-roaming, traveller-deluding fairy woman,   F 360
[So that] some sorry wight more feeble and misguided [than
    thyself],
Take thy head and thine ear and thy life's career from thee,
Unless thou get for me and bring me here   C 650
The head of the Little Man and the head of the Big Man.'   H 1377

Chaidh [1] e dachaidh is leag e a uileann air a' bhord,
is thug e osann as. 'Osann mhic rìgh fo gheasan,' ars an
t-uachdaran, 'ma's ann airson a' chluas a thoirt dhiomsa
a tha thu ag osnaich, an leabhara, tha toil do ghnothuich
agad.'

'Ma tà, droch comhdhail ort, a thrusdair, nam biodh
mo chlaidheamh aig mo làimh, chuirinn a' chluas eile
dhìot, chionn dùil a bhi agad fhéin gun rachainn-sa a
dh'osnaich airson a' chluas a thoirt dìot.'

'Ciod è na geasan a chuir i ort an dràsd?' arsa
Ladhar [Dubh].

'Ceann an Fhir Bhig is ceann an Fhir Mhóir a thoirt
d'a h-ionnsuigh,' ars Iain.

'O! creididh mi sin gu math,' arsa Ladhar [Dubh].
'Tha rìoghachd aig an Fhear Bheag da fhéin, is tha rìoghachd
aig an Fhear Mhór da fhéin, is tha ise gun rìoghachd idir
is tha i feuchainn an cuir i thusa gu bàs, feuch am faigh
i an Fhraing a bhi aice dhi fhéin. Ach falbhaidh thusa
air an turus sin, is chan fhalbh mise comhla riut idir, ach
fanaidh mise a' dìon na rìoghachd an so gu ceann latha
is bliadhna, is mura till thusa an ceann latha is bliadhna,
cuiridh mise an rìoghachd so 'na teinidh, chor nach téid
rìgh eile oirre gu bràth.'

Dh'fhalbh Iain Og, is bheairtich e soitheach.

Z 72·1

Z 85*

THUG E A TOISEACH RI MUIR 'S A DEIREADH RI TÌR,
Thog e na siùil bhaidealacha, bhàna,
An aghaidh nan crann fada, fulangach,
[Le soirbheas beag, ciuin, lag, laghach,
O mhullach nam beann 's o àirde na h-eirthire,]
Nach fàgadh slat gun lùbadh, seòl gun reubadh,
A ruith na fairge plucanaiche, cnapanaiche,
Neòil ghuirme Lochlannach— [2]
An fhaochag bheag liath a bhiodh an grunnd an aigeil,

---

[1] It is not said that the hero lays counter-spells upon the Cailleach on this occasion. But the sequel makes it certain that he did.

[2] Meaning of this line very uncertain. A similar and usually very broken line occurs in most 'seafaring runs,' but no satisfactory explanation has been given. See an 'arming run' in *W. H. Tales*, ii., No. 35, and 'sailing runs,' *ibid.*, ii., No. 52; iii., pp. 283 or 267, 213 or 227. *Waifs and Strays*, ii., pp. 61, 349. *Trans. Gael. Soc. Inverness*, xiii., p. 70. The lines between square brackets have been supplied from 'seafaring runs' in other tales, in order to make sense.

He [1] went home, lent his elbow on the table, and heaved a sigh. 'The sigh of a king's son under spells,' said the governor, 'if it is for having cut off mine ear thou art sighing, by the book, it serves thee right.'

'Now, may evil encounter thee, rascal; had I my glaive at my hand, I would cut off thine other ear, merely for thinking that I would so much as sigh for having cut off any ear of thine.'

'What spells has she laid upon thee now?' said [Black] Toe.

'To bring her the head of the Little Man and the head of the Big Man,' said Iain.

'O! I can well believe that,' said [Black] Toe. 'The Little Man has a kingdom to himself, and the Big Man also has a kingdom to himself, but she has no kingdom at all, and so she is casting about to put thee to death if she can, to see if she can get France for herself. Do thou, however, set forth on that quest. But I, I shall certainly not go with thee; I shall remain here for a year and a day Z 72·1 guarding the kingdom; and unless thou return at the end of a year and a day, I shall set this kingdom on fire, so that no other king shall ever assume lordship over it.'

Iain went off, and equipped a ship.

HE SET HER STEM TO THE SEA AND HER STERN TO THE LAND,   Z 85*
He hoisted the spreading, snowy sails,
Against the tall tough masts,
[There was a slight breeze, mild, faint, and pleasant,
That came from the hill-tops and heights of the seaboard,
A breeze] that would leave no yard unbent, or sail untorn,
While scouring the billowing, surging sea.
The blue clouds of Lochlann [2]— ·
The little gray sea-shell that lay at the bottom of the abyss,

See Dr Geo. Henderson, *Norse Influence*, p. 145, and Dr D. Hyde, *Beside the Fire*, p. 105 ('*the fulparnee and the folpornee*'). For other 'seafaring runs' see *Waifs and Strays*, ii., p. 448; iv., pp. 139, 140, 150, 176, 177, 244. *W. H. Tales*, iv., p. 129 or 140. *Trans. Gael. Soc. Inverness*, xv., p. 57; xxv., p. 232 (a fragmentary seafaring run), from which it appears that it was the great size of a hero that enabled him to be in the bows, stern, and amidships simultaneously. *An Gàidheal* (1876), v., p. 262. *Celtic Review*, ii., p. 147; iii., p. 261. *Larminie*, pp. 50, 67, 91, 253. *Scottish Gaelic Studies*, i., pp. 160, 164. *Rosg Gàidhlig*, p. 82, 1st ed.

Bhiodh i glagadaich air a h-ùrlar—
['S gun sgoilteadh i coinnlein cruaidh coirce
Roimh a toiseach],
Aig fheobhas 's a bha an gille 'ga stiuireadh:
Gun dèanadh e stiuir 'na deireadh,
Ball 'na toiseach, beairt 'na buillsgein.
Gach ball a bhiodh fuasgailte gun ceangladh e,
'S gach ball a bhiodh ceangailte gum fuasgladh e.
Bha e an sin a' seòladh, agus ag astarachadh,
Agus a' sìor-imeachd.

Dh' amais fearann ris, agus bha an soirbheas a' dol
seachad air an fhearann, ach a' dol seachad air maol [?]
an fhearainn, chaidh i 'na bròn fiatha.
Ach sùil gun tug Iain uaidh, ciod è chunnaic e ach
iasgair mór ag iasgach air creig.
Chaidh an soitheach car teann air a' charraig air an
G 318*   robh an t-iasgair ag obair. Dh'fhalbh an t-iasgair, agus
thilg e na driamlaichean a mach, agus chuir e an sàs 'san
t-soitheach iad, is thilg e air feur glas air a chùl i.[1]

'Ma tà, droch comhdhail ort, a thrusdair bhodaich!'
ars Iain, 'dol a chur mo shoithich an so!'
'Ma tà, droch comhdhail ort fhéin, a thrusdair
bhalaich!' ars am bodach, 'tighinn cho dlùth air a' chreig,
is dol a chur an éisg air falbh orm! Ciod è an gnothuch
a bha agad tighinn ann?'
'Leigidh mise fhaicinn duit,' ars Iain, 'gum bi e glé
dhuilich dhuit, agus nach bi ach glé bheagan a nasgaidh
agad, mo shoitheach a chur an so.'—'Feuch ris,' ars am
bodach.
Thòisich am bodach is am balach an so, is ghabh iad
an dàil a chéile.

F 943   DHÈANADH IAD BOGAN AIR A' CHREAGAN,
Z 85*   Agus creagan air a' bhogan,
An t-àite a b' àirde rachadh iad fodha,
Rachadh iad fodha gu an glùinean,

---

[1] A giant deals thus with a creel containing a hero whom he had hauled
up out of a cavern in *W. H. Tales*, i., No. 7. For a hostile, black, and gigantic
fisherman, and for an angling giant, see *ibid.* intro., c. or xciv; iii., pp. 12, 15, or
21, 24. *Waifs and Strays*, ii., pp. 263, 473; iii., pp. 161, 291. In other tales

Would rattle and clank against the ship's planks—
[And she would split a fine hard oaten straw
With her prow]
So excellently did the lad steer her :
For he could steer her from the stern,
Coil a rope in the bow, and manage her tackling amidships.
Every loose rope['s end when need was] he would secure,
And every fastened one cast loose.
And there he was sailing, and scudding along,
And ever steadily advancing.

He now sighted land, but the breeze was moving past it. But after passing the bluff [?] end of the land, the wind dropped and it became a dead calm.

But on looking about, what should Iain see but a great fisherman fishing from a rock.

The ship went rather close to the rock where the fisherman was at work. The fisherman, setting himself in G 318* motion, flung out his lines, fixed them in the vessel, and [pulling it out of the water] cast it behind him upon the green grass.[1]

'Well, may evil encounter thee, thou rascal bodach !' said Iain, 'for having thrown my vessel here.'

'Well then, may evil meet thee thyself, thou rascal loon !' said the bodach, 'for coming so close to the rock, and driving the fish away from me ! What business hadst thou to come here ?'

'I will let thee see,' said Iain, 'how hardly it shall go with thee, and how little thou shalt profit for having thrown my ship here.'—'Try it,' [2] said the bodach.

Then did the bodach and the lad set to, and attacked each other furiously.

THEY MADE A MARSH OF THE ROCK,   F 943
And a rock of the marsh,   Z 85*
Where they sank least deeply into the earth,
They would sink to their knees,

magic clews of thread are used by a giant or a Cailleach to capture fugitives who are fleeing in ships.—*Ibid.*, p. 291. *W. H. Tales*, i., No. 2, var. 8; ii., No. 46, var. 2. Rev. J. G. Campbell, *Superstitions*, p. 119.
[2] See what thou canst do.

'S an t-àite bu doimhne rachadh iad fodha
Rachadh iad fodha gu an sùilean !
Smuainich Iain gun robh e goirid o a nàimhdean
'S fad o a chàirdean.
Thug e an togail shunndach, shanntach, aighearach ud air
    a' bhodach,
'S thilg e air a dhruim e.

'Tha mi air do ghoile, a bhodaich: ciod è t' éirig?'
ars Iain.
'Tha thu an sin. Chan 'eil éirig agam; is dona is
fhiach duit mo bhàs. Is fhearr dhuit mi a bhualadh buille
leat na mo bhàs. Bheir mise mionnan duit air t' armaibh,

Q 82
N 812

aona bhuille bhuaileas mi, gur ann leat a bhuaileas mi e, 's
nach buail mi gin gu bràth 'nad aghaidh.'

'Is e sin is fhearr leamsa,' ars Iain.
'Ach their mi so riut,' ars am bodach, 'chan 'eil duine
agamsa ri a ghrad-mharbhadh gu bràth, ach cha mhór
a bhios aige ri ràdh an déidh mo làimhe.' [1]

Mhionnaich am bodach an sin do Iain air faobhar a
arm, is dh' iarr e a leigeil 'na sheasamh.

C 432·2*

'Cha leig mi 'nad sheasamh thu gus am bi fios 'm,
ciod è as ainm duit,' ars Iain.
'Is è as ainm domh Donnchadh Mac Brian Gàrraidh,'
ars am bodach.
'Tha fear de'n ainm agam a cheana,' ars Iain.
'Tha fios 'm gu bheil,' ars am bodach : 'tha Ladhar

D 2151

[Dubh] mo bhràthair, agad. Rinn e fiath feadh an
t-saoghail an los mise a chur ann ad charaibh. Tha a
dhà uibhir de gheasachd aige is a tha agamsa, is thig esan
an so a nochd,[2] 's mura faic e gun d'fhalbh mise, cha bhi
tuilleadh saoghail agam, agus is éiginn domhsa falbh
comhla riutsa, a nis.'
Dh' fhalbh iad an so, is chaidh iad air bòrd, is bhuail

---

[1] This is the second time that the magnanimous hero accepts an oath of
fealty from his former foe, and admits him to mercy. The terms of service
are apparently to be qualified by what seems to be a bloodthirsty request on
the part of the bodach to be allowed to torture his prisoners.

And where they sank most deeply,
They would sink to their eyes.
And now Iain remembered that he was close to his foes
And far from his friends.
So he gave the bodach such a cheerful, eager, merry
    heave,
And threw him down on his back.

'I am over thy throat, thou bodach; what ransom
hast thou?' said Iain.

'Thou art over me indeed. But I have no ransom;
and to thee my death were worse than useless. For me
to strike a blow on thy behalf were better gain to thee
than my death. I'll swear to thee by thy weapons, that
whatever blow I strike, I'll strike for thee, and that I'll   Q 82
never strike a single blow against thee.'   N 812

'That is what I would prefer,' said Iain.

'But I will say this to thee,' said the bodach, 'I am
never to be obliged to kill a man suddenly, but he whom
I handle will not have much to say after I have dealt with
him.' [1]

The bodach then swore to Iain by the edge of his
weapons, and asked to be allowed to rise.

'I will not let thee rise till I know what thy name is,'   C 432·2*
said Iain.

'My name is Duncan MacBrian Gàrraidh,' said the
bodach.

'I have a man of that name already,' said Iain.

'I know thou hast,' said the bodach: 'thou hast [Black]
Toe, my brother. He caused a great calm to spread over   D 2151
the world in order to bring me within thy reach. He
knows twice as much magic as I do; he will come here
to-night,[2] and unless he sees that I have left, I shall live no
longer; so I must now go along with thee.'

Hereupon they set off, and went on board, and applied

---

[2] This implies that Black Toe left the kingdom of France, though he had
previously announced his intention of staying in it to guard it.

iad air astarachadh is air imeachd gus an do ràinig iad
Rìoghachd nam Fear Móra.[1]

BHUAIL IAD BEUM SGÉITHE—
Cath, air neo comhrag,
Air neo ceann an Fhir Mhóir
A chur a mach d'an ionnsuigh.

Is e siod an rud a gheibheadh iad—
Cath, air neo comhrag,
'S cha b'e ceann an Fhir Mhóir.

Chuireadh dithis dhaoine a mach 'nan comhdhail.
Thòisich iad orra, is cha b'fhada bha Iain a' cur as do'n
fhear aige fhéin.
'Tionndaidh ris an fhear so is cuir as da,' arsa
Donnchadh.
'An [= nach?] do mharbh thu fhéin fhathast e?' ars Iain.
'Nach d' innis mi duit cheana mar a bha sin?' arsa
Donnchadh.
Chuir Iain crìoch air an fhear eile.

Bhuail iad an darna uair beum sgéithe—
Cath, air neo comhrag,
Air neo ceann an Fhir Mhóir a chur a mach d'an ionnsuigh.

'Nach gòrach mise,' ars am Fear Mór, 'is nach fhaca
mise fear mór no beag riamh nach rachadh agam air, a
bhi cosd mo dhaoine mar so.'
Chaidh e fhéin a mach an sin.
'Ma tà,' ars Iain Og, 'tha am fear so fiadhaich [2] ri a
fhaicinn, co dhiùbh.'
Thòisich Iain is e fhéin air a chéile, is bha Iain ag
obair air cho math is a dh' fhaodadh e leis a' chlaidheamh.
Thòisich Donnchadh air a chùl, is ghearr e dlocan a
bac na h-easgaid, dlocan eile as an t-sliasaid, dlocan eile
as a chaol-druim, air alt is gun do rinn e ceumannan
staighreach air, dìreach gu eadar dà shlinnean an Fhir
Mhóir![3]   Fhuair e eadar a dhà shlinnean, agus leag e e,

---

[1] or Giants. Such a kingdom occurs in *Waifs and Strays*, iv., p. 175. The
Isle ⸴' Eigg is still called *Eilean nam Ban Móra*, the Isle of the Big Women, or
Giantesses (*cf.* Martin's *Description*).

themselves to hard travelling and fast going until they came to the Kingdom of the Big Men.[1]   F 122*

THEY SOUNDED A BOOMING CHALLENGE, CLASHING THEIR SHIELDS—   Z 85*
[Demanding] a battle, or else a combat,
Or else that the head of the Big Man
Should be sent out to them.

This is what they should have—
A battle, or else a combat,
But not the head of the Big Man.

Two men were sent out to encounter them. They began fighting with them, and Iain was not long in killing his man.

'Turn thee now to this one, and kill him,' said Duncan.

'Hast thou not killed him yet ?' said Iain.

'Have I not told thee already how the matter stands ?' said Duncan.

So Iain put an end to the other enemy also.

A second time they boomed out a shield-clashing challenge—   Z 85*
[Demanding] a battle, or else a combat,
Or else that the Big Man's head should be sent out to them.

'How foolish am I,' said the Big Man, 'to be spending my men thus, considering that I never yet saw any man, big or little, that I could not manage.'

And then out he came himself.

'Well, well,' said Iain Og, 'this one, at any rate, is terrible [2] to see.'

Iain and he attacked each other, and Iain plied his sword against him as hard as he was able.

Duncan also attacked him in the rear, and cut a collop out of him from the crook of the hough, and another out of his thigh, and another out of the small of his back, so that he cut a staircase out of the Big Man up to [the region]   G 153*
between the two shoulder-blades ! [3] He got up between

---

[2] Epithets are very rare in these tales.
[3] For cutting a similar staircase, see *W. H. Tales*, iii., No. 75.

is thilg Iain an ceann deth.   Chuir e siod air a ghualainn,
G 510   is dh' fhalbh iad a dh' iarraidh ceann an Fhir Bhig.

F 123*   Ràinig iad rìoghachd an Fhir Bhig.

Z 85*   BHUAIL IAD BEUM SGÉITHE—
Cath, air neo comhrag,
Air neo ceann an Fhir Bhig a chur a mach d'an ionnsuigh.

Siod an rud a gheibheadh iad,—
Cath, air neo comhrag,
'S cha b'e ceann an Fhir Bhig.

Chuireadh a mach dithis d'an ionnsuigh, is mharbh
Iain a fhear fhéin.   'Tionndaidh ris an fhear so, is marbh
e,' arsa Donnchadh.   Chuir Iain crìoch air an fhear ud
cuideachd.

'Is mi tha gòrach,' ars am Fear Beag, 'a bhi cosd mo
chuid daoine, is nach fhaca mi fear mór no beag riamh
nach rachadh agam air.'   Chaidh e a mach, is mharbh
iad esan, mar a mharbh iad am Fear Mór, is thug iad dheth
an ceann.

Thill iad dachaidh do'n Fhraing [anns an t-soitheach].
An uair a bha iad a' nochdadh ris an rìoghachd, chunnaic
iad toit os an cionn.

'Ciod è an toit a tha an siod?' arsa Iain.

P 361·2   'Tha an siod Ladhar Dubh, is e cur rìoghachd na
Frainge 'na teinidh.   Tha latha is bliadhna air dol seachad,
is bha e smuaineachadh nach tilleadh thusa tuilleadh.[1]
Thoir tuilleadh astair do'n t-soitheach, is gun cumamaid
Ladhair [Dubh] air ais.'

Thug Iain tuilleadh astair do'n t-soitheach.

'Ciod e an t-astar tha aig an t-soitheach?' arsa
Donnchadh.

'Tha i cho luath ris a' ghaoith luaith Mhàirt,' ars Iain.

'Thoir tuilleadh astair di fhathast,' arsa Donnchadh.
Thug Iain tuilleadh astair di.

---

[1] The faithful henchman, despairing of his master's return, had determined
that no one else should have the kingdom of France.   The King of Lochlann's
witch-daughter sets fire to the ancient Scottish pine-forests in various tales
so that the smoke of the burning spreads all over the country.—Dr A.

his two shoulder-blades, and felled him, and Iain swept
off his head.   He laid it on his shoulder, and then they set   G 510
forth to fetch the head of the Little Man.

They arrived at the kingdom of the Little Man.   F 123*

THEY SOUNDED A BOOMING SHIELD-CLASHING CHALLENGE—   Z 85*
[Demanding] a battle, or else a combat,
Or else, that the Little Man's head should be sent out to them.

This was what they should have—
A battle, or else a combat,
But not the head of the Little Man.

Two men were now sent out to them, and Iain killed
his. 'Turn now to this one, and kill him,' said Duncan.
Iain put an end to that one also.

"Tis I who am foolish,' said the Little Man, 'to be
spending my men thus, considering that I never saw any
man, big or little, whom I could not manage.'   Out he
came, and they killed him, as they had killed the Big Man,
and took off his head.

They now returned home to France [in the vessel].
But when they were coming in sight of it, they noticed
smoke floating over their heads.

'What smoke can that be ?' said Iain.

'That is Black Toe's doing; he is giving the kingdom   P 361·2
of France to the flames. A day and a year have gone
past, and he was beginning to think that thou wouldst
return no more.[1]   Give the vessel more way, that we may
restrain [Black] Toe.'

Iain gave the vessel more way.

'What speed has the vessel now ?' said Duncan.

'She is as swift as the swift March wind,' said Iain.

'Give her more way yet,' said Duncan.   Iain gave her
more way.

Carmichael's *Deirdre*, p. 149.   *Trans. Gael. Soc. Inverness*, xxvi., p. 277.   *An Deò
Gréine*, ix., p. 149.   *Waifs and Strays*, v., p. 101.   Dr George Henderson, *The
Celtic Dragon Myth*, xxii.   *The Norse Influence*, p. 278.

'Seall ciod è tuilleadh astair a tha aice a nis !' arsa Donnchadh.

'Tha i na's luaithe na a' ghaoth luath Mhàirt,' arsa Iain.

'Chan fhoghainn sin fhathast. Seall a rithist ciod e an t-astar a tha aice,' arsa Donnchadh.

D 2122·3   'Tha i cho luath ri aigne nam ban baoth,' arsa Iain.

D 1521·2   'Foghnaidh sin,' arsa Donnchadh.[1]
Ràinig iad tìr, is cha robh iad fad air ruigheachd an uair a mhothaich Ladhar [Dubh] dhaibh. Thòisich e air cur as do'n teine, is bu duiliche dha a cur as, na a toirt beò. Choinnich Ladhar [Dubh] aig a' chladach iad.

'Seadh, a Dhonnchaidh ! tha thu ann !'

'Tha,' arsa Donnchadh.

'Ma tà,' arsa Ladhar [Dubh], 'bha mise 'nad thigh an oidhche dh'fhalbh thu.'

'Bha fios agam fhéin gum biodh,' arsa Donnchadh.

'Falbhaidh tusa nis, Iain, is bheir thu leat ceann an Fhir Mhóir, is tilgidh tu air beulaibh na Caillich e. Abair gu bheil an ceann an siod aice, is gu bheil thu glé sgìth air a shàilibh, is na can facal tuilleadh rithe,' [arsa Ladhar Dubh].[2]

Dh'fhalbh e far an robh a' Chailleach, is thilg e ceann an Fhir Mhóir air a beulaibh.

E 55·1·1*   'Sin e agad,' ars Iain, 'is tha mi seachd sgìth dheth.'
E 67*   Dh'fhalbh e, is cha tug e feairt oirre, is i ag eubhach ris gu tuilleadh seanchais a dhèanamh ris.

An là-'r-na-mhàireach, thuirt Ladhar [Dubh] ris, 'Bheir thu leat ceann an Fhir Bhig an diugh ann ad achlais. Ruigidh tu a' Chailleach, is bheir thu móran modha dhi, is their thu rithe gu bheil thu ag iarraidh maitheanais oirre airson na rinn thu de mhìomhodh oirre an dé, is nam biodh i fhéin cho math is gun tigeadh i a

---

[1] For similar acceleration of a boat's speed, see *Waifs and Strays*, ii., pp. 351, 487. *An Gàidheal* (1924), xix., p. 114.   D. C. MacPherson, *An Duanaire*, p. 97. Dr W. J. Watson, *Rosg Gàidhlig*, p. 83.   *Witchcraft*, pp. 19, 20. *Folk-Lore*, xiv., pp. 301-2. *Celtic Review*, iii., p. 261. In *W. H. Tales*, ii., No. 52, var. (no number) a hero runs up a mast 'faster than a mad woman's tongue.' See Nicolson's *Gaelic Proverbs*, p. 142—'Cho luath ri aigne nam ban baoth. As swift as the fancy

'Look and see how much more way she has now !'
said Duncan.

'She is swifter than the swift March wind,' said Iain.

'That will not yet suffice. See how much way she has
now,' said Duncan.

'She is as swift as the fancy of foolish women,' said Iain. D 2122·3

'That will do,' said Duncan.[1] D 1521·2

They came to land, but had not long arrived, when
[Black] Toe noticed them. He began to put out the fire,
but found it more difficult to put out than to kindle. He
met them at the shore.

'Ha ! Duncan ! art thou there ?'

'I am,' said Duncan.

'Well then,' said [Black] Toe, 'I was in thy house the
night thou didst go away.'

'Well I knew thou wouldst be,' said Duncan.

'Go thou now, Iain, take the head of the Big Man with
thee, and cast it down before the Cailleach. Say that she
has now got the head, and that thou art very tired of it,
but say not a word more,' [said Black Toe].[2]

So he went off to the place where the Cailleach was,
and threw the head of the Big Man down before her.

'There thou hast it,' said Iain, 'and I am seven times E 55·1·1*
tired of it.' Then he went away, and though she was E 67*
shouting at him to hold further speech with her, he took
no notice.

On the morrow, [Black] Toe said to him,

'To-day thou shalt take the head of the Little Man with
thee tucked under thy arm. Go to the Cailleach, show
her much politeness, and say that thou art seeking forgiveness from her for the discourtesy thou didst do her yesterday,
and [ask her] if she would be so good as to come over and

---

of foolish women.' Compare Thor's attempt to run against Thought. For
other expressions of speed, see *Waifs and Strays*, i., pp. 49, 52 n, 82, 83 n; ii.,
p. 351.

[2] The faithful henchman evidently realized that too much talking would
revive or resuscitate the old Cailleach sooner than was desirable.

E 55·1·1* nall is an ceann a thoirt á t'achlais. Tòisichidh ise air
tighinn a nall chugad, is ma rinn thusa cuimse riamh air
an t-saoghal—tha e agad ri a dhèanamh air an t-siubhal
sin! Buailidh tu an ceann oirre ann an taobh a' chinn
aice. Chan 'eil dad air an t-saoghal gu ise a mharbhadh
Z 312   ach ceann a bràthar fhéin.' [1]

Dh'fhalbh Iain an so far an robh a' Chailleach. Ghabh
e a lethsgeul airson a bhi cho mìomhodhail roimhe, is
thuirt e rithe, nam b'e a toil e, an ceann a thoirt a achlais.

G 275   An uair a bha ise tighinn far an robh e, tharruing e an
·1·1*   ceann, is bhuail e an taobh a' chinn i, is mharbh e i.

'Tha a h-uile gnothuch a nis seachad,' arsa Ladhar
[Dubh]. 'Faodaidh tusa, a Dhonnchaidh, dol dachaidh
do t' àite fhéin is ma théid dragh ort, bidh thu freagarrach.
Fanaidh mise comhla ri Iain.'

'From Roderick MacNeill, labourer, Glen, Barra. Heard it
from many old men of whom are those already mentioned.'
For the names of these old men, see No. 11, by the same
reciter.

---

[1] For killing by a blow on the head, using the head of another character
for a weapon, see p. 40 n, No. 2 (MS. vol. x., No. 203). It will be observed that
when she is presented with the head of the Big Man, the Cailleach is able to
call after the hero, but does not seem able to pursue him. On presenting
her with the second head, that of the Little Man, she is so far revived that
she is able to move towards him. It is clear that she was gradually reviving
or resuscitating from some previous state of disintegration, and that this
reviving was the result of the hero's talking to her, and that had he talked
to her long enough, her resuscitation would have been complete. From all
this, we must conclude that before setting out on her last errands, the hero
must have counter-be-spelled her in the usual way to remain where she was
and to refrain from food and drink, until his return. Unfortunately, either
the reciter or the scribe forgot to record that he did so. The double visit
to the Cailleach is unique. The fact that she is twice resuscitated is also
unique. See Appendix, p. 508.

take the head from under thine arm. Then will she begin E 55·1·1*
to come over to thee, and if ever in the world thou didst
take good aim—that is what thou then hast to do ! Strike
her on the side of her head with the head of the Little Man.
In all the world there is nothing that can kill her but the
head of her own brother !' [1]   Z 312

Thereupon Iain went over to the Cailleach. He
excused himself for having been so unmannerly before,
and asked her, if it were her pleasure, to take the head
from under his arm.

When she was coming over to him, he, swinging the head G 275
round hard, struck her on the side of her own head with it, ·1·1*
and killed her.

'Everything is now over and finished,' said [Black]
Toe. 'Thou, Duncan, mayest go home to thine own place,
and if anything trouble thee, thou wilt be equal to it. I
will stay along with Iain.'

NOTES

MS. vol. x., No. 31. Scribe, Hector MacLean. On the flyleaf
of the MS. Campbell has written: 'One of the regular Highland
stories which have nothing earthly to do with books of any kind that
I ever read—quite peculiar.'

A story, similar in some ways but not in others, is 'Séarlus, Mac
Rí na Frainnce,' *Béaloideas*, ii., p. 134.

In cutting off the Governor's ear for refusing to give him his father's
weapons, the young hero gives an earnest of his future prowess, and
a proof that he is conscious of his royal prerogative which places him
above ordinary obligations, and entitles him to treat his subjects as his
own personal property.

In J. H. Simpson's *Poems of Oisín, Bàrd of Erin*, p. 203, a big giant
gives Diarmuid 'a golden apple which will kill anything you throw
it at, and then come back again to your hand.' Diarmuid forthwith
tests the golden apple on the giant's own head, and ascertains that
his statement was correct. See also *W. H. Tales, introd.*, lxxxi or lxxv.—
'There is a gruagach who has a golden apple which is thrown at all
comers, and unless they are able to catch it they die; when it is caught
and thrown back by the hero, Gruagach an Ubhail [the Gruagach
of the Apple] dies. There is a game called cluich an ubhail, the
apple play, which seems to have been a deadly game, whatever it was.'
Heroes who fight each other also use an 'apple,' probably of brass or

other metal—'The apple of the juggler, throwing it and catching it into each other's laps, frightfully, furiously, bloodily, groaning, hurtfully.' (*W. H. Tales*, ii., No. 52. Professor W. J. Watson, *Rosg Gàidhlig*, pp. 94, 214.) The game is also played with a 'venomous' apple (*Waifs and Strays*, ii., pp. 87, 91). For the 'apple-feat' of Cuchulainn, see *Celtic Review*, i., p. 368.

There are several versions of the strange incident of resuscitation. Two instances of it occur in this tale. In the first instance the hero allows the enemy not only to re-materialize but also to lay further commands upon him. His doing so is very much in keeping with his magnanimity and forbearance, and is therefore an artistic touch of imagination. So much can be seen on the surface, but there is probably some deeper significance in this part of the matter, whatever that significance may be. But the fact that he does not kill after resuscitation has been completed, but allows the enemy to lay further spells upon him, is still more significant and unique. It does not seem to occur in any other tale.

Equally exceptional is that story of the Queen of Lochlann living underground. Her relationship to the hero's two henchmen, that of aunt, is also very singular. And who the two henchmen really represent remains a puzzle.

The hero's magnanimity and generosity is illustrated on six occasions. He wins in the first game or gamble with Black Toe, and also in the first game or gamble with the Cailleach, but does not avail himself of his victory on either occasion. He overcomes Black Toe in one fight, and Black Toe's brother in another fight, but on each occasion admits his late foe to mercy, and allows him to become a retainer or henchman. On the occasion of the Cailleach's first resuscitation, he does not kill her, but allows her to revive and lay further spells upon him. Finally, he only accepts a modest fraction of the King of Erin's proffered bounty. (For a similarly magnanimous hero, see *W. H. Tales*, ii., No. 51.)

Whether the hero obtained the kingdom of France is not said, but it may be inferred that he did.

Hector MacLean, the scribe, whose euhemerizing mind believed that these tales had been originally composed for the laudable purpose of inculcating moral lessons, has a note about the old witch at the end of this story. The note begins thus :—

'The Cailleach G[h]las is a complete material representation of moral delinquency, the impersonation of passion and intellect without a spark of moral principle. She is one-eyed. So is the mind without moral perception. It has but one eye. It perceives the agreement and disagreement of things but not right and wrong.' And so forth. His other notes are in much the same spirit. 'The deer pet here is, no doubt, a figurative representation of follies and delusive pleasures which have so often ruined kings,' etc.

One wonders why different supernatural characters desire to possess the heads or the swords of their relations. The only story that appears to hint at any reason whatever is called 'Eachtra air an Sgolóig agus air an nGruagach Ruadh,' The History of the Farmer and the Red Gruagach, where the Red Gruagach wants his brother's sword. The reason given is ordinary common covetousness. See *The Gaelic Journal*, iv., p. 28 (1890, Dublin). But this reason seems unconvincing, especially when one remembers that possession of the things coveted is, in Scottish tales, always fatal. In Irish tales this is not always so.

AN DÀ CHRAOIBH GHAOIL

No. 18.   [*Vol. x., No. 32*]

Aarne-Thompson, No. 966 (A-T, p. 233)

BHA duine uasal bochd ann, agus bha trì nigheanan aige, agus thuirt an té b'aosda latha, 'Is e an smaointinn a tha agam, athair, gum falbh mi uaibh air mhuinntearas, gun téid mi dha'm chosnadh.'
'Ciod è is coireach ris an sin?' ars a h-athair.
'Chan 'eil mi 'gam fhaotainn fhìn coltach ri cloinn eile tha mi faicinn an so,' ars ise.
'Cha tàinig aois duit a bhi coltach ri cloinn eile. An uair a thig thu gu h-aois, bidh thu coltach riu.'
'Thàinig mise gu h-aois n'a[s] leòir, is chan 'eil sibhse sealltuinn orm o'n a shiubhail mo mhàthair.'
Cheangail i a h-aodach suas is dh'fhalbh i.
An uair a dh'fhalbh i, cha robh i faighinn maighstir. Shiubhail i gach àite 'san dùthaich sin, is chaidh i do dhùthaich eile. Am beul na h-oidhche, thachair duine uasal oirre aig ceann an tighe aige fhìn.
Rinn i fasdadh ris an duine uasal, is chaidh i leis a stigh. Cha robh i ach beagan ùine a stigh, an uair a chuireadh umhail nach fanadh mac an duine uasail as an t-seòmar aice. Cha robh aige ach an aon mhac. Thug a athair an aghaidh air a' ghille airson a bhi dol do sheòmar na nighinn. 'Tha naidheachdan cho éibhinn aice, is tha i fhìn cho laghach,' ars a mhac, 'ach chan 'eil dad de dhroch nì sam bith eadaruinn.'
Uine as a dhéidh so, thuirt a h-aon de an luchd-muinntir a bha stigh ri a h-aon eile, 'Chuala mise ràn leanaibh ann an seòmar na nighinn.' Chuala an nighean bheag e, agus dh'innis i do a màthair e. 'Cuisd, a thrusdair,' ars a màthair, 'ga bualadh mu'n bheul, 'ciod e an seanchas a tha agad mar sin!'—'Tha seanchas agam a dh'fhaodas a bhi agam,' ars am pàisde.

THE TWO LOVE TREES

No. 18.   *[Vol. x., No. 32]*

Aarne-Thompson, No. 966 (A-T, p. 233)

THERE was a poor gentleman who had three daughters, and the eldest said one day, 'What I think, father, is that I will leave you to seek service, and go and earn my own living.'

'What is the cause of that ?' said her father.

'Well, it seems to me that I am not like other children that I see about here,' quoth she.

'Thou art not yet of an age to be like other children. When thou comest to some age, thou wilt be like them.'

'I have come to age enough, but you give me no consideration since my mother died.'

She made a bundle of her clothes, and went off.

She travelled but could not find a master at once. She traversed every place in that country, and then went to another country. One evening, at night-fall, a gentleman met her at the end of his own house.

She took service with the gentleman, and went indoors with him. She had not been there but for a short time when it was noticed that the gentleman's son would not stay away from her room. The gentleman had but one son. His father took the lad to task for going to the young woman's room. 'But she has such cheerful stories, and is so nice herself too,' said his son, 'and there is nothing whatever between us that is wrong.'

Some time after that, one of the servants who were indoors said to another, 'I heard the cry of a child in the girl's room.' The little daughter heard it, and told her mother. 'Hush, thou scapegrace,' quoth her mother, striking her on the mouth, 'how canst thou talk in that way !'— 'I say what I very well may say,' replied the child.

Dh'innis a bhean do'n duine e aig a thràth-nòin. 'Na bi togail droch sgeoil air an nighinn as fhearr a chunnaic mi riamh,' ars esan, 'is coma leam a leithid sin de sheanchas. Cha d'aithnich sinn air a h-obair riamh e, is nam bitheadh a leithid sin ann, cha b'urrainn di a fhalach.' Ars a bhean, 'Chan 'eil teagamh nach fhaodadh a leithid a bhi ann.'—Ars esan, 'Gheibh mise a mach an ceartuair. Iarraidh mise oirre dol air astar glé fhada le litir, is ma tha a leithid sin ann, chan fhalbh i.' Chuir e brath oirre is thàinig i. 'Is e an gnothach a bha agam riut,' ars esan, 'tha mi 'gad chur a so le litir, agus cha tig thu a nochd. Tha an t-astar fada. A bheil thu deònach falbh?' 'Tha, ach bheir sibh uair dàil domh?' 'Bheir,' ars esan, 'ged a dh'iarradh tu a dhà.' An ceann uair, thàinig i. 'Am bheil sibh deiseil?' ars i ris an duine uasal. 'Tha,' ars an duine uasal. Thug an duine uasal dhi an litir, is dh'fhalbh i.

Dh'fhalbh bean an duine uasail, is fhuair i iuchair, is dh'fhosgail i an dorus aice an uair a dh'fhalbh i. Ciod e fhuair i ach leanabh gille, is e gàireachdaich is a' togail a làmhan rithe anns an leabaidh aice-se. Bha aotroman [làn bainne] a' slaodadh ris, agus sine 'na bheul 'ga deòghal. Thog bean an duine uasail e, is thug i leatha e. Chruinnich a h-uile duine a stigh mun cuairt air. Chuireadh brath air an duine uasal, is thàinig e. Cha robh fios aig an duine uasal ciod è dhèanadh e ris. Chan fhac e leanabh riamh cho brèagh ris. 'Nach e tha coltach rium-sa?' ars esan. 'Air na chunnaic sibh riamh, na canaibh facal ris a' mhaighdinn-sheòmair, is na cuiribh duilichinn sam bith oirre. Tha mi glé thoilichte an gille a bhi ann.' Thàinig ise am beul na h-oidhche air sia uairean an latha sin fhìn. Rinn i coiseachd dà latha an aon. Ghabh i do'n t-seòmar an uair a thàinig i, 's cha d'fhuair i an leanabh a stigh an sin anns an t-seòmar. Bha i fas nàrach. Arsa bean an duine uasail [ris], 'Falbh d'a h-iarraidh.' Chaidh an duine uasal a stigh far an robh i.

The wife told her husband at dinner time. 'Don't be raising a bad report about the best lass I ever saw,' said he, 'I dislike that kind of talk. We never saw any sign of it in her work, and had there been such a thing, she could not have hidden it.'

Said his wife, 'But there certainly might have been such a thing.'—Quoth he, 'I will find out at once. I will ask her to go a long way with a letter, and then if such a thing is the case, she will not go.'

He sent word for her and she came.

'The errand that I have for thee,' said he, 'is that I am sending thee forth with a letter, and thou wilt not be back to-night, for the journey is long. Art willing to go?'

'I am, but will ye not give me an hour's grace?'

'Yes, I will,' said he, 'even if thou hadst asked for two.'

At the end of an hour, she came to him. 'Are ye ready?' she said to the gentleman. 'I am,' said the gentleman. The gentleman gave her the letter, and she set off.

The gentleman's wife went and got a key, and opened her door when she had gone. What did she find but a baby boy, laughing and lifting his hands to her, in the girl's bed. A bladder [full of milk] was tied to him, and he had a teat in his mouth which he was sucking. The gentleman's wife lifted him up and took him off with her. Everyone indoors gathered round about the baby. Word was sent for the gentleman and he came.

Well, the gentleman did not know what he should do with the baby. He had never seen a child so handsome as he. 'Is he not just like myself?' quoth he. 'For all ye ever saw [= for any sake] don't say a word to the chambermaid, and do not cause her any vexation. I am very pleased that there is a boy.'

But she came back at night-fall, in six hours, that very same day. She had done two days' walking in one. She went to the room when she came back, and did not find the child there. She felt covered with shame. Said the gentleman's wife to him, 'Go and fetch her.' The gentleman went to where she was.

'Tha thu air tighinn,' ars esan, 'cha b'fhada bha thu air do thurus.'

'Cha b'fhada, le'r cead. Cha robh mi fada idir.'

'Seadh,' ars esan, 'na bi cho nàrach is a tha thu, ged a fhuair mise a mach ort e.'

'Tha mi fad ás an rathad. Tha mi 'g iarraidh maitheanais.'

'Cha robh mise latha riamh cho mór mu do dhéinibh [1] is a tha mi,' ars esan; 'thig a mach a sin, is gabh a dh' ionnsuigh do leanaibh.' Thug e leis i, is chuir e do'n t-seòmar aige fhìn i far an robh an leanabh.

'Thàinig thu,' arsa bean an duine uasail.

'Thàinig,' ars ise.

'Cha robh mise latha riamh cho mór mu do dhéinibh is a tha mi.' Shìn i an so dhi an leanabh.

'Cha bhi e fada agad,' arsa bean an duine uasail: 'gheibh mise banaltrum gus an aire thoirt da.'

Chuir bean an duine uasail an so brath air banaltrum. Thàinig banaltrum, agus thug ise an leanabh di.

'Luthaigidh [2] mise mo mhac duit, is na bi fo mhulad sam bith,' ars an duine uasal ris an nighinn.

Bhruidhinn an duine uasal ri maighstir soithich a bha 'san acarsaid mar a dh'éirich do a mhac.

'Is e an rud a nì thu. Bheir mise do mhac leam,' arsa maighstir an t-soithich; 'cuir thusa a nuas an so e le litir, air a leithid so de latha.'

Chuir an duine uasal a mhac a sìos le litir. An uair a fhuair esan an gille air bòrd, thug e òrdan na siùil a chur ris an t-soitheach. Thug e gu ruige na h-Innsean e, is bha aonta seachd bliadhna air.

Bha e 'na ghille-bùth anns na h-Innsibh. Bha e cur litrichean chun na nighinn, is bha ise cur litrichean d'a ionnsuigh-san.

Choinnich an duine uasal am posta latha. 'A bheil litir agad a bheanas do'n tigh agamsa?' ars e ris a' phosta.

---

[1] So MS.   [2] For lughasaichidh.

'Thou hast come back,' said he, 'thou wert not long on thy journey.'

'I was not, with your leave. I was not long at all.'

'Yes,' said he, 'do not be so shamefaced as thou art, though I have found thee out.'

'I have gone very far astray. I ask forgiveness.'

'But I was never before so proud of thee as I am now,' quoth he, 'come away from here, and go to thy child.' He took her with him, and sent her to his own room where the child was.

'Thou hast come,' quoth the gentleman's wife.

'I have,' said she.

'I was never so proud of thee any day as I am now,' [said the gentleman's wife], and here she handed her the child.

'Thou shalt not have him long,' she continued: 'I shall get a nurse to take care of him.'

So the wife of the gentleman sent word for a nurse. A nurse came, and she gave her the child.

'I will permit thee to have my son, so be not at all grieved,' quoth the gentleman to the young woman [= the heroine].

The gentleman spoke to the master of a ship that was in the anchorage, and told him what had happened to his son.

'This is what thou must do. I will take thy son with me,' said the shipmaster; 'do thou send him down here with a letter, on such and such a day.'

The gentleman sent his son down with a letter. When K 978 he got the lad on board, he gave orders to set the vessel's sails. He took him to the Indies, and he was apprenticed for seven years.

He was a shop-boy in the Indies. He used to send letters to the young woman and she was sending letters to him.

Now the gentleman met the postman one day. 'Hast thou any letter that belongs to my house?' said he to the post.

'Tha litir agam leis [1] a' mhaighdinn sheòmair,' ars am posta.

'Bheir thu domhsa i ann an so. Giùlainidh mi fhìn dachaidh i, agus pàidhidh mi fhìn thu,' [ars an duine uasal, agus] sgrìobh e té eile, is chuir e naidheachd bàis a' ghille innte. An latha bu chòir do'n phosta tighinn, thug e (an duine uasal) an litir da. 'So,' ars esan, 'bheir thu an litir sin do'n mhaighdinn-sheòmair agamsa.' Chaidh am posta a dh' ionnsuigh na maighdinn seòmair leis an litir. Dh'fhosgail a' mhaighdeann sheòmair an litir, is fhuair i naidheachd a bhàis-san innte. Cha tugteadh an so facal a ceann na maighdinn-sheòmair. Thuirt an duine uasal latha rithe:—

'Tha mi ag aithneachadh rud-eigin ort. Cha chreid mi nach' eil rud-eigin ort, mum biodh tu cho muladach is a tha thu o chionn trì làithean. Fhuair mise litir mu mo mhac, agus dh'eug e.'

'O ! fhuair mise litir cuideachd,' ars ise: 'is ann is fhearr dhuinn cunntas a dhèanamh, is gum falbhainn.'

'Chan fhalbh thu as mo thigh idir, is na cuireadh siod air falbh idir thu. Na bi falbh idir, is gabh mo chomhairle fhìn agus comhairle sam bith a bheir mise ort: is math leam gu math thu.'

'Is ciod è a' chomhairle a tha sibh a' toirt orm ?' ars ise. 'Tha,' ars esan, 'pòsaidh thu mo bhràthair ged a tha e sean. Tha móran de chuid an t-saoghail aige. Ged a tha e sean, gabhaidh tu mo chomhairle-sa, is pòsaidh tu e.' [3]

Dh'fhalbh e is chuir e brath air a bhràthair, is laigh iad air an nighinn chor is gun do phòs iad.

Is e ochd seachduinnean a bha an gille gun tighinn as

---

[1] *leis* is the regular word in saying *a letter for* somebody, though *gu* is also used.

[2] The incidents concerning the coming of the postman are not quite clear. The first time the postman came the gentleman took the letter and did not give it to the girl; the next time the postman came the gentleman gave him a letter which he himself had composed during the interval, and

'I have a letter for the chambermaid,' said the postman.

'Thou shalt give it to me here. I will carry it home myself, and I will pay thee,' [quoth the gentleman, but] he wrote another, and put in it tidings of the lad's death. 　K 1851

The day that the postman was due to come, he (the gentleman) gave him the letter.[2] 'Here,' said he, 'give thou that letter to my chambermaid.'

The postman went to the chambermaid with the letter. The chambermaid opened the letter, and found the news of his death inside it. Not a word could now be got from the chambermaid's mouth, so one day the gentleman said to her:—

'I notice that there is something on thy mind. I will never believe but that there is something the matter with thee, or thou wouldst never have been so mournful as thou hast been for the last three days. I have had a letter about my son, and he is dead.'

'O! I got a letter also,' quoth she, 'we had better have a reckoning in order that I may go.'

'Thou shalt not go out of my house at all, and let not this matter drive thee away. Do not go at all but take my advice and any advice whatever that I give thee; I wish thee well.'

'And what is the advice you are giving me?' quoth she.

'It is this,' said he, 'thou shalt marry my brother, though he be old. He has abundance of the world's goods. Though he be old, thou shalt take my advice, and marry him.'[3]

He went and sent word for his brother, and they both urged the girl and worked upon her feelings till they married.

After this, eight weeks elapsed before the lad returned.

gave it to the postman to deliver so as to make the letter seem as genuine as possible.

[3] The gentleman's advice is singular. He wants to turn his daughter-in-law into his sister-in-law, in order probably to separate the lovers, and in order perhaps that his grandson might inherit his brother's property. Or he may have another intention—venting his spite against her.

a dhéidh so. An ceann ochd seachduinnean, thàinig e,
agus dh'fhaighnich e an uair a thàinig e dhachaidh, càite
an robh ise.

'Phòs i sin bràthair t'athar o'n a dh'fhalbh thu, is cha
robh i brath fuireach riutsa,' ars iad ris.

T 30

Thàinig a h-uile duine riamh a bha 'sa bhaile dh'a
choimhead an uair a thàinig e. An uair a thàinig ise far
an robh e, rug iad air làmhan air a chéile, is thòisich iad
air caoineadh.

'Ciod e thug dhuit pòsadh, gus an tàinig mi?' ars esan.

'Fhuair mi litir do bhàis,' ars ise.

'Cha d'fhuair,' ars esan.

'Fhuair,' ars ise. Shìn i an litir da.

'O,' ars esan, 'is e m'athair a rinn so. Tha m'athair
dona,' ars esan.

'Tha an t-ám agam,' ars ise, 'bhi falbh a sìos do'n tigh.'

'Théid mise sìos far am bi thu an uair a chaidleas na
daoine, is fàgaidh tu an dorus mór fosgailte agus dorus an
t-seòmair.'

'Fàgaidh,' ars ise.

Chaidh esan a sìos an uair a chaidil na daoine. Chaidh
e do'n t-seòmar aice-se, is chuir e a làmh oirre-se, is i bhos
an taobh so de'n leaba.

Thug ise ràn aisde, agus dh'éigh i do'n bhodach an
taobh eile. 'Eirich, a dhuine, agus cuid-eigin feadh an
tighe.'

'Is fuathasach [so],' ars am bodach, 'd è an rànaich no an
caoineadh a tha ort? Am bi thu a h-uile h-oidhche
mar sin?'

Chuir esan a làmh a rithist oirre, is thug ise ràn a
rithist aisde, e a dh'éirigh gu h-ealamh.

Dh'éirich am bodach air an t-siubhal so, agus fhuair
e mac a bhràthar marbh ri taobh na leapa.

'A Dhia! cobhair orm!' ars esan, 'tha mac mo
bhràthar marbh an so aig ceann na leapa! O!' ars
esan, 'crochar mi! Abraidh iad gur h-ann gu do
choimhead a thàinig e agus crochar mi!'

At the end of the eight weeks he arrived, and when he came home he enquired where she was.

'Yon lass married thy father's brother since thou left, and she did not intend waiting for thee,' said they to him.

Every man in the town came to see him when he arrived. But when she came up to where he was, they caught each other's hands, and began to cry. T 30

'What caused thee to marry, before I came?' said he.

'I had news of thy death,' she replied.

'No, thou couldst not have had,' said he.

'But I had,' said she, and handed the letter to him.

'O,' said he, 'it is my father who has done this. My father is wicked,' said he.

'It is time for me,' said she, 'to be going away home.'

'When people are all asleep, I will come to thee wherever thou art, and do thou leave the big door and the door of the room open.'

'I will do so,' she said.

He went accordingly when the people were all asleep. He went to her room, and put his hand upon her, she being on the outside of the bed.

But she gave a shriek, and called to the old man on the other side of the bed. 'Rise, goodman, someone is going about the house.'

'This is dreadful,' said the old man, 'what art thou screaming and crying for? Art thou thus every night?'

Presently again, he laid his hand upon her, and again she gave a shriek, saying that the old man was to rise instantly.

This time the old man arose, and found his brother's son dead by the side of the bed.

'O God! help me!' said he, 'for here is my brother's son dead at the bedside! O!' said he, 'they will hang me! They will say that it is to see thee he came, and I shall be hanged!'

'Ma tà,' ars ise, 'is e as fhearr dhuit a dhèanamh, falbh
leis agus a fhàgail ann an tigh a athar.'

Dh'fhalbh e leis air a mhuin, agus dh'fhàg e anns an
t-seòmar aige fhìn e ann an tigh a athar.
Thill e an so dachaidh, agus fhuair e ise marbh anns an
leaba.—Thog e i, is dh'fheuch e i feuch an robh an anail
innte, is cha robh.
Ràinig e tigh a bhràthar, agus bhuail e anns an uinneig
mu mheadhon oidhche.
'Có tha bualadh anns an uinneig?' ars a bhràthair.
'Tha mise,' ars esan.
'Ciod è so? Ciod è tha cur ort an uair a thàinig thu
mu mheadhon oidhche?' ars a bhràthair.
'O, is coma sin domh!' ars esan, 'is coma sin domhsa!
Fhuair mi do mhac fhìn marbh aig taobh na leapa agam
fhín air a' mhionaid. Ghiùlain mi air mo mhuin e, is
dh'fhàg mi 'na sheòmar fhìn e. An uair a thill mi sìos,
fhuair mi a' bhean agam fhìn marbh anns an leaba gun
anam.'
'Am faod mi do chreidsinn?' ars a bhràthair.
'Faodaidh,' ars esan.
Chaidh iad a suas, is fhuair iad e mar a dh'fhàg bràthair
a athar e 'na leabaidh fhìn marbh.
Chaidh iad an so sìos do'n tigh aige-san, is fhuair iad
a bhean marbh anns an leapa.
An là-'r-na-mhàireach thiodhlaiceadh iad.

Cha leigeadh an duine uasal a mhac fhìn agus ise anns
an aon uaigh.
Chuireadh ise an taobh a muigh de ghàradh cladh an
duine uasail, is thiodhlaiceadh a mhac fo a lic fhín.

An ceann ùine, dh'fhàs craobh as gach uaigh, is chuir
E 631·0·1 iad trì chuir dhiubh mu a chéile.

From Roderick MacLean, tailor, Ken Tangval, Barra, who learnt
it from a mason at Petty, Inverness, but does not recollect
his name.

'Well then,' said she, 'what thou hadst better do, is to take him with thee, and leave him in his father's house.'

He accordingly carried him away on his back, and left him in his own room in his father's house.

He then returned home, and found *her* dead in the bed. —He lifted her up, and felt her to see if there were any breath in her, but there was none.

He went to his brother's house, and knocked at the window about midnight.

'Who is knocking at the window?' said his brother.

'It is I,' said he.

'What's all this? What is troubling thee, that thou comest at midnight?' said his brother.

'O! it is a dreadful thing for me!' quoth he, 'it is a dreadful thing for me! For I have just found thine own son dead at the side of my own bed this minute. I carried him here on my back, and left him in his own room. When I returned, I found my own wife dead in the bed, her soul having departed.'

'May I really credit thee?' quoth his brother.

'Thou mayest indeed,' said he.

They went up and found the son dead in his own bed, where his uncle had placed him.

And upon going down to the brother's house, they found his wife dead in the bed.

On the morrow, they [the two young lovers] were buried.

But the gentleman would not allow her to rest in the same grave as his son.

So *she* was buried outside the wall of the gentleman's burial ground, but his son was buried under the gentleman's own tombstone.

In the course of time, a tree grew out of each grave, and twined themselves thrice round each other. E 631·0·1

NOTES

MS. vol. x., No. 32.   Scribe, Hector MacLean.   Narrator, Roderick MacLean, tailor [Isle of Barra].

One of the few Gaelic folk-tales that may be called tragic, as most of the tales have a happy ending, except in the case of some of the Fenian tales.

The story is in essence a common English ballad theme; two parted lovers die of grief and plants of some kind grow out of their graves and entwine.   For a Celtic parallel, however, see Carmichael's *Deirdire*, p. 111, and *Béaloideas*, ii., p. 209.

AN NIGHEAN A REICEADH

No. 19.   *Campbell MS. Vol. x., No. 33*

Aarne-Thompson, No. 930

BHA duine bochd ann agus bha seachdnar chloinne aige.
Thàinig duine uasal an rathad, is thuirt e ris gur h-ann
aige bha a' chlann. Thuirt e gun robh na leòir aige, agus
droch cothrom aige air an togail, is iad air dhroch bhiadh
is aodach.

'An creic [1] thu a h-aon diubh?' ars an duine uasal.
'Creicidh,' ars esan. 'Tha gu leòir agam diùbh.'
'Cha chreic,' ars a bhean.
'Creicidh,' ars esan.

H 491·2*   Thairg e fichead punnd Sasunnach air an t-aon [2] a
S 210   b'òige—leanabh caileig. Cha robh a màthair deònach a
K 2015   creic, ach bha a h-athair. Fhuair e an t-airgiod, is fhuair
M 371   an duine uasal am pàisde. Chuir e fleanainn timchioll
S 142   oirre, agus bha e dol seachad air linne muilleir anmoch
'san oidhche. Thilg e 's an linne i.[3]
'Cha bhi mi 'ga giùlan n'as fhaide,' ars esan.

An uair a bha am muillear a' leigeil uisge air a'
mhuileann an glasadh an latha, 'd è chunnaic e ach pìos
R 131·2   fleanainn cùl na còmhla. Thug e làmh air an fhleanainn,
is 'd è fhuair e ach leanabh ann, is i a' deoghal an fhleanainn,
is am fleanainn air snàmh air an uisge.

Shìn e dachaidh leatha, is thug e dh'a bhean i, is chuir
e ainm [t]roimh an bhaile gun do thuisleadh a bhean,
is gun do rug i leanabh nighinn da an raoir. Cha do

---

[1] I have retained the forms *creic, creicidh, cha chreic, reiceadh,* as they stood
in the MS. In the title the word is *reiceadh.* See p. 226 *n.*

[2] The preservation of the 't' of the article before a noun beginning with a
vowel, in an oblique case, is remarkable.

THE LASS WHO WAS SOLD

No. 19.   *[Vol. x., No. 33]*

Aarne-Thompson, No. 930

THERE was once a poor man who had seven children. A gentleman came that way, who remarked to him that he indeed had a family. The poor man replied that he had plenty, though there was only a poor chance of bringing them up, so that the children themselves were but poorly fed and poorly clothed.

'Wilt thou sell one of them?' quoth the gentleman.

'I will,' he replied. 'I have enough of them.'

'Thou shalt not sell any,' said his wife.

'Ah ! but I will,' said he.

The gentleman offered twenty pounds sterling for the youngest—a girl child. Her mother was not willing to sell her, but her father was. The poor man got the money, and the gentleman got the lassie. He wrapped her in flannel, and when he was going past a mill-pond late at night, he threw her in.[3]

'I will not carry her any farther,' said he.

In the gray dawning of the day, when the miller was letting the water into the mill, what should he see but a piece of flannel behind the sluice-gate. He caught hold of the flannel, and what should he find there but a child; she was sucking the flannel, and the flannel itself was floating on the water.

He made off home with her, and gave her to his wife, and sent a report through the town that his wife had been delivered, and that she had borne him a baby girl last

H 491·2*

S 210

K 2015

M 371

S 142

R 131·2

---

[3] Plainly the story is mutilated, for no reason is given for this cruelty. The gentleman obviously had heard from someone what the girl's destiny was, and tried to interfere, with the usual ill-success. Contrast Grimm No. 29.

thachair dhi clann a bhi aice. Thàinig móran mhnathan
a stigh a choimhead oirre, is bha esan leòmach agus leanabh
nighinn air a bhreith dha.

An ceann dà bhliadhna dheug 'na dhéidh sin, có
thàinig mun cuairt ach coigreach. Thuirt e ris a' mhuillear,
'Nach brèagh an nighean a th' agad an so feadh an tighe !'
'Tha i glé bhrèagh,' ars am muillear.
'D è an aois a tha an nighean sin agad?' ars an coigreach
ris a' mhuillear.
'Tha i,' ars esan, 'dusan bliadhna.'
'Is leamsa an nighean sin,' ars esan ris a' mhuillear.
'Ma tà, cha leat fhathast i, co-dhiùbh,' ars am muillear
bochd; 'is leamsa i gun teagamh.'
'Tha mise ag ràdh riut gur leamsa i,' ars an coigreach,
'is air a leithid so de latha gun do cheannaich mise i o
dhuine 'na leithid so de àite, airson fichead punnd
Sasunnach is gun do chaith mi anns an uisge agadsa i,
agus fhuair thusa anns an uisge i, is bha thu cur a mach
gum bu leat fhìn i.'
B'éiginn da gum faigheadh e i. Dh'fhalbh e an là-'r-
na-mhàireach, is thug e leis ise air a chùl air muin an eich,
is bha am muillear agus a bhean a' rànaich as an déidh,
is cha dèanadh sin feum daibh.

Dh'fhalbh e, is bha e falbh os cionn na mara, is gum
bu rathad olc a bha e gabhail os cionn na mara. Cha robh
an t-each deònach an rathad a ghabhail a bha e 'ga
thabhairt, is bha esan 'ga chur air aghaidh gun taing.
'D è 'n rathad a tha thu 'gabhail mar sin leis an each?'
ars ise.

'Theirig thusa bhàrr muin an eich, is cuiridh mise
sìos leis a' chreig so thu, air chor is nach fhaigh mise greim
ort tuillidh, is nach fhaic mi thu,' ars esan.
'Dh'aithnich mi sin ort, gur h-e toil a bh'agad sin a
dhèanamh, o'n a thàinig an latha. Ach 'd è am math a
nì e dhuit mise a chur leis a' chreig so? Chan fhàg sin
n'as fhearr thu, mise a chur leis a'chreig so,' ars ise.
'Is toileachadh leam fhìn, thusa a chur leis an so,' ars
esan.

H 1510
H 1535

night. She had never had any children. Many women came in to see her, and he was proud of having had a baby girl born to him.

Twelve years afterwards, who should come that way but a stranger. He said to the miller, 'What a pretty girl thou hast about the house !'

'She is very pretty,' quoth the miller.

'What age is that daughter of thine?' quoth the stranger to the miller.

'She is,' said he, 'twelve years old.'

'The lassie is mine,' said the other to the miller.

'Not yet, at all events,' said the poor miller; 'she is mine, and no doubt about it.'

'I tell thee she is mine,' said the stranger, 'and that on such and such a day I bought her from a man in such and such a place for twenty pounds sterling. I threw her into that mill-pond of thine, and there in the water didst thou find her, and hast been publishing it abroad that she belonged to thee.'

He insisted on having the child, and when he departed on the morrow, he took her up behind him on horseback, leaving the miller and his wife weeping and screaming, though that availed them nothing.

He started off, and travelled along a road that lay above the sea, and a bad road he took above the sea. The horse was not willing to take the road he was following, but he continued to urge it on against its will.

'Why dost thou take this road with the horse [*lit.* what road art thou taking in that way with the horse]?' she asked.

'Get thee down off the horse's back, and I'll cast thee H 1510 down this rock, so that I may never have anything to do H 1535 with thee again, nor see thee,' said he.

'Ever since the day came, I knew by thy look that that was thy intention. But what good will it do thee to throw me down this rock? Throwing me down this rock will not leave thee any better off,' said she.

'It gives me pleasure to throw thee down here,' he replied.

'Tha mise ag iarraidh mar aon fhàbhar ort, gun mo mharbhadh, is dèan aon ghnothach a th' agad rium, gun mo mharbhadh,' ars ise.

'An dèan thu mar so rium?' ars esan.

'D è sin?' ars ise.

Thug e fàinne òir bhàrr a mheòir. 'A bheil thu faicinn an fhàinne ud?' ars esan.

'Tha,' ars ise.

'Tha m'ainm anns an fhàinne ud,' ars esan. 'Mionnaich air an fhàinne ud nach faic mise thusa tuillidh. Tha mi dol dh'a thilgeil a mach air a' mhuir.'

'Is mór bàigh duine ris an anam,' [1] ars ise.

Mhionnaich i an so air an fhàinne nach faiceadh e ise tuillidh, gus am faiceadh e am fàinne bha e dol a chaitheamh a mach air a' mhuir. Mhionnaich ise.

Rug e an sin air an fhàinne, agus chaith e cho fada 'sa b'urrainn da a mach air an fhairge e.

Dh'fhàg iad beannachd aig a chéile, agus thill ise air a h-ais.

Thachair tigh duine uasail oirre, mu shia uairean 's an oidhche, is chaidh i a stigh do'n chearn. Dh'fhasdaidh an duine uasal i, is bha i aige trì bliadhna, is bha i còrdadh ris gu math.

An ceann nan trì bliadhna, có chunnaic i tighinn, ach esan.

Bha iad aig iasgach bhodach an oidhche roimhe sin. Bha ise a' sgoltadh nam bodach is i 'na còcaire, is 'd è leum a goile a' bhodaich ach fàinne! Sheall i air an fhàinne, is bha a ainm-san ann, is chuir i mu a meur e.

An là-'r-na-mhàireach, thàinig esan comhla ris an duine uasal eile gu a dhinneir. Dh'aithnich ise esan glé mhath, ach cha do leig i dad oirre.

An déidh na dinneireach, bha e falbh, is dh'fhàg e beannachd aig an duine uasal eile.

'Trobhad an so, a nighean. Tha turus agam riut.'

Fhreagair i e, is chaidh i far an robh e aig ceann an tighe.

---

[1] See Nicolson's *Gaelic Proverbs*, p. 216.

'I ask thee only one favour—not to kill me.   Do anything to me thou hast to do, but kill me not,' said she.

'Well, wilt thou do this for me?' he said.

'What is that?' said she.

He took a golden ring off his finger.   'Seest thou that ring?' said he.

'Yes, I do,' said she.

'My name is [inscribed] in that ring,' said he.   'Swear by that ring that I shall never see thee more.   I am going M 112 to throw it out into the sea.'

'Great is a man's love for his life,' she replied.[1]

And thereupon she swore by the ring that he should never see her more, until he saw the ring he was going to fling out into the sea.   Yes, she swore.

Then he took the ring, and flung it out into the sea as far as he could.

They left a farewell blessing with each other, and she turned back.

She came to a gentleman's house, about six o'clock in the evening, and went into the kitchen.   The gentleman engaged her, and she was with him for three years, and she pleased him right well.

At the end of three years, whom did she see coming but him [who had purchased her].

They had been fishing for cod the night before; and when splitting the cod open, she being a cook, what should leap out of the inside of the fish, but a ring !   She examined B 548·2·1 the ring, and there was his name on it.   So she put the ring on her finger.

On the morrow, he came to his dinner along with the other gentleman.   Well did she recognize him, but she did not make any sign that she knew him.

After dinner, when he was going away, he left a blessing with the other gentleman.

'Come hither, lass.   I have something to say to thee.'

She complied, and went to the end of the house where he was.

'Seadh,' ars esan, 'nach do mhionnaich thusa dhomhsa, o chionn a leithid so dè bhliadhnachan, nach faicinn thu gus am faicinn am fàinne a thilg mi a mach air a mhuir?'

'Mhionnaich,' ars ise. 'D è tha thu ag iarraidh a dhèanamh ort fhìn, a nis?' ars esan. 'Am bheil thu faicinn an fhàinne a chaidh thu fhéin a thilgeil a mach?' ars ise, is i 'ga thoirt bhàrr a meòir. 'D è mar a fhuair thu am fàinne?' ars esan. 'So a cheart fhàinne a thilg mise a mach. Is fìor sin. Chan urrainn dhomhsa cur as duit, is dh'fhiach mi ris. Ach chan fhàg mise n'as fhaide an so thu,' ars esan, is e a' bualadh a bhois air a gualainn. 'Théid thu a stigh, is gheibh thu do phàidheadh o'n duine uasal. Cha bhi thu n'as fhaide aige. Pòsaidh mi thu. Théid mi fhéin a stigh, agus sgrìobhaidh mi litir, is cuiridh mi do Dhùn-Eideann thu, a dh'ionnsachadh sgoile.'

Chaidh i stigh, is dh'iarr i a tuarasdal, is fhuair i siod.

Sgrìobh esan leatha litir chun a bhràthar ann an Dùn-Eideann.

'Falbhaidh thu nis,' ars esan, 'gu ruig Dùn-Eideann. Tha mo bhràthair ann. Bithidh thu latha is bliadhna ann an sgoil comhla ris na nigheanan aige fhìn. Ann an ceann bliadhna, ruigidh mise thu agus pòsaidh mi thu.'

Thug e dhi an litir. Dh'fhalbh i leis an litir, is bha i gabhail air a h-aghaidh, is an taobh a muigh de Ghlaschu, chaidh i do thigh tuathanaich, agus an oidhche a' tighinn oirre.

'Có as a thàinig a' chaileag nach 'eil mi ag aithneachadh?' ars an tuathanach. 'Is e caileag Ghàidhealach a th'annam-sa,' ars ise.

Thàinig an so treiseag de'n oidhche. 'D è an naidheachd as fhearr a th'aig a'chaileig Ghàidhealaich duinn a nochd?' ars an tuathanach. 'D è dh'éirich duit fhìn a dh'innseas tu dhuinn?'

'Tha naidheachdan gu leòir agam orm fhìn,' ars ise. Dh'innis i mar a dh'éirich dhi, o thoiseach gu deireadh.

'Well,' said he, 'didst thou not swear to me, such and
such a number of years ago, that I should not see thee till
I saw the ring I threw out into the sea?'

'Yes, I did,' said she.

'What dost thou wish to have done to thee now?'
said he.

'Seest thou the ring that thou thyself didst throw away
of set purpose?' said she, taking it off her finger.

'How didst thou get the ring?' said he. 'This is indeed
the very ring that I threw away. That is true enough.
It is a fact that I cannot kill thee, and I have had a try at
it. But I will not leave thee any longer here,' said he,
striking the palm of his hand on her shoulder. 'Thou
shalt go in, and get thy wages from the gentleman. Thou
shalt be with him no longer, for I will marry thee. I shall
go in myself, and write a letter, and send thee to Edinburgh,
to be taught and educated.'

In she went, asked for her wages, and got them.

He wrote a letter which she was to take with her to his
brother in Edinburgh.

'Thou shalt now go,' said he, 'to Edinburgh. My
brother is there. Thou wilt remain in the school for a
year and a day along with his own daughters. At the end
of the year, I shall come and marry thee.'

He gave her the letter, and she went off with it. She
journeyed on, until, when on the outskirts of Glasgow,
night began to overtake her, and she went into a farmer's
house.

'Whence comes the lassie whom I do not recognize?'
said the farmer.

'I am a Gaelic lassie,' she replied.

When some short portion of the night had gone by,
'What is the best news that the Gaelic lassie has for us
to-night?' asked the farmer. 'Has anything ever happened
to thee thou mightest tell us?'

'I have plenty of tales to tell thee about myself,' said she.
And she told him what had happened to her, from first
to last.

'Agus is e a chuir an litir leat an dràst?' ars an
tuathanach.

'Is e,' ars ise. 'Tha e an déis deagh cheann a dhèanamh
rium an dràsd. Thug e an litir so domh.'

'Nam biodh tu cho math is a leigeil fhaicinn 'domh,'
ars an tuathanach. Leig i fhaicinn an litir da.

'Am bi thu airson domh an litir fhosgladh?' ars esan.

'Bhur toil fhìn,' ars ise.

Dh'fhosgail e an litir. 'A bheil fios agad 'd è tha 's
an litir ?' ars an tuathanach.

'Chan 'eil,' ars ise.

'Tha, anns an litir,' ars esan, ' "o'n a dh'fhairtlich
ormsa cur as do'n chaileig so, an uair a ruigeas i thu, croch
i." Ach sgrìobhaidh mise litir duit-sa 'na h-àite so, air
chor is gun gabh a bhràthair cùram dhiot.'

'Cha leig an t-eagal domh dol air m'aghaidh idir,' ars ise.

'Chan e sin as fhearr duit,' ars an tuathanach.
'Theagamh gum faigh esan greim ort a rithist. Ach
théid thu air t'aghaidh, agus sgrìobhaidh mise litir duit.'

Sgrìobh e litir dhi, is chuir e 'san litir—'Tha mise a'
cur litir chugad-sa, a bhràthair, agus tha mi ag earbsa na
caileig so riut, agus gabhaidh tu cùram dhi. Is i caileag
as fhearr a shuidh air a h-aodach riamh. Chan 'eil a leithid
eile ann. Cha bu rud leamsa ionnsachadh na Gàidheal-
tachd a thoirt di, ach a cur do Dhùn-Eideann gu sgoil
agus foghlum. Na biodh ionnsachadh aig bean uasal an
Dùn-Eideann nach bi aice, agus an ceann na bliadhna,
ruigidh mise thu, agus tha mi ri a pòsadh.' Ghlas e an
litir, agus shìn e dhi i. Chaidil i an oidhche sin an tigh an
tuathanaich.

K 511

K 1851

An là-'r-na-mhàireach, dh'fhàg i beannachd aig an
tuathanach, is thug i buidheachas da airson a choibhneis
is dh'fhalbh i.

Ràinig i Dùn-Eideann. Chaidh i gu tigh a bhràthar-
san, is e 'na dhuine uasal mór an Dùn-Eideann. An uair
a chaidh i a stigh, shìn i an litir do a h-aon de a nigheanan-
san anns a' chearn. Bha trì nigheanan aige. Dh'fhalbh

'And it is he who sent the letter with thee on this occasion ?' said the farmer.

'Yes, it is,' said she. 'He has begun to treat me well now. He gave me this letter.'

'If thou wouldst be so good as to let me see it,' said the farmer. So she showed him the letter.

'Art thou desirous that I should open it ?' said he.

'As you yourself please,' said she.

He opened the letter. 'Dost thou know what is in the letter ?' said the farmer.

'No, I do not,' said she.

'This,' said he.—" 'All my efforts to kill this lass having failed, thou art to hang her when she arrives." But I will write thee another letter in the place of this, in such a vein that his brother will take care of thee.'

'But fear will not allow me to go any farther,' said she.

'To go no farther were not the best thing for thee to do,' quoth the farmer, 'for perhaps he may get a hold of thee again. But do thou push forward, and I will write a letter for thee.'

So he wrote a letter, and put in it—'I am writing a letter to thee, brother, entrusting this lass to thee. Take care of her. She is the best lass that ever sat on her clothes. K 511 Such another as she does not exist. I thought that such learning as is to be found in the Gaeldom was not sufficient to give her—it were a mere nothing, so I have determined to send her to Edinburgh for schooling and education. K 1851 Let there be no accomplishment that the ladies of Edinburgh have that she does not learn also, and at the end of a year I will visit thee, and then I am to marry her.' He sealed [*lit.* locked] the letter, and handed it to her, and that night she slept in the farmer's house.

On the morrow, she left a farewell blessing with the farmer, gave him thanks for his kindness, and set out.

She arrived at Edinburgh, and went to the house of his (her persecutor's) brother who was a gentleman of note there. When she went in, she handed the letter to one of his daughters, who were at the time in the kitchen. He

an nighean leis an litir gu a h-athair. Dh'fhosgail e an
litir, is leugh e i. 'O,' ars esan, an uair a leugh e an litir,
'a nuas a' chaileag.' Thugadh a nuas i, is an t-aodach a
b'fhearr a bha a stigh, chuireadh uimpe e.

Chuireadh do'n sgoil i. Cha robh i fada anns an sgoil,
an uair a bha i toirt bràigh-ghill [1] air a h-uile gin a bha
innte, is bha i na b'fhearr na a' chlann aige fhìn. Chuir
e gu sgoil fhuaigheil i, is an uair a bha i treis 's an sgoil
fhuaigheil, chuir e do sgoil dhannsaidh i. Thug e
ionnsachadh bean uasail cho mór 'sa bha an Dùn-Eideann
di.

An ceann na bliadhna, ràinig esan. Agus ciod è an t-àm
a ràinig e, ach an uair a bha bàl aig mnathan uaisle is aig
daoine uaisle móra.

Chaidh brath an so oirre-se, is air trì nigheanan an
duine uasail dha'n bhàl, [agus chaidh iad ann.]

'Nuair a bha esan treis a stigh [ann an tigh a bhràthar,]
dh'fhaighnich e de a bhràthair, c'àite an robh a nigheanan.

'Tha iad am bàl mór a nochd, iad fhìn is a' bhean
uasal mhór a chuir thu fhín an so.'

'D è a' bhean uasal a bha an sin?' ars esan.

'Nach 'eil [2] a' bhean uasal a chuir thu fhìn an so, gu
sgoil agus ionnsachadh a thoirt di?' ars a bhràthair.

'O,' ars esan, 'an i sin an té a chuir mi ad ionnsuigh
airson a crochadh? O'n a dh'fhairtlich i ormsa, chuir
mi chugad-sa i airson a crochadh! Cha robh dàil ri bhi
aice ach aon latha!'

'Is ann a fhuair mise litir uait, airson sgoil is ionnsachadh a thoirt di, cho math is a bhiodh aig aona bhean
uasal an Dùn-Eideann.'

Thòisich iad an so ri cothachadh air a chéile. 'O nach
do rinn thusa sin, crochaidh mise i am màireach.'

---

[1] 'bràigh-ghill, substituted for beatadh, an English corruption used by reciter.'
Note in MS.
[2] The copula verb is implied (though not expressed) in the question.
Yet the answer is given with the substantive verb. This is the regular thing

had three daughters. The lass took the letter to her father. He opened it and read it. 'O,' said he, when he had read it, 'bring the girl here.' She was brought accordingly, and they arrayed her in the best clothes there were in the house.

She was sent to school, but was not long there before she surpassed everyone in it, and was even better than the gentleman's own children. He sent her to a school for needlework and when she had spent a while there, he sent her to a school for dancing. He gave her such an education as would have been given to the greatest lady in Edinburgh.

At the end of a year, he (her persecutor) arrived. And at what time should he come, but when the great ladies and gentlemen were having a ball.

At this juncture, word was sent for her and for the gentleman's three daughters to go to the ball [and they went there accordingly.]

When he had been a while in the house [in his brother's house,] he enquired of his brother, where his daughters were.

'They are at the great ball to-night, both they and the great lady that thou didst send here.'

'What lady was that?' said he.

'Why, the lady thou thyself didst send here, to be taught and educated,' said his brother.

'O,' said he, 'is that the one I sent to thee to have hanged? She baffled me completely, and so I sent her to thee to have her hanged! She was only to have one day's respite!'

'Why, but I received a letter from thee, to give her schooling and education, which was to be as good as that of any lady in Edinburgh.'

Then they began to contend with each other. 'Since thou didst not hang her, I will hang her to-morrow.'

in questions and answers of this particular kind. But it constitutes an exception to the general rule, which is, that whatever verb appears in any question must appear also in the answer.

'Is beag a bhiodh a [1] chridhe agad a crochadh an diugh,' ars a bhràthair. Shìn e dha a litir fhìn. 'Sin agad an litir a chuir thu chugam-sa.' Dh'fheuch e an litir. 'Dh'fhairtlich i ormsa,' ars esan. Dh'fhalbh e fhéin agus a bhràthair do'n bhàl. Cha robh bean uasal anns a' bhàl air nach robh i toirt bràigh-ghill. Bha i cho math air an dannsadh. Chuir bain-tighearna cho mór is a bha a stigh litir dh'a h-ionnsuigh nam biodh i cho math agus a freagairt gum biodh i taingeil di.

Chaidh ise agus na trì nigheanan eile dhachaidh, is chaidh esan agus a bhràthair dhachaidh an uair a sgaoil am bàl.

Chuir esan brath oirre an là-'r-na-mhàireach. Thàinig i far an robh e. 'Seadh,' ars esan, 'tha thu beò fhathast.'

'Tha mise beò fhathast,' ars ise.

'Am bheil eagal ort,' ars esan, 'gun croch mi thu?'

'Cha bhiodh a chridhe agad sgàth a dhèanamh ormsa, gun tighinn air mo chrochadh.'

'Smuainich mi gun d'fhàirtlich thu orm,' ars esan. 'Is e an aon fhichead sin a phàidh thu air mo shon, a tha thu cur as mo leth. Bheirinnsa an diugh ceud duit, an àite an fhichead sin a phàidh thu air mo shon. Bheir mise suas do luchd lagha Dhùn-Eideann an rud a bha thu dèanamh orm, agus beiridh iad ort, agus gabhaidh iad cùram dhiot, agus cuiridh iad bliadhna a [2] phriosan ort. Chan 'eil bean uasal ann an Dùn-Eideann as fhearr ionnsachadh na mise an diugh, agus gabhaidh iad m'fhacal.'

'Uist! fuirich sàmhach,' ars esan. 'Tha mi ag iarraidh móran maitheanais ort. Tha mi smaointeachadh agam fhìn gun do luathasaich Nì Maith dhomh thu, agus bhithinn 'nad chomain nam pòsadh tu mi.'

'Tha eagal agam romhad,' ars ise.

'Bheir mise mo mhionnan duit nach dèan mi coire ort am feasd.'

Phòs iad, agus bha móran de uaislean Dhùin-

[1] = de.   [2] = de.

'Scarcely wouldst thou be allowed to hang her to-day,' quoth his brother, and handed him his own letter. 'There's the letter thou didst send me.'

He examined the letter. 'She has baffled me,' said he. He and his brother then went to the ball. There was no lady at the ball whom she did not surpass. And she was so good at dancing. One of the greatest ladies in the place sent her a letter, saying that if she would be so good as to answer it, she would be obliged to her.

She and the three other lassies presently went home. He and his brother went home when the ball broke up.

He sent word for her on the morrow, and she went to the place where he was. 'So then,' said he, 'thou art alive still.'

'Yes, I am alive still,' she answered.

'Art thou not afraid,' said he, 'that I will hang thee?'

'Thou wouldst not be allowed to do anything at all to me, let alone hang me.'

'I realize that thou hast baffled me,' said he.

'What thou art now laying to my charge, is, that trifling twenty [pounds] that thou didst pay for me. But I could give thee to-day a hundred instead of that twenty thou didst pay for me. I will give up to the lawyers of Edinburgh an account of what thou hast done to me, and they will seize thee, and take thee into custody, and lay thee in prison for a year. There is not a lady in Edinburgh to-day better educated than I am, and they will all take my word.'

'Whisht! be quiet,' said he. 'I entreat thee to grant me a great forgiveness. I think within myself, that the Good Thing has vouchsafed thee to me, and if thou wouldst marry me, I would be indebted to thee.'

'I am afraid of thee,' said she.

'I give thee my oath and swear that I will never harm thee.'

So they married, and many of the nobles of Edinburgh

Eideann aig a' bhanais. Cheannaich iad móran de thighean, agus cha robh a bheag ann an Dùn-Eideann cho beairteach riu.

> 'From Roderick MacLean, tailor, Ken Tangval, Barra. Heard it from many old men, some of whom are mentioned already. Alexander MacPherson, one of those from whom he heard it, is still living, and is about 80 years of age.' The tale was obtained in 1859. The scribe was Hector MacLean.

NOTES

MS. vol. x., No. 33. Campbell calls this story 'old but altered to modern ideas. Half novel, half tale—has a flavour of books.' In his Gaelic List he says of No. 33—'Novel: good.'

Mr C. J. Inglis has kindly informed me that the story theme is undoubtedly old, and there are numerous variants in European folk-lore. An excellent English parallel is given in Henderson's *Folk-Lore of Northern Counties*, Appendix by S. Baring Gould. The story is known as 'the Fish and the Ring,' and emanates from Yorkshire. The incidents are less modernized.

were present at the wedding. They bought many houses, and there were not any people in Edinburgh as rich as they.

Related Tales

Grimm, No. 29, joins this story to *Fios na Mionaid Fortanaich* (MS. vol. xi., No. 268).

Larminie, p. 174. R. Nisbet Bain, *Russian Fairy Tales*, p. 252. *Celtic Magazine*, xiii., p. 189.

The substitution of forged letters occurs in MS. vol. xi., No. 191 (*Celtic Monthly*, May 1917) and in No. 20 (MS. vol. x., No. 34) following.

The practice of buying people occurs in No. 20 (MS. vol. x., No. 34), and in *W. H. Tales*, ii., No. 18. The person purchased had few rights or none. The buyer had absolute jurisdiction, and in our story, buys expressly to kill his purchase. The heroine seems to admit the buyer's rights, but advances a counter-claim, based upon the increase in her value. She can produce an amount much larger than the original price.

AN LEANABH GUN BHAISTEADH

No. 20. [*Vol. x., No. 34*]

Aarne-Thompson, No. 706

BHA Rìgh ann roimhe so, agus bha [e] 'na bhantraich, agus phòs e Banrighinn eile.

S 31 Bha aige o'n cheud Bhanrighinn nighean agus gille. Bhiodh e anns a bheinn-sheilge a' sealg a h-uile latha.

Thug ise air an nighinn mionnachadh, nuair a dh'
K 1933 fhalbh a h-athair, nach innseadh i nì a chìtheadh i 'ga dhèanamh no a dhèanadh i fhéin, do dhuine chaidh a bhaisteadh.

M 113* 'Mionnaich domh-sa,' ars a' Bhanrighinn, 'air a' chlaidheamh so, nach innis thu facal de na chì thu 'ga dhèanamh, no de na bheir mi ort fhéin a dhèanamh, [do dhuine chaidh a bhaisteadh].'

'Nuair a mhionnaich i, rug a' Bhanrighinn air a' chlaidheamh, is thilg i an ceann de mhac an Rìgh. Is e a b'òige na an nighean; is e seachd bliadhna a dh' aois a
K 2155·1 bha e. Rùisg i làmhan a pheathar, is *rub* i an fhuil riutha.

'Nuair a thàinig a h-athair as a' bheinn-sheilge, dh' fhaighnich e an robh naidheachd aig a' Bhanrighinn, is e breith air làimh oirre.

'Tha sin agam,' ars ise, is i toirt a mach neapaigin poca, is i tòiseachadh air caoineadh.

'D è an naidheachd a th' agad ?'

'Tha do nighean an déidh do mhac a mharbhadh, o'n a dh'fhalbh thu.'

Chuir e brath air a nighinn.

'Chuir mise ann an seòmar i, is ghlas mi i, gus an tilleadh tu.'

THE UNCHRISTENED CHILD

No. 20. [*Vol. x., No. 34*]

Aarne-Thompson, No. 706

THERE was formerly a King, who being a widower, married another Queen. He had a daughter and a son by the first Queen. He used to go to the hill of hunting every day.

She [the second Queen], caused the daughter, when her S 31 father was away, to swear that whatever she might see being done, or whatever she (the Queen) might do, she K 1933 would never tell about it to any person who had been baptized.

'Swear to me,' said the Queen, 'on this sword, that M 113* thou wilt not tell a word of what thou seest being done, nor a word of what I shall make thee do, [to anyone who has ever been baptized].'

When she had sworn, the Queen took the sword, and struck off the head of the King's Son, who was younger than the daughter, his age being seven years. The Queen then bared the hands of his sister, and rubbed them with K 2155·1 the blood.[1]

When the father came home from the hunting-hill, he enquired if the Queen had news, at the same time taking her by the hand.

'That I have,' said she, taking out a kerchief, and beginning to cry.

'What news hast thou ?'

'Thy daughter has killed thy son, after thou didst go out.'

He sent for the girl.

'I have put her in a room, and locked her in till thou shouldst return.'

---

[1] Did the child wear gloves, or simply long sleeves, which the Queen turned back over her arm ?

Thàinig an nighean, is a làmhan làn fala.

'Ciod a thug dhuit do bhràthair a mharbhadh?' ars an Rìgh.

'Is fheudar éisdeachd ris an sin,' [1] ars ise, agus i crathadh a cinn.

Ars a' Bhanrighinn, 'Croch i, a Rìgh.'

'Tha smaointean tighinn fodham do chrochadh, agus an uair a sheallas mise ort, is mór leam do chrochadh,' ars an Rìgh.

An là-'r-na-mhàireach, chaidh an Rìgh do'n bheinn-sheilge, is an uair a dh'fhalbh e, chuir a' Bhanrighinn teine ris na craobhan ùbhlan.

Nuair a thill an Rìgh, ars e,

'Ciod è an naidheachd a th'aig a' Bhanrighinn?'

'Tha naidheachd, gun do chuir an nighean a h-uile gin de na craobhan ùbhlan ri theinidh.'

Chuir an Rìgh brath air an nighinn, agus thuirt e rithe, c'arson a rinn i siod.

'Is fheudar éisdeachd ris an sin,' ars ise, agus i a' crathadh a cinn.

'Tha mi 'g iarraidh ort a crochadh; cuiridh i an lùchairt ri theinidh cuideachd,' ars a' Bhanrighinn. 'Leigidh sinn siod leatha fhathast,' ars an Rìgh.

An là-'r-na-mhàireach, chaidh an Rìgh do'n bheinn-sheilge, agus an uair a thill e air ais, ars e ris a' Bhanrighinn, 'Ciod è an naidheachd a tha aig a' Bhanrighinn?'

Z 71·1   'Naidheachd gu leòir. Tha'n gàradh 'na smàl teine; tha do nighean an déidh teine a chur ris a h-uile nì a th'ann.' An fheadh is a bha an Rìgh 'sa' bheinn-sheilge, chuir i fhéin teine ris gach ni bha 'sa ghàradh.

'Seadh, a nighean, ciod e an call a tha thu brath a dhèanamh air an Rìgh, t'athair?'

'Is fheudar éisdeachd ris an sin,' ars ise, agus i a' crathadh a cinn.

Chuir e an òrdugh. Bheairtich e each, agus chaidh e air a mhuin, agus chuir e ise air a chùl. Dh'fhalbh e an so leatha, agus bha e falbh fada leatha. Ràinig e far an

---

[1] *Cf.* for idiom, *éisd do bheul*, let thy mouth listen = be quiet; *éisd* = whisht.

The lassie came with her hands covered with blood.

'What caused thee to kill thy brother?' quoth the King.

'I must listen to that [without replying],'[1] said she, shaking her head.

Said the Queen, 'Hang her, O King.'

'I feel greatly inclined to hang thee, but then when I look at thee,' quoth the King, 'I am reluctant to hang thee.[2]

On the morrow, the King went to the hunting-hill, and when he had gone, the Queen set fire to the apple trees.

When the King returned he said,

'What news hath the Queen?'

'The news is, that the girl has set fire to everyone of the apple trees.'

The King sent word for the girl, and asked her why she had done that.

'I must listen to that [without replying],' said she, shaking her head.

'I ask thee to hang her, she will set the palace on fire too,' said the Queen. 'We will forgive her this offence, also,' said the King.

On the morrow the King went to the hunting-hill, and when he returned he said to the Queen, 'What news hath the Queen?'

'News enough. The garden has been burnt to a cinder; Z 71·1 thy daughter has set fire to everything in it.' While the King was in the hunting-hill, she herself had set fire to everything in the garden.

'Well, my daughter, why dost thou wish to inflict loss on the King, thy father?'

'I must listen to that [without replying,]' said she, shaking her head.

So the King made ready. He harnessed a horse, mounted it, and took her up behind him; then he went off with her, and a long way did he travel with her. He

---

[2] *Lit.* Thy hanging is a great matter with me.

robh craobhan móra coille, agus thàinig e air làr, far an
robh na craobhan sin.

Chunnaic e té bu mhó na chéile de na craobhan, agus
thug e suas ise an àird innte. Ars e rithe an sin, 'An
Q451·1 làmh a rinn an cron, cuiridh mise dhìot i.' Thilg e dhì
Q451·9 an làmh [dheas] o'n ghualainn. Thug e dhì a' chìoch
dheas. Dh'fhàg e an siod i, is bha e fhéin a' dol a sìos as
S143 a' chraoibh.
M431 'Ma tà,' ars ise, 'tha mise ag iarraidh [1] bior droighinn
a dhol anns a' bhonn agad-sa, nach toir duine as, gus
D1765 an toir mo dheas làmh as e.'
Chaidh bior droighinn 'na bhonn mun deachaidh am
facal ás a beul, anns an robh trì òirlich air fad.
Bha acarsaid a sìos o'n àite anns an robh i, agus bha
soitheach air ùr thighinn a stigh innte. Bha fear a'
sealltuinn uaidh le gloine as an t-soitheach.

Ciod è chunnaic e, ach ise anns a' chraoibh, agus i
N711·1 sileadh fala. 'Tha mi faicinn boireannaich ann am bàrr
craoibh, agus i sileadh fala, bhàrrachd air an sin, as a com.'
Thàinig bàta a nall, agus thug iad as a' chraoibh i,
agus thug iad leò air bòrd i. Bha léigh air bòrd air an
t-soitheach, agus cha robh e fad a' leigheas nan lotan.

Bha gille ionnsuichte air bòrd, a bha thall thairis, agus
'd è rinn e ach gaol a ghabhail oirre. Bhruidhinn e ris an
nighinn an so, gum b'fhearr di falbh leis fhéin, gun robh e
an déis gaol a ghabhail oirre.
'Cha dèan mise móran maith diot, agus cha dèan mi
móran feum dhuit.'
'Oh !' ars esan, 'ged nach 'eil móran de'n t-saoghal
againn, cuiridh Nì Maith [2] rud oirnn. Is fhearr dhuit
falbh leam fhéin; tha gaol mór agam ort.'
Dh'fhalbh i an so leis, agus chuir iad bàta gu tìr leotha.
Ghabh iad air an aghaidh, agus bha iad a' falbh gus an
do ràinig iad tigh a mhàthar-san. [Phòs iad.]

---

[1] The name or names of the supernatural power or powers who is or are
prayed to, invoked, or "ordered," never transpire. See pp. 198, 343.

arrived at a place where there were mighty forest trees; and he lighted to the ground where those trees were.

He noticed that one of the trees was bigger than the others; he ascended it taking her with him. Then said he to her, 'The hand that did the evil will I strike off thee,' Q451·1 and he cut her right arm off from the shoulder. He struck off her right breast also. He left her there, and Q451·9 began descending from the tree.   S143

'Well,' said she, 'I pray [1] that a bramble thorn shall M431 go into thy heel, and that no one shall ever take it out, D1765 till my right hand does so.'

And, or ever the word had gone out of her mouth, a bramble thorn, three inches long, pierced his heel.

Down below the place where she was, there was an anchorage, and a vessel in it, that had but lately arrived. There was a man in the vessel, who was looking abroad with a glass.

What did he espy but the young woman in the tree, N711·1 dripping with blood. 'I see a woman in the top of a tree, and moreover, blood is dripping from her body.'

A boat came over, and they took her down from the tree, and brought her with them on board. There was a doctor on board the vessel, and he was not long healing the wounds.

There was a well educated youth on board, who had been abroad, and what did he do but set his heart on her. So he spoke to her, saying that she had better go off with him, that he had fallen in love with her.

'I shall not get much good by thee, and I shall not be of much use to thee.'

'Oh !' quoth he, 'though we have not much of world's gear, the Good Being [2] will send us something. Thou hadst better go with me. I have great love for thee.'

She went off with him, and they sent them ashore in a boat. They pressed forward, and continued their journey until they reached his mother's house. [They married.]

---

[2] *Lit.* the Good Thing.

Bha esan ri dol thairis a rithist leis an t-soitheach.
'Nuair a dh'fhalbh e, thuirt e, 'A mhàthair! gleidhidh
tusa am boirionnach so, gus an till mise; chan 'eil orm
ach trì bliadhna thall.'

'O,' ars a mhàthair, 'is mise nì sin; is ann is maith
leamsa i bhi comhla rium.'

Sheòl e air an t-soitheach cheudna a null.

An ceann trì ràithean, thuisleadh le leanabh gille ise.
Bha litir a' tighinn d'a h-ionnsuigh, gach darna pocaid
a thigeadh.

*   *   *   *   *   *

'Nuair a chaidh an Rìgh dhachaidh, dh'innis e do'n
Bhanrighinn mar a rinn e.

An là-'r-na-mhàireach, thàinig an Rìgh is a' Bhanrighinn,
feuch an robh i beò. 'Nuair a thàinig iad gus an àite, cha
d'fhuair iad ann idir i. Thuirt an Rìgh ris a' Bhanrighinn,
'Thug cuid-eiginn as i.'

As a dhéidh sin, bha a' Bhanrighinn daonnan a' feòrach
a mach, gus an d'fhuair i mach far an robh i, agus ciod e
bu chor di. Thuig i gun robh i pòsda, is gun robh litir a'
tighinn thairis d'a h-ionnsuigh, is a' dol thairis uaithe.

Goirid an déidh ise bhi air a h-asaid, ciod è rinn i
[a' Bhanrighinn] ach am post a choinneachadh. 'Feuchaidh
tu a h-uile litir a th'agad dhomh-sa, is gheibh thu ginidh,'
ars ise ris a' phosta.

Dh'fheuch am posta a h-uile litir a bha aige dhi, is
fhuair ise litir uaidhe-san a dh'ionnsuigh a mhàthar. Bha
'san litir, 'Gabh cùram de'n bhoirionnach an am a h-asaid,
agus gabh cùram de'n leanabh; air neò, mur bi i a stigh
air mo chionn-sa, chan fhaic thu mise am feasd.'

K 2117
T 551·3
K 2115
K 1851 Sgrìobh ise an àite na té sin mar gun sgrìobhadh a
mhàthair chuige i. 'Is iongantach am boirionnach so.
Tha ceann coinein, agus coluinn cait air a' phàisde.'

Bha i coinneachadh a' phosta agus a' seilltuinn air na
litrichean a bha tighinn, agus an uair a thàinig litir air a

He had to go abroad again with the vessel. When departing, he said, 'Mother ! keep thou this woman till I return. There are only three more years now that I have to spend abroad.'

'O,' quoth the mother, 'certainly I will; indeed, I am only too glad to have her with me.'

He sailed away on the same vessel.

At the end of three quarters of a year, she was delivered of a baby boy. A letter used to come for her [from him] by every other packet boat that came.

*   *   *   *   *   *

When the King went home, he told the Queen what he had done.

On the morrow, the King and Queen came to see if the girl were alive. When they came to the place, they did not find her there at all. The King said to the Queen, 'Some one or other has taken her away.'

So after that, the Queen was always enquiring on all sides, until she found out where the King's daughter was, and what her circumstances were. She became aware that she was married, and that she was receiving letters from abroad, and was sending others back.

A little while after the King's daughter had been delivered, what did the Queen do but go and meet the postman. 'Show me every letter that thou hast, and I will give thee a guinea,' said she to the postman.

The postman showed her every letter he had, and she found a letter from him [the young man who was abroad] to his mother. In the letter was written, 'Take care of her when she is being delivered, and take care of the child, for if she be not there against my coming, thou shalt never see me again.'

The Queen wrote in reply to [1] that one, [making it appear] as if his mother had written to him. 'This woman is strange indeed: the child has the head of a rabbit, and the body of a cat.'   K 2117   T 551·3   K 2115   K 1851

So the Queen used to meet the post, and look at the letters that came, and when a letter came back from him

[1] *Lit.* in place of.

h-ais uaidhe-san, fhuair i i, agus thug i ginidh do'n phosta.
Is bha, anns an litir so, 'Ge b'e bith seòrsa tha aice, gabh
cùram deth.'

Dh'fhalbh a' Bhanrighinn, agus sgrìobh i litir an àite
na té sin, agus chuir i innte, 'Cuir a mach air an spot i,
air neò chan fhaic thu mise am feasd.'
Fhuair a mhàthair an litir. Thòisich i air caoineadh,
agus sheall i oirre-se, agus duileachas oirre, an rud a bha
'san litir. 'Ciod e fàth ur caoineadh, a bhean chòir?'
ars ise.
'Chan 'eil móran, ach so dhuit fhéin an litir a th'agam
an so.'
Rug i air an litir, agus leugh i i.
'Cha chuir mise ur mac a dhìth oirbh-se idir. Togaibh an
leanabh so air mo mhuin, agus giùlanaidh mi air falbh e.'
Chuir i an leanabh ann an lùb a' bhreacain, agus
cheangail i gu maith e. An là-'r-na-mhàireach, mu dheich
uairean, dh'fhalbh i a tigh na caillich.

Bha i treis mhaith a' coiseachd.
Thàinig pathadh oirre, is bha i gabhail rathad
lòintichean boga, feuch am faigheadh i uisge. Bha i air
tiormachadh leis a' phathadh, is cha robh i faighinn boinne.
Cha robh fios aice ciod è dhèanadh i.
Nochd tigh duine uasail di, agus dh'aithnich i gum
biodh tobar goirid da.
Sheas i treis aig ceann tigh an duine uasail, agus ciod
è chunnaic i ach tobar agus ceann air. Bha an tobar
domhain mór, agus soitheach anns an tobar gu deoch òl as.

Bha i cumail an leanaibh gu h-àrd, is am pathadh oirre,
is ciod è rinn an leanabh ach dol thar a cinn anns an tobar.
Cha b'urrainn di ruigsinn air an leanabh, agus an làmh
eile a dhìth oirre.

Dh'éigh guth os a cionn. 'A bhoirionnaich a tha 'nad
éiginn,—sìn do làmh dheas, agus beir air do leanabh ás
an tobar.'

Shìn i an làmh dheas, agus rug i air an leanabh.

she got it, and gave the postman a guinea. And there
was written in this letter, 'Whatever kind of creature she
has, take care of it.'

The Queen went, and wrote a letter which she substituted
for this one, and put in it, 'Put her out on the spot, otherwise thou shalt see me no more.'

His mother got the letter. She began to cry and she
looked at her (her daughter-in-law) for the mother was
very sorrowful about the letter. 'What is the cause of
thy crying, Kind Woman?' said she (her daughter-in-law).

'Not very much, but there, see for thyself the letter I
have here.'

She took the letter, and read it.

'I will never be the cause of your losing your son. Lift
this child up on to my back, and I will carry him away.'

She put the child into the neuk of her plaid, and secured
it there firmly. On the morrow, about ten o'clock, she
left the old woman's house.   S 410

She was a good while walking.

Thirst came upon her, and she was keeping to soft
marshy places to see if she could find water. At last she
began to be parched with thirst, yet could she not find a
drop of water. She knew not what to do.

A gentleman's house came in sight, and she knew there
would be a well within a short distance of it.

She stood for a while at the end of the gentleman's
house, and what did she see but a well with a lid on it.
The well was deep and big, and there was a vessel in it to
drink out of.

She had hoisted the child high up [on her shoulders],
and she was very thirsty, and what should happen but that
the child shot over her head into the well; and she was
quite unable to get a hold of the child, her other hand
being wanting.

A voice called from above, 'Thou woman, who art so
sore distressed—stretch forth thy right hand, and take thy
child out of the well.'

She stretched forth her right hand, and took hold of the   D 2161·
child.   3·2

E 782
Q 140
Q 61

'Bheir thu a mach a nis do chìoch dheas, is bheir thu do'n leanabh i. Gach nì rinneadh ort, bha thu leagte ris, agus fhuair thu iochd o'n Tighearna.'

Shuidh i, is thug i a mach a' chìoch dheas, agus thug i do'n leanabh i. Ghlan i i fhéin aig an tobar, is chìr i a ceann.

Thàinig bean-mhuinntir a mach as an tigh mhór, agus dh'innis i an uair a thill i a stigh, gur h-ann aig an tobar a bha an aona bhoirionnach a bu bhrèagha a chunnaic i riamh.

Thàinig bean an duine uasail a mach, agus thug i dachaidh am boirionnach. Ghabh iad tlachd mór dhith leis cho brèagha 's a bha i fhéin is an leanabh a bha aice.

'Bhithinn fada ann ad chomain,' arsa bean an duine uasail, 'nam fuiricheadh tu leinn fhéin, chionn tha pàisde agam, agus bheathaicheadh tu le chéile iad.'

Dh'fhuirich i an tigh an duine uasail, agus bha an dà leanabh aice 'gam beathachadh. Cha robh ionnsachadh aig boirionnach sam bith nach robh aice, agus bha i còrdadh gu h-anabarrach maith riutha. Bha i trì bliadhna anns an tigh so, is cha leigeadh iad air falbh i.

Bha iad a muigh, i fhéin is an luchd muinntir latha, is ciod è chunnaic i tighinn ach gille òg, is ghabh e a nall far an robh iad-san. 'Ciod è bhur naidheachd, a nigheanan òga?' ars an gille.

'Chan 'eil againn móran; ciod è naidheachd a' choigrich?' ars ise.

'Is è naidheachd dhomh,' ars esan, 'gu bheil mi, o chionn trì bliadhna, air thòrachd boirionnaich, is gur tu fhéin is coltaiche rithe a chunnaic mi fhathast, ach tha eadar-dhealachadh eadàr am boirionnach a tha mise ag iarraidh, agus thu fhéin.'

¹ This is almost the only instance of the Sacred Name being used in these tales. It is probably a Christian touch, and we may suppose that in some remote version the restoration of the lost members was ascribed to the fairy or goddess of the well. In English List No. 343 (see Notes), an old woman meets the heroine, says something (an incantation?) which Islay had forgotten, and restores her lost members. But there is nothing about a

'Bring forth now thy right breast and give thou it to E 782
the child. Everything that was done to thee, thou wert Q 140
resigned to it, and thou hast obtained mercy from the Q 61
Lord.' [1]

She sat down and brought forth the right breast, and
gave it to the child. She washed herself at the well, and
combed her head.

A servant came out from the big house, who when she
went back indoors, told that there was at the well the most
beautiful woman she had ever seen.

The gentleman's wife came forth, and took the woman
indoors. They were greatly pleased with her, because of
her great beauty, and the beauty of the child she had
with her.

'I would be greatly indebted to thee,' quoth the wife
of the gentleman, 'if thou wouldst stay with us, for I have
a child, and thou couldst feed them together.'

She stayed in the gentleman's house, and had the two
children to feed. There was no womanly accomplishment
that she did not possess, and she was on excellent terms
with them, pleasing them very well. She spent three years
in this house, and they would not allow her to go away.

They were out one day, she and the servants, and
whom did she see approaching but a young man, and he
came over to the place where they were. 'What is your
news, young women?' asked the young man.

'We have not much news; what news hath the stranger?'
said she.

'My news is this,' said he, 'that I am, and have been
for three years, seeking for a certain woman, and that
thou art the most like her that I have seen yet: but there
is a certain difference between the woman that I seek,
and thee.'

well in No. 343, though Campbell, in his summary of the story (*W. H. Tales*,
iii., last page) says that the heroine recovered 'by the help of a poor woman
and through the agency of a well.' He has confused No. 343 with MS.
vol. x., No. 34. See also *Scottish Gaelic Studies*, iii., p. 186. Finding a beautiful
woman at a well also occurs, *W. H. Tales*, i., No. 2. D. MacKenzie, 'Children
and Wells,' *Folk-Lore*, xiii.

'Ciod è am boirionnach a tha thu ag iarraidh, mar sin ?' ars ise.

'Tha mi 'g iarraidh boirionnaich a dh'fhàg mi a stigh le mo mhàthair, an uair a chaidh mi thairis do na h-Innsean; is an uair a thill mi, cha d'fhuair mi i.'

'Agus an robh i pòsda riut ?'

'Bha,' ars esan.

'Tha an oidhche agad, a ghille mhaith, gu falbh as an so an nochd. Ach ciod è an comharra a bh'agad oirre ?' ars ise.

'Bha comharra gu leòir oirre—bha comharra gu leòir oirre—cha robh an làmh [dheas] oirre, is cha robh a' chìoch dheas oirre. Bha comharra gu leòir an sin,' ars esan.

'Tha 'n làmh dheas agus a' chìoch dheas orm-sa: thig thu dachaidh comhla rium féin a nochd do thigh an duine uasail so shuas; fuirichidh tu ann, is e do bheatha ann,' ars ise.

Chaidh e leò chun an tighe, agus ghabhadh roimhe gu coibhneil an sin.

An là-'r-na-mhàireach, an déidh a thràth-mhaidne a ghabhail, bha e airson a bhi falbh. Bha ise air fàs gu maith miadhail air.[1]

'Is ann is fhearr dhuit fuireach an diugh fhathast,' ars ise.

'Chan fhuirichinn an fhad ud fhéin, mura bhith gu bheil mi 'gad fhaighinn coltach ris a' bhoirionnach a tha mi 'g iarraidh.' Thug i air fuireach an latha sin.

Dh'innis i do'n duine uasal, is d'a mhnaoi o thoiseach gu deireadh, gur e a fear a bha an siod air tighinn. Cha robh i a' leigeil dad sam bith oirre ris-san.

'Ciod è bheireadh tu do dhuine dh'innseadh dhuit far a bheil am boirionnach sin ?'

'Bu mhór sin, nam biodh e agam,' ars esan.

Bha e tighinn dlùth air ám dol a laighe, agus chaidh esan a laighe.

'Is fhearr dhuit,' ars bean an duine uasail, 'dol sìos,

---

[1] MS. *mìomhail*, rude, which does not fit the rest of the story, and is obviously a mistake, for *mìomhail* would be followed, not by *air* but by *ris*.

'What manner of woman art thou seeking thus?' said she.

'I am seeking a woman that I left at home with my mother when I went abroad to the Indies ; but when I returned, I found she had gone.'

'And was she married to thee?'

'She was,' said he.

'Thou hast the whole night before thee, good lad, in which to go away from here. But what marks of recognition hadst thou of her?' said she.

'There were marks enough about her—there were marks enough about her—she wanted the [right] hand, and the right breast. Those were marks enough,' said he. H 57

'I have both the right hand and the right breast; come thou home with me to-night to the house of this gentleman yonder: thou shalt stay there, and be made welcome,' said she.

He went with them to the house, and was kindly treated there.

On the morrow after taking his breakfast, he made ready to go. She had meanwhile become very fond of him.[1]

'Thou hadst much better stay here for to-day too,' said she.

'I would not have stayed even as long as this, were it not that I found thee so like the woman I am seeking.' However she made him stay for that day.

She told the gentleman and his wife everything from beginning to end, and that it was her husband who had come. But to him she did not yet disclose anything.

'What wouldst thou give to anyone who would tell thee where that woman is?'

'Much would I give, if I had it,' said he.

It was coming near the time for going to bed, and he went to bed.

'Thou hadst better,' said the gentleman's wife [to the

agus dol a laighe comhla ris, agus innseadh gur tu a th'ann, agus théid sinn fhéin sìos as do dhéidh.'

Chaidh i sìos. 'An deach thu a laighe, ghille òig?' ars ise.

'Chaidh,' ars esan.

Có bha aig cùl an doruis ach an duine uasal, is a bhean-uasal.

'Is cinnteach nach misde thu duine comhla riut anns an leaba,' ars ise.

'Chan 'eil mi airson duine sam bith comhla rium an dràst, co dhiùbh,' ars esan.

Bha an duine uasal is a bhean gu bhi marbh le gàireachdaich.

'Seadh,' ars ise, 'a bheil thu toirt pàidhidh sam bith dhomh-sa airson brath a thoirt duit mu'n bhoirionnach sin a tha thu ag iarraidh?'

'Chan 'eil móran pàidhidh agam fhéin, an déidh a bhi siubhal o chionn trì bliadhna, ach nan cuireadh Nì Maith orm e, bhithinn deònach pàidheadh.'

'Is mise a th'ann!—a cheart bhoirionnach a bha'n sin!'

'O! cha tù!'

'O! is mi. C'arson a chuir thu fhéin litir chugam-sa mi ghabhail air falbh, is gun a bhi a stigh an uair a thilleadh tu?' ars ise.

'Cha do chuir mise [an] [1] litir chugad idir,' ars esan. 'Thàinig litir o mo mhàthair gun robh leanabh agad, agus ceann coinein agus com cait aige.'

'Cha tàinig,' ars ise.

'Tha an litir an so fhathast,' ars esan, [agus leig e fhaicinn di i].

'Is fìor sin. Is i an aon té rinn an cron mu thoiseach is a rinn e mu dheireadh,' ars ise.

Dh'aithnich iad an so, gur h-e na breugan a bha anns na litrichean.

'Eirich, a ghille mhaith, as fhearr a chunnaic mi riamh, agus nì mise banais air ais [2] duit ann an so, a nochd,' [ars an duine uasal].

---

[1] *mise litir, mise an litir,* are indistinguishable in rapid speech; *the letter* is apparently the meaning here.

King's daughter], 'go down and go to bed with him; tell him that it is thou, and we will go along after thee.'

Away she went. 'Hast thou gone to bed, young man ?' quoth she.

'I have,' said he.

Now who was at the back of the door, but the gentleman and the lady.

'Surely thou wilt be none the worse of someone being with thee in the bed,' said she.

'I will not have anybody along with me just now, anyhow,' said he.

The gentleman and his wife were nearly dead with laughing.

'Come,' quoth she, 'art thou going to give me any reward for telling thee tidings about the woman that thou art seeking ?'

'I have not much to pay with, for I have been travelling these three years, but if the Good Being should send me the wherewithal, I would be willing to pay.'

'I am she ! I am indeed that very woman !'

'O no ! thou art not !'

'O ! but I am ! But why didst thou send me a letter [telling me] to go away, and not to be at home at the time of thy return ?' quoth she.

'I did not send thee the letter at all,' quoth he. 'But a letter came to me from my mother [saying] that thou hadst a child with a rabbit's head and a cat's body.'

'Surely no such letter came to you,' said she.

'But I have the letter here yet,' said he, [and showed it to her].

'It is only too true. The woman who worked the first wrong is the same as the one who did the last,' said she.

They now realized that the letters were but lies.

'Arise, thou good lad, the best I ever saw, and I will make a re-wedding [2] for thee in this very place to-night,' [said the gentleman].

---

[2] *bainis air ais*, a wedding in return, similar in idiom to *pàidheadh air ais*, a repayment, to pay back.

Dh' éirich e, is rinneadh cuirm chridheil a chur air dòigh, is chuir iad seachad an oidhche gu sunndach.

* * * * * *

Bha aig an Rìgh, o'n chaidh am bior 'na chois, pàipearan feadh a h-uile h-àite, léigh sam bith a leighseadh e, gum bu leis an dara leth de'n rìoghachd ri a bheò, is an rìoghachd uile an déidh a bhàis.

An là-'r-na-mhàireach, bha iad-san a falbh á tigh an duine uasail. Bha duilichinn mhór air, an déidh i bhi 'ga fhàgail, leis cho maith is a bha i 'còrdadh ris. Bha an leanabh gille aice trì bliadhna a dh'aois, agus e gun bhaisteadh.
Ghabh iad rompa gu tigh an Rìgh.

Bha feadhainn a muigh a' feitheamh aig tigh an Rìgh a h-uile latha, feuch có thigeadh an rathad a leighseadh e.

'Bha mi fhéin, uair,' ars ise, 'agus bha beagan leigheis agam. Iarraidh mi a stigh; cha lughaide gun tig sonas orm fhathast.'

Sgrìobh i litir chun an dorsair gum bu bhan-léigh i a thug fada ann an àiteachan fòghlum leighis 'ga h-ionnsachadh, 'agus,' ars ise, 'cha bhi mi fuireach ri mac rìgh no ridire, mura leig sibh a stigh air an uair mi.'

Chuireadh litir air a h-ais, i a thighinn a stigh.
Cha rachadh sealladh dhith a stigh, mura rachadh an dithis dhaoine uaisle bha comhla rithe, a stigh. Fhuair iad a stigh , agus thug i a mac leatha ri a taobh. Fhuair iad àite suidhe, is shuidhe ise faisg air an leabaidh aige-san.

'Seadh, a dhuine chòir,' ars ise, 'tha thu 'nad shìneadh an so, is tha mi cluinntinn gum bu mhór am beud e.'

---

¹ Who 'they' are is uncertain. Later on, the heroine seems to be accompanied by two gentlemen, as well as by her baby boy. One of the two gentlemen must have been her husband. If the other was her late master, then the next sentence, to the effect that he was grieved 'after' she had left

He arose, and a merry feast was prepared, and they passed the night cheerfully.

*   *   *   *   *   *

Now the King, ever since the thorn had gone into his foot, had had papers abroad in every place, that any doctor who should heal him, should have half the kingdom during the King's life, and all the kingdom after his death. H 1292·4 Q 112

On the morrow, they [1] departed from the house of the gentleman. He was exceedingly grieved after she had left him, because she had pleased him so greatly. She had her baby boy with her. He was three years of age, and had not been baptized.

They pressed on their way [straight] to the King's House.

Outside the King's house there were people waiting every day, to see if any should come that way who might be able to heal him.

[When they arrived] she said, 'At one time of my life, I had some skill of healing. I will seek admittance, my chance of getting happiness will not thereby be rendered less likely.'

She wrote a letter to the door-keeper that she was a woman doctor who had spent a long time in medical schools studying medicine, 'and,' quoth she, 'I will wait for neither king's son nor knight's, if you do not let me in at once.'

A letter was sent back that she was to come in.

But not a step [2] would she take into the house unless the two gentlemen, who were with her, went in also. Well, they got in, and she took her son in with her by her side. They got seats, and she herself sat close to the King's bed.

'Yes, honest man,' quoth she, 'prone art thou lying here, and I hear that it is a very great pity.'

---

him, must be construed as looking forward to some later occasion, when she finally did part from him to follow her husband's fortunes.

[2] *Lit.* not a sight of her would go in.

'Tha mi an déidh mo chuid de'n t-saoghal a chosd ri mo leigheas,' ars esan.

'Thàinig mise airson a dhèanamh dhuibh: is ban-lighiche mi.'

'Is fada bha thu gun tighinn, nan dèanadh tu feum domh-sa,' ars esan.

[Ars ise,] 'C'à'm bheil a' Bhanrighinn? Cuiribh a nuas an so i, mun tòisich mi.'

Thàinig a' Bhan-righinn a nuas.

'Suidh thusa ann an sin, a leanaibh! tha mise dol a dh'innseadh naidheachd duit-sa, a leanaibh—agus faodaidh sibh-se, a dhaoine uaisle, éisdeachd, ach chan ann duibh a tha mi dol d'a innseadh idir, ach do mo mhac fhéin.

H 13
K 2312·1*

H 11·1

'Bha Banrighinn aon uair air a' chrùn an siod, agus bha dithis dhaltachan [2] aice, mac agus nighean. Is i an nighean a b'aosda na am mac. Bha an Rìgh anns a' bheinn-sheilge latha. Thug a' Bhanrighinn air an nighinn mionnachadh, an uair a bha an Rìgh air falbh, ge b'e ni chìtheadh i ise dèanamh, nach innseadh i do dhuine chaidh a bhaisteadh. Tha mise, a leanaibh! 'ga innseadh dhuit-se: cha deachaidh do bhaisteadh fhathast. Is mi fhéin a' cheart bhoirionnach a bh'ann. Chaidh an Rìgh do'n bheinn-sheilge. An uair a bha e air falbh, rug i air mo bhràthair, is thilg i an ceann deth leis a' chlaidheamh. Shuath i, an sin, an fhuil ri mo làmhan-sa. Sin agaibh, a dhaoine uaisle, mo naidheachd-sa. Is mise do nighean. Cuir a nall do làmh, agus feuch mo chìoch dheas agus mo làmh dheas orm.' [3]

V 81

Chuir e a nall an sin a chas air a glùn. Thug ise prìn airgid [4] a mach as a broilleach. Chuir i ris a' bhior e, is leum am bior 'na h-uchd.

D 1182
D 1500·1

'Faodaidh sibh, a nis dol a mach, a spaisdearachd.'

'Ciod è,' ars esan, 'a nì sinn ris a' Bhanrighinn?'

Q 413

'Nì, a crochadh gun dàil, aig dà uair dheug am

---

[1] *i.e.* it is a pity thou didst not come long ago.

[2] For this translation of *daltachan*, see Nicolson's *Gaelic Proverbs*, p. 101. 'Cha dual do rath a bhi air dalta spìocaid. The step-child of a scrub has a bad lot.'

[3] The heroine leaves a good deal of her story untold. She ought also

'I have spent all my worldly wealth in trying to get myself healed,' said he.

'I have come on purpose to accomplish the matter for you; I am a woman doctor.'

'If thou canst do me any good, thou hast been a long time coming,' [1] said the King.

[Said she,] 'Where is the Queen? Send her here, before I begin.'

The Queen came.

'Sit thou there, child! I am going to tell thee a tale, child,—and ye, gentlemen, may listen, but it is not to you I am going to tell the tale at all, but to mine own son. H 13
K 2312·1*

'There was once a certain crowned Queen, and she had two step-children,[2] a boy and a girl. The girl was older than the boy. One day the King was in the hunting-hill. When the King was away, the Queen made the lassie swear that whatever thing she saw her do, she would not tell to any man who had ever been baptized. Child! I am telling thee, for thou hast not yet been baptized, and I am the very woman in question. The King went to the hunting-hill. When he was away, the Queen seized on my brother, and struck his head off with the sword. Then she rubbed the blood over my hands. There you now have my story, gentlemen. I am thy daughter,' [said she to the King.] 'Stretch forth thy hand, and behold my right breast and my right hand in their places.' [3]
H 11·1
V 81

The King then stretched forth his foot, and laid it on her knee. She took a silver pin [4] from her bosom, and placed it up against the thorn, and the thorn leapt out into her lap.
D 1182
D 1500·1

'Ye may now go out, and walk.'

'What,' said he (the King), 'shall we do to the Queen?'

'What we will do is to hang her without delay, at Q 413

to say to the King, 'Stretch forth thy foot.' And in saying, 'There you have my story, gentlemen'—she breaks through her own plan of addressing her child, and mars the intended effect. Corruption is probably responsible.

[4] Apparently, a silver pin had magnetic power. Silver has magic power in one or two other stories.

màireach, agus an uair thig i bhàrr na croiche, teine chur
Q414·3 rithe, agus an luath aice leigeil leis a' ghaoith.'

An là-'r-na-mhàireach, rinneadh siod.

'Seadh, a Rìgh, ciod e tha sibh a lughasaicheadh [2]
dhomh-sa, a nis ?'
'A Nighean na Banrigh a b'fhearr a sheas fo chrùn,
is leat uile gu léir an rìoghachd. Théid t'fhear éigheach
'na rìgh. Cha bhi gnothuch agam-sa ris an rìoghachd
tuilleadh, chan 'eil annam ach seann duine.'
Dh'éigheadh 'na rìgh esan. Chuir ise fios air an duine
uasal aig an robh i cosnadh, agus thug i oighreachd fearainn
da. Chuir esan brath air a mhàthair an so, is bha i leò
anns an lùchairt rìoghail.

[1] Executions in these tales always take place at noon.   See also *Larminie*,
p. 186, and this book, p. 81.
[2] There is also the form *lughaigeachadh* and *lughaigeachduinn*.

NOTES

MS. vol. x., No. 34.   Note at end of MS. 'From Roderick MacLean,
tailor [Barra], who learnt it from Alexander McPherson about 88 years
ago.   McPherson is still living, and is about 80 years of age.   He
lives at no great distance from the reciter, but is now bedridden and
unable to recite himself.'
On the flyleaf, Islay has written:—

'An leanabh gun bhaisteadh No 34.   Gaelic Index—pages 352
to 372; Barra MS.—Printers Index.—Hector Boyd, Barra—[Scribe]
Hector MacLean, July /59.   Unchristened daughter with the hand
cut off.   See Journal [MS. vol. xiii.] for the version got at Polchar
by J. F. C.—Compare Grimm, Handless Maiden.'

twelve o'clock to-morrow,[1] and when she is taken off the gallows, she shall be set on fire, and her ashes scattered Q 414·3 to the winds.'

On the morrow, that was done accordingly.

'Yes, O King ! what are ye going to grant me, now ?'

'Thou daughter of the best Queen that ever supported a crown, the entire Kingdom is thine. Thy husband shall be proclaimed King. I will have nothing to do with the Kingdom any more, for I am but an old man.'

He (the hero) was proclaimed King. She on her part, sent word for the gentleman in whose service she had been,[3] and she gave him a landed estate. He (the hero) sent word for his mother, and she lived with them in the royal palace.

[3] This sentence seems to show that the heroine's former master did not enter the palace with her.

A more accurate description of the story surely were—'The Handless Woman and her Unchristened Child.'

'The version got at Polchar' is No. 343, English List, of which Islay says:—'A very good version—differs from Grimm.' He summarized it at end of W. H. Tales, iii., where he connects some of the incidents with some in 'Nighean Rìgh fo Thuinn,' ibid., No. 86. See Index, p. xxxv.

Similar Narratives: — Dr Hyde, Beside the Fire, pp. 167, 194. Béaloideas, iii., p. 84, and pp. 473 (No. 6), 500; iv., pp. 46, 168; vii., p. 167.

AN DUINE BOCHD, BEAIRTEACH

Aarne-Thompson, Nos. 935^{xx}, 726^x, 449^x

BHA duine bochd ann, agus cha robh aige ach tasdan 'san latha, is bha e cho bochd. Bha e latha de na laithean ag obair, is thàinig dà dhuine uasal an rathad. 'An saoil mi fhìn,' ars an darna fear ris an fhear eile, 'an dèanadh airgiod an duine so beairteach?'

'Ma tà, cha dèanadh,' ars am fear eile, 'bhitheadh e cho math dhuit cnap luaidhe a thoirt da.'

'Feuchaidh mi ris, co dhiùbh, is bheir mi dà cheud punnd Sasunnach da, air chor is gum pàidh e dhomh fhìn iad an ceann na bliadhna.'

Chaidh an duine uasal far an robh an duine bochd, is thug e da an dà cheud punnd Sasunnach, is cha robh pòca no àite aige an cuireadh e e, ach seana churrachd craicinn a bha mu a cheann.

Bha e falbh dachaidh is a' dol troimh choillidh, is bha e faicinn eòin a' seòladh os a chionn daonnan. Aon de na h-uairean, thàinig an t-eun, is thog e leis an currachd craicinn is an t-airgiod ann. Bha e an sin na bu mhiosa na bha e riamh, is chaill e a phàidheadh latha. Thuirt e ris a' mhnaoi gur ann gu tinn a dh'fhàs e ris an obair. An la-'r-na-mhàireach, chaidh e chun na h-oibre. Bha e an obair mar sin gus an tàinig ceann na bliadhna, agus thadhail an dà dhuine uasal aige. 'Nach fhaic thu Domhnall shìos ud ag obair?' ars an dara duine uasal. Dh'iarr iad suas e. 'Seadh, am bheil mo chuid airgid agad an diugh, a Dhomhnaill?' ars an duine uasal.

'Chan 'eil,' ars esan. Dh'innis e mar a dh'éirich dha. 'Bheir mi dà cheud eile dhuit am bliadhna, is biodh iad agad domh an ceann na bliadhna.' Thug an duine uasal an dà cheud do Dhomhnall, agus dh'fhalbh e dhachaidh. Cha robh àite a stigh a chumadh iad ach sean chrogan beag a bhiodh a' cumail càthaidh. Chuir Domhnall an dà cheud anns a' chrogan.

Thàinig marsanda an là-'r-na-mhàireach a bha creic [shoithichean] crèadha. Bha each aige, agus dh'iarr e a'

THE POOR RICH MAN

No. 21.   [*Vol. x., No. 35*]

Aarne-Thompson, Nos. 935[xx]*, 726*[x]*, 449*[x]

THERE was once a poor man, who had only a shilling a day, and he was so poor. One day when he was working, two gentlemen came that way. 'I wonder,' said one of the gentle- N 66 men to the other, 'whether money would make this man rich?'

'Well then, it would not,' said the other, 'thou mightest as well give him a lump of lead.'

'I shall try it, anyhow, and I shall give him two hundred pounds sterling, on condition that he shall pay them back to me at the end of a year.'

The gentleman went over to where the poor man was, and gave him the two hundred pounds sterling. But the poor man had neither pocket nor place in which to put it, nothing but an old skin cap that he wore on his head.

When going home and passing through a wood, he noticed a bird that was continually hovering over his head. On one N 183 occasion, the bird swooped down, and carried off the skin cap N 527 and the money in it as well. The poor man was then worse off than ever, and lost his pay for that day as well. He told his wife that he had become ill while at work. The next day, however, he went to work. He continued in work in that way until the end of the year came round, and the two gentlemen came to see him. 'Dost thou not see Donald working down there?' said one of the gentlemen. They asked him to come over to them. 'Well, hast thou got my money with thee to-day, Donald?' said the gentleman.

'I have not,' said he, and related what had happened to him. 'I will give thee two hundred more this year, and see thou hast them ready for me at the end of the year.' The gentleman gave Donald the two hundred, and Donald went home. He had no place in the house that would hold the two hundred but a little old jar that used to hold husks of corn. So Donald put the two hundred in the jar.

On the morrow came a merchant who was selling earthenware vessels. He had a horse, and he asked her (the poor

chàth a bha anns a' chrogan oirre-se, is gum faigheadh i soitheach
air a son.   Thug i da an crogan is a' chàth mar a bha e, is an
dà cheud ann am measg na càtha.   An uair a thàinig esan
dachaidh, dh'fhaighnich e c'à'n robh an crogan.   Thuirt ise
J 2093·1   gun tug i seachad airson soithich e.   'Chan fhaod e bhi gun
do rinn thu sin is mo dhà cheud punnd Sasunnach ann?' ars
esan.   'Cha robh is cha bhi sin agadsa, dà cheud punnd
Sasunnach!'   'Bha,' ars esan.   'Cha robh,' ars ise.   Cha robh
a chridhe aige facal a ràdh.   Dh'fhalbh e an là-'r-na-mhàireach
a dh'ionnsuigh na h-oibre.

An ceann na bliadhna, thàinig an dithis dhaoine uaisle.
Bha iad shuas os a chionn, is esan ag obair, is dh'eubh iad ris.
'Seadh,' ars an duine uasal, 'a bheil mo dhà cheud punnd
Sasunnach agad am bliadhna?'—'Chan 'eil,' ars esan.
Chuir an duine uasal eile a làmh 'na phòca, is thug e cnap
luaidhe as, is thug e siod do Dhomhnall.   'So,' ars esan, 'gléidh
sin.'   Ghléidh e e, is an uair a chaidh e dachaidh, thilg e thar
a' bhalla a stigh e.

Thàinig bean iasgair an rathad, is dh'fheòraich i de bhean
Dhomhnaill an robh sgàth aice.   Thuirt ise gun robh.   Thug
i dhi pìos luaidhe, is fhuair i gealladh uaipe gum faigheadh i
beathach éisg.   Thàinig bean an iasgair goirid 'na dhéidh
sin, agus trosg mór leatha a dh'ionnsuigh bean Dhomhnaill.
N 66   Rug i air an trosg, is thòisich i air a sgoltadh, is an uair a bha
B 107   i 'ga sgoltadh, leum meall a bhroinn.   Thàinig bean òircheaird
a stigh, agus dh'fheuch bean Dhomhnaill an cnap di.   Dh'
aithnich ise ciod è a bh'ann.   'Thoir domh e, agus gheabh thu
punnd air.'   'Cha toir,' ars ise, 'bidh Domhnall a' trod rium,
ma bheir mi seachad gun fhios da e.'   'Bheir mi dhuit dà phunnd
Shasunnach air,' arsa bean an òircheaird.   'Cha toir mi seachad
idir e—chan fhaigh thu idir e gus an tig e fhìn,' arsa bean
Dhomhnaill.   'An uair a thig an t-òircheard dachaidh, cuiridh
mise a nuas dh'a cheannach e,' arsa bean an òircheaird.
Dh'fhalbh i dhachaidh, is dh'innis i d'a fear mu'n chnap.
Thàinig an t-òircheard, agus dh'fheuch e e, agus is e cnap
daoimean a bh'ann.   Thug e deich mìle de òr buailt' air,
agus uibhir eile an uair a bhuaileadh e e.

---

¹ This is a very idiomatic expression, which cannot be satisfactorily
translated.   The literal translation is 'He had not the heart to say a word,'
but the actual meaning is that the man was brow-beaten into silence.   'Chan
'eil a chridhe agad sin a dhèanamh' = 'You are strictly forbidden [by the
speaker or some third person] to do that.'

man's wife) for the husks in the jar [and said] that she should
have an earthenware dish in return for the husks. She gave
him the jar with the husks in it just as it was, and the two
hundred pounds amongst the husks. When he (the poor man)
came home, he enquired where the jar was. She said that J 2093·1
she had given it away for an earthenware dish. 'It cannot
be that thou hast given it away with my two hundred pounds
sterling in it as well ?' said he. 'Two hundred pounds sterling !
that thou never didst have, and never wilt !' 'But I did have
them,' said he. 'Thou didst not,' said she. He was not allowed
to say a word.[1] And the next day he went to work.

At the end of the year, the two gentlemen came. They stood
on some ground that was higher than where he was working and
called to him. 'Well,' said the gentleman, 'hast thou my two
hundred pounds sterling ready this year ?'—'I have not,' said he.
The other gentleman put his hand in his pocket, fetched
out a lump of lead, and gave Donald that. 'Here,' said he,
'keep that.' Donald took it, and when he got home, threw
it over the inner wall.[2]

A fisherman's wife came that way, and asked Donald's
wife if she had anything. She said she had, and gave her a
bit of lead, and got a promise from her in return that she should
have a fish [to eat]. The fisherman's wife returned a little
while afterwards, with a large codfish which was for Donald's
wife. She laid hold of the cod, and began to split it open, N 66
and while doing so, a lump of something fell out of the inside B 107
of it. A goldsmith's wife came in, and Donald's wife showed
her the lump. She recognized what it was. 'Give it to me,
and thou shalt have a pound for it.' 'I will not,' she replied,
'Donald will scold me if I give it away without his knowledge.'
'I will give thee two pounds sterling for it,' said the goldsmith's
wife. 'I will not give it away at all—thou shalt not have it
at all until Donald comes himself,' said Donald's wife. 'When
the goldsmith comes home, I will send him along to buy it,'
replied the goldsmith's wife. Off she went home, and told
her husband about the lump. The goldsmith came, and
examined it, and behold, it was a diamond nugget. He gave
ten thousand pounds of beaten (or coined ?) gold for it, and as
much again when he had beaten it (the gold).[3]

---

[2] Presumably a party wall, which in Highland cots does not always reach
to the roof.

[3] Ten thousand was all he had beaten, but as he was going to pay twenty
thousand he had to beat more.

Ghabh Domhnull 'na cheann gun rachadh e a shealgaireachd.
Thug e leis gunna, is bha e dol troimh choillidh. Bha e sealltuinn
os a chionn, agus chunnaic e eun beag. Loisg e air, agus thuit
an t-eun a nuas, agus an ceap aig Domhnall agus an dà cheud
punnd Sasunnach ann. 'So an t-eun a thug an dà cheud
punnd Sasunnach uam, agus fhuair mi a nis iad,' arsa Domhnall.
A' tilleadh dhachaidh, bha e dol seachad air stàbull. Sheall
e a stigh, agus chunnaic e an seana chrogan a bha aige cùl
an doruis, agus a' chàth 'na bhroinn. Chaidh e a stigh, is
chuir e làmh ann, agus fhuair e a dhà cheud punnd Sasunnach
'na ghrunnd. 'So,' ars esan, 'an dà cheud punnd Sasunnach
a thug a' bhean agamsa seachad am measg na càtha.' Bha
e a nis 'na dhuine beairteach, is thòisich e air togail caisteil
mhóir. Thog e e, is cha robh a leithid 'san rìoghachd.

N 183

Bha an rìgh an so a' dol a choimhead air. Bha sia stàtan
leis, agus fear comhairleachaidh. Thachair dall air, agus
thairg e an déirc da. 'Cha ghabh mi i,' ars an dall ris an
rìgh, 'gus am buail thu trì stràcan de bhata orm.' 'Cha
bhuail,' ars an rìgh, 'tha thu dona gu leòir a cheana, ged nach
téid mise gu do bhualadh.' 'Mura buail, cha ghabh mise
sgàth,' ars an dall. Thug an rìgh trì stràcan de bhata dha,
is ghabh e an déirc.

Ghabh an rìgh air falbh. Cha deachaidh e fad air aghaidh,
an uair a chunnaic e fear air muin làire glaise, agus cuip aige,
is e ag éirigh oirre, is e dol mun cuairt air bun craoibhe, is
gun e 'ga leigeil air a h-aghaidh idir. 'Is ciod è is coireach
nach 'eil thu leigeil na làire air a h-aghaidh gun a bhi dol
mun cuairt mar sin leatha?' ars an rìgh. 'Chan 'eil agad ach
a bhi 'ga fhaighneachd gus am faigh thu brath,' ars am fear
a bha air muin na làire.

Ghabh an rìgh air falbh. Chunnaic e an so an caisteal a
bu bhrèagha chunnaic duine riamh air an rìoghachd aige
fhìn. Bha càin air fear sam bith a thogadh caisteal gun ordan
an rìgh. Ghabh e a null, is cha robh duine timchioll air ach
aon chlachair. 'A bheil ainm agad air an duine leis an leis
an tigh so?' ars an rìgh ris a' chlachair. 'Cha chuala mise
riamh ach an duine bochd, beairteach,' ars esan.—' Chan 'eil
dad de choltas na bochduinn air a'chaisteal a tha an so.'
Thill an rìgh dachaidh.

An là-'r-na-mhàireach, chuir e a fhear comhairleachaidh
a dh'iarraidh an doill, is fhir na làire, agus an duine bhochd,
bheairtich. Chaidh am fear comhairleachaidh far an robh

Donald now took it into his head that he would go hunting. He took a gun with him, and went through a forest. Looking upwards, he saw a little bird. He fired at it, and down fell the bird, and with it fell Donald's cap and the two hundred pounds sterling in it. 'This is the bird that stole the two hundred pounds sterling from me, but I have got them back again now,' said Donald. When going home, he passed by a stable. He peeped in, and saw that old jar of his at the back of the door, with the husks inside it. In he went, and putting in his hand, found the two hundred pounds sterling at the bottom of the jar. 'Here,' said he, 'are the two hundred pounds sterling which my wife gave away among the husks.' He was now a rich man, and began to build a great castle. And he built it too, and the like of that castle was not to be found in the kingdom. N 183

So now the King was coming to see him. The King had six nobles with him, and a counsellor. He met a blind man, and offered him alms. 'I will not take alms,' said the blind man to the King, 'until thou hast given me three blows with a stick.' 'I will not strike thee,' said the King, 'thou art in a bad enough case as it is, even if I refrain from striking thee.' 'If thou strike me not, I will not accept a thing.' So the King gave him three strokes with a stick, and the blind man then accepted alms.

The King went on. He had not gone far, when he saw a man seated on the back of a gray mare, with a whip in his hand; he was beating her and going round and round a tree trunk, and preventing her from going on. 'Why is it that thou dost not allow the mare to go on, but art going round about with her in that way?' said the King. 'Thou hast nothing for it but to go on asking till thou find out,' said the man on the back of the mare.

The King went away. He next saw the most beautiful castle that any one had ever seen, and in his own kingdom too. Now, any man who built a castle without the King's command was to be fined. He went over towards it, but there was nobody about but a solitary mason. 'Dost thou know the name of the man who owns this house?' said the King to the mason. 'I never heard him called anything but the poor rich man,' replied the mason.—'There is not the slightest appearance of poverty about this castle.' And the King returned home.

On the morrow, the King sent his counsellor to fetch the blind man, the man with the mare, and the poor rich man. The counsellor went to them, and told them that the King wanted

iad, is thuirt e riu gun robh an rìgh 'gan iarraidh. Dh'fhalbh iad comhla ris 'nan triùir far an robh an rìgh. Chaidh iad a stigh, is shuidh iad 'sa' chidsin. Dh'fhosgail an rìgh dorus a sheòmair, is dh'iarr e orra éirigh sìos. 'Ma tà, cha téid,' ars an duine bochd, beairteach,' bu mhath an gnothuch duinne gum faigheamaid bruidhinn diot 'nad chidsin, gun tighinn air dol do do rùm.' 'Cha ruig thu leas sin [a ràdh,] tha rùm cho math ris an fhear so agad fhìn.' Chaidh iad a sìos an sin.

'Seadh, a dhoill,' ars an rìgh, 'innis domhsa ciod è bu choireach nach gabhadh thu an déirc gus am buailinn trì stràcan de bhata ort ?'

'Ma tà, air ur làimh-se, 's air mo dhà làimh fhìn, gun dèan mise sin,' ars an dall. 'Bha mise 'nam mharsanda mór roimhe, agus dh'fhalbh mi le cóig càmhalan deug a dh'iarraidh bathair. Choinnich fear mi air an rathad ris an canadh iad Mathan, agus thuirt e rium nan tugainn da cóig de na càmhalan, gun tugadh e dhomh sac chàich de òr. Thug mi dha na cóig càmhalan, is thug e dhomh sac an deich de òr.[1] Chaidh mi gu tilleadh dhachaidh leò. Is ann a' dol a choimhead caraid a bha esan leis an òr is leis na càmhalan. Thill mi as a dhéidh. 'Thoir dhomh,' arsa mise, 'an cóigeamh camhal; bu mhath an gnothuch a dhol a choimhead caraid a ceithir fhìn.' Thug e dhomh an cóigeamh fear, agus thill mi leis. Cha robh aig Mathan nì sam bith a dh'iarrteadh air r'a dhiùltadh. Cha robh Mathan fad air falbh, an uair a chaidh mi air m' ais a rithist. 'Bu mhath an gnothuch,' arsa mise, 'trì fhìn a thoirt a choimhead caraid, ged a bheireadh tu an ceathramh fear domhsa.' Thug e dhomh an ceathramh fear, agus thill mi, ach chaidh mi air m'ais a rithist.

J 514·3*

'Bu mhath an gnothuch,' arsa mise ri Mathan, 'dithis fhìn a thoirt a choimhead caraid, ged a bheireadh tu dhomhsa an treas fear.' Thug e siod dhomh. Chaidh mi air m' ais a rithist, is dh'iarr mi fear eile, is fhuair mi siod, is cha robh aig Mathan ach an t-aon. Thill mi a rithist, is thuirt mi ris gum bu mhath an gnothuch a dhol a choimhead caraid làn pocain, ged a bheireadh e dhomhsa am fear eile. Thug e siod domh. Chunnaic mi bocsa aige. Thill mi a dh'iarraidh a' bhocsa. 'Chan òr a th' anns a' bhocsa,' ars esan. 'Seadh,' ars esan,
'ach tha rud ann, is ma shuathas tu ri do shùil e, chì thu fad do

D 1825
·4·1
Q 338
D 1331
·3·1

sheallaidh de an talamh làn òir.'[2] Dh'fhalbh e, is shuath e ri mo shùil e, is chunnaic mi fad mo sheallaidh de'n talamh làn òir. 'Suath ris an t-sùil eile e,' arsa mise. 'Ma shuathas,

---

[1] *sac* = burden.   [2] The meaning of the Gaelic is uncertain.

them. So the three of them went off with him to visit the King.
They went in and sat down in the kitchen. The King opened
the door of his own room, and desired them to rise and walk in.
'Well then, we will not go in,' said the poor rich man, 'it is a
great thing for us merely to get speech of thee in thy kitchen,
without dreaming of entering thine own room.' 'Thou needest
not say that, for thou thyself hast a room as good as this.'
Thereupon they entered his room.

'Well now, thou blind man,' said the King, 'tell me why it
was that thou wouldst not accept alms until I had given thee
three blows with a stick ?'

'Well then, by your hand, and by my own two hands, I
will indeed do that,' said the blind man. 'I was a great
merchant in past times, and I once set forth with fifteen camels
to procure merchandise. On the road I met a man whom they
called Mahon, and he told me that if I would give him five of
the camels, he would give me as much gold as the rest could
carry. I gave him the five camels, and he gave me as much
gold as the remaining ten could carry. I started off to return
home with them. He was going with the gold and the camels
to see a friend. I turned and went after him. 'Give me,'
said I, 'the fifth camel; when going to see a friend four camels
are quite good enough.' He gave me the fifth camel, and I
returned with the animal. Now Mahon was bound not to
refuse to part with anything that was asked of him. Mahon
had not gone far, when I went after him again. 'It were quite
good enough,' said I, ' to have even three camels with thee
when going to see a friend, even if thou gavest me the fourth
camel.' He gave me the fourth, and I returned with it, but
I went after him again.

'It were amply sufficient,' said I to Mahon, 'to have two
camels with thee when going to see a friend, though thou J 514·3*
wouldst give me the third.' He gave me the third. But I
went back after him again, and asked for another, and got
that, and now Mahon had only the one. I returned again,
and said to him that a sack, full of things, would be quite
enough when going to see a friend, even if he gave me the other
camel. He gave me the camel. I had noticed that he had a
box, and returned after him again to get the box. 'It is not
gold that is in the box,' said he: 'no, but there is something in it,
which is such that if thou dost rub thine eye with it, thou shalt
see that the earth as far as thine eye can reach is full of gold.' ² D 1825
                                                                        ·4·1
He went, and rubbed my eye with it, and I saw the earth full Q 338

chan fhaic thu leus gu bràth tuilleadh,' ars esan.   Smuainich mi
gur h-ann a bha e cur mar fhiachaibh orm.   Dh'iarr mi air a
shuathadh ris an t-sùil eile.   Shuath e an so ri mo shùil eile e,
D 1822   is chan fhaca mise leus riamh tuilleadh.   Sgaoil na càmhalan
air feadh an t-saoghail, is chan fhaca mise gin riamh dhiubh.
Q 338   Is mise am fear a dhall an sannt.'

'Seadh, a dhuine bhochd bheairtich, innis domhsa 'd è 'n
reuson an tugadh an t-ainm ort?'   Dh'innis e da a h-uile
dòigh mar a thachair da.

'Seadh, a mharcaiche na làire glaise, innis thusa dhomh
ciod è bu choireach duit a ràdh rium mi bhi faighneachd gus
am faighinn brath?'

'Ma tà, innsidh mise sin duibh, a rìgh.   Bha mise ann am
mhac marsanda gu math beairteach, agus fhuair mi sgoil agus
ionnsachadh glé mhath.   Phòs mi bean uasal mhór, is cha
d'ith i sgàth riamh ach na dh'ith i le pluc prìne.   Cha robh
oidhche a rachainn a laighe nach tugadh i deoch chadail
domh, is cha dùisginn gus am biodh e naoi uairean 'sa' mhaduinn
am màireach.   Bha mi an siod oidhche de na h-oidhchean,
is chuir mi romham nach òlainn an deoch.   An uair a thug i
dhomh i, dhoirt mi sìos am broilleach mo léine i, is leig mi
orm gun robh mi 'nam chadal.   Rug i air dhà chluais orm,
is leig i am buille ud domh ris an leabaidh.   Thug i dìom a
h-uile snàthainn de'n aodach, is tharruing i a nall mi air an
ùrlar, is am buille fhuair mo cheann-sa, cha d'fhuair ceann
riamh a leithid.   Rug i an sin orm, is thilg i do'n leabaidh mi,
is chuir i an t-aodach orm.

Ghabh i a mach an dorus cho luath is a b'urrainn di, is
an uair a chaidh ise a mach, dh'éirich mise, is chaidh mi a
mach as a déidh, feuch am faicinn c'à'n robh i dol.   Cha
b'fhada bha i gus an do thachair cù oirre ris an canadh iad an
cù rùta,[1] agus rinn iad coinneamh ri chéile.   Dh'fhalbh iad
do'n chladh, is thòisich iad air cladhach uaighe.   Thug iad
G 20   corp as an uaigh, agus thòisich iad r'a itheadh.   Bha mi fhín
a' gabhail ealla riu, 's cha robh fhios agam ciod è dhèanainn an
uair a chunnaic mi ise 'g itheadh a'chuirp.   An uair a bha iad
sgìth an sin, dh'fhalbh iad, is ruith mise air thoiseach oirre-se,
is chaidh mi do'n leabaidh, is leig mi orm gun robh mi 'nam
chadal.   Thàinig ise a stigh as mo dhéidh, is chaidh [i] do'n
leabaidh air mo chùl.   An uair a dh'éirich mi, cha do leig
mi dad orm rithe-se.   Dh'éirich ise, is dheasaich i biadh, is
chuir i air a' bhòrd e.   Shuidh i aig a' bhòrd, is rug i air prìne,

---

[1] Probably a dog used to herd rams.   *Rùta* means a ram.

of gold as far as my eye could see. 'Rub the other eye with it,' D 1331
said I. 'If I do, thou wilt never again see another glimpse of ·3·1
anything,' said he. I thought that he was only fooling [daring ?]
me. I asked him to rub the other eye with it. Thereupon
he applied it to my other eye, and I never saw another glimmer D 1822
again. The camels scattered over the world, and I never saw
one of them again. I am he who was blinded by greed.' Q 338

'Yes now, thou poor rich man, tell me the reason why
that name was given thee ?' The poor rich man told the
King everything that had happened to him.

'Well now, thou rider of the gray mare, tell me what was
the cause of thy saying to me to continue asking till I found
out ?'

'Well then, I will tell thee that, oh King. I was a merchant's
son, and very wealthy, and I received a very good schooling and
education. I married a great lady, who never ate anything
at all but what she could pick up with a pin's head. There
was never a night that I went to bed that she would not give
me a sleeping draught, so that I used not to awake until nine
o'clock the next morning. But on a night of nights, I determined
not to drink the draught. When she gave it to me, I spilt it
down inside the front of my shirt, and then pretended to be
asleep. She took me by the two ears, and gave me such a
bang against the bed. She took every stitch of clothing off me,
and dragged me across the floor, and the blow that my head
got, no head ever got the like. Then she seized me, pitched
me into the bed, and put the clothes on me again.

She then went out of the door as quickly as she could, and
when she had gone, I rose, and went out after her, to try if
I could see where she was going. It was not long till she fell
in with a dog which they called the ram-dog,[1] and they held
a meeting together. They went off to the churchyard, and
began digging a grave. Out of the grave they fetched up a
body, and began to eat it. I was taking stock of them, but G 20
I did not know what to do when I saw her eating the body.
When they were tired, they went away, and I ran on ahead
of her, and went to bed and pretended to be asleep. She
came in after me, and coming to bed, lay down behind me.
When I arose, I did not then disclose to her that I knew anything. She arose, prepared food and put it on the table. She
sat down to table, picked up a pin, and began to eat with the
head of the pin. 'Come on and begin,' said I, 'take thy food

is thòisich i ri itheadh le pluc prìne. 'Siuthad,' arsa mise,
'gabh do bhiadh mar is còir dhuit a ghabhail, agus fios agamsa
nach ann le pluc prìne tha thu 'g itheadh na tha 'gad bheo-
thachadh, agus cuimhnich an dìol a rinn thu ormsa an raoir.
Chunnaic mise far an deach thusa agus an cù rùta.'

G 200   Cha dubhairt i facal. Dh'éirich i o'n bhòrd, is chaidh i a
null chun a' phreas. Thug i a nall crogan beag, dubh, is

D 566·2* bhuail i dorn air os cionn mo chinn, agus leum mi 'nam chù
D 141   glas. Rug i air slat, is bhuail i trì slachdan dith orm, is chuir
i a mach as an tigh mi. Cha robh fios 'm ciod è dhèanainn,

K 2213·6 is ged a bha mi 'nam chù, bha tùr duine annam. Chaidh mi
D 682·3   gu cidsin duine uasail. Thàinig gille a mach gus an dorus.
D 683·2   'Gu dearbh,' ars esan, 'is e cù duine uasail a tha a muigh ud.'
Thàinig na gillean air fad a mach a shealltuinn orm, is [bha]
fear a chanadh—'is e cù duine uasail a th' ann,' is fear a
chanadh—'chan eadh.'—'Ma tà,' arsa fear de na gillean,
'caithidh mise cnàimh feòla ann an lòn d'a ionnsuigh, is ma's
e cù duine uasail a th' ann, cha tog e e.' Dh'fhalbh e a stigh,
's thàinig e a mach is cnàimh aige. Dh'eubh e orm fhín, is
chaith e an cnàimh anns an lòn. Chaidh mi a null, is chuir
mi mo shròn ris, is cha do thog mi idir e. 'Nach dubhairt mi
ruibh gur h-e cù duine uasail a bh' ann,' ars esan. Chaidh
e a stigh, is thàinig e a mach is truinnsear leis agus brot is feòil
ann am ionnsuigh. Dh'ith mi siod. An uair a dh'ith mi e,
smuainich mi ged a bha duine ann a bheireadh dhomh, gun
robh duine ann a bhuaileadh mi.

Ghabh mi air falbh is ràinig mi bùth, is bha an gille-bùth a
mach mu'n dorus. Rinn e fead rium fhìn is chaidh mi far an
robh e. Thòisich e an sin air dèanamh dhìom, is air rud a
thoirt domh, is bha mi fad trì oidhchean comhla ris an fhear
sin. Bha e latha cunntas airgid, is bha móran de airgiod math
is dona aige am measg a chéile. Dh'aithnich mi air nach robh
sgoil ro mhath aige. Chaidh mi far an robh e, is chuir mi le
mo spòig an t-airgiod math air an darna taobh, is an t-airgiod
dona air an taobh eile. Dh'aithnich an gille gun d'aithnich
mi fhìn eadar an t-airgiod math is an t-airgiod dona. Thòisich e
air dèanamh dhìom. Cha do rinn e ach an t-airgiod a phasgadh,
an uair a thàinig boirionnach dachaidh. Cheannaich i fiach
puinnd Shasunnaich de aodach. Is e airgiod geal a bha
aice. 'Feuch nach 'eil droch airgiod agad,' ars an gille-bùth
rithe. 'Chan 'eil sgillinn,' ars ise. 'Ma thà,' ars esan,
'aithnichidh mo chù e, is cuiridh e an dà airgiod air leth.'
Chuir i an t-airgiod air a' bhòrd.

as thou oughtest to take it.   I know that it is not with the head
of a pin thou dost eat enough to keep thee alive, and remember
how thou didst treat me last night.   I saw where thou didst
go with the ram-dog.'

    She said not a word.   But getting up from the table, she   G 200
went over to a press.   Thence she brought forth a little black
jar, and coming over to me, held the jar over my head, struck   D 566·2*
it with her fist, and I instantly became a gray dog.   She seized   D 141
a switch, struck me with it three times, and drove me out of
the house.   I knew not what to do; but though I was now a   K 2213·6
dog, I still had my human sense.   I went to the kitchen of a   D 682·3
gentleman.   A gillie came out to the door.   'Certainly,' said   D 683·2
he, 'it is a gentleman's dog that is out there.'   All the gillies
in the place came out to look at me.   One of them said—
'it is a gentleman's dog,' and another said—'no, it is not.'—
'Well,' said another, 'I will throw him a bone with some meat
on it.   I will throw it into a puddle, and if it is a gentleman's
dog, he will not touch it.'   He went indoors, and came out
again with a bone.   He called me, and threw the bone into the
puddle.   I went over to it, put my nose to it, but did not pick
it up at all.   'Did I not tell you that it was a gentleman's dog,'
said the gillie.   He went indoors again, and came out with a
plate with some soup and meat in it for me.   I ate it up.
When I had eaten it, I reflected that though there were some
men who would give me something, there were some who
would beat me.
    I went away and came to a shop.   The shop-boy was
outside at the door.   He whistled to me, and I went up to
him.   He began to make much of me and to give me things,
and I spent three nights with that fellow.   One day he was
counting money, and he had a great deal of good and bad money
mixed together.   I could see that he was not well educated.
So I went up to him, and with my paw, I placed the good
money on one side and the bad on the other.   He realized
that I knew the difference between good money and bad.
He began to pet me.   He had scarcely packed up the money,
when a woman came to the place.   She purchased clothes to
the value of one pound sterling.   The money she had was
silver money.   'See that thou hast no bad money there,' said
the shop-boy to her.   'Not a penny of it is bad money,' said
she.   'If it is bad,' said he, 'my dog will know, and he will
separate the two kinds.'   So she laid the money on the table.

Chaidh mise suas, is chuir mi an t-airgiod dona air an darna taobh is an t-airgiod math air an taobh eile. 'Nach seall thu siod a nis,' ars an gille-bùth.—'B'fhearr leam gun creiceadh tu an cù sin rium fhìn, is bheirinn duit a leithid so air.' 'Cha chreic; is mór a ghabhainn [1] [mun dèanainn sin]. Cha ghabhainn dà cheud punnd Sasunnach air.'

An uair a dh'fhalbh ise, chaidh mise a mach as an tigh. Chunnaic ise mi fhìn, is rinn i fead rium, is bha nàire orm falbh as a déidh; ach smuainich mi gum biodh i glé mhath dhomh an uair a bha i tairgse mo cheannach, agus lean mi i. Chaidh i dachaidh, is chaidh mi fhìn a stigh comhla rithe. Cha robh a stigh ach aon nighean a bha aice. Thuirt i ri a nighinn, 'Thug mi sgoil is ionnsachadh dhuit, is cho cinnteach 's a tha

H 62   mise 'ga ràdh riut, is e duine a tha 'sa' chù so, is thoir o na geasan e.'

'Ma tà, ma thug thu sin domhsa, sgoil is ionnsachadh, b'e sin an droch sgoil,' ars an nighean.

D 683·2   'Dèan thusa,' ars ise, 'an rud a tha mise ag iarraidh ort, có dhiùbh.' Dh'fhalbh an nighean, is chaidh i a null gu preas, is thug i a nall ceart tomhas a' chrogain a bhuaileadh orm roimhid. Bhuail i dorn air a' chrogan os cionn mullach

D 771·5*   mo chinn, agus leum mi ann am dhuine. 'Taing do Nì Math gun d'fhuair mise bhi mar a bha mi roimhid,' arsa mi fhìn. 'Ciod è,' arsa mise, 'an aon rathad air am faigh mise a leithid a dhèanamh air a' mhnaoi a dh'fhàg mise mar siod is a rinn ise ormsa?'

'Tha, gheibh thu an crogan so uamsa,' ars an nighean,

D 1765   'is cuiridh tu dhìot do dhà bhròig an uair a théid thu a stigh air an dorus. Théid thu gu fàilidh suas an t-ùrlar, is bidh ise aig an teine, is i 'ga garadh fhìn is a cùl ris an dorus, agus

D 566·2*   buailidh tu an crogan os cionn mullach a cinn, agus òrdaichidh [4]
D 131   tu i bhi agad 'na làir ghlais, agus bidh i ann an sin.'

Rinn mise sin, a rìgh ! Leum mi air muin na làire glaise, is ghabh mi leatha gu bun na craoibhe. Cha tug mi [a] toil

G 275   di, is cha do leig mi air a h-aghaidh i, ach a bhi dol mun cuairt leatha timchioll bun na craoibhe. An latha sin a choinnich thu mi, cha robh ùine agam, ach a ràdh riut a bhi dol air t'aghaidh [5] gus am faigheadh thu brath, is an robh dad coire an sin?' 'Cha robh dad coire ann, gun teagamh,' ars an rìgh.

---

[1] *Lit.* I would take a lot [before I would do that.]
[2] *Lit.* bring him from the spells.
D 566·2*   [3] Not quite correct. When changing him into a dog, his wife struck a jar, not him. Afterwards, she struck him with a switch, it is true, but not with a jar.

I went forward, and put the bad money on the one side, and the good on the other. 'There—dost thou see that now,' said the shop-boy.—'I wish thou wouldst sell me that dog; I would give thee so much for him.' 'I will not sell him; I would think twice before doing that.[1] I would not sell him for two hundred pounds sterling.'

When she had gone away, I went out of the house. She saw me, and whistled to me, and I felt ashamed to go after her ; but I reflected that seeing she had offered to buy me, she would probably be very good to me, and so I followed her. She went home, and I went indoors along with her. There was nobody there but her only daughter. She said to her daughter, 'I gave thee schooling and education, and as sure as I tell thee, this dog is really a man, so disenchant him.'[2]   H 62

'Well, if thou didst give me schooling and education, that was the bad schooling,' said the lass.

'Do thou,' she answered, 'the thing I ask of thee, in any case.' The lass went across to a press, and brought over a jar exactly like the one with which I had been struck before.[3] Holding it above my head, she struck the jar with her fist, and I instantly became a man. 'Thanks be to the Good Thing that I have got to be as I was before,' said I. 'What,' said I, 'is the best plan to enable me to do to the woman who put me in that condition the same as she did to me ?'   D 683·2

D 771·5*

'Why, thou shalt have this jar from me,' said the daughter, 'and thou shalt [go home] and put off thy two shoes when thou goest in at the door. Thou shalt move stealthily up the room, where she will be. She will be at the fire warming herself, with her back to the door, and thou shalt strike the jar above her head, and thou shalt order [4] that she be turned into a gray mare for thee, and a gray mare is what she shall become.'   D 1765

D 566·2*

D 131

All those things did I do, oh King ! I leaped on the back of the gray mare, and went off with her to the trunk of the tree. I did not let her have her own way, neither did I let her go forward, but forced her to keep going round the tree trunk. The day thou didst meet me, I had no time for anything, but to tell thee to go forward [5] until thou shouldst find out, and was there anything wrong in doing that ?' 'Undoubtedly, there was nothing wrong in doing so,' said the King.   G 275

---

[4] order. See Note, p. 312.
[5] Again, not quite correct.

'Ach a dhoill ! a dhall an sannt,' ars an rìgh, 'bidh thusa comhla riumsa fhad is a bhios tu beò. A dhuine bhochd, bheairtich ! theirig thusa dhachaidh, is cuir do chaisteal an òrdan cho math is a dh'fhaodas tu; chan iarr mise sgillinn ort air a shon am feasd. Agus a mharcaiche na làire glaise! falbh thusa is marcaich an làir ghlas cho math is a dh'fhaodas tu, is na caomhain a cnàmhan—tha cead agad o'n rìgh.'

NOTES

MS. vol. x., No. 35. The reciter was Hector Boyd of Barra. The last page of the MS. is headed 'Na Tri Bantraichean,' The Three Widows. It was by the same reciter, and was published by Islay in *W. H. Tales*, ii., No. 39, in 1860.

On the flyleaf of this tale, Islay has written as follows:—

'An duine Bochd Beairteach.

No. 35 Gaelic Index.

Page[s] 374 to 394.   Barra MSS.

The poor rich man.—This is clearly from the *Arabian Nights* [the tale of Sidi Numan] and as clearly not taken directly from the book, all the incidents are in the book and no incidents are introduced from other sources, but the manners and customs are all western. The fish is a cod—Bran [? Brem ?] becomes chaff, the kite is a bird—the gh[o]ul is *ca rata* [*cù rùta* in MS., *i.e.* the ram dog]. The style varies from other tales—Camels remain—in short this must be *Arabian Nights*, but at second or third hand.'

Other tales, obviously from the *Arabian Nights*, have found their way into the Highlands. See No. 13 (MS. vol. x., No. 26) and MS. vol. x., No. 105, and MS. vol. xi., Nos. 327, 383. For the latter, see

'But thou blind man! whom greed did blind,' said the King, 'do thou dwell with me as long as thou livest. Thou poor rich man! do thou go home, and put thy castle in as good order as thou canst; never will I require a penny from thee for it. And thou, oh rider of the gray mare! go and ride her as hard as thou canst, and spare not her bones—from the King thou hast received permission.'

'Ròlais Cailleach na Cuinneige,' J. G. McKay, *The Wizard's Gillie*, p. 48. A study of tales such as these, coming back through the oral tradition of the people, may be of assistance in understanding their dissemination and origin. See M. Gaster, *Folk-Lore*, xxxv., p. 208. Other tales, however, are known to have travelled from the West to the East. Mrs H. H. Spoer (Miss A. Goodrich-Freer) has heard of *Jane Eyre* and *Robinson Crusoe* as coffee-house tales told in the East, *ibid.*, xxxvi., p. 298.

Dr George Henderson (*Norse Influence*, pp. 294, 334) gives the Gaelic original and an English translation of a tale called 'The adventures or legendary history of King Magnus.' The tale is undoubtedly the History of the Second Religious Mendicant from the *Arabian Nights*, though probably at second or third hand. But Dr Henderson, misled by the fact that the tale has been attached to the name of the famous Norse king, seems to think it constitutes evidence of Norse influence. The occurrence of the word *Sultan* in the tale ought to have been enough to direct Dr Henderson's attention away from Norway.

Some of the incidents in this tale, No. 21 (MS. vol. x., No. 35). resemble those in a tale from the Panjab given in *Folk-Lore*, xxxii., pp. 211-213.

NA TRÌ LÉINTEAN CANAICH

No. 22.   [*Vol. x., No. 37*]

Aarne-Thompson, No. 451

BHA rìgh an siod roimhe ann, agus bha triuir mhac agus
aon nighean aige. Shiubhail a bhean air. Bha e bliadhna
no dhà an déidh a bàis gun phòsadh. Smuainich e an
so gum b'fhearr da pòsadh, ach bha eagal air gum biodh
a' bhean dona do'n chloinn. Ach is e an rud a rinn e——

Z 85*

        Thog e tigh dhaibh,
        Anns a' bheinn-sheilge,
        Air chùl gaoithe,
        'S air aghaidh gréine,
        Far am faiceadh iad a h-uile duine,
        'S nach fhaiceadh duine iad.

Phòs e an so, agus bha bean aige a stigh. Bha an
gnothach a' còrdadh ris glé mhaith. Bhiodh e an so
a' dol do'n bheinn-sheilge, agus a h-uile h-eun a mharbhadh
e, dh'fhàgadh e aig a' chloinn e.

Bha nighean aige ris a' mhnaoi ùir, is cha robh meas
sam bith aca oirre leis cho grannda is a bha i. Is i an
Nighean Mhaol Charrach a theireadh iad rithe. Dh'fhàs
an nighean cho mór is gum biodh i ag obair leis an t-
searbhanta chòcaire a stigh.

Latha de na làithean, dh'fhalbh an Rìgh do'n bheinn-

G 200   sheilge, agus thàinig an Iochlach Urlair [1] dhachaidh.

'Tha thusa an sin, a chreutair ghòraich,' [ars ise ri
dara Bean an Rìgh], 'is dùil agad-sa nach 'eil duine is
docha leis an Rìgh na thù—ach thà.

Z 85*

        Tha a thriuir mhac,
        'S a aon nighean,
        Ann an grianan éibhinn, aighearach,

---

[1] A domestic witch. See p. 493.

THE THREE SHIRTS OF CANACH DOWN

No. 22.   *[Vol. x., No. 37]*

Aarne-Thompson, No. 451

THERE was formerly a King who had three sons and one daughter. His wife died, and for a year or two after her death, he remained unmarried. He then came to the conclusion that it would be better for him to marry [again], but he feared the wife would be unkind to the children. So what he did was this—

> He built them a house,   Z 85*
> In the hunting-hill,
> At the back of the wind,
> And facing the sun,
> Whence they could see everyone,
> None seeing them.

So he then married, and now he had a wife at home. The matter pleased him right well. And he used to go hunting in the hill, and every bird he killed, he used to leave with the children.

He had a daughter by the new wife, but no one had any liking or respect for her, because she was so ugly. They used to call her the Bald Scurvy Lass. She grew so big that she used to work indoors with the cook.

But on a day of days, the King having gone to the hunting-hill, the Iochlach Urlair [1] came to the house.   G 200

'There thou art, thou silly creature,' [said she to the King's second Wife], 'and thou thinkest that there is no one of whom the King is so fond as he is of thee. But there are.

> There are three sons of his,   Z 85*
> And an only daughter,
> Who dwell in a fine sunny mansion, so merry,

Air chùl gaoithe,
'S air aghaidh gréine,
Far am faic iad a h-uile duine,
'S nach fhaic duine iad.'

'D è an dòigh air am faigh mise dachaidh iad?' arsa Bean an Rìgh.
'Ma tà,' ars ise, 'innsidh mi sin duit. Nuair a bhios esan a' tighinn as a' bheinn-sheilge, biodh duine agad a mach a' coimhead gus am bi e tighinn a stigh an dorus. Biodh do bheul agad làn fhìon dearg, agus cuiridh tu a mach e an uair a thig esan a stigh. Feòraichidh esan 'd è tha ort, agus canaidh tu gu bheil fuil do chridhe 'ga chur a mach air do bheul. Canaidh esan an sin, 'd è an rud a léighseas tu, is canaidh thusa gur h-ann aige fhéin a tha siod. Canaidh esan 'd è an rud a bhiodh aige-san nach fhaigheadh thusa. Canaidh thusa gur h-ann aige fhéin a tha do léigheas. Canaidh esan an sin, rud sam bith a tha aige-san, gu bheil e deònach a thoirt seachad. Iarraidh thusa an sin air, a làmh a thoirt duit, agus bheir esan duit a làmh. Canaidh thusa ris an sin, gur h-e a thriuir mhac agus a nighean a thoirt dhachaidh a léighseas tu.'

Thàinig an Rìgh dachaidh. Bha ise is am fìon aice 'na beul, mar a dh'iarr an Iochlach Urlair oirre. Spùt i a mach mu choinneamh an Rìgh e. 'Ciod è a th'ort?' ars an Rìgh.
'Tha fuil mo chridhe 'ga chur a mach air mo bheul,' ars ise.
'Ciod è léighseadh thu?' ars an Rìgh.

'Is ann agad fhéin a tha sin,' ars ise.
'Ciod è bhiodh agam-sa nach fhaigheadh thu?' ars esan.
'Tha mo léigheas agad fhéin,' ars ise.

'Rud sam bith a th'agam-sa nì feum dhuit, tha mi deònach a thoirt seachad,' ars an Rìgh.
'Thoir dhomh do làmh,' ars ise.

> At the back of the wind,
> And facing the sun,
> Whence they can see everyone,
> None seeing them.'

'How can I have them brought home here?' said the S 31 King's Wife.

'Well then,' said she, 'I will tell thee how. When the King is coming home from the hunting-hill, have thou a man outside watching, until the King is just coming in at the door. Have a mouthful of red wine in thy mouth, and do thou spue it out when he comes in. He will ask what ails thee, and thou shalt say that thy very heart's blood is coming up and being driven out through thy mouth. He will then ask if there be anything that would heal thee, and thou shalt say that there is, and that it is he himself who has it. He will then ask what there could be of his which thou shouldst not have. Thou shalt reply [and repeat] that it is he himself who has the power of healing thee. He will then say that anything whatsoever he has, he is willing to give. Then thou shalt ask him to give thee his hand upon it, and he will give thee his hand. And thou shalt then tell him that if his three sons and his daughter were brought home, it would heal thee.'

The King came home. She had the wine in her mouth all ready as the Iochlach Urlair had told her, and she spued it out before the King. 'What ails thee?' said the King.

'My very heart's blood is coming up and being driven out through my mouth,' she said.

'Is there anything that would heal thee?' said the King.

'There is something, and that thou hast thyself,' said she.

'And what could there be of mine that thou shouldst not have?' said he.

'It is thou thyself who hast the power to heal me,' she repeated.

'Anything whatsoever of mine that will do thee good, that am I willing to give,' said the King.

'Give me thy hand upon it,' she answered.

'So,' ars esan.

'Is e do thriuir mhac agus do nighean a thighinn dachaidh, a dhèanadh feum dhomh,' ars ise.

H 1212

'Beannachd duit-sa, agus mallachd do bheul t'ionn-sachaidh. Is i an Iochlach Urlair a dh'innis sin duit-sa. Mura bhith nach 'eil breug aig an Rìgh r'a dhèanamh, cha tugainn-sa feairt ort-sa.'

M 203

Dh'fhalbh e, agus bheairtich e ceithir eich le'n cuid diallaidean, agus chuir e a h-aon air falbh a dh'iarraidh na cloinne. Thàinig a' chlann an sin dachaidh, is iad a' caoineadh is a' rànaich a' tighinn.

Dh'fhalbh an Rìgh an là-'r-na-mhàireach do'n bheinn-sheilge. Nuair a dh'fhalbh e, chuir a' Bhanrighinn fios air an Iochlach Urlair. 'Ciod è an aon dòigh air am faigh mi cur as daibh a nis ?'

'Ma gheibh mi pàidheadh maith, cuiridh mi as daibh luath gu leòir,' ars an Iochlach Urlair.

'Ciod è am pàidheadh a bhios an sin ?' arsa Bean an Rìgh.

K 170

'Tha,' ars ise, 'làn aillean mo dhà chluais de chlòimh, agus na thiobhaicheas² an crogan dubh de mhin, agus na thanaicheas e de ìm.'

'Ciod è uibhir 'sa bhitheas an sin ?'

'Na lìonas aillean mo dhà chluais de chlòimh—is e sin, toradh seachd tighean chaorach fad seachd bliadhna; agus toradh seachd grainnsichean fad seachd bliadhna, na thiobhaicheas an crogan dubh de mhin—agus toradh seachd tighean cruidh fad seachd bliadhna, na thanaicheas e de ìm.'⁵

Z 71·5

'Gheibh thu siod,' ars a Bhan-righinn.

---

¹ Other Gaelic curses are directed towards the eyes, as in English.
² Dial. for *thiughaicheas*.
³ = could be squeezed into.
⁴ = as would make the meal thin.

K 170

⁵ Though the terms demanded by the witch sound innocent enough, they form in reality a series of riddles, each of which probably embodied at one time a play upon words which is now lost. But it is clear that each has a meaning deeper than appears on the surface, and is designed to entrap

'Here is my hand,' said he.

'Well then, this is what would do me good,' said she; —'the coming home of thy three sons and thy daughter.'   H 1212

'A blessing to thee, but a curse on the mouth of thy teacher.[1] It is the Iochlach Urlair who instructed thee. Were it not that the King must act no lie, I would not M 203 pay thee any heed.'

He bestirred himself, harnessed four horses and saddled them, and sent someone off to fetch the children. And home came the children, crying and lamenting as they came.

On the morrow, the King went to the hunting-hill. When he had gone, the Queen sent word for the Iochlach Urlair. 'What is the best plan by means of which I can now get rid of them?'

'If I get good payment, I will soon destroy them,' quoth the Iochlach Urlair.

'What sort of payment would it be?' said the King's Wife.

'Why,' said she, 'as much wool as would fill the outer hollows [?] of my two ears, as much meal as would thicken[3] K 170 my little black crock, and as much butter as would make it thin.'[4]

'How much would that be?'

'To fill the outer hollows of my two ears with wool would take as much as seven sheep-houses could produce in seven years; to cram the little black crock full of meal would take as much as seven granaries could supply for seven years—and to thin out the meal in the crock with butter would take as much as seven cow-houses could Z 71·5 produce in seven years.'[5]

'That shalt thou have,' said the Queen.

the Queen into granting extravagant concessions (see Appendix II., p. 499). In more ancient versions of the tale, the Queen probably acceded to the terms, before ascertaining what the cunning witch intended by them. Similar payment is demanded by the witch in the following tale, No. 25 (MS. vol. x., No. 47), p. 411. But the explanation of the play upon the words has been lost from that instance also. An echo of the terms is to be seen in MS. vol. x., No. 97.

'Cuir thusa a nall iad, a lìon h-aon is aon a dh'iarraidh
na cìre mìne,' ars an Iochlach Urlair.

*   *   *   *   *   *

Chuir i am fear a b'aosda dhiùbh a null an toiseach.

H 1347*   'Tha mo mhuime [1] ag iarraidh na cìre mìne,' ars esan,
[an uair a ràinig e an Iochlach Urlair].
'Ma tà,' ars an Iochlach Urlair, 'gheabh thu sin, a
mhic màthair mo ghaoil, agus athair mo ghràidh! Is
tric a bha mi ag imlich nam miasan is nam poitean aig
teine t'athar fhéin! [2]   Siod i fo chois an fhuirm ud thall.' [3]

D 1254   Dh'éirich e, is thug e làmh air a' chìr mhìn a thoirt
D 683·2   o chois an fhuirme. Bhuail ise an sin, an slacan druidheachd
D 565·2   air 'san druim, is leum e 'na chù glas a mach air an uinneig.
D 141

Thuirt a mhuime an sin ris an fhear a bu mheadhonaiche,
'Falbh thusa a dh'iarraidh na cìre mìne, a ghaoil, dhomh-
sa. Cha do ràinig am fear ud, ach fantuinn a dhèanamh
coire an àite air choireigin.'

Dh'fhalbh e, is ràinig e an dorus, agus dh'éigh e anns
an dorus gun robh a mhuime ag iarraidh na cìre mìne.
'Is tusa a gheibh sin, a mhic màthair mo ghaoil agus athair
mo ghràidh! Is tric a bha mi ag imlich nam miasan is
nam poitean 'nam shuidhe aig teine t'athar fhéin! Siod
i fo chois an fhuirm ud thall.' An uair a chrom e dh'a
D 565·2   toirt o chois an fhuirm, bhuail ise an slacan air 'san druim,
D 141   is leum e 'na chù glas a mach air an uinneig, mar a rinn
am fear eile.

Thachair an aon nì do'n treas fear.
Bha an nighean a' faicinn aig an uinneig mar a thachair
d'a bràithrean. Chuireadh ise air son na cìre cuideachd.
An uair a bha i cromadh dh'a toirt leatha, thug a' chailleach

---

[1] *mhàthair*, mother, in MS.
[2] See *Superstitions*, p. 282.
[3] A strange place for a comb. Yet the fact does not appear to arouse
D 1072·1   any suspicions in the mind of the eldest son. The witch may have put the
comb at the foot of the bench in order to make more sure of her stroke. Or
some other significance may attach to the matter. Combs were very magical

'Then do thou send the children hither, one by one, to fetch the fine comb,' said the Iochlach Urlair.

*   *   *   *   *   *

The Queen sent the eldest one thither first. 'My step-mother [1] wants the fine comb,' said he, [when he H 1347* arrived at the Iochlach Urlair's].

'Well then,' said the Iochlach Urlair, 'that shalt thou have, thou son of the mother whom I loved and of the father whom I cherished ! Many a time have I licked the dishes and pots at thine own father's fireside.[2] See— there is the comb at the foot of yonder bench.' [3]

He arose, and attempted to take the fine comb from D 1254 where it lay at the foot of the bench. But she, with her D 683·2 wizard wand, struck him on the back, and out of the D 565·2 window he sprang, changed into a gray coloured hound. D 141

His step-mother then said to the second lad, 'Do thou go and fetch the fine comb, my love, for me. That other fellow never got there at all, but must have stopped some-where or other to do some mischief.'

He set off, and upon arriving at the door, called out that his step-mother wanted the fine comb. 'It is thou who shalt have it, thou son of the mother whom I loved, and of the father whom I cherished ! Many a time have I licked the dishes and the pots when sitting at thine own father's fireside ! See—there is the comb under the foot of yonder bench.' But when he bent down to pick it up from where it lay at the foot of the bench, she struck him on the back with her wizard wand, and out of the window D 565·2 he sprang in the shape of a gray hound, just as the other D 141 had done.

The same thing happened to the third lad.

Now the daughter had been looking on from the window and had seen what had happened to her brothers. She also was sent for the comb. When she was bending down

things. See *W. H. Tales*, iv., Index; and MS. vol. x., Nos. 126, 159. In MS. vol. x., No. 126, the heroine lays the witch low by striking her in the eye with an 'unravelling' comb, which her enemy had refused to accept from her. See *Survivals*, p. 293 and *W. H. Tales*, iii., p. 206 or 220. 'Chìr mi a chìrean da' (*Robertson*, 415 c/43), literally 'I combed his crests for him,' meaning 'I humbled him, triumphed over him.'

P 253·2   làmh air an t-slacan. Rug ise air làimh oirre, is spìon i
G 270   an làmh o'n ghàirdean aice.[1]

R 158   Ghabh i air falbh feuch am faiceadh i a bràithrean.

Z 85*   Bha neòil dhubha na h-oidhche tighinn,
'S neòil gheala an latha falbh,
'S ma bha, cha bu tàmh dhì-se.

Chunnaic i tigh air ùrlar glinne. Ghabh i dìreach a
dh'ionnsuigh an tighe.

Z 85*   Cha robh duine a stigh san tigh.
Bha teine beag, bòidheach,
Air a thogail de ghual,
Agus clobha ruith timchioll air,
'S a h-uile sradag
D 1601   A thuiteadh ás an teine,
·24*   Thogadh an clobha leis féin i.

Cha b'fhada bha i a stigh, an uair thàinig Bean a'
F 347   Chòta Chaoil Uaine,[2] dhachaidh. Dh'fhaighnich i ciod
è an naidheachd a bha aig a' bhana-chòigrich.
'Ma tà,' ars ise, 'chan 'eil móran agam-sa, mura faigh
mi agad fhéin e.'
'Tha naidheachd agam gum faca mi do thriuir
bhràithrean a' falbh an so 'nan trì choin ghlasa.'
'Tha an t-ám agam bhi falbh, feuch am faic mi iad.'
'Ma tà, cha téid; bidh thu an so féin a nochd.'
Dh'fhan i an oidhche sin còmhla rithe.
Dh' éirich i moch 'sa' mhaduinn, is rinn i biadh deiseil
do'n nighinn. Dh' iarr i ionnsachadh air an rathad.

D 1065·2   'Tha bròg agam-sa an so, agus cumaidh i dìreach air
D 1313   an rathad thu gus an ruig thu tigh mo pheathar, agus
·13*

---

[1] The window was presumably in the King's house. The ability to see
from there what was going on, shows that the witch's hut was close to the
royal residence. Some tales definitely say as much. The exploit of pulling
the witch's hand off her arm suggests that the daughter knew something of
witchcraft. Compare *Béaloideas*, iii., p. 302—'The *bean sidhe* cries for a family
D 1072·1   when some member is about to die. . . . She carries a comb and is always
combing her long hair. A traveller will never lift a comb from the road.
C 543*   John Power says he knew a "traveller" who lifted a comb, which he saw on

to pick it up and take it away, the old witch laid hold of P 253·2
the wizard wand.   But seizing her by the hand, the lass G 270
tore her hand right off her arm.[1]

She then set out to try and find her brothers.   R 158

> The black clouds of night were coming on,   Z 85*
> And the white clouds of day were departing,
> But even so, for her there was no rest.

She spied a house at the bottom of a glen, and went
straight towards it.

> Not a soul was there within.   Z 85*
> But a fire there was, a bonnie wee fire,
> All built of coal,
> And round and o'er it ran a tongs,
> And every little sparkling coal
> That from out the fire did fall,   D 1601
> The tongs of itself picked up again.   ·24*

She had not been long indoors, when home came the
Dame of the Fine Green Kirtle.[2]   She asked what news the F 347
stranger-woman had.

'Well then,' replied the King's Daughter, 'not much
news have I, unless I get some from thee.'

'My news is that I have seen thy three brothers wandering
about here in the shape of three gray hounds.'

'Then it is time for me to be off, to see if I can find them.'

'Nay then, do not go: thou shalt just stay here to-night.'
So she stayed that night with her.

The Dame rose early in the morning, and made food
ready for the lass.   The lass asked to be directed on her
road.

'I have a shoe here, which will keep thee straight and D 1065·2
on the right road till thou reach my sister's house; when D 1313
·13*

---

the road.   That night, the *bean sidhe* came to his fire, and he handed the
comb to her with a tongs.   If he had taken it in his hand to give to her, she
would have taken his hand from him.'

[2] A name for a fairy woman, usually friendly, but in *Waifs and Strays*, ii.,
pp. 338, 485, and *W. H. Tales*, ii., No. 51, she lays spells upon the hero to search
for her through the world and go through dangerous adventures on her
account, like the heroines in MS. vol. xi., Nos. 185, 216.   She is unwarrantably
pressed into the service of Gaelic myth in MS. vol. x., No. 105.

an uair a ruigeas, tionndaidh thu a h-aghaidh an taobh
D 1602·4 a thàinig i, agus thig a' bhròg dhachaidh leatha féin.'

Dh'fhalbh i, is cha do stad i gus an do ràinig i tigh
H 1235 piuthar a' bhoirionnaich a dh'fhàg i. Chuir i dhith an
sin a' bhròg, agus thionndaidh a h-aghaidh an taobh a
thàinig i, agus chaidh a' bhròg dhachaidh leatha féin.
Chaidh i an so a stigh.

Z 85*
Cha robh duine a stigh.
Bha teine beag, bòidheach,
Air a thogail de ghual,
Agus clobha ruith timchioll air,
Agus a h-uile sradag
A thuiteadh ás an teine,
D 1601·
Thogadh an clobha leis féin i.
24*

Cha b'fhada [bha i a stigh] an uair a thàinig Bean a'
Chòta Chaoil Uaine dhachaidh. 'Ciod è an naidheachd
a tha aig a' bhana-choigreach?'
['Ma tà,' ars ise, 'chan 'eil móran agamsa mura faigh
mi agad fhéin e.' 'Tha naidheachd agam gum faca mi
do thriuir bhràithrean a' falbh an so 'nan trì choin ghlasa.'
'Tha an t-ám agam a bhi falbh, feuch am faic mi iad.'
'Ma tà, cha téid—bidh thu an so fhéin a nochd.' Dh'fhan
i an oidhche sin còmhla rithe. Dh'éirich i moch 'sa'
mhaduinn, is rinn i biadh deiseil do'n nighinn. Dh'iarr
i ionnsachadh air an rathad.]

'So bròg, agus bheir i air an rathad thu. Coinnichidh
H 1235 tu seann duine mór [2] air aghaidh a' bhruthaich ud thall,
N 825·2 agus an uair a chì thu e, tionndaidh thu aghaidh na
D 1602·4 bròige an taobh a thàinig i, agus thig a' bhròg dhachaidh
leatha fhéin.'
Ghabh i air falbh, agus choisich i gus an do ràinig i

---

[1] Both in this tale and in No. 123 there are two magic fires.

[2] Instead of the usual three female characters or three male characters
to speed the hero or heroine on his or her way, we have in this tale two
Dames of the Fine Green Kirtle, and one old man: and instead of three
magical foot-gear all of the same kind, we have on the first two occasions
a magic shoe, and on the third a fine hempen string, which in this tale seems

thou hast arrived there, thou shalt turn the front of the shoe towards the way it came, and the shoe will then come home of itself.'

D 1602·4

She started off, and never stopped until she arrived at the house of the sister of the woman she had left. Then putting off the shoe, she turned its point the way it had come, and the shoe went off home of itself. Then she went in.

H 1235

> Not a soul was there within.
> But a fire there was, a bonnie wee fire,
> All built of coal.
> And round and o'er it ran a tongs,
> And every little sparkling coal
> That from out the fire did fall,
> The tongs of itself picked up again.[1]

Z 85*

D 1601·
24*

She had not been in long, when home came the Dame of the Fine Green Kirtle. 'What news has the stranger-woman?'

['Well then,' said she, 'not much news have I, unless I get some from thee.' 'My news is that I have seen thy three brothers wandering about here in the shape of three gray hounds.' 'Then it is time for me to be off, to see if I can find them.' 'Nay then, do not go—thou shalt just stay here to-night.' So she stayed that night with her. The Dame rose early in the morning, and made food ready for the lass. The lass asked to be directed on the road.]

'Here is a shoe, which will take thee along the road. Thou wilt meet an old man, an old and mighty man,[2] on the face of yonder brae, and when thou seest him, turn the point [3] of the shoe towards the way it came, and it will then come home of itself.'

H 1235

N 825·2

D 1602·4

Away she went, and she walked until she came to where

---

to have nothing magic about it. In *Trans. Gael. Soc. Inverness*, xvi., p. 121, three old men speed the hero on his way by giving him respectively magic foot-gear, a magic hank of thread, and a carrying eagle. In Dr D. Hyde, *Beside the Fire*, p. 129, three friendly old women and one friendly old man appear to speed the hero.

   [3] *Lit.* the face.

far an robh an seann duine, is an uair a ràinig, chuir i
dhì a' bhròg, agus thionndaidh i a h-aghaidh an taobh a
thàinig i, agus chaidh a' bhròg dhachaidh leatha féin.
'Ciod è,' ars an seann duine, 'an naidheachd a tha
aig a' bhana-choigrich?'
'Chan 'eil a bheag, mura faigh mi agad fhéin e.'
'Tha aon naidheachd agam-sa, gu bheil do thriuir
bhràithrean a' gabhail còmhnuidh anns an uaimh ud
thall.'
'Ciod è mar a gheibh mi dol d'an ionnsuigh?'
'Tha sreang chaol chainbe agamsa an so, is ceanglaidh
tu ri do làimh i, [is gleidhidh mise an ceann eile aice,] is

D 1313
·1·2*
R 121·5

ma bhitheas tu gabhail an rathaid chearr, bheir mise
draghadh oirre, is gabhaidh tu dìreach gu beul na h-
uamha.'
Ghabh i gu beul na h-uamha. Dh'fhuasgail i an t-
sreang bhàrr a làimhe, is tharruing esan dh'a ionnsuigh i.

Chaidh i a stigh, is bha bòrd an sin, agus bha trì
cupannan [1] air, cupan beag, cupan mór, is cupan
meadhonach, agus iad làn fìona.   Bha, mu a meur, fàinne

H 94·4

a bha aig a màthair, agus ainm a màthar air, agus chuir i
anns a' chupan a bu lugha e.   Chaidh i fhéin am falach fo
itean eun a bhiodh aca-san 'gan itheadh a stigh.

D 630
D 531
D 720

Cha b'fhada bha i ann, an uair a thàinig a triuir
bhràithrean dhachaidh 'nan coin [ghlasa].   Thilg iad
diùbh na cochuill a bha orra, is bha iad 'nan daoine.[2]

L 10

Rug a h-uile fear air a chupan féin, is thòisich iad air
òl an fhìona, agus an uair a dh'òl am fear a b'òige a' chuid
mu dheireadh de'n fhìon, thug am fàinne gliong air na
fiaclan aige, is dh'fheuch e am fàinne.[3]

---

[1] MS. *chupannan*.

[2] Apparently, the brothers are able, either when at home or during
night-time, to recover themselves temporarily from the spells, by putting off
the covering or *cochull* which each wore.   Enchantment and disenchantment
are sometimes plainly equivalent to donning and doffing the hide of some

the old man was, and when she got there, she put off the
shoe, and turned the point of it towards the way it had
come, and the shoe went off home of itself.

'What,' said the old man, 'is the news that the stranger-
woman has ?'

'None at all, unless I get some from thee.'

'I have indeed one piece of news. It is that thy three
brothers are dwelling in the cave over yonder.'

'How shall I manage to get to them ?'

'Thus. I have here a fine hempen string which thou
shalt tie to thy hand, [while I will hold the other end of
it,] and if thou go the wrong road, I will give the string a   D 1313
pull, and in this way thou shalt go straight to the mouth   ·1·2*
of the cave.'   R 121·5

Thus she came to the mouth of the cave. Then she
loosed the string from her hand, and the old man drew it
back to himself again.

Into the cave she went. In it there was a table with
three cups standing on it, a little cup, a big cup, and a
medium sized cup, and all of them full of wine. Now she
had on her finger a ring which had been her mother's,
and had her mother's name on it, and this she put into   H 94·4
the smallest cup. Then she hid herself under a lot of
feathers, the feathers of the birds which they [her brothers]
had had to eat there.

She had not been there long, when her three
brothers came home in the form of [gray] hounds. They   D 630
cast off the coverings they were wearing, and became   D 531
men.[2]   D 720

Each of them took up his own cup, and began to drink
the wine, and when the youngest had drunk off the last   L 10
of his wine, the ring clinked against his teeth. He examined
the ring.[3]

---

animal. See Islay's English List, No. 329, and *Folk-Lore*, xlvi., p. 335. And
this book, p. 496.

[3] For dropping a ring in a glass in order to bring about recognition, see
Waifs and Strays, v., p. 21; ii., p. 157.

'Gu dearbh,' ars esan, 'ge b'e àite a bheil mo phiuthar-sa, is e am fàinne a bha aig mo mhàthair-sa a tha an so.' Dh'fhalbh iad an so, agus rannsuich iad an uaimh, agus fhuair iad ise fo na h-itean. Ghabh iad an sàs innte 'ga pògadh, is iad cho toilichte a faicinn. Bha iad an sin ag innseadh dhì mar a dh'éirich dhaibh, agus an seòrsa tighinn beò a bha aca. Dh'fhaighnich i dhiùbh an so, an robh rud sam bith a bheireadh bho na geasan iad.

D 965·12* Thuirt iadsan gun robh, ach gun robh e glé dhoirbh a dhèanamh. Thuirt iad gur h-e bheireadh bho na geasan
D 753·1 iad, léine am fear a dhèanamh dhaibh de chanach an
D 758 t-sléibhe,[1] agus gun fhacal cainnt a thighinn á a ceann gus an cuireadh i na léintean umpa-san an déidh an dèanamh.

P 253·2 Dh'fhalbh ise, is dh'fhàg i beannachd aca. Thug i leatha trì pocannan, is ràinig i sliabh anns an robh canach pailt, is thòisich i air an lìonadh. An uair a bha na pocannan làn aice, chunnaic i marcaiche a' tighinn. Ghabh e d'a h-ionnsuigh. Có bha an so ach rìgh, is cha robh e pòsda idir.

N 711 Bhruidhinn e rithe, is cha dubhairt i facal ris. Ghabh e gaol a chridhe oirre. Rinn e comharraidhean di
T 42·1 am biodh i deònach a phòsadh. Rinn i comharraidhean da nach dèanadh i fhéin dad, is i bodhar, balbh. Rinn esan comharraidhean di, ged nach dèanadh i sìon am feasd ach a bhi 'ga choimhead, gun robh e deònach a pòsadh. Rinn ise comharra da an so, o'n a bha e fhéin cho deònach, nach robh na b'fhearr aice r'a fhaotuinn.

Dh'fhalbh e, is thog e leis i fhéin agus na trì pocannan air muin an eich, agus ràinig e an rìoghachd aige fhéin. Fhuair e pearsa eaglais, agus phòs iad.

Bhiodh ise ag obair air snìomh canach an t-sléibhe a h-uile latha, agus gun facal cainnte a' tighinn as a ceann. An ceann ùine, rug i leanabh mic da, agus bha a' bhean-ghlùin seachduinn 'na caithris ris an leanabh. An ceann
G 261·1 na seachduinn, chaidil i, is chuir i an leanabh 'sa' chreathaill.

---

[1] Canach down, called in MacPherson's *Ossian* 'the down of Cana.' The white fluffy growth, something like wool, borne upon the cotton-sedge plant

'Truly,' said he, 'wherever my sister is, this is the ring that my mother had.' Thereupon they began to ransack the cave, and found her under the feathers. They swooped down upon her, and began kissing her, and right pleased they were to see her. They then began telling her how things had fared with them, and what sort of a life they led. At this point, she asked them if there were any way of recovering them from the spells.

They replied that there was, but that it was a very difficult thing to do. They said that if she made them each a shirt of the down of the moorland canach,[1] and never allowed a single word of speech to pass her lips until she herself, after making the shirts, had put them on them, it would recover them from the spells. D 965·12* D 753·1 D 758

She departed, leaving a farewell blessing with them. She took three sacks with her, and went to a mountain moor where the canach down was plentiful, and began filling the sacks. When she had filled the sacks, she saw a rider coming. He made towards her. Who should it be but a King and he was unmarried. P 253·2

He addressed her, but not a word would she say to him. He fell in love with her, and loved her with all his heart. He asked her by signs if she would be willing to marry him, and she made signs to him that she could do nothing, being deaf and dumb. So he made signs to her that even if she never did anything but simply look at him, he was willing to marry her. So then she made a sign to him, that as he was so willing, there could be no better fate for her. N 711 T 42·1

He went, and lifted her and the three sacks on to the horse's back, and setting forth, arrived in his own kingdom. He got a parson, and they wedded.

She continued to spin and spin the moorland canach, working industriously every day, but never permitting a word to come from her lips. At the end of some time, she bore a baby boy to the King, and for a week a midwife watched over the child and never slept. At the end of the

---

or cat's-tail, *Eriophorum vaginatum*. It appears in several tales, and was powerful against enchantments. See Notes.

Chunnaic an té a bha snìomh, Làmh a' tighinn a stigh air an uinneig, is a' toirt leatha an leanaibh, is cha dubhairt i facal, ged a bha e cruaidh leatha. B'fhearr leatha a bràithrean a thoirt bho na geasan.

Dhùisg a' bhean-ghlùine, is cha robh sgeul air a' phàisde, is cha robh fios aice 'd è dhèanadh i.

Bha coileach beag a stigh, is rug i air, is mharbh i e, is chuir i an fhuil ann an cupan, agus shuath i an fhuil ri K 2155·1 beul na Ban-righinn.

Chaidh i sìos, an so, far an robh an Rìgh. 'Nach olc K 2116 am boirionnach i siod,' ars ise ris an Rìgh, 'an uair a tha ·1·1 i ag itheadh a gineil fhéin !'

'A bheil i 'ga dhèanamh sin?' ars esan.

'Tha,' ars ise.

'U !' ars esan, 'chan 'eil i ach gòrach; leigidh sinn leatha sin fhathast.'

Bha ise ag obair air figheadh canach an t-sléibhe, is cha robh i leigeil dad oirre, agus an uair a thàinig an darna h-ám oirre, rug i leanabh mic eile, agus is i an aon bhean-ghlùin a thugadh dh'a h-ionnsaigh.

Bha a' bhean-ghlùin an so, a' cur roimpe nach caidleadh i, fhad is a bhiodh i a stigh.

An ceann na seachduinn, thàinig an cadal oirre mar a rinn e roimhe.

Cha b'fhada bha i 'na cadal, an uair a thàinig Cràg[1] G 261·1 a stigh air an uinneig, is a thug i leatha an leanabh.

Dhùisg i an so, 's cha robh sgeul aice air an leanabh. Bha piseag chait a stigh, is dh'fhalbh i, is mharbh i i, [is chuir i an fhuil ann an cupan,] agus shuath i an fhuil ri K 2155·1 beul na Banrighinn. Chaidh i stigh far an robh an Rìgh. 'Nach olc am boirionnach siod,' ars ise ris an Rìgh, '[an K 2116 uair a tha i] ag itheadh a gineil féin !' ['A bheil i ·1·1 'ga dhèanamh sin?' ars esan. 'Thà,' ars ise.] 'U,' ars

---

[1] *làmh*, a human hand, is the word used before. Cràg or Cròg, a term of contempt for the human hand, and used of an animal's paw, is the word generally used in this incident.

week, the midwife put the child into a cradle, and fell asleep. But she [the Queen] who was still spinning and spinning, saw a Hand come in through the window, and G 261·1 take the child away. Yet though she felt it bitterly hard, never a word did she utter. For she longed to recover her brothers from the spells.

The midwife awoke, but there was no sign of the child, and she knew not what to do.

There was a little cockerel indoors, and she seized it and killed it, put the blood in a little cup, and rubbed it upon the Queen's mouth. K 2155·1

She then went off to the King. 'What a wicked woman that is,' said she to the King, 'to eat her own offspring.' K 2116 ·1·1

'Does she indeed do that?' said he.

'Yes, she does,' replied the woman.

'U!' he said, 'she is silly, that is all, we will forgive her that for the present.'

She continued working and weaving the canach down, without [uttering a word or] giving any hint or disclosing anything, and when her hour came again for the second time, she bore another son, but the midwife they brought to her was the same one as before.

The midwife now resolved not to sleep, as long as ever she was in the house.

But at the end of a week, sleep came upon her, as it had done before.

She had not been long asleep, when a Claw-like Hand [1] came in through the window and took the child away with it. G 261·1

Then the midwife awoke, but she could find no sign of the child. There was a little kitten indoors, and she went and killed it, [and put the blood into a little cup], and rubbed it upon the Queen's mouth. She then went in to where K 2155·1 the King was. 'What a wicked woman that is,' said she to the King, 'to eat her own offspring!' ['Does she K 2116 indeed do so?' said the King. 'Yes, she does,' replied ·1·1

esan, 'chan 'eil i ach gòrach; leigidh sinn leatha sin
fhathast.'

Bha ise a' snìomh is a' fígheadh canach an t-sléibhe,
is cha robh i ag ràdh facal cainnte. An treas uair, thuisleadh
i air leanabh mic eile, agus chuir a' bhean-ghlùin roimpe,
nach caidleadh i idir air an t-siubhal so.

Ach an ceann na seachduinn, thàinig an cadal oirre
mar a b' àbhaist. Cha robh i fada 'na cadal, an uair a
G 261·1 thàinig Cràg a stigh air an uinneig, is a thug i leatha an
leanabh as a' chreathaill. Dhùisg a' bhean-ghlùine, is an
uair a thug i làmh air an leanabh, cha robh sgeul air.

Rug i air cuilean beag coin [1] a bha a stigh, is mharbh
K 2155·1 i e, [is chuir i an fhuil ann an cupan,] agus shuath i an
fhuil ri beul na Banrighinn. Chaidh i a stigh an so far
an robh an Rìgh, agus thuirt e rithe ciod è an naidheachd
a bha aice, is thuirt i gun robh droch naidheachd, gum
b'olc am boirionnach a bha aige an uair a bha i ag itheadh
K 2116 a gineil féin.
·1·1 ['A bheil i 'ga dhèanamh sin?' ars an Rìgh.
'Thà,' ars ise.]
'Coma leatsa; leigidh sinn dàil leatha an diugh, ach
bidh sinn a' falbh dh'a crochadh am màireach.'
D 753·1 Bha ise an uair sin, is bha na léintean ullamh
aice.
Dh'fhalbh iad, an là-'r-na-mhàireach, is chruinnich a
h-uile duine a bha 'san rìoghachd gus iad a dh'fhaotainn
R 175 an cuid de'n spors an ám a bhi crochadh na Banrighinn;
agus an uair a chuireadh fios air a h-uile duine, chuireadh
fios air na trì choin ghlasa a bha 'san uaimh. Thàinig iad
an so air muin each, 'nan trì gillean òga, agus bha balachan
beag leis a h-uile fear aca.

Sgaoil ise na léintean, agus ghabh i 'nan coinnimh
dh'am pògadh. Dh'iarr i air an fhear a bu shine a chuid
aodaich a chur dheth. Rinn e siod, is chuir ise air an
léine.

---

[1] For this incident, see *Folk-Lore*, xxxi., p. 157, and *Béaloideas*, ii., p. 400.

the woman.] 'U !' he said, 'she is only silly: still, we will forgive her for the present.'

But the Queen continued to spin and spin and weave the canach down, without ever uttering a word. She was delivered of another baby boy for the third time, and the midwife was quite determined that she certainly would not sleep on this occasion.

But at the end of a week, sleep came over her as usual. She had not been long asleep, when a Claw-like Hand   G 261·1
came in through the window, and took the child out of the cradle and went off with it. The midwife awoke, but when she went to take the child, there was no sign of it.

She seized a little puppy dog [1] that was indoors, killed it, [and having put the blood in a little cup,] rubbed it   K 2155·1
over the Queen's mouth. Then she went in to where the King was, and he asked her what news she had, and she said she had bad news, that the woman he had was so wicked as to eat her own offspring.

   K 2116 ·1·1

['Does she indeed do so ?' said the King.

'Yes, she does,' she replied.]

'Very well then; we will allow her a respite for to-day, but we will set about hanging her to-morrow.'

But by this time, the Queen had the shirts ready.   D 753·1

On the morrow people were stirring, and every person in the kingdom gathered together, in order to have their share of the sport when the Queen was being hanged;   R 175
and when word had been sent for everyone, word was also sent for the three gray hounds who lived in the cave. And those three came, all on horseback, in the form of three young men, each of them bringing a little boy with him.

Then the Queen spread out the shirts, and went to meet them and kiss them. She asked the eldest young man to put off his clothes. He did so, and she arrayed him in one of the shirts.

'Meal is caith do léine mhìn, a bhràthair,' ars ise.[1]

'Meal thusa do shlàinte, a phiuthar,' ars esan.
Dh'iarr i an sin air an fhear mheadhonach [a chuid aodaich] a chur dheth. Rinn e siod, is chuir i air an léine. 'Meal is caith do léine mhìn, a bhràthair,' ars ise. 'Meal thusa do shlàinte, a phiuthar,' ars esan.

Dh' iarr i air an fhear a b'òige [a chuid] aoda[i]ch a chur dheth. Rinn e siod, is chuir i air an léine. 'Meal [is caith] do léine mhìn, a bhràthair,' ars ise. 'Meal thusa do shlàinte, a phiuthar,' ars esan.

'Is sinne,' ars iadsan, 'a bha toirt air falbh na cloinne agadsa mar siod, air eagal gum briseadh cainnt orra an ám a bhi 'gan cur a laighe. Tha do thriuir chloinne an so.'[2]
Chreid an Rìgh so, agus bha e fuathasach toilichte an uair a chunnaic e a' chlann.
Chaidh clann an Rìgh an so dhachaidh, agus rug an Rìgh air a' bhean-ghlùine a bha aige fhéin, is thug e leis i [còmhla ri a bhean féin] gus an do ràinig e athair na mnà, agus dh'innis a bhean fhéin da mar a rinn an Iochlach Urlair orra, agus am muime.

G 275·3   Rug iad orra 'nan triùir, [an Iochlach Urlair, am muime, agus a' bhean-ghlùin,] agus thog iad téine, agus

D 1812·
5·1·11*

[1] It was thought ominous if a woman chanced to be the first person to congratulate a man on wearing new clothes.—*Waifs and Strays*, iv., p. 276. Rev. J. G. Campbell, *Superstitions*, p. 231. In this tale the belief does not seem to be regarded. The brothers recover human form, and the heroine breaks silence, *before* the donning of the magic shirts, two incidents which are contrary to the conditions of success laid down by the brothers earlier in the tale. In the closely related tale MS. vol. x., No. 126, the brothers, who are there turned into stags, lose all human sense in the process; but their condition experiences a nicely graduated series of improvements, for when the heroine hits the witch in the eye with a comb, they recover human sense and know what they are about. When their father finds them in the wilderness they recover human form, except as regards their heads, which remain cervine and antlered; when their sister finds them, and (probably) supplies them with the blood they had lost, their heads (apparently) become human once more, except for the antlers which still surmount them; and finally, when they put on the canach shirts the antlers, the last vestige of animal form, fall off; and then,

'May thou enjoy thy soft fine-spun shirt, and [live long enough to] wear it out, brother,' said she.[1]

'May thou enjoy thy health, sister,' said he.

Then she asked the next eldest to put off [his clothes]. He did so, and she arrayed him in one of the shirts. 'May thou enjoy thy soft fine-spun shirt, and [live long enough to] wear it out, brother,' said she. 'May thou enjoy thy health, sister,' said he.

She asked the youngest one to put off his clothes. He did so, and she put one of the shirts on him. 'May thou enjoy thy soft fine-spun shirt, and [live long enough to] wear it out, brother,' said she. 'May thou enjoy thy health, sister,' said he.

'It is we,' said they, 'who took thy children away as we did, for fear that they would break silence and speak when being put to bed. Here are thy three children for thee.' [2]

The King believed this, and was overjoyed when he saw his children.

The children of the King hereupon went home, and the King seized that midwife of his, and taking her [and his own wife] with him, went to his father-in-law's, for his wife had told him how they [her brothers and she] had been treated by the Iochlach Urlair and their step-mother.

They [3] seized the three of them [the Iochlach Urlair, their step-mother, and the midwife], and they built a fire G 275·3

---

but not till then, does the heroine speak. In this account (No. 22), however, there is no gradation in the process of disenchantment: the brothers seem to be able to put off canine form, either at night or when at home. Then again they are gray hounds when sent for to attend their sister's execution; but when they come upon the scene they come in the form of young men without any trace of animal shape, though the last part of the process of disenchantment, viz., the putting on of the shirts, was not yet accomplished.

[2] If the children spoke in their mother's hearing, she might have been betrayed into speaking to them in return, which would have invalidated the magic of the shirts of canach down. In this tale and others it was essential that the mother should keep complete silence and remain quite dumb during the long period of her labours; in other tales it is only essential for her to keep silence regarding some particular fact, or to refrain from divulging something.

[3] Impersonal use of pronoun = The three of them were seized.

Q414·3

loisg iad iad. An déidh do na cnàimhean aca bhi air an losgadh le teine, phronn iad iad, agus leig iad an luaith le gaoith.

Thill a' Bhan-righinn òg dhachaidh, agus a cuid m[h]ac is a fear; agus bha i bruidhinn ris tuilleadh fhad 'sa bha e beò, is bha e fuathasach toilichte. Cha leigeadh e beanghlùine no duine 'na còir.

NOTES

MS. vol. x., No. 37. Reciter, Hector Boyd, Barra. The scribe was probably Hector MacLean. On the flyleaf, Islay has written:—
'37. Na trì Leantean Canaich. No. 37. Gaelic Index. The Three Cannach Shirts. The same as the 12 wild ducks, full of genuine West Country ideas and evidently not taken from any one book. It has a character of its own. To be translated.'
Similars. MS. vol. x., No. 126.—*Béaloideas*, i., p. 120. *Larminie*, p. 179, 'Gilla of the Enchantments,' where the shirts are made of ivy leaves. Ivy was a plant of magic power.

D965·12*

In *Trans. Gael. Soc. Inverness*, v., p. 32, a father has three sons who are changed into three beautiful white hounds or wolves. The father induces a Princess to summon bands of women together who are to gather and weave, etc., enough canach down to make a shirt for each son. The shirts are left on a hill above the father's house, and are taken away at night by the three white animals, when no one is looking. A week afterwards, the three sons come to their father's house in their own proper bodies. How they manage to put the shirts on does not transpire. The canach down appears in this version as *caineachan an t-sléibhe; na léinntean caineachain*, the canach shirts. In MS. vol. x., No. 126, the word is written in the MS. as *canaichean*.

The following is *litteratim* from *Robertson*, Note-book No. 415A, art. caineachan:—
'caineachan (*ai* as *e*) a kind of grass that grows in moss and is liked by cattle in April. Cf. *canoch*. Cf. *cain'chean*, down, moss crops. McL[eod] & D[ewar]. *can'chean*, cotton grass, Lit[tle] Loch [Broom]. (*Canaichean*, cotton grass, Lit[tle] Loch). "caoin-cheann." Cameron, *Names of Plants*.' See perhaps *Folk-Lore*, xxxiii., p. 263.

In a Canadian Gaelic paper, *MacTalla* (1899), vii., p. 338 (Sydney, Cape Breton), appeared a summary of a tale in which a prince suffers enchantment, and is metamorphosed into a creature that was neither like man nor beast. There was no recovering his natural shape, unless some young woman made him three canach shirts. One shirt apparently was not enough. Many a young woman began the task, but only one of them was persevering enough to finish. She won the King's son, and well deserved to do so, etc.

One of the *geasan* or spells that Diarmaid laid upon Gràinne was that she was not to come near him, clothed or unclothed. But she and burnt them. After their bones had been burnt with fire, they ground them to powder, and let the ashes fly Q 414·3 with the wind.

The young Queen, and her sons, and her husband, returned home; and ever after and as long as she lived she held converse with him, and he was delighted. And neither midwife nor man would he allow to come near her.

attained her end by coming to him arrayed in a dress of the *canach* down, and it seems to have been held that her doing so did not involve any infraction of the *geasan.—Waifs and Strays*, iv., p. 52. A very similar incident occurs in 'The Sage Damsel,' *Russian Fairy Tales*, R. Nisbet Bain.

In *W. H. Tales*, i., No. 14, a girl refuses to marry her suitor (who was her father) unless he procured for her a gown of the *canach* down, or as it is there called, the 'moorland canach,' or 'canach an t-sléibhe.'

Shirts given by three fairy women to three giants, endow each of the latter with the strength of one hundred men.—*Waifs and Strays*, iv., pp. 182, 218. Whether these shirts are of canach down or not, is not said.

A woman makes a shirt for Fionn, *ibid.*, pp. 227, 264. It fits him like a glove. This and other matters enable her to identify him. No clue is given as to the material of which the shirt is made.

The fluffy little balls of white wool or cotton that grow on the canach plant (*i.e.* the cotton-sedge plant or cat's-tail) become detached from the plant in time, and then begin to float upon the wind. To judge from the riddle given below, these fluffy little white balls were believed to be emanations from, or manifestations of, witches. A similar belief was held regarding snowflakes, which in their fluffiness and whiteness so strongly resemble the down of the canach; for children are told that the snowflakes are the *Doideagan*, or the *Mull Witches* going to a meeting of witches. (They appear in some tales as a unity, *Doideag*, or *An Doideag Mhuileach*, *The Mull Witch*, or perhaps *The Mull Goddess*.)

Toimhseachan (Riddle).

Tha Mogan molach, molach,
Sìor shiubhal a' mhonaidh;   H 530
Cha dath gobhair, no caoire,
No dath d'aoine,[1] th'air Mogan molach.
    Canach an t-sléibhe.
    Ceò an t-sléibhe.

An Gàidheal (1872), i., pp. 62, 95.

[1] *MacTalla*, vii., p. 306, gives 'dath dhaoine' (colour of men), which is probably the correct reading.

D 965·12*

> Mockan,[1] so rough and shaggy,
> Is aye traversing the moor;
> But the colour of neither goat nor sheep,
> Nor of men has Mockan shaggy.
> [Solution.]   Canach of the hills.
> The mist of the hills.

Moganach, from *mogan*, is also applied to another product of the vegetable world, in the following *toimhseachan*, or riddles.

> 'Bean bheag, mhoganach,
> Suidhidh i taganach,
> Bidh i torach h-uile bliadhna,
> 'S bidh laogh beag, geal aice.
> Cnù.'   *An Gàidheal* (1873), ii., pp. 86, 117.

> A little wife in mockans,
> Sitting very baggily,
> Fruitful every year she'll be,
> And a wee white calf she'll have.
> A nut.

The nut, peeping out of its surrounding foliage, seemed perhaps, in its partial uncoveredness, to be wearing mockans.[2] The 'wee white calf' was doubtless the kernel.   Compare an Irish riddle from Dr Douglas Hyde's *Beside the Fire*, p. 171:—

> 'On the top of the tree
> See the little man red,
> A stone in his belly,
> A cap on his head.
> Haw.'

Another white product of the vegetable world, good against magic, was:—

'*Clòimh-chat*, s.m. catkin, cat-wool, inflorescence of the birch, beech, willow, etc.   The catkin wool was twined into a 3-ply cord, and that into a circle, to safeguard against unseen powers.'—*Am Faclair*.

For *canach* in place-names, see Professor W. J. Watson, *Celtic Review*, vi., p. 240.

[1] *Mogan*, pronounced *mockan*, means a toeless or footless stocking.   Many characters derive their names from their foot-gear, or from their feet, or from the character of their gait.   See MS. vol. x., Nos. 31 and 97.   The daughter of the Mull Doideag was called Mogan Dubh or Black Mockan, *W. H. Tales*, English List, No. 400: Mogan Dearg MacIachair is a hero in MS. vol. xi., No. 185.

[2] The velvet on a deer's horns was also called *mogan*, probably for a similar reason.

AN DÀ SGIOBAIR

No. 23.

Aarne-Thompson, No. 1651

BHA dithis sgiobairean shoithichean ann, a bha 'nan companaich gu math mór aig a chéile. Bha iad a' seòladh a mach as an aon phort, agus bha soitheach aig a h-uile fear dhiubh. Thuisleadh na mnathan aca, agus bha mac aig an darna té, agus nighean aig an té eile. Thuirt a h-aon de na sgiobairean gum bu mhath an gnothuch am pòsadh. 'Tha e glé cheart,' ars am fear eile.

T 112*
T 69·2
Thug iad dachaidh pearsa eaglais. Bhaisteadh a' chlann agus phòsadh iad. Sgrìobh a h-uile fear 'na leabhar fhìn briathran a' phòsaidh. Thill gach fear do a shoitheach air ais. Sheòl athair a' ghille do'n Tuirc, agus bhàsaich e an sin.

L 111·3
An uair a chuala luchd an ainbhfiach[1] iomradh air a bhàs, thàinig iad agus cha d'fhàg iad mìr aig a' bhalach no aig a mhàthair. Bha ise an sin cho bochd is nach b'urrainn di sgoil a thoirt do'n ghille. Bha esan an so a' fàs, is e gun aodach, gun dòigh, is gun sgoil, gun ionnsachadh aige 'ga fhaotainn. An uair a bha crìonnachd a' tighinn ann agus mothachadh, bha e faicinn mar a bha a' chùis.

L 101
'A mhàthair,' ars esan, 'tha mi 'gam fhaicinn fhìn cho bochd, tha mi gun aodach, gun sgoil, is tha mi smaointeachadh falbh a dh'iarraidh an fhortain, feuch ciod è

K 2296*
[1] Other tales of this kind make it probable that there was only one creditor, and that he was the partner of the deceased. He usually appropriates the goods of the deceased, leaving the widow and her son with nothing. He next separates the children, by sending the boy on a voyage on which he

THE TWO SKIPPERS

No. 23.   *[Vol. x., No. 40]*

Aarne-Thompson, No. 1651

THERE were two ships' skippers who were boon companions.
They used to sail from the same port and possessed a vessel
each.

Their wives were delivered, and one of them had a son,
and the other a daughter.

One of the skippers suggested that it would be an
excellent plan to marry the two children to one another.

'It is a good plan,' quoth the other.

So they brought home a clergyman. Then the children   T 112*
were baptized and married.   T 69·2

Each man wrote the marriage vows in his own book,
and each returned back to his vessel.

The father of the lad sailed to Turkey, and died there.

When his creditors [1] heard the report of his death, they
came and took everything away, leaving the lad and his   L 111·3
mother without a scrap or a bite.

She was then reduced to such poverty, that she was
unable to give the lad schooling.

Yet there he was, growing up, and neither clothes,
means, schooling nor education was he getting.

When sense and discretion began to come to him,
he began to see how matters were.

'Mother,' said he, 'I perceive myself to be very poor;   L 101
I have neither clothes nor schooling, so I am now thinking
of departing in search of fortune, and try what it will

hopes he will be drowned. This he does in order that his own daughter
may marry elsewhere and in more advantageous circumstances. That this
must have once been the trend of events in this story is probable from the
words with which his daughter upbraids him later on in the story.

chuireas e orm. Chan fhaigh mi dad an so, co dhiùbh: leis an sin, is fhearr dhomh falbh feuch ciod è chuireas am fortan [1] orm.'

B'fhearr le a mhàthair e a dh'fhuireach aice fhìn, na dh'fhalbh.

'Seachainn,' ars ise, 'seòladaireachd, is gur h-ann ris an t-seòladaireachd a thog t'athair a cheann, is gur h-i a chuir as da.'

Dh'fhalbh an gille, is dh'fhàg e beannachd aig a mhàthair. Ciod è an t-ám a bha ann, ach an t-Earrach.

Bha frasan sneachda agus fuachd ann.

Ciod è an rathad a ghabh e, ach rathad tighe companach a athar, agus e air éirigh suas anns an t-saoghal.

Bha ochd luingeas marsandachd aige a' tarruing as na h-Innsean, agus as gach àite, agus bha ochd bùithean air tìr aige.

Cha robh aig an fhear shoithichean mhór a bha an so ach aon nighean.

Ghabh e a stigh do'n chearn.

Dh'éirich am boirionnach agus dh'iarr i air suidhe. Cha tug i làmh air biadh no deoch a thoirt da, agus an uair a rinn e a gharadh an so, thogair e gu falbh, agus dh'fhalbh e.

N 825·3 Ciod e thòisich an seana bhoirionnach a bha a stigh, ach ri caoineadh.

Có bha 'sa chearn ach nighean fir an tighe, 'Ciod è sin ort?' ars ise ris a' bhoirionnach.

'Chan 'eil móran orm fhìn de thinneas no de ghoirteas,' ars ise, 'ach na smaointinnean a tha tighinn fa-near domh.'

'Ciod è na smaointinnean a tha tighinn fa-near duit? As an so cha téid mi gus an innis thu dhomh ciod e na smaointinnean a tha tighinn fa-near duit,' arsa nighean fear an tighe ris an t-seana bhoirionnach.

'Tha mi smaointeachadh an gille bha an siod, gun robh uair eile is nan tigeadh e, nach ann mar siod a leigteadh air falbh e.'

[1] Am Fortan, the Good Luck, is often used to mean *Providence*.

bring me. There is nothing for me here, and therefore
I had better depart and see what fortune [1] sends me.'

His mother would have much preferred him to stay
with her than to depart.

'Avoid,' said she, 'sailoring; it was sailoring by which
thy father prospered, and it was sailoring that killed him.'

The lad set out, leaving a farewell blessing with his
mother. Now what time of year was it but Spring.

It was cold, and there were showers of snow.

What road did he take, but the road that led to the house
of his father's friend, who had now risen in the world.

This man had eight merchant ships trading with the
Indies and with every other place, and he had eight store-
houses on land.

Now this great shipowner had only one daughter.

The lad went into the kitchen.

The woman asked him to be seated. She made no
move to offer him either food or drink, so when he had
now warmed himself, he desired to go, and he went.

What should an old woman who was indoors begin to N 825·3
do but weep.

Who happened to be in the kitchen, but the goodman's
daughter. 'What's troubling thee?' said she to the
woman.

'Of illness or pain there is very little troubling me,'
quoth she, 'it is the thoughts that come before me that
trouble me.'

'What are the thoughts that come before thee? I will
not go hence till thou tell me what the thoughts are that
come before thee,' said the daughter of the house to the
old woman.

'I am thinking about yon lad; for there was a time, and
a different time, and had he come then, it is not thus he
would have been allowed to depart.'

'Ciod è an reuson a th'agad air an sin?' arsa nighean
fear an tighe.

'Chan urrainn mise dad a ràdh de reusan sam
bith: ach theirigeadh sibhse suas do sheòmar bhur
n-athar agus tairnibh a mach seotal, is gheibh sibh
leabhar beag an sin, agus na briathran a bha eadar an
dà athair, gheibh sibh a mach an sin iad,' ars an seana
bhoirionnach.

'Falbh thusa cho luath is a rinn thu riamh, agus éigh
ris, agus thoir air ais e,' arsa nighean fir an tighe ris a'
bhoirionnach [eile].

Dh'éigh i ris, agus thill am balach air ais. Thug i
biadh agus deoch dha.

Dh'fhalbh an nighean agus faighear an leabhar, is
gabhar a stigh do'n t-seòmar far an robh am balach ri a
bhiadh.

T 91·7 'Gabh do bhiadh, a laochain. C'àite a bheil thu
dol?' ars ise.

'Tha mi dol a dh'iarraidh an fhortain. Tha ciall is
crìonnachd a' tighinn chugam is chan 'eil annam ach mac
mnatha bochda,' ars am balach.

'Is a bheil sgoil agad?' ars ise.

'Chan 'eil,' ars esan.

'D è mar a gheibh thu sgoil?' ars ise.

'Chan 'eil fhios 'm,' ars esan.

'S a bheil sgillinn airgid agad?' ars ise.

'Chan 'eil,' ars esan.

'A bheil fios agad ciod è am feum a dhèanadh thu
de airgiod, nam faigheadh tu e?' ars ise.

'Tha,' ars esan, 'ach chan 'eil mi dol a dh'iarraidh air
duine sam bith, is gun fhios 'm nach tuiteadh dhomh
fhìn gum faighinn e.'

'So dhuit leabhar—agus bi a' falbh leis an leabhar,
agus a h-uile duine choinnicheas air an rathad mhór thu,
iarraidh thu air leasan a thoirt duit; agus so dhuit ochd
puinnd Shasunnach, agus an ceann na bliadhna thig
chugamsa, agus m'ochd puinnd Shasunnach fhìn agad
domh, agus ma nì thu fhìn rud sam bith leis na h-ochd
puinnd Shasunnach, is leat fhìn e. Ceannaichidh tu

'What reason hast thou for thinking that?' said the daughter of the house.

'I cannot say a word about any reason: but go you up to your father's room, pull out a drawer, and there you will find a little book in which are written the covenant vows between the two fathers. You will find out from that,' said the old woman.

'Go thou as quickly as ever thou didst anything, halloo after him, and bring him back,' said the daughter of the house to the [other] woman.

She shouted after him, and the lad came back again. She gave him food and drink.

The daughter of the house went away to get the book, and came to the kitchen where the lad was eating.

'Take thy food, my hero. Where art going?' quoth she. T 91·7

'I am going to seek fortune. Sense and discretion have come to me, and I am only the son of a poor woman,' quoth the lad.

'And hast thou any schooling?' said she.

'I have not,' said he.

'How wilt thou get schooling?' said she.

'I know not,' said he.

'And hast thou never a penny of siller?' said she.

'I have not,' said he.

'Dost know what use thou wouldst make of money if thou hadst it?' said she.

'I do know,' said he, 'but I am not going to ask of any man, for I don't know but what I may happen to get it for myself.'

'Here is a book for thee—carry it about with thee, and every man that meets thee on the high road, ask him to give thee a lesson; and here are eight pounds sterling for thee. At the end of a year, come back to me, having my eight pounds sterling ready for me. If thou make anything with the eight pounds sterling, it shall belong to thee. Thou shalt buy needles, knives, rings and thimbles; and

snàthadan, agus sgianan, agus fàinneachan agus meurain; agus falbhaidh tu leis an sin, feuch ciod è am feum a nì thu,' ars ise.

Dh'fhàg iad beannachd aig a chéile, agus dh'fhalbh esan.

N 410   Thug e leis na h-ochd puinnd Shasunnach is an leabhar, agus a h-uile duine a choinnicheadh e, dh' iarradh e leasan air, air chor is gun robh e faotainn leasain o na h-uile duine a b'urrainn a thoirt da, agus an ceann na bliadhna, rinn e fichead punnd Sasunnach leis an ochd.

Thàinig e far an robh ise.

'Seadh, an tàinig thu?' ars ise.

'Thàinig,' ars esan.

Chuireadh biadh is deoch air a bheulaibh is shuidh i fhìn mu'n bhòrd làimh ris. 'A bheil thu tighinn air t'aghaidh gu math 'san sgoil?' ars ise.

'Thà,' ars esan, 'nì mi mo ghnothuch fhìn 's gach àite an téid mi.'

'A bheil mo chuid airgid agad domhsa a nis?' ars ise.

'Thà,' ars esan, 'agus taing mhór duit air a shon.' Rug e air an airgiod, agus chuir e ochd puinnd Shasunnach air a' bhòrd.

'Ciod è sin agad fhìn 'na dhéidh sin?'

'Dà phunnd deug Shasunnach,' ars esan.

'Is math a rinn thu,' ars ise.

'Tha mi toilichte, co dhiùbh, gun d'fhuair thusa do chuid fhìn,' ars esan.

'Chan ann mar sin a bhitheas, ach gleidhidh tu an ochd, agus so dhuit dà fhichead punnd Sasunnach eile, agus bidh an sin trì fichead agad, agus thig do m'ionnsuigh-sa an ceann na bliadhna le m'ochd agus le mo dhà fhichead punnd Sasunnach.'

Dh'fhàg iad beannachd aig a chéile, is dh'fhalbh esan.

N 421·1   Cheannaich e fiach an trì fichead puinnd Shasunnach de bhathar. Bha e falbh leis o àite gu h-àite, agus an ceann na bliadhna, bha dà cheud gu leth punnd Sasunnach aige. Chaidh e an sin far an robh ise.

'Seadh, an tàinig thu?' ars ise.

thou shalt go about with these and try what thou canst do,'
said she.

They left farewell blessings with each other, and he set
off.

He took the eight pounds sterling and the book, and N 410
he asked every man he met for a lesson; thus he was getting
lessons from all who were able to give them to him, and,
at the end of a year, he had made twenty pounds sterling
by means of the eight.

He returned to her again.

'Well, hast thou come ?' said she.

'I have,' said he.

Food and drink were set before him, and she sat at
the table near him.   'Art coming on well, at the schooling ?'
said she.

'I am,' said he, 'I can transact my own matters in every
place I visit.'

'Hast thou brought me my money now ?' said she.

'I have,' he replied, 'and many thanks to thee for it.'
He took out the money, and laid eight pounds sterling on
the table.

'And what hast thou there besides that ?'

'Twelve pounds sterling,' said he.

'Thou hast done well,' quoth she.

'I am glad, in any case, that thou hast gotten thine
own back,' said he.

'The matter shall not rest so. See—keep thou the
eight, and here are two score pounds sterling more for
thee, and thou wilt have three score then, and thou must
come to me at the end of a year with my eight and my
two score pounds sterling.'

They left farewell blessings with each other, and he
set off.

He bought goods to the value of three score pounds N 421·1
sterling.   He was travelling about with them from place
to place, and, at the end of a year, he had two hundred
and fifty pounds sterling.   He then returned to her again.

'Ah ! hast thou come ?' said she.

'Thàinig,' ars esan.

'D è mar a thàinig thu air t'aghaidh o'n a dh'fhàg thu roimhe mi ?' ars ise.

'Thàinig gu math !' ars esan.

'D è mar a tha thu dèanamh leis an sgoil ?' ars ise.

'Tha gu math,' ars esan.

'Ciod è a's motha a rinn thu ?' ars ise.

'Tha, dà cheud gu leth punnd Sasunnach agam,' ars esan.

'Rinn thu gu math, gu dearbh,' ars ise. 'Gheibh thu dà cheud gu leth eile leis an dà cheud gu leth sin, agus théid thu agus ceannaichidh tu bathar agus cairtean, agus sgeadaichidh tu thu fhìn gu math, agus an uair a bhios a h-uile nì deas agad, thig leis a' bhathar anns na cairtean gu tigh m'athar far am bi mise, am beul na h-oidhche, agus iarraidh tu àite do'n bhathar, agus fuireach car na h-oidhche sin.'

Dh'fhalbh esan an sin, agus cheannaich e bathar agus cairtean, agus chuir e e fhìn ann an sgeadachadh iomlan, agus feasgar a bha an sin, ghabh e a dh'ionnsuigh tigh a h-athar-se leis a' bhathar. Chuir e brath a stigh a dh'ionnsuigh fear an tighe, nam biodh e cho math is gun tugadh e àite d'a chuid bathair an oidhche sin, gum fanadh e, o'n a bha e cho anmoch.

K 1954

Thuirt fear an tighe nach robh àite aige d'a bhathar.

'Mo nàire agus mo leaghadh,' ars a nighean, 'an ann a' brath an coigreach a leigeil as a' bhaile gun àite a thoirt d'a chuid bathair ! Falbh sibhse a mach, no cuiribh brath a mach gum faigh e àite.'

Chaidh brath a mach àite a thoirt do'n bhathar, agus thàinig esan a stigh.

Bha e fhìn is fear an tighe gu math mór a stigh comhla, is cha robh fios aig a' ghille air an t-saoghal 'd è mar a bha, ach bha fios aice-se.

Ars ise ris, a leth-taobh, 'Nis, tha ochd luingeas aig m'athair, agus tha ceithir a tha dùil aige nach tig gu bràth, agus thàinig ceithir a cheana dhiubh, agus fhuair mise pàipearan nan luingeas nach tàinig an dé, agus tha iad

'I have,' he replied.

'How hast thou prospered since I last saw thee ?' said she.

'I have prospered well !' he said.

'And how art thou doing at the schooling ?' said she.

'Very well,' said he.

'What is the most thou hast made ?' said she.

'Why, two hundred and fifty pounds sterling,' said he.

'Thou hast indeed done well,' quoth she. 'Thou shalt get two hundred and fifty more with that two hundred and fifty, and thou shalt go and buy goods and carts. Then dress thyself well and brawly, and when thou hast everything ready, come at night-fall with the goods in the carts to my father's house where I shall be, and do thou ask him for room for thy goods, and for leave to stay for that night.'

Away he went, purchased goods and carts, and arrayed himself in a dress that was perfection, and went one evening to her father's house with the goods. He sent word in to the goodman of the house that if he would be kind enough to give his merchandise room for that night, K 1954 he would stay, as it was so late.

The goodman replied that he had no room for his goods.

'My shame and my melting,' said his daughter, 'wouldst thou then let the stranger depart from the place without giving his goods any room ! No, go yourself out, or send out word that he shall have room.'

Word was sent out that the merchandise was to be given house-room, and he (the hero) came in.

He and the goodman began to get on exceedingly well, and the lad did not know in the world what had happened (between her and her father ?) but she knew.

Said she to him, privately, 'Now, my father hath eight ships, four of which he never expects to return. The other four of them have come already. See now, yesterday, I obtained the papers concerning those which have not sàbhailte. Thig thusa mu'n cuairt air, cho math 's is urrainn thu an déidh an tràth-fheasgair; is feuch an ceannaich thu an té as sine dhiubh, chionn tha i ro luachmhor.'

An déidh an tràth-nòin, bha e fhéin agus fear-an-tighe a' bruidhinn mu na soithichean. 'Tha móran calltachd a' dol air a' bhliadhna so,' ars an gille.

'Tha,' arsa fear an tighe, 'tha ceithir luingeas agam fhéin air falbh, agus chan 'eil dùil agam gun tig iad gu bràth, agus is iad ceithir soithichean a b'fheudalacha a bha agam.'

'Tha mi fhéin coma ged a cheannaichinn an té as sine dhiubh. Ma thig i, thigeadh, is mura tig, biodh i caillte. Bheir mi trì cheud punnd Sasunnach air thuiteamas oirre,' ars an gille.

'Is leat i,' arsa fear an tighe. Chunnt esan na trì cheud punnd Sasunnach air a' bhòrd, agus thog fear an tighe iad.

An uair a bha an long reicte, thàinig ise a nuas, agus thilg i na paipearan air a' bhòrd air beulaibh a h-athar.

'Dona dona rinn thu orm,' ars a h-athair rithe.

'Ciod è rinn mi oirbh?' ars ise.

'Tha mi an déidh an soitheach is fiachalaiche a tha agam a reic, agus gun nì 'na corp ach sìoda is a h-uile seud as fhearr na chéile as na h-Innsean,' ars esan.

'Ma tha sibh a' gabhail aithreachais,' ars an gille, 'leigidh mise an soitheach agaibh fhéin, mar a bha i roimhe.'

Cha b'fhiach leis an fhear mhór gun gabhadh e an soitheach. 'Ma tà, cha ghabh mise i; biodh i agad fhéin, tha gu leòir de chuid an t-saoghail agam-sa, as a h-ioghnais,' ars esan.

An là-'r-na-mhàireach, thàinig an soitheach, is chuireadh air tìr am bathar, agus b'e sin am bathar fiachail. Reic e am bathar, agus cheannaich e luchd guail, agus chuir e air bòrd e, agus sheòl e leis do'n Tuirc. Chaidh e air

come, and these ships are safe. After dinner, bring the
conversation round to that matter as well as thou art able,
and see if thou canst buy the oldest ship, because she is
very valuable.'

After dinner, he and the goodman were talking about
the vessels. 'There is a good deal of loss going on this
year,' said the lad.

'There is,' quoth the goodman; 'I myself have four
ships abroad, and I do not expect they will ever come
again, and they were the four most precious vessels I had.'

'I really don't mind if I buy the oldest one of them.
If she comes, let her come, and if she comes not, let her
be lost. I will give thee three hundred pounds sterling
for her on chance,' quoth the lad.

'She's thine,' said the goodman. He counted the
three hundred pounds sterling down on the table, and the
goodman picked them up.

When the ship had been sold, the daughter came
forward, and threw the papers on the table before her
father.

'Badly, badly, hast thou treated me,' said her father to
her.

'What have I done to you?' said she.

'I have just sold the most valuable ship that I had, in
the hold of which there was nothing but silk and all sorts
of jewels from the Indies, each thing more precious than
another,' quoth he.

'If you repent the bargain,' quoth the lad, 'I will let
the vessel remain with you as it was before.'

But the great man would not condescend to take back
the vessel. 'Oh no, however that may be, I will not take
her; let her be yours. I have plenty of world's gear without
her,' quoth he.

On the morrow the vessel came, and the goods were
sent ashore, and they were valuable goods indeed. He
sold the goods, and purchased a cargo of coal, put it on
board, and sailed with it to Turkey. He went ashore, and

tìr is dh'amais e air fear tigh-sheinnse mhóir, agus reic
e an gual ris airson [na h-]uibhir de òr. Chuir fear an
tigh-sheinnse gu a thràth-nòin e. Chaidh e ann.

An uair a chaidh e a stigh do'n t-seòmar bhìdh, bha
dà fhear-mhuinntir dheug an sin a' fritheal do'n bhòrd.
Chunnaic e a dhà dheug de bhodaich ghlas a' tighinn
a nuas, agus bata aig a h-uile fear riamh dhiubh.

'Na bi gabhail iongantais,' arsa fear an tigh-sheinnse,
'tha creutairean anns an àite so fuireach anns na tuill,
agus cho luath is a mhothaicheas iad àileadh a' bhìdh,
bidh iad aige, agus feumaidh daoine bhi feitheamh orra
mar so le bataichean 'gan cumail air falbh, fhad is a bhios
sinn aig ar biadh.'

'Dèanaibh foighidinn bheag,' ars esan, 'agus na beanaibh
do ur biadh.'

N 411·1   Chaidh e do'n t-soitheach, is thug e a nuas cat.

'Gleidhibh ur cuid bhataichean,' ars esan.

[Thàinig na radain a mach.] Thòisich an cat air
marbhadh, agus thòisich iadsan air gabhail am bìdh.
Cha tigeadh na radain a mach as na tuill mu dheireadh,
leis an eagal a bha orra.

'Ma tà,' arsa fear an tighe-sheinnse, 'o'n a bha thusa
cho còir agus am beathach so a thoirt do m'ionnsuigh,
bheir mise duitse each a bhios agad a' marcachd nach
robh riamh a leithid anns a' Chrìosdachd, agus nach
deachaidh riamh a leithid ann.'

Chuir e sìos an t-each gus an luing, agus thug e a nuas
a h-aon eile de na cait.

'Siod fear boirionn agus fear firionn,' [1] ars esan, 'agus
sìolaichidh iad feadh na rìoghachd uile.'

'Ma tà,' arsa fear an tigh-sheinnse, 'o'n a thug thusa
sin domhsa, bheir mise duitse srian òir agus diallaid airgid
a bhios agad a' marcachd feadh na Crìosdachd.'

Chuir e siod chun an t-soithich, is thòisich iad ri òl.

---

[1] An interesting case of stating gender.

happened to come across a man who owned a great change-house, and to him he sold the coal for a great deal of gold. The change-house man gave him an invitation to dinner, and he went accordingly.

When he entered the banqueting-room, there were twelve serving-men serving at the table.

He also saw twelve others, twelve gray-haired old men, who came forward, and each and everyone of them carried a stick.

'Do not be astonished,' said the man of the change-house, 'there are creatures in this place that dwell in holes, and as soon as ever they perceive the smell of food, they are at it, so that it is necessary to have men watching for them with sticks to keep them away while we are at our meals.'

'Have a little patience,' said the lad, 'and do not touch your food.'

He went to the vessel, and brought back a cat.   N 411·1

'Put away your sticks,' said he.

[Rats came forth.] The cat began to kill, and the people began to partake of the food.

At last the rats would not come out of the holes, with the fear that possessed them.

'Well then,' quoth the man of the change-house, 'seeing that thou hast been so good as to bring this beast to me, I will give thee a horse that thou shalt have to ride, the like of which never was in Christendom, neither did such an animal ever go there.'

He sent the horse down to the ship, and he brought back another of the cats.

'There is a female, and there a male,'[1] quoth he, 'and they will breed and multiply throughout the kingdom.'

'Well then,' said the man of the change-house, 'since thou hast given me that as well I will give thee a golden rein and silver saddle with which to ride through Christendom.'

He sent the things to the vessel, and they began drinking.

Bha esan a' fàs blàth, is dh'fhalbh e a mach gu ceann an tighe. Chuala e bruidhinn fo'n chloich-stéidh.[1]

'An ann a' brath éirigh duit mar a dh'éirich do t'athair ? A bheil fhios agad có tha bruidhinn riut ?' ars an guth.

'Chan 'eil,' ars esan. 'Tha t'athair,' ars an guth; 'mharbh iad mise an so. Theirig a stigh. Cha dearg an dram ort ach mar gum bitheadh an t-uisge fuar 'nad bheul. Cho loma luath is a thuiteas fear an tigh-sheinnse leis an dram, ruig do shoitheach, gearr na cabaill, agus bi falbh.'

E 366

Rinn e mar a dh'iarr an guth air. Sheòl e gu ruig Albainn.

Chaidh e air tìr, agus thug e leis an t-each, is an t-srian, is an diallaid.

Ràinig e far an robh a mhàthair. Ghabh e a stigh. Dh'iarr e fuireachd an oidhche sin.

Thuirt i ris nach b'àite duine uasail a bha an siod idir; nach robh an siod ach àite bochd, gum b'fhearr dha dol do thigh an fhir-luingeis a bha shuas an siod.

'An robh mac agad fhéin riamh ?' ars e rithe.

'Bha,' ars ise.

'An gabhadh tu mise air a shon ?'

'Cha ghabhadh,' ars ise; 'cha b'e a chionn is nach fhaodainn ur gabhail air a shon.'

'Chan fhaigh thu gin air a shon gu bràth ach mise, agus ma bha thusa am bothan bochd riamh, bidh thu an tigh beairteach a nis. [Is mise do mhac.]'

Shìn e a làmh dhi,[3] agus thug e tigh an duine uasail air.

Bha ise, an sin, an déidh leanabh a bhi aice air a chionn.

Dh'fhàs am bodach cho trom, bochd, tinn, agus dùil aige gur mac dìolain a bha aig a nighinn, is nach fhaigheadh e a mach a athair.[4]

[1] Help from a dead parent is a common enough incident in folk-tale, but not very frequent in our collection. See *Waifs and Strays*, ii., p. 73.

[2] *Lit.* 'it was not for lack of not being able to take you for him' (*i.e.* because of resemblance she saw).   [3] In filial recognition ?

[4] This sentence shows that the reciter himself thought (1) that the children

He presently began to get warm with drinking, and went out of doors to the end of the house. He heard speaking from beneath the key-stone.[1]

'Dost thou wish that what happened to thy father should happen to thee too? Dost thou know who is speaking to thee?' said the voice.

'I do not,' he replied.

'It is thy father,' said the voice; 'they murdered me here. But go in, for the dram will not affect thee more E 366 than if it were merely cold water in thy mouth. As soon as ever the man of the change-house falls down drunk, go to thy vessel, cut thy cables, and begone.'

He did as the voice commanded him, and sailed to Scotland.

He landed, taking with him the horse, the rein and the saddle.

He came to the place where his mother was, and going in, asked for leave to stay there that night.

She told him that it was not a gentleman's house at all; that it was but a poor place, and that he had better go to the house of the shipowner that was up yonder.

'Hadst thou ever a son?' said he to her.

'I had,' said she.

'Wouldst thou accept me in his place?'

'I would not,' said she; 'not that I might not mistake you for him.' [2]

'Thou shalt never have another for him, but me; and if thou hast always been in a poor bothy, thou shalt be in a rich house now. [I am thy son.]'

He stretched out his hand to her,[3] and then betook himself to the house of the gentleman (his wife's father).

Now she [the heroine] had just had a child by him.

The old man had become heavy-hearted, poorly, and ill, for he thought it was a bastard son she had, whose father he would never be able to discover.[4]

were as much bound by the contract of marriage mentioned at the beginning of the tale as they would have been if they themselves had contracted themselves when of age and with their eyes open; (2) that they had therefore been lawfully and thoroughly married; and (3) that their child was, in consequence, legitimate.

[An uair a ràinig e tigh an duine uasail, bha làmhan sgaoilte aice roimhe.]
'An là-'r-na-mhàireach,' ars ise, 'théid mise agus m'athair a ghabhail sràide far am bi thu a' cur a mach an luchd.'
An là-'r-na-mhàireach, thòisich e air cur a mach an luchd. Bha bùth aige air a chur a suas air tìr, agus bha an t-òr air a chur a stigh do'n bhùth so ann am pocannan, agus beul a h-uile poc air a fhàgail fosgailte.
Bha e fhéin 'na shuidhe shuas an ceann a' bhùth, is e a' sgrìobhadh.
Dh'iarr ise air a h-athair dol a ghabhail sràide leatha, agus chunnaic iad am bùth.[1]
Ghabh iad suas d'a ionnsuigh, 's nach b'àbhaist daibh a leithid fhaicinn.
Dh'iarr ise air a h-athair dol a stigh do'n bhùth, agus ghabh iad a stigh.
Thug esan sùil a sìos seachad, agus dh'iarr e orra suidhe.

Shuidh iad air na pocaichean, agus thug am bodach fainear gun robh iad làn òir.
'M'athair,' ars ise, 'nach iarr sibh air an fhear so mise a phòsadh ?'
'Cha phòsadh am fear ud nighean an rìgh is fhearr a bha riamh air an t-saoghal, agus na tha an so de òr aige,' ars am bodach.
Dh'iarr i air a rithist e, is cha charaicheadh a h-athair.

'A bhodaich,' ars ise, 'rinn thu orm-sa mar a rinn thu, a chionn gun robh esan bochd agus thusa beairteach. Tha mise pòsda a cheana aige—tha do leabhar an siod, is do bhriathran ann.'
Chaidh iad suas chun an tighe, agus bhaisteadh an gille,[3] agus bha toil-inntinn mhór aca.

---

[1] *Bùth* is usually, if not always, feminine in the Outer Hebrides.
[2] This version of the Married Children theme does not say what it was that the man had done to his daughter. He had probably tried his best to separate her from her lover, to whom she had been married when an infant.
[3] Getting the child baptized—a great point. No wise man will mention the name of his child till it has been baptized. See No. 20, Notes. Up to

[Upon coming to the gentleman's house, she welcomed him with open arms.]

'On the morrow,' said she, 'my father and I will take a walk, past the place where thou art unloading the cargo.'

On the morrow, he began to unload the cargo. He had had a shop built on land, and gold was being sent in to this shop in sacks, and the mouth of every sack left open.

He himself was sitting there managing the shop, and writing.

She asked her father to go and take a walk with her, and they saw the shop.

They went up towards it, for they were not used to see such a shop as that.

She asked her father to go into the shop, and in they went.

He [the hero] looked down the shop to the outer end of it, and asked them to be seated.

They took seats on the bags, and the old man noticed that they were full of gold.

'My father,' said she, 'will you not ask this man to marry me?'

'That man would never marry the daughter of the best king that ever was in the world, seeing what a lot of gold he has here,' quoth the old man.

Again she asked him to do so, but her father would not alter his mind.

'Old man,' said she, 'what thou didst to me,[2] thou didst because he was poor and thou rich. But already am I married to him.—See, there is thy book, and thine own vows written in it.'

They went up to the house, the baby boy was baptized,[3] and they were very happy.

---

now the child has been considered a disgrace; but as soon as the parents are discovered to have been legitimately married, the child becomes respectable; it may now be baptized, and then take its place in the social world. For baptism, see No. 20 (MS. vol. x., No. 34 and MS. vol. x., No. 83). Fionn's Aunt is delighted when he is baptized.—*Celtic Review*, ii., p. 358. See *W. H. Tales*, iii., pp. 383 or 399.

NOTES

MS. vol. x., No. 40. Scribe: probably Hector MacLean. On the flyleaf, Islay has written:—'Alexander MacNeil, Fisherman, Ken Tangval, Barra, who learnt it from Alasdair MacRuaraidh Bhàin.

The two Skippers. To be translated. Like other stories already got in Gaelic and from Gaelic—answers to Whittington and his cat and Grimm's version, varies from both the English and German stories and resembles the other Gaelic stories closely.

See "How Cats went first to Spain—MacCraw's version." ' See MS. vol. x., No. 73.

INFANT MARRIAGE

The following incidents, in fairly similar sequence, are found in several Gaelic tales.

Two men, fathers, usually merchants, contract that the infant son of the one and the infant daughter of the other, shall wed when they come of age. Each father keeps a copy of the marriage contract.

T 69·2 The children are left in total ignorance of the contract.

One of the men, usually the one who has the son, presently dies.

K 2296* The other man, in treacherous violation of the joint contract, determines to convert the goods of his dead friend to his own use, settle them on his own daughter, and have her eventually married, not to the original bridegroom, but to some other suitor whose riches shall make him, in the worldly view of the treacherous man, more of a match for her.

The treacherous man sometimes takes his dead friend's son into his household and employ, but presently finds that the boy is getting very fond of his daughter, and she of him. In order, therefore, to carry out his wicked scheme, he determines to send the boy away to foreign parts, on some perilous adventure. In several stories, he gives

H 1211 the sailors orders to throw him overboard, or maroon him. Sometimes
H 931 the boy is to be slain upon arrival.

In some tales, it happens that before the hero can set out on his dangerous journeys, he and the heroine discover their respective marriage lines in the desks of their respective fathers, and shyly show them to each other. In other tales the young people are drawn towards each other naturally, and do not discover the contracts till late in the tale.

In any case, the heroine always befriends the hero, even to her father's undoing.

Thus the boy naturally becomes the hero of the piece ; but though his various adventures, and the plots and letters forged against him by the enemy keep him for a long while away from home and beauty, he is of course rescued from every danger, comes safely out of every

K 1616 predicament, and in most versions arrives home just in time to prevent some rival from marrying his rightful love. In this version, No. 23 (MS. vol. x., No. 40), no rival is mentioned, but the ending is none the less happy.

The young people always think it a point of honour to carry out the contract of marriage. Accordingly they wed. Though the contract was entered into on their behalf by proxy, when they were too young either to consent or to object, or indeed to know anything about it, they always regard the contract as being as binding as if they themselves, when of age to do so, and with their eyes open, had been the parties who had entered into it.

In MS. vol. x., No. 154, the hero, who had been contracted as a child to the heroine is shipwrecked. In MS. vol. xi., No. 191, he is thrown overboard. Sometimes he is marooned.[1] These incidents seem to illustrate the Caithness belief recorded in *Folk-Lore*, xiv., p. 304. 'It was thought unlucky to allow a bridegroom on board a fishing-boat; and from the time he is contracted until he is married, he is not allowed on board.' A similar belief is recorded for Fife in Folk-Lore Society's *County Folk-Lore* (1914), vii., p. 419; in *Trans. Gael Soc. Inverness*, xiv., p. 245, and Islay's English List, No. 267. In sending the hero on sea voyages, as the heroine's father does in some tales, he probably thought that such an unlucky person as a contracted bridegroom would be sure to come to grief, if he once got on board a boat. See also No. 111 English List and *Celtic Magazine*, xiii., p. 110.

The custom of infant marriage was known among some of the North American Indian tribes, according to Mr Robert W. Chambers, who says in his book *The Hidden Children*:—

'For among the Iroquois and their adopted captives, there are both girls and boys who are spoken of as "Hidden Persons" or "Hidden Children." They are called Ta-neh-u-weh-too, which means "hidden in the husks," like ears of corn.

'And the reason is this—a mother for one cause or another, or perhaps for none at all, decides to make of her unborn baby a Hidden Child. And so when born, the child is instantly given to distant foster-parents, and by them hidden, and remains so concealed until adolescence. And, being considered by birth pure and unpolluted, a girl and boy thus hidden are expected to marry, return to their people when informed by their foster-parents of the truth, and bring a fresh, innocent, and uncontaminated strain into their clan and tribe.' From this it is clear that among the Amerindians the children thus destined to marry each other are kept in ignorance of the fact until marriageable; that they are sent to distant places, and kept apart from each other; and that these conditions are observed, not with any intention of violating the marriage contract, but rather in pursuance of it, for care is taken to bring them together again. Whereas the separating of the children in the Gaelic tales is in violation of contract, and with intent to keep them apart for ever. For to judge the tales superficially, had it not been for the death of one of the fathers, and the desire of the surviving father to possess himself of the goods of the dead, the Gaelic

---

[1] Marooning is a frequent incident.—*W. H. Tales*, i., No. 10, var. 3; ii., Nos. 32 and 52. *Waifs and Strays*, v., p. 18. *An Deò Gréine*, viii., p. 181. *Trans. Gael. Soc. Inverness*, xxv., p. 182. This book, p. 34 n.

S 145

children would probably have always lived near each other until marriageable. This becomes very clear from No. 73, MS. vol. x., where the children are neighbours till they are each eighteen years old, at which time they were to have been informed of the contract. The Mashona of Southern Rhodesia also had a custom of pledging children in marriage. See *The Times Literary Supplement*, 11th October 1928, p. 733.

The incident of a young woman cheating her father in the matter of selling his ships occurs in a very different story, *Waifs and Strays*, ii., p. 318.—A young woman kills her father for the hero's sake, *ibid.*, iii., pp. 160-161. A young woman cheats her father, a giant, in *W. H. Tales*, i., No. 2. Another cheats her father in MS. vol. xi., No. 268. The cheating is always done for the benefit of the hero, but the circumstances under which she acts, vary widely. In tales of the Married Children theme, she doubtless feels herself justified, inasmuch as her father had done his best to rob her lover, and separate him from her.

Of the following themes observable in this story, viz.:—

T 69.2	Infant Marriage,
K 2296*	The Fraudulent Partner,
E 341	The Grateful Dead (Aarne-Thompson, No. 506),
	Dick Whittington and his Cat (Stith Thompson N 411·1),

two or more occur, or can be deduced as having occurred, in the following tales:—

Islay's MS. vol. xvi. (Journal, 1870), opposite p. 76.
W. H. Tales, ii., No. 32 (summarized *Folk-Lore*, ix., p. 235).
Islay's English List, No. 111.
Islay's Gaelic List, Nos. 14, 40, 73, 154, 191, 268, 299.
Larminie, pp. 115, 256.

See also *Béaloideas*, iii., pp. 43 and 143, item P284; iv., p. 292.

In some of these tales occur the incidents connected with the bride's *K 1371·2* disguising herself in order that her father, failing to recognize her, shall unwittingly give her away, as in 'Baillie Lunnainn,' *W. H. Tales*, i., No. 17b (see Addendum, p. xxxvi.), and *Larminie*, p. 115, 'The Servant of Poverty,' two tales which contain a surprising number of parallel incidents. See p. 186, and Addendum, No. 35 (14).

MAC A' BHREABADAIR [1]

No. 24.   *[Vol. x., No. 44]*

Aarne-Thompson, No. 401

BHA Breabadair ann an caisteal anns an Stochd Stachd [?] [2]
agus bhiodh e daonnan ag iasgach. Bha e fàs sean, agus
bhiodh e cur a mhic a dh'iasgach 'na àite. Cha robh a
mhac cho toilichte aig an iasgach agus a bha a athair.

Chaidh e oidhche a shealgaireachd, is e smaointicheadh
gur h-e bu bhuannachdaiche na 'n [t-]iasgach. An uair
a bha e treis a' falbh, a' sealltuinn airson beathaich no
eòin a mharbhadh e, ciod è chunnaic e ach duine mór,
dorcha.

An uair a chunnaic e an duine mór dorcha so, dh'fhàg
e am bàta anns a' Ghleann air fad.[3] Ghabh e a nuas
[t]roimh Eirisgeidh, agus ghabh e air ais gu ruige Salltraigh.
Choisich e sìos [t]roimh Uibhist air fad, gus an d'ràinig
e Loch nam Madadh.[4]

Ghabh e as a sin gu ruig an t-Eilean Sgitheanach.
Dh'fhàg e an t-Eilean Sgitheanach, is chaidh e gu tìr-
mór. An uair a ràinig e tìr-mór, ghabh e air falbh is
choisich e a h-uile ceum gu Dùn Eideann. An uair a
rainig e Dùn Eideann, fhuair e gunna is cù agus boineid
ianadair.

An ceud stad a rinn e, choinnich duine uasal e.

'An sealgair thu ?' ars an duine uasal.

'Bidh mi ag obair rithe,' ars esan.

'Ma's sealgair thu, gabhaidh tu fasdadh uamsa, agus

---

[1] In Uist, 'breabadaireachd,' *i.e.* weaving, was considered the lowest
possible calling in which a man could take part, and the reciter, in making
his hero the son of a weaver at the start and the king's son-in-law at the finish,
wishes to emphasize the greatness of his hero, who ascends from one social
extreme to the other. Why the old weaver was so devoted to fishing, unless
it was because he desired to have a calling more manly than weaving, does
not appear, nor are we told how it was that he lived in a castle.

THE WEAVER'S SON [1]

Aarne-Thompson, No. 401

THERE was once a Weaver in a castle in the Stochd Stachd
[?],[2] who used to be always fishing.   He was growing old,
and so began to send his son to fish in his stead.   His son L 101
was not so fond of the fishing as his father was.

One night he went out to hunt, thinking that that
would be more profitable than fishing.   After wandering
about for some time looking for a beast or bird that he
might kill, what should he see but a big dark man.

Upon seeing this big dark man,[3] he abandoned the
boat entirely and left it in the Glen.   He went down
through Eriskay, and back as far as Salltraigh.   Then he
walked away right through Uist, until he came to Loch
Maddy.[4]

From there he went to the Isle of Skye.   He next left
the Isle of Skye, and went to the mainland.   Upon coming
to the mainland, he set forth again, and walked every step
of the way to Edinburgh.   Upon reaching Edinburgh, he
procured a gun, a dog, and a fowler's bonnet.

The first stay he made, he met a gentleman.

'Art thou a hunter ?' said the gentleman.

'I do work at it [= hunting],' said he.

'If thou art a hunter, thou shalt take hire from me, and

---

[2] Possibly the Stack Isles, between Barra and S. Uist.

[3] The big dark man is brought into the story without any apparent reason
or connection.

[4] *slos, lit.* downwards, would be used by a man at the south end of S. Uist
in speaking of a journey to Loch Maddy in N. Uist, *i.e.* from the high ground
of S. Uist to the flats of N. Uist.   'The Glen' is not specified, and the geography
seems uncertain.

bheir mi deagh thuarasdal duit. Dèan stad gus an till mi,'
ars an duine uasal, is e 'ga fhàgail. Stad an sealgair.
An ceann treis, thàinig duine uasal eile. 'An e so an
sealgair?' ars esan; 'dèan fasdadh rium, is bheir mi
deagh thuarasdal duit.'
'Chan fhaod mi; bha duine uasal eile a' bruidhinn
rium,' ars esan, 'is gheall mi feitheamh.'
An uair a b'fhada leis a bha an duine uasal eile gun
tighinn, rinn e fasdadh ris an fhear so.
'Is e an gille agam fhéin a bha bruidhinn riut roimhe,'[1]
ars an duine uasal.

Bha an sin fear-gleidhidh aig an duine uasal air a
oighreachd, is chuir e brath chun a mhaighstir airson
sealgair a chur dh'a ionnsuigh. Chuir an duine uasal an
sealgair chun an fhir-ghleidhidh. Bha aige ri dol a h-uile
h-oidhche a shealg féidh a bha an sin. Dh'fhùirich e aig
caillich aig nach robh ach aon mhac, ris an canadh iad
an Gille Glas.

D 712·7
D 114
·1·1*

A' cheud oidhche a chaidh e a mach, chunnaic e am
fiadh, agus an uair a thug e làmh air losgadh, thionndaidh
e 'na bhoirionnach.[2]

Chaidh e mach an ath-oidhche, agus chunnaic e am
fiadh, agus an uair a thug e làmh air losgadh, thionndaidh
e 'na bhoirionnach. Chaidh e a mach an treas oidhche
agus chunnaic e am fiadh, agus thionndaidh e 'na bhoirionnach an uair a thug e làmh air losgadh mar a b'àbhaist.

Smuaintich e nach tilleadh e a làmh air an turus so,
agus loisg e air a' bhoirionnach.[3] Dh'fhan am boirionnach
far an robh i, is chaidh esan a bhruidhinn rithe. Dh'iarr
i air a coinneachadh 'san eaglais an ath-oidhche. Thuirt
e gun coinnicheadh. Dhealaich e rithe is chaidh e
dhachaidh.

Cha robh toil aig a' chaillich aig an robh e fuireachd
e [dh'] a fàgail, a thaobh gun robh buannachd aice ann,
agus thuirt i ri a mac gun robh an siod deoch chadail,

---

[1] MS. roimhid.

[2] Campbell of Islay seems to have classed this kind of incident as a piece
of shape-shifting and magical, and to have thought that the act of looking
over the iron sights of the gun was the counter-acting magic action that broke

I will give thee good wages. Wait till I come back,' said the gentleman, and he left him. The hunter waited. At the end of a while, another gentleman came. 'Is this the hunter?' said he; 'take service with me, and I will give thee good wages.'

'I may not do so; another gentleman has already been speaking to me,' he replied, 'and I promised to wait.'

When he thought the other gentleman was long of coming, he took service with this last one.

'It is my own servant who was speaking to thee before,' said the gentleman.

The gentleman had a keeper on his estate, and he had sent word to his master to send him a hunter. The gentleman [accordingly] sent the hunter to the keeper. The hunter had to go every night to hunt a certain deer. He lodged with an old woman, who had only one son, whom they called the Gille Glas.

The first night he went out, he saw the deer, but just when he was about to fire, it turned into a woman.[2]   D 712·7
    D 114
    ·1·1*

He went out the next night, and saw the deer, but when about to fire, it turned into a woman. He went out the third night, and saw the deer, but it turned into a woman as usual when he attempted to fire.

He determined not to hold his hand on this occasion, so he fired at the woman.[3] The woman stayed where she was, and he went up to her to speak to her. She asked him to meet her in the church the next night. He said he would, and then parted from her, and went home.

The old woman with whom he lodged did not wish him to leave her, because she was profiting by him; so she told her son that there was a sleeping draught in such and

the spells, and enabled the hunter to see that he was aiming at a woman and not at a deer (*W. H. Tales*, intro., lxix or lxxv). But the story originated long before the invention of guns.

[3] His shot does not seem to have touched her.

agus e [dh'] a toirt leis, is a toirt da an uair a thigeadh am
pathadh air, is gun tuiteadh e 'na chadal, is nach fhaigheadh
am boirionnach bruidhinn deth.

An ath-oidhche, dh'fhalbh esan do'n eaglais, agus
dh'fhalbh mac na cailliche leis. Shuidh e a' feitheamh
a' bhoirionnaich, agus cha robh e fada 'na shuidhe, an
uair a bhuail am pathadh e. Dh'iarr e air a' Ghille
Ghlas deoch a thoirt da. Thug an Gille Glas siod da;
agus an uair a dh'òl e an deoch, thuit e 'na chadal.

Thàinig carbad gus an eaglais, agus thàinig boirionnach
brèagha as a' charbad. Thàinig i a stigh far an robh
esan, is bha i feuchainn ri a dhùsgadh, ach cha b'urrainn
di.[1] Sheinn i ceòl cianail, is cha chluinneadh e diog.
Dh'fhalbh i an so, is dh'fhàg i brath, e dh'a coinneachadh
an siod an ath-oidhche.

An uair a dh'fhalbh i, dhùisg esan, is bha e fo
mhìothlachd mór a thaobh mar a dh'éirich dha.

Chaidh e an ath-oidhche a rithisd do'n eaglais a
choinneachadh a' bhoirionnaich. Shuidh e 'ga feitheamh,
agus cha robh e fada 'ga feitheamh an uair a thàinig am
pathadh air. Dh'iarr e air a' Ghille Ghlas deoch a thoirt
da.

Thug an Gille Glas siod da, agus an uair a dh'òl e an
deoch, thuit e 'na chadal. Cha robh e fada 'na chadal,
an uair a thàinig carbad gus an eaglais, is a thàinig
boirionnach brèagha a mach ás. Thàinig i a stigh far an
robh esan, is bha i feuchainn r'a dhùsgadh, is cha b'urrainn
di. Sheinn i ceòl cianail, is cha chluinneadh e diog.

Dh'fhalbh i an so, is dh'fhàg i brath e dh'a coinneachadh
an siod an ath-oidhche. An uair a dh'fhalbh i, dhùisg
esan, is bha e fo mhìothlachd mór a thaobh mar a dh'éirich
dha.

Smaointich e nach òladh e an deoch tuilleadh. Chaidh
e do'n eaglais an treas oidhche; is a thaobh nach òladh
e'n deoch, chuir an Gille Glas prìn ann an earball a chòta,
is chaidil e. Cha robh e fada 'na chadal, an uair a thàinig

D 1364·7

D 1972

D 1364·15

---

[1] In the *Waifs and Strays* version (ii., pp. 126, 458) the magic paraphernalia
employed for making the hero sleep is the sleeping pin. Its effect is so great

such a place, and that he was to take it with him and give it to the hunter when he should become thirsty, so D 1364·7 that he should fall asleep, and thus the woman should not get speech of him.

The next night, the hunter set out for the church, and the old woman's son went with him. He sat down to watch for the woman, but had not been long sitting when he was smitten with thirst. He asked [her son] the Gille Glas to give him a drink. The Gille Glas gave him the drink; but when he had drunk it, he fell asleep.

A chariot came to the church, and a handsome woman got out of the chariot. She came in to where the hunter was, and kept trying to awaken him, but could not.[1] She D 1972 sang a piteous song, but he never heard a syllable. She then departed, leaving word that he was to meet her there the next night.

When she had gone, he awoke, and was greatly depressed at what had happened to him.

On the next night, he went to the church again in order to meet her. He sat down to await her, but had not been waiting long when he became thirsty. He asked the Gille Glas to give him a drink.

The Gille Glas gave him one accordingly, but when he had drunk it, he fell asleep. He had not been long asleep, when a chariot came to the church, and a handsome woman got out of it. She came in and went up to him, and kept trying to awaken him, but could not. She sang a piteous song, but he could not hear a syllable.

She thereupon departed, and left word that he was to meet her there the next night. When she had gone, he awoke, and was greatly depressed on account of what had happened to him.

He determined that he would not drink that draught again. So the third night, when he went to the church, the Gille Glas, because he would not drink the draught, put a pin in the tail of his coat [with the result that] he

that the united strength of three people is unable to raise the hero from the ground.

carbad gus an eaglais, is a thàinig boirionnach brèagha a
mach as.

Thàinig i a stigh far an robh esan, is bha i feuchainn
ri a dhùsgadh, is cha b'urrainn di. Sheinn i ceòl brèagha,
cianail, is cha chluinneadh e diog. An uair a chunnaic
ise nach dùisgeadh e, rug i air a ghunna, agus sgrìobh i
air gur e an Gille Glas, agus a mhàthair, a bha cur
buidseachais air.[1] Sheinn i ceòl cianail, is ghabh i air
falbh.

Cha robh i fada air falbh, an uair a dhùisg esan, is
bha e fo mhìothlachd mór a thaobh mar a dh'éirich dha.
An uair a chaidh e dhachaidh, sheall e air a ghunna, is
chunnaic e an sgrìobhadh. An uair a chunnaic e e,
G 275·1·2* tharruing e an gunna, is chuir e an t-eanchainn as a'
Ghille Ghlas, is as a mhàthair.

H 1385·5 Ghabh e air falbh,[2] agus am beul an fheasgair, chunnaic
e tigh. Chaidh e chun an tighe, agus choinnich fear an
tighe e.

'An e so an sealgair?' arsa fear an tighe.

'Is mi,' ars esan.

'Nach mi-fhortanach nach robh thu an so an raoir!
nam bitheadh, bu mhac sona thu! Is tu thug Nighean
Rìgh an Eilein Mhóir o na geasan?' arsa fear an tighe.[3]

'Is mi,' arsa Mac a' Bhreabadair.

'Fanaidh tu an so fhéin a nochd.'

Dh'fhan e an oidhche sin, is chaidh e a laighe. Moch
'sa' mhaduinn, dh'éirich e is dh'fhàg e beannachd aig fear
an tighe, is ghabh e air falbh. 'Bidh tu an tigh mo
bhràthar mheadhonaich-sa an nochd,' arsa fear an tighe.

Bha e a' gabhail air aghart fad an latha, agus am beul
an fheasgair, chunnaic e tigh.

Chaidh e chun an tighe, agus choinnich fear an tighe e.

---

[1] She writes her name 'under his arm' in *W. H. Tales*, ii., No. 44. For
the hero's information, a heroine writes something on his sword in *W. H. Tales*,
iii., p. 228 or p. 214.

slept. He had not been long asleep, when a chariot came D 1364·15
to the church, and a handsome woman came out of it.

She entered the church and went up to where he was
sleeping, and kept trying to awaken him, but she could
not. She sang a beautiful mournful melody, but not a
word did he hear. When she saw that he could not be
awakened, she took up his gun, and wrote upon it that it
was the Gille Glas and his mother, who had been be-
witching him.[1] She sang a mournful melody, and departed.

She had not long been gone, when he awoke, and he
was greatly depressed at what had happened to him.
Upon going home, he happened to look at the gun, and
he saw the writing. Upon seeing it, he [swung up] the
gun, and bringing it down again, dashed out the brains G 275·1·2*
of the Gille Glas and his mother.

He set out,[2] and in the mouth of evening, saw a house. H 1385·5
He went up to it, and the gudeman of the house met him.

'Is this the hunter?' said the gudeman.

'It is, I am he,' he replied.

'How unfortunate it is that thou wert not here last
night! if only thou hadst been here then, thou wouldst
have been a lucky, happy fellow! It is thou who didst
deliver the Daughter of the King of the Great Isle from
enchantment?' said the gudeman.[3]

'Yes, it is I,' said the Weaver's Son.

'Then thou must stay here to-night, in this very place.'

He stayed there that night accordingly, and went to
bed. Early in the morning he arose, left a farewell blessing
with the gudeman, and departed. 'To-night thou wilt be
in the house of my middle brother [i.e. one who in point
of age comes between me and another brother],' said the
gudeman.

He pressed on and on all day long, and in the mouth
of the evening, he saw a house.

He went up to the house, and the gudeman met him.

[2] He set out in order to find the lady, but the MS. fails to say so.
[3] In other versions he undergoes death or torments in order to deliver
the lady from spells. But these incidents have dropped out of this story.

H 1235 'An e so an sealgair ?' arsa fear an tighe.

'Is mi,' ars an sealgair.

'Nach mi-fhortanach nach robh thu an so an raoir! nam bitheadh, bu mhac sona thu! Is tu thug Nighean Rìgh an Eilein Mhóir o na geasan ?' arsa fear an tighe.

'Is mi,' arsa Mac a' Bhreabadair.

'Fanaidh tu an so fhéin a nochd,' arsa fear an tighe.

Dh'fhan e an oidhche sin, agus chaidh e a laighe.

Moch 'sa' mhaduinn dh'éirich e, is dh'fhàg e beannachd aig fear an tighe, is ghabh e air falbh.

'Bidh tu an tigh mo bhràthar as òige an nochd,' arsa fear an tighe.

Bha e gabhail air aghart gus an tàinig am feasgar, agus am beul an fheasgair, chunnaic e tigh. Chaidh e chun an tighe, is choinnich fear an tighe e.

'An e so an sealgair ?' &c.[1]

Moch 's a' mhaduinn, dh'éirich e.

'Nis,' arsa fear an tighe, 'chan 'eil dol n'as fhaide agad. Tha am boirionnach sin fada thar iomall an t-saoghail a' fuireachd. Aon uair anns a' bhliadhna, tha gìre-

R 322·1* mhìneach [2] a' tighinn as an eilean. Tha nead aice air an taobh so. Ma ghabhas tu de mhisnich dol ann an seiche, agus dol do'n nead, nì sam bith marbh a gheabh [i] ann, bheir i leatha e.'

Dh'[fhàg] e fhéin agus fear an tighe beannachd aig a chéile, agus dh'fhalbh e.

Ràinig e far an robh nead na gìre-mhìnich. Chaidh
K 1861·1 e anns an t-seiche. An uair a chunnaic a' ghìre-mhìneach
B 552 e, thog i leatha do'n nead e, is dh'fhàg i ann e. Bha
K 932 dà isean anns an nead. Rug e orra, is thilg e leis a' chreig

_____
[1] &c., so in MS.

[2] For the Geera-veenuch, see p. 12 n. The Great Isle where the bird
B 31·1 lived is one of the Happy Isles or Isles of the Blest, supposed to be situated
an immense way out in the western ocean, or beyond the edge of the world.
A 692 The heroine is the daughter of the King of the Great Isle. In the corresponding

'Is this the hunter ?' said the gudeman.   H 1235

'Yes; I am he,' said the hunter.

'How unfortunate it is that thou wert not here last
night ! if only thou hadst been here then, what a happy
lucky fellow thou wouldst have been ! It is thou who
didst deliver the Daughter of the King of the Great Isle
from enchantment ?' said the gudeman.

'Yes, it is I,' said the Weaver's Son.

'Then it is in this very place that thou must stay
to-night,' said the gudeman.

So he stayed that night, and went to bed.

Early in the morning he arose, left a farewell blessing
with the gudeman, and departed.

'Thou wilt be in the house of my youngest brother
to-night,' quoth the gudeman.

He pressed on and on until evening came, and in the
mouth of the evening, he saw a house. He went up to
the house, and the gudeman of the house met him.

'Is this the hunter ?' &c.[1]

Early in the morning, he arose.

'Now,' quoth the gudeman, 'thou hast not to go any
farther. That woman lives far beyond the edge of the
world. Once a year, [a bird called] a geera-veenuch [2]
comes from the island, [the Great Isle]. The bird has a
nest on this side [of the water]. If thou hast courage
enough to get into a skin or hide, [thou canst] get to the
nest, [for the bird will think that the hide is a dead animal],   R 322·1*
and she always carries away with her any dead thing she
finds.'

He and the gudeman left farewell blessings with each
other, and he set off.

He came to the place where the geera-veenuch's nest
was. He got inside the hide. When the geera-veenuch   K 1861·1
saw him, she picked him up and carried him away with   B 552
her to the nest, and left him there. There were two young   K 932

tales in *W. H. Tales*, ii., No. 44 (Campbell gave this one the same number!),
the heroine is the daughter either of the King of Lochlann or of the King of
the Kingdom of Town-under-Waves, one of the names of one of the Happy
Isles. She is either a goddess or a priestess, to judge by her ancestry.

iad. An uair a thill a' ghìre-mhìneach, is nach d'fhuair
i na h-iseanan anns an nead, thog i leatha e g'a fhàgail anns
a' chuan.

An uair a leig i as anns a' chuan e, rug e air casan oirre,
is lean e ri a dà chois, gus an d'ràinig i an t-Eilean. Chaidh
i os cionn tòrr chlach leis. An uair a leig e as a casan,
thuit e air an tòrr chlach, is chaidh a dhochann gu goirt,
agus bha e 'na shìneadh a' sileadh fala an sin.[1]

An uair a chaidh e air ghluasad, thachair abhainn air.
Lean e air aghaidh taobh an uillt, agus chunnaic e mu
a choinnimh aitreabh mhór. Ghabh e air aghaidh gu
bothan beag a chunnaic e a leth-taobh, agus ciod è bha an
sin ach tigh cailliche. An uair a chunnaic i mar a bha
e air a lot, chaidh i a dh'iarraidh cheirean da. Có air a
chaidh i a dh'iarraidh a' cheirean [sic], ach air Nighean
T 32   Rìgh an Eilein [Mhóir]. Fhuair i an ceirean uaithe, agus
gach nì bhiodh freagarrach air a shon. Chuir i ris an
ceirean, is bha i a' cumail gach bìdh is dighe ris a bhiodh
maith airson a thoirt air aghaidh, is bha i faotuinn a h-uile
nì a dh'iarradh i dha, bho Nighean an Rìgh.

Bha e tighinn air aghart gu brèagha, agus ann an ùine
gun a bhi fada, bha e leighiste. 'Tha mi an déidh cosgais
gu leòir a chur air a' bhean-uasail sin a nis,' ars e ris a'
chaillich, 'ach tha aon fhàinne an so, is thoir d'a h-ionnsuigh
e, agus gleidheadh i e.'
Is ise a thug am fàinne so dha roimhid.

Ràinig a' chailleach Nighean an Rìgh, is thug i dhì am
fàinne, is thuirt i rithe, gun robh an siod fàinne a chuir
am fear a bha a stigh aice-se d'a h-ionnsuigh (Mac
a' Bhreabadair). Rug i air an fhàinne.

---

[1] 'Anyone who will take the trouble to watch, may see hoodies on the
shores of the Western Isles, at low tide, flying up into the air and dropping
down again. It will be found that they are trying to drop large stranded
muscles [mussels] and other shells on the stones on the beach; and if left

ones in the nest. He seized them, and threw them down the rock. When the geera-veenuch returned, and found no young ones in the nest, she picked him up and carried him away with her intending to leave him in the sea.

When she let him go in order to drop him in the sea, he seized her by her two feet, and held on until she came to the Isle. She flew on and was presently hovering above a heap of stones, with him [still hanging to her]. When he let go of her feet, he fell upon the heap of stones; he was sorely injured, and there he lay, dripping blood.[1]

When he managed to get moving again, he chanced on a river. He continued to press on by the side of the burn, and [at last] he saw before him a big building. He went forward and came to a little hut that he saw at one side, and what was it but an old woman's house. When she saw how [badly] he was wounded, she went off to procure some plasters for him. To whom should she go to get plaster but to the Daughter of the King of the [Great] Isle. From her she obtained plaster and everything else that could be suitable in his case. She put the plaster on him, and kept him supplied with every kind of food and drink that would help him to progress and get well. And everything she needed for him, she obtained from the King's Daughter.

He was coming on splendidly, and in no long time, he was healed. 'I have now put that noble lady to expense enough,' said he to the old woman, 'but I have one ring here, take it to her, and let her keep it.'

It was she [the King's Daughter] who had given him this ring on a previous occasion.

The old woman went and saw the King's Daughter, and gave her the ring, telling her that it was a ring which the man who lived in her house, had sent her (the Weaver's Son). She took the ring [in her hand].

T 32

to their own devices, they will go on till they succeed in cracking the shell, and extracting the inhabitant.'—*W. H. Tales*, i., No. 17*a*, Fable 13. The secretary bird does the same with the tortoise, and the magic bird in this story wishes to do the same with our hero.

Am[1] Moire fhìn, ghrad-aithnich i e. Ghabh i sìos
far an robh e—Mac a' Bhreabadair! Chuir i a làmh 'na
poca, agus thug i sporan gobhlach a mach làn òir.[2] Thug
i siod da, agus dh'iarr i air e fhéin a chur ann an uidheam.
Ghabh e a mach, agus cheannaich e each agus deis'
aodaich. Sgrìobh e litir chun an Rìgh gun robh an siod
Breatunnach, a bha ag iarraidh cuid na h-oidhche air.

Chuir an Rìgh brath dh'a ionnsuigh, gum b'e a bheatha.
Chuir e air an deise, is chaidh e air muin an eich, is ghabh
e chun tigh an Rìgh.   Mhothaich iad a' tighinn e.
'An e siod am Breatunnach?' ars an Rìgh.
'O! is è,' ars an Nighean; 'siod am fear a thug mis'
o na geasan.'
'Is furasda sin aithneachadh; is brèagha an duine e,'
ars an Rìgh.
An uair a ràinig e, thugadh a dh'ionnsuigh an lùchairt
e, agus thugadh a stigh air bharraibh bas e.[3]
Cha robh ach nach pòsadh ise gin ach è. Bha an
Rìgh ro dheònach. Chòrd a choslas ris cho maith.
Fhuaradh pears' eaglais, agus phòs Nighean Rìgh an Eilein
Mhóir agus Mac a' Bhreabadair.

Bha banais éibhinn shunndach aca. Bha òl is ceòl
is dannsadh ann; agus is fhada bha cuimhne air banais
Mac a' Bhreabadair agus Nighean Rìgh an Eilein Mhóir.
Bha e fhéin 'na rìgh an déidh bàs a athar-chéile; agus
bha e fhéin, is a' Bhainrighinn fada beò ann am mór
thoil-inntinn.

Taken down at Polachàr [sic] South Uist from the recitation of
Patrick Smith, tenant, South Boisdale, South Uist, who heard
this and other tales often recited by Neil MacDonald, tenant,
who died about twelve years ago at an advanced age: heard
it also from Angus Smith, South Boisdale, and numerous
others: reciter says it was very common in his younger days.

By Mary herself, she recognized it instantly. Down H 94
she went to where he was—the Weaver's Son ! She put T 96
her hand in her pocket, and brought out a double-ended
purse [2] full of gold. That she gave him, and desired him
to dress and equip himself in style. Out he went, and
bought a horse and a dress. And he wrote a letter to the
King, [saying] that there was a certain Briton in the place,
who requested him to give him a night's entertainment.

The King sent him word that he should be welcome.
He put on the dress, mounted the horse, and went to the
King's house. People observed him coming.

'Is that the Briton ?' said the King.

'O ! yes, it is,' said the Daughter; 'that is the man
who delivered me from the enchantments.'

'That is easy to see; he is a fine looking man,' said the
King.

When he arrived, he was brought up to the palace, and
carried in on upturned palms.[3]

Nothing would now do, but she must marry him and
no one else. The King was very willing. His appearance
had pleased him so well. A churchman was brought, and
the Daughter of the King of the Great Isle, and the Weaver's
Son, wedded.

A right merry wedding had they and a cheery. There
was drinking and music and dancing; and the wedding
of the Weaver's Son and the Daughter of the King of the L 161
Great Isle was long remembered. The Weaver's Son
himself became King after the death of his father-in-law;
and he and the Queen lived long and in great happiness.

[1] ? Air Moire.
[2] The double-ended, or more literally, forked purse, consisted of a long
slender bag, with two ends, in each of which money could be deposited.
Two rings, sliding up and down the bag, secured the money in place. For
the recognition incident, see *Scottish Gaelic Studies*, iii., p. 186.
[3] 'air bharraibh bas': *bas*, genitive plural, as in Cruachan Beann, Dùn
Bretann, etc. Campbell wrongly thought this was a phrase wrongly used.
He translated it as 'deadly points,' and supposed it to mean that the hero
was borne aloft and carried in upon spears. But see *W. H. Tales*, ii., p. 92
or p. 77 ; iii., p. 124 or p. 138.

NOTES

MS. vol. x., No. 44. Scribe, probably Hector MacLean. On the flyleaf, Islay has written:—

'Mac a'Bhreabadair. Gaelic Index No. 44.
From Patrick Smith, South Boisdale, South Uist, July or August 1859.
He learned it from other old men: see within.
The Weaver's Son, the huntsman, of which there are several versions.
It is in no book that I know. Patrick Smith. S. Uist.
See Journal for MacFie's version, and
MacCraw's ditto [MS. vol. xiii., Nos. 329, 349].'

In his Gaelic List, Islay calls this story a 'Version of No. IV,' an inadvertence for XLIV, *W. H. Tales*, ii. For other versions, see his English List, Nos. 329, 349.

Shooting at an alternating deer-woman occurs in these, and in *Trans. Gael. Soc. Inverness*, xvi., p. 214.—Shooting at a deer which when killed turns out to be a woman, occurs in *Superstitions*, p. 126.—Shooting at a *fairy* who had adopted the mortal rôle of a deer occurs *ibid.*, p. 109, and *Scottish Celtic Review* (1885), p. 269. See also *W. H. Tales*, intro., lxxv or lxix, and *Folk-Lore*, xliii., p. 144.

D 114
·1·1*

Another instance of an alternating deer-woman is to be found in the Maiden or Gruagach and the deer which occur in *W. H. Tales*, ii., No. 38. In that tale their connection is not obvious, but they are identified in a version preserved in *Norse Influence*, p. 290. The old Lochaber deer-goddess, *Cailleach Beinne Bhric*, sometimes took the form of a gray deer. (See Principal J. C. Shairp, *Glen Desseray*, pp. 110,

A 440
·1·1*

271, and J. G. McKay on 'The Deer-Cult and the Deer-Goddess Cult of the Ancient Caledonians,' *Folk-Lore*, xliii., p. 144.)

The following group of tales approximate in theme to No. 24 very closely, with the exception that the opening incidents concerning the alternating deer-woman do not appear, but are superseded by incidents concerning three soldiers who desert from the army—an obviously modern corruption, not even three hundred years old.

The Blue Mountains, *An Deò Greine* (1922), xvii., pp. 173, 181; xviii., pp. 13, 29, 40.
The Kingdom of the Green Mountains, *Waifs and Strays*, ii., pp. 126, 458.
The Dwarfs or Pigmies, *Trans. Gael. Soc. Inverness*, xvi., p. 111.
Nighean Rìgh an Tulaich Ghuirm, the Daughter of the King of the Green Hillock, MS. vol. ix., No. 209.

For several incidents in these, see Aarne-Thompson, No. 400. In the first of these, the old woman and her son have been utterly forgotten. The sleeping-pin is stuck into the hero's coat by a ' little fair gillie ' who, we are told, was sent to the hero by the heroine. Obviously, the reciter remembered that the gillie had been sent by someone, and having forgotten the old woman, foolishly made the heroine send him, the very thing of course, which the heroine would never have done. In the other versions, an 'elfin woman' appears, or else the old woman and her son. And the fact that they appear at all is inexplicable, unless we suppose that the opening incidents originally concerned an alternating deer-woman, and not three deserters.

In *Waifs and Strays*, ii., p. 139, the reason of the old woman's hostility to the hero appears to be that she hoped her son might supersede the hero as a suitor for the heroine's hand. But a more likely clue is given in our No. 24, where the reason is that the old woman was profiting by him; she did not wish to lose (presumably) the venison and game the hunter used to bring home.

In tales in which a mortal man marries a fairy, or a seal-woman, or a swan-maiden, or a mermaid, the marriage always comes at the beginning of the story. He desires the marriage as a rule, and she, if a fairy, does also, though she leaves him as soon as he breaks the taboos she lays upon him. In other cases, she does not desire marriage, and leaves him as soon as she can. These tales belong to a large and varied class in which man has dealings with supernaturals. But in the case of a man marrying a deer-woman, she desires marriage as much as he does; she is not forced into it. The only obligation under which she lays him is to search for her. And the marriage comes at the end of the story, and they live happily ever after, and never dream of separating, in which matters the story differs fundamentally from tales of marriage with a supernatural. Therefore the woman in this story is no supernatural, but a mortal woman of solid flesh and blood. See *Béaloideas*, vii., p. 53.

SMEURAN DUBHA 'S AN FHAOILLTEACH

No. 25.   [Vol. x., No. 47]

Aarne-Thompson, No. 953

BHA Rìgh air Eirinn uair, agus air a' cheud leanabh-gille
a bha aig a' Bhainrighinn, shiubhail i.

'A nis, a Rìgh shaoghalta,'[1] ars ise, 'pòsaidh tu a rithist.'

'Cha phòs, cha phòs, m'eudail,' ars esan.

Chaidh cóig cóigean na h-Éireann a chruinneachadh,
gus an d'fhuaradh cóig paisde deug a bha air an aon
aois ri [Iain] Mac an Rìgh, a chumail cuideachd ris, agus
Z 71·10   cóig banaltruman deug chum frithealadh orra.[2]

Phòs an Rìgh saoghalta so againn a rithist. [Bha
Bainrighinn òg ùr a stigh aige.]

Bha Mac an Rìgh a' tighinn as an sgoil latha de na
laithean, agus na cóig sgoilearan deug còmhla ris, is iad
ag iomain rompa dhachaidh.

G 200   'O ! hoth !' ars a' Chailleach Chearc, agus i a' tachairt
air a' Bhainrighinn òig eile so, 'a Bhainrighinn dhona,
dhòlach,[3] ged a bhiodh sliochd agadsa, tha rìgh òg saoghalta
eile an so, a' tighinn mu do choinnimh an ceartuair; cha
duilich dhuit a aithneachadh; tha e ag iomain le caman
òir is le ball airgid; ach airson duais gle bhig, bheirinn
H 1211   seòladh dhuit air cur as da,' ars a' Chailleach Chearc.

S 31   'Ciod è an duais a bhiodh tu ag iarraidh ?' thuirt ise.
K 170   'Làn mo bhalgain duibh de chlòimh, agus làn mo
chrogain duibh de ìm, agus fad agus leud mo bhròige
de staoig.'[4]

---

[1] Earthly King; probably a Christian addition, distinguishing him from
the Heavenly King.

[2] In No. 17 (MS. vol. x., No. 31) the King of Erin has *sixteen* foster-brothers.
Both fifteen and sixteen are numbers which express completeness, totality.

[3] In some tales Islay makes these words, 'dhona, gho[bh]lach,' and

BRAMBLE BERRIES IN FEBRUARY

No. 25.   *[Vol. x., No. 47]*

Aarne-Thompson, *No. 953*

THERE was a King over Erin once, whose Queen died, when her first male-child was born.

'Now, my earthly King,'[1] said she, 'thou wilt marry again.'

'No, no, I will not marry, my treasure,' said he.

The [people of the] five fifths [= provinces] of Erin were gathered together, until fifteen children had been found, who were all of the same age as [Iain] the King's Son. They were to keep him company, and there were fifteen nurses to attend upon them.[2]   Z 71·10

Well, this earthly King of ours married again. [He now had a young Queen at home, a new one.]

One day the King's Son came out of school, accompanied by the fifteen scholars, and they were all playing at shinty and driving the ball before them on their way home.

'O ! hoh !' quoth the Hen Wife, happening to meet   G 200 this other young Queen, 'thou luckless, wretched[3] Queen, even if thou ever shouldst have children, there is coming towards thee at this very moment another young earthly king; it will not be difficult for thee to recognize him, for he is playing shinty with a golden club and a silver ball; yet for a very small reward I would shew thee how to make away with him,' says the Hen Wife.   H 1211

'What reward wouldst thou ask ?' said the Queen.   S 31

'As much wool as my little black bag would hold, as   K 170 much butter as my little black crock would hold, and the length and breadth of my shoe in steak.'[4]

translates, 'thou bad, straddling Queen.' See notes, at end of No. 46, *W. H. Tales*, ii.

[4] The curious rewards about to be bargained for, are similar to those demanded by other extortionate witches. Greed on the part of individual witches may very well have been one of the causes that led to the downfall of witchcraft as a state power. See pp. 351, 499, and *Béaloideas*, iv., p. 46.

'Ciod è làn do bhalgain duibh de chlòimh?' thuirt a'Bhainrighinn.

'Is e làn mo bhalgain duibh de chlòimh, na théid a lomadh air do [thighean]-lomaidh gu ceann sheachd bliadhna.'

'UBH! UBH!' ars ise, 'is mór am balgan a tha agad; ach ged a tha e mór féin, gheibh thu sin.—Agus ciod è làn do chrogain duibh [de ìm]?'

'Is e làn mo chrogain duibh, na théid a dhèanamh de ìm air do bhuaile gu ceann sheachd bliadhna.'

'UBH! UBH! is mór an crogan a tha agad; ach ged a tha e mór féin, gheibh thu sin; agus [ciod è] fad is leud do bhròige de staoig?'

'Is e fad is leud mo bhròige de staoig na théid a mharbhadh 'nad thigh-spadaidh gu ceann sheachd bliadhna.'

'UBH! UBH! is uamhasach a' bhròg i; ach mór ge'm bheil, gheibh thu sin.'

H 935   Arsa Cailleach nan Cearc,

Z 85*   'CUIR THUSA, MA TÀ,
            MAR CHROISIBH IS MAR GHEASAIBH AIR,
D 1273   [Is mar naoidh buaraichean
            mnatha-sìdhe siùbhlaiche seachranaiche,
F 360   An] gille maol carrach,
            As miosa na a ghille-bhròg fhéin,
            A thoirt a chinn
            Is a ch[a]omh-bheatha dheth,
            Is lodan gun dol as a bhròig,
            No tàmh air a shùil,
C 650   [Is far an caidil e aon oidhche
            Nach caidil e a dhà,]
H 530   Gus am faigh e dhuit-sa
H 1378   AM FIODH NACH 'EIL CAM NO DÌREACH.' [1]
·1*

[Chuir a' Bhainrighinn fios air Iain, Mac an Rìgh, chuice. Thàinig e, is thuirt i ris,

---

[1] The *siùbhlaichean* or *ruitheachan* or *runs*, become much fuller in detail towards the end of the MS. than at the beginning; this suggests that as the reciter, John MacDonald the Tinker, warmed to his work, his memory quickened also. The defective *siùbhlaichean* have been expanded in accordance with the later and more perfect examples. The restorations are indicated by

'How much wool would fill thy little black bag?' said the Queen.

'To fill my little black bag would take as much wool as is shorn in thy shearing-houses in seven years.'

'Oov! oov!' quoth she, 'that little bag of thine is very big; but big though it be, thou shalt have all that. And how much butter would fill thy little black crock?'

'To fill my little black crock would take all the butter that is made in thy cow-houses in seven years.'

'Oov! oov! that little crock of thine is very big; but big though it be, thou shalt have all that; and what is the length and breadth of thy shoe in steak?'

'The length and breadth of my shoe in steak is as much as is killed in thy slaughter-house in seven years.'

'Oov! oov! that is indeed an awful shoe; but big though it be, thou shalt have all that.'

So the Hen Wife answered,   H 935

'Do thou then bind him strictly,   Z 85*
    bind him by crosses and spells,
[Under pain of being struck by the nine cow-fetters   D 1273
    of the busily-roaming fairy-woman, misleader-of-travellers, F 360
And under pain of] having his head
And his dear life taken from him
By any crop-eared, rough-skinned wretch,
Worse even than his own shoe-gillie—
That he drain not water from his shoe,
Neither give rest to his eyes,
[And that where he sleep one night   C 650
He sleep not two,]
Unless and until he get for thee,   H 530
The wood that is neither bent nor straight.' [1]   H 1378
                                                 ·1*

[The Queen sent for Iain, the Son of the King, to come to her. He came and she said to him,

square brackets. The *siubhal* in this case is an incantation, for the meaning of which, see p. 230, note. In the English translation it was necessary, for the purpose of making all clear, to place some of the lines of the incantation in an order different from that of the Gaelic original. See App. p. 504.

Z 85*   'THA MISE CUR
                    MAR CHROISIBH IS MAR GHEASAIBH ORT,
D 1273   Is mar naoidh buaraichean
F 360   mnatha-sìdhe, siùbhlaiche, seachranaiche,
              An gille maol, carrach,
              As miosa na do ghille bhròg fhéin,
              A thoirt do chinn
              Is do ch[a]omh-bheatha dhìot,
              Is lodan gun dol as do bhròig,
              No tàmh air do shùil,
              Is far an caidil thu aon oidhche,
              Nach caidil thu a dhà,
C 650   Gus am faigh thu dhomh-sa
H 1378   AM FIODH NACH 'EIL CAM NO DÌREACH.']
·1*

Z 85*   DH'FHALBH IAIN N'AS FAIDE
              N' as urrainn domh-sa innseadh dhuibh-se,
              No sibh-se innseadh dhomh-sa,
              [Ged a bhiomaid ag innseadh
              Gus an tràth so a màireach,]
              Gus an robh na h-eòin bheaga,
               Bhuchullach, bhachallach,
              A' gabhail tàimh
              Ann an innseagan beaga bòidheach,[1]
              Air gach taobh de'n rathad mhór,
               Ach ged a bha,
               Cha robh tàmh airson Iain bhochd,
               [Mac Rìgh Eireann.]
              Chunnaic e an so solus beag, fada uaith,
              Is ge b'fhada uaith,
              Cha b'fhada 'ga ruigheachd e.

      Chaidh e a stigh. 'Ai! Ai! a Mhic Rìgh Éireann,'
N 825·3 arsa bean an tighe, 'thig a nuas; ciod e ghluais bho'n
bhaile thu? Is mise piuthar do mhàthar; innis domh.'
      Dh'innis e di.
      Thug i biadh is deoch dha, agus nigh i a chasan le
bùrn is bainne, agus thiormaich i iad le brat sìoda sròil;
[chuir i a luighe e,] agus chuir i a' Chruit Chànanaich
D 1231   Chiùil aig a cheann, gus am b'ann a b' fhearr a gheibheadh
D 1364·24 e cadal.

        [1] *innseagan*, holmlets, little wooded fields, or patches of arable land.
A fragment of this *siubhal* occurs *W. H. Tales*, ii., No. 52, in a variant contributed

'I BIND THEE STRICTLY   Z 85*
   BIND THEE BY CROSSES AND SPELLS,
Under pain of being struck by the nine cow-fetters   D 1273
   of the busily-roaming fairy-woman, deluder-of-travellers, F 360
And under pain of having thy head
And thy dear life taken from thee
By any crop-eared, rough-skinned wretch,
Worse even than thine own shoe-gillie,—
That thou drain not water from thy shoe,
Neither give rest to thine eye,
And that where thou sleepest one night,
Thou sleep not two,
Unless and until thou get for me   C 650
THE WOOD THAT IS NEITHER BENT NOR STRAIGHT.']   H 1378
                                                    ·1*

   AWAY WENT IAIN FARTHER   Z 85*
   Than I am able to tell you,
   Or you to tell me,
   [Even though we went on telling
   Till this time to-morrow,]
   Until the wee small birdies,
   So crested and melodious,
   Were going off to rest
   In the holmlets small and pretty,[1]
   That were on either side of the great high-road,
   But still, though they were going to rest,
   Rest for poor Iain there was none,
   [No rest for the Son of Erin's King.]
   And now he saw a little light, a long way from him,
   But a long way from him though it was,
   He was not long in reaching it.

In he went. 'Ai! Ai! thou Son of Erin's King,'
cried the goodwife, 'come forward; what has moved thee N 825·3
to leave home? I am thy mother's sister; so tell me.'
   He told her.
   Then she gave him food and drink, and washed his
feet with water and milk, and dried them with a sheet of
silk and satin; [she put him to bed,] and at his head she
placed the Humming Harp of Harmony, that he might the D 1231
better slumber.[2]   D 1364·24

by the same reciter. For other runs of this description see *Waifs and Strays*,
ii., p. 497; iii., p. 311. *W. H. Tales*, ii., Nos. 44, 51.
   [2] See No. 29 (MS. vol. x., No. 54) p. 471, and MS. vol. x., No. 121.

H 1378·
1·*

Dar a thàinig a' mhaduinn, thug i sloc sàbhaidh oirre,
agus lìon i balgan beag de mhin an t-sàbhaidh, is thug i
dha e, is thuirt i ris,
'Thoir so do'n Bhainrighinn dhona, dhòlaich, a chuir
na geasan ort.'
Phill e an sin, agus thuirt a' Bhainrighinn [is i 'ga
fhaicinn chuice a nìos an rathad] thuirt i ri Cailleach nan
Cearc,[1] 'Tha an t-òganach so a' pilltinn, le làn balg[ain]
de mhin sàibh.'

H 935

'Ach,' arsa Cailleach nan Cearc,

Z 85*
D 1273

'Cuiridh tu air falbh a rithist e,
Agus mar chroisibh is mar gheasaibh air,
[Is mar naoidh buaraichean

F 360

mnatha sìdhe, siùbhlaiche, seachranaiche,
An] gille maol, carrach,
As miosa na a ghille-bh ròg fhéin,
A thoirt a chinn
Is a ch[a]omh-bheatha dheth,
Lodan gun dol ás a bh ròig,
No tàmh air a shùil,
[Is far an caidil e aon oidhche

C 650

Nach caidil e a dhà,
Gus am faigh e dhuit-sa

H 1023·3

Smeuran Dubha 'san Fhaoillteach.'[2]

Chuir a' Bhainrighinn fios air Iain chuice.   Thàinig e,
agus thuirt i ris,

Z 85*
D 1273

'Cuiridh mi air falbh a rithist thu,
Agus mar chroisibh 's mar gheasaibh ort,
'S mar naoidh buaraichean

F 360

mnatha sìdhe, siùbhlaiche, seachranaiche,
An gille maol, carrach,
As miosa na do ghille bh ròg fhéin,
A thoirt do chinn
'S do chaomh-bheatha dhìot,
Lodan gun dol ás do bhròig,
No tàmh air do shùil,]
'S far an caidil thu aon oidhche,

C 650

Nach caidil thu a dhà,
Gus am faigh thu dhomh-sa

H 1023·3

Smeuran Dubha 'san Fhaoillteach.'

1 A' Chailleach Chearc, in MS. up to this point.
2 A proverb: for the meaning, see Notes, p. 432.

When the morning came, she betook herself to a saw pit, H 1378
.filled a little bag with sawdust, and gave it to him, saying, ·1*

'Give this to that wicked and mischievous Queen, who
bound the spells upon thee.'

He then returned, and the Queen [who saw him coming
towards her up the road] said to the Hen Wife, 'Here comes
that youth back again, with a bag full of sawdust.'

'But,' said the Hen Wife, H 935

'THOU SHALT SEND HIM AWAY AGAIN, Z 85*
Binding him by crosses and spells, D 1273
[Under pain of being struck by the nine cow-fetters
    of the busily-roaming fairy-woman, misleader-of-wayfarers F 360
And under pain of] having his head
And his dear life taken from him
By any crop-eared, rough-skinned wretch,
Worse even than his own shoe-gillie,—
That he drain not water from his shoe,
Neither give rest to his eyes,
[And that where he sleep one night,
He sleep not two, C 650
Unless and until he get for thee
BRAMBLE BERRIES IN FEBRUARY.'[2] H 1023·3

The Queen sent for Iain to come to her.   He came,
and she said to him,

'I WILL SEND THEE AWAY AGAIN, Z 85*
Binding thee by crosses and spells, D 1273
Under pain of being struck by the nine cow-fetters F 360
    of the busily-roaming fairy-woman, misleader-of-wayfarers,
And under pain of having thy head
And thy dear life taken from thee
By any crop-eared, rough-skinned wretch,
Worse even than thine own shoe-gillie,—
That thou drain not water from thy shoe
Neither give rest to thine eye,]
And that where thou sleep one night,
Thou sleep not two, C 650
Unless and until thou get for me
BRAMBLE BERRIES IN FEBRUARY.' H 1023·3

Z 85*

DH'FHALBH IAIN N'AS FAIDE
N' as urrainn domh-sa innseadh dhuibh-se,
No sibhse innseadh dhomh-sa,
[Ged a bhiomaid ag innseadh
Gus an tràth so a màireach,
Gus an robh na h-eòin bheaga,
Bhuchullach, bhachallach,
A' gabhail tàimh
Ann an innseagan beag, bòidheach,
Air gach taobh de'n rathad mhór,
Ach ged a bha,
Cha robh tàmh airson Iain bhochd,
Mac Rìgh Éireann,
Agus stad cha d'rinneadh leis,]
Gus an d'ràinig e
Tigh piuthar a mhàthar,
[Agus a dh'innis e dhi
Gun robh e an tòir air
SMEURAN DUBHA 'SAN FHAOILLTEACH.]

'Och! och! Iain bhochd!' ars ise, 'tha eagal orm-sa
Z 71·5 nach pill thu-sa; is iomadh rìgh agus ridire a chaidh air
Z 130·3* an tòir, is cha do phill duine riamh a dh'innseadh an sgeòil;
F 971·5 chan 'eil na smeuran so a' fàs ann an àite air bith fo sheachd
G 11·2 rionnagan ruadh an t-saoghail, ach an seòmar a tha aig
F 686·2* trì famhairean; tha iad a' cinntinn an sin le teas nan
G 691·1* corp [a thaisg na famhairean anns an t-seòmar sin].'

Ach tàmh no clos cha b'urrainn do Iain fhaotainn.
Thug e na buinn as, gus an d'ràinig e tigh nam famhairean.
F 771·4·1 Cho luath 's a chaidh e a stigh, chunnaic e boirionnach
brèagha 'na suidhe, 's i a' cumha is a' caoidh, agus naoidhean
ri a taobh.
'O! a Mhic Rìgh Eireann,' ars ise, 'ciod è thug an so
thu? Bidh tu marbh an nochd.'

['Cha dèan tùirse ach truaghan,' ars Iain: ach cha
b' fhada bha e an sin, an uair a chualas stioram, starum,
stararaich a' tighinn aig na famhairean. Bha fìor-thalamh
a' dol a measg a chéile, agus crith a' tighinn fo'n ursainn
is fo shuidheachain an tighe, clachan beaga a' dannsadh

Away went Iain farther   Z 85*
Than I am able to tell you,
Or you to tell me,
[Even though we went on telling
Till this time to-morrow,
Until the wee small birdies,
So crested and melodious,
Were going off to rest
In the holmlets small and pretty,
That were on either side of the great high road,
But still, though they were going to rest,
Rest for poor Iain there was none,
No rest for the Son of Erin's King,
And never a stop was made by him,]
Until he had at last reached
His mother's sister's house,
[And had told her
That he was seeking for
Bramble Berries in February.]

'Och ! och ! poor Iain !' said she, 'I fear me that thou
wilt never return; many a king and many a knight has
there been who set out to get them, but no man ever   Z 71·5
returned to tell the tale; nowhere under the seven red stars   Z 130·3*
of the universe do those berries grow, except in a room   F 971·5
belonging to three giants; they grow there because of the   G 11·2
heat of the corpses [which the giants have stored up in   F 686·2*
that room].'   G 691·1*

So neither rest nor peace might Iain get. He took to
his heels, and hastened thence, and travelled until he came
to the house of the giants. When he went in, he saw a   F 771·4·1
handsome woman seated there, weeping and lamenting,
and at her side a babe.

'O ! Son of the King of Erin,' said she, 'what has
brought thee here ? Thou wilt be a dead man
to-night.'

['Only a poor wretch makes moan,' replied Iain ; but
he had not long been there, when the giants were heard
coming, stamping, tramping, battering. The very earth
was convulsed, the door-posts and supports of the house
quivered to their foundations, the little stones danced

ri clachan móra, is clachan móra a' dannsadh ri clachan beaga.]

Chunnacas na fir mhóra a' tighinn, agus shìn Iain e fhéin am measg nan corp, is bha e lìonadh a phòcannan leis na smeuran.

Dar a thàinig na famhairean dachaidh, bha cailleach mharbh [1] a' slaodadh ri geinneag còta gach fir aca. Thug iad seòrsa dathaidh dhaibh, is rinn iad an tràth-feasgair orra.

G 691·1* Anns a' mhaduinn am màireach, dh'ith iad na dh'fhàg iad de na cailleachan, ach dh'iarr am famhair a bu mhó air an fhamhair a bu lugha, e a dhol suas agus staoig a
G 86 thoirt as a' chorp a b'ùire 's a bu reamhra gheibheadh e. Thug e an stiall ud á Iain, bho a chruachan sìos gu a ghlùn.

'Fòil ! fòil !' arsa am fear mór, 'is e so feòil as fhearr a dh'ith mi riamh—falbh a suas agus thoir a nuas sliosag eile as a' chorp cheudna, agus tilg 'san togsaid uisge e, 'ga chumail ùr gus am pill sinn.'

[Agus o'n a bha an t-olc an dàn do Iain, chaidh sliosag eile a thoirt as, agus chaidh e fhéin a thilgeil anns an togsaid uisge.]

Dh'fhalbh na famhairean an so a shealg. [Ma dh'fhalbh, cha b'ann gun fhios do Iain, agus thàinig e as an togsaid,] agus dar a bha Iain eadar dà dhorus,[2]
G 400 is e falbh, thàinig fear de na famhairean air thòir saighid a dhìochuimhnich e, agus choinnich e Iain.

'Ho ! hoth ! fhir eile,' ars am famhair, 'is fada bho'n a bha dùil agam riut; bha 'san fhàistneachd gun tigeadh thu [3] ach cha mhath tha fhios agam ciod è nì mi riut; chan fhiach leam d'ithe.'

---

[1] In *Waifs and Strays*, iii., p. 284, brings 'a dead old woman for his own supper, and a fresh-water salmon for that of the King's daughter.' The *cailleach mharbh*, or dead old woman, is probably the black sea bream, called in English *the old wife*, because the head of the fish bears a striking resemblance to the head of an old woman wearing a mutch. The *cailleach mharbh* was the usual repast for a giant. See MS. vol. x., Nos. 121, 126, and *W. H. Tales*, i., No. 6. This suggests that some of these giants may be connected with the

against the big ones, and the big stones danced against
the little ones.]

The great fellows could now be seen coming, and Iain
went and lay down amongst the bodies, and began filling
his pockets with the bramble berries.

Home came the giants with a dead old woman [1] hanging
to the coat button of each of them. They gave them a
sort of singeing, and then made their supper off them.

In the morning, having eaten what they had left of G 691·1*
the carlins, the biggest giant desired the smallest one to
go up and cut a steak out of the freshest and fattest body he G 86
could find. [This he did,] and oh! what a slice did he
take out of Iain, from his hip right down to his knee.

'Gently! bide a wee!' said the big giant, 'this is the
best flesh I ever ate—go up and bring down another slice
out of the same body, and throw the body itself into the
water-butt, to keep it fresh till we return.'

[And so, as Iain was fated to suffer evil, another slice
was cut out of him, and he himself was thrown into the
hogshead of water.]

The giants hereupon went off to hunt. [But if they did,
this was not without Iain's knowledge, and so he came
out of the hogshead,] but just when he was in the passage
between the two doors,[2] and about to flee, one of the giants
came back to fetch an arrow he had forgotten, and met G 400
Iain there.

'Ho! hoh! thou other man,' quoth the giant, 'long
have I been expecting thee; it was in the prophecies [3]
that thou shouldst come, but I know not very well what to
do with thee; I would not condescend to eat thee.'

---

sea, and therefore possibly relations of the Tuairisgeal. See Nos. 1, 2 (MS.
vol. viii., Nos. 106, 203). See *Béaloideas*, vii., p. 220.

[2] *eadar-dà-dhorus* = the passage or space between the outer door and the
kitchen door: *eadar-dà-bhì* = between the two door-posts, in the doorway.
In *Trans. Gael. Soc. Inverness*, xix., p. 31, occurs *eadar dhà bhì a's dorus*.

[3] Giants frequently inform heroes that their meeting had been prophesied.
See tale MS. vol. x., No. 97, and *W. H. Tales*, i., No. 5; iii., No. 57.
Waifs and Strays, ii., p. 357; iii., p. 299.

Ach is e a bh'ann, gun do cheangail iad ris na h-eich e, agus leig iad na coin mhóra as a dhéidh, agus dar a shaoil leo gun robh Iain marbh, thilg iad thar creig e.

An uair a fhuair am boirionnach na famhairean air falbh, thug i na buinn aisde mar a b'fhearr a dh'fhaodadh i, agus dar a thàinig na famhairean dachaidh, is a chunnaic iad gun d'fhalbh am boirionnach, chuir iad na coin mhóra air a luirg; ach cha leanadh iad ach an lorg a rinn Iain le a fhuil, gus an d'ràinig iad mullach na creige. Bha na famhairean ann an corruich mhóir ris na coin, agus is e a bh'ann, gun do thilg iad saighead trompa, is mharbh iad iad. [Agus thàir am boirionnach as le a beatha.]

Ciod è thachair a bhi 'sa chreig thar an do thilgeadh Iain ach nead iolaire, is tuitear e 'san nead. Dh' ith Iain iseanan na h-iolaire leis an acras, agus gach oidhche bha an iolaire 'ga chumail blàth a' toirt feòla is sìthne chuige.

Ach ghabh e sgìos a bhi 'san nead, agus oidhche de na h-oidhcheanan agus an iolaire 'na cadal, cheangail Iain e fhéin ri a spògan le a ghallois [1] is le a chràbhat, agus dar a dhùisg i, dh'fhalbh i is Iain a' slaodadh rithe, agus an ceud àite anns an do stad i, b'ann an gàradh mór athair Iain ann an rìoghachd Eireann.

'Nis,' ars Iain, 'a bheathaich bhochd, bho'n a rinn thusa so dhomhsa, cha dèan mise cron air bith ortsa,' is dh'fhuasgail Iain e fhéin, is chaidh e a stigh do thigh a athar [is na smeuran dubha aige].

Bha iongantas uamhasach air gach neach smeuran dubha fhaicinn mu'n am ud de'n bhliadhna.

Dh'fhalbh a' Bhainrighinn do thigh Cailleach nan Cearc, agus dh'innis i dhì gun tàinig am fleasgach ud dachaidh a rithist, agus na smeuran aige.

'Ai ! Ai !' arsa Cailleach nan Cearc, 'is cinnteach gu bheil n'as miosa na e fhéin 'ga chuideachadh; ach cuir thusa air falbh aon uair eile e,

---

[1] 'galais,' in An t-Ogha Mór, p. 80, by Aonghas MacDhonnachaidh (Glasgow, 1913).

And so what they did was to tie him to horses, and set great hounds after him, and when they thought that he was dead, they threw him over a rock.

Q 415
·I ·2*

Now when the woman saw that the giants had gone, she took to her heels as hard as she could, and when the giants came home and found that the woman had gone, they set the great hounds on her track; but the great hounds would follow nothing but the track Iain had made with his blood, and they followed it until they reached the top of the rock. The giants were therefore in a great rage with the hounds, and so they shot them through with arrows, transfixing and killing them. [But the woman escaped with her life.]

Now what should there be in the rock over which Iain had been thrown but an eagle's nest, and into this nest he fell. He ate the eagle's young ones in his hunger, and every night the eagle used to keep him warm, and bring him flesh and venison.

R 322*

But Iain got tired of being in the nest, and upon a night of nights when the eagle was asleep, he tied himself to her claws with his braces and cravat, and when she awoke she went off with him hanging to her. The first place at which she stopped was the great garden of Iain's father, in the Kingdom of Erin.

B 542·I·I

' Now,' quoth Iain, 'thou poor creature, since thou hast done this for me, I will do no harm whatever to thee.' Then he freed himself, and entered his father's house, [taking the bramble berries with him].

Tremendous was the astonishment that all felt at seeing bramble berries at that time of year.

H 1023·3

The Queen went to the Hen Wife's house, and told her that that young fellow had come home again, and had brought the berries with him.

'Ai ! Ai !' quoth the Hen Wife, 'it must be that there are some helping him who are worse than even he himself; but do thou send him away once more,

H 935

Z 85* IS CUIR MAR CHROISIBH IS MAR GHEASAIBH AIR,
D 1273 Is mar naoidh buaraiche mnatha-sìdhe,
F 360 [siùbhlaiche, seachranaiche,
        An] gille maol, carrach,
        As miosa na a ghille-bhròg fhéin,
        A thoirt a chinn
        'S a ch[a]omh-bheatha dheth,
        Nach téid lodan as a bhròig,
        No tàmh air a shùil,
        Is nach caidil e dà oidhche
        Far an caidil e a h-aon,
C 650   Gus am faigh e dhuit-se
H 1154 STEUD CHOIRE CHIARRAICH,[1]

oir,' ars ise,

B 181·1 'Beiridh ise air a' ghaoith luaith Mhàirt,
         'S a' ghaoth luath Mhàirt, cha bheir i oirre.'

[Chuir a' Bhainrighinn fios air Iain d'a h-ionnsuigh,
agus chuir i na croisean is na geasan air, mar a dh'àithn
Cailleach nan Cearc. Ach mar nach deachaidh siod air
mhi-thapadh do Iain,]

Z 85*   'A BHEAN,' ars esan,

H 951·1* 'THA MISE CUR DE CHROISIBH
D 1273   IS DE GHEASAIBH ORT-SA,
D 5·1   Gum bi cas agad air an tigh mhór,
          Is cas air a' chearn,
          Do leth-phluic làn min eòrna,
          Is do leth-phluic eile làn bùirn is salainn,
          Iteag geòidh 'na do shròin,
          Is gach taobh a stiùireas a' ghaoth,
          Gun stiùir i thusa,
          GUS AM PILL MISE.'[2]

'Croisean air do gheasaibh, a bhalaich,' ars ise.[3]

---

[1] As will be seen, this last be-spelling *siubhal* or *run* is the most perfect
example.
[2] The hero, in self-defence, fights the enemy with her own weapons.
For an Irish instance of a hero's counter-be-spelling, see Jeremiah Curtin,
Hero Tales of Ireland, p. 463. See also Appendix, p. 507.
[3] *i.e.* withdraw thy spells—retract, revoke thy words. The hero's counter-
spells are so drastic, that the enemy would like him to abrogate or rescind
them, and restore things to the *status quo ante*. But the hero will have none
of her suggestions, and insists upon events taking their course in accordance

AND DO THOU LAY UPON HIM AS CROSSES, CROSSES AND BINDING-SPELLS, Z 85*
Upon pain of being struck by the nine cowfetters of the fairy- D 1273
    woman, [wildly-roaming, wayfarer-deluding,] F 360
And upon pain of having his head
And his dear life taken from him
By any crop-eared, rough-skinned wretch,
Worse even than his own shoe gillie,—
That he drain not water from his shoe,
Nor even give rest to his eye,
And that where he sleep one night
He sleep not two,
Unless and until he get for thee C 650
THE STEED OF CORRIE CIARRACH,[1] H 1154

for,' said she,

    'That steed can overtake the swift March wind, B 181·1
    But the swift March wind cannot overtake her.'

[The Queen sent word for Iain to come to her, and
she bound the crosses and spells upon him as the Hen
Wife had commanded. But as Iain was not to be daunted
by that,]

    'WOMAN,' said he, Z 85*

        'ON THEE DO I LAY AS CROSSES, H 951·1*
            AS CROSSES AND HARD-BINDING SPELLS, D 1273
        That thou stand with one foot on the palace, D 5·1
        And thine other foot set on the kitchen,
        Have thy one cheek with barley meal filled,
        With salt and with water the other,
        Have a goose feather fixed in thy nose,
        And be twisted and steered by the wind,
        In whichever direction it veer
            TILL I RETURN.' [2]

'[Counteracting] crosses be upon thy spells, thou loon,'
said she.[3]

with the terms originally laid down. The Queen apparently fulfils her
part, being as much bound by the hero's spells as he is by hers. The Queen's
expression, 'Croisean air do gheasaibh,' may be compared with—

    Tha siod air a chroiseadh.
    That has been crossed, *i.e.* forbidden, interdicted,

and with two proverbs given by *Nicolson*, pp. 155, 156,

    ' Croiseam sgiorradh ! The cross between me and mishap !
    Croiseam thu ! The cross be between us !'

'Cha chroisean is cha gheasan, ach mar siod,' ars esan.

Z 85*

DH'FHALBH ESAN A NIS N'AS FAIDE
N' as urrainn domh-sa innseadh dhuit-sa,
No thusa innseadh dhomh-sa,
Ged a bhiomaid ag innseadh
Gus an tràth so a màireach,
[Gus an robh na h-eòin bheaga,
Bhuchullach, bhachallach,
A' gabhail tàimh
Ann an innseagan beaga bòidheach,
Air gach taobh de'n rathad mhór,
Ach ged a bhà,]
Cha robh tàmh air son Iain bhochd,
Mac Rìgh Eireann,
[Agus stad cha d'rinneadh leis,]
Gus mu dheireadh thall an d'ràinig e
Tigh famhair.

'Ma tà, a ghille òig,' ars am famhair, 'ciod air a tha thusa math?'

'Tha mi 'nam ghille-stàbuill math.'

G 452*
H 901·1

'Is sin an rud air a bheil feum mór agamsa,' ars am famhair; 'an fear a bha agam mu dheireadh, sin a cheann air an stob thall.'

G 462

Bha Iain a' taitinn ris an fhamhair gu ro-mhath, ach coma leat, thuirt Iain ris fhéin, 'Feuchaidh mi ri falbh,' agus oidhche de na h-oidhchean, falbhar Iain leis an Steud a bha aig an fhamhair anns an stàbull, agus 'sa

G 610

mhaduinn am màireach, dar a dh'éirich am famhair, bha Iain air chall, agus bha an Steud air falbh.

D 1225
R 350

Shéid am famhair an fheadag, is ma bha Iain [agus an Steud] luath a' falbh, bu sheachd luaithe air ais iad.

'Ho! hoth! ha! hath! a Mhic Rìgh Eireann,' ars am fear mór, 'bha 'san fhàisneachd gun robh thu tighinn g'a goid; chan 'eil fhios agam an ann do na coin mhóra a bheir mi thu 'sa' mhaduinn, no a chuireas mi thu fo shileadh nan lòchran.' Ach cheangail e Iain, is thilg e ann an cùil na mòine e.

'There shall be neither crosses nor spells, but as has been said,' said he.

> AWAY HE NOW WENT FARTHER   Z 85*
> Than I am able to tell thee,
> Or thou to tell me,
> Even though we went on telling
> Till this time to-morrow,
> [Until the wee small birdies,
> So crested and melodious,
> Were going off to rest
> In the holmlets small and pretty,
> That were on either side of the great high road,
> But still, though they were going to rest,]
> Rest for poor Iain there was none,
> No rest for the Son of Erin's King,
> [And never a stop was made by him,]
> Until at length and at last he came
> To a giant's house.

'Well, young lad,' quoth the giant, 'what art thou good at ?'

'I am good as a stable-boy.'

'I have great need of that same,' quoth the giant;   G 452*
'there on yonder stake is the head of the last one I had.'   H 901·1

Iain pleased the giant very much, but never mind,   G 462
Iain said to himself, 'I will try to make off,' and on a night of nights, off he goes with the Steed that the giant had in the stable. The next morning when the giant arose, Iain   G 610
was not to be found, and the Steed was gone.

The giant blew his whistle, and quickly though Iain   D 1225
[and the Steed] had gone away, they were seven times   R 350
quicker returning.

'Ho ! hoh ! ha ! hah ! thou Son of the King of Erin,' said the great fellow, 'it was foretold in the prophecies that thou wert to come and steal the Steed; I do not know yet whether I will give thee in the morning to the great hounds, or whether I will put thee under the drippings of the lamps.' And he trussed Iain up, and pitched him into the peat corner.

Anns a' mhaduinn, thug e a mach e.

'Tha mi am barail,' thuirt esan, 'gun cuir mi fo shileadh nan lòchran thu,' agus a cheud bhoinne thuit, ghearr e troigh na coise dheth.[1]

Q 451·2

'An robh thu riamh ann an càs bu mhó na sin, Iain?' thuirt esan.

'Moire! bha mi an càs na bu mhó na so cuideachd, is thàinig mi as.'

R 153·3·3   ·'Innis domh an càs, Iain, is cumaidh mi boinne dhìot.'

'Chaidh mi a dh'iarraidh an fhiodha sin nach 'eil cam no dìreach, is air leam gun robh an càs gu math cruadalach;' ach leig e [le] boinne eile tuiteam, is ghearr e a chas bho'n ghlùn.

'An robh thu an càs riamh cho cruaidh so, Iain?' 'Moire, bha! chaidh [mi] a dh'iarraidh SMEURAN DUBHA 'SAN FHAOILLTEACH, agus rug na famhairean orm, [is thug iad dà shliosaig asam,] is thilg iad ann an togsaid uisge mi; [is cheangail iad ris na h-eich mi, is leig iad na coin mhóra rium;] 'na dhéidh sin thilg iad thar creig mi, is bha mi naoidh latha is naoidh oidhchean ann an nead iolaire, ged a tha mi an diugh fo do làimh-sa gun tròcair.'

'A chrochaire na croiche!' arsa màthair an fhir mhóir, 'sin agad am fear a shàbhail thusa agus mise bho na

N 763*   famhairean, agus thu 'nad leanabh beag!'[2]

'Marbhaisg oirbh, a bhean! carson nach d'innis sibh sin domh-sa na bu luaithe?'

E 102   Thug e an sin tarruing air an t-searraig ìocshlaint, is
D 1500   rinn e Iain cho ùr fallain is a bha e riamh.
·1·19

Fhuair Iain an so a roghainn de nigheanan an fhamhair, agus Steud Choire Chiarraich is a dìollaid air a h-òradh,

---

[1] Torture. See Notes.

[2] Similar questions, answers, incidents, similar curtailing of his experiences by hero and similar interposition on the part of the woman he had saved, occur in tales of the Conall Crà-Bhuidhe group; see *W. H. Tales*, i., Nos. 5, 6, 7. It is possible that these incidents have been imported into this story from other tales. Otherwise, we must assume that giants grow up very quickly, seeing that this particular giant, who when a child was saved by the hero in the course of his second labour, has attained during the course of the third

In the morning, the giant took him out.

'I think,' said he, 'that I will put thee under the drippings of the lamps,' and [so he did, and] the first drop that fell, cut Iain's foot right off.[1]   Q 451·2

'Wert thou ever in a worse strait than that, Iain?' said he.

'By Mary! I was in a worse strait than even this, but I escaped.'

'Tell me about that strait, Iain, and I will keep the drop   R 153·3·3 from falling on thee.'

'Why, I went to seek for the wood that is neither crooked nor straight, and that was a case, methinks, of very great hardship;' but the giant let another drop fall, and cut his leg off from his knee.

'Wert thou ever in as hard a strait as this, Iain?'

'By Mary, I was! I went once to seek for BRAMBLE BERRIES IN FEBRUARY, and giants caught me [and took two slices out of me,] and threw me into a hogshead of water; [they also tied me to horses, and set the great hounds at me;] after that they threw me over a rock, and I was nine days and nine nights in the nest of an eagle, though I am to-day in thy merciless clutches.'

'Thou gallows-hangman!' said the giant's mother, 'see! this is the very man who saved thee and me from the   N 763* giants, when thou wert but a tiny baby!'[2]

'Death-wrappings be upon ye, woman! why did ye not tell me that sooner?'

Then the giant brought forth the vessel of healing   E 102 balsam, and [with it] he made Iain as free of wounds and   D 1500 as well as ever he had been.   ·1·19

Thereupon, Iain got his choice of the giant's daughters; and the Steed of Corrie Ciarrach, whose saddle was all

labour such a considerable measure of maturity as to have daughters of his own, one of whom the hero marries. Heroes marry the daughters of giants in several tales, but not, as in this case, with the giant's consent. Social relations between giants and men are implied in several tales. See *W. H. Tales*, i., Nos. 2 and 9. Giants, heroes and knights are associated in *Trans. Gael. Soc. Inverness*, xxxiv., p. 43. Giants and robbers in No. 13 (MS. vol. x., No. 26).

is an t-Slabhruidh Eisdeachd,[1] agus a cheud chrathadh a thug e air an t-Slabhruidh, chuala iad ann an cóig cóigibh na h-Eireann [i], is an Drochaid Cheudaibh na[m] Maithean.[2]

[Chuir Iain a chas thairis air an Steud, agus Moire! b'i an curaidh i; agus thug e Nighean an Fhamhair a suas air a chùl, agus bha iad a' cumail air 'nan steudaibh a' dol dachaidh.][3]

Nis, bho'n a dh'fhalbh Iain bho'n tigh, laigh a athair air a leabaidh dhubhaich, agus chaill e trian de a neart, is trian de a léirsinn, is trian de a chlaistneachd; agus mar a bha Iain a' dlùthachadh air an tigh, fhuair a athair trian de a neart, is trian de a léirsinn is trian de a chlaistneachd, agus dar a bha e a stigh air ùrlar a' bhaile, leum a athair as a leabaidh dhubhaich, cho ùr, fallain 'sa bha e riamh.[4]

'Hu! huth!' ars an seann duine, 'ma tha mo mhac-sa beò, tha e a stigh air ùrlar a' bhaile an diugh.'

Thàinig Iain am fradharc a' bhaile, agus thuit a mhuime 'na smal bochd bho mhullach bàrr mór a'chaisteil.[5]

Phòs Iain an so Nighean an Fhamhair, agus rinn iad banais mhór ghreadhnach, a mhair dà fhichead là is dà fhichead oidhche.

Agus chuir iad sia daoine deug do'n choillidh dharaich, a ghearradh glas daraich, agus rinn iad teine mór, is thilg

D 2161
'4·10·4*

D 2061
·1·1

Z 71·10

P 653·1*

[1] At public assemblies, the Chain of Audience was shaken, probably several times, for the purpose of demanding silence and procuring a hearing. An echo of this ancient practice is perhaps to be traced in the modern idiom 'air a' cheud chrathadh rithe' = at the first blush of the thing, at the first opportunity, *lit.* at the first shaking in connection with the thing. See *An Gàidheal* (1877), vi., p. 238. In *Seanchaidh na Traghad*, p. 42 (Iain MacCormaic, published Æneas MacKay, Stirling, 1911), *ris* is used instead of *rithe*. For the practice of chain-shaking, see Dr D. Hyde, *Beside the Fire*, p. 181—'there are three chains in the palace, one of gold, one of silver, and one of findrinny (a kind of metal, perhaps bronze) which are shaken to seat the people at the banquet, and to secure their silence; but whoever spoke after the gold chain had been shaken, did it on pain of his head.'

[2] It is for 'Triocha Céad na Midhe' (of Meath). In the Cantred of Land belonging to the Nobles.—*Celtic Review*, i., p. 128. See Dr A. Carmichael's

gilded, that did he also receive, as well as the Chain of
Audience.[1] And the very first shake that he gave the
Chain, people heard it in the five provinces of Erin, and in
the Bridge of the Hundreds of the Nobles.[2]

[Iain threw his leg over the Steed, and by Mary!
she was the champion; and he took the Giant's Daughter
up behind him, and home they went, riding hard.][3]

Now ever since Iain had left home, his father had
been lying on a bed of sorrow, having lost a third of
his strength, a third of his sight, and a third of his
hearing; but as Iain was drawing nearer home, his D 2161
father recovered the third of his strength, and the third ·4·10·4*
of his sight, and the third of his hearing, until at last,
upon his [Iain's] entering into home territory, his father
sprang from off his bed of sorrow, as fresh and well as
ever he had been.[4]

'Hu! huh!' said the old man, 'if my son indeed live,
'tis into the domain of his own homeland he's come this
day.'

Iain now came within sight of the home farm, and
thereupon his step-mother crumbled miserably to dust and D 2061
fell down, down from the top of the great castle tower.[5] ·1·1

So Iain married the Giant's Daughter, and they
celebrated a great magnificent wedding, a wedding which
lasted forty days and forty nights.

And they sent sixteen men to the oak forest to cut Z 71·10
green oak [faggots], and they made a big fire, and threw

Deirdire, p. 152. 'Triúcha chéud,' in the older language. See *Rosg Gàidhlig*,
p. 285 (292). Other corruptions are (1) Drochaid cheudan na maith,
(2) Drochaid cheudan nam Mith, (3) Drochaid shaor ann an Lochlainn.—
W. H. Tales, i., pp. 174, 304, or 178, 313; ii., pp. 183 or 197. (4) Drochaid-
nan-Teud, *An Gàidheal*, (1876), v., pp. 261-2. (5) Drochaid nan ceud,
(6) Drochaid nan ceudan, (7) Drochaid Cheudna na Mith, *Trans. Gael. Soc.
Inverness*, xiii., pp. 72, 83.

[3] *Lit.* they were keeping at it, as steeds, the horse and the two riders being
all classed as steeds. For this paragraph, interpolated for the sake of connection, see *An Gàidheal* (1875), iv., p. 308.

[4] See for this incident, *Celtic Review*, vi., p. 374. *Waifs and Strays*, iv.,
pp. 21, 27, 84. *Trans. Gael. Soc. Inverness*, xxxiv., p. 49, and MS. vol. x.,
No. 126. Something similar will be found in *Celtic Review*, i., p. 172.

[5] As does the *muime* in *W. H. Tales*, ii., No. 46.

G 275·3   iad a' Chailleach [Chearc] 'na theis meadhon, is bha i
Q 414   ag éigheach is a' sgreuchail dar a dh'fhàg mise iad.

From John McDonald, Tinker, Inveraray.
Collected by Hector Urquhart.

NOTES

MS. vol. x., No. 47. On the flyleaf of the MS. Islay has written:—

'47. Smeuran Dubh ['s]an Fhaoi[l]teach. Unlike any of the others at first: old, for it is a proverb, has relatives in German and in Norse and a bad version of Cath nan Eun [*recte* Conall Crà Bhuidhe, *W. H. Tales*, i., No. 5]. Heard from John Tinker at Inveraray . . . [?] see Notes.' Islay calls the story 'wild—good.'—*W. H. Tales*, iv., p. 405, and refers to it, *ibid.*, i., intro., xxxvii or xliv.

John Tinker also recited the published tales Nos. 9, 31, 42, 46, 52, or versions of them. Also Nos. 46 and 68 of MS. vol. x., and 274, 275 of MS. vol. xi. All his tales are racy and un-Anglicized, and therefore nearer the primitive. A family of West Highland tinkers, who were almost certainly his descendants, and who were well acquainted with Shelta, Romanes, Gaelic and English, were encountered by Dr Fearon Ranking in August 1890. See *Trans. Gael. Soc. Inverness*, xxiv., p. 431.

H 1023·3   For the meaning of the title, see Nicolson's *Gaelic Proverbs*, pp. 51, 349.
F 971·5   'B'e sin na smiaran-dubha 'san Fhaoilleach. *That were the bramble berries in February.* Said of anything out of season.'

'Smiaran dubha 's an Fhaoilleach, 'us uibhean fhaoileag a's t-Earrach. *Bramble berries in February, and sea-gull eggs in Spring.* Things out of season.'

The season of Faoillteach was divided into two halves, F. Geamhraidh and F. Earraich, the F. of Winter, and the F. of Spring. According to some authorities, the first half was the last fortnight of January, the second the first fortnight of February.

A version of No. 25 (MS. vol. x., No. 47) occurs in Islay's English List, No. 304. It is so much condensed as to be scarcely more than a summary.

In two stories, 'Mórag an Rìgh,' *ibid.*, MS. vol. ix., No. 124, and in

---

[1] See *Celtic Review*, iv., pp. 80, 90, 'Imtheachd na Tromdhaimhe,' Life of St Kentigern, c. 37.

[2] Curiously enough there appeared in *The Daily Mail* of 7th February 1930, the following letter to the Editor : 'Sir, while at my work felling trees in the noted Selsdon Woods I discovered these blackberries, which I considered most interesting, as in 55 years' experience I have never before seen ripe and ripening blackberries in February.—W. J. LANE [of] Cosy Corner, Selsdon Park, Sanderstead, Surrey.' (Mr Lane sent to *The Daily Mail* several sprays of ripe blackberries, a photo of which was printed with the letter.)

the [Hen] Wife into the very middle of it, and she was G 275·3
still shouting and screaming when I left them [all].   Q 414

' Gruagach an Eilein,' *Celtic Magazine*, xiii., pp. 416, 486, 496, a wicked
stepmother sends a heroine in quest of bramble berries in February.
The heroine obtains them, but her rival fails. The incidents in both
tales differ from each other and from this tale (No. 25, MS. vol. x.,
No. 47), but are related to Nos. 14 and 43 (*W. H. Tales*, i. and ii.)
and No. 308, Islay's MS. vol. xi. See also *Béaloideas*, vii., p. 159.

The Cliar Sheanchain,[1] a bardic company, which travelled about
all over the country, used to ask for 'Smeuran Dubha 'sna Faoillich
Earraich,' 'ripe brambles in the beginning of spring,' when they
came to the house where they intended to stay. They were entitled
to hospitable entertainment until their demand was complied with
or they chose to depart. On their making the usual demand at a
house in Badcall, at Little Lochbroom, one spring day, the goodman
led them to his cornyard to a bush which he had covered with his
oilskin coat in autumn (a painfully modern touch), and he presented F 971·5
them then and there with ripe brambles. Sorely put out by this untoward occurrence they left the place, travelled on and were drowned.—
Trans. Gael. Soc. Inverness, xxvi., p. 298; xxix., p. 201; xxxii., p. 296.
Bàrdachd Ghàidhlig, xvii. *Celtic Review*, iv. pp. 80-88; viii., p. 321.
Waifs and Strays, ii. pp. 207, 465.[2] *Celtic Magazine*, iii., p. 179.

Campbell gives a riddle about sawdust, *W. H. Tales*, ii., No. 50.   H 1378
'2. What is the wood that is not bent nor straight?   ·1*
    Sawdust. It is neither bent nor straight.   H 530

This riddle forms part of a very long and curious story which I heard
told at Inveraray, at Easter, 1859, and which is written down.' He
also says in reference to a story in which Fionn made a fire of sawdust,
'The incident of sawdust as wood that grew and is neither crooked nor
straight, is proverbial in the Highlands,' *ibid.*, iii., p. 352 *n*,[3] or p. 336 *n*.

[3] For other versions of Fionn and the fire of sawdust, see *Waifs and Strays*,
iv., pp. 16-28. *Celtic Review*, i., p. 360; ii., p. 270. The fire is said to have
been made of augur [= auger] dust and the 'hearts' of feathers, *ibid.*, ii., p. 15;
this looks like some further riddle similar to that about the auger-dust given
in Nicolson, p. 153—'Co dhiùbh 's fhusa bata dheanamh de'n ghuairne mu
ghuairn, no cuaille de'n ghiùrne mu ghiùrn? *Whether is it easier to make, a
stick of the quill-pith, or a stake of the auger-dust?* This is another version of
Tweedledum and Tweedledee, the phrases used having reference to the use
of a turning-lathe.'

S 180 ff   *Torture.*—Trussing a man up so that his toes were brought up to
his ears, his hands being tied (presumably) behind his back, is frequently
referred to in Scottish Gaelic tales as 'putting the binding of the three
(or five) smalls upon him'; the 'smalls' are (1) the smalls or slenders
of the fists, *i.e.* the wrists, (2) the smalls or slenders of the feet, *i.e.* the
ankles, and lastly (3) the small of the back. See *W. H. Tales*, i., pp. 140-1,
or 144-5 ; ii., pp. 444, 453, 474, or 460, 468, 490. 'Four smalls' is the
expression in *W. H. Tales*, ii., No. 29, and in *Trans. Gael. Soc. Inverness*,
xxv., p. 241; *Waifs and Strays*, ii., pp. 49, 445, and 'five smalls,' *ibid.*, iv.,
pp. 73, 128. When in this position, it was said that the victim's great
toes were whispering in his ears. See *W. H. Tales*, ii., No. 52, where
a hero, who had overcome his enemy, binds him before cutting his
head off, so that 'the thumb of his foot gave a warning to the root
of his ear.' In MS. vol. xi., No. 185, an enemy is bound so that his
two great toes give warnings to his two ears. See also *Celtic Review*,
iii., p. 357. See also *Larminie*, p. 51, where Bioultach brings the *five*
slenders of his enemy together very tightly, 'so that the toes of his
feet gave conversation to the holes of his ears, and no conversation did
they give him but the height of mischief and misfortune.' See also
Rosg Gàidhlig, p. 210. For a curious modern French military example
of this torture, 'la crapaudine,' see *Zeits. für Celtic Phil.*, vi. Band, i.
Heft, pp. 181, 186, 188. In *W. H. Tales*, i., No. 7, Notes, Campbell
of Islay says: 'It seems to have been the part of a brave man to submit
without flinching, to have his wrists and ankles tied to the small of
his back, and be "tightened" and tortured; and then to recite his deeds
as an Indian brave might do.' Though the wrists might have been
tied to the small of the back, Islay is probably speaking inadvertently
in saying that the ankles were tied to the same part. In all the tales
that I can remember, if the position of the feet is mentioned at all,
it is to represent the toes as being close to the ears when this kind of
torture was being inflicted. In *Celtic Review*, vi., p. 368, people threaten
to tie a hero in a *cuibheall bhall*, *i.e.* a wheel of ropes, which may have
been a development of the trussing up by the three smalls. See also
Larminie, p. 41.

The posture in which the big toes are made to meet the ears appears
elsewhere as being one which a juggler might assume. In John
MacFadyen's delightful *Sgeulaiche nan Caol*, p. 173, a *gille dubh nan car*,
or black lad of the twists or tricks, in order apparently to show his
skill in magic athletics, leaps upon the top of one of the house rafters,
and having put his two big toes in his two ears, spins round as fast
as a whirligig. This he does in a sitting position. He also performs
the strange feat of using his left big toe as a pivot by thrusting it into a
hole in a joist, and then spinning round on it. A reference to this sort
of magic feat is probably to be seen in a verse in Dr K. N. MacDonald's
Puirt-a-Beul, p. 22.

Q 416   After 'the binding of the three smalls' had been 'strictly and straitly
·1·2*   laid upon him,' the prisoner might be kicked over several rafters, seven
or eight sometimes.—*Celtic Review*, vi., pp 369, 374; iii., pp. 353, 357.
W. H. Tales, ii., No. 52. Professor W. J. Watson, *Rosg Gàidhlig*, pp. 92,

97, 216. *Trans. Gael. Soc. Inverness*, xxv., p. 241. *Waifs and Strays*, ii., pp. 85, 453.

Sometimes, instead of being kicked over the rafters, the victim was banged under the table or into the 'peat corner' or 'amongst dogs, and cats and pigs.' But he was sometimes subjected to still further torture. In Dr George Henderson's *Celtic Dragon Myth*, p. 165, heroes are placed 'fo shileadh na lòchraidh 's fo ròs nan coinnlean,' *i.e.* under the drippings of the lamps and the resin of the (pine) candles.[1] 'To be under the drippings of the lamps and under the feet of the big dogs'—'to be tied roundly like a ball' and 'to be under the sparks of the bellows,'—or to be 'under the drippings of the waxen torches,' are some of the expressions which refer to this kind of torture in *W. H. Tales*, ii., Nos. 52, 46, var. 4; iii., pp. 235, 270, or 250, 285. In Larminie's *West Irish Folk Tales*, p. 74, a hero is thrown under 'the molten torrent,' every drop of which goes 'from the fat to the marrow, and from the marrow to the inmost marrow.' The torture is also described as the drops of a molten torrent which go through the bone of a hero, *ibid.*, pp. 48, 49, 254. See also *Waifs and Strays*, iii., p. 264.

In a tale preserved in J. H. Simpson's *Poems of Oisin, Bard of Erin*, p. 200, we read how this torture was applied to Fionn; 'with the leash of a stag hound they tied fast the toes of his feet to his two ears, and then put him under Hella na Reighta (*Drop of the kingdom*) [?] a drop from which, falling on the skin, goes through to the bone, and the drop which reaches the bone pierces afterwards to the marrow. Under this he passed a year and a day without relief of any kind.' Simpson says in a note: 'It is hard to tell what sort of an instrument or engine of torture this was; the person from whose lips I took down this tale suggested that it was most likely a *shower bath of sulphuric acid !!* pleasant certainly !'

In *Zeitschrift für Celt. Phil.*, i., p. 489, par. 21, a character says he will not give the information required of him 'until I am tied as fast and tight as are the flaming hounds (?),[2] until my small toe makes whispers to my ear, and until the drop which is in the top of my head is forced through my great toe; until the dropping of a king's candle is brought on me, so that it goes from the marrow to the *smintan* and from the *smintan* to the *smantan*.' The Irish for 'the dropping of a king's candle' is given as 'sileadh na righ-choindle (rae-choindle?),' and this is referred to in the following note, *ibid.*, p. 492. See Dinneen's *Irish Dictionary*, art. 'riogh-choinneal,' a palace candle, *i.e.* one of the largest size.

'*Sileadh na rae-choindle* (§ 21). This phrase was thus explained by a neighbour of mine. A candle used to be lighted for the punishment

---

[1] Henderson unaccountably translates—'Beneath the drippings from the black (sooty) rafters and the resin of the (pine) candles.'

[2] *Zeitschrift*, p. 482, 'ceangal na gcù gcaor,' the binding of the flaming hounds, is of course a misunderstanding of 'ceangal na gcúig gcaol,' *i.e.* the binding of the five smalls. I owe this information to the kindness of Professor Watson.

of wicked people after their death, each drop of which, as it fell on the head of the wicked, burnt its way through the soul until it came out through the lowest part. Even to this day in parts of Connemara, when a person is in extreme agony, they say: "Atá sileadh na rae-choindle air." ' Thus is religion coloured by popular traditions.

But Professor T. F. O'Rahilly, *Gadelica*, i., p. 275 (Dublin, 1913), explains the matter. He says: 'The name *rí(o)gh-choinneal*, otherwise *coinneal rígh-thighe*, was given to a candle 'of enormous size, with a great bushy wick,' which it was usual in ancient Ireland to keep burning at night in the presence of a king or chief. 'In the palace it was placed high over his head; during war it blazed outside his tent-door; and on night-marches it was borne before him.' . . . In connection with the *rígh-choinnle* there is an interesting point which seems to have hitherto escaped attention. If we may trust the evidence of several romances (no unsafe guides in such matters) the custom formerly existed of placing a bound captive, whom it was wished to punish or torture, under the dripping of one of these "royal candles" all night long.' The Professor gives many instances of this torture from Irish tales.

A *crann soillse* appears in a tale in *Béaloideas*, iii., pp. 474, 501. It was used as a beacon to guide people home, and is probably an instance of the *rí(o)gh-choinneal*.

In *W. H. Tales*, iii., p. 235 or 250, Conall says to a man so tortured, 'Thou man that art beneath, wert thou ever before in strait or extremity as great as to be lying under the great board, under the drippings of the waxen torches of the King of Lochlann and mine?' Thus is Professor O'Rahilly's statement confirmed from a Scottish Gaelic source, which represents two princes as having each a royal candle of his own.

In tale No. 229, Gaelic List, MS. vol. xi. (see *An Gàidheal*, 1927, p. 58), a farmer who was drawing some beer from a barrel noticed that a pig had wandered into the house. In his hurry to drive the animal away, he forgets to turn off the beer tap, with the result that the beer runs away to waste. The Gaelic expression used in this connection is that the beer was 'a' sileadh air a chreuchdan,' *lit.* was dripping on his wounds. The metaphor may have arisen from the custom of placing a prisoner or captive where the drippings of a torch would fall on his wounds. See also *Béaloideas*, vii., pp. 130, 183.

DÌOL-DÉIRCE DHÙN-EIDEANN

BHA, ann an Dùn-Eideann aig oisinn sràide, seann duine
fad thrì bliadhna, is cha d'fhuair iad riamh a mach ciod è
an seòrsa duine a bh'ann. Bha e air a chomhdach le
lùirich mhóir bho mhullach a chinn gu bonn a bhrògan.
[Bu dìol-déirce e.]

Thall aig oisinn na sràide far am biodh e 'na sheasamh,
bha bùth aig gille de mhuinntir Inbhir-nis. Bhiodh an
dìol-déirce so agus an ad aige 'na làimh, ag iarraidh bonn-
a-sé. Bha fear na bùth 'toirt sé sgillinn dha a h-uile là
a thachair e ris. Ach an ceann trì bliadhna, dhùnadh a
bhùth air a' Ghàidheal. [Bha e air thuar tuiteam bhàrr
a chasan, agus gun rachadh an t-aran a bhristeadh 'na
bheul.]

Bha e fad seachduinn air ais agus air adhart, is gun e
faighinn nan daoine gu còrdadh.

Dh'amais dha dol seachad air an dìol-déirce, agus chuir
e sé-sgillinn 'na aid. Thug an dìol-déirce sùil air, is thuirt
e ris, 'Tha mi faicinn gu bheil do bhùth air a dùnadh ort.'
Chuir e a làmh 'na bhroilleach, is air dha sin a dhèanamh,
chunnaic an Gàidheal an t-aodach a bu bhrèagha a bha
ri a fhaicinn air an dìol-déirce fo'n lùirich. Thug e a mach
peann agus sgrìobh e *loine*, shìn e dha i, ag ràdh, 'Ge b'e
àite 'san iarr sin ort a dhol, bi ann.'

Dh' fhalbh am fear so mar le suarachas o'n dìol-déirce
a dh' ionnsuigh a àite chòmhnuidh fhéin.

Air an là-'r-na-mhàireach, air dha bhi dol a mach,
chuir e a làmh 'na phocaid, 's thachair *loine* an dìol-déirce
ris; leugh e i, is dh' iarr i air dol gu a leithid so a dh' àite.

[Chaidh e ann agus] an uair a ràinig e an dorus, thuirt
e ris fhéin, 'Cha deachaidh dìol-déirce riamh a steach air
a leithid so de thigh brèagh.'

THE BEGGAR OF EDINBURGH

No. 26.   [*Vol. x., No. 49*]

THERE was in Edinburgh at the corner of a street, an old
man who had stood there for three years.   But what kind
of man he was, people had never been able to find out.
He was clad in a long cloak from the top of his head to the
soles of his shoes.   [He was a beggar.]

Opposite, at the corner of the street where he used to
stand, was a shop kept by a man of the people of Inverness.
Now the beggar used to stand with his hat in his hand,
asking for a halfpenny, and the man of the shop used to
give him a sixpence every time he met him.   But at the
end of three years, the Gael's [the Inverness man's] shop
was closed against him.   [It looked as if he would be ruined,
and the very bread would be broken in his mouth.]

For a week he was going to and fro [from one man
to another], but was unable to get people [his customers
or creditors] to come to terms with him.

He happened to pass the beggar, and he put a sixpence
in his hat.   The beggar looked at him, and said, 'I see
thy shop is closed against thee.'   He then put his hand in
his bosom, and when he did so, the Gael saw that under
his rags, the beggar was wearing the finest clothes that
there were to be seen.   However, the beggar took out a
pen and wrote a line, and handed it to him, saying, Q42
'Wherever that bids thee go, go.'

The shopkeeper left the beggar as if with contempt,
and went away to his own dwelling-place.

The next day, as he was going out, he put his hand
in his pocket, and there he found the beggar's note.   He
read it.   It told him to go to such and such a place.

[He went there] but when he came to the door, he said
to himself, 'No beggar ever entered so beautiful a house as
this.'

Bha e ann an iomachomhairle ciod è dhèanadh e.
Chunnaic e sreang, tharruing e i, is bhuail e clag. Dh'
fhosgail an dorus, agus thuirt am fear-frithealaidh ris,
'A bheil gnothach agad an so ?'

'Tà, chan 'eil fhios agam; tha mi am barail gu
bheil mi air mo mhealladh, ach tha *loine* agam o dhuine
tha mi smaointeachadh nach tàinig riamh a stigh an so.'
Thàinig an sin nighean òg uasal a nuas; thug e dhi
an *loine*. 'Tha so ceart gu leòir,' ars ise, 'chugainn [1] far
a bheil fear an tighe, is e leughadh 'san t-seòmar sheanchais.'

Dh' fhalbh e is chaidh e a steach. Nuair a chunnaic
e fear an tighe, bha e air a nàrachadh buileach.
'Seadh, a bheil gnothuch agad riumsa, mo [2] ghille
maith ?' arsa fear-an-tighe.
'Tà, chan 'eil fhios agam, ach tha *loine* an so a dh'
innseas ma thà.'
Leugh an duine-uasal i; rinn e gàire; 'tha thu ceart
gu leòir, dèan suidhe an sin.' Bhuail e clag; thàinig
nighean òg a nuas. 'Cuir nìthean maith air a' bhòrd,'
ars esan. Rinn i sin.
'Feuch t' fhear-dùthcha fhéin, an t-uisge-beatha,' ars
an duine-uasal ris a' Ghàidheal, 'is cuidich thu fhéin.'
Rinn e sin.
'Tha mi faicinn gu bheil thu mi-thoilichte airson do
bhùth. Chan 'eil thu idir a' faighinn nan daoine gu
còrdadh. Ciod è, tha thu am barail a cheannaicheadh i
uile ?'
'Tha mi smaointicheadh,' ars an gille [fear na bùth],
'gun dèanadh ceithir mìle a' chùis.' Thionndaidh an
duine-uasal ris an àite-sgrìobhaidh; sgrìobh e litir. 'Falbh,'
ars esan, 'gu àite an ionmhais (Bank) [*sic*] Rìoghail: ge
b'e air bith freagairt a gheibh thu, thig leis dh' am
ionnsuigh-sa.'
Rinn an gille so. [Ràinig e am Bank.] An uair a

---

[1] *Chugainn* (in MS. *thugainn*) = [it is] towards us, coming towards us
= we had better, it behoves us. *Cf.* English (slang), it is up to us. *Cf.*
Tha tighinn fodham, it is coming under me = I intend to, I am thinking of.
Possibly *tiugainn*, not *thugainn*, is meant.

He was in two minds and had many doubts as to what he should do. But seeing a string, he pulled it, and rang a bell. The door opened, and an attendant asked him, 'Hast thou any business or errand here?'

'Indeed, I scarcely know. I think I must be mistaken; still, I have a note here from a certain man, who I scarcely think ever entered this house.'

At this moment a young lady came forward. To her he handed the note. 'This is quite right,' said she. 'We had better go where the master of the house is; he is reading in the drawing-room.'

The shopman went in. But upon seeing the master of the house he felt utterly abashed.

'Well, hast thou business with me, my good fellow?' said the master of the house.

'Indeed, I scarcely know, but I have a note here, which will tell if I have.'

The gentleman read it. He laughed, 'Thou art quite right; sit down there.' He rang a bell, and a young woman appeared. 'Put good things on the table,' said he. She did so.

'Behold thine own countryman, the whiskey,' said the gentleman to the Gael; 'help thyself.' He did so.

'I see thou art sad and concerned about thy shop. Thou art not able to get people to come to terms. What, thinkest thou, would buy it outright?'

'I think,' said the man of the booth, 'that four thousand would do it.' The gentleman turned to his writing desk, and he wrote a letter. 'Go to the Royal Bank,' said he, 'and whatever answer thou gettest, bring it to me.'

The man of the shop did so. [He arrived at the Bank.]

---

² *Mo ghille maith*: an adjective in the vocative is not aspirated, if '*mo*, my,' be present. Compare, *mo rùn geal dìleas*, where no inflexion or aspiration whatever appears, though the case seems to be vocative.

leugh am 'Banker' an litir, thuirt e, 'Is ann aige tha an earbsa asad.'

Dh' iarr e air na cléirich ceithir mìle a chunntas; rinn iad sin agus dh' fhalbh e leò.

Ràinig e an duine-uasal. 'Tha mi faicinn gun d' fhuair thu siod.' Sgrìobh e litir a rithisd, thug e dha i, agus ginidh (21/-) [sic]. 'Thoir sin,' ars esan, 'do fhear-bualadh a' chluig, chum 's gun iarradh e orra coinneachadh riut !'

Rinn an gille sin.

Phill e air ais, agus thuirt an duine-uasal ris, 'Tha mi smaointicheadh gur còir dhomh a nis do shé-sgillinn a phàidheadh. Biodh fios agad gura mise dìol-déirce mór a' Chanongate. Is iomadh sé-sgillinn a chuir thu 'nam aid. Dh' fhàgadh mise 'nam bhantraich agus aon nighean agam, is thàinig mi gu bochduinn. Smaointich mi gum b'e siod dòigh a b' fhearr gu mo dhèanamh beairteach, gus mo nighean a thogail mar bhean-uasail, agus tha i mar sin, cho maith ri a màthrach.[1] Cha do thachair uasal no ìosal riamh rium a bha cho cunbhalach 'na thabhartas riutsa. Nis, falbhaidh sinn agus coinnichidh sinn na fearaibh.'[2]

Chaidh iad a mach. Bha each aig an dorus 'ga[m] feitheamh. Ràinig iad na daoine. Thuirt an duine-uasal riu, 'Ciod è a tha sibh a' dèanamh air a' ghille chòir so 'ga chumail 'na thàmh? Ciod è a dh' iarradh sibh air a thigh 's na tha 'na bhroinn? Ceannaichidh mise e.'

Bhualadh a mach air ceithir mìle e. [Cheannaich an dìol-déirce e.] Thug e an iuchair do 'n Ghàidheal.

'Falbh a nis,' ars esan, 'agus faigh dà chléireach agus fear 'sa 'bhaile, agus ruig mise a rithist.' Rinn e sin.

'Nis,' arsa an duine-uasal, 'tha do shé-sgilling pàidhte.

---

[1] *Màthrach*, alternative genitive; the sentence probably stood originally in some such form as the following, 'a comh maith a màthrach,' in which *maith*, excellence, being a noun, governed its following noun in the genitive. Cf. *Mac na màthrach* = his mother's son, *i.e.* like mother, like son.

When the Banker had read the letter, he said, 'What great faith he must have in thee.'

The Banker told the clerks to count out four thousand pounds. They did so, and the shopman departed with the money.

He went back to the gentleman. 'Well, thou hast got that, I see.' He wrote another letter, and gave it to him, along with a guinea. 'Give that to the bell-ringer [town crier],' said he, 'that he may ask them [*i.e.* thy clients] to meet thee.'

The shopman did so.

When he returned, the gentleman said to him, 'I think I ought now to pay back thy sixpences. Know that I am the big beggar of the Canongate. Many a sixpence didst thou put in my hat. I was left a widower, with one daughter, and I came to poverty. I determined that that plan [the plan known to us both, *i.e.* begging] would be the best way of making myself rich, that my daughter might be brought up as a gentlewoman, and such she now is, as much so as her mother was. I never met either gentle or simple so regular in his gifts as thyself. Now then, we will be off and meet these men [thy clients].'

They went out. There was a horse at the door waiting for them. They met the people [the clients or customers of the Inverness man]. The gentleman said to them, 'What do you intend doing to this honest fellow by keeping him idle ? What do you want for his house and all that is in it ? I will buy it all.'

It was valued at four thousand pounds. [The beggar purchased it.] He gave the key to the Gael.

'Go now,' said he, 'and get two clerks and a man from the town, and come and see me again.' He did so accordingly.

'Now,' said the gentleman, 'thy sixpences are paid.

---

² *na fearaibh* is frequently used as a nominative and accusative plural, as well as a dative plural.

Chan 'eil agam ach aon nighean. Is e do leithid de dhuine bha a dhìth oirre airson companach pòsda dhi. Pòsaidh tu i. Tha móran fearainn agamsa 'sna h-Innsean, agus deich mìle punnd Sasunnach air chùl sin,—is leat e uile. Sgrìobh a nis a dh' ionnsuigh gach neach a dh' iarras mise, chum iad a bhi an so a màireach, 'n là[th]rach ur [1] pòsaidh.'

Thachair am pòsadh, agus bha greadhnachas mór aca. Bha iad cho sona ri dithis a chaidh còmhla riamh. Chuir an duine-uasal a shaoghal seachad gu socair, sona, maille ris a' chàraid òig, agus bha gach cùis a' soirbheachadh leò.

From J. F. Campbell's MS. Collections, MS. vol. x., No. 49.

This tale was collected in Benbecula in 1859. Donald MacDonald MacCharles Macintyre recited it. D. Torrie wrote it down. Campbell says of it, 'About a poor beggar in Edinburgh. Something like the Blind Beggar of Bethnal Green, so far as I remember that ballad.'

There is another but a very poor version of this tale in MS. vol. xi., No. 272.

I have only one daughter. Thou art the very sort of man
that she needed for a husband. Thou shalt marry her. N 826
I have much land in the Indies, and ten thousand pounds
sterling besides—it is all thine. Write now to everyone
that I desire, so that they may be here to-morrow, and
be present at your wedding.'

The wedding took place, and they had great doings.
They were as happy as any pair that were ever joined.
The gentleman passed his life at his ease, happy and
contented, along with the young couple, and everything
prospered with them.

[1] *ur*, your—in MS. *air*, or *ar*,= our. Some writers habitually use *ar*
to mean both 'our' and 'your,' to the great loss of the language.

AN DUINE A THUG RIS A' MHÈAIRLE, AGUS A CHREACH MÈAIRLICH

No. 27. [*Vol. x., No. 50*]

BHA duine gasda ann an Sruighlea a bha air tuarasdal là. Bha e aig aon am bho Dhi-luain gu Di-Sathurna, agus cha d'fhuair e duine a dh'fhaighnich gu car e. Oidhche Di-Sathurna bha e 'ga fhaicinn fhéin ann an càs [1]—cha robh fhios aige ciod è dhèanadh e.

Smuainich e gun rachadh e a dh'ionnsuigh aon de'n fheadhainn o'm b' àbhaist da bhi ceannachd. Ràinig se e, ach cha d'fhuair e nì uaidh. An uair a phill e dhachaidh, thuirt e ri a bhean, 'Théid mi a mach, agus tòisichidh mi ris a' mhèairle.'
Dh'fhalbh e gun sgian, gun bhata air a shiubhal. Ràinig e toll, agus sheas e an sin. An tiota beag, chunnaic e marcaiche a' tighinn. Rug e air an each, agus thuirt e ris an duine, 'Thoir dhomh-sa na tha air do shiubhal.'

'Có leis bheir thu uam e,' ars am marcaiche, 'is thu gun airm agad? Tha mi faicinn nach 'eil thu ach aineolach 'sa' cheaird.'
'Tha mi; cha robh mi riamh rithe gus a nochd.'
Thuirt am marcaiche ris, 'Innsidh mise dhuit an dòigh air a' mhèairle.' Thug e dha sgian. 'Falbh agus gearr bata 'sa 'choillidh, agus a cheud duine a thig, buail mu'n chluais e. Ma bhitheas rud aige, is leat-sa e.'
Ghearr e bata agus sheas e, ach cha robh neach a' tighinn. Chunnaic e an sin marcaiche. Smuainich e comhairle an fhir a dh'fhalbh a ghabhail. Thàinig am marcaiche; bhuail se e, agus mharbh se e [ar leis fhéin]. Shìn an t-each air falbh, agus am poc airgid air a mhuin.

---

[1] *streis* in MS. = English *straits* ?

446

THE MAN WHO TOOK TO ROBBING, AND ROBBED ROBBERS

No. 27.   [*Vol. x., No. 50*]

THERE was a fine fellow in Stirling who lived by a daily wage. But there came a time when he spent a whole week from Monday to Saturday without finding anyone who asked him to do a single hand's turn. On Saturday night he found himself in a sad plight,[1] and did not know what to do.

So he thought he would go to one of the people from whom he was accustomed to buy. He went and saw him, but got nothing from him. So when he returned home, he said to his wife, 'I will go out, and take to robbing.'

Off he went, but without taking so much as a knife or a stick about him. He came to a hollow, and stationed himself there. In a little while, he saw a horseman coming. He seized the horse, and said to the rider, 'Give me all thou hast about thee.'

'With what wilt thou take it from me?' said the rider, 'seeing that thou hast no weapon? I perceive thou art but a novice to thy trade.'

'That I am. I never took to it till to-night.'

The rider replied to him, 'I will tell thee the way to rob.' Here he gave him a knife. 'Go and cut a cudgel in the wood, and the first man who comes along, hit him over the ear. If he have aught, it is thine.'

So he cut himself a cudgel, and stood ready, but [at first] no one was coming. Then he saw a horseman coming. He determined to take the advice of the man who had lately left him. When the horseman came up, he struck him, and [as he thought] killed him. But the horse bolted, with a bag of money on its back.

An uair a chunnaic esan an duine marbh, ghabh e
eagal, is thug e an saoghal fo a cheann. Bhris e bhàrr
an rathaid, agus chaidh e a steach do'n choillidh. Chunnaic
e an sin uinneag, agus mùig sholuis ann. Chaidh e a
steach. Cha robh duine ann. Chunnaic e móran
choireachan làn feòla aig an teinidh. Dh'aithnich e gun
robh daoine ri tighinn. An uair a dh'ith e pàirt de'n
bhiadh, chaidh e am falach fo fhiodh a bha an ceann shìos
an tighe.

Cha b'fhada gus an d'fhosgail an dorus, agus thàinig
móran daoine a stigh fo airm. Chaidh iad suas, agus
dh'ith iad am biadh.

Bha iad cho sona airson na rinn iad fad na seachduinn.
Thòisich iad ri cunntas an airgid, is bha cóig ceud punnd
Sasunnach aca. Bha annas orra nach robh am fear a
dh'fhàg iad a stigh a' tighinn; ach lean iad air òl, agus
thuit iad 'nan cadal.

Chuala am fear [bochd] a bha am falach éigheach a'
tighinn a dh'ionnsuigh an doruis—thàinig duine a steach,
agus a aodann làn fala. Dhùisg fear aca-san, agus thàinig
e far an robh an duine leòinte. 'Ciod è dh'éirich dhuit?'
ars esan.

'Is coma sin: bhuaileadh mi [1] an dé: gun robh am
mail coach a' falbh le trì mìle do Bhannc Dhùn-Éideann;
dh'fhalbh mi as a dhéidh [agus fhuair mi an t-airgiod]. An
uair a bha mi dol seachad air an drochaid, thachair duine
rium, is bhuail e mi 'sa' chluais: thuit mi, is bha dùil
aige-san gun robh mi marbh; shìn e a mach leis an each
agus an trì mìle.'

Thug iad suas e, agus nigh iad a chreuchdan. Chaidil
iad uile 'na dhéidh sin. An uair a chunnaic am fear
[bochd] a bha am falach so, chaidh e suas, agus thug e
leis an cóig ceud is dh'fhalbh e.

Aig a' gheata, thachair each a' mhèairlich ris, agus

---

[1] The sentence should probably read : "Chuala mi an dè gun robh am
mail-coach," etc., *i.e.* " I heard yesterday that the mail-coach," etc.

When he saw the man dead there, he became afraid, and set off to wander through the world [as an outcast]. He turned off the road, and plunged into the forest. He then saw a window in which a dim misty light was shining. He went in. But there was no one there. But at the fireside he saw many cauldrons full of flesh-meat. He realized that people were coming. So when he had eaten some of the meat, he went and hid under some wood at the outer end of the house.

It was not long until the door opened, and in came a great number of armed men. They went to the inner end of the house, and took their food.

They were very pleased with what they had accomplished during the week. They began to count their money, and found they had five hundred pounds sterling. [They said] they thought it strange that the man whom they had left in the house was not coming; however, they went on drinking, and fell asleep.

The [poor] man who was in hiding heard a shouting coming towards the door—and in came a man whose face was covered with blood. One of the others awoke, and came over to the wounded man. 'What has happened to thee?' said he.

'It matters little: I was assaulted [1] yesterday: [it was known] that the mail-coach was to go with three thousand pounds to the Bank of Edinburgh; I went after it [and got the money]. When I was going over the bridge, a man met me, and struck me over the ear; I fell, and he thought I was dead; and he dashed away with the horse and the three thousand pounds.'

They fetched him up to the inner end of the house, and washed his wounds. After that, they all went to sleep. When the [poor] man who was in hiding saw that they were asleep, he went up to the inner end of the house, took the five hundred pounds and went off.

At the gate, he met the robber's horse with the three

K 306·2*

an trì mìle air a mhuin. Thàinig e dhachaidh [air muin an eich].

Thuirt a bhean ris, 'Is beag a rinn thu o'n a dh'fhalbh thu.'

'Rinn mi gu math,' ars esan, is e a' tilgeil a' phoca air a' bhòrd. Dh'innis e dhi gach nì.

'Na buin do an trì mìle,' ars a bhean, 'ach airgiod nam mèairleach, thoir leat ginidh dheth, agus ruig fear de do sheann luchd-malairt,[1] is faigh rud dhuit féin is do do phàisdean.'

Ràinig e, is chan éireadh e [an seann fhear malairt] as an leabaidh. Phill e dhachaidh. 'Thàinig thu,' ars a bhean, 'is gun dad agad agus airgiod agad—ach tiugainn thusa maille riumsa far a bheil am Bàillidh.'

Bha e 'na chadal. Bhuail iad aig an uinneig. Leigeadh a steach iad, is ràinig iad am Bàillidh. Mar a rinn am marsanta air, is mar a fhuair e an t-airgiod, dh'innis iad da.

Sgrìobh am Bàillidh a dh'ionnsuigh a' mharsanta, agus dh'iarr e air tighinn far an robh esan. Fhuair am Bàillidh dà mhaor-sìth, agus chuir e iad air falbh leis an duine [bhochd] a dh'ionnsuigh fear na bùth. Ràinig iad, agus chuir iad air a chois e. 'Thoir[2] do'n duine [bhochd] so na tha e ag iarraidh,' ars iad-san, 'air neo bheir sinne do'n lagh thu.'

Riaraich fear na bùth an duine bochd, oir bha eagal aige roimh 'n Bhàillidh.

Anns a' mhaduinn Di-Luain, thàinig an duine bochd leis an airgiod a dh'ionnsuigh a' Bhàillidh. Thuirt am Bàillidh ris, 'Is leat féin airgiod nam mèairleach, ach airgiod Dhùn-Éideann, gleidhidh mi e, gus am faigh mi fios bho'n Bhannca, ciod è nì mi ris.'

Thàinig fios uaidh an t-airgiod a chur do'n Bhannca a rithist, agus riadh trì bliadhna thoirt do'n duine [bhochd] dheth.

Dh'innis am Bàillidh so do'n duine [bhochd], is thaitinn e ris gu math. Chuir am Bàillidh air a dhòigh e, is

---

[1] *luchd dealigidh* in MS.   [2] *bheir* in MS.

thousand pounds on its back. So he went home [on horseback].

His wife said to him, 'Thou hast not done much since thou didst go away.'

'Nay, I have done well,' said he, throwing the bag on the table. He told her everything.

'Touch not the three thousand,' said his wife, 'but of the robbers' money take a guinea, and go and see one of thine old dealers, and get something for thyself and thy children.'

He went, but [the old dealer] would not even get up out of bed. So he returned home. 'Thou hast come back,' said his wife, 'bringing nothing with thee, though thou certainly hast money—but do thou come with me to the Baillie's.'

The Baillie was asleep. They knocked at the window. They were let in, and came to the Baillie. They told him how the merchant had treated him, and how he had got the money.

The Baillie wrote to the merchant, and told him to come to him. The Baillie then got two policemen, and sent them off with the [poor] man to the shopkeeper. When they got there, they made him get up. 'Give this [poor] man all he wants,' said they, 'or else we will take thee to the law.'

The shopkeeper satisfied the poor man's wants, for he was afraid of the Baillie.

On Monday morning, the poor man, bringing the money with him, went to the Baillie's. The Baillie said to him, 'The robbers' money is thine, but the money belonging to Edinburgh I will keep, till I hear from the Bank what I am to do with it.'

Word came from the Bank to send the money back to the Bank again, and three years' interest on it was to be given to the [poor] man.

The Baillie told this to the [poor] man, and he was greatly pleased at it. The Baillie set his affairs in order

cheannaich e tigh mór dha ann an Dùn-Éideann, anns
an robh e reic gach seòrsa dibhe, agus bha e fhéin is a
theaghlach an còmhnuidh ann, fhad agus a bha iad beò;
bha gach nì a' soirbheachadh leò, agus bha iad riamh fo
chomain mhóir do'n Bhàillidh [airson] mar a rinn e riutha.

NOTES

MS. vol. x., No. 50. Probably from the same man who recited
No. 26 (MS. vol. x., No. 49).

The character who appears only once in the tale, and then only
in order to teach the hero how to steal, may, in some more ancient
version, have been magical, for he probably knew beforehand that
the robber of the mail-coach would be the first person the hero would
meet. There is no other sign of anything magical in the story. As
to the robbers, nothing appears to be known as to their ultimate fate,
or what they did when they discovered the loss of the five hundred
pounds.

for him, and bought a big house for him in Edinburgh, where
he sold every kind of drink, and he and his family dwelt
there as long as they lived; everything went well with
them, and they were ever under a great obligation to the
Baillie for what he had done for them.

Nicolson, *Gaelic Proverbs*, p. 391, gives a verse appropriate to this
tale:—

> 'Mèirle 'dheanamh air a'mhèirleach,
> Gu'm b'e sin a'mhèirle bhorb;
> Cha'n'eil taobh a théid a'mèirleach,
> Nach'eil meirleach air a lorg,'

of which the following is a translation:—

> To commit robbery upon a robber,
> That were a wild and drastic robbery indeed;
> There is no direction that a robber can go,
> That another robber will not be on his track.

Sruighlea, Stirling, *Faclair MhicDhomhnuill*. In the MS. *Strilla*.
I have also seen it spelt *Struibhle* and *Striveling*. Campbell of Islay
thought the word was meant for Australia, for he has written on the
flyleaf, 'Story of a man who took to robbing and robbed robbers—
scene laid in Astrilla—? Australia.'

UISDEAN MÒR MAC GILLE PHÀDRUIG AGUS A' GHOBHAR MHAOL BHUIDHE

No. 28. [*Vol. x., No. 53a*]

BHA duine ainmeil bha chòmhnuidh timchioll Leitir Iù no na Laidean Lìn, do'm b'ainm Uisdean Mór Mac Gille Phàdruig.[1] Bha e uair-eiginn a' siubhal ann an taobh tuath Siorramachd Rois. Do bhrìgh gun robh an duine so 'na cheatharnach agus a' giùlan armachd gach taobh a rachadh e, is e na h-ionadan bu chunnartaiche is a b'oillteile le muinntir eile bu taitniche leis-san a bhi siubhal. Bha e déidheil air bhi coinneachadh ris gach seòrsa de fhuathan (no, mar a theirear, uadh-bhéistean).

Tha monadh ann an Gearrloch ris an abrar an Tom Buidhe, agus alltan a' ruith a leth-taobh ris. Cha mhór a ghabhadh an rathad sin, moch no anmoch, nach fhaiceadh an aon sealladh, gobhar mhór ribheagach, fheusagach, a bha toirt mór éiginn do'n luchd siubhail, [a' marbhadh cuid, agus a' cur cuid eile a cochull a cridhe leis an eagal,] [2] agus bha mór iomradh air a' Ghobhar Mhaol Bhuidhe a bha air Tom Buidhe Ghearrloch.

Chuala Uisdean Mór mu thimchioll na béisde, agus chuir e roimhe dol 'na comhdhail, gun umhail, gun amharus.

Chaidh e air aghart gu math tràth a dh'ionnsuigh a' mhonaidh, agus air dha teachd gu bun an Tuim, chaidh e a steach do thigh breabadair a bha chòmhnuidh an sin 'san am am Bràigh Thòrasdail [ris an abradh iad breabadair nan casan buidhe]. Bha am breabadair a' fighe air a bheairt an uair a chaidh Uisdean a stigh. Thòisich am breabadair agus Uisdean air co-labhairt. Ars am breaba-

---

[1] Big Hugh or Big Hutcheon, the Son of the Servant of Patrick. The last part of the name usually appears in English as *Paterson*.
[2] See Notes.

UISDEAN MÓR MAC GILLE PHÀDRUIG AND THE HORNLESS YELLOW GOAT

No. 28.   *[Vol. x., No. 53a]*

THERE was a famous man who dwelt near Letter-ewe or the Laidean Lìn, called Uisdean Mór Mac Gille Phàdruig.[1] He was once on a time travelling in the north of Ross-shire. Because this man was a champion, and carried arms wherever he went, it was the most dangerous places and places which other people dreaded most that he best liked to wander about in. He had a passion for encountering bogles of all sorts, (or, as they are also called, monsters).

There is a mountain moor in Gearrloch (= Gairloch) which is called the Tom Buidhe, by the side of which runs a little brook. There were few who took that road, early or late, who did not see the same sight, a great shaggy, bearded goat, who harassed travellers exceedingly, [killing some, and driving others out of the husks of their hearts with fear].[2] The Yellow Hornless Goat who lived on the Tom Buidhe in Gearrloch was very celebrated.

Uisdean Mór heard about the monster, and he determined to go and encounter it, careless of danger, and undoubting.

He proceeded pretty early in the day to the moor, and on coming to the foot of the Tom, he went into the house of a weaver who dwelt there at the time in Bràigh Thòrasdail (upland of Torrisdale) [whom they called the weaver of the yellow feet]. The weaver was weaving at his loom when Uisdean went in. The weaver and Uisdean entered into conversation. Said the weaver, 'Is it to the Tom

dair, 'An ann a dh'ionnsuigh an Tuim Bhuidhe tha thu dol ?'—Fhreagair Uisdean, 'Is ann.'

'Nach 'eil eagal ort gun tachair a' Ghobhar Bhuidhe ort ?'

'O, chan 'eil,' deir Uisdean.

'Có leis a dh'fheuchas tu rithe ?'

'Feuchaidh mi an claidheamh oirre.'

'Ciod è mura tig e as an truaill duit?' deir am breabadair.

D 2072
·0·1

'Mura tig, feuchaidh mi an gunna oirre,' fhreagair Uisdean.

'Ciod è,' deir am breabadair, 'mura loisg ise srad duit?'

'Mura loisg,' fhreagair Uisdean, 'feuchaidh mi Catrìona, piuthar mo sheanmhathar, oirre.'[1] [Agus air gach arm a dh'ainmich Uisdean, chuir am breabadair rosad, ach air a' bhiodaig cha b' urrainn da rosad a leagail, agus gur e Catrìona, piuthar a sheanmhathar, a bha aig Uisdean oirre.]

C 432·3*

Air do Uisdean so a ràdh, ghabh e air aghart a dh' ionnsuigh an Tuim le ceum iullagach sunndach, agus ràinig e an t-allt am beul an anmoich. Air dha teachd a dh'ionnsuigh an uillt, chuala e nì-eiginn coslach ri meigeadaich goibhre, nì a chuir mór iongnadh air. Tharruing e air aghart a dh'ionnsuigh an àth an coinneamh na h-uadhbheist. 'An e do mheann a tha bhuait, a chleideach ?' labhair Uisdean.

'Ma's è,' fhreagair a' ghobhair, 'fhuair mi a nis e.'

'Chan fhaodar gun d'fhuair fhathast,' arsa Uisdean.

Air dhaibh so a ràdh, tharruing iad am fagus d'a chéile.

Thug Uisdean tarruing air a' chlaidheamh, ach cha tigeadh e as an truaill. Cha mhó bheireadh an gunna srad !

---

[1] What is probably a similar answer occurs in *W. H. Tales*, ii., No. 46, Var. 2, where the hero says : 'My grandmother, on the hinderside of Alba, is here, and will come to help me.' This is probably a mistranslation of a badly written Gaelic sentence which may have run somewhat thus: 'Tha mo sheanmhàthair an so, air taobh cùil an Albannaich'—'My grandmother, (= my dirk) on the hinder-side of the Scot, is here.' The dirk is also referred to as 'my grandmother's sister,' see *Witchcraft*, p. 184. When encountering

Buidhe thou art going?'—Uisdean answered, 'Yes, it is.'

'Hast thou no fear of meeting the Yellow Goat?'

'O, no, I have not,' said Uisdean.

'What weapon wilt thou try against her first?'

'I will try what the sword can do to her.'

'What if the sword will not come out of the sheath for thee?' said the weaver.

'If it will not, I will take the gun to her, and try that,' answered Uisdean.

'What,' said the weaver, 'if the gun will not fire a spark for thee?'

'If it will not fire,' answered Uisdean, 'I will see what Catrìona, my grandmother's sister, can do to her.' [1] [And upon every weapon that Uisdean mentioned, the weaver laid a spell, but on the dirk he could lay no spell, because Uisdean had styled it Catrìona, his grandmother's sister.]

Having said this, Uisdean pressed on to the Tom with a jaunty cheerful step, and arrived at the brook as dusk was coming on. Upon coming up to the brook, he heard something like the bleating of a goat, a matter which astonished him greatly. But he pressed on to the ford to meet the monster. 'Is it thy kid which thou dost want, thou shaggy one?' said Uisdean.

'If it be,' answered the goat, 'I have got it now.'

'Not yet—it cannot be that thou hast got it yet,' said Uisdean.

When they had said this much, they drew near to each other.

Uisdean tugged at his sword, but it would not come out of the sheath. Neither would the gun give a spark!

D 2072
·0·1

C 432·3*

---

an evil thing, one should also carefully refrain from calling one's weapons or dogs by their correct names. *Z. C.*, i., p. 337. In one version the hero says, 'tha cobhair an Cruachan,' *i.e.* there is help in Cruachan Beann. But *cruachan* also means *hip*, and Uisdean is referring of course (as does another hero in the Dundee Gaelic Society's *Celtic Annual*, 1916, p. 83) to the dirk he carried about him, dangling from his hip. See *Survivals*, p. 176. For a somewhat similar tale, see *Folk-Lore*, xxxiii., p. 309.

An sin rug a' ghobhar air, agus chuir i gu a ghlùn
e, ag ràdh ris—'Uisdein Mhóir, Mhic Ghille Phàdruig,
do bheò cha téid as.'

'A bhiastag odhar nan alltan,' fhreagair esan, 'agad
chan 'eil fios.'

'C'àite, a nise, a bheil Catrìona, piuthar do sheanmhathar, a làmh thapaidh?'[1] deir a' ghobhar, agus i a'
saoilsinn gun d'fhuair i làmh an uachdair air.

'Tapadh leat! is tu a b'fhearr cuimhne,' fhreagair
Uisdean, a' toirt tarruing air a' bhiodaig, agus a' toirt
sàthadh fuilteach de'n lann chruadhach do'n bheist anns
a' bhroinn.   Air ball thug a' ghobhar ás.

Air do Uisdean sealltuinn timchioll air, phill e gu tigh
a' bhreabadair.   Chaidh e a steach gu cròdha, agus dh'
fharraid e c'àite an robh fear an tighe.

Thuirt [iad] gu'n robh e 'na laighe gu tinn.

'Feumaidh mise a fhaicinn,' arsa Uisdean, a' leum
thairis air gach ceap-tuislidh gus an d'ràinig e leabaidh
a' bhreabadair.   [Ach cha robh e 'na leabaidh, agus an
uair a las Uisdean solus, fhuair e e] 'na laighe fo'n bheairt,
a' sileadh na fala.

Dh'iarr e air a' bhreabadair gun sealladh e a chreuchdan
da gu h-aithghearr.   [Rinn e sin,] agus dh'aithnich e
D 134
G 252
gum b'e am breabadair a' ghobhar an uair a chunnaic e
lot na biodaige 'na bhroinn.[2]

['Ma's tù a rinn na h-uiread calldach air an Tom
Bhuidhe, cha téid thu n'as fhaide,' arsa Uisdean.]   Agus
an àite iocshlàinte a chàradh ri a chreuchdan, is ann a
thug Uisdean sàthadh bàis do'n bhreabadair, [is mharbh
e fo a bheairt fhéin e,] agus air ball ghabh e a thurus.

[Agus cha do mharbhadh duine le gobhair no le fuath
air an Tom Bhuidhe riamh o'n uair sin.]

[1] *Lit.* Oh clever hand !

[2] Incident of a character bearing about with him or showing on his own
proper person when in his normal state, a wound corresponding in position
to that received while in the metamorphosed state.   Compare the case of
the fox who had turned himself into a sword, *W. H. Tales,* ii., No. 46, Var. 4.
When referring to the manner in which a giant had used him when in sword-

Then, the goat seized him, and brought him to his knees, saying to him—'Uisdean Mór, Mac Gille Phàdruig, thou shalt not go hence alive.'

'Thou vile dun beast of the brooks,' he answered, 'little dost thou know about it.'

'Where, now, is Catrìona, thy grandmother's sister, thou active expert champion?' [1] said the goat, thinking that she had got the upper hand of him.

'Good luck be thine, thanks to thee! 'tis thou who hast the better memory,' answered Uisdean, drawing his dirk, and giving the brute a murderous stab of the steel blade in its stomach. Instantly the goat fled (or vanished?).

Uisdean, after looking round about him, [and seeing nothing?] returned to the house of the weaver. He went in, resolutely inflexible, and enquired where the man of the house was.

[They] said that he was in bed, lying ill.

'I needs must see him,' said Uisdean, and leaped over every obstacle until he came to the bed of the weaver. [But he was not in his bed, and when Uisdean had struck a light, he found him] lying under the loom, dripping blood.

He desired the weaver to show him his wounds at once. [He did so,] and when Uisdean saw the wound the dirk had made in his belly, he realized that the weaver was the same person as the goat.[2]

D 134
G 252

['If it be thou who hast caused so much loss on the Tom Buidhe, thou shalt not go further any longer,' quoth Uisdean.] And instead of applying any salve to his wounds, he gave the weaver a death stab, [killed him under his own loom], and instantly went his ways.

[And no man has ever been killed by goat or bogle on the Tom Buidhe since then.]

shape, the fox says: 'When he [the giant] seized me, with the first blow he cut the tree all but a small bit of bark; and look thyself there is no tooth in the door of my mouth which that filth of a Bodach has not broken.' In this case the teeth of the fox correspond to the teeth, which in old Gaelic lore constituted the edge of a weapon. See also Professor Sir John Rhys, *Celtic Folk-Lore*, ii., p. 260.

NOTES

MS. vol. x., No. 53 (A) 'Uisdean Mór Mac Gille Phàdruig,' and MS. vol. x., No. 67 (A), 'A' Ghobhar Mhaol Bhuidhe.' In one of the cancelled lists at the beginning of MS. vol. x., Islay says in effect that these two tales also appear as Nos. 11 and 12 of his Gaelic List. Though no signature appears on either of the MS. of these tales, and though no locality is mentioned, one of them, it is impossible to say which, is probably the one recited by Alexander MacDonald, Inverasdale, Gairloch, Ross-shire, mentioned in *W. H. Tales*, ii., No. 30, Var. 10.

The two tales have been fused in order to avoid needless repetition, as they are almost exactly the same. In order to assist the sense, some of the sentences in Var. 9 of No. 30 (*W. H. Tales*, ii.) have been brought in.

No. 53 (B) also called 'Uisdean Mór Mac Gille Phàdraig' is not mentioned in Islay's Gaelic List. It is the same as No. 7, Var. 4 (*W. H. Tales*, i.), which was recited by the said Alexander MacDonald. From the latter variant, and from Var. 9, we learn that the hero's profession was a strange one—being that of a bogle-slayer. The doughty deeds of a somewhat similar character, who was 'a skilful and fearless pacifier of restless ghosts' are related in *Trans. Gael. Soc. Inverness*, xxvi., p. 35.

Two versions of this tale, given by Uilleam MacCoinnich, of Edinburgh, appeared in the *Transactions of the Glasgow Gaelic Society*, 1899. In one of these the hero calls his dirk Beathag, his mother's sister. Whereupon the weaver, using the spell called *Fàth fithe*, vanishes, to meet the hero later on in goat-shape, and attack him with its two horns.[1] In due course the goat receives the fatal stab, and falls; but when the hero goes to lift it up and pitch it into the waterfall, he finds that the dead thing in his hands is the body of the Yellow-footed Weaver.

In the other version, after pitching the goat down the waterfall, the hero goes back to the house of the weaver, whom he finds wounded and dripping blood. The hero does not stab him again, and the weaver dies that night of his wound. Both these versions are very like the fused versions given above.

For another variant, see *Celtic Magazine*, ii., p. 467.

Another version is given in *Trans. Gael. Soc. Inverness*, xxvi., p. 279, and is quoted here. It comes from the west of Ross-shire.

---

[1] In other versions the goat wrestles with the hero and is said to be *maol*, hornless, but not said to be yellow. For the spell and incantations variously called *Fàth fithe, fith fath*, etc., see *Carmina Gadelica*, ii., p. 22. *Trans. Gael. Soc. Inverness*, viii., p. 127; xiv., p. 264; xvii., p. 225. Windisch, *Wörterbuch*, p. 535. Kuno Meyer, *Ancient Irish Poetry*, pp. 25, 111. Dr George Henderson, *Survivals*, pp. 11, 12 n, 221. *Silva Gad.*, i., p. 201; ii., p. 228. *Irische Texte*, iv., pp. 143, 318. For the connected *fiad*, a veil, see *ibid.*, p. 402. For *fath*, see *Revue Celtique*, xx., p. 146.

'Casan Buidhe.

Casan Buidhe, Yellow Legs, the famous wizard of Garve, is also called sometimes Breabadair nan casa buidhe—Weaver with the yellow legs. In his time the Black Water had the reputation of drowning more men than all the other rivers in the country, and showed a marked preference for men likely to have well-filled purses, such as drovers and pedlars. Not only did Casan Buidhe lie under suspicion, but the very means he employed to compass people's death without laying his hands upon them were whispered. He decked himself out in the hide and horns of a buck, and when people were in the middle of the ford he presented himself in this guise, ramping and threatening them on the bank. They, seeing Satan, as they supposed, awaiting them, were panic-stricken, lost their heads, and were carried away by the river and drowned. The last person he tried to frighten was the smith, Mackay. Instead of taking fright at the apparition, the valorous and mighty smith stormed the bank, laid violent hands on the wizard, and gave him such a mauling as incapacitated him from ever again repeating the same villainy.

In a Lochbroom version of the story, the weaver is represented as making murderous attacks in mid-stream on people fording the Black Water, and meeting his fate by being dirked by Uisdean Mac Ille Phàdruig, an intended victim, and the strongest man ever reared in Lochbroom.

The story of the yellow-shanked weaver, with local adaptations and variations in detail, is told in many places. A version, of which the scene is laid in the Urquhart district, appears in Mr William Mackay's 'Urquhart and Glenmoriston'; others lay the scene in Badenoch, Skye, etc.'

We learn also that Casan Buidhe was said to have had a son, one Donald Grant, who could charm the deer from the hill and make them follow him where he would, and that he was given to the practice of witchcraft.—*Trans. Gael. Soc. Inverness,* xxvi., pp. 284-5.

R. L. Stevenson had also heard of this story. See his *Catriona,* chap. xv.

MAC GILLE MHAOIL NA CRUIT

CHAN 'eil e an comas domh ainm an duine mu bheil mi dol a labhairt a thoirt [seachad], a thaobh is gu bheil fada o'n a bha an duine ann—ach b' fhear de'n chinneadh Dhomhnallach e. Is ann ri linn nan ceud uachdaran de Chloinn Choinnich a bhi air Gearrloch a bha e. B'e a àite còmhnuidh Inbhir-Asdail ann an Gearrloch.

Bha an Domhnallach 'na dhuine aig an robh mór thogradh ri eachdraidh na Féinne.

Air dha bhi oidhche gheamhraidh àraidh 'na shuidhe làimh ris an teinidh, thàinig duine bochd a dh' ionnsuigh a thighe a dh' fheòraich am faigheadh [e] cead tàimh air son oidhche. Mar bu ghnàthach leis na Gàidheil, thuirte gum faigheadh. Air do'n choigreach suidhe sìos, ghradthòisich fear an tighe air feòraich a sgeòil, agus air faighneachd ris mu thimchiòll na Féinne.

An uair a thòisich an comhradh, fhuair an Domhnallach sgeul air an Fhéinn nach robh aige riamh. Ach cha deach an comhradh fad air aghart, an uair a dh'fheòraich fear an tighe brath a ainme.

Fhreagair an coigreach gun robh 'Mac Gille Mhaoil na Cruit' mar ainm air.

Chan eudar nach do chuir an t-ainm mór ioghnadh air fear an tighe; ach co dhiùbh, cha deach fear de'n dithis gu leabaidh gus an tàinig an latha—Mac Gille Mhaoil na Cruit ag innseadh mu dhéidhinn na Féinne [fad na h-oidhche].

Dh' fhuirich e an còrr de'n gheamhradh an tigh an Domhnallaich, agus sgeul ùr [aige] na h-uile h-oidhche mu'n Fhéinn. Mar sin gus an tàinig obair an Earraich 's an treabhaidh. Aig ceann gach sgrìob, bha sgeul ùr aig Mac Gille Mhaoil mu'n Fhéinn. Bha an Domhnallach

MACMILLAN THE HARPIST

IT is not in my power to give the name of the man about whom I am going to speak, because it is so long since he lived—but he was one of the MacDonald clan. He lived at the time that the chieftains of Clan MacKenzie first became lords over Gairloch, and his dwelling-place was in Inverasdale in Gairloch.

This MacDonald was a man who took great delight in the history of the Fiann (or Fenians).

On a certain winter night he was sitting by the fireside, when a poor man came to his house who asked if he might have leave to stay for the night. As was the custom with the Gael, MacDonald gave him leave. Upon the stranger sitting down, the gudeman at once began to ask him for news, and to enquire of him concerning the Fiann.

At the very beginning of the colloquy, MacDonald obtained from the other a tale about the Fiann he had never heard before; but the conversation had not proceeded very far, when the gudeman requested to know the other's name.

The stranger answered that Macmillan the Harpist was his name.

Such a name could not but astonish the gudeman of the house very much; but whether or no, neither of the two went to bed till the day broke—Macmillan the Harpist telling legends about the Fiann [all night long].

He stayed for the rest of the winter in the MacDonald's house, and recited a new story about the Fiann every night. And so it went on until Spring and the labours of Springtime and ploughing came. At the end of every furrow, Macmillan had a new story about the Fiann. Every time

a' sìor ràdh, 'Is truagh nach [mi] bha beò r'a linn; is mi
dh' fhàgadh gach nì agus a leanadh iad,' an uair a dh'
innseadh am fear eile dha sgeul mu'n treubhantas agus mu
na cruadalan a bha tachairt riu.

Bho'n a bha an Domhnallach ag obair air an latha,
bhiodh e sgìth an am na h-oidhche. Uime sin, is e Mac
Gille Mhaoil na Cruit a bha saodachadh nan each [mu
fheasgar] leis an robh e ruigsinn cho fad ri Feadan Mór
Locha Dring, sean àite còmhnuidh na Féinne.[1]

Bu ghnàthach leis, oidhche mu seach, gum biodh an
latha ann, mun tigeadh e air ais; agus mar bu trice, bhiodh
sgeul ùr aige an latha sin mu'n Fhéinn. Bha an
Domhnallach a' sìor leantail nam briathran, gur bochd
nach robh e beò 'nan linn gus am faiceadh e iad.

Thuirt Mac Gille Mhaoil ris mu dheireadh, nan
saoileadh e gun seasadh e ri am faicinn, e a dhol maille
ris-san an nochd, is gun tugadh esan dha sealladh dhiùbh.

Feasgar na h-ath oidhche, chaidh iad air an aghart le
chéile a shaodachadh nan each. Dh' fhàg iad na h-eich
air Achadh na Féithe Dìrich, agus chaidh iad fad air an
aghart gu ruig an Fhéith Mhór.

Air dhaibh suidhe, thuirt Mac Gille Mhaoil ris an
Domhnallach—'Nise, tha eagal ormsa gu bheil thu cho
lag 'nad inntinn is nach seas thu ri am faicinn.'

Fhreagair an Domhnallach gur e sheasadh.

F 875·1*   Air dha so a ràdh, thuirt Mac Gille Mhaoil na Cruit
ris, 'Leag sìos do cheann am fagus domh, a chum['s] gun
ceangail mi e.' [Agus cheangail e suas a cheann, gu teann
teàruinte.]

E 384*   An sin thug e a mach feadag, agus leig e sgal; is b'e
D 1225   sin an sgal ! shaoil an Domhnallach gun deach a cheann
'na mhìribh !

[1] In this runnel the Féinn kept the cauldron, which the witch Cuilisg
ran away with.—Professor W. J. Watson, *Place Names of Ross and Cromarty*,
p. 230.

he told MacDonald a story about their heroism and the desperate adventures that they used to have, MacDonald would say, 'Pity 'tis that I did not live in their generation; 'tis I who would have left all and followed them.'

As MacDonald used to work during the day, he used to be tired at night-time. Thus it came to pass that Macmillan the Harpist was the one who used to drive the horses out [in the evening], and he used to go with them as far as the Great Runnel of Loch Dring, an old habitation of the Fiann.[1]

Every alternate night it was his custom to wait until day came before returning; and usually on that day he would bring some new tale about the Fiann. [Upon hearing them] MacDonald would always reiterate the same words, that it was a pity he had not lived in their time, that he might have beheld them.

At last Macmillan told him that if he thought he could endure to look upon them, he should go with him that very night, when he would grant him to see them in a vision.

Next evening they accordingly set out together to drive the horses. They left the animals in Achadh na Féithe Dìrich, but themselves went a long way farther on, as far as the Féith Mhór.

When they had sat down, Macmillan said to MacDonald —'Now, I greatly fear that thou art so weak in mind that thou wilt not be able to endure the sight of them.'

MacDonald answered that he was the very man who could endure it.

Upon his saying this, Macmillan the Harpist said to him, 'Lay thy head down near me, that I may bind it F 875·1* up.' [And bind it up he did, firmly and safely.]

Then did he produce a whistle, and blew a blast; and E 384* what a blast ! MacDonald felt as if his head had split to D 1225 pieces !

Dh'fheòraich e am b'urrainn da a cheann a thogail.
F 875·1* Thuirt e gum b'urrainn. An sin, leig e an ath sgal, agus
mar an ceudna an ath té, gus mu dheireadh an robh ceann
an Domhnallaich an inbhe bhi spealgte. Dh'iarr Mac
Gille Mhaoil air a cheann a thogail.

Air togail a chinn da, sheall e sìos an leathad còmhnard
E 502 a bha fa chomhair, agus chunnaic e na daoine a' teachd
fo làn àrmachd—agus b'e sin na daoine! le an coin air
loimhnean—agus b'e sin na coin! Air dhaibh a bhi
tighinn dìreach, bha an Domhnallach ag amharc gu geur
orra, ach am feadh a tharruing iad am fagus da, thòisich
e air fannachadh, chaill e a fhaireachadh, agus bha e ann
an cadal trom car sealain, a thaobh gun robh an sealladh
cho mór is nach robh e an comas da a ghiùlan.

An uair a dhùisg e as a shuain, cha robh duine aige ach
Mac Gille Mhaoil na Cruit 'na aonar, a' gul os a chionn,
agus a' dòrtadh uisge air a aghaidh.

'A dhuine bhochd!' labhair Mac Gille Mhaoil, 'is tu
a chaill air nach b'urrainn thu seasamh ri labhairt ris
na fir ud! Siod agad na gaisgich nach tig tuilleadh air
comharradh corraige dhuit-sa no dhomhsa!'

An sin dh' éirich iad, agus dh' imich iad dhachaidh
gu dubhach, brònach. B' e còmhradh Mhic Ghille Mhaoil
air an t-sràid: 'A dhuine bhochd! nach b' urrainn seasamh
ri còmhradh a chumail ris na fir ud a bheireadh dhuit
buaidh chòmhraidh, is mar an ceudna buaidh seilge [1] a
b' fheairrd thu féin is do shliochd as do dhéidh.'

An sin thàinig iad dhachaidh, agus tha e air aithris
gun do bhàsaich Mac Gille Mhaoil na Cruit an ceann
bheagan laithean 'na dhéidh so. Chaidh e anns *a' mheud*
D 55·1 *mhóir*, mun do bhàsaich e; bha a cheann a' ruigheachd
aon cheann an t-sabhail (far am bu ghnàth leis a bhi

---

[1] Success in oratory and in hunting. Compare the gift of success when
abroad or in company, 'buaidh cnuic is codhalach,' the gift that the Glaistig
of Lianachan in the fine legend of that name offers her captor if he will

Macmillan then asked him if he were able to raise his head. MacDonald replied that he could. Then F 875·1* Macmillan blew another blast, and yet another, till at last MacDonald's head was nearly shattered. [Finally] Macmillan desired him to raise his head.

So MacDonald lifted his head and looked away down E 502 the level slope that lay before him; and then, indeed, he saw men approaching, men armed to the teeth—and ah! but they were the men! and with them came their hounds on leash—and what hounds they were, too! Onwards they came, straight on, and keenly did MacDonald bend his glance upon them the while; but when they began to draw nearer he began to grow faint, and then losing all consciousness, sank for a little while into a deep sleep, for the vision had been so tremendous that he had not been able to endure it.

When he awoke from his swoon, there was no one with him but Macmillan the Harpist, who was weeping over him and pouring water on his face.

'Alas! unhappy man!' said Macmillan, 'how great a loss hast thou suffered through not being able to endure speech with those champions! Know then that those were the heroes who will never come again, never, neither at the beckoning of thy finger, nor yet of mine!'

Then they arose, and darkly and sadly they went home. On the way Macmillan conversed, but the burden of all he said was this: 'Alas for thee, unhappy man! who wast not able to endure speech with those heroes. For they would have bestowed upon thee the gift of success both in oratory and in hunting [1]; a gift that would have wrought great good, both to thee and to thy descendants after thee.'

Then they came home, and it is said that a few days later Macmillan the Harpist died. Before he died he grew to a *gigantic size*: so great that his head reached to D 55·1 one end of the barn (where he used to sleep), and his feet to the other. It was thus impossible to lift him up or to

restore her her freedom.—MacPherson's *Duanaire*, p. 123. *Celtic Review*, v., p. 253.

laighe), agus a chasan an ceann eile.—Mar so, bha e
do-dhèanta a thogail no a fhaotainn slàn a mach as an
t-sabhal; uime sin, b'éiginn a ghearradh 'na cheathramhan
a chum a fhaotainn a mach is a adhlacadh. Mar so,
V 63 dh' adhlaic an Domhnallach a chorp mar a b'fhearr a
dh'fhaodadh e.

An uair a chuala Uachdaran Ghearrloch mu thimchioll
a bhàis, thuirt e nam biodh fios aige gun do chaochail e,
gun rachadh barrachd cosdais a dhèanamh mu thimchioll
a thiodhlacaidh; nach b'e an t-ainm ceart a thug e seachad
air féin; nach b'e Mac Gille Mhaoil na Cruit a bh'ann,
ach Biolair Uasal MacFhinn.[1]

Is ann de iarmad eachdraidh an Domhnallaich so a
tha na bheil ri a fhaotainn ann an Gearrloch de eachdraidh
na Féinne. Bu chòir a ainmeachadh gu bheil corp Mhic
Ghille Mhaoil na Cruit an tasgaidh ann an cnocan air
fearann an tigh sgoile, aig Inbhir-Asdail, an ear-thuath
air an tigh, bho'm bheil mar ainm air a' chnocan gus an
latha 'n diugh, To[bh]tag Mhic Ghille Mhaoil.

Donald Macdonald, Travelling Tinsmith (?).
A Gairloch story.

NOTES

MS. vol. x., No. 54. In the Gaelic List the title is given as 'Mac
'ille Mhore na cruit.' The MS., however, gives 'Mhaoil' everywhere,
and never gives 'Mhore.'

This is one of a number of tales from Gairloch of which Campbell
of Islay says:—'This lot got from various sources by different school-
masters, through Osgood Hanbury Mackenzie, but the collectors,
after a time, struck work, one saying that he would write no more
lies for the whole estate.' See Islay's Gaelic List, Nos. 53-61. W. H.
Tales, iv., end.

Mac Gille Mhaoil na Cruit, literally The Son of the Tonsured
or Shaven (or Bald, or Crop-eared) Servant (or Devotee or Aspirant)
of the Crowd (or Harp.)—This name deserves some notice, if only
because it astonished the goodman MacDonald in our story. At
first sight it seems to be one of the religious names that date from

convey him whole out of the barn; so they had to divide him into quarters in order to take him out to bury him. In this way did MacDonald bury his body, buried it as V 63 best he might.

When the Laird of Gairloch heard about his death, he said that had he known he had died, more money should have been expended over his burial; that the name he had given himself was not the right one; for he was not Macmillan the Harpist at all, but Noble Watercress, Son of Fionn.[1]

All that is still extant in Gairloch of the history of the Fiann is taken from the remains of this MacDonald's collection of tales. It ought to be mentioned that the body of Macmillan the Harpist is in Inverasdale, in the keeping of a little hill that is situated on the school-house land, and to the north-east of the house. From this circumstance the hill to this very day is called MACMILLAN'S MOUND.

---

[1] Other members of the Fenian host had two names.—*Celtic Review*, i., pp. 205, 207, 354; vii., p. 347.

---

early Church times, of which names there are many in modern Gaelic, such as—

Mac Gille Chrìosd, The Son of Christ's Slave or Votary;
Mac Gille Chaluim, The Son of St Columba's Servant;
Mac Gille Iosa, the Son of the Servant of Jesus;
Maol Iosa, The Tonsured (Servant) of Jesus;
Maol Chaluim, The Shaven (Devotee) of St Columba.

In the mangled forms of these names that appear in English, *e.g.* Gilchrist, Malcolmson, Gillies and MacLeish, Malise, Malcolm, a good deal of their original meaning is lost. Mac Gille Mhaoil itself (as well as Mac Mhaolain, the Son of The Tonsured) both appear in English as. Mac Millan.

One feels justified, however, in suspecting that in our tale, if not in other cases, the name Mac Gille Mhaoil na Cruit is of pagan or pre-Christian origin. For our story, though very touching, is most thoroughly pagan in incident. In the first place, no Christian would call himself the Devotee of the Harp, but rather the Votary of a Saint. Then the cognate name 'Maolan' is compared by Doctor MacBain with the Ogham *Mailagni* which, it is to be presumed, is pre-Christian. Then in many old Gaelic tales, undoubtedly of pre-Christian origin, various supernaturals flourish, who are described as being *maol*, *carrach*, 'bald, or crop-eared, or tonsured, and scurvy or rough-skinned.' They are usually, though not always,[1] the villains of the piece, frequently also the offspring of the enemy, or of a witch or of some mysterious bogle. These characters possibly represent pagan devotees who, in the happy days of the ancient Celtic religion, had been the respected officials of various pagan institutions, to the service of which they had been dedicated by tonsure and scarification. (Campbell himself thought that his peasant collectors were right when they told him that the mysterious Gruagach of these tales was once a Druid, or a professor or master of arts.—*W. H. Tales*, intro., xciii. Perhaps 'The Slave of the Lamp' in *Aladdin* had a genesis similar to that of *The Devotee of the Harp*. Creatures that are the 'slaves' of a magic snuff-box appear in *W. H. Tales*, ii., No. 44.) But with the appearance in the land of a new faith, gradually gaining ground and destined to blot out the older for ever, people would begin to use the word *maol*, not with the respectable meaning of 'tonsured,' but with the other meaning of 'bald,' and apply it to the devotees of the older faith in contempt. Similarly, the word *carrach*, originally implying scarification, the honourable mark of dedication, took on the contemptible meaning of 'scurvy' or 'rough-skinned.' At the same time the belief in witchcraft, and in the authority of the witch who had once been a great power in the State, began to decline, and this is borne out by the evidence of the old Gaelic [2] tales, in which the wicked witches are usually worsted. In passing, it may well be said of these tales that when they seem to be merely extravagant and idle accounts of impossible events and exploits, they are frequently fairly good records of pagan ritual or magic, though corrupted and garbled by successive generations of story-tellers, for whom the tales had lost their original meaning because the ancient rites to which they referred were no longer practised or known.

We may imagine then, that among the pagan Gael, those who had

---

[1] See *W. H. Tales*, i., No. 17, and vars.

[2] It may be interesting to remember that the earlier prophets of Israel, the *nebiim* or ecstatics of the more ancient times, fell under contempt and died out as a class, to be succeeded by nobler men such as Elijah, Isaiah and others. See Hermann Gunkel, 'The Secret Experiences of the Prophets,' in *The Expositor*, May, June, July, 1924. In meaning, *nebiim* may be compared with the Manchu word Saman, or Shaman, *one who is excited*; it is applied in Siberia to a sorcerer or magician. See W. Bonser, in *Folk-Lore*, xxxv., p. 55.

devoted themselves to the arts would practise various tonsures in order to indicate the nature of their calling. The votaries of any particular muse would most certainly have wooed her with the whole-hearted devotion peculiar to the Celt, and 'Mac Gille Mhaoil na Cruit' is probably an instance. Close cropping or shaving the hair of the head was the symbol of thralldom (see *Rosg Gàidhlig*, p. 216); in the case before us, the hero is the thrall of the harp, that is, he is someone who was devoted to the art of playing on the instrument.

In No. 25 (MS. vol. x., No. 47) a hero's mother's sister puts the Humming Harp of Harmony at his bed-head that he might the better D 1231 sleep. Sir Olave O'Corn had another such harp, which he took with him when sailing the seas.—*Trans. Gael. Soc. Inverness*, xiii., p. 70, from which I here translate :—

> A harp had he of music softly murmuring,
> That played sweet tunes and slumber melodies,
> So sweet that in no fairy hill or eminence,
> Or fairy cavern (?) 'neath the swelling waves,
> Or even in Mananan's dwelling-house,
> Were whispered lullabies more beautiful.
> E'en wounded men in heavy sleep 't would lay,
> Women in travail too, and fairy dames.

For the Highland harp, see *Celtic Review*, i., p. 182; viii., p. 341. *Trans. Gael. Soc. Inverness*, xxxiii., p. 279. The instrument was probably at one time looked upon as something unusually magical.[1]

A' Chlarsach Urlair, The Harp of the Floor, was the name of a domestic witch, whose duties were probably witchcraft and harping.—*Trans. Gael. Soc. Inverness*, xxv., p. 218. See p. 497.

An unfriendly harper appears in *W. H. Tales*, ii., No. 52, and *Celtic Review*, iii., p. 349 ; and some magical and unfriendly ones in *Waifs and Strays*, ii., pp. 367, 488 ; iv., pp. 247-8. *Rosg Gàidhlig*, p. 92. *Trans. Gael. Soc. Inverness*, xv., p. 60.

Three harpers from Lochlann, who are also magicians, run away with a bride, and perform impossible feats in 'The Red-lipped Maiden.' See *Norse Influence*, p. 290.

A' Chruit Chiùil, or The Harp of Music is the confederate of the child-stealing giant in the Eigg version of The Tuairisgeal (see p. 25). Its music lulls the watchers to sleep. In *Waifs and Strays*, iv., p. 205, it is a Musical Harper who does so. See also *ibid.*, ii., pp. 451, 488.

Again in No. 306, MS. vol. xi., the Harp of Music appears in the open. At sight of it, everyone flees, but no reason is given for the terror it inspires. The question now arises—how came the harp to have such ominous associations ? The bagpipes never have.

That the hero spends alternate nights in an old habitation of the Fiann is, of course, in order to hold communication with the ghosts

---

[1] This is probably the explanation of Macdonald's surprise—not the man's name (MacGille Mhaoil or Macmillan) but the fact that he was a harpist, which was shown by the epithet 'na Cruit.'

of his fellow-heroes, and to hear more tales of the Fenian saga, which he might afterwards recite to MacDonald.

D 1225
E 384*

The head-splitting whistle or chanter or hammer [1] occurs in *W. H. Tales*, ii., No. 31, Var. 5. Islay's English List, No. 115. *An Gàidheal*, (1875), iv., pp. 11, 81. *Waifs and Strays*, iii., p. 274. An elk-bone is used to whistle with, *ibid.*, iv., p. 83 ; sometimes a shield is used (presumably as an instrument of percussion), *ibid.*, p. 212.

E 380
F 404

For instances of summoning up the spirits of the dead: Islay's English List, Nos. 1, 12, 175, 283, 387. *Witchcraft*, p. 200. Summoning up the worst gillie and hound that the Fenians had, and various herds of deer as well.—*An Deò Gréine*, xv., p. 181. Summoning the ghosts (?) of cats at the 'Taghairm.'—*Superstitions*, p. 304.

All the Fenian heroes were giants, so that gigantic stature was quite in keeping with the character of Mac Gille Mhaoil the Harpist. But the attainment of such stature by sudden growth, and as a preliminary to death, is unusual and wild. The words *a' mheud mhóir*, (underlined in the MS.), also mean *pride, dropsy*. *A' mheud mhór gun chur leatha* means *pride, boasting, with nothing to support it*.

Dismemberment occurs in *The Celtic Dragon Myth*, p. 120.

---

[1] *An t-ord*, the hammer, is a corruption of *dord Fiann*, the Fenian chant.

DONNCHADH EILEIN IÙ AGUS AN GILLE GLAS

No. 30.   *Campbell MS. Vol. x., No. 55*

BHA duine ann an Eilean Iù do'm b'ainm Donnchadh. Bha mar an ceudna seirbhiseach aige, ach cha robh brath a ainm agamsa. Bha Donnchadh air a mheas 'na dhuine cothromach 'na latha féin.

Thàinig an sin droch earrach a chum fad air ais an obair ghnàthaichte.

An uair a thòisich an aimsir air fàs beagan na bu chiuine, bha Donnchadh a' faicinn móran aige r'a dhèanamh. An ceud latha chaidh e a mach, thòisich e air gearan is ag ràdh, nam faigheadh e fear eile ri a thuarasdalachadh, gum biodh e toilichte.

An ceann tacain, thàinig gille caol glas, gus an ionad anns an robh Donnchadh, [agus dh'iarr e a fhasdadh air Donnchadh]. Dh'fheòraich Donnchadh dheth ciod an duais a ghabhadh e airson tòiseachadh air an ruamhar maille ri a ghille féin.

Thuirt e nach iarradh e móran 'sam bith. 'Ma bheir thu dhomhsa,' ars esan, 'làn mo ròpa de fhaoigh [1] an uair a thig am Foghar, tòisichidh mi.'—'Sin bheir mi dhuit,' fhreagair Donnchadh. Le so chòrd iad.

A thaobh gun robh an t-àite fad o'n tigh, chuireadh am biadh do'n ionnsuigh. Ghabh na fir am biadh, agus thuirt an Gille Glas ri gille Dhonnchaidh, 'Gabhaidh sinn ar n-anail car tacain.' Chaidil na fir le chéile.

An uair a dhùisg iad, bha e tarruing gu math ri feasgar. Ghabh na fir an dinnear, agus an sin, thòisich iad air obair. Bha móran aca ri dhèanamh, achadh de ghlas thalamh r'a

---

[1] *faoigh*, an asking for aid in the shape of corn, wool, and sometimes cattle, a custom once very common: *faoigh eòrna*, a begging for barley.

DUNCAN OF EWE ISLE AND THE
SALLOW LAD

No. 30.   *Campbell MS. Vol. x., No. 55*

THERE lived a man in Ewe Isle by name Duncan. He also
had a servant, but I have no knowledge of the servant's
name. In his own day, Duncan was looked upon as a
man who was well to do.

There came a springtime, when the weather was so bad,
that the customary work was kept a long way back.

When the weather began to get a little milder, Duncan
began to see that there was a great deal of work for him to
do. The first day he went out, he began grumbling and
saying, that if he could get hold of another man whom he
could hire, he would be satisfied.

In the course of a short time, there came a slender   N 810
sallow lad to the place where Duncan was [and asked him
to hire him]. So Duncan asked him what wages he
would want to begin the digging with his own lad.

He replied that he would not want much at all. 'If
thou wilt bestow upon me,' he said, 'when harvest comes,
as much gift [corn] [1] as I can tie up in my rope, I will
begin.'—'That will I certainly give thee,' answered Duncan.
Thereupon, they struck the bargain.

As the place [where the digging was to be done] was
far from the house, their food used to be sent out to them.
The men took their food, and the Sallow Lad said to
Duncan's lad, 'We will take our ease for a short spell.'
So both the men went to sleep.

When they awoke, it was drawing well on towards
evening. They took their dinner, and then began work.
There was a great deal for them to do, a whole field of fallow

ruamhar. Ach is e a ruamhradh an Gille Glas ! Bha
aon fhacal mór, math aige ri gille Dhonnchaidh:—'Bhuait,
a ghille Dhonnchaidh !' ¹ agus air cho math 'sa ruamhradh
gille Dhonnchaidh, cha bhiodh aige ach aon phloc air a
thionndadh de'n t-sreath, an uair a bhiodh an Gille Glas
air ais. Mun tàinig an oidhche, bha an t-àite air a
ruamhar !

Bha gach nì gu ro mhath gus an tàinig am Foghar.
Aig am na buana, chaidh an t-àite a bhuain maille ris a'
chuid eile. Thàinig an Gille Glas le taod 'na làimh, agus
gun dàil, ghrad thòisich e ri a lìonadh a arbhar an achaidh.
K 174·1* Bha e a' cur ann agus a' cur ann,² gus mu dheireadh an
deachaidh na bha air an achadh anns an taod !

Dar a chunnaic Donnchadh gun robh a chuid uile anns
an aon ghad, ghlaodh e—

Z 85*   'Aoine a threabh mi,
           Aoine a chuir mi,
           Aoine a bhuain mi;
F 382   Fhir a dh'òrduich na trì Aoineachan,
           Na leig mo chuid uile 'san aon ghad-ghuailne !'

An sin, labhair an Gille Glas—

           'An uair is teinne an gad-guailne,
              is ann is dualaiche dha briseadh.'

Le so, bhris an taod—ach an uair a bhrist, cha robh sguab
Q 585 air an achadh, ach na bha air an aon phloc a thionndaidh gille Dhonnchaidh !

Alexander MacDonald, Inverasdale [Loch Ewe, Ross-shire].

¹ *Lit.* from thee, oh gillie of Duncan ! probably elliptical for *cur bhuait e*,
put it from thee, *i.e.* get it done, get it past and over. Compare *thig bhuait*,

land to dig. But the Sallow Lad was the boy to dig !
And [while they were working] he continually shouted at
Duncan's gillie, one great clinching phrase—'Play up, thou
Duncan's lad !' [1] Yet no matter how hard Duncan's lad
dug, he could never get more than one clod of his furrow
turned, before the Sallow Lad [had finished his furrow and]
was back again. And before the night came, the whole
field had been dug !

However, everything went well until Autumn. When
reaping time came, the field was reaped along with the
other parts [of the farm]. Then came the Sallow Lad with
a rope of withies in his hand, and without any delay, he
[laid it on the ground and] began filling it with [*i.e.* piling
upon it] the corn of the field. He kept on adding to it K 174·1*
and adding to it [2] until at last all the corn that there was in
that field had been bound up in that rope !

When Duncan saw that all he had, had been tied up in
one withy, he cried—

'On Friday I ploughed,   Z 85*
On Friday I sowed,
On Friday I reaped;
O Thou who didst ordain the three Fridays,   F 382
Let not my all be carried off in a single shoulder-withe !'

Then spoke the Sallow Lad, and said—

' When the shoulder-withe is tightest,
the more likely it is to break.'

At this the rope broke—but when it did so, there was not Q 585
one sheaf of corn left on the field, save only what had
grown on those single clods that Duncan's lad had turned.

---

thigbhuat, come from thee (a challenge to fight); also an encouragement in
shinty.
   [2] *Lit.* putting into it and putting into it.

NOTES

MS. vol. x., No. 55. Scribe unknown: probably a schoolmaster. Ewe Isle is in Loch Ewe, Ross-shire.

Similar tales.—(1) *Trans. Gael. Soc. Inverness*, xxvi., pp. 272-5; xxxiv., p. 175. (2) *Am Bàrd*, p. 50 (Alasdair Camshron and I. MacA. Moffatt-Pender; Edinburgh, U. M. Urchardainn agus a Mhac, 1926). (3) *Waifs and Strays*, iii., pp. 216, 297. (4) *Superstitions*, p. 97.

For the story in general, *cf.* the article of M. M. Banks in *Études Celtiques* (September 1938) on *The Three Màrts*.

In Similars 1 and 2, as in this story, No 30 (MS. vol. x., No. 55), the verse mentions Friday as the day of the week on which the various agricultural operations were performed, whilst in Similars 3 and 4, *Màrt* (or Tuesday) is the day mentioned.

Nicolson (*Gaelic Proverbs*, pp. 26, 242, 413) makes *Màrt* the day on which sowing was to be done. But *Màrt* meant not only (1) Tuesday but also (2) the month of March, and (3) 'the fit time for doing any particular part of agricultural work' (*Waifs and Strays*, iii., p. 298). *Màrt-cuir* was the fit time for sowing, beginning on 12th April, ending on Mayday (Old Style). *Màrt-fuine*, the fit time of baking, began on 12th August. ('It was so called because no part of the growing corn was cut and the meal made from it baked into bread before that day arrived.') *Màrt-buana*, or the fit time of reaping, began on 12th September. *Waifs and Strays*, v., p. 124, says that *Màrt* denotes any busy time of the year, there being a *màrt* in harvest (*Màrt Fogharaidh*) and another in Spring (*Màrt Earraich*). *Superstitions*, p. 88, speaks of a *màrt cur an t-sìl* or seed-time, and a *màrt buain*, or harvest. See also *Witchcraft*, p. 255. *Folk-Tales and Fairy Lore*, pp. 229, 328. *Dwelly's Dictionary*, art. *màrt*. Dr A. Carmichael, *Carmina Gadelica*, i., p. 245. *Béaloideas*, iii., p. 144. Some of these references concern *Coileach Dubh a' Mhàirt*, a black cock hatched in March from a cock and hen hatched in a previous March, whose crow was sovereign against evil. A dog born in a *Màrt* was also greatly valued. Whether the *Màrts* in Similars 3 and 4 meant *Tuesday* or a suitable 'agricultural' period, remains uncertain.

The version in *Am Bàrd* contains a very remarkable incident, not known to me as occurring elsewhere. When the digging was over, the farmer asked his supernatural helper to come in and have some food. But the other replies that food was not in the bargain. This probably suggests merely that he would run no risk of voiding his contract; he agreed to *tuarastal*, not *biadh agus tuarastal*.

In other versions, the Sallow Lad vanishes magically, but leaves all the corn behind him on the field, which is the more likely ending.

GILLE DUBH LOCHA DRING [1]

BHA fear uair-eiginn ann an Asaint mu Thuath do'm
b'ainm Mac an Air. Tha e air aithris gum b'e an duine
F 305 so athair a' Ghille Dhuibh, agus gum b'e bean-shìdh a
bu mhàthair da,[2] ach co dhiùbh, bha an Gille Dubh r'a
fhaicinn caochladh amannan air monaidhean na Gàidheal-
tachd, gu h-àraidh an Locha Dring ann an Gearrloch.
Bha fear Maol-Moire MacRath a chòmhnuidh uair-
eigin ann an Sannda Ghearrloch, a bhiodh a' dol gu
àirigh le a chuid spréidh an Locha Dring. Bha caileag
aige 'na seirbhiseach do'm b'ainm An Coisiche Mór.
Chaidh aon de chrodh an duine so air chall, agus dh'
fhalbh a bhean g'a h-iarraidh. Air do'n Choisiche bhi
gabhail fadachd nach robh a banamhaighstir a' tighinn
dhachaidh, dh'fhalbh i fhéin mar an ceudna. Ach air do
phàisdean a bu nighean do Mhaol-Moire a bhi gabhail
iongnaidh nach robh aon chuid a màthair no An Coisiche
a' pilltinn, thug i as an déidh; ach cha b'fhada chaidh am
pàisde, an uair a chaidh i air seacharan anns a' choillidh.
An sin, thachair an Gille Dubh rithe le currachd mór
chóinntich, air a ceangal le crios luachrach mu a cheann.
Lìon e a h-uchd làn de lusan,[3] agus thuirt e rithe gun robh
F 403·2 a màthair agus An Coisiche air dol dachaidh leis a' bhoin.
An sin chuir e air an rathad dachaidh i gu sàbhailt.

     Bha duine mór fiadhaich air chuairt ann an Gearrloch
a' toirt a bheò de an tuath, do'm b'ainm Murchadh
Ministeir. Bha Murchadh 'na dhuine anabarrach làidir,

---

¹ Gille, or lad, is the name of many a male supernatural. Loch Dring
was an ancient resort of the Fenians. See No. 29 (MS. vol. x., No. 54.)
² The Urisks were also said to be the offspring of unions between mortals
F 305 and fairies.—Rev. J. G. Campbell, *Superstitions*, p. 195.
³ The *Glaistig*, and another creature called *Connal*, were also said to be

THE BLACK LAD OF LOCH DRING[1]

THERE was once a man of North Assynt whose name was
Mac an Air.   It was said that this man was the father, and
that a fairy-woman was the mother of the Black Lad [of F 305
Loch Dring],[2] but whether or no, the Black Lad has been
seen on various occasions on the moors of the Highlands,
particularly in the district of Loch Dring in Gairloch.

There was another man called Mulmoire MacRath
who dwelt at one time in Sannda of Gairloch, who [in the
summer time] used to take his herds to the sheilings in the
district of Loch Dring.   He had a lassie for a servant whose
name was Big Speedy-Foot (*lit.* The Big Walker).   One of
this man's cattle went astray, and so his wife went in search
of it.   When Big Speedy-Foot grew weary of waiting for
her mistress, and was beginning to think she was never
coming back home, she also set forth.   A certain little child,
a daughter of Mulmoire's, beginning to wonder because
neither her mother nor Big Speedy-Foot were returning,
set forth after them ; but the child had not gone far,
when she got lost in the woods.   Then it was that the
Black Lad, wearing a great headdress made of moss, which
was bound about his head with a fillet of rushes, met her.
He filled her arms full of flowers,[3] and told her that her
mother and Big Speedy-Foot had got home again and had
brought the cow with them.   He then set her safely on the F 403·2
road home.

There used to be a big wild sort of man wandering
about Gairloch called Murdoch the Minister, who lived on
the peasantry.[4]   Murdoch was an exceedingly strong, wild

kind to children.—*Celtic Review*, v., pp. 62, 65.   The terrible *Coluinn gun Cheann*,
or Headless Body of Morar, never did harm to either women or children.—
W. H. Tales, ii., No. 30, Var. 5.

[4] The Gaelic means that Murdoch forced the peasantry to contribute to
his maintenance.

fiadhaich, a' giùlan lùirich mhóir nach robh an comas do
neach sam bith eile a ghiùlan. Thachair dha bhi gabhail
a' mhonaidh: thàinig an oidhche air ann an Locha Dring,
agus b'éiginn da tàmh a ghabhail an sin ann am bothan
fàs. Bha Murchadh cho làidir is gun laigheadh e fo
tharbh mór, fiadhaich,[1] a bhiodh a' gabhail air an t-sluagh,
agus o'm biodh gach aon a' teicheadh, gus an sguireadh e
dheth leis féin. Choinnich an Gille Dubh Murchadh an
oidhche so, agus bha cath searbh eatorra, ach chan innseadh
Murchadh ach beagan mu a thimchioll. Theireadh e
uairean gun robh sùilean a' Ghille Dhuibh cho leathann
ris na miasan. Thòisich muinntir ri farraid dheth: 'An
do ghabh thu eagal, a Mhurchaidh?'[2]

F 402·1·2

'Bha aobhar an eagail ann, nam biodh fios có a ghabhadh
e,' fhreagradh Murchadh.[3]

Bha Locha Dring 'na àirigh aig Fear Shannda, agus
tharla, air dha bhi siubhal a' mhonaidh, gun tàinig an
oidhche air, agus gum b'éiginn da a cur seachad anns
a' bhothan àirigh. Air dha bhi ro thartmhor, cha dèanadh
bainne a phathadh a chasg: uime sin, dh'iarr e air aon de
a sheirbhisich a dhol airson deoch an uisge gu Tobar
Dringaig:—ach cha rachadh aon diùbh ann le eagal a'
Ghille Dhuibh. An uair a dhiùlt iad uile, b'éiginn da
féin falbh; agus a réir mo sgeula-sa, cha tàinig e air ais gu
beul an latha. Cha d'fhuair neach 'sam bith a mach an
comhrag a bha eadar e féin 's an Gille Dubh: ach co dhiùbh,
chan fhacas an Gille Dubh an Locha Dring gu ùine mhóir
as déidh so. Bha e air aithris gun tug e gealladh de'n
Ghille Dhubh gum fàgadh e an t-àite; agus 'na dhéidh
so, gur h-ann an Asaint (dùthaich a athar) a bha an Gille
Dubh r'a fhaicinn.

Ach fada an déidh bàis Fhir Shannda, bha buachaille
spréidhe ann an Locha Dring, do'm b'ainm Eachann Mór
Bodhar, mu'm bheil e air a aithris gum faca e fhéin is a

---

[1] Lie down in front of it, *i.e.* let it worry him.

[2] There is many a Highland tale of some bogle who was for a long time
the terror of the countryside until some champion met and overcame it.
See No. 28 (MS. vol. x., No. 53A.)

man, who wore a suit of armour heavier than anyone else could wear. On one occasion when roaming over the mountains, night overtook him when in the Loch Dring district, and he was obliged to seek rest in a deserted bothy. There was a certain great fierce bull, that used to attack people, and from which everyone used to flee ; but Murdoch was so strong that he would wrestle with it [1] until the animal of its own accord, ceased raging. On the night in question the Black Lad met Murdoch, and there was a bitter fight F 402·1·2 between them, but it is very little that Murdoch would ever tell about it. He would sometimes remark that the Black Lad's eyes were as broad as plates. And people began to ask him 'Wert thou afraid, Murdoch ?' [2]

'There certainly was cause of fear,' Murdoch would answer, 'if there had been anyone to feel it.[3]

The Laird of Sannda had Loch Dring for a summer grazing place or sheiling. He happened to be passing over the mountains once, when night overtook him, and he was obliged to pass it in the sheiling bothy. He was so thirsty that milk could not quench his thirst: he therefore asked one of his servants to go the Well of Dringag for a drink of water ; but not one of them would go for fear of the Black Lad. When they all refused, he was obliged to go himself; and according to the story I heard, he did not come back till daybreak. No one ever found out what sort of a fight took place between him and the Black Lad: but in any case, the Black Lad was not seen in the Loch Dring district for a long time afterwards. It was said that the Laird of Sannda wrung a promise from the Black Lad to leave the place; and that thereafter it was in Assynt (his father's country) that the Black Lad was to be seen.

But long after the death of the Laird of Sannda, there was a cattle-herd in the Loch Dring district, called Big Deaf Hector, of whom it is related that he himself and his

---

[3] *Lit.* 'Didst thou take fear, Murdoch ?'—'The cause of fear was there, if it could be known who would feel it.'

theaghlach an Gille Dubh mun cuairt do'n tigh, na bu
trice na aon uair. Ach co dhiùbh, an uair a chuala am
bàrd an sgeul, sheinn e mar a leanas [1] :—

> Don. McDonald.　}
> Wm. McRae, Cove.　} [Reciters.]
> John McLennan.　}

The scribe was probably a schoolmaster.

NOTES.

MS. vol. x., No. 56. John H. Dixon, in his *Gairloch* (Edinburgh,
1886), says that the Black Lad of Loch Dring 'was generally regarded
as a beneficent fairy. He never spoke to anyone, except to a little
girl named Jessie MacRae, whose home was at Loch a Druing [*sic*].
She was lost in the woods one summer night; the Gille Dubh came to
her, treated her with great kindness, and took her safely home again
next morning.' See also 'Conall,' *Celtic Review*, v., p. 64.

family had seen the Black Lad about the house, more than once. However, when a certain bard heard the tale, he sang the following [1] :—

We take the opportunity of adding to this volume the following items, which are not stories, as containing interesting and curious information about the supernatural beings of popular Gaelic belief. They are bound up after No. 7 (MS. vol. x., No. 16).

[1] The song to the Black Lad which is bound up after this item is too disconnected to be intelligible. Another song to a neighbour is bound up next, equally unintelligible. The two songs are therefore not printed here.

A' BHANTRACH

No. 31a.   *[MS. Vol. x., No. 17a]*

Aarne-Thompson, No. 311

THIS tale has been summarized by Islay in *W. H. Tales*, ii., No. 41, Var. 2. For the Gaelic, see *Béaloideas*, (1934), iv., p. 396. It has some resemblances to 'Peerifool,' *Folk-Lore*, i., p. 302. See also *Folk-Lore Record* (1881), iv., p. 152. At the end of the MS. of No. 17(A), Hector MacLean has added the following note:—

'Got these four tales [Nos. 35, 6, 7, 36, MS. vol. x., Nos. 14, 15, 16, 17] from Hugh MacIndear [*sic*] an old man at Bowmore [Islay] who can recite a great many more. The last is a version of one I have sent you already. I do not know if they be quite of the kind to suit your purpose. MacIndeoir [*sic*] borders upon eighty, is very poor, and I think has had no education, or extremely little. He tells me he learnt them long ago from one Angus Brown who lived at the place where John McIntyre the wright lately resided.

AN DONN MARA MÓR MACMHOIREIN

No. 31b.   *[MS. Vol. x., No Number]*

F 531·2   BHA e cho àrd ri craoibh an coillidh, ach cha robh coire sam bith ann. Bhiodh e falbh is e glaodhaich 'Steó hó ! na bà 'sa ghart.'[1]

---

[1] This creature evidently wished, like the Glaistig, to assist mortals by keeping the cattle away from the crops. I have no further information about

THE WIDOW

No. 31a.   *[MS. Vol. x., No. 17a]*

Aarne-Thompson, No. 311

THIS Brown was known by the sobriquet of Aonghas Gruama [Angus the Grim] and very queer anecdotes are told of him, which I do not doubt you must [have] heard yourself. MacIndeoir [*sic*] was able to play the pipes in his day: his father was considered an excellent piper and his son Dugald is allowed to be one of the best pipers in the island [Islay]. He is a firm believer in the wonders related in the stories, in fairies, giants, and hobgoblins. The following are some things that he related to me with great gravity and deep conviction.

> An Donn Mara Mor MacMhoirein.
> An Sac Bac [= Bàn].
> A' Ghlaisrig.'

These three items do not appear in Islay's Gaelic List. The sheet on which they are written is numbered 13, but the items themselves bear no numbers. I have therefore numbered them 31*a*, 31*b*, 31*c*, 31*d*. For Aonghas Gruama, see *W. H. Tales*, No. 41, Notes, and *Trans. Gael. Soc. Inverness*, xxv., pp. 187, 262. Angus was a carter, and used to tell his tales when driving in his cart. He it was who recited the long version (*b*) of No. 5 (MS. vol. x., No. 10), this book, to the father of the man who recited it for Campbell of Islay.

THE GREAT BROWN MACMORRAN (OR MORRISON) OF THE SEA (?)

No. 31b.   *[MS. Vol. x., No Number]*

HE was as tall as a tree in the forest, but there was no F 531·2 harm in him at all. He used to go about shouting, 'Steó hó ! the cows are in the corn.' [1]

him. My translation of his name is conjectural. But there is a tale about apparently similar beings in *Urquhart and Glenmoriston*, pp. 425, 577.

AN SAC BÀN

No. 31c.   [MS. Vol. x., No Number]

F 495·1*   BHIODH an Sac Bàn 'ga roladh fhé[in] ro[i]mh chasan
dhaoine is 'gan leagail, agus an sin a' dol air am muin, is
D 1193   'gan leudachadh is 'gam mort.

NOTES

'An Sac Bac' in title only.

There is a tale in *Trans. Gael. Soc. Inverness*, xx., p. 58, which informs
us that the White Sack was a spirit. The tale is to the effect that a
woman whose son was courting a servant girl, being jealous of the girl,
determined to get rid of her, and for that purpose sent her to the Creagan
Change House to buy some drink. As far as can be guessed from the
tale, she sent her after dark. The road passed the Dell or Hollow of
the White Sack, a place which people did not like to frequent after
dark. On the way the girl found the White Sack's *luman* (a coarse
covering or sackcloth) the garment from which he probably got his
name. The girl knew that the White Sack could do nothing without
his *luman*, and so she gave it to the goodwife of the Change House,
telling her to keep it until she thought she, the girl, had had time
to get home. She then set off home, but after leaving the Change
House the White Sack, who had found out (how is not said) that the
goodwife had possession of his *luman*, came to the Change House, and
banged so furiously at the door that the goodwife, greatly afraid,
delivered up to him his property. He now gave chase to the girl.
Her lover saw her coming home pursued by the White Sack, and
stood in the doorway to catch her. Pursuer and pursued arrived
together, but though the lover managed to drag her away from the

A' GHLAISRIG [1]

No. 31d.   [MS. Vol. x., No Number]

F 600·1*   BEAN mhór a bhiodh gu bitheanta ann am bealaichean
ghàraidhean a' cur eagail air eich.

[1] This feminine creature's name is usually spelt Glaistig. She used to
haunt cattle- and sheep-folds, and do domestic work about the house. See
Rev. J. G. Campbell's *Superstitions*, p. 155, foll. Her frightening of the horses
was probably done to prevent them straying through the gaps in the dykes,
and damaging the crops of those to whose houses she had attached herself.

THE WHITE SACK

No. 31c.   *[MS. Vol. x., No Number]*

THE White Sack used to roll itself round (*lit.* before) men's   F 495·1*
feet, bringing them down; then getting on top of them, it
used to flatten them out and murder them.   D 1193

enemy, the White Sack got a hold of the girl's plaid or other wrapping,
and she died of fright. The jealous woman who had sent her on
her dangerous errand was greatly grieved, and never had a peaceful
conscience afterwards. The White Sack's attack upon the door in
order to recover his *luman* does not agree with the statement that he
could do nothing without the *luman*.

The Sac Bàn is mentioned as something in which nobody believes
nowadays, in *An Cuairtear* (1842), ii., p. 263.

In William Livingstone's *Gaelic Poems*, pp. 214, 215, the bard speaks
of the Sac Bàn and other bogles as chasing people. These are the
only other references to the Sac Bàn known to me.

There is, however, a tale about a man who, alarmed at the motions
of a black sheep, put a silver sixpence in his gun, and on the animal's
coming near enough, took aim. 'The black sheep instantly became a
woman, whom he recognized, with a drugget coat wrapped about her
head.'—*Witchcraft*, p. 30. Perhaps this was a *Black* Sack, or another
variety of the same genus of bogle. The mermaid, the swan-maiden,
the seal, the enchanted wolf or stag, and many other creatures have
cochullan or coverings, or 'husks,' or hides, the donning and doffing of
which enables them to assume animal or human shape at will, or as
spells direct or permit (see p. 358 *n*).

THE GLAISHRIG OR GLAISTIG

No. 31d.   *[MS. Vol. x., No Number]*

A BIG woman who used frequently to stand in gaps in the   F 600·1*
dykes, frightening horses.

She was, generally speaking, harmless. Robertson, MS. Book 420, p. 14
(Arran), has a note to the effect that the 'Caointeach,' or weeping female,
'Bodach a' Chipein,' or the Old Man with a Peg, and the 'Glaisrig' or gray
one, were all friendly spirits that took a deep interest in the affairs of man,
and seemed much affected at the prospect [spectacle ?] of human grief.

APPENDICES

APPENDIX I

A' Chailleach Chearc, or
Cailleach nan Cearc, or
The Hen-Wife

G 200

This domestic witch figures in very many tales, more often as an enemy, but sometimes as a friend. She usually lives in or near the royal residence.

In a story in *Waifs and Strays*, iii., p. 222, the story-teller gravely says: 'landlords . . . valued poultry so highly that they were in the habit of keeping about them a shrewd woman whom people called the Hen-Wife.' In Scotland, primitive man must have had a hard fight to wring a living from Nature. We can easily understand that he would apply to magic for assistance, and that the services of a witch would be eagerly sought after. And if her magic succeeded or appeared to succeed in the management of poultry, she would soon become a person of importance. Hence the prominence of the Hen-Wife in so many tales. There is no such a person as a Hen-wizard.

The Hen-Wife shows signs of having once been, not a mere farm-servant but an official of considerable power and importance. She belongs to the wide domain of woman's magic, which centres usually about agriculture, but could perfectly well be associated also with the breeding of the smaller domesticated creatures. When the Highlanders became cattle-breeders, a new state of affairs commenced. Cattle are the province of men and boys the world over, even milking and the preparation of dairy produce being by no means left to or even shared by women. Hence if there was to be cattle-magic at all, it would be men's magic. That is why there is no witch who bears any name which might be translated as 'Cattle-wife.' The only witch who was 'famed at home and abroad, far and wide, for her skill among cows and cattle,' and who 'was said to possess every variety of dairy knowledge in her father's kingdom' was a Norse witch. See *Waifs and Strays*, v., p. 101; *Norse Influence*, p. 278; *An Deò Gréine*, ix., p. 149. This Norse witch was called *Dubh*

a' Ghiuthais, or *Fir Black,* because the smoke of the fir forests
to which she set fire made her face black. Some witches
do indeed bargain for farm produce as the price of their
services (this book, p. 498), and some have an abundance of
wealth, which in former times meant cattle (*Scottish Gaelic
Studies,* iii., p. 23). But knowledge of the charms, incantations,
and magic of all kinds, which were brought into requisition
when dealing with cattle, was common property, and never
gave rise to the institution of a particular class of witch.

Cattle hardly ever act a magical part in any tale, except in
MS. Vol. x., No. 117.

APPENDIX II

AN EACHRAIS-URLAIR

G 200

THE FLOOR-MISCHIEF

THE Eachrais-Urlair, a curious and very interesting witch,
is sometimes found acting alone, or acting with, or acting
against, the Hen-Wife. In the modern forms of folk-tales
she strongly resembles the Hen-Wife. But the names under
which she appears vary so much, that it is probable that she
represents several weird characters who have coalesced.

An Eachrais-Urlair, Englished as 'Trouble-the-House,' *Scottish
Celtic Review* (1881), i., p. 74: as 'Confusion of the floor,' [1] Rev. J. G.
Campbell's *Superstitions,* p. 282: as 'Cantrips' in *Celtic Magazine,* xiii.,
pp. 455, 494, where she is a benevolent character. Occurs also in
Celtic Review, vi., p. 369.

'The evil genius by whom this transformation [metamorphosis] is
effected is very frequently the *Eachrais u[r]lair.* This witch, who is
the embodiment of domestic strife and discord, enters on the scene
whenever the exigencies of the tale require it, and with a stroke of her
enchanter's wand—the *slachdan druidheachd*—the dark deed is done.'—
Trans. Gael. Soc. Inverness, xix., p. 45.

Earchlais ùrlair, No. 3 (MS. Vol. x., No. 2), p. 54.
Eachlaraiche, -ùrlair, Eachlair-, Eachalair- -ùlair, or -ùrlair,
(MS. Vol. x., No. 126).

---

[1] *ùrlair,* of the floor. This word is also the second element in the names
of various retainers and menials. See John Macfadyen, *Sgeulaiche nan Caol,*
pp. 164, 165 (Sinclair, Glasgow) for *am Freiceadan-ùrlair, am freiceadan fuar-
dhorus, am freiceadan fuar,* the floor-sentry or indoor-warden or usher, the cold-
door or outside-door warden or usher. Cf. *gille-fuachd,* best-man or groom's
man, *Réiteach Móraig,* p. 6 (Sinclair, Glasgow). See *MacMhaighstir Alasdair,*
p. 179, *seisir gu fearas-ùrlair,* six fellows to act as deck-hands about the ship.

APPENDIX II 493

Eachlach Urlair, No. 2 (MS. Vol. viii., No. 203).
Iochlach Urlair, No. 22 (MS. Vol. x., No. 37), and MS.
Vol. x., No. 121.
Iorasglach Urlair, *Waifs and Strays*, iii., p. 280.
Clarsach Urlair, *Trans. Gael. Soc. Inverness*, xxv., p. 218.
Achlas Urlair (Tiree),[1] *Celtic Magazine*, xiii., p. 495.

'Eachlach Urláir [2]

In one of the poems in Ac. na Senórach, the following quatrain
occurs (ed. Stokes, ll. 586-7):

> Dá trian do mhíne re mnáibh
> is re hechlachuib urláir;
> re haes dána dénta duan;
> nárbhat dian re daescarshluagh.

[Two-thirds of thy gentleness be shown to women
and to creepers on the floor; *i.e.* little children;
likewise to men of art that make the *duans*;
and be not violent to the common people.]

O'Grady (*Silva Gadelica*, ii., p. 115) renders *echlachuib urláir* here
by 'creepers on the floor [*i.e.* little children].'

Stokes (p. 277) renders the phrase literally by 'messengers
on the floor,' and quotes O'Grady's explanation.

The phrase also occurs in the Glenmasan MS., *Celtic Review*,
ii., p. 32 : 'mo mogaid agus m'echlacha urlair,' translated by
Mackinnon 'my slaves and my little children.'

Another instance occurs in Cath Finntraga (ed. Meyer,
l. 639): 'is imdha taisteallach sibhail 7 echlach urrlair o
ingeanaibh righ 7 rofhlatha Eirenn ag feitheam do comlann
[*leg.* chomlainn].' Here Meyer renders *echlach urrlair* as
'horseman' simply; but O'Grady (*Phil. Soc. Trans.*, 1885-7,
p. 647) explains it as 'a mounted messenger belonging to the
teaghlach (household).'

This last explanation of the phrase comes nearest, I think,
to the correct one. The word *echlach*, though derived from
ech [a horse], means little more than 'messenger,' and in later
times at least it came to be nearly synonymous with *giolla*,
servant, attendant. *Cf.* 'ro bhádar triar eachlach, i. giollaidhe,
aco,' *Oss. Soc.*, iii., p. 126. Hence *eachlacha urláir* = household servants, menials. For this use of *urlár*, *cf.* 'Penates'

[1] Cf. *eachrann, achrann*, entanglement.—*Scottish Gaelic Studies* (1926), i.,
p. 34.
[2] From *Eriu*, ix., p. 15 (Dublin, 1921-23). By Professor T. F. O'Rahilly.

rendered by Begly (531 *b*) *dée úrláir*, *i.e.* household gods: *a riocht gósda nó sbrid-úrláir*, *i.e.* in the shape of a ghost or family spirit, D. do Barra's Corraghliocas na mBan; and the present day *baiste úrláir*, lay baptism, *i.e.* baptism performed at home (and by a layman) in case of emergency.

The expression *eachlach urláir* has also survived in folk-tales, though in a corrupted form. For Ireland, I have only one example, namely, in *Eachtra Ghiolla an Fhiugha*, a folk-tale which was given literary form something over a century ago; *ionnus gurab lia fleadh . . . ná mar do bhí fear ná buidheann chum a chaithte, de ghadhair, de mhná, de choileáin agus d'athalaisg urlair* [1] (I[rish] T[exts] S[ociety], i., pp. 6-8). In Scottish folk-tales the name is applied in a variety of forms, to a very wicked witch who helps the cruel stepmother to do away with her [step-]children.[2] This witch is called *eachrais-urlair* in folk-tales recorded by [Rev.] J. G. Campbell (*Celtic Review*, vi., p. 364; *The Scottish Celtic Review*, 1881, p. 67); *eachrais ulair* in a tale in *T. I[nverness] G[aelic] Soc.*, xiv., p. 143; *eachalair* (and *eachlaraiche*) *úrlair* in a tale from J. F. C.'s Collections, pub. in *An Sgeulaiche*, iii., p. 65 *seq.*[3] [MS. Vol. x., No. 126].

The Scottish *eachrais úrlair* has been translated by J. G. C[ampbell] as the Trouble-the-house, *lit.* Confusion of the Floor. In this form of the phrase *eachlach* has been assimilated to the Sc. *eachrais*, confusion, disturbance, which is doubtless to be equated with the M.I. *echrais*, a sally (Stokes, *Cath Cath.*, *q.v.* for reff.), a rapid movement in a fight (*Eriu*, viii., p. 61, and p. 44 w). The alternative form *eachalair úrlair* is probably the origin of MacAlpine's [Dict.] *eachlair*, a brutish fellow. *Cf.* also Dinneen's [Dict.] *eachlais*, a lazy slovenly woman, a slattern (used also of a man) which is probably due similarly to an Irish corruption of the same phrase (*cf.* the Irish form *athalaisg*, supra).

The degradation of meaning which *eachlach urláir*, originally a menial servant, has undergone in Scottish Gaelic particularly,

---

[1] For *thl<chl*. *cf.* the spelling *ethlach* in the Laud 610 version of Ac. Sen., *passim*. *Cf.* also *bathlach* (Sc. *balach*<M.I. *bachlach*: n.pl. is already *bathlaich* in Laud 610 (Ac. Sen. l. 3795).

[2] *Cf.* J. G. C., *Superstitions of the Scottish Highlands*, p. 282.

[3] In corresponding Irish folk-tales, the woman who helps the stepmother is called simply the Hen-Wife, [this is sometimes the case in Scottish tales also] (*cf.* Larminie, *West Irish Folk Tales*, p. 179; Curtin's *Hero Tales of Ireland*, p. 94) in Irish *Cailleach na gcearc* (*Irishl. M. Nuadhad*, 1910, p. 35) [in Scottish tales *Cailleach nan Cearc*, or *A'Chailleach Chearc*]. In J. F. Campbell's tale in *An Sgeulaiche*, both the *Cailleach nan Cearc* and the *eachalair úrlair* are introduced, and both help the stepmother.

is paralleled not only by the history of such words as *villain*, *boor*, *knave*, and *churl*, but also by such native words as *amhas*, a hired soldier, which in popular use has come to mean a fierce, cruel man, and M.I. *aitheach*, a plebeian, which has given the M.I. (*f*)*athach*, a giant.'

In the Glenmasan MS. also occurs the expression *min-daéine*, *i.e.* little folk, who may be the same as the messengers of the floor. If the witch, the Eachlach Urlair, can be proved to be a degradation of the creeper on the floor, some change in social custom is probably to be deduced. A similar degradation has overtaken the *druineach*, formerly meaning probably an embroideress (as it means in Irish to-day), or else a cultivator of the soil, or else a recluse,[1] but nowadays meaning a female bogle, and applied to the earth-beating cailleach of spring.[2]

The natural history of this strange and shadowy creature, the Eachrais Urlair, is too mysterious to be uninteresting. Like the Hen-Wife, she often lives either in or near the royal residence,[3] and the second element in her name *ùrlair* (= of the floor) shows that her character was domestic. The tales in which she and other witches, as well as feminine supernaturals of all kinds come upon the scene, are far more numerous than tales about wizards and masculine bogles, a fact which is eloquent of the magical reputation of women at the time when the traditions of these strange beings originated.

The Eachrais-Urlair was probably at one time an important official of the royal retinue, a distinguished member of society, a time-honoured institution. She probably continued in the discharge of her duties, whatever they were, until some social change occurred when the status of sorceress began to suffer loss. The degradation of the Eachrais-Urlair, and of witches generally, naturally followed. Glimpses of the change may be seen in many a story, where some sorceress who appears at the beginning as a person of power and influence is, in

---

[1] Professor W. J. Watson, *Rosg Gàidhlig*, p. 266 or 273, and *Place Names of Ross and Cromarty*, lxxxv.

[2] *An Gàidheal* (1875), iv., p. 147.

[3] So does the *gruagach* in *W. H. Tales*, i., No. 1, and the inimical banshee in 'Na h-Amhuisgean,' *Trans. Gael. Soc. Inverness*, xvi., p. 120. In this last tale, as well as in a tale, given *ibid.*, xxv., pp. 184, 235, and in other tales, the Amhuisgean or Awisks or Avasks, whom Islay calls 'savage guards,' also live in a den near the palace, *W. H. Tales*, iii., p. 220 or 235. In Islay's MS. Vol. xi., No. 177, a king keeps a pet Awisk, or berserker ruffian, in a den. For these see Dr Alex. Carmichael, *Deirdre*, p. 77, and Larminie, p. 77. For Irish instances, see *Béaloideas*, i., p. 104, and *Temair Breg*, p. 269—'Duma na mBan-amus, Mound of the She-mercenaries.' See also p. 354 *n*.

the end, defeated by some hero and burnt. In some tales
he does not burn her, but vanquishes her by a blow, or by
magical action, or by crushing her bones, or by beheading
her. He usually succeeds in proving to her that masculine
magic was quite as good as feminine.

The Rev. J. G. Campbell, in his *Superstitions of the Scottish
Highlands*, p. 281, says: 'In nursery and winter evening tales
(*sgialachdun 'us ur-sgeulun*) the machinery of spells is largely
made use of. In the former class of tales, they are usually
imposed on king's children by an old woman dwelling near the
palace, called "Trouble-the-house" (*Eachrais ùrlair, lit.* confusion
of the floor). Her house is the favourite place for the king's
children to meet their lovers. She has a divining rod (*slacan
druidheachd*), by a blow from which she can convert people into
rocks, seals, swans, wolves, etc., and this shape they must keep
until they are freed by the same rod. Nothing else can deliver
them from the spell.

'The story usually runs that the king is married a second
time. His daughter by the first marriage is very handsome,
and has a smooth comb (*cìr mhìn*) which makes her hair, when
combed by it, shed gold and precious gems. The daughters
by the second marriage are ugly and ill-natured. When they
comb their hair, there is a shower of fleas and frogs. Their
mother bribes Trouble-the-house to lay spells on the daughter
of the first marriage. Unless the princess enters the house, the
old woman is powerless to do this. One day the beautiful
princess passes near the house, and is kindly and civilly asked
to enter. "Come you in," says the designing hag, " often did I
lick the platters and pick the bones in your father's house,"
["*Is tric a bha mise 'g imlich na[m] mias agus a' lomadh nan cnàmh
an tigh t'athar*"].[1] Misled by this artful talk, the princess enters,
is struck with the magic rod, and converted into a swan.

'It is a popular saying that seals and swans are "king's children
under enchantments" (*clann rìgh fo gheasaibh*). On lonely
mountain meres, where the presence of man is seldom seen,
swans have been observed putting off their coverings (*cochull*) [2]
and assuming their proper shape of beautiful princesses in their
endeavours to free themselves from the spells. This, however,
is impossible till the magician, who imposed them, takes them
away, and the princesses are obliged to resume their coverings
again.'

In 'Rìgh Eirionn 's a dhà mhac,' *Celtic Review*, vi., p. 365,

---

[1] This is what the witch actually says in MS. Vol. x., No. 126.
[2] *cochull.* See this book, pp. 358 *n*, 489.

when the Eachrais comes to incite the queen stepmother against her stepchildren, the stepmother replies that it pleases her just as well to think that the children of the first marriage should inherit their father's estates as that her own children should. But the Eachrais continuing importunate, the queen at last consents to the poisoning of her stepson. Later on, the Eachrais is seen urging *Fionn* to encompass the death of the hero, the stepson, but he, of course, is always one too many for her.

In *Trans. Gael. Soc. Inverness*, xxv., p. 218, we read of '*A*' *Chlarsach Urlair*,' *i.e.* the Harp of the Floor. Campbell of Islay speaks of her (*ibid.*, p. 183) as a harper, and on the same page as a witch; whether she played on the harp, or performed divination by its means, or did both, or what her business in life was beyond sorcery or harping, does not appear.

The *Iorasglach - ùrlair* who can transform herself into a buzzard, and probably into anything else she chose, is friendly to a hero in two tales, and gives him the advice that saves him. See *Waifs and Strays*, iii., pp. 89, 233. The Rev. James MacDougall, who gives these two tales from the recitation of Alexander Cameron, Ardnamurchan, says (*ibid.*, p. 280) that the sorceress in question 'is described as an old haggard-looking woman, who is careless of her person and of her dress. Her hair is dishevelled, and the skirt of her garment hangs down unequally. Hence an untidy person is still called "Iorasglach." Her favourite posture is sitting on the floor.[1] Hence another name she bears, *Clàrsach-ùrlair*. According to the version I first heard, she struck, before she gave forth her responses, the ground three times, as if she would thus summon to her help the Underworld power or powers from whom she received her inspiration.' In identifying her with the *Clàrsach-ùrlair*, or Harp of the Floor, the Rev. James MacDougall may be correct, but the reason he gives scarcely seems sufficient. He goes on to say that he cannot tell whether the *Iorasglach-ùrlair* is the same character as the *Eachrais-ùrlair*. That the term *Iorasglach* now connotes a dishevelled appearance, shows how far the sorceress had fallen from her former dignity.[2] She may well be the venerable representative of some pre-Celtic race. In striking the ground, she resembles those who, in classical times, invoked the chthonian powers as in *Iliad*, ix., 568. Modern Zulu sorcerers,

---

[1] Squatting on the floor seems to have been a favourite posture with other witches.—*Folk-Lore*, xliii., p. 158, and *Scottish Gaelic Studies*, iii., p. 39.

[2] In Dr Keith Norman MacDonald's *Gesto Collection of Highland Music*, p. 145 (1895, Leipzig), there is a Strathspey called 'Sproilac, An untidy witch.'

when invoking spirits, do just the same. Apparently the same method was employed among the ancient Hebrews. See *Superstitions*, p. 8.

That she was sometimes an official of the reigning king is shown by the fact that in 'The Knight of the Green Vesture' (*Waifs and Strays*, iii., p. 222) the Iorasglach Urlair acts as a nurse who, having saved a child from slaughter, passes it off as her own offspring and brings it up as such, until the time comes for its proper state and rank to be revealed. Such a tale would only be told by friends of the sorceress, who wished to represent her favourably, and who were also friends and co-retainers of the family whose child it was she had saved. The thought suggests that in wicked stepmother tales, the unfriendly Hen-Wife, and the *Eachrais-ùrlair* or Cantrips, were 'wise women' or sorceresses, whom the second or step-mother queen had brought with her when leaving her own clan or tribe and settling among the clan of the king, her husband. But this would probably imply that these strangers displaced the king's native retainers, who would probably include the original local Hen-Wife or other witch or witches. At first sight this seems hardly likely. But that such a super-session of native retainers by strangers did occasionally take place seems possible from stories Nos. 47, 97, 121, 126 (MS. Vol. x.), where his mother's sister, or else his *muime* (foster-mother) helps the hero against his stepmother's confederate, the Hen-Wife or the Eachrais.

K 170   Whatever the variety of the witch happens to be, the terms she demands for her services in getting rid of the second queen's stepchildren are sometimes very curious and extortionate. See pp. 351, 411. The terms have been lost from No. 126 (MS. Vol. x.). Other instances occur in *W. H. Tales*, i., intro., lxxxix or xcv, *Trans. Gael. Soc. Inverness*, xxv., pp. 183, 218, and *Waifs and Strays*, iii., p. 77. In dealing with this last example, the Rev. James MacDougall has the following important note (*ibid.*, p. 277).

'The Hen-Wife is here presented in her usual character of mischief-maker. . . . Her request is so put that it looks moderate enough. She wants only the full of the little black jar of meal and butter, etc. Her terms should then be accepted by the queen, and not, as in the tale [and as in Nos. 22, 25 (MS. Vol. x., Nos. 37, 47)], after the extent of her demands are made known. These terms form a series of riddles, but their solution is omitted. A similar incident, however, occurs in "Conn Eda" in *Folk and Fairy Tales of the Irish Peasantry* (Camelot series), and the solution of the request made there may be virtually that of the first part of the request made here. The Hen-Wife in "Conn Eda" requested that the cavity of her arms should be filled with wool, and that the hole she would bore with her distaff should be filled with red wheat. Her request was granted. She "thereupon stood in the door of her hut, and bending her arm into a circle with her side, directed the royal attendants to thrust the wool into her house through her arm, until all the available space within was filled with wool. She then got on the roof of her brother's house, and having made a hole through it with her distaff, caused red wheat to be spilled through it until that [house] was filled up to the roof with red wheat."' (For similar 'Crafty Bargains,' see *Folk-Lore*, xliv., p. 310.) It is likely enough that a witch would, when opportunity presented itself, trick her patron into granting extortionate requests, which her patron would fear to refuse. Greed on the part of a witch may very well have been one of the causes which led to the downfall of witchcraft.

Whatever material paraphernalia a witch possesses, her equipment included an ability for repartee and apt answers, which was as much a part of her stock-in-trade as it was that of a bard or of a satirist. Yet occasionally witches meet their match, and various stories tell us of ordinary mortals blessed with abundant mother-wit, who defeat witches at their own game of repartee, and drive them away. Witches, however, were not the only ones who suffered humiliation after this manner. Fairies and other supernaturals, and even bards, are sometimes outwitted and outshone by ordinary mortals whom they had numbered among their inferiors. Mortals are also to be seen in some tales defeating witches by adopting their methods and employing their own charms or incantations against themselves. See *Scottish Gaelic Studies*, iii., pp. 10-51 (Humphrey Milford).

In two stories a witch describes herself as a member of a sisterhood (see Islay's English List, No. 279). In other tales witches are private individuals, who practised their art at their own pleasure and not as the officials of a king.

APPENDIX III

A' MHUIME, or,

S 31
F 311·1
P 272

1. The stepmother.
2. The godmother as in No. 83 (MS. Vol. x.)
3. The foster-mother or wet-nurse.

THE *Muime* is unfriendly when the meaning is stepmother, but friendly and devoted when the meaning is foster-mother, for among the Gael the tie of fosterage was held to be five times stronger than any tie of blood-relationship. See Nicolson's *Gaelic Proverbs*, p. 155:—

'Comh-dhaltas gu ciad, 'us càirdeas gu fichead.
Fostership to a hundred, kindred to twenty.'

The intensity of the mutual attachment between foster-mother and foster-child is a motive in many a Highland story. The tie of fosterage seems to have even included the father of the hero's wet-nurse, and to have made him also an ally of the hero's. See No. 97 (MS. Vol. x.)

Sponsorship, or god-parentship, of which a notable instance occurs in No. 83 (Vol. x.), was not so strong a tie as fosterage. See Nicolson, who gives the following (p. 365):—

'Theid trian daltachd ri goistidheachd.
A third of fostership goes to sponsorship.

This means that the bond to a foster-father is three times as strong as that to a godfather.'

There is another word for stepmother, *leas-mhàthair*, and another for nurse, *ban-altrum*, but these words are seldom used in these tales. The word *leth-bhràthair*, half-brother, is also seldom used, and the only instances of it that I remember are to be found in Nos. 97, 126, and *Waifs and Strays*. ii., p. 272. In most tales, two half-brothers, the sons of two queens by the same father, are spoken of as brothers.[1] (This runs counter

---

[1] The Irish words *bràthair*, a kinsman, a cousin, a relative, and *dearbhràthair*, a brother (apparently for *dearbh-bhràthair* and apparently meaning *a real brother*) suggest that ideas regarding family relationships in Ireland differed from the corresponding ideas in Scotland. Other differences between the Irish and Scottish folk-lore exist. The rivalry between the lupine and equine cults ended in Ireland with victory for the lupine; in Scotland the equine was victorious. I have reason to believe that the deer-cult died out in Ireland long before it did so in Scotland. Thus the trend of developments differed for the two countries.

to the regular rule commemorated by the proverb, 'Chan abair mi mo bhràthair ach ris a'mhac a rug mo mhàthair,' I will not call any man my brother except the son whom my mother bore, Nicolson, p. 105.)

For A' Mhuime, see *Trans. Gael. Soc. Inverness*, xxxii., pp. 275-290.

The foster-mother or wet-nurse is also sometimes spoken of as *A'Mhuime-chìche*, or the breast-foster-mother.

Dalta na cìche deise, or the foster-child of the right breast, is a term probably indicating that the person referred to was held in especial honour by his foster-mother. A hero will sometimes compel an otherwise unfriendly feminine supernatural to become his foster-mother and accept him as a foster-son, thereby changing her disposition towards him and making her friendly. To achieve this end he springs upon her unawares and from behind, and conveying the nipple of her right breast to his lips, calls heaven and earth to witness that he is a T 671 fosterer of her right breast. His action, if it is to be looked upon as symbolical, is all the more effectual, and it implies that she has suckled him, and has therefore, willingly or unwillingly, become his foster-mother. For examples of this wild incident, see my monograph on *A'Bhean Nighe* (*Guth na Bliadhna*, ix., p. 195, Alex. MacLaren & Sons, Glasgow).[1] If she admitted his claim, she was bound by the tie of fosterage to support and assist him in all his undertakings to the utmost of her power.

The relationship between foster-mother and foster-child appears to have been more than usually magical. In *The Black Dwarf*, chap. vii., Sir Walter Scott speaks of the nurse as being 'a person then of great consequence in all families in Scotland, whether of the higher or middling classes.' In the same chapter, stout Hobbie Elliot, when travelling homeward and nearing his journey's end, is greatly perturbed at observing on the road before him, at some distance from his house, his old nurse Annaple; he deems the incident a sure omen of D 1812 disaster, and his apprehensions are justified by the ruin and ·5·1·7 desolation he finds before him when at last he reaches home.

---

[1] Another instance will be found in Islay's MS. Vol. xi., No. 224, where a fairy foster-mother, whose services had been secured in the manner noted above, speaks of having a *master*. This supports the theory set forth in my monograph, that legends of the *Bean-Nighe*, which represent her as involuntarily suckling grown men, may reflect a memory of a race of invaders who made slaves of the aboriginals, and caused the women of the conquered to become nurses to the children of the conquerors. Fosterage may also very well represent an attempt to patch up feuds between rival nationalities and a desire for peaceful amalgamation.

Again, Lochiel curses his foster-mother for meeting him in the road early in the morning, deeming that when on important business she was an unlucky person to meet at such a time of day and at the distance of five miles from home. In one sense she was certainly unlucky, for she brought with her bad news, news of treachery, and had gone to meet him only in order to put him on his guard. The hero listens to her advice and takes counter-measures that enable him to get the better of his enemy. See Islay's MS. Vol. i. (purple-covered series) and MS. Vol. xi., No. 179 (erroneously numbered 180 in his Gaelic List). It is strange that a wet-nurse or foster-mother should be deemed an unlucky person for her foster-child to meet at a distance from home, seeing that the tie of affection between them was far stronger than any tie of blood relationship.

The two instances given show that this superstition existed both in the Highlands and the Lowlands. In seeking to account for it, it is necessary to review certain other matters. First of all, the position or status of a mother with regard to her children must be considered. In several Scottish Gaelic tales, mothers seem to have absolute control over their sons. In some stories she beats her only son; a thing never done by the father. In innumerable other tales a mother, before her hero-son sets out on his adventures, offers him the choice of two things : on the one hand, a big bannock or the bigger half of a bannock accompanied by her curse ; on the other hand, a small bannock or the smaller half of a bannock with her blessing. The son who chooses the larger allowance of bannock and her curse is always unsuccessful.[1] But the son who prizes his mother's blessing so much that he is content with the smaller allowance of bannock, is always successful. In *W. H. Tales*, i., No. 17, a heroine who chooses the small half of the bannock, is successful, because 'her mother's blessing came and freed her' whenever she was in trouble. In No. 2, Var. 6, occurs a hero who was called 'Mother's Blessing' because 'he was so good,' and who was as successful as good. The frequency of these incidents, though tedious from the general reader's point of view, is of great significance to the folk-lorist, for they illustrate the immense importance of the mother and the great powers of magic over her children with which she was supposed to be endowed. It is further to be remarked that a father never

J 229·3

---

[1] The power of a mother's curse and its dreadful results may be seen in the tale of the Will o' the Wisp (An Teine Mór).—*Witchcraft*, p. 171. *Folk-Lore*, viii., p. 227; xxxiii., p. 317. *Trans. Gael. Soc. Inverness*, xix., p. 161. This book, p. 49.

figures in these incidents.   Indeed, in the generality of tales, fathers figure far less often and are far less important than mothers.[1] In Wales, 'The Mothers' and 'The Blessing of the Mothers' (*Y Mamau, Bendith Y Mamau*) are actually names for the fairies.   And there is no doubt that the fairies of Western European folk-lore have much in common with the old Mother Goddesses [2] (*Matres, Matronae*) to whom various monuments and inscriptions have been found both in Britain and on the Continent. The subject is a big one, but enough has been said to suggest that the mothers of a tribe were probably at one time supposed to be possessed of an unusual amount of magical power over their children.

The next thing to be considered is the great strength of the tie of fosterage expressed in the saying already quoted— *'Fostership to a hundred, kindred to twenty.'*   At the back of this article in the social creed, there must have been at one time a magical, supernatural, or religious sanction of supreme force. Only so can the depth, strength, and sacred character of the thing be explained.   And it may be fairly deduced that if the relationship of a mother to her son was magical or supernatural, there must have been five times as much magic or supernaturalness in the relationship that bound the foster-mother to her foster-child.

If fosterage was supposed to bring a fresh strain of uncontaminated blood into a clan, the reason of the magical relation of the foster-mother to her foster-child becomes at once apparent.   But I have no evidence that this idea obtained among the Gael.[3]   It is enough for the moment to observe that a foster-mother must have stood in a supremely magical relationship to her foster-son.   Now as we never hear either of a natural mother or of a foster-mother travelling, we may perhaps infer that the place of such persons was deemed to be in the home; that their presence abroad was contrary to use or propriety, and that that was why meeting one's foster-mother at even a little distance from home was deemed ominous.   Here again there is only conjecture.   But there may have been another factor in the matter.   To meet a supernatural was always D 1812· ominous.   To meet the ancient deer-goddess, the Cailleach of 5·1·7

[1] The fact suggests that the state of society in which Highland folk-tales originated was matriarchal. That feminine supernaturals are far more numerous than masculine points to the same conclusion.

[2] For these goddessses, see Professor Sir E. Anwyl, Ancient Celtic Goddesses, *Celtic Review*, iii., p. 26; M. Ihm in Roscher's *Lexikon*, ii, 246[4] sqq; Canon MacCulloch in Chantepie de la Saussaye, *Lehrbuch d. Religionsgesch.*, ii., p. 606.

[3] See *More W. H. Tales*, i., p. 391.

Ben Breck, Lochaber, was ominous. To meet a spectre, a solitary deer separated from the herd, a water-horse, and many other creatures supposed to be magically or supernaturally endowed, was also ominous.[1] Hence probably the ominousness of meeting one's foster-mother when abroad; for it meant meeting a person whose relationship to one's self, whatever it may have been to others, was magical or supernatural in the highest degree.

In No. 97 (MS. Vol. x.) appear an unfriendly stepmother and a friendly foster-mother.

In *More W. H. Tales*, i., No. 22, an unfriendly witch and unfriendly stepmother appear. The rôle of the friendly foster-mother is taken by the Dame of the Fine Green Kirtle, who is usually a friendly fairy.

See *ibid.*, No. 25, where the two unfriendly characters again appear, the rôle of the friendly foster-mother being taken by a friendly mother's sister.

APPENDIX IV

D 1273
E o—
E 199
Z 85*
H 951·1*

BE-SPELLING AND COUNTER-BE-SPELLING INCANTATIONS— RESUSCITATION

IN Highland lore occasionally occurs the incident of a witch or a wizard conjuring or be-spelling a hero to the performance of some task or the undertaking of some quest. The method of procedure was to utter a mysterious incantation in which the performance of the task specified was enjoined upon the hero by certain spells or charms of apparently great power, the mere enunciation of which forced the hero, willy-nilly, to do as bidden. If he failed he was threatened with 'the losses of the year,'[2] *i.e.* with the force of all the disasters that might happen

---

[1] To meet the fairy-woman, or some variety of fairy-woman is, in some tales, very ominous. In others, fairies of both sexes encounter mortals without anything untoward taking place.

[2] The losses of the year. The expression may be connected with various superstitions. At *Samhain* (All Hallowe'en) Queen Meave used to ascertain from her magicians and poets whether the year was to be prosperous for her or not, *Silva Gad.*, i., p. 179; ii., p. 202. For the expulsion of evil spirits and for otherwise purging the premises at Hallowe'en, see *An Deò Gréine*, January 1914, p. 53. 'When the Highland home was cleaned out at Hogmanay . . . the ill-luck of the past year was supposed to be driven out, and everything was ready for a fresh start; and to prevent the powers of evil again entering, first the Bible was placed above the door during the last hours of the year, and the cat kept inside, so that if by any mishap an unlucky first-foot should dare to enter in spite of this, the evil could be got rid

during the year's progress.[1] The dreaded fairy-woman is also invoked against him. If he failed, she was to meet him, and strike him with the nine cow-fetters which she carried. It must be explained here that even the ordinary cow-fetter or cow-spancel of ordinary mortals was a most ominous instrument, though its function was the very innocent one of keeping a cow quiet while being milked.[2] It was placed upon the animal's hind-legs. The fairy-woman's cow-fetters with which she secured the hind-legs of any deer she was about to milk, were still more deadly than those of mortals. If struck by them a hero was supposed to be rendered so awkward and silly, so fey and unlucky, that the veriest scum of the populace would be able to overcome him in battle, and take his ear, and his head, and his means of life from him. With these awful and shameful calamities hanging over him, every hero of course did his best to obey the enemy's behests.[3]

In some instances the hero is be-spelled to his task by a feminine character who is friendly, or at least not unfriendly. In some of these instances the hero eventually marries her. But in the instances about to be examined, it is an enemy who be-spells him.[4] The incidents which take place later on, when

of by throwing out the cat, for poor pussy was supposed to be able to carry out with it all the mischief which such a person was supposed to bring in,' *Trans. Gael. Soc. Inverness*, xxi., p. 71. Compare the following from County Kerry. 'The cat was missing three days, and Kate, discussing the probability of his having gone for good, said: "Ah, well! the harm of the year go with him," ' *Folk-Lore*, xxxi., p. 236. The cat apparently carried the losses of the year about with it.

[1] In *W. H. Tales*, i., No. 1, the words *mar sheisean na bliadhna* (*i.e.* as the session of the year) occur. They seem to refer to the modern practice of citing persons to 'compear' before the dreaded Kirk Session. But they may be corruptions of *mar easbhuidhean na bliadhna*, i.e. as the losses of the year.

[2] Professor Rose has kindly suggested to me that the fact that it bound something may have made it magically dangerous. The Flamen Dialis might not have anything about him which suggested a knot. The Greek word καταδέω, 'I bind down,' means 'I be-spell.'

[3] The spells pronounced by a Highland witch would not injure the person adjured, provided he carried out the tasks laid upon him. The Highland spells thus differed fundamentally from the Welsh oath, called *tynghed*, which, says Sir John Rhys, 'effects blindly the ruin of the sworn man's health, regardless of his conduct. At any rate, that is the interpretation which I am forced to put on what I have been told,' *Celtic Folk-Lore*, ii., p. 648.

[4] See p. 230 *n*, for a list of these, and a good example. The be-spelling of the heroine by her foster-mother, and the spells which the heroine alleges in No. 126 (MS. Vol. x.), probably belong to a different category. But the incidents of the be-spelling there are obscure, and no conclusion can be based on them.

the hero, having performed all the tasks, returns to his task-master or task-mistress to report progress, are very curious and have certain significant implications.[1]

It may be taken for granted that such incantations or be-spelling 'runs' as have come down to us, are but fragments of the old original charms, though containing a good deal of their spirit, and some at least of the old phrases. But with the exception of two cases occurring in Nos. 1, 2, where it is reasonable to suppose that forgetfulness on the part of reciter or scribe is to blame (p. 19 n), the two antagonists, the enemy and the hero, both punctiliously observe the terms of the conditions laid upon them. From this it is evident that the geasan or spells were deemed to be of a peculiarly binding or compelling character. Perhaps they had a religious sanction and were enforced by some magic or religious rite now lost. The only trace of any such thing is the reference to the fairy-woman, who in many cases is a goddess of the mounds or hillocks, though in others probably the ghost of a dead deer. At all events the enemy, whether witch, or giant, is invariably as completely subject to the compelling power of the spells as the hero is.

I have said that the two antagonists, the enemy and the hero, both punctiliously observe the terms of the conditions laid upon them. This applies to those tales in which it appears to occur to the hero as an afterthought that he might take up his ill-wisher's own weapons and turn them against him; in other words, that he might, by using similar spells and incanta-tions, compel his enemy to accept or come under, conditions far more dire than those with which he himself had been saddled. Thus the hero takes the first step towards turning

---

[1] Professor R. A. S. Macalister says (*Temair Breg*, p. 362): 'One of the most curious and perplexing phenomena in all Irish literature is the power, nowhere explained, which people seem to have possessed of imposing *gessa* [=spells] on others. Gráinde puts a *geis* [= spell] 'of the ridge of druidry,' *i.e.* apparently a particularly strong and bind-ing *geis* on Diarmait to elope, with her; and Diarmait is obliged to do so, though it is much against his will. It is obvious that all human relations would have been impossible had the process been so simple as is described. Gráinde must have done something else, which the sense of propriety felt by the Christian chronicler prevented him from recording—performed a gesture, secured some magical instrument, or what-not—in order to make her *gessa* effective.' Apparently, reference to the fairy-woman with her nine cow-fetters with which she secured her deer has been lost from Irish lore, a circumstance confirming my theory that the deer-cult died out in Ireland long before it died out in the Highlands (*Folk-Lore*, xliii., p. 151).

the tide of battle in his own favour and getting even with his enemy.[1]

With the intention then, of 'dishing' his enemy, the hero conjures him or her to remain where he or she is, in some absurdly uncomfortable attitude, and without food or drink. He or she is either to keep motionless, or to be twisted about by the wind whichever way it veer, and to suffer various other impossible inconveniences—one cheek for instance, is to be kept full of meal, and the other full of water and salt, and a goose feather is to be fixed in the nose (see p. 425, this book), and in that plight and condition the enemy is to remain until the hero returns. The hero of course hopes that when he does return, the other will be in such a weak and parlous state that there will be no difficulty in settling accounts with him or her. In one story the enemy is be-spelled to keep running until the hero returns, an equally satisfactory way of dealing with him.—*Trans. Gael. Soc. Inverness*, xxv., pp. 214, 228. D 5·1

In some tales the enemy, dismayed at the prospect of death by privation, offers to cry quits, but the other always refuses. See *Trans. Gael. Soc. Inverness*, xxv., p. 214. *W. H. Tales*, ii., No. 51, p. 420 or 434. *Waifs and Strays*, iv., p. 233. *Scottish Celtic Review* (1881), p. 678. This book, p. 425.

Details of this incident vary from story to story. Thus in the Eigg version of the Tuairisgeal, *Trans. Gael. Soc. Inverness*, xxxiv., p. 19, the enemy be-spells the hero to fetch the story of the Great Tuairisgeal's death. The hero in his turn be-spells the enemy to remain in one position, with his head leaning on

---

[1] Gràinne be-spells Diarmaid and Diarmaid counter-be-spells Gràinne in *W. H. Tales*, iii., No. 60. Two witches appear to use charms and counter-charms against each other, and also engage in a verbal battle in D. C. MacPherson's *An Duanaire*, p. 42. But in neither of these cases does the strife quite resemble the instances of counter-be-spelling examined here. The belief that apt and ready answers threw off the spells of witches and frustrated their evil intentions offers no parallel. Neither does the belief that evil-wishes could be counteracted by a *tu quoque* from a bystander—'The fruit of your wish be on your own body' (Rev. J. G. Campbell, *Superstitions*, p. 281). The interesting point about the be-spelling incidents examined in this section is that they take the form of commands, inexorable commands, which must be obeyed, and which could not be cancelled save by the person who gave them, *Superstitions*, p. 283. The idea that the enemy's own spells might be turned against himself may have arisen independently in many places. An instance is given by Mr J. H. Hutton, *Folk-Lore*, xxxiv., p. 160. 'Again I am reminded of my childhood and a much-tried Yorkshire nurse-maid who would sometimes, when particularly exasperated, threaten as a last resort, when all else failed, to "look over" my "head." I remember, too, how upset she was when I used her own expression against her. It was a really serious thing to say.'

his hand, and to take no food or drink until his return. Even if the enemy's bones are scattered abroad, the hero is to recite the story. The hero departs, performs the tasks, returns and recites the story over the enemy's decayed remains. While doing this, the enemy re-materializes until he is once more present in the flesh with his head leaning on his hand. The recitation finishes at this point, and before the enemy can rise, the hero strikes off his head. In other versions the command to recite the story, even if the enemy were dead, is omitted ; but comparison suggests that it was once there. In *Scottish Celtic Review* (1881), i., p. 141 (Rev. J. G. Campbell), the enemy rises clear of the hillock on which he had been be-spelled to remain. The hero then beheads him. In this version, as the Rev. J. G. Campbell notes, the enemy is himself a son of the Great Tuairisgeal, and if he had been allowed to rise from the hillock would have been irresistible. But even with Campbell's emendations this version is very corrupt, for it does not say that the enemy had decayed or sunk into the ground, as he apparently had. In No. 2 (p. 29 *n*) the incident of the gaming is lost. In both Nos. 1 and 2 (pp. 19, 41), after the hero's successful return, nothing is said as to reciting any story : instead, he is instructed to shout at his enemy thrice. Possibly in the original story both recitation and shouting occurred. In another story, No. 17 (MS. Vol. x., No. 31) the enemy is a one-eyed, one-armed, one-legged Cailleach. By the time the hero returns, she has crumbled to dust. She rises from the dead when the story has been completely recited and, most unusually, is left unharmed by him. She then be-spells him to fetch certain heads, and is presumably, though the story fails to say so, counter-be-spelled by him, to remain where she was without food or drink. When he returns with the heads he visits her with one of them, leaves it with her and addresses her with certain discourteous phrases prescribed by his magic henchman who tells him he is not to say a word more, which significantly suggests that his henchman knew that too much talking would revive her sooner than was desirable. He visits her again next day, apologises for his rudeness of yesterday, and invites her to come and take the second head from him. She is now so far revived that she is able to move towards him, but he kills her by striking her on the head with one of the task-heads. In *W. H. Tales*, ii., No. 51, a Cailleach be-spells Fionn and sets him to tasks in which the hero must needs assist him. It is not said that she be-spelled the hero as well, but the sequel makes it clear that she did, and that she be-spelled him also to recite

E 55·1·1*
E 31

the tales of his adventures on his return. By the time they return it is implied, though not said, that she had crumbled to dust, or at all events had died. Recitation causes her to rise again and again, but every time she does so the hero breaks her bones until, presumably, he has completely killed her. In *Trans. Gael. Soc. Inverness*, xxv., p. 214, the counter-spell on the enemy is that he is to keep running about. He begins running and continues doing so until the hero returns. He does not decay, though deprived by the counter-spell of food and drink. While the hero is reciting he falls asleep. The hero finishes his recitation and then, but not till then, beheads him. In *W. H. Tales*, i., No. 1, the hero has to fetch a sword, not a story. On his return he finds his enemy just where he had left him, suggesting that he had counter-be-spelled him to remain there. In *ibid.*, ii., No. 46, the enemy, a *muime* or stepmother, sends the hero for a bird. He counter-be-spells her to remain in an extraordinary position till his return. She does not wither away. On his return he protects himself against her by turning towards her the edge of a 'sword of light,' which he had got in the course of his adventures. This counteracts her glance, which otherwise would have made him fall like a faggot of firewood. She then falls like a faggot herself. In No. 25 (MS. Vol. x., No. 47), p. 431, the mere return of the hero makes his *muime* crumble and fall. The suddenness of her collapse may be compared with the collapse of persons in various tales, who in a few seconds or moments crumble to dust when the magic, which had kept them whole during some extraordinarily long period of time, ceases to operate (*e.g.* on return from fairyland). *Cf.* also No. 46 above. Perhaps we may suppose that in these cases the effects of all the deprivations which the *muime* had had to undergo came upon her at once.

The belief lying at the back of these incidents seems to be that even when a person had crumbled to pieces, no matter whether buried in the grave or resting above-ground, still, provided that his dust or bones or remains were present, he was not so thoroughly dead but that he might be resurrected by the employment of the right kind of magic. For a not dissimilar idea, see Donald Mackinnon, *Descriptive Catalogue of Gaelic MSS.*, p. 220, where Fergus MacRoich appears from his grave and tells a watcher the story of the Táin Bó Cúailnge. For other accounts of this, see *Celtic Review*, iv., pp. 82, 91.

If we may judge from three of the versions of the Tuairisgeal, from the two instances in this book (pp. 19, 41) and from the instance in No. 51, *W. H. Tales*, ii., the belief was that the process of becoming present in the body would be gradual; it would merely keep step with, or follow close upon the act of recitation, so that if recitation stopped, redintegration would also stop; but if, on the other hand, recitation progressed, redintegration would also progress and would become more and more perfect, until finally, if the recital lasted long enough, or if it were duly completed (it is not certain which of these alternatives was the essential one), redintegration would also be duly completed. Thus in both versions of the Tuairisgeal given in this book the hero, before despatching his enemy, allows him to resume life to the full, and in the same place and in the precise posture in which he had been when laying life down (pp. 19, 41). The posture in question, that of lying prone and leaning the head on the hand, the elbow being supported on the ground, is spoken of in Gaelic as being 'on the elbow' (*air an uilinn*). It is frequently used, and indicates that though the person is still alive, he is in a decrepit condition.   However, in allowing the enemy to revive completely, as in the case of the Cailleach in No. 17 (p. 261), and (though less obviously) in the case of the Cailleach in No. 51 (*W. H. Tales*) a feeling for the fitness of things may perhaps be detected, a desire that the hiatus in the life of the enemy, and the gap in the continuity of the story, should be effectually bridged over, and be brought up square and level with the original *status quo* before proceeding further. But there was also probably a desire for something more practical than mere artistry or congruity.   There may have been a dim surmise that it was vain to try to despatch an enemy who was only partially resuscitated: he was not all there to despatch.[1] Before he could be completely despatched, his complete resuscitation was necessary, and the fact that the stages in the process of resuscitation are graduated, points to such a climax as the desideratum.   There is evidence, however, that

[1] There was a belief that magic could *not* have any effect upon persons who had not been baptized, and therefore wanted a name; they were not all there, *Trans. Gael. Soc. Inverness*, xvii., p. 229.   The heroine who, on p. 327 (this book) tells a tale of disaster to her child whom she had carefully kept unbaptized, takes advantage of this, for the supernatural powers will bring disaster upon a person who listens to a tale of disaster, but not upon one who has not been baptized and therefore has no name.   Again, persons wanting an ear or other member could not be injured by the magic of the *corp creadha*, or clay corpse, *Witchcraft*, pp. 46-49.   Even things which had been unshipped, or disarranged, or put out of gear, or which were not in their normal places, could not be harmed by the fairies, *Waifs and Strays*, i., pp. 54, 70, and *Superstitions*, pp. 19, 35, 74, 232.   Contrast the belief that children who had not been baptized, were liable to be stolen by the fairies, *Waifs and Strays*, v., pp. 141, 145.

this idea eventually underwent modification or corruption. See the Rev. J. G. Campbell's amended account of the resuscitation incident on p. 508.

But there seems to have been another belief (whether more ancient than the foregoing or later cannot be determined here), a belief that even decapitation did not necessarily mean death, if the severed head were placed in juxtaposition with the body. There are several tales in which a hero is advised to keep his sword for two days on the neck of the witch or giant he has E 783 decapitated until the spinal marrow froze; or he is advised to remain in person for the same time between the head and the body, and keep them apart until the blood froze, thus preventing them from effecting a junction; otherwise the head would resume its original position on the body from which it had been severed, and the enemy would then be able to recommence hostilities (p. 38 n). In No. 2 (MS. Vol. viii., No. 203) the G 635·1 incident occurs twice: in MS. Vol. x., No. 158, once. In these instances the hero, after beheading the enemy whom he himself had resuscitated, has to remain in person for two days and two nights between the head and the body until the spinal marrow froze, after which they could never unite again.

That mere dismemberment, whether caused by decay or by violence, was not enough to kill outright appears to be the thought at the back of an incident on p. 259, where the bones of the king's slain foster-brothers are placed in a vessel of poison, in order presumably, to make them more thoroughly dead. Even that, apparently, could be counteracted, for the foster-brothers are revived or resuscitated when their bones are removed from the vessel of poison and placed in a vessel of balsam.

The Tuairisgeal stories, the story of the Cailleach in No. 17 (MS. Vol. x., No. 31) (p. 273), and the story of the Cailleach in No. 51 (W. H. Tales, ii.) seem to show that one of the essentials of resuscitation was the presence of the remains or the bones of the desiccated person. Presumably all the bones were necessary for the purpose, otherwise the resuscitated body would not be intact and complete. Presumably also, all the bones of the king's foster-brothers in the story noted above were necessary, ere complete resuscitation of the persons could be accomplished. But there are instances of another belief, a belief that resuscitation was still possible, even when dismemberment and destruction had been carried so far that only one bone or other small portion of the original body remained. Thus in the Islay version of the Tuairisgeal (Trans. Gael. Soc. Inverness, xxv., p. 214) the young giant be-spells the hero to fetch, not only the story concerning the old giant's death, but also one of the old giant's bones. Similarly, in *W. H. Tales*, ii., No. 51, when the pet deer belonging to the old Cailleach is captured, the Cailleach begs the hero who has captured it to give her the full of her fist of its bristles, or a mouthful of its broth, or a morsel of its flesh. Later on, Fionn remarks that if a morsel of its flesh remained uncooked, or if a drop of the broth in which it was boiling fell into the fire, the animal would arise and be as it had been before. The reason why the young giant wanted one of his father's bones, or why the old Cailleach should beg for some part of her favourite animal, is from the last instance quite clear, for possession of these things would have made resuscitation possible. The natural deduction from such a set of ideas was, that the only way of getting rid of a witch or other dangerous member of society was to burn them to ashes, for then none of their original substance remained. Boiling such individuals was apparently ineffectual. See p. 221.

It is clear that there was a belief that magic could restore the dead, provided that some part or emanation of the dead body could be procured upon which to base operations. Conversely, the common belief was held that a part of a living body was enough to work magic upon to the detriment of the whole. Even a piece of clothing was enough. *Cf.* MS. Vol. x., No. 151. For non-Gaelic parallels, see W. H. R. Rivers in *Folk-Lore*, xxxi., pp. 48-69, and *ibid.*, p. 332; xxxii., p. 137; xxxiv., p. 29; xxxv., p. 111. E. S. Hartland, *Science of Fairy Tales*, pp. 29, 50, 54. Contrast the belief already noted that the absence or loss of a part prevented magic from obtaining power over the whole (*Witchcraft*, pp. 46-49).

Though redintegrating magic or resuscitating magic was so powerful, its power is, sometimes at least, limited or modified by the sympathetic variety. In No. 43, *W. H. Tales*, ii., the sheep that comes to life again after being slaughtered does so because her bones had been gathered together and rolled up in her skin. But she comes with a halting step, because her 'little hoofs' had been forgotten and had not been included with her other bones.[1] Here clearly, the preservation of the

---

[1] See No. 28 (MS. Vol. x., No. 53*a*, p. 458 *n.*). Similarly, whatever wounds a character receives in his metamorphosed state, occur in the same region of the body when he resumes his normal state. John Macfadyen pokes fun at this belief when he makes one of his characters say that if, when in hare-form, the ear of a witch had been shot off, the witch when in human form would be wanting that ear. Whereupon a half-wit enquires what would have been the case if the tail had been the part that had been shot off the hare, and receives for answer that he is asking too many questions. *An t-Eileanach*, p. 302 (MacLaren and Sons, Glasgow).

bones is an essential to resuscitation, and in this respect the tale reveals a conception of the matter similar to that revealed in the incident of reviving slain heroes by placing their recovered bones in a vessel of balsam. On the other hand, if magic could, from a portion only, restore the dead body completely and in all respects, it is strange that it could not restore the 'little hoofs.'

Resuscitating the dead by means of shouting at them resembles, though it is not quite parallel to, the many versions of the tale about arousing the sleeping Fenians. The legend usually runs that they were sleeping in a cave at the mouth of which hung a horn, or other magic apparatus, three blasts on which would deliver them from the spells under which they lay. A traveller found the cave one day, and peeping in, saw the huge champions and their huge hounds stretched asleep inside the cave. He blew a blast on the horn, and hounds and men all moved. He blew a second blast, and the champions all sat up on their elbows, as does the Tuairisgeal in the tales noted above. But their aspect was so terrible, and the howling of their hounds was so awful, that the traveller fled. The Fenians are therefore still resting on their elbows, waiting for the third blast that shall revive them completely. In some versions it is not a horn but the *gurra fiodha* (the wooden whistle) or the *dord Fianna* (the Fenian's chanter) upon which the blasts were blown, or else it was *an t-slabhruidh éisdeachd* (the Chain of Audience, see p. 430 n.) which had to be shaken to awaken the heroes. It is to be observed that the case of the Fenians differs from the other cases considered above. In these legends the Fenians are always represented as being present each in his own proper person and intact, but asleep. They are never spoken of as having crumbled to dust. The number of blasts on the horn necessary to make them awake, so far as to sit up on their elbows, is only two. Whereas in tales Nos. 1 and 2 (MS. Vol. viii., Nos. 106 and 203) (taking these two tales at their face value, and ignoring for the moment the probability that the incident of recital has been dropped out or forgotten) the number of shouts necessary to make the decayed enemy sit up on his elbow is three. It is possible, however, that the corruption to be seen in the resuscitation incident in these two tales (pp. 19, 41) is due to the influence of the tales about awakening the Fenians.[1]

The marginal references:
F 531·6
·13·1
E 55·3·1*
E 502

---

[1] For the awakening of the Fenians, see Nicolson's *Gaelic Proverbs*, p. 28. *Waifs and Strays*, iii., p. 74; iv., p. 4. *An Gàidheal* (1873), ii., p. 241. Sometimes the tale is told of Thomas the Rhymer, *W. H. Tales*, iii., p. 85 or 97; E 502

In another tale three head-splitting blasts on a whistle or
D 1225 chanter cause the Fenians, or their ghosts, to appear (p. 467).
In some of the versions of 'Oisean after the Feen,' *i.e.* Ossian, the
survivor of the Fenians (*W. H. Tales*, ii., No. 31 ; *An Deò Gréine*,
xv., p. 181), three head-splitting blasts on a whistle, or three
terrific shouts cause three herds of deer, or the ghosts of three
such herds, to appear. Whether these are instances of bodily
resuscitation, or whether they are instances of the calling up of
spirits from the dead, is very uncertain.

For other instances of summoning up the dead, see p. 472.

E 80 Other modes of resuscitation were (1) sprinkling water from
a magic well, often situated in one of the Isles of the Blest ;
E 115 (2) sprinkling balsam or applying balsam. (3) In *W. H. Tales*,
ii., No. 44, a deer shakes *sol* (wax) from her ear on a dead hero,
and revives him.

See also *Trans. Gael. Soc. Inverness*, xxviii., p. 169.

iv., p. 35 or 37. Rev. J. G. Campbell, *Superstitions*, p. 270. Rev. Alex. Stewart
or 'Nether Lochaber,' *Twixt Ben Nevis and Glen Coe*, p. 45. *Celtic Monthly*,
xxiv., pp. 76, 91. But according to other legends Fionn himself, instead of
sleeping in a cave, is supposed to be in fairyland. Confusion of ideas as to
the life after death are known to exist in other countries. See *Folk-Lore*,
xxxiv., p. 250; xxxv., p. 142. However, the cave may correspond to the
A 661·1 Danish Valhall, p. 243 *n*.

SUBJECT INDEX

A'Chailleach Chearc, 491
adventures of Champion, xxxvi
Æsop, 146
aged man, 31
Alasdair, the Son of the Emperor, 169
Amerindians, 391
A' Mhuime, 500
Angus the Grim, 487
antlers, 199, 201
apple, 275 n.
apple game, 253, 275 n.
apples, red, 199, 201
Arabian Nights, 344 n.
awful appearance, 97

Baillie, 185, 451
Baillidh Lunnainn, xxxvi, 185 n., 392
Bald Scurvy Lass, 347
ball (dance), 303
balsam, 259, 429
band for neck, 219
band of soldiers, 165
Bank, Royal, 441
Banks, M. M., 478
baptism, 309, 389
battle, 93, 103, 247, 269, 271
beautiful castle, 335
beautiful woman, 69
bed-sheet, 129
Beggar of Edinburgh, 439
begging, 75
be-spelling, 504
be-spelling "run," 5, 231, 237, 261, 413, 415, 417, 425
bet, 135, 139
big beast, 133
Big Rory, 65
Big Speedy-Foot, 481
Billy, 119
bird, 29, 141, 189, 331, 335, 403, 423 (see Gìre-Mhìneach)
bird language, 169, 226
bird's heart, 189
Bird's Liver, 189
bird's prophecy, 169, 181

Black Knight, 9, 45
Black Knight's Daughter, 45
Black Lad of Loch Dring, 481
Black Lass of Ragged Clout, 55
Black Toe, 235
blind man, 335
blinding, 339
blood, 363
blood-hounds, 13, 35
blowing steam, 251, 257
Blue-eyed Hawk, 21, 45
blue filly, 69
Blue Mountains, 408
boar, 252 n.
boar riding, 59
Bodach, 211, 231
body snatching, 127
bog, 105
bogle slayer, 455, 460
boiling water, 221
bottle of water, 55
Bràigh Thòrasdail, 455
Bramble berries in February, 411, 417, 432
breaking leg, 69
bridegroom, 135
bridegroom, unlucky, 391
Bridge of the Hundreds, 431
Briton, 407
broad low road, 33
broth, 13, 37
bull fair, 219

calumniated dog or wolf, 15, 37
calumniated wife, 361, 363, 365
camels, 337
Canach Down, 347, 369
cap for travel, 205
carters, 123
carts, 123
castle, 215, 335
cat, 385
Catrìona, 457
cauldron(s), 17, 41, 221, 249, 251, 464 n.
cave, 249, 359
chaff, 344

515

Chain of Audience, 431
chair, spiked, 59
chairs, gold, silver, 11, 33
challenge "run," 245, 247, 269, 271
Champion, 53, 231
change-house, 79, 121, 159
chanter, 472
chariot, 181, 399
chasing "run," 248 n., 255
cheek filled with barley meal, 425
child, 37, 93, 279
child selling, 293
child stealing, 13, 37, 363, 365
child with animal head, 315, 323
children of King, 347, 367
chimney, 121
church, 399
churchyard, 127, 339
Ciuthach, 167 n.
Clan MacKenzie, 463
Claw Hand, 13, 15, 37, 39, 363, 365
clergyman, 175
Cliar Sheanchain, xv, 433
clump of rushes, 17, 33, 41, 69
cockerel, 15, 363
College of Magic, 216 n.
comb, -ing, 9, 353, 355 n.
coracle, 71
Cormac's Advice to his Son, xxxv
corpse(s), 127, 419
Corra Chriosag, 105
covenant vows, 377
cow, 105
cow-fetters (see be-spelling "runs"), 505
cow's hide and horns, 121
cradle, 31
crì-bhìnneach, 35 ; see Gìre-Mhìneach
crop-eared wolf, 14 n., 37
Cro-veenich, 141 ; see Gìre-Mhìneach
Cruachan Beann, 457 n.
Cuilisg, 464 n.
cup, 363
cups, three, 359
cut off arm, 15, 39, 313

Dame of Fine Green Kirtle, 355
daughter cheats father, 392

Daughter of Donald of unjust laws, 115
Daughter of King of France, xxxv
Daughter of King of Great Isle, 401
Daughter of King Under Waves, xxxvi, 403 n.
dead old woman, 420 n.
decay of enemy, 19, 41, 261, 273 n., 431, 508
deer-cult, 209
deer-woman, 397, 408
Delving Bodach, 105
Diarmaid, 368, 507 n.
Dick Whittington, 392
dirk, 457
disenchant, 17, 41, 343, 401
disguise, 176 n., 186 n., 392
dish of tongues (twice), 143
dismemberment, 469, 472
distinguished, 153
dog, 217, 341
dog fair, 217
Doideag, 369
Donald, 331
Donald Scholar, 169
Donn Mara Mór MacMhoirein, 486
door, 109
doorkeeper, 241
dord Fiann, 472
dove, 29, 215, 217
dreaming, 95
dress, 177, 186, 381
drink up sea, 137
drippings of lamps, 429, 427, 435
Duncan of Ewe Isle, 475
Duncan MacBrian Gàrraidh, 267
Dwarfs, 408

Eachdraidh a' Cheatharnaich, xxxvi
Eachlach Urlair, 35, 493
Eachrais Urlair, 492
eagle, 423 (see Gìre-Mhìneach)
ear, cutting off, 14 n., 37 n., 231
Earl of Antrim, 69
ears, 434
eating grass, 199
Edinburgh, 85, 299, 395
Eilean Iarthuath, 70 n.
emetic, 197

Emperor, 169
Emperor of Rome, 87
Empress of Rome, 89
Eriskay, 395
Evnissyen, 166 n.
Ewan MacAlk, 63
executions, 81 n., 328 n.

fair-haired lad, 97
Fair Knight, 7, 29
fairy woman, 231 n., 355 n., 413,
    415, 417, 425, 481, 504 n., 505
famine, 75, 133
farmer, 75
Féith Mhór, 465
Fenian chant, 472 n.
Fenians, 99, 463, 472, 513
Fiann, 463
fifteen bellows, 225
fifteen eels, 223
fifteen foster brothers, 411
fifteen tinkers, 223
fighting "run," 247, 269, 271
filly, 69, 199, 203, 239 (see
    palfrey)
fine big man, 79
Fionn MacCumhail, 99
fire "run," 355, 357
fisherman, 265
flogging, 89
Floor Mischief, 35, 55, 492
food, 206, 207
forged letters, 285, 301, 307 n.,
    315, 323
forty thieves, 166 n.
fosterage, 500
foster brothers, 249, 411
foster mother, 500
fox, red, 225
France, 87, 229
Fraoch, 115
fraudulent partner, 392
French vessel, 87
frenzy, 97
Friday, 477, 478 n.

Gaelic lassie, 299
Gairloch, 463
gambling, 3, 5, 231, 235
game of the apple, 253
game of the notch, 253
garden burnt, 311
Gearrloch, 455, 463

Geere - veenach,   see   Gìre -
    Mhìneach
general, 161
ghoul, 339
giant, 2 n., 21, 45, 264 n., 427 (see
    S-T Classification, G.)
giants, 153
giants and robbers, 429 n.
Gille Glas, 397
Gìre-Mhìneach, 12 n., 13, 35,
    141, 403 (see eagle, 423)
Glasgow, 299
Glashrig or Glaistig, 489
Glen Arm, 99
Goat, hornless, yellow, 455
godmother, 500
golden chair, 11, 33
golden club, 411
golden ring, 223
goldsmith, 333
Goll, 101
Good Hearing, 53
Good Thing, 81, 225, 313 n., 343
goose feather, 425
governor, 229
Gràinne, 167 n., 368, 507 n.
grandmother's sister, 457
grateful dead, 392
Gray Cailleach, 235, 239
gray coloured hound, 353
gray filly, 199, 203
gray haired old man, 49
Gray Hound (short-tailed) of
    Green Wood, 21
gray mare, 335
great age, 31
Great Brown MacMorran of the
    Sea, 487
great carter, 161
great castle, 215
great Champion Bodach, 231,
    235
great gentleman, 93
Great Gulp, 49, 55
great hounds, 157
great rowan tree, 95
great sea monster, 97
Great Tuairisgeal, 3, 29
great wedding, 69
Great Wizard, 221
Greece, 5, 29, 41, 133
Green Isle (see Happy Isles),
    197
Green Mountains, 408

green well, 55
greyhound, 141
Grinder of Mill, 65
growth after death, 467

hairy as a goat, 93
Hand, Claw-like, 13, 15, 37, 39, 363, 365
hand through window, 363
Handsome Lazy Lass, 149
hanging, 81, 365
Happy Isles, 49 *n.* (and probably 55), 70 *n.*, 197, 205 *n.*, 402 *n.*
Hard Haunches, 53
hare, 69
Harp, 415, 471, 497
Harris, 85
haunches, 53, 153
Hawk of Slieve Brat, 21, 45
head of Big Man, 261
head of Little Man, 261
healing balsam, 259, 429
healing leg, 71
healing "run," 71 *n.*
heap of bones, 19, 43, 508
heap of dead drift, 261
heart's blood, 349
helpers, 51, 53, 55, 356 *n.*
Hen Wife, 411, 491
high narrow road, 33
hip, 457 *n.*
hiring, 75, 133
honey sweet berries, 115
horse (*see* steed), 123, 219
horse fair, 219
Horse with White Trews, 65
hospitality, 73 *n.*, 216 *n.*
host and guest, 73 *n.*, 216 *n.*
house building "run," 347
house in skies, 139
How Great Tuairisgeal was put to death, 3
Humming Harp of Harmony, 415
hundred bowmen, 243
hundred crowders, 243
hundred spearmen, 243
hunter, 395
husband, wretched old, 79

Iain, 75
Iain Og, Son of the King of France, 229

Indies, voyage to, 283
infant marriage, 373, 390, 392
Inverasdale, 463
Iochlach Urlair, 347, 493
Iosbadaidh, 131
Ireland, 93
Island, N.W. of the Great World, 71
[Islay] Farmer's Son, 85
Isle of Women, 49
Isles (*see* Happy)
ivy shirts, 368

jar of husks, 331
jar of magic, 341, 343

kail stump, 107
Kane's Leg, 69
kicking over rafters, 434
kill husband, 79
king, 347
king and dumb girl, 361
king widower, 309
King of Erin, 3, 29, 411
King of France, 229
King of France's daughter, xxxv
King Green Hillock's daughter, 408
King of Ireland, 69, 73, 93
King of the Isle of the Women, 49
King of Lochlin, 73 *n.*
king's candle, 435
king's daughter, 49
king's joy and woe, 237
Kingdom of Big Men, 269
Kingdom of the Green Mountains, 408
kingdom on fire, 263, 271
knights, 7, 9, 29

language of birds, 169, 226
lark, 63
Lass who was sold, 293
lawman, 79
letters, *see* forged letters
Lewis, 70 *n.*
life or soul, 23, 45, 223 *n.*, 225, 227
lights, 206, 207
little beasts, 133
little black bag, 411
little black crock, 351, 411
Little Rory, 65
liver, 206, 207

Llychlyn, 243 n.
loaf, 77, 83
Loch Dring, 465, 481
Loch Luaim, 115
Loch Maddy, 395
London, 85
London Baillie, xxxvi, 185 n.,
     392,
Lord, the, 319
lovers' meeting, 287, 323

Macalister, Prof. R. A. S., 506 n.
Mac an Air, 481
Macdonald clan, 463
MacMillan the Harpist, 463
magic fire " run," 355, 357
magic wand, 17, 35, 41, 353
Mahon, 337
maid-servant, 121
man in woman's dress, 151
Man who took to Robbing, 447
marks of recognition, 321
marooning, 13, 35 n., 199, 391 n.
Màrts, the Three, 478
Matres, 503
Matronae, 503
merchandise, 161
merchant, 161, 337
message, 281
mill pond, 293
miller, 293
midwife, 361, 363, 365, 367
midwives, three, 13, 15, 37, 39
mogan, 369, 370
money, good and bad, 341
monster, 97, 115
Mór, Daughter of Smùid, 63
mother's blessing, 49, 502
mother's sister, 415
much butter, 351, 411
much meal, 351
much steak, 413
much wool, 351, 411
Mull witch, 369
Mulmoire MacRath, 481
murder, 79, 387
Murdoch Minister, 481
music, 13 n., 36 n., 415, 471

naming, 456 n.
ne'er do well, 211
nightfall " run," 355
Nimble Shanks, 53
nine bottles of wine, 9

nine loaves, 9
nobleman, 153
Noble Watercress, 469
North Assynt, 481
North-West Island of Great
     World, 71

O'Cròleagann, 69
old man in cradle, 31
old mighty man, 357
old woman, 375, 397, 421
Old Woman of the Bothy, 65
one daughter, 347
One-eyed Man, 63
Otter of Rapid Stream, 21, 44 n.
outer hollows of ears, 351

palfrey (see filly), 3, 29
parted lovers, 283, 315
pedlars, 77
pedlar's pack, 93
pet deer, 249, 255
Pigmies, 408
poke full of peats, 105
poor gentleman, 279
poor man, 105, 293
Poor Rich Man, 331
Priest Speckled Boy, 63
prophecies, 168, 181, 421 n., 427
purse, 193
purse, double ended, 407 n.
pursuit of wife, 21, 43

Queen Meave, 504 n.
Queen of Lochlann, 243
Queen of Rome, 85

rabbit, 123
Ragh Monaidh, 105
ram-dog, 339
ransom, 235, 259
rats, 385
recognition, 29 n., 37, 97, 217, 321,
     327, 343, 359, 407
recovery of health, 431
rein, 31, 221, 223
restoration, 207
resuscitation, 504
riddles, 369, 370, 417, 433 n.
ring, 219, 223, 297, 359, 405
robbers, 77, 111, 135, 153, 249, 447
robber's horse, 447, 449
roc (see Gìre-Mhìneach)
roof, 13, 15, 37, 39

Royal Bank, 441
"runs," *see* the Stith Thompson
  Classification, Z 85*, p. 537
rushes, 17, 33, 41, 69

sack(s), 161, 489
sailing "run," 263
Sallow Lad, 475
Salltraigh, 395
Samhanaich, 2 *n.*
Sannda of Gairloch, 481
sawdust, 433
Scouring Gray Blast of Spring,
  105, 109, 113 *n.*
scrape tongue, 111
seal, 93, 102 *n.*
second Queen, 309 (*see* stepmother)
seeming devil, 123
selling child, 293, 307 *n.*
sergeant, 85
set fire to apple trees, 311
sex-shifting, 209
shamrock, 193 *n.*
shape-shifting, 215 (*see* transformation)
shepherd, 99
shinty, 411
ship, 13
ship for sea or land, 49
shirts, 75, 361, 365, 368 *n.*
shoe, 355
Short-tailed Gray Hound, 21
Short-tailed Hound of Wood, 45
sigh, 237, 263
signs, converse by, 361
silence, 14 *n.*, 361, 367 *n.*
silver ball, 411
silver chair, 11, 33
silver pin, 327
sixteen foster brothers, 249
sixteen men, 431
six years old, 229
skinning boar, 251, 257
skull of horse, 57
Skye, 395
sleeping draught, 397, 399
sleeping pin, 399
smalls, three, 434
smithy, 93
soldiers, 85, 165
Son of the Sea, 93
soul, separable, 23, 45, 223 *n.*, 225,
  227

spears, 167
speed of vessel, 271, 273
spiked chair, 59
spinal marrow, 38 *n.*, 41, 511
spinning canach, 361
Spirit of Eld, xxxv
sporran full of gold, 189
squatting, 497 *n.*
stairs in giant's back, 269
stakes, unnamed, 3, 5, 231, 235
  (and *see* 73 *n.*)
steak, 413
Steed of Corrie Ciarrach, 425
stepmother, 13, 35, 189, 309, 347,
  411, 500
Stirling, 447
Stochd Stachd, 395
stockings, 75
storm of *croachachan*, 155
story telling, 11, 31, 71, 73 *n.*,
  110 *n.*, 133, 299
Straight Aim, 55
string, 359
summoning the dead, 472
swear by ring, 297
swear secrecy, 309
swift March wind, 273, 425
sword of light, 17, 39

tartan cloak, 79
Tale of Kane's Leg, 69
telling tales (*see* story telling)
ten robbers, 153
Thatcher of Kiln, 65
thieving, 119
thorn in foot, 313
three bottles of wine, 9
Three Counsels, 75
three cups, 359
three daughters, 93
three giants, 419
three lads, 131
three loaves, 9
three Màrts, 478
three robbers, 111
Three Shirts of Canach, 347
three sons, 13, 35, 347
three wolves, 13, 35
throwing bones, 253
toes, 434
Tom Buidhe, 455
Tonsured One, 468 *n.*
torture, 434

transformation, *see* Stith Thompson Classification, Do-D 699, p. 526
travelling "run," 43, 415, 419, 427
Tuairisgeal, The Great, 3, 29
Tuairisgeal, The Young, 3, 21, 41
Tuesday, 478
Turkey, 373
twelve old men, 385
twenty pounds, 211
twenty-four tales, 73
two fathers, 373
two hundred pounds, 331
Two Love Trees, 279
Two Skippers, 373

Uisdean Mór MacGìlle Phàdruig and the Hornless Yellow Goat, xxxvi, 454
Uist, 395
unbaptized child, 325
unchristened child, 309
underground dwelling, 242 *n.*, 514 *n.*

Valhalla, 243 *n.*, 514 *n.*
victorious younger son, 51, 131, 195, 359
voice from above, 317

wager, 135-139
wages in loaf, 77, 83
watchers, 97
water-cress, 199, 469

water-horse, 206
weaver, 105, 459
Weaver's Son, 395
wedding party, 133
well, 55, 317
Well of Dringag, 483
whip, 89, 203
whiskey, 125
whistle, 153, 165, 427, 465, 472, 514
White Knight, 7
White Sack, 489
Widow, xxxvi, 487
widow's son, 49
wild boar, 251, 257
wild boar riding, 57
witch, 13, 35, 41, 55, 235, 341, 347, 353, 411, 491-499
witch's terms, 351, 411
witch wand, *see* magic wand
Wizard's Gillie, 211
wood neither bent nor straight, 413, 433
wool, 351, 411
Wren in Rock, 65
wrestling "run," 233, 265
writing on gun, 401

yawl, 17, 39
Yellow Legs, 461
Y Mamau, 503
Young King of Greece, 11, 29
Young Tuairisgeal, 3, 21, 41